Computer Communications and Networks

For other titles published in this series, go to
http://www.springer.com/

The **Computer Communications and Networks** series is a range of textbooks, monographs and handbooks. It sets out to provide students, researchers and non-specialists alike with a sure grounding in current knowledge, together with comprehensible access to the latest developments in computer communications and networking.

Emphasis is placed on clear and explanatory styles that support a tutorial approach, so that even the most complex of topics is presented in a lucid and intelligible manner.

Ian J. Taylor   Andrew B. Harrison

From P2P and Grids to Services on the Web

Evolving Distributed Communities

Second Edition

Ian Taylor, BSc, PhD
Andrew Harrison, BA, MSc, PhD
School of Computer Science, Cardiff University, UK

Series Editor
Professor A.J. Sammes, BSc, MPhil, PhD, FBCS, CEng
CISM Group, Cranfield University,
RMCS, Shrivenham, Swindon SN6 8LA, UK

CCN Series ISSN 1617-7975
ISBN 978-1-4471-5761-8 2nd edition
ISBN 978-1-85233-869-5 1st edition
DOI 10.1007/978-1-00084800-123-7
ISBN 978-1-84800-123-7 (eBook) 2nd edition

British Library Cataloguing in Publication Data
A catalogue record for this book is available from the British Library

Softcover re-print of the Hardcover 2nd edition 2009
First published 2004
Second edition 2009

Printed on acid-free paper

9 8 7 6 5 4 3 2 1

springer.com

Adina, I thank you for your support and encouragement during the writing of this book, amidst a somewhat *laborious* time as my words fell ever more quickly off the end of these chapters. And as one delivery ended, another began – to George, our son.

Ian

To P & U again (sigh). I will now keep my promise to break my worst habit.

Andrew

Preface

Over the past several years, Internet users have changed in their usage patterns from predominately client/server-based Web server interactions to also involving the use of more decentralized applications, where they contribute more equally in the role of the application as a whole, and further to distributed communities based around the Web. Distributed systems take many forms, appear in many areas and range from truly decentralized systems, like Gnutella, Skype and Jxta, centrally indexed brokered systems like Web services and Jini and centrally coordinated systems like SETI@home.

From P2P and Grids and Services on the Web Evolving Distributed Communities provides a comprehensive overview of the emerging trends in peer-to-peer (P2P), distributed objects, Web Services, the Web, and Grid computing technologies, which have redefined the way we think about distributed computing and the Internet. The book has four main themes: distributed environments, protocols and architectures for applications, protocols and architectures focusing on middleware and finally deployment of these middleware systems, providing real-world examples of their usage.

Within the context of applications, examples of the many diverse architectures are provided including: decentralized systems like Gnutella, Freenet and in terms of data distribution, BitTorrent; brokered ones like Napster; and centralized applications like SETI@home, as well as the core technologies used by the Web. For middleware, the book covers Jxta, as a programming infrastructure for P2P computing, core Web Services protocols, Grid computing paradigms, e.g., Globus and OGSA, distributed-object architectures, e.g., Jini, and recent developments on the Web including Microformats, Ajax, the Atom protocols and the Web Application Description Language. Each technology is described in detail, including source code where appropriate.

To maintain coherency, each system is discussed in terms of the generalized taxonomy and transport and data format protocols, which are outlined in the first part of the book. This taxonomy serves as a placeholder for the systems presented in the book and gives an overview of the organizational differences between the various approaches. Most of the systems are discussed at a high level, particularly addressing the organization and topologies of the distributed resources. However, some (e.g., Jxta, Jini, Web Services, the Atom syndication and publishing protocols, and to some extent Gnutella) are discussed in much more detail, giving practical programming tutorials for their use. Security is paramount throughout and introduced with a dedicated chapter outlining the many approaches to security within distributed systems.

Why did we decide to write this book?

The first edition of this book was written for Ian's lecture course in the School of Computer Science at Cardiff University on *Distributed Systems*. However, for this second edition, we wanted to make the scope more broad to not only include more recent advances in distributed systems technologies, such as BitTorrent and Web 2.0, but also to focus on the underlying protocols for the Web, discovery and data transport. So:

Who should read this book?

This book, we believe, has a wide-ranging scope. It was initially written for BSc students, with an extensive computing background, and MSc students, who have little or no prior computing experience, i.e., some students had never written a line of code in their lives! Therefore, this book should appeal to people with various computer programming abilities, to the casual reader who is simply interested in the recent advances in the distributed systems world, and even those who resent the invasion of distributed computing into their lives. This book provides an easy-to-follow path through the maze of often conflicting architectures and paradigms.

Readers will learn about the various distributed systems that are available today. For a designer of new applications, this will provide a good reference. For students, this text would accompany any course on distributed computing to give a broader context of the subject area. For a casual reader, interested in P2P, Web Services, the Web or Grid computing, the book will give a broad overview of the field and specifics about how such systems operate in practice without delving into the low-level details. For example, to both casual and programming-level readers, all chapters will be of interest, except some parts of the Gnutella chapter and some sections of the deployment chapters, which are more tuned to the lower-level mechanisms and therefore targeted more to programmers.

Organization

Chapter 1: Introduction: In this chapter, an introduction is given into distributed systems, paying particular attention to the role of middleware. A taxonomy is constructed for distributed systems ranging on a scale from centralized to decentralized depending on how resources or services are organized, discovered and how they communicate with each other. This will serve as an underlying theme for the understanding of the various applications and middleware discussed in this book.

Chapter 2: Discovery Protocols: This chapter discusses the local and global mechanisms for the discovery of services across the Internet. It provides a foundation for the middleware and applications because each employs some aspect of discovery in their implementation. We describe both the Unicast protocols (UDP and TCP) and the Multicast protocol by providing some detail about how each operates. We then conclude with a brief description of SLP, which is a protocol that makes use of these underlying protocols and directory services for discovering services on a network.

Chapter 3: Structured Document Types: This chapter provides an overview of the related technologies of XML, HTML and XHTML. These technologies are widely used across many distributed systems and hence are referred to frequently throughout the book. A description of the primary technologies used to model and validate these documents is also provided.

Chapter 4: Distributed Security Techniques: This chapter covers the basic elements of security in a distributed system. It covers the various ways that a third party can gain access to data and the design issues involved in building a distributed security system. It then gives a basic overview of cryptography and describes the various ways in which secure channels can be set up, using public-key pairs or by using symmetric keys, e.g., shared secret keys or session keys. Finally, secure mobile code is discussed within the concept of sandboxing.

Chapter 5: The Web: This chapter describes how the Web came into being and what its underlying principles and technologies are including the use of Uniform Resource Identifiers, Hypermedia and the Hypertext Transfer Protocol. The architectural style of Representational State Transfer (REST) which is derived from observations of the Web is also described. The Web is the most ubiquitous distributed system of all and therefore has influenced many of the systems described in this book, both architecturally and technologically. The advent of Web 2.0 has re-ignited interest in the Web as a distributed platform from areas that did not previously consider it feasible.

Chapter 6: Peer-2-Peer Environments: This chapter gives a brief history of client/server and peer-to-peer computing. The current P2P definition is stated and specifics of the P2P environment that distinguish it from client/server are provided: e.g., transient nodes, multi-hop, NAT, firewalls, etc. Several examples of P2P technologies are given, along with application scenarios for their use and categorizations of their behaviour within the taxonomy described in the first chapter.

Chapter 7: Web Services: This chapter introduces the concept of machine-to-machine communication and how this fits in with the existing Web technologies and future scopes. This leads onto a high-level overview of

Web Services, which illustrates the core concepts without getting bogged down with the deployment details.

Chapter 8: Distributed Objects and Agent Technologies: This chapter provides a brief introduction to distributed objects, using CORBA as an example, as well as the related field of Mobile Agents. The relationship between three important abstractions used in distributed systems, namely, Objects, Services and Resources, is also discussed, providing the reader with an understanding of the underlying differences between different architectural styles.

Chapter 9: Grid Computing: This chapter introduces the idea of a computational Grid environment, which is typically composed of a number of heterogeneous resources that may be owned and managed by different administrators. The concept of a "virtual organization" is discussed along with its security model, which employs a single sign-on mechanism. The Globus toolkit, the reference implementation that can be used to program computational Grids, is then outlined giving some typical scenarios.

Chapter 19: On the Horizon: This chapter provides a glimpse into possible future environments based on technologies that are already being deployed; specifically cloud computing infrastructures and ubiquitous systems, as well as conjectures by particular current commentators on where distributed systems are likely to lead in the coming decade.

Chapter 10: Gnutella: This chapter combines a conceptual overview of Gnutella and the details of the actual Gnutella protocol specification. Many empirical studies are then outlined that illustrate the behaviour of the Gnutella network in practice and show the many issues which need to be overcome in order for this decentralized structure to succeed. Finally, the advantages and disadvantages of this approach are discussed.

Chapter 11: Scalability: In this chapter, we look at scalability issues by analysing the manner in which peers are organized within popular P2P networks, using both structured and unstructured approaches. First, we look at social networks and compare these against their P2P counterparts. We then explore the use of decentralized P2P networks within the context of file sharing and how and why hybrid (centralized/decentralized) networks are used. We then discuss distributed hash table technology, which offers a more structured approach to this problem.

Chapter 12: Freenet: This chapter gives a concise description of the Freenet distributed information storage system, which is a real-world example of how the various technologies, so far discussed, can be integrated and used within a single system. For example: Freenet is designed to work within a P2P environment; it addresses scalability through the use of an adaptive routing algorithm that creates a centralized/decentralized network topology dynamically; and it addresses a number of privacy issues by using a combination of hash functions and public/private key encryption.

Chapter 13: BitTorrent: This chapter describes the BitTorrent protocol. It discusses how BitTorrent uses a tracker to create a group or swarm for a particular file which dynamically updates the information about the peers in the network who have interest in downloading the particular file. As more participants join the group, more pieces are downloaded, thus creating more sources for the pieces of the file on the distributed network. This, in turn, provides more download sources for peer, to make multiple TCP connections to in order to increase their download bandwidth for a particular file.

Chapter 14: Jini: This chapter gives an overview of Jini, which provides an example of a distributed-object-based technology. A background is given into the development of Jini and into the network plug-and-play manner in which Jini accesses distributed objects. The discovery of look up servers, searching and using Jini services is described in detail and advanced Jini issues such as leasing and events are discussed.

Chapter 15: Jxta: This chapter introduces Jxta that provides a set of open, generalized, P2P protocols to allow any connected device (cell phone to PDA, PC to server) on the network to communicate and collaborate. An overview of the motivation behind Jxta is given followed by a description of its key concepts. Finally, a detailed overview of the six Jxta protocols is given.

Chapter 16: Web Services Protocols: This chapter describes the core specifications that underpin Web Services technologies. Specifically, three core technologies are discussed in detail: SOAP for wrapping XML messages within an envelope, WSDL for representing the Web Services interface description, and UDDI for storing indexes of the locations of Web services. An overview of some of the most important specifications that build on top of these is also provided, particularly the use of WS-Addressing.

Chapter 17: OGSA: This chapter discusses the Open Grid Service Architecture (OGSA), which extends Web Services into the Grid computing arena by using WSDL to achieve self-descriptive, discoverable services that can be referenced during their lifetime, i.e., maintain state. OGSI is discussed, which provides an implementation of the OGSA ideas. This is followed by OGSI's supercessor, WS-RF, which translates the OGSI definitions into representations that are compatible with other emerging Web service standards.

Chapter 18: Web 2.0: This chapter describes the underlying principles of Web 2.0 and how it differs from earlier approaches to developing successful activities across the Web. An overview of a variety of technologies is given including Ajax, Microformats, some exemplary service APIs, the Atom Syndication Format and Publishing Protocols, as well as the Web Application Description Language.

Chapter 20: Distributed Object Deployment Using Jini: This chapter describes how one would use Jini in practice. This is illustrated through several simple RMI and Jini applications that describe how the individual parts and protocols fit together and give a good context for the Jini chapter and how the deployment differs from other systems discussed in this book.

Chapter 21: P2P Deployment Using Jxta: This chapter uses several Jxta programming examples to illustrate some issues of programming and operating within a P2P environment. A number of key practical issues, such as out-of-date advertisements and peer configuration, which have to be dealt with in any P2P application are discussed and illustrated by outlining the potential solutions employed by Jxta.

Chapter 22: Web Services Deployment: This chapter describes an approach to developing a Web Service and service client. Issues such as the use of complex types in service operations are addressed, as well as different client-side mechanisms for dealing with these complex types in the context of programming language defined entities.

Chapter 23: Web Deployment Using Atom: This chapter takes the Web Service developed in Chapter 22 and exposes the same capability using the Atom Publishing Protocol. The aim is to show how a Protocol like Atom can be used to execute services beyond the typical syndication scenarios associated with Feeds.

Disclaimer

Within this book, we draw on a number of examples from file-sharing programs, such as Napster, Gnutella (e.g., Limewire), KaZaA to name a few. The reason for this is to illustrate the different approaches in the organization of distributed systems in a computational scientific context. Under no circumstances, using this text, are we endorsing or supporting any or all of these file-sharing applications in their legal battles concerning copyright issues.

Our focus here is on the use of this infrastructure in many other scientific situations where there is no question of their legality. We can learn a lot from such applications when designing future Grids and P2P systems, both from a computational science aspect and from a social aspect, in the sense of how users behave as computing peers within such a system, i.e., do they share or not? These studies give us insight about how we may approach the scalability issues in future distributed systems.

English Spelling

The spelling of some words in British English should (perhaps) be with an 's'; however, in almost all related literature in this field, these words are spelt with a 'z', e.g., organize, centralize, etc. For this new edition, therefore, we decided to stay with the use an amalgamation of American English and British English, known as mid-Atlantic English... Therefore, for the set of such words, we will use the 'z' form. These include derivatives of: authorize, centralize, decentralize, generalize, maximize, minimize, organize, quantize, serialize, specialize, standardize, utilize, virtualize and visualize. Otherwise, we will use the British English spelling, e.g., advertise, characterise, conceptualise, customise, realise, recognise, stabilise, etc. Interestingly, however, even the Oxford Concise English Dictionary lists many of these words in their 'z' form...

Acknowledgements

We would like to thank a number of people who helped us with various aspects for this book. Ian would like to thank, in particular, Adina Riposan-Taylor for her support and Joe Macker and Brian Adamson for their dissemination of the little orange book! Also, many thanks to the numerous contributors to motivation over the years including but not limited to Mr. and Mrs. Taylor, Paula Gardiner, Angela Harrison, Alex Hardisty, Jon Giddy, Ian Downard, Omer Rana, Andre Merzky, Andrei Hutanu, Bernard Schutz, Ed Seidel, Gabrielle Allen, Ian Kelley, Rion Dooley, Jason Novotny, Ian Wang, Matthew Shields, Michael Russell, Oliver Wehrens, Felix Hupfeld, Rick Jones, Sheldon Gardner, Thilo Kielmann, Jarek Nabrzyski, Sathya, Tom Goodale, David Walker, Kelly Davis, Hartmut Kaiser, Dave Angulo, Alex Gray and Krzysztof Kurowski.

Cardiff, UK
May 2008

Ian Taylor
Andrew Harrison

Contents

Part I Common Themes

1 **Introduction** 3
 1.1 Introduction to Distributed Systems 5
 1.2 Terminology 7
 1.3 Centralized and Decentralized Systems 9
  1.3.1 Resource Discovery 10
  1.3.2 Resource Availability 11
  1.3.3 Resource Communication 13
 1.4 Taxonomy Dependency Considerations 14
 1.5 Examples of Distributed Applications 17
  1.5.1 The Web: Decentralized 17
  1.5.2 A Stand-Alone Web Server: Centralized 18
  1.5.3 SETI@home: Centralized 20
  1.5.4 Napster: Brokered 21
  1.5.5 Gnutella: Decentralized 21
 1.6 Examples of Middleware 23
  1.6.1 J2EE and JMS: Centralized 23
  1.6.2 Jini: Brokered 23
  1.6.3 Web Services: Brokered 24
  1.6.4 Jxta: Decentralized 25
 1.7 Conclusion 26

2 **Discovery Protocols** 27
 2.1 Service and Directory Discovery 27
 2.2 Unicast Addressing 29
  2.2.1 UDP 30
  2.2.2 TCP 30
 2.3 IP Multicast Addressing 32
  2.3.1 Multicast Grouping 33
  2.3.2 Multicast Distribution Trees 34

2.3.3 Reverse Path Forwarding 34
2.4 Service Location Protocol 35
2.5 Conclusion 37

3 Structured Document Types 39
3.1 HTML 40
3.2 XML 43
3.3 XHTML 46
3.4 Document Modelling and Validation 48
3.4.1 Document Type Definition 48
3.4.2 XML Schema 51
3.4.3 RELAX NG 56
3.5 Conclusion 60

4 Distributed Security Techniques 61
4.1 Introduction 62
4.2 Design Issues 63
4.2.1 Focus of Data Control 64
4.2.2 Layering of Security Mechanisms 65
4.2.3 Simplicity 66
4.3 Cryptography 67
4.3.1 Basics of Cryptography 67
4.3.2 Types of Encryption 68
4.3.3 Symmetric Cryptosystem 69
4.3.4 Asymmetric Cryptosystem 69
4.3.5 Hash Functions 70
4.4 Signing Messages with a Digital Signature 71
4.5 Secure Channels 72
4.5.1 Secure Channels Using Symmetric Keys 73
4.5.2 Secure Channels Using Public/Private Keys 74
4.6 Secure Mobile Code: Creating a Sandbox 75
4.7 Conclusion 77

Part II Distributed Environments

5 The Web 81
5.1 Introduction 81
5.2 The Dawn of the Web 82
5.3 Naming Things in a Uniform Way 83
5.3.1 URI Templates 86
5.4 A Shared Representation of Things 89
5.5 Hypertext Transfer Protocol 90
5.5.1 HTTP and Security 92
5.6 Representational State Transfer 94

5.6.1 Client-Server 95
5.6.2 Statelessness 95
5.6.3 Caching 96
5.6.4 Uniform Interface 97
5.6.5 Layering 100
5.6.6 Code-on-Demand 100
5.7 The Semantic Web 101
5.8 Conclusion 105

6 Peer-2-Peer Environments 107
6.1 What Is Peer to Peer? 108
6.1.1 Historical Peer to Peer 108
6.1.2 The Shift to New Internet Users 109
6.2 Modern Definition of Peer to Peer 110
6.2.1 Social Impacts of P2P 113
6.3 The P2P Environment 115
6.3.1 Hubs, Switches, Bridges, Access Points and Routers 115
6.3.2 NAT Systems 117
6.3.3 Firewalls 118
6.3.4 P2P Overlay Networks 119
6.4 P2P Example Applications 119
6.4.1 MP3 File Sharing with Napster 120
6.4.2 File Sharing with Gnutella 121
6.5 True P2P and Good Distributed Design 122
6.6 Related Projects: Volunteer Computing 123
6.6.1 Distributed Computing Using SETI@home 124
6.6.2 BOINC 124
6.7 Conclusion 125

7 Web Services 127
7.1 Introduction 127
7.1.1 Looking Forward: What Do We Need? 128
7.1.2 Representing Data and Semantics 130
7.2 Web Services 132
7.2.1 A Minimal Web Service 132
7.2.2 Web Services Architecture 133
7.2.3 Web Services Development 135
7.3 Service-Oriented Architecture 136
7.3.1 A Web Service SOA 136
7.4 Conclusion 138

8 Distributed Objects and Agent Technologies ... 139
8.1 What Are Distributed Objects? ... 140
8.2 CORBA ... 141
8.3 Mobile Agents ... 143
8.4 Objects, Services and Resources ... 145
8.4.1 Objects ... 145
8.4.2 Resources ... 146
8.4.3 Services ... 146
8.5 Distributing Objects Using Java ... 148
8.5.1 Remote Method Invocation ... 149
8.5.2 Java Serialization ... 150
8.6 Conclusion ... 153

9 Grid Computing ... 155
9.1 The Grid Dream ... 155
9.2 Social Perspective ... 156
9.3 History of the Grid ... 157
9.3.1 The First Generation ... 158
9.3.2 The Second Generation ... 159
9.3.3 The Third Generation ... 161
9.4 The Grid Computing Architecture ... 162
9.4.1 Virtual Organizations and the Sharing of Resources ... 163
9.5 To Be or Not to Be a Grid: These Are the Criteria... ... 166
9.5.1 Centralized Control ... 166
9.5.2 Standard, Open, General-Purpose Protocols ... 167
9.5.3 Quality of Service ... 168
9.6 Types of Grid ... 168
9.7 The Globus Toolkit 2.x ... 169
9.7.1 Globus Tools ... 170
9.7.2 Security ... 171
9.7.3 Information Services ... 172
9.7.4 Data Management ... 174
9.7.5 Resource Management ... 174
9.8 Comments and Conclusion ... 176

Part III Protocols and Architectures I — P2P Applications

10 Gnutella ... 181
10.1 History of Gnutella ... 181
10.2 What Is Gnutella? ... 183
10.3 A Gnutella Scenario ... 185
10.3.1 Discovering Peers ... 185
10.3.2 Gnutella in Operation ... 186
10.3.3 Searching Within Gnutella ... 187

10.4 Gnutella 0.4 Protocol Description 187
10.4.1 Gnutella Descriptors 188
10.4.2 Gnutella Descriptor Header 189
10.4.3 Gnutella Payload: Ping 190
10.4.4 Gnutella Payload: Pong 190
10.4.5 Gnutella Payload: Query 191
10.4.6 Gnutella Payload: QueryHit 191
10.4.7 Gnutella Payload: Push 192
10.5 File Downloads 193
10.6 Gnutella Implementations 194
10.7 More Information 195
10.8 Conclusion 195

11 Scalability 197
11.1 Performance in P2P Networks 198
11.2 Unstructured P2P 199
11.2.1 Social Networks 200
11.2.2 Combining Network Topologies 202
11.2.3 The Convergence of the Napster and Gnutella Approaches 204
11.2.4 Gnutella Research Experiments 207
11.3 The Structured P2P Approach 208
11.3.1 Structure of a DHT Network 209
11.4 Further Reading 210
11.5 Conclusion 211

12 Freenet 213
12.1 Introduction 214
12.2 Freenet Routing 214
12.2.1 Populating the Freenet Network 214
12.2.2 Self-Organizing Adaptive Behaviour in Freenet 215
12.2.3 Requesting Files 217
12.2.4 Similarities with Other Peer Organization Techniques . . 218
12.3 Freenet Keys 219
12.3.1 Keyword-Signed Keys 219
12.3.2 Signed-Subspace Keys 220
12.3.3 Content-Hash Keys 221
12.3.4 Clustering Keys 223
12.4 Joining the Network 223
12.5 Conclusion 224

13 BitTorrent 227
13.1 What Is BitTorrent? 228
13.2 The BitTorrent Protocol 229
13.2.1 Terminology 229

13.2.2 Entities in a BitTorrent Application 230
13.2.3 Bencoding and Torrent Metafiles 231
13.2.4 The Tracker and File Downloading 232
13.3 BitTorrent, Inc. 234
13.4 Conclusion 235

Part IV Protocols and Architectures II — Middleware

14 Jini 239
14.1 Jini 240
14.1.1 Setting the Scene 240
14.2 Jini Architecture 241
14.2.1 Jini in Operation 242
14.3 Registering and Using Jini Services 245
14.3.1 Discovery: Finding Lookup Services 245
14.3.2 Join: Registering a Service (Jini Service) 246
14.3.3 Lookup: Finding and Using Services (Jini Client) 247
14.4 Jini: Tying Things Together 249
14.5 Organization of Jini Services 250
14.5.1 Events 250
14.6 Conclusion 251

15 Jxta 253
15.1 Background: Why Was Project Jxta Started? 253
15.1.1 Interoperability 254
15.1.2 Platform Independence 254
15.1.3 Ubiquity 255
15.2 Jxta Overview 256
15.2.1 The Jxta Architecture 257
15.2.2 Jxta Peers 257
15.2.3 Identifiers 258
15.2.4 Advertisements 259
15.2.5 Messages 259
15.2.6 Modules 260
15.3 Jxta Network Overlay 260
15.3.1 Peer Groups 260
15.3.2 Rendezvous Nodes 261
15.3.3 Pipes 262
15.3.4 Relay Nodes 264
15.4 The Jxta Protocols 264
15.4.1 The Peer Discovery Protocol 264
15.4.2 The Peer Resolver Protocol 265
15.4.3 The Peer Information Protocol 266
15.4.4 The Pipe Binding Protocol 266

15.4.5 The Endpoint Routing Protocol 266
15.4.6 The Rendezvous Protocol 266
15.5 A Jxta Scenario: Fitting Things Together 266
15.6 Jxta Environment Considerations 267
15.6.1 Security 267
15.6.2 NAT and Firewalls 268
15.7 Comment 268
15.8 Conclusion 268

16 Web Services Protocols 269
16.1 SOAP 270
16.1.1 Just Like Sending a Letter 270
16.1.2 Web Services Architecture with SOAP 272
16.1.3 The Anatomy of a SOAP Message 273
16.2 WSDL 275
16.2.1 Service Description 276
16.2.2 Implementation Details 277
16.2.3 Anatomy of a WSDL Document 278
16.3 UDDI 281
16.4 WS-Extensions 284
16.4.1 WS-Addressing 284
16.4.2 WS-Policy 286
16.4.3 Security Specifications 286
16.4.4 WS-Transfer 287
16.4.5 WS-Eventing 288
16.4.6 WS-ReliableMessaging 288
16.4.7 WS-Coordination 289
16.5 Conclusion 289

17 OGSA 291
17.1 OGSA 292
17.1.1 Grid Services 292
17.1.2 Virtual Services 294
17.1.3 OGSA Architecture 295
17.2 OGSI 296
17.2.1 Globus Toolkit, Version 3 298
17.3 WS-RF 299
17.3.1 Problems with OGSI 300
17.3.2 The Specifications 301
17.3.3 WS-Resources 302
17.3.4 WS-ResourceProperties 302
17.3.5 WS-Notification 305
17.3.6 The Future of WS-RF 306
17.4 Higher Level Interfaces 307
17.4.1 Job Submission Description Language 307

17.4.2 Basic Execution Service ... 309
17.5 Conclusion ... 312

18 Web 2.0 ... 313
18.1 The Web as Platform ... 314
18.1.1 The Long Tail ... 316
18.2 Technologies and APIs ... 318
18.2.1 Ajax (formerly AJAX) ... 318
18.2.2 Application Programming Interfaces (APIs) ... 322
18.2.3 Microformats ... 325
18.2.4 Syndication ... 327
18.2.5 Web Application Description Language ... 334
18.3 Conclusion ... 337

19 On the Horizon ... 339
19.1 Computing in the Cloud ... 339
19.2 Ubiquitous Computing ... 341
19.2.1 *Everyware* ... 343
19.2.2 Spimes ... 345
19.3 Conclusion ... 346

Part V Deployment

20 Distributed Object Deployment Using Jini ... 349
20.1 RMI Security ... 349
20.2 An RMI Application ... 350
20.2.1 The Java Proxy ... 350
20.2.2 The Server ... 351
20.2.3 The Client ... 353
20.2.4 Setting Up the Environment ... 355
20.3 A Jini Application ... 355
20.3.1 The Remote Interface ... 356
20.3.2 The Server ... 356
20.3.3 The Client ... 358
20.4 Running Jini Applications ... 360
20.4.1 HTTP Server ... 360
20.4.2 RMID Daemon ... 361
20.4.3 The Jini Lookup Service ... 361
20.4.4 Running the Service ... 361
20.5 Conclusion ... 362

21 P2P Deployment Using Jxta ... 363
21.1 Example One: Starting the Jxta Platform ... 364
21.1.1 Peer Configuration Using Jxta ... 365
21.1.2 Using the Jxta Configurator ... 366
21.2 Example Two: Using Jxta Pipes ... 369
21.2.1 Running the Examples ... 377
21.3 P2P Environment: The Jxta Approach ... 378
21.3.1 Jxta and P2P Advert Availability ... 378
21.3.2 Expiration of Adverts ... 379
21.4 Conclusion ... 380

22 Web Services Deployment ... 381
22.1 Data Binding ... 382
22.2 Setup ... 383
22.3 Container Classes ... 384
22.3.1 VEvent Class ... 384
22.3.2 VCard Class ... 387
22.4 Server Implementation ... 390
22.5 Service WSDL ... 395
22.6 Client Implementation ... 397
22.6.1 Standard Client ... 398
22.6.2 Dynamic Client ... 404
22.7 Conclusion ... 409

23 Web Deployment Using Atom ... 411
23.1 Setup ... 412
23.2 Utility Classes ... 413
23.3 The Atom Server ... 414
23.4 Atom Client ... 421
23.5 Running the Service and Client ... 425
23.6 Conclusion ... 428
23.7 Ancillary Code ... 428

A Want to Find Out More? ... 435
A.1 The Web ... 435
A.2 Web 2.0 ... 436
A.3 Web Services ... 436
A.4 Grid Computing ... 437
A.5 P2P Tools and Software ... 438
A.6 Distributed Object Systems ... 440
A.7 Underlying Transport and Discovery Protocols ... 440

B RSA Algorithm 441

References 443

Index 455

Errata 463

Part I

Common Themes

1 Introduction

> *"A distributed system is one in which the failure of a computer you didn't even know existed can render your own computer unusable."*
> *Leslie Lamport*

The field of distributed systems is characterized by rapid change and conflicting ideologies, approaches and vested interests. In its short history it has seen a number of different paradigms gaining interest and adoption before being vanquished by newer, more virile, movements. However, when a technology fades from the limelight, it often re-emerges at a later date under a new banner. As a result, there is a continuous intermixing of core, reusable concepts, with new innovations.

In the 1990s, there were two primary approaches to distributed systems. The Web represented a human-oriented, distributed information space rather than a computing program [1]. On the other hand, distributed object technologies such as CORBA [2] and DCOM [3] were primarily attempting to create distributed environments that seamlessly emulated local computer applications while providing the benefits of access to networked resources. But despite the initial vision of the Web as a space which many would contribute to, publishing became the preserve of the few with most users merely accessing data, not creating it. Meanwhile distributed object systems were growing in terms of their capabilities but becoming more heavyweight, proprietary and complex in the process.

Just after the turn of the millennium, there was an explosion of applications and middleware employing the use of new techniques, including peer-to-peer (P2P) and Grid-computing technologies. P2P was addressing issues that had arisen from the immense growth of the Internet and the Web, in particular, how the many, who were mere consumers of Web information, might be able to contribute in more active ways. Grid computing, on the other hand, was considering how to integrate the vast processing and data storage capabilities becoming available to governments and institutions on a massive scale.

By 2001, P2P had become ingrained in current grass-roots Internet culture through applications like Gnutella [4], Napster [5] and BitTorrent [6]. It appeared in several popular magazines including the *Red Herring* and *Wired*, and was frequently quoted as being crowned by *Fortune* as one of the four technologies that will shape the Internet's future. The popularity of P2P spread through to academic and industrial circles, being propelled by media and widespread debate both in the courtroom and out. However, such enormous hype and controversy has led to the mistrust of such technology as a serious distributed systems platform for future computing, but in reality, there is significant substance as we shall see. Nowadays, however, P2P is less of a buzzword in marketing and more of a grown-up technology offering numerous scalable techniques for distributed systems and much research has been conducted in order to apply these techniques in many different areas.

In parallel, there was an overwhelming interest in Grid computing, which attempted to build the infrastructure to enable on-demand computing in a similar fashion to the way we access other utilities now, e.g., electricity. Further, the introduction of the Open Grid Services Architecture (OGSA) [7] has aligned this vision with the technological machine-to-machine capabilities of Web Services (see Chapter 7). This convergence has gained a significant input from both commercial and non-commercial organizations ([8] and [9]) and has a firm grounding in standardized Web technologies, which could perhaps even lead to the kind of ubiquitous uptake necessary for such an infrastructure to be globally deployed.

Big *S*, little *s*

There is still no consensus on whether services that use the technologies of SOAP and WSDL should be called Web Services *with an uppercase 'S' or not. For the sake of clarity, in this book we use the term* Web Services *to mean those components that employ SOAP, WSDL and other related specifications. The term* Web services *(with a lowercase 's') we take to mean a broader set of services that utilize Web technologies in some way, for example interfaces defined using HTTP methods.*

Although the underlying philosophies of Grid computing and P2P are different, they both are attempting to solve the same problem, that is, to create a *virtual overlay* [10] over the existing Internet to enable collaboration and sharing of resources [11]. However, in implementation, the approaches differ greatly. Whilst Grid computing connects virtual organizations [12] that can cooperate in a collaborative fashion, P2P connects individual users using highly transient devices and computers living at the *edges of the Internet* [13] (i.e., behind NAT, firewalls, etc).

After the dot-com bubble burst in 2001, new concepts of what the Web could and should be were evolving — what is now collectively termed Web 2.0. These new concepts were based on themes such as participation, mass publication and lightweight, scalable services. While some P2P technologies were being aligned with Web 2.0 such as BitTorrent, in general the development of social networking sites such as MySpace [14] and Facebook [15] and the explosion of weblogs were scratching the itches that previous P2P technologies had been satisfying. This time around, however, the underlying topologies were highly centralized, with traffic moving from many users to a few highly popular sites and services.

While the Web was reinventing itself, the business community was spending time creating the next-generation specifications that would address the problems of distributed object technologies, in the guise of Web Services and Service-Oriented Architecture. These began to attract a lot of interest, but also had their detractors, in particular because Web Services use the Web but do not make use of its underlying principles. The resulting SOAP versus REST battle was a bitter argument about what the Web is, what it can be used for, and how it should be used. By 2006 the battle had ended in a truce rather than a resounding victory for either side.

The name of this edition of the book *Evolving Distributed Communities* comes from the growing understanding that different approaches and paradigms are suited to the communities that require them. As distributed technologies become more mature and are applied in more complex scenarios and situations, it may be that divisions between approaches are less starkly drawn allowing hybrid and integrated solutions to emerge. In this book, therefore, the key influential technologies are addressed that will help to shape the next-generation Internet. P2P and distributed object-based technologies, through to the promised pervasive deployment of Grid computing combined with Web services, both in SOAP and RESTful incarnations, will be needed in order to address the fundamental issues of creating a scalable ubiquitous next-generation computing infrastructure. Specifically, a comprehensive overview of current distributed-systems technologies is given, covering environments, such as the Web (Chapter 5), P2P (Chapter 6), Web Services (Chapter 7), Distributed Objects (Chapter 8) and Grid computing (Chapter 9). We then cover a number of P2P applications (Gnutella, Freenet, BitTorrent) and scalability considerations in Chapters 10 to 13. We then take a look at a number of middleware toolkits and approaches in Chapters 14 through 18. Finally, we present examples of deployment of these middleware toolkits in Chapters 20 to 23.

1.1 Introduction to Distributed Systems

> *"A distributed system is a collection of independent computers that appears to its users as a single coherent system."[16]*

There are two aspects to such a system: hardware and software. The hardware machines must be autonomous and the software must be organized in such a way as to make the users think that they are dealing with a single system. Expanding on these fundamentals, distributed systems typically have the following characteristics; they should:

- be capable of dealing with heterogeneous devices, i.e., various vendors, software stacks and operating systems should be able to interoperate
- be easy to expand and scale
- be permanently available (even though parts of it may not be)
- hide communication from the users.

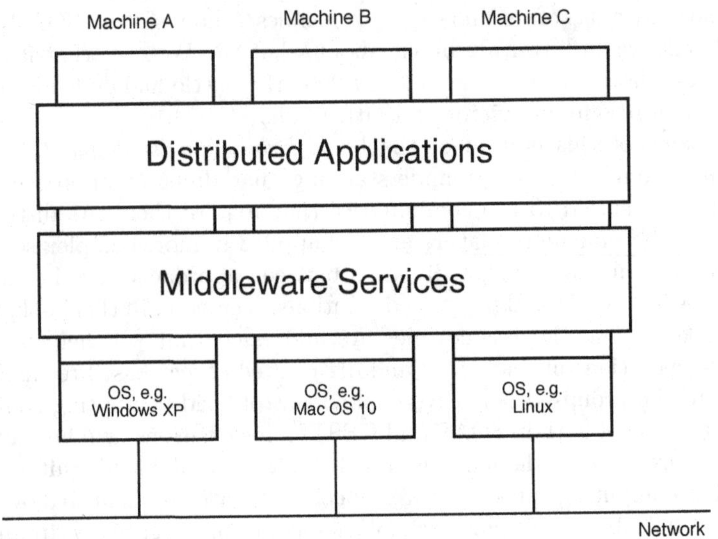

Fig. 1.1. The role of **middleware** in a distributed system; it hides the underlying infrastructure away from the application and user level.

In order for a distributed system to support a collection of heterogeneous computers and networks while offering a single system view, the software stack is often divided into two layers. At the higher layers, there are applications (and users) and at the lower layer there is **middleware**, which interacts with the underlying networks and computer systems to give applications and users the transparency they need (see Fig. 1.1).

Middleware abstracts the underlying mechanisms and protocols from the application developer and provides a collection of high-level capabilities to make it easier for programmers to develop and deploy their applications. For example, within the middleware layer, there may be simple abstract communication calls that do not specify which underlying mechanisms they actually use, e.g., TCP/IP, UDP, Bluetooth, etc. Such concrete deployment bindings are often decided at run time through configuration files or dynamically, thereby being dependent on the particular deployment environment.

Middleware therefore provides the *virtual overlay* across the distributed resources to enable transparent deployment across the underlying infrastructures. In this book, we will take a look at a number of different approaches in designing the middleware abstraction layer by identifying the kinds of capabilities that are exposed by the various types.

1.2 Terminology

Often, a number of terms are used to define a device or capability on a distributed network, e.g., node, resource, peer, agent, service, server, etc. In this section, common definitions are given which are used throughout this book. The definitions presented here do represent a compromise, however, because often certain distributed entities are not identified in all systems in the same way. Therefore, wherever appropriate, the terminology provided here is given within the context of the system they are described within. The terms are defined as follows:

- **Resource:** any hardware or software entity being represented or shared on a distributed network. For example, a resource could be any of the following: a computer; a file storage system; a file; a communication channel; a service, i.e., algorithm/function call; and so on.
- **Node:** a generic term used to represent any device on a distributed network. A node that performs one (or more) capabilities is often exposed as a service.
- **Client:** is a consumer of information, e.g., a Web browser.
- **Server:** is a provider of information, e.g., a Web server or a peer offering a file-sharing service.
- **Service:** can be seen as "a network-enabled entity that provides some capability" [7]; e.g., a simple Web server could just provide a remote HTTP file-retrieval service. A single device can expose several capabilities as individual services.
- **Peer:** a peer is a device that acts as both a consumer and provider of information.

Figure 1.2 organizes these terms by associating relationships between the various terminologies. Here, we can see that any *device* is a entity on the network. Devices can also be referred to in many different ways, e.g., a node, computer, PDA, peer, etc. Each *device* can run any number of *clients*, *servers*, *services* or *peers*. A peer is a special kind of node, which acts as both a client and a server.

There is often confusion about the term *resource*. The easiest way to think of a resource is any capability that is shared on a distributed network. Resources can be exposed in a number of ways and can also be used to represent

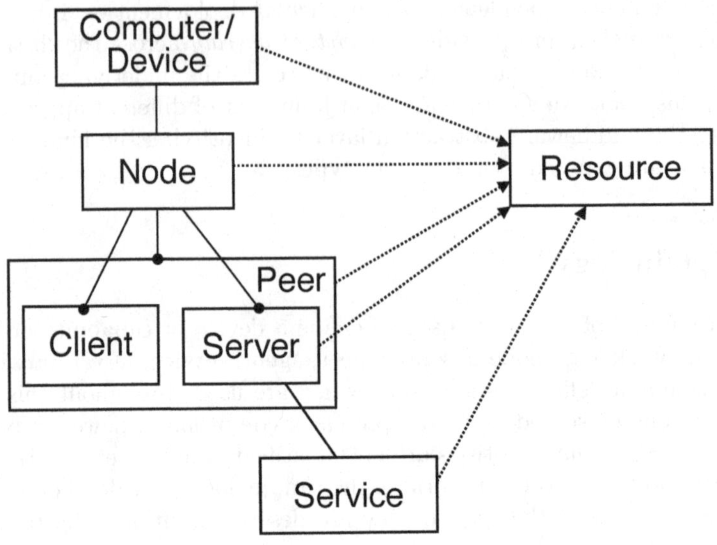

Fig. 1.2. An overview of the terms used to describe distributed resources.

a number of physical or virtual entities. For example, you can share the following resources: files, CPU cycles, storage capabilities (i.e., a file system), a service, e.g., a Web server, and so on. Therefore, everything in Figure 1.2 is a resource except a client, who generally does not make anything available to share.

A service is a software entity that can be used to represent resources, and therefore capabilities, on a network. There are numerous examples, e.g., Web servers, Web Services, services on the Web, Jini services, Jxta peers providing a service, and so on. In simple terms, services can be thought of as the network counterparts of local function calls. Services receive a request (just like the arguments to a function call) and (optionally) return a response (as do local function calls). To illustrate this analogy, consider the functionality of a simplified HTTP Web server, which serves HTML files: it receives a request for an HTML file and returns the contents of that file, if found, to the client. If this was implemented as a local function call in Java, it might look something like this:

String getWebPage(String httpfile)

This simple function call takes a file-name argument (including the protocol and directory, e.g., http://www.awebsite.com/mydir/myfilename.html) and it returns the contents of that local file within a Java *String* object.

This is analogous to the real world counterpart; that is, the user would provide an HTTP address (e.g., *http://www.google.com/index.html*) and this would be converted into a remote request to the specified Web server (e.g., http://www.google.com) with the requested file (index.html). The entire process would involve the use of the DNS (Domain Name Service) and perhaps some back-end services for generating content, but the client (e.g., the Web browser) performs the same operation as our simple local reader and then renders the information in a specific way for the user, i.e., using HTML.

1.3 Centralized and Decentralized Systems

In this section, the middleware and systems outlined in this book are classified onto a taxonomy according to a scale ranging between centralized and decentralized. The distributed architectures are divided into categories that define an axis on the comparison space. On one side of this spectrum, we have completely centralized systems, e.g., typical client/server-based systems, and on the other side, we have completely decentralized systems, e.g., Gnutella. In the center, where the majority of systems live, is a mix of the two extremes in the form of hybrid systems, e.g., brokered, where a system may broker the functionality or communication request to another service. This taxonomy sets the scene for the specifics of each system which will be outlined in the chapters to follow and serves as a simple look-up table for determining a system's high-level behaviour.

Boundaries in any distributed taxonomy, however, are not simple and there are a number of factors that can determine the centralized nature of a system. Even systems that are considered fully decentralized can, in practice, employ some degree of centralization, albeit often in a self-organizing fashion [17]. Typically, decentralized systems adopt immense redundancy, both in the discovering of information and content, by dynamically repeating information across many other peers on the network.

Broadly speaking, there are three areas that determine whether a system is centralized or decentralized:

- Resource Discovery
- Resource Availability
- Resource Communication

All three are dependent on both demand, i.e., the number of users for a system, and the environment they are operating within, e.g., a wireless environment might need to be more redundancy than a wired one. Another important consideration, therefore, to bear in mind as we talk about the degree of centralization of systems is that of scalability. When we say a resource is centralized, we do not mean to imply that there is only one server serving the information; rather, we mean that there are a fixed number of servers (or even possibly one) providing the information to the consumers and this is unrelated to the number of clients requiring access to this resource. Obviously, there are many levels of granularities here and hence the adoption of a sliding scale, illustrating the various levels on a resource-organization continuum.

1.3.1 Resource Discovery

Within any distributed system, there needs to be a mechanism for discovering resources. A service which supplies discovery information is called a *discovery service* (e.g., DNS, Jini Lookup, Jxta Rendezvous, JNDI, UDDI, etc.). There are a number of mechanisms for discovering resources, which are often highly dependent on the type of application or middleware. For example, resource discovery can be organized centrally, e.g., UDDI, or decentrally, e.g., Gnutella.

> **What's in a Name?**
> *Domain names are used to locate hosts because they are easier to remember than IP addresses and because the name does not represent an actual address. Hence machines that are physically unconnected can be logically grouped by name, and the IP address that is mapped to a name can change. A domain name is made up of* ***labels*** *separated by dots (e.g.,* ***www.cs.cf.ac.uk****). The rightmost label is the top level domain (****uk****). Each subsequent label moving from right to left represents a subdomain of the top level domain. A domain may contain more than one subdomain. For example,* ***uk*** *contains* ***co*** *and* ***ac*** *amongst others. Likewise,* ***co.uk*** *and* ***ac.uk*** *contain many subdomains. Hence a domain namespace can be divided into a tree with the top level domain as the root, and its subdomains as child nodes. Each node in the domain name tree is served by an authoritative DNS nameserver. DNS nameservers publish information about the domains under their authority and the nameservers of any domains beneath them in the tree. When resolving a domain name, these servers associated with the labels in the address are iteratively queried for either a DNS server beneath it, or the IP address of the requested host. In practice, caching of known nameservers plays an important role in reducing the amount of queries made to the system.*

Discovery is typically a two-stage process. First, the discovery service needs to be located; then the relevant information is retrieved. The mechanism of how the information is retrieved can be highly decentralized (as in the lower layers of DNS), even though access to the discovery service is centralized. Here, we are concerned about the discovery mechanism as a whole. Therefore, a system that has centralized access to a decentralized search is factored by its lowest common denominator, i.e., the centralized access. There are two examples given below that illustrate this.

As our first example, let's consider the very low-level operation of DNS which is used to look up an Internet IP address. DNS works in much the same way as a telephone book. You give a DNS an Internet site name (e.g., www.cs.cf.ac.uk) and DNS returns to you the Internet Protocol (IP) address (e.g., 131.251.49.190) for locating this site. In the same way as you keep a list of name/number pairs on your mobile phone, DNS keeps a list of name/IP number pairs.

DNS is not centralized in structure but the access to the discovery service certainly is because there are generally only a couple of specified hosts that act as DNS servers. Typically, users specify a small number of DNS servers (e.g., one or two), which are narrow relative to the number of services available to it. If these servers go down, then access to DNS information is disabled. However, behind this small gateway of hosts, the storage of DNS information is massively hierarchical, employing an efficient decentralized look-up mechanism that is spread amongst many hosts.

Another illustration here is the Web site Google. Google is a centralized Web server in the sense that there is only one Google machine (at a specific time) that binds to the address http://www.google.com. When we ask DNS to provide the Google address, using "nslookup", it says that there is a "non-authoritative answer" and it returns several addresses including, at the time of writing, the IP address 216.239.59.104, which will allow you to contact a Google server directly. Google is a Web search engine that is used by millions of people daily and consequently it stores a massive number of entries. To access this information, it relies on a back-end database that uses a large parallel cluster of machines to provide the service. Therefore, the access and storage of this information, from a user's perspective, is somewhat centralized but from a search or computational perspective, it is certainly distributed across many machines.

These two examples are simple but somewhat illustrative of the high-level organisation of discovery components. Most middleware systems, however, typically use more sophisticated mechanisms and can involve the use of a combination of discovery techniques, such as directory services and multicast. These techniques are described in detail in Chapter 2.

1.3.2 Resource Availability

Another important factor is the availability of resources. Again, Web servers fall into the centralized category here because there is generally only one IP address that hosts a particular site. If that machine goes down, then the Web site is unavailable. Of course, machines could be made fault tolerant by replicating the Web site and employing some internal switching mechanisms but in most cases, the availability of the IP address remains the same.

Other systems, however, use a more decentralized approach by offering many duplicate services that can perform the same functionality. Resource availability is tied in closely to resource discovery. There are many examples here but to illustrate various availability levels, let's briefly consider the sharing of files on the Internet through the use of three approaches, which are illustrated in Fig. 1.3:

- MP3.com

- Napster
- Gnutella.

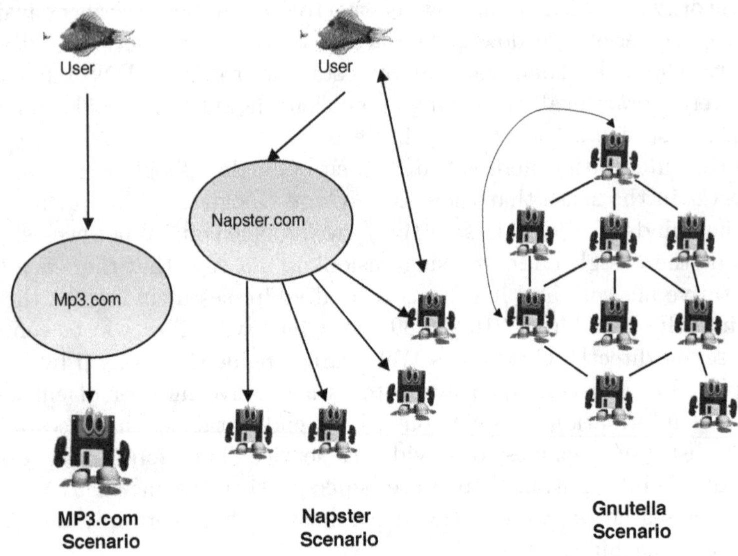

Fig. 1.3. A comparison of service availability from centralized, brokered and decentralized systems.

MP3.com contains a number of MP3 files that are stored locally at (or behind) the Web site. If the Web site or the hard disk(s) containing the database goes down, then users have no access to the content.

In the Napster model, on the other hand, MP3 files are stored on the actual users' machines and *napster.com* is used as a massive index (or meeting place) for connecting users. Users connect to Napster to search for the files they desire and thereafter connect to users directly to download the file. Therefore, each MP3 file is distributed across a number of servers making it more reliable against failure.

However, as the search is centralized, it is dependent on the availability of the main Web site; i.e., if the Web site goes down, then access to the MP3 files would also be lost. Interestingly, the difference between MP3.com and Napster is smaller than you may think: one centralizes the files, whilst the other centralizes the addresses of the files. Either is susceptible to failure if the Web site goes down. The difference in Napster's case is that, if the Web site goes down, then current users can still finish downloading the current files they have discovered since the communication is decentralized from the main search engine. Therefore, if a user has already located the file and initiated the download process, then the availability of the Web site does not matter and they can quite happily carry on using the service (but not search for more files).

Third, let's consider the Gnutella model. Gnutella does not have a centralized search facility nor a central storage facility for the files. Each user in the network runs a *servent* (a client and a server), which allows him/her to act as both a provider and consumer of information (as in Napster) but furthermore acts as a search facility also. Servents search for other files by contacting other servents they are connected to, and these servents connect to the servents they are connected to and so on. Therefore, if any of the servents are unavailable, users can almost certainly still reach the file they require (assuming it is available at all).

Here, therefore, it is important to insert redundancy in both the discovery and availability of the resources for a system to be truly robust against single-point failure. Often, when there are a number of duplicated resources available but the discovery of such resources is centralized, we call this a brokered system; i.e., the discovery service brokers the request to another service. Some examples of brokered systems include Napster, Jini, ICQ and Corba.

1.3.3 Resource Communication

The last factor is that of resource communication. There are two methods of communication between resources of a distributed system:

1. **Brokered Communication**: where the communication is always passed through a central server and therefore a resource does not have to reference the other resource directly.
2. **Point-to-Point (or Peer-to-Peer) Communication**: this involves a direct connection (although this connection may be multi-hop) between the sender and the receiver. In this case, the sender is aware of the receiver's location.

Both forms of communication have their implications on the centralized nature of the systems. In the first case for brokered communication, there is always a central server which passes the information between one resource and another (i.e., centralized). Further, it is almost certainly the case that such systems are centralized from the resource discovery and availability standpoints also, since this level of communication implies fundamental central organization. Some examples here are J2EE, JMS chat and many publish/subscribe systems.

Second, there are many systems that use point-to-point connections, e.g., Napster and Gnutella, but so do Web servers! Therefore, this category is split horizontally across the scale and the significance here is in the centralization of the communication with respect to the types of connections.

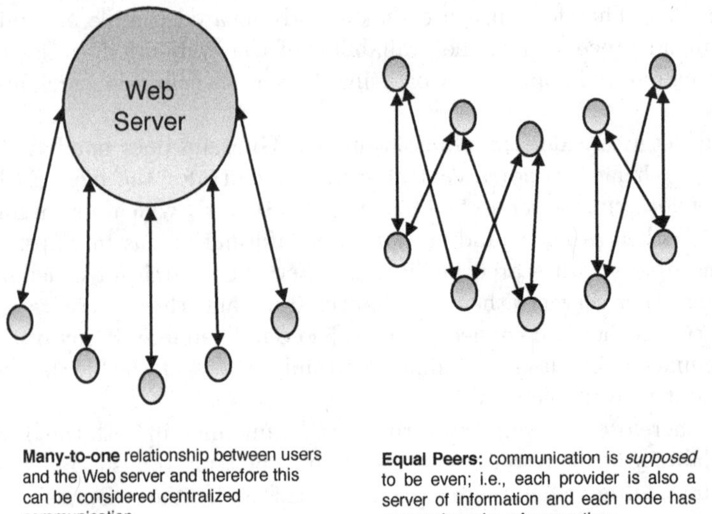

Web
Server
Many-to-one relationship between users and the Web server and therefore this can be considered centralized communication
Equal Peers: communication is *supposed* to be even; i.e., each provider is also a server of information and each node has an equal number of connections

Fig. 1.4. The centralization of communication: a truly decentralized system would have even connections across hosts, rather than a many-to-one type of connectivity.

For example, in the Web server example, communication always originates from the user. There exists a **many-to-one** relationship between users and the Web server and therefore this is considered centralized communication. This is illustrated in Fig. 1.4, where an obvious centralized communication pattern is seen for the Web server case.

However, in more decentralized systems, such as Napster and Gnutella, communication is more evenly distributed across the resources; i.e., each provider of information is also a server of information, and therefore the connectivity leans more towards a one-to-one connectivity rather than many-to-one. This equal distribution across the resource (known as equal peers) decentralizes communication across the entire system. However, in practice this is almost never the case because of the behavioural patterns depicted by users of such networks; e.g., some users do not share files and others share many (see Section 11.2.4).

1.4 Taxonomy Dependency Considerations

There are strong dependencies between resource availability, discovery and communication, which are important in the application of the taxonomy to real-world systems. For example, the Web as a whole contains examples that range from centralized usage to completely decentralized usage. Whilst access to one Web site by many users might be considered centralized, such activity is happening in parallel over multiple sites by multiple users simultaneously. Therefore, the Web can be classified differently depending on the granularity of one's view and the activity that is being addressed. Consider the following two Web scenarios:

- Find and download the Safari Web browser application.
- Find and read news items about a particular headline.

In the first case, the availability is centralized as downloading the application is restricted to *http://www.mac.com*. However, the discovery to this resource is still decentralized; that is, there are many search sites that have the location of the download page for the Safari browser. Does this mean therefore that this scenario is decentralized overall? Not always, because in most cases **resource discovery is dependent on resource availability**. Therefore, as a general rule, discovery is bound by availability — the more decentralized the availability, the more likely it will be that discovery is also more decentralized. Likewise the degree of centralization of resource communication is also bound by the availability. For example, while a system may be globally highly decentralized in terms of communication, high demand for a particular resource located on a single node will push the overall communication pattern towards a centralized architecture.

In the second example, availability is decentralized because there are almost certainly a number of sites that have news articles about the story that you are interested in (each with different content, e.g., The Times, Washington Post, Daily Mail and so on). Therefore, the level of decentralization of discovery of these Web locations will be reflected in the increased availability of the resource. Further, communication is also somewhat decentralized because many users can connect to these different Web sites simultaneously. However, even in this example, the ratio between the number of users and the servers is relatively high; that is, the number of consumers is far larger than the resource availability (i.e., the articles). It follows therefore that in cases where the cardinality of the consumers far outweighs the cardinality of the suppliers, such a system approaches a somewhat centralized architecture. These dependencies are outlined in Figure 1.5.

The point of choosing a particular distributed architecture is really about the issue of scalability. As long as the load that servers can bear meets the demand of consumers, then the network will scale proportionally. However, demand may not be continuous or even easily predictable, making system design more complex. For example, certain systems may have predictable peaks in demand, such as enrollment day at a university, or an annual online tax filing deadline. Other systems may provide services that must respond to unexpected events such as freak weather conditions or large-scale medical emergencies. It is not uncommon that such systems struggle when demand rises

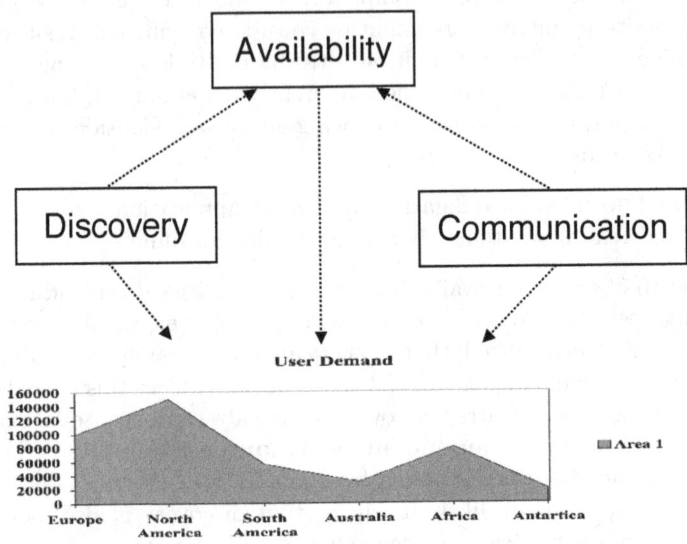

Fig. 1.5. Dependency of taxonomy criteria. Both communication and discovery are dependent on the availability of resources and the design of a distributed system as a whole is dependent on usage characteristics.

because the system has been designed against the common usage patterns, not the exceptional.

Furthermore, scalability can also be considered in terms of cost. High demand for centrally available, and potentially large resources, requires serious financial muscle. For example, the content delivery network provider, Limelight Networks, was reportedly receiving a monthly income from YouTube of 4 million dollars in 2006 [18]. Hence systems and applications that cannot sustain high income will crack under the strain of centralized resource communication.

The decision therefore in considering which architecture to employ depends completely on the ratios and numbers of consumers versus providers of information, hence the lower part of the dependency diagram in Figure 1.5. If this ratio is manageable, then the network will scale. However, as numbers of participants get extremely large or if the data served becomes large then this choosing the correct distributed architecture becomes very much more of an issue. P2P applications, for example, employ a decentralized mechanism because the size of data shared (5Mb to 2 GB) and the numbers of consumers (millions) mean that attention must be paid to the distribution of the resources and such a ratio may well not work well. Scalability issues are discussed in more detail in Chapter 11.

In the next section, we present a number of examples and employ a simplification by implying application-specific ratios for the individual approximate scores by pre-considering usage patterns before grading. The scores for each application and middleware, however, are indicative and by no means do the scales represent precise measurements.

1.5 Examples of Distributed Applications

In this section, the criteria defining the taxonomy are applied to several well-known examples of existing distributed applications and middleware. The examples given here serve as a point of reference for each chapter that describes the particular application or middleware in more detail.

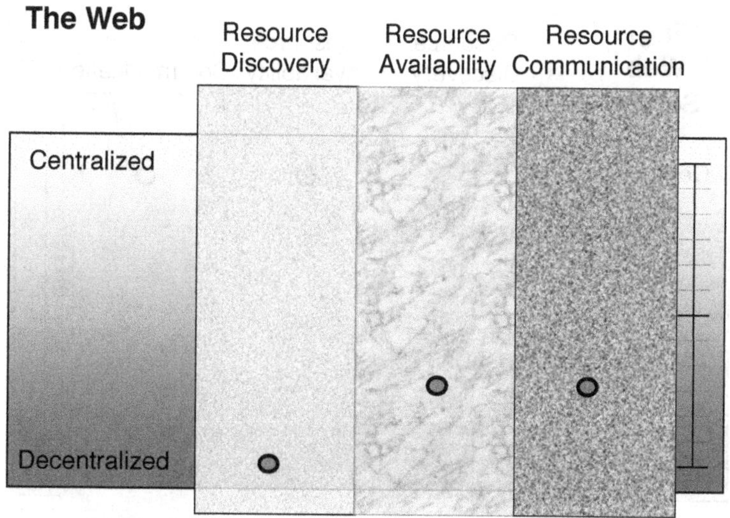

Fig. 1.6. Taxonomy for the Web.

1.5.1 The Web: Decentralized

As discussed in the previous section the Web is a completely decentralized set of resources and dependent completely on the Web application that is being deployed using it. For example, as we will see in BitTorrent in Chapter 13, the Web is used to search and launch multiple BitTorrent clients and servers that interact in a completely decentralized fashion and are coordinated on a per file basis (as groups) using the BitTorrent trackers. Alternatively, Web sites that are accessed primarily by multiple users in a many-to-one relationship are far more central in their dependencies for interaction. Hence, in reality the Web can represent any combination of the taxonomy. Here, we show a more specific and yet general applicable example when the Web is used to search for news articles. Here, there are far more users than sources for the data, hence not completely decentralized in terms of the dependency between entities but still the system as a whole offers a scalable solution with a general high availability of the data sources through multiple news Web sites.

1.5.2 A Stand-Alone Web Server: Centralized

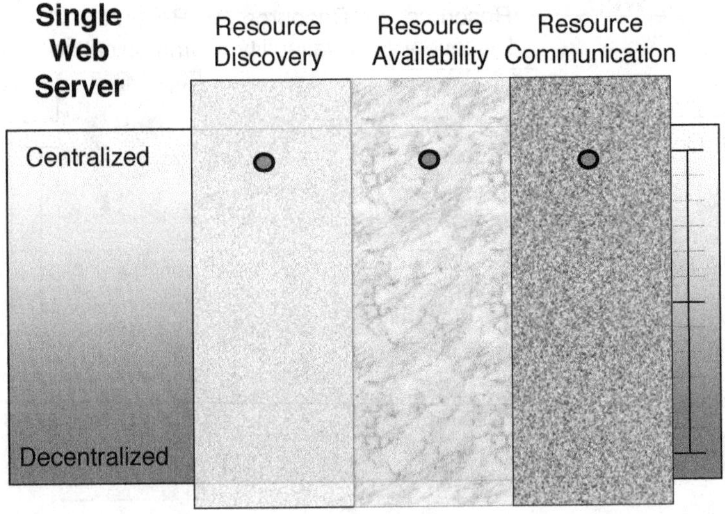

Fig. 1.7. Taxonomy for a Web server.

A good example of a centralized system is a Web server. Clients (i.e., users) use their Web browser to navigate Web pages on one or more Web sites. Each Web site is static to the particular domain with which it is associated. A Web server therefore in this sense is centralized in every sense. It has centralized discovery (through DNS), it is either available or not and all communication is centralized to the particular Web server being contacted. Communication is point to point but there is a many-to-one relationship between the users of this service and the server itself.

The circles in Fig. 1.7 show the position where a Web server lies on the centralized/decentralized scale for the three categories listed: resource discovery, resource availability and resource communication. The scale at the right-hand side of this graph indicates the broad granularity of our measurements (finer levels would not really change the outcome much anyway) but somewhere around the mid-point would denote the brokered case.

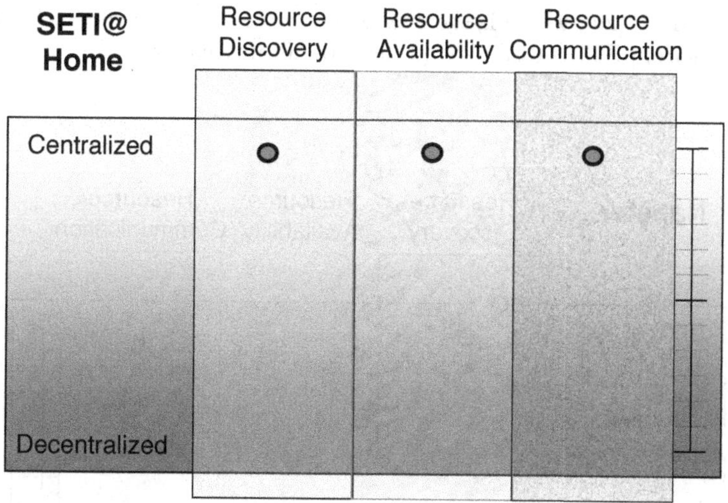

Fig. 1.8. Taxonomy for SETI@home.

With brokering, typically one service brokers the request to another. DNS does not fall into this category since it has no intrinsic functionality or semantics itself. Web forwarding is a kind of brokering in this sense but this is a one-to-one forwarding. Typically, brokering involves making a decision about where to broker the request and therefore typically, there are many services offering the same functionality from which to choose. Communication can also be brokered by the server acting as a coordinator between the sender and receiver.

1.5.3 SETI@home: Centralized

SETI@home (Search for Extraterrestrial Intelligence) [19] is a project that analyses data from a radio telescope to search for signs of extraterrestrial life. Each user who takes part in this project downloads a data set and executes some signal-processing tasks. The actual program is implemented as a screen saver and therefore only operates when the computer is idle. The SETI@home project has used over a billion years of CPU time at the time of writing.

Here, the entire system is run from the SETI@home Web site. Users download the code and also the data when they are available to process. Therefore, the discovery is centralized (DNS) and the communication is centralized to the Web site. Resource availability is also centralized because without the availability of the Web site, the many SETI nodes cannot do anything since they need this server to download the next chunk of data. This taxonomy also applies to BOINC [20], which is the new open source release of the SETI@home infrastructure. SETI is discussed in more detail in Chapter 6.

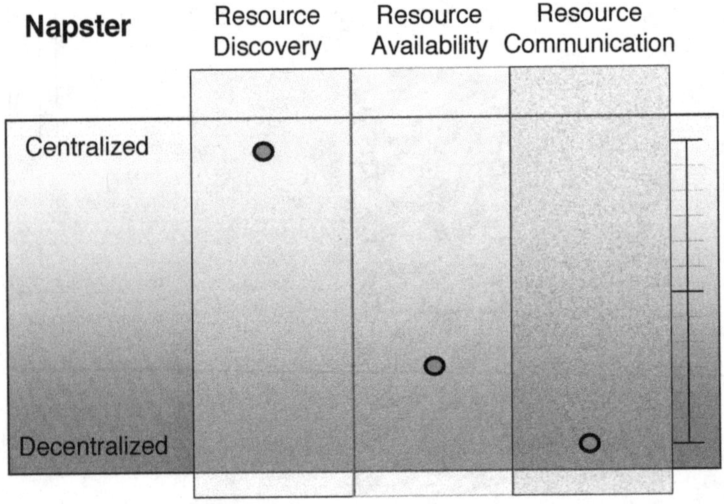

Fig. 1.9. Taxonomy for Napster.

1.5.4 Napster: Brokered

A good example of a brokered system is Napster [5]. Napster stores information about the location of peers and music files in a centralized way but then lets the peers communicate directly when they transfer files.

Here therefore, the discovery and availability are centralized through the Napster Web site but the communication between the peers is decentralized. However, the availability of the resources (i.e., files) is less centralized to a degree because users can still download the file even if the Napster server goes down. However, users cannot search for new resources when the Web site is unavailable and therefore limited in this respect. Napster is described in more detail in Chapter 6.

1.5.5 Gnutella: Decentralized

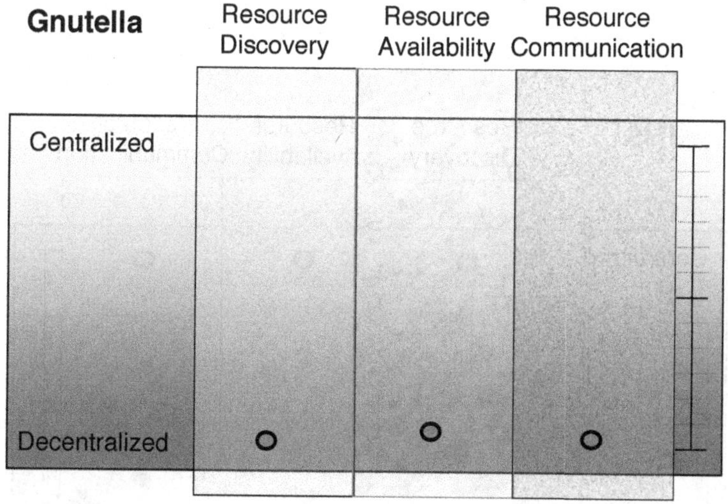

Fig. 1.10. Taxonomy for Gnutella.

A popular example of a decentralized system is Gnutella [4] where discovery, availability and communication are completely decentralized over the network. Gnutella is discussed in detail in Chapter 10.

In theory, Gnutella is completely decentralized but in practice is this really true? Decentralized networks are inherently self-organizing and so it is not only possible but indeed very likely that strong servers of information (the so-called super-peers in Gnutella) could easily turn a decentralized network into a semi-centralized one when peers contain an uneven amount of content. Whether this is achieved by behavioural patterns or by artificially creating a centralized-decentralized structure, the resulting network is no longer completely decentralized. This is discussed in detail in Chapter 11.

It is no coincidence, for example, that this evolution of hybrid decentralized and centralized systems echoes the evolution of other types of systems such as Usenet [21]. The history of Usenet shows us that peer-to-peer (decentralization) and client/server (centralization) are not mutually exclusive. Usenet was originally peer-to-peer. Sites connected via a modem and agreed to exchange information (news and mail) with each other (UUCP). However, over time, it became obvious that certain sites had better servers than others and these sites went on to form the Usenet backbone. Today, the volume of Usenet is enormous and servers on the backbone can elect how much information they want to serve and they get added to the Usenet network in a decentralized fashion. Even the addition of new newsgroups is not centralized as users have to vote for a newsgroup before it gets initiated.

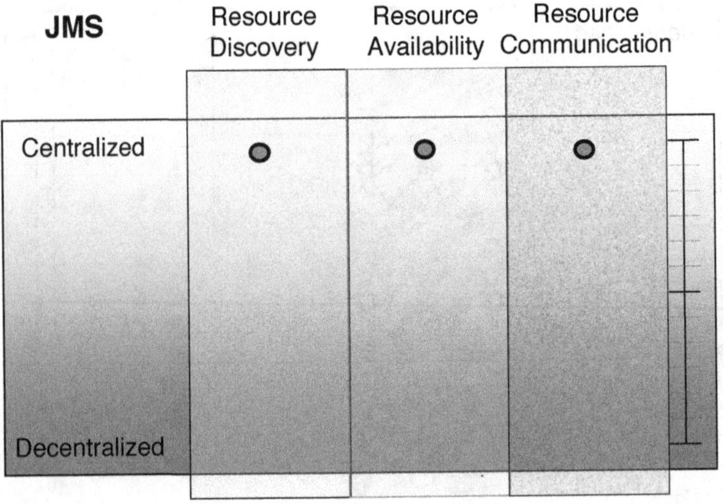

Fig. 1.11. Taxonomy for JMS.

1.6 Examples of Middleware

1.6.1 J2EE and JMS: Centralized

The Java development kit enterprise edition J2EE [22] is an example of a centrally controlled system. Here, one Web site is the manager of all interaction between clients. Clients in the Java Messaging System (JMS) do not know the whereabouts of other clients because this knowledge is stored within the central manager on the J2EE server. The entire system is based around a Web site and therefore the discovery is central.

JMS is used as a publish/subscribe mechanism within the J2EE environment (amongst other things) and is quite typical of other messaging systems, e.g., ICQ where messages are brokered through a central server in order to get to their destination. Therefore, the communication is brokered through the Web site. Further, there is only one copy of the Web site (typically these are quite complicated to set up) and therefore the availability is centralized also.

1.6.2 Jini: Brokered

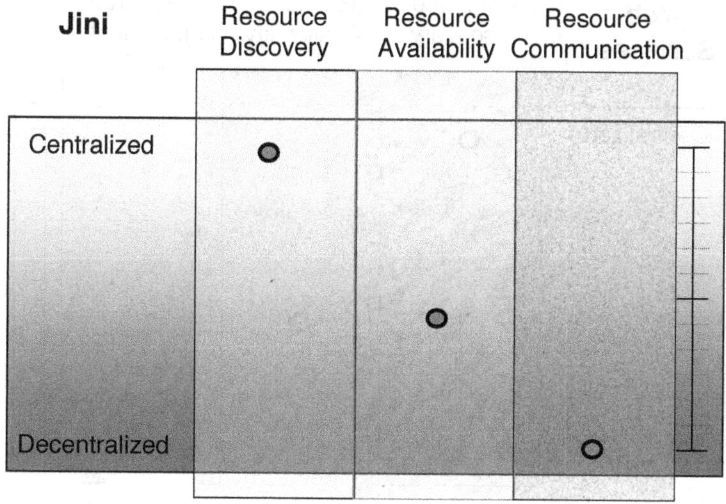

Fig. 1.12. Taxonomy for Jini.

Jini [23] allows Java objects to become network-enabled services that can be distributed in a network 'plug and play' manner. In a running Jini system, there are three main players. There is a service, such as a printer, a supercomputer running a software service, etc. There is a client which would like to make use of this service. Third, there is a lookup service (service locator) which acts as a broker/trader/locator between services and clients. Jini is discussed in detail in Chapters 14 and 20.

Jini is another example of a brokered system. Jini clients find out about services by using the lookup server. The lookup server brokers the request to a matching service and thereafter the communication takes place directly between the client and services. Therefore, the availability is centralized in the sense that it is dependent on the Jini lookup service but on the other hand, once a client discovers a service it wishes to use, the client and service can carry on communicating without the availability of the lookup service. Therefore, as in previous brokered systems, the availability is better than a strict centralized system.

1.6.3 Web Services: Brokered

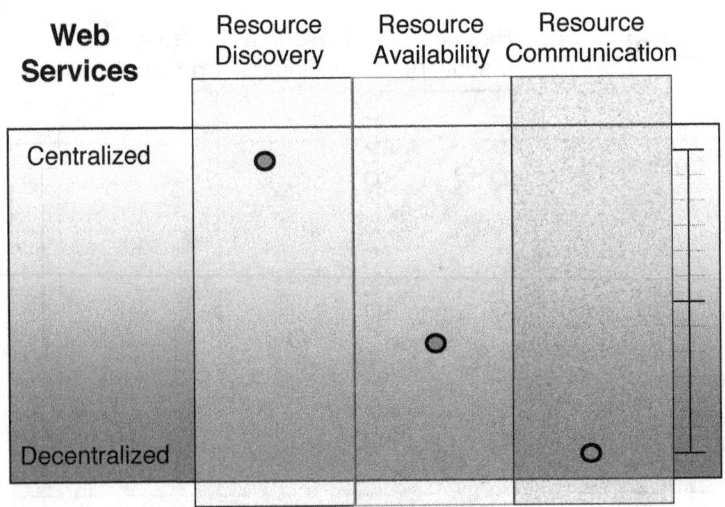

Fig. 1.13. Taxonomy for Web Services.

At the core of the Web Services model is the notion of a service, which can be described, discovered and invoked using standard XML technologies such as SOAP, WSDL and UDDI. Conventionally, Web Services are described by a WSDL document, advertised and discovered using a UDDI server and invoked with a message conforming to the SOAP specification.

Web Services therefore use the same brokered model as other systems, such as Napster, Jini or CORBA, and therefore have a similar taxonomy to those systems. However, Web Services differentiates itself by being based completely on open standards that have gained enormous support from thousands of companies and have been adopted by several communities, including the OGF. Web Services are discussed in detail in Chapters 7, 16, 22 and 17.

1.6.4 Jxta: Decentralized

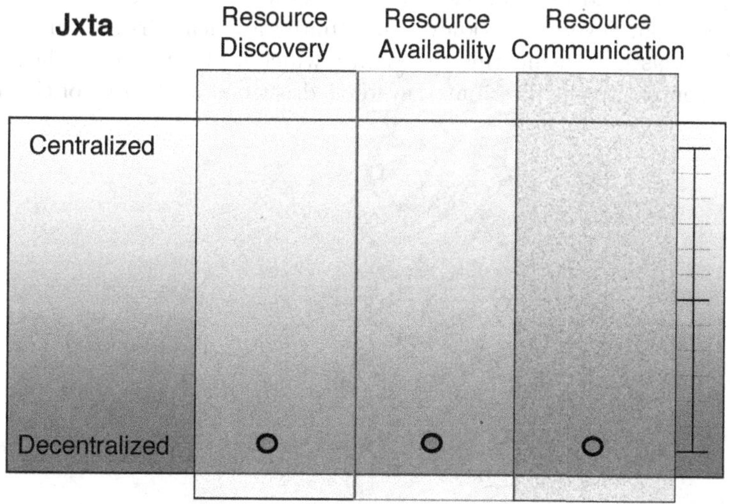

Fig. 1.14. Taxonomy for JXTA.

Project Jxta [24] defines a set of protocols that can be used to construct peer-to-peer systems using any of the centralized, brokered and decentralized approaches but its main aim is to facilitate the creation of decentralized systems. Jxta's goal is to develop basic building blocks and services to enable P2P applications for interested groups of peers. Jxta will be discussed, both conceptually and from a programmer's perspective in Chapters 15 and 21, respectively.

Jxta can support any level of centralization/decentralization but its main focus (and hence power) is to facilitate the development of decentralized applications. Therefore, in this context, Jxta peers can be located in a decentralized fashion; they have much redundancy in their availability and their communication is point to point and therefore no central control authority is needed for their operation.

1.7 Conclusion

In this chapter, the critical components of any distributed system were outlined concentrating particularly on the role of *middleware*. Distributed-systems terminology was introduced, along with notion of a service, which will be used frequently within this book. We then discussed a taxonomy for distributed systems based on a scale ranging from centralized to decentralized, which factored in resource discovery, resource availability and resource communication. Several well-known distributed applications and middleware have been classified using this taxonomy, which will serve as a placeholder and give context to the distributed systems described in the rest of this book.

2

Discovery Protocols

> *"I do not seek. I find." Pablo Picasso (1881-1973)*

As outlined in the taxonomy in the previous chapter, a major theme that needs to be addressed amongst many of the distributed architectures and protocols we talk about in this book is the concept of discovery in both the Intranet and Internet scale domains. Some systems keep this simple by providing a central lookup point in the network but such a scheme, although convenient, is often not scalable to larger networks. Therefore, different mechanisms are needed in order to create a manageable discovery backbone for the automation of the discovery process. In this chapter, we discuss some of the common techniques that are used for discovery and describe the underlying protocols that these techniques rely on.

2.1 Service and Directory Discovery

There are a number of different mechanisms that offer approaches to service discovery. Often such mechanisms are ingrained into middleware (e.g., Jxta and Jini) and form part of the core toolkit. Behind the scenes, however, there are two main techniques that are used: *multicast* for discovery within sub-networks; and *unicast* for connection to specific *service directories*, which contain look-up tables or directories of services available on the network.[1] Multicast is very convenient for Intranet use but is not, at the time of writing, supported at the Internet scale. Therefore, generally service directories are used in order to provide centralized or federated lookup tables. The use of directories further involves two phases in the service discovery process. First,

[1] Although other protocols are adopted in some cases, e.g., Anycast.

a user or service provider discovers a service directory, then he or she searches the particular service directory or directories to locate the desired service or services.

Despite the way these protocols are used, they appear in some form in most of the distributed applications and middleware that exist today. For example, a service directory: in Jini is called the LUS (lookup server); in a super-peer network, it is a super-peer; in Napster, it is the central Napster server; in Jxta, it is a rendezvous; in the Service Location Protocol (SLP), it is called a directory agent or DA; and in Web services, UDDI may be used as the directory service. Often multicast and unicast are used in conjunction with each other. For example, in Intranets, an entity could use multicast to auto-detect the location of a service directory address on the network. A number of systems use this approach (e.g., Jxta, Rendezvous, Zeroconf, Jini, SLP and so on). Depending on the scalability requirements, an application may even choose to opt out of using a service directory and simply use multicast to auto-configure connections between clients and servers directly to form direct peer-to-peer connections. In this discovery mode, multicast can be used two ways: in passive or active discovery. In passive discovery, servers multicast their service advertisements periodically and clients listen out for those advertisements. Once clients receive these advertisements, they are matched with services they wish to use (often called the matchmaking process). In active discovery, the opposite happens. Clients multicast their service search requests or queries, and servers listen for them. If a server has a matching service for the query, then the server will unicast its service advertisement to the client.

For Internet scalability, however, often some form of service advert caching through the use of service repositories or directories is needed in order to scale past systems containing more than a few hundred nodes. In this directory-centric service discovery model, directory services cache service advertisements from multiple servers, and provide a centralized service lookup table for the network (or part of the network). The majority of distributed applications or systems use an architecture which ranges from a centralized and brokered (hybrid) service directory scheme, to using multiple service directories arranged either statically or dynamically across the system. These architectures were described in the previous chapter and will be discussed through the remainder of this book. The algorithm specifying how service directories are arranged is at the core of the scalability of a distributed system, and many techniques have been proposed and are used in systems today (see Chapter 11 for more information). In the next two sections we provide an overview of two core protocols and Internet protocol (IP) standards they depend on, e.g., UDP and TCP.

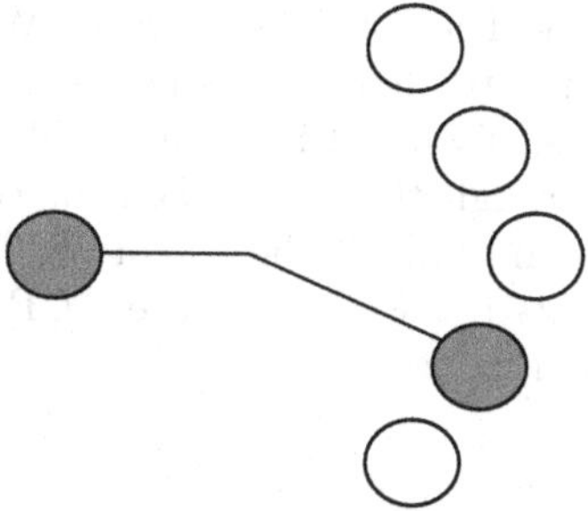

Fig. 2.1. A unicast connection is made between two peers, a sender and a receiver of the packet.

2.2 Unicast Addressing

IP addresses that are assigned a unique identifier to a specific host are referred to as unicast addresses. In simple terms, therefore, unicast means that you are connecting and sending information packets to a single destination as shown in Figure 2.1. However, a unicast address can be used as a source or destination address in an IP datagram. A sender inserts a unicast address in the destination address field in an IP datagram when a packet is sent out to the network, indicating who (and where) the packet should be delivered to. *Unicast* is derived from the word *broadcast*, which is the exact opposite, namely, broadcast sends to every host on the network (as shown in Figure 2.2), unicast only sends to one. Unicast connections often are used in the discovery process within distributed systems to specify and connect to a directory server in the discovery process. As example of a unicast address is 131.251.45.22, which was an address of the old mail server in the School of Physics at Cardiff University, UK.

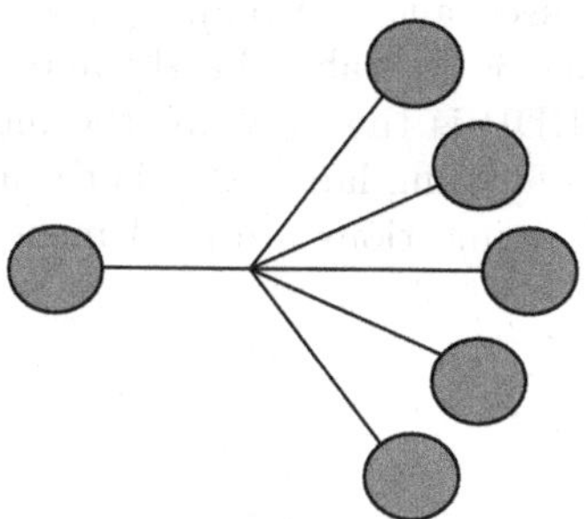

Fig. 2.2. A broadcast connection floods the network and sends a packet to all hosts.

Examples of using a unicast approach to discovery are: for the connection to a Napster server for the discovery of files in a P2P network, described in

Chapter 6; UDDI, a protocol for the discovery of Web Services, described in Chapter 7; for connecting to Rendezvous nodes discussed in Chapter 15; and for Jini lookup servers, discussed in Chapter 14. Unicast addresses can be connection-oriented, through the use of TCP or connectionless by using UDP. However, most systems employ the use of TCP for specifying unicast connections wihin distributed systems because TCP is more reliable than UDP, as outlined in Section 2.2.2.

2.2.1 UDP

The User Datagram Protocol[2] (UDP) was proposed in 1980 [25] and is one of the core protocols of the Internet protocol suite. Distributed applications send messages, called datagrams, to one another by specifying a destination address in the IP header. UDP is connectionless, meaning that prior relationships between nodes do not have to be set up beforehand in order to send UDP packets, as in TCP. Packets are sent out to the network and the IP routing ensures delivery to its destination if the links are congestion free. If there is congestion, packets are simply dropped. The UDP protocol therefore has no control mechanisms for guaranteeing reliability or for sequencing the ordering of the arrival of packets. Datagrams can arrive in any order or go missing en route without notice. However, the simplicity of the protocol makes it very efficient and can be far faster than TCP and for some applications, therefore, it is preferred.

An example of a range of applications that use UDP would be those situations where time-sensitive data is more important than guaranteed delivery; that is, it is better for a packet to be dropped than to be delayed. Streaming audio or video applications (e.g., Voice over IP (VoIP) or IPTV) therefore will often base their implementations on UDP. Another example concerns networks of extremely low bandwidth where TCP's control mechanisms can be too severe and restrict the full utilisation of the network bandwidth. In such cases, UDP is often used and can be integrated with reliability at the application level also if that is desirable. Lastly, and most importantly from a discovery perspective, UDP is the basis for the multicast protocol. UDP is supported in most programming languages. For example, in the Java programming language UDP connections are implemented in *java.net* and are called *DatagramSocket*.

2.2.2 TCP

The Transmission Control Protocol[3] (TCP) [26] provides fairly reliable transfers and it attempts to deliver the packets in order at their destination. This

---

[2] Sometimes called the Universal Datagram Protocol.

[3] Sometimes referred to as the TCP/IP protocol suite.

makes it very suitable for any application which would like to transfer a sequence of bytes (e.g., a file transfer, an e-mail or the Web) to its destination in a somewhat reliable and sequential fashion. TCP is the most ubiquitous protocol on today's Internet and is used by many of the Internet applications that we use on an everyday basis. The Web is built on TCP/IP as HTTP uses TCP to manage the individual conversations between Web clients and Web servers by dividing the HTTP messages into smaller pieces and delivering them in order at the destination.

TCP employs the use of a number of events and controls to implement its behaviour and it is therefore far more complicated an implementation than UDP. Briefly, TCP therefore includes the following features:

1. Connection Oriented: When a TCP connection is created, the underlying protocol implemented a handshake mechanism in order to establish a TCP connection. TCP connections therefore have state and have a lifetime until they are disconnected. The procedure is broadly as follows. A client sends a *SYN* packet to the desired location, the TCP server, which is a minimal 40-byte packet which contains the sender's and destination addresses. When the server receives this packet it will respond with an *ACK* packet, which is an acknowledgement of the server's willingness to *accept* the connection.
2. Multiple TCP Connections: The connection request at the server is implemented using an *accept()* method. A TCP server can block an accept call or use an asynchronous event to indicate that the server should accept the connection. Once accepted, the server typically spawns a new thread and creates a socket to manage this new connection. A server therefore generally acts as a listener and multi-plexor for managing multiple TCP connections and brokers these requests to actual TCP sockets that create a one-to-one TCP relationship with the client.
3. Data Control Mechanisms: attempt to deliver data in a reliable in-order fashion and therefore employ the use of *ACKs* to acknowledge delivery of packets as and when they arrive. The TCP receiver also implements a buffer that is used to slot the packets in the correct order before data is delivered to the application. Therefore, even though data might arrive in the incorrect order in the first instance, the packets are re-ordered before being passed to the application.
4. TCP Events: Most C++ TCP implementations allow an application to attach itself as a listener to a socket.[4] Since sockets can be senders and/or receivers of information, clients and servers receive events based on their role in the TCP connection. A client TCP socket (or the socket that is

[4] Java is a notable exception here. Rather than using TCP events, Java programmers who use java.net must block rather than be notified when something happens at the socket level. This approach is simple but highly restrictive from an optimisation sense, not to mention from an efficiency sense because an application must use threads.

brokered to deal with the incoming connection at the server) therefore can receive Connect, Send, Receive and Disconnected events. Briefly, a client is notified of a Connect event, when it receives an ACK back from the server indicating that the server has accepted the connection request. A Send event is passed to the client when the data has been sent to the server (either using edge- or level-trigger mechanisms) and after a connect event has been received. A Receive event is received by the client when data has arrived and is ready for collection (for asynchronous notification) and a Disconnected event means that the connection has been terminated. A server in the TCP implementation generally acts as a broker to create new sockets for dealing with new connections and therefore it is typically only interested in receiving Accept and Receive events. When a client has requested a connection (by sending a SYN packet), the server passes an Accept event to the listener for server connections. The application can use this event in order to call the *accept()* socket method in order to accept this connection (however, in Java this behaviour is implemented through a blocking call to the *ServerSocket* accept method). Thereafter, a server socket can be notified with a Receive event when data has arrived and is ready for collection.

2.3 IP Multicast Addressing

> **David Clark on multicast**
>
> *David D. Clark, chief protocol architect in the development of the Internet, and chair of the Internet Activities Board, which later became the Internet Architecture Board, commented on multicast: "You put packets in one end, and the network conspires to deliver them to anyone who asks."*

Internet Protocol multicast [27] delivers UDP packets (data) to multiple receivers that have previously joined a **multicast group**, by efficiently routing and duplicating data at specific routers (chosen algorithmically depending on the particular scheme) that identify more than one receiver downstream in their tree. Receivers are arranged within a group, which is represented by an address, and anyone on the network can send data to that group address in order to send data to all of its members. Multicast is designed so that neither the sender nor any of the receivers take on the extra burden of making copies of the data; rather, the data is routed and duplicated at the router level, which makes it an extremely efficient form of data distribution from a source to many destinations. Multicast therefore is useful in a number of Internet applications, including video and audio conferencing, distance learning, distribution of software, stocks and quotes, and news.

The key elements in the multicast protocol will be described in the following sections: the **multicast group address** concept; **reverse path forwarding**; and the construction of the **multicast distribution tree.**

2.3.1 Multicast Grouping

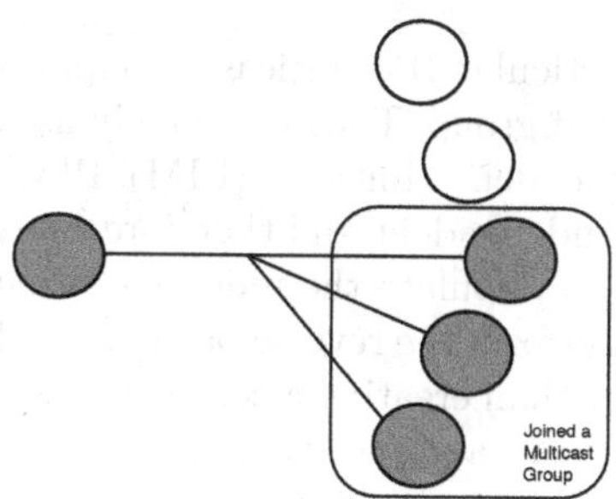

Fig. 2.3. Using multicast, a packet is sent to all the members of a particular multicast group.

Multicast is based on the concept of a group. A group address in a particular range of IP addresses (reserved for multicast) is specified and then people interested in receiving or sending data *join* that particular group, as illustrated in Figure 2.3. The membership of a multicast group is dynamic and therefore hosts may "join" and "leave" a group at any time. There are no restrictions on the number of members in a multicast group and a host may be a member of more than one group at a time. Further, a host does not need to be a member of a group in order to send datagrams to it; that is, you can send standard UDP packets to a multicast address and it will send it to all the members of a group.

The Internet Assigned Numbers Authority (IANA) [28] controls the assignment of IP multicast addresses and assigned the old class D address space for IP multicast. This has the following range of addresses:

- The broad range is from 224.0.0.0 to 239.255.255.255.
- Addresses 224.0.0.1, 224.0.0.2, 224.0.0.5, 224.0.0.6 and 224.0.0.12 are reserved for linked local addressing.
- Addresses 224.0.1.0 through 238.255.255.255 are called globally scoped and can be used for multicasting data between organizations (global addresses). However, some of these addresses have been reserved for certain applications, e.g., 224.0.1.1 has been reserved for the Network Time Protocol (NTP).
- However, RFC 2770 [29] proposes that the 238.0.0.0/8 range of addresses are reserved for statically allocating multicast addresses with global scope for organizations.

- Addresses in the range 239.0.0.0 to 239.255.255.255 contain limited scope or administratively scoped addresses (local addresses). These are reserved for use on your local network by organizations and therefore routers generally do not allow the flow of data to these addresses to go beyond the user-defined domain.

2.3.2 Multicast Distribution Trees

When receivers join a particular IP multicast group, a **multicast distribution tree** is created for that group. The most widely used protocol for creating this tree is Protocol Independent Multicast (PIM). PIM gets its name because it is IP routing protocol-independent and therefore can use whichever unicast routing protocol is used to populate the unicast routing table. PIM uses the unicast routing table to perform the reverse path forwarding (RPF), described in the next section, rather than creating a completely separate multicast routing table and it does not send and receive multicast routing updates between routers like other routing protocols do.

There are many different flavors of PIM: Sparse Mode (SM), Dense Mode (DM), Source Specific Mode (SSM) and Bidirectional Mode (Bidir). At the time of writing, PIM-SM was the most widely deployed but SSM and Bidir have been developed more recently, and seem to be simpler and more scalable. PIM Sparse Mode (PIM-SM) uses a pull model to deliver multicast traffic and is defined in RFC 2362 [30]. Only networks that have active receivers that have explicitly requested the data will be forwarded the traffic. PIM-SM begins by using a shared distribution tree that employs the use of a single common root placed at some chosen point in the network. This shared root is called the rendezvous point (RP). Traffic begins flowing down the shared tree and then if a router along this tree determines there is a better path to the source, the router closest to the receiver can send a join message toward the source and then reroute the traffic along this path by creating a so-called optimized source distribution tree.

2.3.3 Reverse Path Forwarding

Reverse path forwarding (RPF) in multicast routing enables routers to correctly forward multicast traffic down the distribution tree. RPF makes use of the existing unicast routing table to determine the upstream and downstream neighbours and ensures loop-free forwarding of multicast packets in multicast routing and to help prevent IP address spoofing in unicast routing.

In multicast RPF routing, the source address is used as a basis for the decision on whether to forward a packet and not on the destination address, which is the case in unicast routing. It uses the existing unicast routing table and generally does not need to employ the use of a specific multicast one. Essentially, it works as follows: when a packet arrives at a router's interface, the router determines whether the packet has arrived on the interface, which is on the *reverse path* back to the source. If the router determines that the packet arrived on the interface that can lead back to the source (by checking matching entries in the routing table for the source IP address), then RPF check succeeds and the packet is forwarded to all interfaces that are interested in receiving multicast packets for this group. If this (RPF) check fails, then the packet is dropped. Since the same multicast packet could reach the same router via multiple interfaces, RPF checking is integral in the decision to forward packets or not.

2.4 Service Location Protocol

The Service Location Protocol (SLP) [31] is a protocol that allows services to be deployed and discovered with minimal configuration. SLP is one of the few standardised protocols for service discovery in existence and gives a more comprehensive solution than many of the middleware toolkits described in this book. For example, Jin and Jxta both employ a combination of multicast, unicast and directory services but they do not provide rules for their network interactions and retrying schemes for enabling fault-tolerant mechanisms to establish connections between these entities. SLP is a far more advanced protocol in these respects and although SLP was primarily designed for local area networks within a single administrative boundary, it provides a good example of how the combined use of unicast, multicast and directory techniques can achieve dynamic deployment and discovery, while at the same time minimizing network traffic and increasing reliability. SLP breaks the deployment and discovery process into three roles:

- User Agent (UA) - a service consumer
- Service Agent (SA) - a service provider
- Directory Agent (DA) - a cache for service advertisements

Each SLP agent type produces and consumes certain types of messages. These agent types can also be scoped. Scopes are simply character strings defining some category, for example, a network proximity or a shared capability, such as *printers*, that are defined by the network administration. They allow communication between nodes to be filtered, for example, a UA with a certain set of scopes will only be able to discover services or DAs whose scopes intersect with its own. Services also have a *type* attribute which again is used for discovery purposes. The service type can have both an abstract and a concrete definition. The URI below shows a hypothetical service endpoint for a printer:

service:printer:ipp://pr99.cf.ac.uk

The *service* scheme defines the endpoint as being a service of some sort. The *printer:ipp* component represents the service type. This has both an abstract definition (*printer*) and a concrete type, (*ipp*). Here, *ipp* identifies the printer as being available using the Internet Printing Protocol. Another printer on the network may have a concrete service type of *lpr*, indicating it is a Line Printer Daemon. Services can also have attributes which are key/value pairs. These can be queried by a UA using a filter expression. The combination of scopes, attributes and service types provides a simple, yet flexible means of describing and querying for services.

A small SLP network may be made up only of SAs and UAs. In this case, when a UA wishes to discover a service, it sends a multicast service request message to the well-known SLP multicast group that all SLP nodes join. This message contains possible scopes, attributes and a desired service type, either abstract, concrete or both. If an SA with a matching service receives the message, it returns a unicast message to the UA containing the URI of the service. A UA may also issue a query for SAs. This results in discovered SAs returning an *SAAdvert*. This advert contains the scopes and attributes of the SA and whether the SA is listening on a TCP connection. By discovering an SA, particularly one that supports TCP, a UA can issue service queries directly to the SA without using the multicast group, thus reducing overall network traffic.

DAs are used to make larger networks more scalable by providing centralized lookup facilities, further reducing the need to continually multicast requests. By default, DAs must support TCP. When UAs and SAs first start up, they multicast a query for DAs. If any are discovered on the network, their *DAAdverts* are cached locally and used in later exchanges. Specifically, an SA that knows of one or more DAs, registers its services with the DA using unicast, and a UA queries for services with the DA, again using unicast.

SLP also supports presence announcement. This further reduces overall network traffic because nodes receive notification of agent availability as it occurs, rather than having to test for availability every time a service query is made. DAs periodically, though relatively infrequently, multicast their presence to the network, sending out their *DAAdvert*. Similarly, they announce their departure from the network. This allows both SAs and UAs to update their view of the network accordingly. The notification and subscription extension to SLP [32] also supports SAs publishing their services to the network. This is particularly useful in networks not supporting DAs. By listening for service adverts with particular scopes, attributes or service types, a UA can be kept informed of available services. When a service is required by a human user, the UA can look in its local cache for matches before sending a query to the network.

When using multicast to retrieve service adverts, SLP uses a convergence algorithm to counteract possible packet loss. Specifically, the request is repeated if no response is received, doubling the wait time on each repeat. Typically, if no responses are received after two attempts, the request is dropped.

When sending responses, both SAs and DAs include their own address in the message. This allows UAs to know whether they have already received a response from the particular node before.

2.5 Conclusion

This chapter discussed the protocols that are typically used for the discovery of services locally or globally across the Internet. They are directly relevant to the applications and middleware discussed in this book because, as described in the previous chapter, each middleware or application employs some aspect of discovery in their implementation. We described both the unicast protocols (UDP and TCP) and the multicast protocol by providing some detail about how each operates. We then concluded with a brief description of SLP, which is a protocol that makes use of these underlying protocols and directory services for discovering services on a network.

3

Structured Document Types

> *"In my experience it's a serious source of interoperability problems when people try to pretend that XML is a data model, not a syntax."*
> *Tim Bray on the xml-dev mailing list, 10 Feb. 2003*

In order to span heterogeneous environments, many distributed systems have looked to means of expressing data in a way that can be interpreted unambiguously and without loss of information by remote nodes irrespective of their operating system or hardware. The Standard Generalized Markup Language (SGML) forms the basis of the most popular of such mechanisms. A markup language is a vocabulary that combines content with notation, or markup. The markup provides a context for the content. SGML has two important properties that make it suitable for use in distributed environments. First it is based on descriptive markup; the markup is designed to annotate the data in terms of its structure, not in terms of what one should *do* with the content. This means no particular processing, and therefore underlying software or hardware, is presumed. Such markup separates data from structure and, by implication, presentation as well because the structural markup can be processed for presentation independently of the data. Second SGML provides a means of associating a marked-up document with a *document type.* Document types are defined in a Document Type Definition (DTD). The DTD is a template against which the marked-up content can be understood, interpreted and validated using an SGML parser.

SGML has spawned several languages that are widely used, in particular Hypertext Markup Language (HTML) and Extensible Markup Language (XML). These are referenced extensively in this book because they are so commonplace. The following sections give an overview of these technologies. Readers may skip these sections now if they are familiar with these languages, or return to them later for clarification.

3.1 HTML

HTML is the primary publishing language of the Web. It was originally developed by Tim Berners-Lee while at the European Organization for Nuclear Research (CERN). Its primary focus is on providing a simple means of displaying information that can be rendered in a human-readable manner. In order to render the HTML, software for converting the HTML into visual components is required, namely a browser. The first browser to really achieve an impact was the Mosaic browser, released in 1993 and developed at the National Center for Supercomputing Applications (NCSA).

HTML uses the standard SGML syntax for separating structure from data through the use of *elements*. Elements are particles of structure in the overall content. The standard syntax for representing an element is by using *tags*. A tag is a pair of angle brackets surrounding the tag name. An element is made up of a start tag and an end tag. The end tag is identified by a forward slash before the tag name. Elements can be nested; that is, one element can contain other elements:

```
<html>
    <head>
    </head>
    <body>
    </body>
</html>
```

and elements can contain textual data, for example:

```
<p>this text is in a paragraph tag.</p>
```

Elements can also contain attributes. These are key=value pairs defined within the tag, for example:

```
<img width="120" height="100" src="images/fido.jpg"/>
```

shows an `<img>` tag with an attribute called `width`. The value of the attribute is `120`. Likewise it has an attribute `height` with a value of `100`. The meaning of these attributes is reasonably self-explanatory; they represent the width and height in pixels of the image to be displayed. The `src` attribute has a value defining where the location of the image file is, relative to where the HTML document is. This allows the browser to locate the image and load it into the rendered page. The `<img>` tag is also an example of an empty, or singleton, tag. Such tags contain neither textual content nor child elements. The forward slash at the end of the tag shows how a singleton tag should close itself off, so that it is not misinterpreted as a start tag with a matching end tag somewhere further on in the document.

The syntax for including comments in HTML; that is, data that is ignored by a parser, is:

```
<!--
Anything between these two character strings is ignored.
-->
```

These simple syntactic rules make machine processing of a document relatively easy. Below is a simple example of an HTML document. Note that the indentation and spacing of the lines has no significance. It is common practice to indent in this way to make the structure more apparent.

```
<html>
    <head>
        <title>My page</title>
    </head>
    <body>
        <h1>The Cat in the Hat</h1><br>
        <p>by Dr Seuss</p>
        <ul>
            <li>Publisher: HarperCollins</li>
            <li>Genre: Childrens Fiction</li>
            <li>Year: 2003</li>
            <li>ISBN: 0-00-7158440</li>
        </ul>
        <br>visit the website
            <a href=http://harpercollins...co.uk>here</a>
    </body>
</html>
```

As can be seen from the example above, HTML provides an enclosing `<html>` tag representing the HTML content as a whole. This tag contains a `<head>` tag and a `<body>` tag. The head tag is used to contain meta information about the content — in the example above, this is the title of the HTML document. There is also a `<meta>` tag available that can contain metadata such as description and keywords for the document. These can be used (and abused) to attract the attention of search engines. The body contains the content of the document. In the example above, the content is a description of a book.

The primary purpose of HTML is to convey presentational information to a browser. It has tags that suggest that the enclosed content should be bold or italic and of a certain font. One can also model common document structures such as headings (e.g., `<h1>` tag above), paragraphs (`<p>` tag), line breaks (`<br>` tag), tables and lists. In the example above, we have an unordered list — the `<ul>` element containing list item (`<li>`) elements.

Crucially, HTML can reference other resources on the network. The `<img>` tag as described above is such an example. In this case, the browser embeds the remote content into the page. To enable user interaction with remote resources, the anchor tag (`<a>`) is used in conjunction with the hyper-ref attribute (`href`), as shown in the example above. This mechanism is what puts the *hyper* in hypertext because an HTML page with links on it provides support for a non-linear progression through states. Unlike a film, for example, in which the state transitions are determined by the director and the editor, and to which the viewer is subject, hypertext allows the user to determine the next state they want to progress to.

Today, if you click on the *View Source* button in your browser you will see two further important properties of HTML documents. First, they can contain or reference style documents, and second they can contain or reference scripts. Style documents, in particular Cascading Style Sheets (CSS), have relieved much of the HTML markup from determining details of presentation. The font tag, for example, is less used today than previously; instead the CSS can be used to define color, font, positioning, borders and much more for HTML tag types, and even for elements with certain attributes. This has the benefit of separating presentational concerns from content structure which is more in keeping with the design concepts underlying SGML. The separation makes it easier to change presentational aspects without manipulating the structure.

Scripting in HTML pages has been dominated by Javascript (nothing to do with the Java programming language). It is the most common scripting language used in HTML pages, originally developed at Netscape. Browsers supporting Javascript give scripts embedded into the HTML access to the document structure of the HTML and events generated by the browser such as a page loading or a user clicking on a link. This allows the script to take certain actions as a result of such events, the most famous of these being the ubiquitous *rollover* in which a user moves their mouse over a link or image triggering a change in color or image. At the time this was a welcome development in making pages more animated and responsive and a significant advance on the abominable `<blink>` tag, which browsers supported by making the text inside the tag flash on and off irritatingly.

HTML evolved over time, and the HTML specifications are as much codifications of common practice, as they are documents laying out new standards that should be adhered to. Hence there are areas of HTML that have remained under-specified and open to interpretation, in order to maintain compatibility with extant versions and documents as well as to ensure consensus from a wide range of stakeholders. Furthermore the rapid growth of the Web and the browser wars of the late 1990s, primarily between Microsoft's Internet Explorer and Netscape's Navigator, led to a deterioration in the quality of HTML that was published. In an effort to gain users, browsers became more and more forgiving of syntactic irregularities in HTML, attempting to parse and render the HTML despite it being very badly written. Likewise the original goal of maintaining a separation between structure and presentation became muddied as Web designers wanted more control over how content is presented. Hence such tags as the `<font>` tag which allow complete control over text rendering became widely used, replacing such tags as `<em>` for emphasis, and `<h1>` for heading which leave rendering decisions to the browser.

Two further problems with HTML frustrated many who were interested in using the Web for exchanging data in a more machine processable way. First,

HTML does not implement the extensibility that SGML supports. Hence, with a fixed set of tags, HTML can only ever render information in a fixed way. Second, not all HTML is *well-formed*. By well-formed, we mean the rules governing the syntactic structure are somewhat loose. For example, the `<p>` and `<li>` (see the example above) tags do not require matching closing tags, although they are themselves opening tags. Likewise the `<br>` tag, which is an empty or singleton tag, is commonly not explicitly closed by including a forward slash after the element name (`<br/>`). This makes machine processing far more complex. While this situation can just about be managed when dealing with a fixed set of tags, the problems would spiral out of control if one wanted to make use of the extensibility of SGML and define one's own tags.

While HTML was perceived as too limited and polluted through its own success and evolution, SGML remained a highly complex specification, reducing the chances of its uptake on the Web. This is where XML enters the fray.

3.2 XML

Extensible Markup Language (XML) is a subset of SGML capability with a focus on making it easy to create and use on the Web. Although specified under the auspices of the World Wide Web Consortium (W3C), XML is now widely used in all manner of situations, from software build systems [33] to graphics engines using Scalable Vector Graphics (SVG), to generating complex graphical user interfaces [34] [35] to the multitude of application configuration files hidden in your file system. Its ease of use and portability have proven to be useful in many contexts.

Like SGML, XML is not really a markup language, but a meta-language for defining markup languages. It provides the syntactic rules for creating languages that must be well-formed and can be validated. When you create an XML document, you define your own tags. As long as the document is well-formed, it is acceptable XML. Because you define your own tags, XML is not limited in what or how it can describe data.

In the HTML example, we had to take our book object and marry it with the existing set of HTML tags to produce something a human might be able to make sense of. However, the HTML is not particularly machine-friendly. For example, if I am a machine and I want to find out the year of publication from the HTML, I have to look through all the tags and read all their content because the tags give me no hint as to what the content inside them is. Then I have to guess that the list item whose content starts with the character string `Year` is probably the publication year. Then I have to split that string and extract the number at the end of it (`2003`). Of course this can be done with lots of clever parsing tricks (known as *scraping*), but there is nothing stopping another page representing the book in an entirely different way; for example, they may use an HTML table as the holding structure, the word `Published` as a column title and the year itself in a table row. This would still be valid HTML. The problem is that HTML has nothing to do with the internal structure or semantics of the data it is describing. Let's define the book that we wrote as HTML in XML instead:

```
<?xml version="1.0"?>
<book>
    <title>The Cat in the Hat</title>
    <author>Dr Seuss</author>
    <isbn>0-00-7158440</isbn>
    <genre>Childrens Fiction</genre>
    <published>2003</published>
    <publisher>
        <name>HarperCollins</name>
        <url>http://harpercollins...co.uk</url>
    </publisher>
</book>
```

Now the machine is happy. The structure of the document reflects the structure of the data it is describing. The tags have names that can be associated with decisions to take while reading the document. When the machine hits the `<published>` tag, it can be told that all the content within the tag represents the year of publication. And if the document references a DTD, and is validated against it, then the machine can be sure that all instances of this book definition will follow the same structure. Unfortunately a human will not be so happy if they happen upon this while surfing the Web. If their browser supports XML, they will at best see what you see above — raw markup.

The flexibility of XML has led to XML languages that are concerned with XML processing and validation. For example, DTDs are less common now for defining the structure of XML documents. Instead XML Schema are used. These are XML documents defining the structure of other XML documents. Likewise, Extensible Stylesheet Language Transformations (XSLT) can be used to convert an XML document into another XML document or any other structured document such as source code. This makes XML documents suitable as meta-representations of data that can be rendered to the most appropriate form on demand, including HTML of course.

While the benefits and usefulness of XML are undoubted, it has some properties that some find disadvantageous. The verbosity of the language is a concern, particularly in the context of distributed computing because of network bandwidth and latency issues. Likewise, the freedom to create user-defined structure has led to a proliferation of document types and schema. This is turn requires new language parsers. Not XML parsers — if the new dialect is valid XML, then any extant parser should work — but rather software components that can interpret the semantics of the new XML language. This is a problem HTML has by and large avoided because of its fixed set of tags.

A further problem with allowing user-defined tags is distinguishing between tags that may have the same name. For example, imagine the bookstore BooksRUS defines a book structure whose root element is called `<book>`. At the same time the bookstore Book-O-Rama also defines a book structure, also with a root element called `<book>`. However, the Book-O-Rama's book structure is subtly different from the BooksRUS structure; it contains an additional `<co-author>` element and a `<booktitle>` tag which is semantically equivalent to BooksRUS's `<title>` tag. How do I tell the difference between the two? How do I validate them?

Tim Bray

Tim Bray was born in 1955 and has worked as a software developer, writer and entrepreneur. He was a major contributor to the XML standard and wrote the first XML processor called "Lark" (short for "LAurens Right Knee" after his wife twisted her knee while he was writing it). More recently he has contributed to the Atom Syndication Format specification.[1]

XML gets around this problem with something called namespaces. Namespaces allow tag names to be qualified by another name — a *namespace*. The reserved attribute `xmlns` is used to specify the namespace associated with a tag:

```
<book xmlns="http://www.booksrus.com">
```

In the above example all child elements of the `<book>` element inherit the namespace `http://www.booksrus.com`. If you want to embed elements from another namespace into a document with an already existent namespace, then a namespace *prefix* can be used. This is simply a shorthand for a full namespace. The prefix can then prepend all elements within a particular namespace. So now the BooksRUS book tag looks like this:

```
<b:book xmlns:b="http://www.booksrus.com">
```

while the Book-O-Rama book tag looks like this:

```
<bs:book xmlns:bs="http://www.book-o-rama.com">
```

[1] Photo and biography summarised from wikipedia `http://en.wikipedia.org/wiki/Tim_Bray`.

In the first example, the `book` tag name is mapped to the namespace `http://www.booksrus.com` via the prefix `b`, and in the second, to the namespace `http://www.book-o-rama.com` via the prefix `bs`. The value of the prefix is not important in itself, as long as it is unique within a document in pointing to a particular namespace. This combination of a tag name, or *local name*, and a namespace is called a *qualified name*.

So now the book structures can be distinguished by their qualified name. This allows each book structure to be independently parsed without confusion and also allows both book structures to inhabit an enclosing document, say a catalogue of books available at different bookstores, with its own defined namespace. This latter property is an important feature because many XML documents import other vocabularies into their own documents, building up composite documents made from a variety of vocabularies. The downside is that the XML has become more complex. Furthermore, many people use namespaces as a means of versioning their structures. Wanton changes to namespaces can lead to versioning nightmares.

3.3 XHTML

XHTML is an attempt to make HTML conform to XML syntactic structure so that the standard publishing language of the Web can benefit from the machine-processability and portability of XML. There are currently three versions of XHTML either standardized, or in the process of becoming so. XHTML 1.0 is really just a reformulation of HTML to comply with XML. This, in short, means that the HTML document must be well-formed, tags must be case sensitive, and singleton tags must be self-closing.

The fact that XHTML 1.0 is valid XML makes it much easier to machine process. However, the nature of HTML tags and their relationship to content means it is still not possible to assign or extract the semantic meaning of content based on the tags which enclose it. This problem has been solved to a degree through the use of the *class* attribute that can be used to decorate tags in HTML. The class attribute is most commonly used in conjunction with CSS to associate presentational information defined in the CSS with arbitrary tags in the HTML document. The value of a class attribute can be anything an author wishes:

```
<p class="my-class">This content is of class my-class</p>
```

The class attribute can also be used in a semantic context. Rather than just using it to define CSS rules, it can be used by processing engines to extract content from an HTML page based on the value of the class attributes. Let us look at our book structure one last time, this time defined using class attributes to identify content.

```
<html xmlns="http://www.w3.org/1999/xhtml">
  <head>
      <title>My Book</title>
  </head>
  <body>
    <div class=book>
      <h1 class=title>The Cat in the Hat</h1>
      <p>by <span class=author>Dr Seuss</span></p>
      <ul>
        <li>Publisher: <span class=pub>
                  HarperCollins</span></li>
        <li>Genre: <span class=genre>Childrens</span></li>
        <li>Year: <span class=year>2003</span></li>
        <li>ISBN: <span class=isbn>0-00-715853</isbn></li>
      </ul>
    </div>
    <p>visit the website at
      <a href=http:/harpercollins...co.uk class=url>
                      http:/harpercollins...co.uk
      </a>
    </p>
  </body>
</html>
```

Here we can see a mixture of both presentational and semantic markup. The `<div>` tag is used to enclose a book structure and given an attribute of `book`. The list items still show useful human readable information, but the `<span>` tag is used to neatly wrap the content that a machine might be interested in, and annotated with class attributes that a machine can parse. We have also removed any unclosed tags. This means the browser is happy, the human is happy, and the machine is pretty happy as well. There's just one thing missing here — namespaces. This is because XHTML can be served as HTML, convincing the browser that it is looking at a piece of HTML. However, not all XHTML is valid HTML because XHTML allows the features supported by XML such as namespaces. Notice the `xmlns` declaration in the `html` tag. A browser will likely not understand this, but in the spirit of tolerance overlook it, and continue. The XHTML 1.0 specification contains guidelines for how to enable XHTML to be accepted by current browsers that only understand HTML. Some argue this is a recipe for disaster.

XHTML 1.1 goes further than 1.0 and defines a modularization mechanism allowing, on the one hand, page authors to advertise their support for a subset of tags, and on the other, to allow extensibility within the context of these modules. Document types can be created by aggregating modules providing a mechanism for both document extensibility but also reuse of modules by different document types. This approach is being taken to facilitate a smoother adoption of Web standards by software components and environments other than the traditional desktop browser, for example mobile and embedded devices. XHTML 2, which is still in draft stage, controversially breaks with the past tolerance of HTML in subsuming less than ideal developments, and instead sets out new mechanisms for defining everything from forms, and events to where links can appear. Concurrently, HTML 5 is also in draft stage. Some involved in this development take the view that XML should remain separate from HTML because they are essentially different technologies. Watch this space...

3.4 Document Modelling and Validation

A major strength of the document types described above, is their ability to be validated against a document definition. The definition acts as a template against which *instance documents* can be tested for compliance. There are currently three common ways of expressing document templates: Document Type Definitions, XML Schema and RELAX NG. The following sections briefly describe these technologies.

3.4.1 Document Type Definition

A Document Type Definition (DTD) provides a simple means of expressing structure and content of a document. It defines a number of components to achieve this. The most commonly used of these are described below.

PCDATA identifies character data that should be parsed. It stands for *parsed character data.*

CDATA identifies character data that should not be parsed by a parser. In a XML document, such data is enclosed in a pair of character sequences identifying that it should be ignored.

```
<![CDATA[
    This content will be ignored by the XML parser.
    It does not have to adhere to XML markup rules.
]]>
```

Entities provide a means of defining values that will be replaced with a different value when the document is parsed. A reference to an entity starts with an ampersand (&), followed by the entity name, followed by a semicolon (;). Typical examples of entity references are characters that may be in the content of an element, but contain characters that are used by the content definition itself, and therefore need to be escaped so as not to be confused with structural data. For example, in XML, < is a reference to the < character and > is a reference to the > character, the entity reference & stands for the ampersand character itself.

Elements describe the structure of a document. In the case of (X)HTML and XML, these are elements defined with angle-brackets, for example:

```
<p>some text.<br/>And some more</p>
```

The DTD element component can describe the name of an element and either a category or allowed content. The category of an element is defined using a DTD keyword. For example, the keyword `EMPTY` describes an element which has no closing element. The `<br/>` tag above is an example of an empty tag. It could be rendered in a DTD as follows:

```
<!ELEMENT br EMPTY>
```

The angle brackets and exclamation mark contain the element declaration defined using the `ELEMENT` keyword. Next, there follows the name of the element. In this case it is `br`. Finally, the keyword `EMPTY` is used to identify this element as having no content, apart from possible attributes. Non-empty elements can either contain character data or child elements. To describe this, the type of content is surrounded with brackets. For example, to describe the `html` element, one might write something like:

```
<!ELEMENT html (head, body)>
```

To describe an element containing character data, for example, the paragraph tag above, you could write:

```
<!ELEMENT p (#PCDATA)>
```

In actual fact the HTML paragraph tag can contain many types of tags as well as textual content. DTDs allow you to model mixed content, as well as simple notions of cardinality based on regular expressions. For example an asterisk (`*`) means zero or more, a plus (`+`) means at least one and a question mark (`?`) means zero or one. For a simple paragraph tag that only accepted text content and any number of break tags, we could write the following (the bar (`|`) being used to define an *or* relationship):

```
<!ELEMENT p (#PCDATA | br)*>
<!ELEMENT br EMPTY>
```

Attributes describe the attributes associated with an element, for example:

```
<img src="../images/fido.jpg"/>
```

defines an image tag with a `src` attribute. This attribute would be declared in a DTD as follows:

```
<!ATTLIST img src CDATA>
```

Here the `ATTLIST` keyword is used to declare the attribute, followed by the element name in which the attribute can occur, i.e. the `img` element, followed by the name of the attribute, i.e., `src`, followed by the allowed content of the attribute, here defined as `CDATA`. An attribute declaration can also contain a default value which may either be an actual character string or one of a set of keywords (`#REQUIRED`, `#IMPLIED` or `#FIXED`). The declaration name is `ATTLIST` because it is actually a list of attributes of a particular element. So, for example, a more complete definition of the HTML `img` element might look as follows:

```
<!ELEMENT img EMPTY>
<!ATTLIST img src CDATA #REQUIRED
              width CDATA #IMPLIED
              height CDATA #IMPLIED
              alt CDATA #IMPLIED>
```

The example below shows a DTD for the `book` structure we defined in XML in Section 3.2.

```
<!ELEMENT book (title, author, isbn, genre, published, publisher)>
<!ELEMENT title (#PCDATA)>
<!ELEMENT author (#PCDATA)>
<!ELEMENT isbn (#PCDATA)>
<!ELEMENT genre (#PCDATA)>
<!ELEMENT published (#PCDATA)>
<!ELEMENT publisher (name, url)>
<!ELEMENT name (#PCDATA)>
<!ELEMENT url (#PCDATA)>
```

A Document Type Declaration, (as opposed to Definition), is used when associating a DTD with document. Typically (X)HTML documents reference a document type they adhere to at the top of the document, for example:

```
<!DOCTYPE HTML PUBLIC
    "-//W3C//DTD HTML 4.0 Transitional//EN"
    "http://www.w3.org/TR/REC-html40/loose.dtd">
```

The declaration contains the name of the document type, (here it is `HTML`), the scope of the type, (here the keyword `PUBLIC` is used to identify the type as being for broad public consumption), the name of the DTD and its location.

DTDs have a number of limitations. As can be seen from the syntax, although attributes are scoped by the elements they appear in, elements are not scoped by their parent elements. This can cause problems when element have the same name. For example, if the XML `book` document had an element called `name` instead of `title`, this would cause a conflict with the `name` element of the publisher element. A further limitation is that not all conditions or structures can be modelled, in particular because of the limited regular expressions supported by DTDs. Perhaps most importantly, DTDs do not support data typing of element content. This is a common requirement of validation. For example, whilst the `genre` element of our `book` document may want to be defined in a lax way to allow almost arbitrary descriptions of various genres, the `published` element should only accept very particular types of content, i.e., a year or possibly a specific data format. The same is true of the `isbn` element and the publisher's url — both require particular character sequences as their values to make sense. Data typing is something that XML Schema is particularly strong on and is described in the following section.

3.4.2 XML Schema

XML Schema [36] is an XML vocabulary used describe XML documents. The content of a schema is defined inside a `schema` element. This element, and all other elements defined by XML Schema are defined in the XML Schema namespace (`http://www.w3.org/2001/XMLSchema`). XML Schema defines a number of core elements that describe XML structure and content:

- An `element` component describes an XML element.
- An `attribute` component describes an attribute of an XML element.
- A `simpleType` component describes a data type whose content can only be character data.
- A `complexType` component describes a data type that can have attributes and whose content can be character data, child elements or mixed content, i.e., character data and child elements.

The latter two components do not directly describe elements in an XML document, but rather how such elements or attributes are structured and what their allowed values are. XML Schema also allows groups of elements and attributes to be defined independently of the `complexType` element, as top level collections. This allows these components to be re-used by various types within the document.

Schema documents, in general, have a target namespace associated with them. This provides a default namespace for elements and types defined in the document. External schema documents can also be included in a document via an `include` element that provides the URI of remote document.

The `element` component has a `name` attribute representing the name of the element and an optional `namespace`. Together, these two values can be used to construct a qualified name (QName) for the element. An element also has a type definition. This is declared *either* through a `type` attribute, which is the QName of a type declaration in the document (either a `complexType` or `simpleType` element), a `ref` attribute, which is the QName of another element declaration, or by a type declaration defined as the child elements of element declaration itself. Beyond this, an element declaration can contain a number of other attributes, expressing qualities such as maximum and minimum occurrences, whether or not the element is allowed to be nil, and whether or not the element declaration is abstract or not. if an element is abstract, then it may not exist in a document directly, but must be derived in some way by other, concrete elements.

Like an `element`, the `attribute` component also has a `name` attribute and an optional `namespace` and a type definition. The type definition is declared in a similar fashion to the `element` component, i.e., via a `type` attribute, a `ref` attribute or directly via its child elements. Unlike an `element`, an `attribute` can only have content that is of a simple type. Beyond this, attributes can also define whether they are required, have a default value or are fixed.

Attribute and element components act as containers for data types. The XML Schema data typing system is based on the object-oriented concept of inheritance. It divides the type space into two main branches — simple types and complex types. At the root of the type tree is the `anyType` structure. The `anyType` type essentially defines nothing about itself and allows any content. Derived from this is the `anySimpleType` type which is the root of those types that are considered simple types. From this are derived the built-in types supported by XML Schema. These include typical programming language primitives such as *string*, *boolean*, *double* and *float*, as well as date and time constructs and miscellaneous useful types representing values such as QNames, URIs, and binary data. Also derived from the `anyType` are user-defined derivations of the built-in types, and user-defined complex types.

A simple type is any data type that has neither element nor attribute content. As such, these types are essentially character strings. XML Schema provides *constraining facets* for restricting the character data of a simple type. For example a `pattern` facet could be applied to a string type to enforce only uppercase letters. The pattern facet uses regular expressions as its value. Likewise, and `enumeration` facet can be applied to restrict allowed content to a particular series of values.

When a schema author wants to define a simple type, she can derive a type from the built-in types. Derivation of simple types takes one of three forms:

- Restriction. The derived type will further restrict the allowed values, i.e., by applying a facet.
- List. The derived type is a list of parent types.
- Union. The derived type is a union of two parent types.

As an example, a simple type representing the playing card suits might be defined as follows:

```
<xsd:schema xmlns:xsd="http://www.w3.org/2001/XMLSchema">
  ...
  <xsd:simpleType name="suits">
    <xsd:restriction base="string">
      <xsd:enumeration value="hearts"/>
      <xsd:enumeration value="diamonds"/>
      <xsd:enumeration value="clubs"/>
      <xsd:enumeration value="spades"/>
    </xsd:restriction>
  </xsd:simpleType>
  ...
</xsd:schema>
```

A simple type representing a clothing size might use the union derivation to allow sizes as both numbers and strings:

```
<xsd:schema xmlns:xsd="http://www.w3.org/2001/XMLSchema">
  ...
  <xsd:simpleType name="size">
    <xsd:union>
      <xsd:simpleType>
        <xsd:restriction base="xsd:positiveInteger">
          <xsd:minInclusive value="8"/>
          <xsd:maxInclusive value="72"/>
        </xsd:restriction>
      </xsd:simpleType>
      <xsd:simpleType>
        <xsd:restriction base="xsd:string">
          <xsd:enumeration value="small"/>
          <xsd:enumeration value="medium"/>
          <xsd:enumeration value="large"/>
        </xsd:restriction>
      </xsd:simpleType>
    </xsd:union>
  </xsd:simpleType>
  ...
</xsd:schema>
```

As can be seen from these examples, the `restriction` element has a `base` attribute that identifies the type from which the definition is derived.

When a schema author needs to create a complex object, potentially containing elements and attributes as well as text, she must define a complex type. A complex type itself, can have two types of content: simple and complex. Simple content can have character data and attributes defined. Complex content additionally contains child elements. Further, this content must be derived in some way from another schema type. The allowed derivations for complex types are:

- Restriction. The derived type will restrict the content model of its parent.
- Extension. The derived type adds further content to the model of its parent.

When the content of a complex type is itself complex, i.e., child elements are being defined, then the child elements can be grouped in certain ways:

- The `sequence` element groups child elements as an ordered list, according to how they are declared in the schema.
- The `all` element groups child elements as a bag, that is, the order they are declared in has no relevance.
- The `choice` element allows either/or relationships to be defined between elements and groups of elements.
- The any element makes all the child elements optional.
- The `group` element allows externally defined collections, i.e., either `sequence`, `all`, any or `choice` elements and their children, to be referenced.

Let's look at some examples to make this clearer. Below are three examples of a measurement structure. The structure defines a value, and the unit of measurement the value is measured in. The first example uses an attribute to define the unit of measurement and extends the `nonNegativeInteger` built-in type. Because no elements are being defined, i.e., only character data and an attribute are defined, this complex type has a content type which is simple. The derivation type is extension because the content model of the parent type (`nonNegativeInteger`) is being extended through the addition of an attribute. Attributes can only ever have a `type` attribute which is a simple type. Here we have used the built-in `string` type for simplicity. The example then defines an `element` component with a `name` attribute of `length` and a `type` attribute pointing to the `measurement1` complex type. Finally, the example shows an instance of the element being used to describe the length of 35cm.

```
<!-- type declaration -->
<xsd:complexType name="measurement1">
 <xsd:simpleContent>
  <xsd:extension base="xsd:nonNegativeInteger">
   <xsd:attribute name="unit" type="xsd:string"/>
  </xsd:extension>
 </xsd:simpleContent>
</xsd:complexType>

<!-- element declaration -->
<xsd:element name="length" type="measurement1"/>

<!-- instance declaration -->
<length unit="cm">35</length>
```

The following version of the measurement structure takes a different approach. It defines its unit of measurement and its value as elements. It derives from the base schema type `anyType`. The derivation method is restriction because the base type allows any content, whereas the measurement structure only allows two elements of particular types. It uses a `sequence` element to group the two elements together. The example then defines an `element` component with a `name` attribute of `length` and a `type` attribute referencing the `measurement2` complex type. The example then shows an instance of the element being used to describe the length of 35cm. The structure of the length element defined using the `measurement2` complex type is different from the length defined using the `measurement1` complex type. In particular, both the unit and the value are represented as named child elements.

```
<!-- type declaration -->
<xsd:complexType name="measurement2">
 <xsd:complexContent>
  <xsd:restriction base="xsd:anyType">
   <xsd:sequence>
```

```
      <xsd:element name="size" type="xsd:nonNegativeInteger"/>
      <xsd:element name="unit" type="xsd:string"/>
     </xsd:sequence>
    </xsd:restriction>
   </xsd:complexContent>
  </xsd:complexType>

  <!-- element declaration -->
  <xsd:element name="length" type="measurement2"/>

  <!-- instance declaration -->
  <length>
    <size>35</size>
    <unit>cm</unit>
  </length>
```

Complex types can extend any user-defined type. Types that do not extend user-defined types automatically extend the base type (anyType). Extending the base type via restriction is a common scenario, so, thankfully, XML Schema allows an abbreviated syntax for describing a type such as the measurement2 type above. Essentially the complexContent and restriction elements are implied if they are omitted from the declaration. Therefore, we can write the previous example type definition as follows:

```
<!-- type declaration -->
<xsd:complexType name="measurement2">
   <xsd:sequence>
    <xsd:element name="size" type="xsd:nonNegativeInteger"/>
    <xsd:element name="unit" type="xsd:string"/>
   </xsd:sequence>
</xsd:complexType>
```

While XML Schema is comprehensive, it is very complex. The details of certain aspects of it, for example, the exact validation rules of the restriction derivation of complex types, are probably only understood by a handful of committed schema hackers. This complexity usually means that writing schema by hand should be avoided. Typically tools are used which take in programming language objects and churn out schema documents. However, even these tools often have incompatibilities between them due to incomplete implementations of the totality of validation possibilities, or different interpretations of ambiguous conditions, such as namespace inheritance of imported schema documents with no target namespace.

Another system that is much simpler and yet addresses most, if not all, of the validation requirements needed on a day-to-day basis, is RELAX NG. The following section provides a brief overview of this technology.

3.4.3 RELAX NG

Just like an XML Schema document, a RELAX NG (REgular LAnguage for XML Next Generation) [37] document is an XML document defining the structure and content of an XML document. However, there are crucial differences between the two approaches. First, RELAX NG (RNG) uses a far simpler data model than XML Schema. Second, RNG can also be written using a non-XML compact syntax which is easy for humans to understand. Third, and possibly most important, it does not directly deal with data typing. Rather, it allows external data typing definitions, e.g., XML Schema documents, to be referenced. This simplifies the data model further. In fact, it forms part of an overall approach to XML validation. Just as Tim Bray's comment at the beginning of this chapter holds true for XML in general, it also holds true for particular XML vocabularies, particularly those concerned with modelling XML itself. The root cause of many of the problems associated with XML Schema is that XML Schema is a data typing system. Data typing is a hugely complex area, and also highly domain dependent because it infuses semantics with syntax. It it therefore extremely difficult to arrive at a data typing system that is both simple and useful, yet generic in its application. RNG takes a syntactic approach to describing XML, steering clear of semantics. In this sense, RNG documents are simply syntactic patterns against which an XML document is matched. This pattern-matching approach allows for greater flexibility. For example, it is possible to create a RNG definition from two arbitrary XML documents that may adhere to different schema. Using a data typing-based approach would make this highly complex because of the semantc dependencies (or lack of them) between documents. The RNG data model is made up a few simple constructs:

- The element is the basic construct of RNG . An element can model both a document, as well as elements within a document. It consists of a name, a context, a set of attributes and an ordered sequence of zero or more children. Each child can be either a character string or another element.
- An element's name is a compound entity representing a QName. It comprises a a local name and a namespace. It it syntactically represented using a `name` attribute for the element's name and an `ns` attribute for the namespace URI. If an `ns` attribute is not defined then the element recursively inherits its namespace from its parent, defaulting to an empty string if none is found.
- The context of an element is made up of a base URI, for example, in the case of an entire document, the location from which the document was retrieved from, and a namespace map. The namespace map maps namespace prefixes used in the element to their URIs.
- An attribute consists of a name (again representing a QName) and a character string representing the attribute's value.

The content of an element is described using child elements. There are a number of allowed patterns. The <text/> tag simply means the element contains a character string with no explicit type. This character string may be empty, or may contain any content that could be interpreted as multiple character strings. If one wanted to define a simple size construct with no data typing one could write:

```
<element name="size">
   <text/>
</element>
```

The <value> tag can be used to define particular allowed content values. This pattern can also have a type attribute. Although RNG steers clear of data typing, it actually contains two built-in types: string and token. Both are just character strings with arbitrary content. The only difference between them is how surrounding whitespace is treated. The string data type matches exactly the character string of an instance document, including space, newline and tab characters that may not actually be integral to the data itself but a consequence of serialization. The token data type matches string values even if they are surrounded by whitespace. Imagine we have a value of "yo ho ho" and an instance document with the characters " yo ho ho". If the value element has a type attribute of string, this will not match, whereas if it has a type attribute of token, it will. The default type of a value element is token. Below is an example of an element representing a unit of measurement with a particular value, and data type of token.

```
<element name="unit">
  <value type="token">cm</value>
</element>
```

Element content can also be defined using the <data> tag. This pattern tries to interpret the contents of the element as some sort of data type. Similar to the value tag, the type of data is expressed using a type attribute. The data pattern interprets content as being a single element with possible child elements. It comes into its own when combined with external data type libraries. This is achieved through a datatypeLibrary attribute that can be placed on an element. When this external library is referenced, the type attribute of the data element can point to data types defined in it.

Elements can, of course, contain other elements as well as attributes. In the previous section we defined a measurement structure using XML Schema in two different ways — one using simple content and the other using complex content. Below is an example of what the attribute-based version might look like if we defined it using RNG. The datatypeLibrary attribute imports the XML Schema built-in types and then gives the element an XML Schema built-in data type of nonNegativeInteger. The unit attribute simply has text as its content.

```
<!-- element declaration -->
<element name="length" xmlns="http://relaxng.org/ns/structure/1.0"
    datatypeLibrary="http://www.w3.org/2001/XMLSchema-datatypes">
  <data type="nonNegativeInteger"/>
  <attribute name="unit">
    <text/>
  </attribute>
</element>

<!-- instance declaration -->
<length unit="cm">35</length>
```

The element-based version of the structure is show below:

```
<!-- type declaration -->
<element name="length" xmlns="http://relaxng.org/ns/structure/1.0"
    datatypeLibrary="http://www.w3.org/2001/XMLSchema-datatypes">
    <element name="size">
        <data type="nonNegativeInteger"/>
    </element>
    <element name="unit">
        <text/>
    </element>
</element>

<!-- instance declaration -->
<length>
  <size>35</size>
  <unit>cm</unit>
</length>
```

One of the strengths of RNG is that elements and attributes are treated similarly. This makes understanding, modelling, parsing and maintaining RNG documents much easier. To change the `unit` value from an element to an attribute, we simply changed its name. Compared to the XML Schema versions, the differences between these two renditions using RNG is much less.

Using the non-XML compact syntax to describe the `length` element would result in the following:

```
element length {
  element size {xsd: nonNegativeInteger},
  element unit {text}
}
```

This makes the structure of the `length` element pretty easy to understand just by looking at the definition. Compare this to full blown XML Schema version, and you begin to understand why RNG is attracting more and more followers.

Below is an example of the book structure we defined in XML in Section 3.2. It imports the XML Schema built-in types using the datatypeLibrary attribute, and then uses these types to more closely define the allowed content of certain elements; in particular the published element content is given a gYear (Gregorian year) type, defined by XML Schema, and the publisher's URL is given an XML Schema type of anyURI.

```
<element name="book" xmlns="http://relaxng.org/ns/structure/1.0"
    datatypeLibrary="http://www.w3.org/2001/XMLSchema-datatypes">
      <element name="title">
         <text/>
      </element>
      <element name="author">
         <text/>
      </element>
      <element name="isbn">
         <text/>
      </element>
      <element name="genre">
         <text/>
      </element>
      <element name="published">
         <data type="gYear"/>
      </element>
      <element name="publisher">
         <element name="name">
           <text/>
         </element>
         <element name="url">
           <data type="anyURI"/>
         </element>
      </element>
</element>
```

Similar to XML Schema, RNG allows different types of groupings of elements. Child elements of the zeroOrMore element can appear zero or more times. Likewise, children defined under the oneOrMore element must appear at least once. A choice element is also available, providing either/or functionality between collections of elements or attributes, as is an optional element, for elements that are not required, and an interleave element, to allow elements to appear in any order.

Further patterns are also supported that echo the capabilities of XML Schema, for example, the list element for defining lists. The enumeration pattern and the union derivation defined by XML Schema can simply be modelled using the RNG's choice element.

RNG also allows groups of elements and attributes to be defined separately from the context in which they may be used. These groups of components, or patterns, can then be referenced from other parts of the document. This allows structures that may be highly complex and even recursive, to be modelled in a clear, reusable manner. A pattern is defined using the define tag:

```
<define name="size-element">
  <element name="size"
    datatypeLibrary="http://www.w3.org/2001/XMLSchema-datatypes">
    <data type="nonNegativeInteger"/>
  </element>
</define>
```

This can now be referenced from elsewhere using the `name` attribute of the `define` element:

```
<element name="length" xmlns="http://relaxng.org/ns/structure/1.0">
    <ref name="size-element"/>
    <element name="unit">
        <text/>
    </element>
</element>
```

Using the `grammar` element defined by RNG, multiple pattern definitions can be grouped together:

```
<grammar xmlns="http://relaxng.org/ns/structure/1.0">
    <start>
      <!-- this is the element that must be matched -->
      <element name="length-element">
        <ref name="size-element"/>
        <ref name="unit-element"/>
      </element>
    </start>
    <!-- other related definitions -->
    <define name="size-element">...</define>
    <define name="unit-element">...</define>
</grammar>
```

The `grammar` structure provides an entry-point into the various definitions, in the form of the `start` element. Parsers will attempt to match against the contents of this element.

3.5 Conclusion

This chapter has provided and overview of three of the most commonly used document types in distributed environments — HTML, XML and XHTML. While these technologies are all related, they have different strengths and weaknesses and are therefore used in different ways by different systems and communities. One commonality between these document types is their ability to be validated against a template. The three primary technologies for achieving this — DTD, XML Schema and RELAX NG — were also introduced.

4

Distributed Security Techniques

> *"Uncertainty is the only certainty there is, and knowing how to live with insecurity is the only security."* John Allen Paulos

This chapter covers the core elements of security in a distributed system. It illustrates the various ways that a third party can gain access to data and gives an overview of the design issues involved in building a distributed security system. Cryptography is introduced, then cryptographic techniques for symmetric and asymmetric encryption/decryption are given, along with a description of one-way hash functions. To demonstrate the use of these underlying techniques we provide an example of how a combination of public/private keys and hash functions can be used to digitally sign a document, e.g., email. Both asymmetric and symmetric secure channels are discussed and scenarios are provided for their use. Finally, the notion of sandboxing is introduced and illustrated through the description of the Java security-manager implementation.

The role and timeliness of this chapter therefore is to provide a security gateway for the middleware and applications that we will discuss in the following chapters, which often use a combination of security techniques. For example, Freenet (Chapter 12) uses many of these techniques extensively for creating keys for the Freenet network, which are used not only for privacy issues, but to actually map from the data content to network location. Further, both Jxta (Chapter 15) and Grid computing (Chapter 9) provide security infrastructures and address authentication issues; and BitTorrent (Chapter 13) makes use of hash functions in order to ensure the integrity of data as it is passed around the network.

This chapter is based on many on-line papers and articles and an excellent overview of distributed-systems security infrastructures, given by Andrew Tanenbaum and Maarten van Steen [16].

4.1 Introduction

Andrew S. Tanenbaum

Andrew Tanenbaum was born in 1944 in New York and grew up in White Plains, New York State. He received both his bachelor's degree (MIT, 1965) and his doctorate (University of California, Berkeley, 1971) in Physics. He moved to the Netherlands with his wife and became professor of computer science at Vrije Universiteit, Amsterdam. He was the author of the free Unix-like operating system for teaching called MINIX and has written many computer science textbooks including several editions of "Distributed Systems: Principles and Paradigms", with his co-author Maarten van Steen, which has a chapter on security that formed the basis for the chapter here.[1]

Security has to be pervasive throughout a system. A single design flaw in the security will render the entire security system useless and therefore great care must be taken in considering the many design choices for the particular system at hand. Security is related to the notion of dependability and a dependable system must be available, reliable, safe and maintainable. Therefore, to address the security of a dependable system, we must provide:

- **Confidentiality:** where authorized access is a necessity.
- **Integrity:** where alterations are only performed by authorized parties, e.g., if we send data from one place to another, we must provide techniques for ensuring that the data has not been modified along the route.

Before we look at the various techniques that can be used to address these issues, let's look at the possible security threats. In brief, there are four types of security threat to computer systems:

1. **Interception:** involves an unauthorized party gaining access to a service or data, e.g., when someone is eavesdropping into a private conversation. Alternatively, interception could also involve somebody making an illegal copy of a file.
2. **Interruption:** happens when a service (or data) becomes unavailable, unusable, destroyed, etc. There are numerous examples: when a file is lost or corrupted, or denial of service through host failure or service attacks.

[1] Photo and biography summarised from wikipedia `http://en.wikipedia.org/wiki/Andrew_S._Tanenbaum`.

3. **Modification:** involves modifying the contents of data or a service without authorization. Therefore, data may become invalid or a service may return a different result than what is expected; e.g., you could rebind a Web service to an alternate implementation or modify database entries.
4. **Fabrication:** involves generating data or an activity that wouldn't normally exist, e.g., adding a password into a password file or database.

A company first needs to define a *Security Policy.* This is a set of rules defining which actions entities, e.g., users, administrators, services, etc., are allowed to take. Once a security policy has been defined, it is possible to define which security mechanisms can be used in order to enforce these criteria. There are four types:

1. **Encryption:** is fundamental to security and involves encoding (encrypting) data into something an attacker cannot understand (i.e., it implements confidentiality).
2. **Authentication:** is used to verify the claimed identity of a user. There are many types of authentication mechanisms, e.g., passwords, digital certificates, etc.
3. **Authorization:** involves checking that a user has the correct permission to perform a particular operation. Typically, authorization is performed after authentication; e.g., in UNIX, even though you have logged on (i.e., authenticated), you still may not have access to certain resources; i.e., you will not be able to write a file in any directory other than your own.
4. **Auditing:** is a passive security measure which tracks or logs the clients that log in and use the system. Auditing can be used to find out who and how a user accessed a particular resource. Auditing is useful in finding out where in the system the security breach happened, which can be used to fix the problem for the future. Further, often if an attacker knows there is such a system in place, this is a good deterrent.

4.2 Design Issues

There are a number of design issues that need to be considered when designing a general-purpose security system. In this section, descriptions of three issues are given [16]:

- **Focus of Data Control:** specifies the level (or position) where the protection for the data or services is provided.
- **Layering of Security:** concentrates on where in the security stack (i.e., within the OSI model) the security focus will be.
- **Simplicity:** focuses on the need for simplicity for any security system. If the security system is not simple to understand, then users will not trust it.

These three issues are described in the following sections.

4.2.1 Focus of Data Control

There are three points where data (or services) can be protected within a distributed system; see Fig. 4.1.

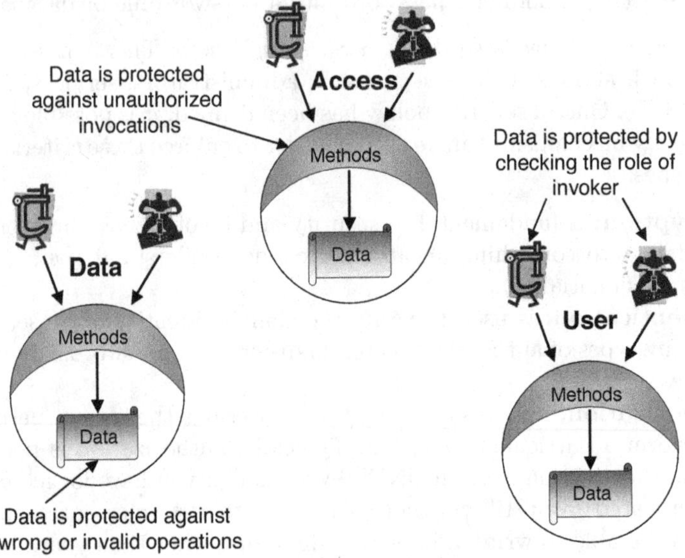

Fig. 4.1. The three approaches for protecting data: at the data, access, or user level. The diagram shows the consequences of each action.

These are at the:

1. **Data Level:** to protect the data directly from wrong or invalid operations (see Fig. 4.1). For example, integrity checks could be implemented within a database each time data is accessed or modified. Another, more familiar example to Java programmers is array-bounds checking, which verifies the legality every time an array item is accessed. If the operation is legal, then access is granted, otherwise an exception is thrown at runtime.
2. **Method Level:** restricts which operations can be applied to the data and by whom. In object-oriented terms, this is equivalent to a set of *accessor* methods on an object, which dictate the types of operations (e.g., setX, getY, etc.) that can be performed on the class's internal data (which could be set private). You may also restrict the access to a database using predefined interfaces. Then, within a method's implementation various types of checks can be performed to ensure the validity of the operation.
3. **User Level:** focuses on the users of the system; i.e., only selected users can have access to the application/data/service regardless of what operations they want to perform. A user role is defined for each user. For example,

on Windows XP, there are two 'user roles': a *Computer Administrator* or *Limited.* A computer administrator can install programs and hardware, make systemwide changes, access and read files, and create and delete user accounts whereas a *Limited* user can only change her own settings, e.g., picture and create, change or remove her own password and files.

4.2.2 Layering of Security Mechanisms

An important design issue for implementing secure systems is to decide at which *level* the security mechanisms should be placed. The *level* positions the security mechanisms within the logical organization of system components, as illustrated in Fig. 4.2. Shown here are the following broad layers: applications, middleware, operating system services, operating system kernel and communications, which illustrate an important separation of general-purpose services from communication.

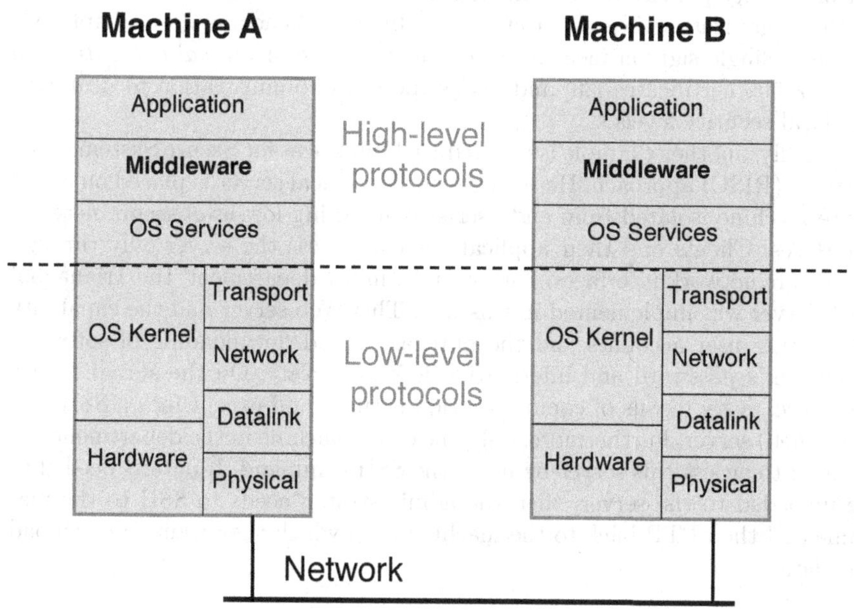

Fig. 4.2. The logical organization of a distributed system into several layers.

Further, it is important to relate this to the notion of trust. A system can be secure but whether a customer trusts it is another matter. Therefore, a crucial factor is to make sure that a client trusts the layer you decided on but further, that he also trusts the layer(s) on which these security services are built.

For example, say Tim on machine A wanted to send a message to Gareth on machine B. If Tim is worried that his confidential message will get interrupted, then he must choose a secure service for doing this. Say, he chooses secure FTP to perform this operation; then he must trust that secure FTP performs the operation it says it does. However, since secure FTP uses SSL (secure sockets layer, secure communication via sockets), Tim needs to trust that SSL is also secure. If he does not, then he may choose another form of secure communication, such as public keys. As a designer of a security system all these factors are important in deciding at which level to place the security mechanisms.

Dependencies between services regarding trust define a Trusted Computer Base (TCB). TCB is the stack of security mechanisms that are needed to enforce a security policy. For example, a security policy implemented at the middleware level relies on the security of the underlying operating systems. If the underlying infrastructure is adequate then the TCB could include the local operating systems at various hosts. Globus [9], for example, defines a set of security policies at the middleware level by defining a set of rules for a virtual organization, i.e., a collection of individuals/machines (see Chapter 9). It uses a single sign-on mechanism through the use of *mutual authentication* using X.509 certificates [38] and leaves the local administration to deal with the local security levels.

Finally, another example is the Reduced Interfaces for Secure System Components (RISC) approach. Here, any security-critical server is placed on a separate machine isolated from end-user systems using low-level secure network interfaces. Clients and their applications can access the server only through the secure network interfaces. For example, in my department, the Triana [39] Web server was implemented in this way. This Web server had the capability of creating user accounts and the purchasing and downloading of software. Each user's password and information is kept private. On the actual server, therefore, every means of communication is turned off except for an SSH (Secure Shell) server. Furthermore, only one other machine in the department can be used to access this server by using the SSH command. If data is needed to be uploaded to the server, then the administrator needs to SSH to the machine and then FTP back to the machine from which they want to download the data.

4.2.3 Simplicity

Simplicity is a key component of any software architecture and therefore, the fewer security mechanisms the better. Users tend to trust systems that are easily understood and trusted to work. If users do not understand the mechanisms, then how can they truly trust them?

Simplicity contributes to the trust that end-users will put into the application and, more importantly, will contribute to convincing the designers that the system has no security holes. The more complicated the system, the harder it is to debug.

Unfortunately, it often is the case that security is an afterthought within the application-development life cycle. Therefore, the designer of the security system must develop security mechanisms around an existing complicated application. This makes it difficult to keep things simple and, consequently, is difficult to trust.

4.3 Cryptography

4.3.1 Basics of Cryptography

Cryptography is fundamental to security in distributed systems. It involves encrypting a message (i.e., scrambling it) before it is sent (so that it remains private) and decrypting it upon arrival before it is read. Encryption and decryption are accomplished by using cryptographic keys as their parameters. All cryptographic systems have the following two core properties:

- the algorithm is publicly known
- and the key is kept private.

The algorithms are written in such a way that it is mathematically intractable to calculate the key from any encrypted text. This ensures the simplicity of cryptography from a user's standpoint because all she needs to provide is a key and the rest is hidden under a well-known trusted algorithm. Keys typically consist of a single number, e.g., a long (64-bit integer).

So, if a user wishes to send a message to another user, she could choose to send this message as it is. However, this message would not be protected at all and could be liable for infringement using any of the mechanisms described in Section 4.1. For example, the message can be intercepted passively (i.e., eavesdropped), or actively by changing the contents of the original text of the message. Using cryptography provides defence from such security threats.

Figure 4.3 shows the basic idea behind cryptography. Here, the original form of the message is called plaintext and the encrypted form is referred to as cyphertext. The input plaintext (P) is transformed into the ciphertext (C) by using an encryption method (E) based on a given key (K); i.e., $C = E_k(P)$. The plaintext is then calculated from the ciphertext by using $P = D_k(C)$. Cryptography enables us to defend from two types of attacks (see Fig. 4.3):

1. **Interception:** would be extremely difficult. Although the user may be able to intercept (i.e., read) the message, he will only see unintelligible scrambled data. He would need to obtain access to the key in order to unlock its contents.

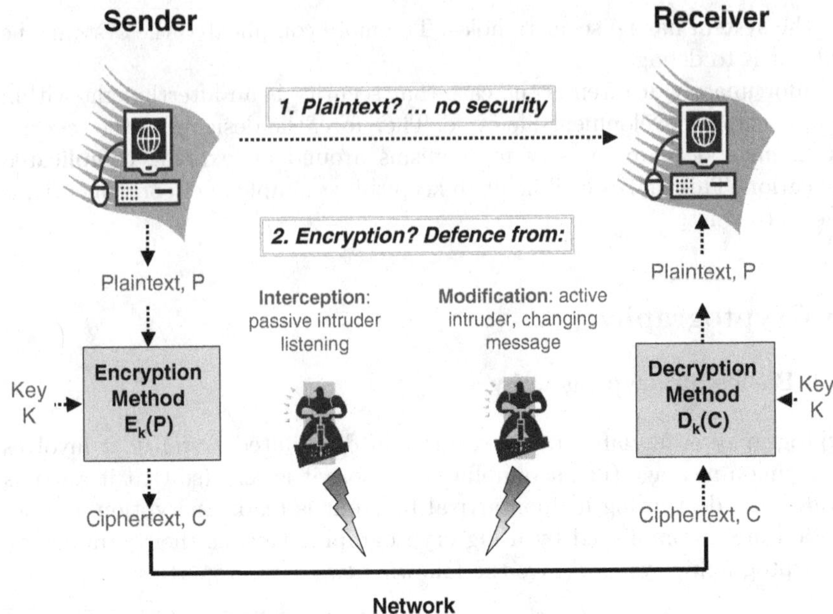

Fig. 4.3. Either a user uses plaintext (no protection) or he can use encryption. This diagram illustrates the basic cryptographic techniques and which protection these give.

2. **Modification:** is even more difficult since the user would not only have to intercept the message (and decrypt it) but he would then have to modify it and encrypt it again so the receiver thinks it has come from the original sender. To do this the modifier would have to know the key and the algorithm used for encryption.

4.3.2 Types of Encryption

A *cryptosystem* is used for the encryption and decryption of data, and has two fundamental approaches, whilst hash functions are one-way mapping of data to keys. Therefore, there are three main categories for encryption:

1. Secret Key (symmetric cryptosystem)
   - single key is used to encrypt and decrypt information
2. Public/Private Key (asymmetric cryptosystem)
   - two keys are used: one for encryption (public key) and one for decryption (private key)
3. One-Way Function (hash function)
   - Information is encrypted to produce a "digest" of the original information that can be used later to prove its authenticity.

4.3.3 Symmetric Cryptosystem

Here, the same key is used for encryption and decryption. Keys can be created in a number of ways: e.g., they can be generated once and used over and over again or they can be generated for each session (using session keys in Section 4.5.1). A good example of a symmetric cryptosystem is the Data Encryption Standard (DES).

The Data Encryption Standard [40] is a widely used method of data encryption using a private (secret) key that was judged so difficult to break by the U.S. government that it was restricted for exportation to other countries. There are 72,000,000,000,000,000 (72 quadrillion) or more possible encryption keys that can be used. For each given message, the key is chosen at random from among this massive range of keys. Like other private key cryptographic methods, both the sender and the receiver must know and use the same private key.

DES applies a 56-bit key to each 64-bit block of data. The process can run in several modes and involves 16 rounds or operations. Although this is considered "strong" encryption, many companies use *triple DES*, which applies three keys in succession. This is not to say that a DES-encrypted message cannot be "broken".

Early in 1997, Rivest-Shamir-Adleman, owners of another encryption approach (RSA [41]), offered a $10,000 reward for breaking a DES message. A cooperative effort on the Internet of over 14,000 computer users trying out various keys finally deciphered the message, discovering the key after running through only 18 quadrillion of the 72 quadrillion possible keys! Few messages sent today with DES encryption are likely to be subject to this kind of codebreaking effort. Other known symmetrical algorithms are:

- DESX (XORed input), GDES (Generalized DES), RDES (Randomized DES): all 168-bit key
- RC2, RC4, RC5: variable length up to 2048 bits
- IDEA is the basis of PGP: 128-bit key
- Blowfish: variable length up to 448 bits

4.3.4 Asymmetric Cryptosystem

In asymmetric cryptosystems (better known as public-key systems), the keys for encryption and decryption are different but together form a unique pair. These two keys are related, but in theory, knowing one key will not help you figure out the other. This key pair is termed the *private key* and the *public key*. The private key is known only to the sender and can also be password protected for enhanced security. The public key, however, can be widely known. Public-private keys can be used in many different ways.

Public-key encryption essentially allows users to identify themselves. They are used to create digital signatures (see Section 4.4), a far more effective version of our handwritten counterpart. They can also be used to encrypt a message for sending to a specific person (using their public key) since only that person can read it (using their private key) and vice versa. A good example of using public-key cryptography is for mutual authentication, described in Section 9.7.2.

One popular example of a public-key system is RSA, named after the inventors Rivest, Shamir and Adleman [41]. The security of RSA is based on the difficulty of factoring large numbers that are the product of two prime numbers. This factoring problem has been studied for hundreds of years and still appears to be intractable. For this reason, people are confident of RSA's security, and it has become fundamental to information security. RSA systems are also easy to use and therefore easy for executives, managers and other decision-makers, who do not have a technical or mathematical background, to understand. RSA is widely used today in many of the encryption applications and protocols in use on the Internet, including:

- Pretty Good Privacy (PGP)
- Secure Sockets Layer (SSL)
- S/MIME, Secure Electronic Transactions (SET)
- Secure Shell (SSH)
- X.509 V.3 certificates as used in Jxta, Globus/OGSA
- RSA is also included in major World Wide Web browsers such as Netscape and Microsoft Internet Explorer. RSA uses modular arithmetic and elementary number theory to do certain computations. It is based on the fact that it is extremely difficult to find the prime factors of large numbers. An overview of the algorithm is given in Appendix B.

4.3.5 Hash Functions

A *hash function* is a mapping of a message from any size input message to a fixed length *hash key*, which is typically far smaller than the original message. A *cryptographically strong* hash key must have the following properties:

- It must be **non-reversible:** You must not be able to construct the original message from the hash key.
- It must be **sensitive to input changes:** It must change significantly with any small change in the input message, even if this change occurs in a single bit. This is also known as the *avalanche effect*; that is, a small change in the input creates a large change in the output.
- It should be **collision resistant:** It should be impractical to find two messages with the same hash key.

Formally, a hash function H takes a message m of arbitrary length as input and produces a bit string h having a fixed bit-length as output.

$$h = H(m)$$

A hash is similar to the extra bits added to a packet in order to perform error correction. Hash functions are one-way functions, meaning that it is unfeasible to find the input m that corresponds to a known output h. This is obvious when you consider the size of the input and output of a hash function. The output is always the same size (e.g., 128-bit) but the input can be of any size (e.g., 16 Mbyte).

MD5 is a good example of a hash function. It was developed by Professor Ronald L. Rivest of MIT. The MD5 algorithm takes as input a message of arbitrary length and produces as output a 128-bit "fingerprint" or "message digest" of the input [42]. It is conjectured that it is computationally unfeasible to produce two different input messages that map to the same output message digest, or key.

Hash functions are typically used within digital-signature algorithms, where a large input file is mapped (and more important, compressed) to create the basis for the signature (see next section). Another example of a hash-function algorithm is the SHA-1 [43] secured hash, used extensively in Chapter 12. SHA-1 keys are non-reversible, collision-resistant and have a good *avalanche effect*. Non-reversibility is a property of hash functions, whilst collision resistant implies that two different input files will not create the same key, and the avalanche effect means that two almost identical input files will create vastly different hash keys. SHA-1 mappings take in one or more blocks of 512 bits (64 bytes) and create a single 160-bit hash key.

Hash functions also provide a mechanism to verify data integrity, and are much more reliable than checksum and many other commonly used methods.

4.4 Signing Messages with a Digital Signature

Asymmetric cryptosystems allow users to *digitally sign messages*, which allows a user to establish his/her identity. A hash function is used to create and verify a digital signature. Hash functions enable the software to create digital signatures that operate on smaller and more predictable amounts of data, but still maintain the integrity of the original message content. Therefore, hash keys provide an extremely concise form of the input data and therefore are extremely efficient to sign digitally. Figure 4.4 illustrates the signing process.

The signer first delimits precisely what is to be signed within the *message* element, i.e., a message, document or data. A hash function is then applied to this message, which results in a hash code (e.g., a 160-bit SHA-1) unique to the message content. This hash result is then transformed into a digital signature using the signer's private key (i.e., it is encrypted). The resulting digital signature is therefore unique to both the message and the private key of the user who created it. The digital signature is typically attached to its

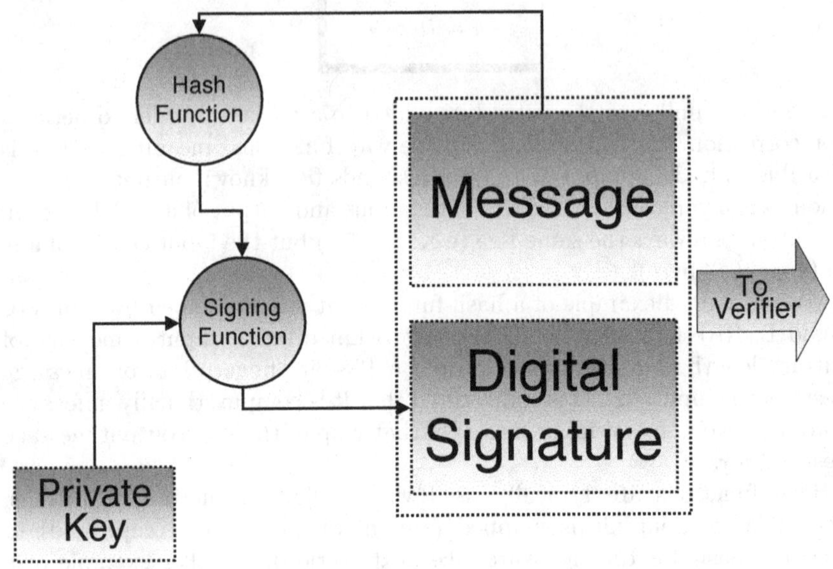

Fig. 4.4. Illustration of a message being signed using an asymmetric cryptosystem and hash functions.

message, either by storing it within a specific format (e.g., X.509 certificate), or transmitted along with the message.

When a user wishes to verify a digital signature (see Fig. 4.5), he/she computes a new hash from the original message using the same hash function as the one used to create the digital signature. The user now can first check whether the key was signed using the signer's private key by using the signer's public key to decrypt the message. If this succeeds, then the user can verify whether this newly computed hash result matches the hash result extracted from the digital signature. If they match, then the verification is complete.

Verification therefore indicates that the digital signature was created using the signer's private key (i.e., he/she is the only person with access to this key) and that the message was not altered since it was signed (because hash collisions are considered mathematically improbable). There exist a number of different mathematical formulas and procedures, but all share this overall operational pattern.

4.5 Secure Channels

The issue of protecting communication between two participants (i.e., a client and a server) can be thought of in terms of setting up a secure channel. There are two methods of encrypting the traffic, described above:

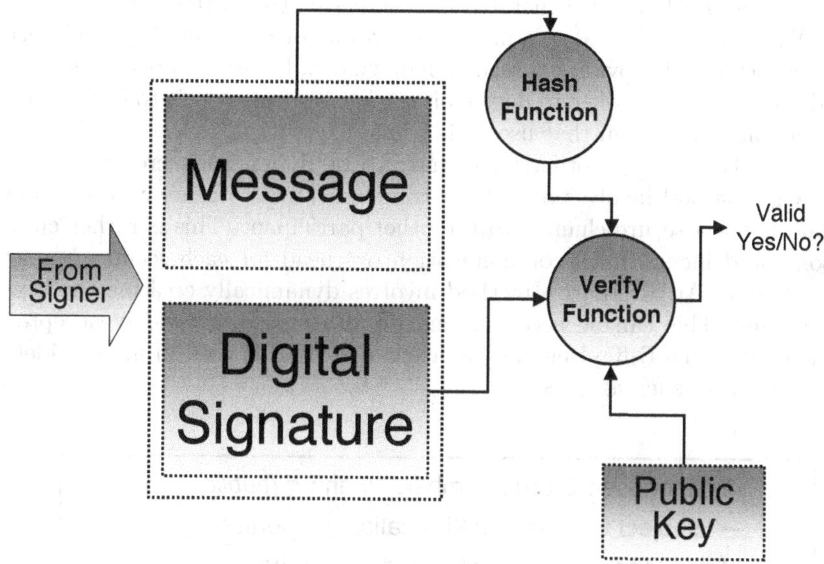

Fig. 4.5. User verification of another user's signature.

- Symmetric key
- Public/private key

The following technologies are examples of secure channels:

- **Secure Socket Layer:** is a standard for encrypted client/server communication between network devices. A network protocol, SSL runs on top of TCP/IP. SSL utilizes several standard network security techniques including public keys, symmetric keys, and certificates. Web sites commonly use SSL to guard private information such as credit card numbers.
- **Transport Layer Security (TLS):** [44] is a protocol that ensures privacy between communicating applications and their users on the Internet. When a server and client communicate, TLS ensures that no third party may eavesdrop or tamper with any message. TLS is the successor to the Secure Sockets Layer.

4.5.1 Secure Channels Using Symmetric Keys

There are two ways of creating keys for secure channels using symmetric keys:

- shared secret keys
- session key

Shared secret keys are generated once and secretly passed to the individuals. This can be achieved in a number of ways. For example, they could use another method of providing a secure channel, e.g., by using public keys, they could telephone each other to decide on the key or even post it to each other. An example of a system that uses this technique is Kerberos.

Session keys, on the other hand, have to be dynamically created at run time. One method involves one of the communicators to generate a key and to send it via a secure channel to the other participant. This is rather cumbersome and incurs much communication overhead for each secure channel to be created. An alternative method involves dynamically creating the keys at run time. This can be accomplished by an elegant and widely accepted method called the Diffie-Hellman key exchange. This is used in many widely used algorithms such as TLS.

1. Both choose 2 large numbers, ***n*** and ***g*** *(public)*
   - subject to certain mathematical properties
2. Tim chooses secret large random number = ***x***
3. Gareth chooses secret large random number = ***y***
4. Tim computes **(g^x) *mod n*** *(public)*
   - virtually impossible to compute *x* from g^x *mod n*
5. Gareth computes **g^y *mod n*** *(public)*
6. They *exchange* public keys **(g^x) *mod n*** and **(g^y) *mod n***
7. Gareth computes **((g^x) *mod n*)^y *mod n* = g^{xy} *mod n***
8. Then, Tim computes **((g^y) *mod n*)^x *mod n* = g^{xy} *mod n***

Both now have the **shared secret key g^{xy} *mod n***

Fig. 4.6. The Diffie-Hellman key exchange algorithm.

Suppose Tim and Gareth want to share a key; then the protocol works according to the algorithm in Fig. 4.6. Using this algorithm ensures that both Tim and Gareth (and only those two) will have the shared secret key g^{xy} mod n. Note that neither of them needs to make his private number (**x** and **y**, respectively) known to the other.

4.5.2 Secure Channels Using Public/Private Keys

Consider the following situation where secure communication is needed: Tim has just sold Gareth a data projector for £750 through a chat room and by using email as their only communication channel. Gareth finally sends Tim a message confirming that he will buy the projector for £750. In addition to authentication there are two other issues:

- Gareth needs to be assured that Tim will not change the sum of £750 specified in his message to something higher.
- Tim needs to be assured that Gareth cannot deny ever having sent the message (if he starts to have second thoughts).

One way to accomplish this is by employing the following mechanism using RSA keys.

1. Gareth encrypts the message using his private key.
2. Gareth also encrypts the message (for privacy) using Tim's public key.
3. Tim can first decrypt the key using his private key and then he can use Gareth's public key to decrypt the original message from Gareth.

If Tim accepts that Gareth's public key is in fact his key, then this can only mean that the message came from Gareth. Furthermore, Gareth knows that Tim has received the message containing the original message because only Tim can open the message as he is the only person who has access to his private key.

4.6 Secure Mobile Code: Creating a Sandbox

Traditionally, you had to trust software before you ran it. You achieved security by being careful only to use software from trusted sources, and by regularly scanning for viruses just to make sure things were safe. Once software obtains access to your system, it has full rein and if it is malicious, it could inflict a great deal of damage as there is little protection, other than certain authorization measures. So, in the traditional security scheme, you tried to prevent malicious code from ever gaining access to your computer in the first place.

The sandbox security model makes it easier to work with software that comes from sources you don't fully trust. Instead of security being established by requiring you to prevent any code you don't trust from ever making its way onto your computer, the sandbox model lets you welcome code from any source. A sandbox is a technique by which a downloaded program is executed in such a way that each of its instructions can be fully controlled. We will take a look at this here by describing the Java sandbox [45].

The Java Sandbox provides a very restricted environment in which to run un-trusted code obtained from the open network. In this sandbox model local code can be trusted to have full access to vital system resources, such as the file system, but downloaded remote code (an applet, for example) is not trusted and can therefore have access only to the limited resources provided inside the sandbox (unless it is signed). For example, an applet prohibits:

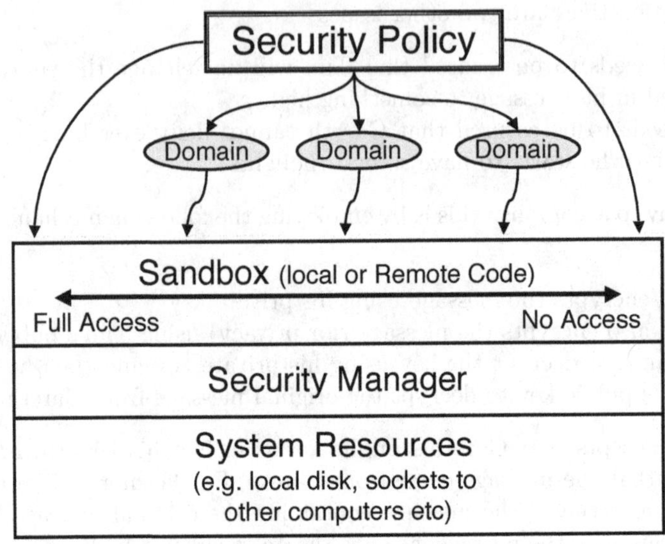

Fig. 4.7. The Java Sandbox, which is implemented using a security manager.

- Reading or writing to the local disk
- Making a network connection to any host, except the host from which the applet came
- Creating a new process
- Loading a new dynamic library and directly calling a native method

By making it impossible for downloaded code to perform certain actions, Java's security model protects the user from the threat of hostile code. A *security manager* (see Fig. 4.7) is responsible for determining which resources can be accessed. All code, regardless of whether it is local or remote, can be subject to a *security policy* enforced by the security manager. The security policy defines the set of permissions available for code from various signers or locations and can be configured by a user or a system administrator. Each permission specifies a permitted access to a particular resource, such as read and write access to a specified file or directory or connect access to a given host and port.

The runtime system organizes code into individual domains, each of which encloses a set of classes whose instances are granted the same set of permissions. A domain can be configured to be equivalent to the sandbox, so applets can still be run in a restricted environment if the user or the administrator so chooses. Applications are run unrestricted by default but can optionally be subject to a security policy. A *signed applet* is treated like local code, with full access to resources, if the public key used to verify the signature is trusted.

The Java sandbox model could potentially be used to implement a secure CPU-sharing infrastructure across a P2P environment and extend the SETI@home idea to create a generalized heterogeneous CPU-sharing environment for Java codes.

4.7 Conclusion

In this chapter, we covered the basics of security in a distributed system. The different types of security breach were discussed, followed by a description of the design issues involved in building a distributed security system.

Cryptography, fundamental to security in distributed systems, was discussed for both the symmetric and asymmetric cases. Hash functions were discussed and combined with asymmetric cryptography techniques to illustrate how a message can be digitally signed.

The concept of a secure channel was introduced, that is, the issue of protecting communication between two participants (i.e., a client and a server). A secure channel can be set up using public key pairs or by using symmetric keys, e.g., shared secret keys or session keys. Finally, Java sandboxing was discussed for protecting the resources to which mobile code may potentially have access.

Part II

Distributed Environments

5

The Web

> *"Usefulness from what is not there." Lao Tse*

5.1 Introduction

In 1959, *The Sound of Music* made its debut on Broadway. The run won numerous awards and the show went on to become one of the most popular musicals in history. The vocal score along with underscoring, comprises about 200 pages of manuscript. In the same year, Miles Davis arrived at Columbia studios to record his seminal album *Kind of Blue.* He did not arrive with 200 pages of black dots. Rather, as Bill Evans writes on the album's liner notes, he *arrived with sketches which indicated to the group what was to be played*, presenting to the other musicians *frameworks which are exquisite in their simplicity and yet contain all that is necessary to stimulate performance with sure reference to the primary conception.*

Miles Davis' approach to composition has much in common with the spirit in which the Web was designed, and is summed up by Tim Berners-Lee's citation of the Lao Tse poem *The Space Within*, the final line of which is given above. The Web has arguably become so ubiquitous, not just because of what it can do, but because of what it does not try to do. The less that is defined, the more potential there is for supporting new ideas. Hence the Web provides a very simple skeleton on which new concepts can be easily hung. The trick, however, is to ensure that new ideas themselves do not shut the door on further invention. Therefore much of the activity of the World Wide Web Consortium (W3C) and other interested parties is in defining what the Web architecture is and how it can be maintained and improved. This is a balancing act between enabling natural evolution and ensuring a consistent approach based on past experience.

Underpinning the Web is the concept of a resource. A resource can be anything — a person, a tax invoice, a photograph, a thought, a country, a political movement, an algorithm — anything that has some bounds and can therefore be identified. The Web makes no restrictions on what resources are allowed onto it. All it defines is how these resources can be exchanged between computers, and hence people. This is the most basic capability of any distributed system — to be able to move resources from one machine to another. To achieve this, the Web supports a few very simple technologies that address:

Resource Naming The Web defines a flexible and extensible means of naming arbitrary resources called Uniform Resource Identifiers (URIs). These are discussed in detail in Section 5.3.

Resource Representation To move arbitrary resources between computers, you need some way of representing them that can be converted into a bit stream and transferred across the network. While a person and an idea can be a resource, neither is naturally amenable to being converted to a series of 0's and 1's. Ideally the representation format is shared and adopted by many, which means it should be easy to generate and easy to interpret. The Web now supports a number of resource representation types. The original and most important of these is Hypertext Markup Language (HTML). The syntax of HTML is described in Chapter 3. Its relation to the design of the Web is described below in Section 5.4.

Resource Transfer Hypertext Transfer Protocol (HTTP) has emerged as the primary transfer mechanism of the Web. HTTP is a client/server, or request/response-based transfer protocol supporting a minimal set of operations for transferring data. HTTP is described in Section 5.5.

Together these core technologies have evolved into a highly powerful mechanism for developing a wide range of distributed applications. After a brief introduction to how the Web came into being, we will look more closely at each in turn.

5.2 The Dawn of the Web

> *"Sites need to be able to interact in one single, universal space." Tim Berners-Lee*

Tim Berners-Lee created the first Web browser in 1990 at CERN in Switzerland, where a few thousand scientists worked using a variety of different computers. He soon found it frustrating to exchange data with different collaborators because he had to log onto the various computers to be able to share information. After writing various similar programs to transfer and convert information from one system to another, he started to think about better ways of achieving this. He then came up with the idea of creating some imaginary information system which everyone could read. He took the existing *hypertext* idea[1] [46] and wrote the first Web browser that connected via DNS and TCP to create the start of the World Wide Web; but that, he says, was the easy bit ... the difficult bit was to get people to join in.

The initial so-called *WorldWideWeb* browser was developed on a NeXT workstation and the first Web server was *nxoc01.cern.ch*, later changing its name to *info.cern.ch*. The following year the Stanford Linear Accelerator Center (SLAC) in California became the first Web server in the USA as the widespread distribution of the software began. In 1992, there were 50 Web servers worldwide; in 1993 NCSA released the first alpha version of Marc Andreessen's "Mosaic for X." Then in October 1994, Berners-Lee founded the World Wide Web Consortium (W3C) for standardizing common protocols to promote the Web's evolution and ensure its interoperability. By this time, the WWW explosion had already set in. For example, Internet users increased from 40 million in 1995 to 150 million in 1998 and 320 million by year 2000. Currently, there are 1.35 billion Internet users using the World Wide Web [47].

Tim Berners-Lee

Sir Timothy John Berners-Lee was born on 8 June 1955 and with the help of Robert Cailliau and a young student staff at CERN implemented the first Web server and browser, that became the birth of the World Wide Web. He is the director of the World Wide Web Consortium (W3C), which overseas its continued development. In December 2004 he accepted a chair in Computer Science at the School of Electronics and Computer Science, University of Southampton, UK, to work on his new project the Semantic Web.[2]

5.3 Naming Things in a Uniform Way

Central to the architecture of the Web is the Uniform Resource Identifier (URI). A URI is a character string which identifies a resource on the Web.

[1] Vannevar Bush was the conceptual creator, laying out the notion of the modern hyperlink in 1945, and in 1965, Ted Nelson coined the word "hypertext."

[2] Photo and biography taken from `http://en.wikipedia.org/wiki/Tim_Berners-Lee`.

URIs provide the Web with a single mechanism for naming arbitrary resources and have a very simple syntax. Let us look at some examples:

- `http://www.google.com`
- `urn:isbn:0-395-36341-1`
- `urn:jxta:uuid:59616261646162614A78746150325033F3BC76`
- `mailto:john.doe@example.com`
- `http://www.bbc.co.uk/weather/`
- `http://www.google.com/search?client=safari&q=web`

Every URI starts with a *scheme* component. In the examples above we have some `http` schemes, a `mailto` scheme used by email clients, and two `urn` schemes. Other schemes are also registered such as `ftp` for the File Transfer Protocol, `sip` for Session Initiation Protocol used mainly for voice over IP communications, even `tel`, representing telephone numbers.

> **What about Ports?**
> *The authority part of a hierarchical HTTP URI actually contains the host address and the port number that the server is listening on. However, by convention, HTTP uses port 80, and if a URI authority component points to a server listening on this well-known port, then it is implied. If the HTTP server were listening on a non-standard port, such as 8080, then the URI would have to reflect this by including the port number in the authority component, after the host component and separated from it by a colon, i.e.,* ***http://www.bbc.co.uk:8080/weather/****.*

URIs are a superset comprising Uniform Resource Names (URNs) and Uniform Resource Locators (URLs). URLs describe a resource in terms of the protocol that is used to access it. This is the case with the http examples and the mailto example above. URNs describe resources according to some other property, for example a unique identifier such as an ISBN. Traditionally URLs and URNs were seen as formal divisions of the URI space. Now you are likely to find the terms URI, URN and URL used almost interchangeably. The primary difference between URNs and URLs is that URLs have some sort of network address in them. This is the case with all the http examples and the mailto example. They contain the host name (google.com, bbc.co.uk and example.com) which can be used by an application to resolve the name to a physical device on the Internet using the Domain Name System (DNS). However, the urn examples could also be resolved to an actual network address as well, using some form of preprocessing of the URI before querying a network resolution service. This is actually the case with the urn:jxta example. The JXTA platform is capable of converting this unique JXTA identifier into a network address for a JXTA peer.

The HTTP scheme is the one most people are most familiar with. It is classed as a hierarchical URI because it contains certain elements that can be distinguished. Taking URI number five from the list above, this can be broken into three separate parts. First the *scheme* — `http` as we know. Second the *authority* — `www.bbc.co.uk`. This is the network addressable content of the URI and is used by the browser to contact the DNS system and resolve the name to a network IP address. Finally this example contains a *path* component — `weather` in this case. The path component is resolved by the host once the browser has found the host using DNS. In other words, the character string `weather` refers to some resource under the authority of the BBC host.

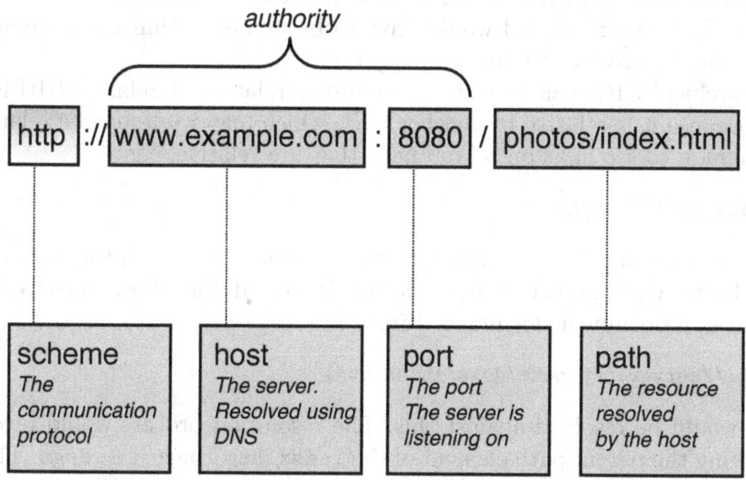

Fig. 5.1. Elements of a hierarchical URI.

HTTP URIs can also contain a *query string.* An example of such a URI is number 6 in the list above. This is the kind of URI you will see if you type a search term into the google home page. The beginning of the query string is denoted by a question mark (`?`). What follows this is a series of key/value pairs separated by an ampersand (`&`). The key and the value of each pair are separated by an equals sign (`=`). Taking the google example above, the URI contains two key/value pairs in the query string:

```
client=safari
```

```
q=web
```

The keys and their values are understood by the server receiving the request. In this example, the key `client` tells google what browser the request is coming from. Here the value is Apple's Safari browser. Google may return content in a different format depending on the browser making the request. The key `q` identifies the actual search term typed in by the user. In this case, the search term was the value `web`.

URIs can also contain a fragment identifier. This is a series of characters at the end of the path element identified by the hash, or sharp, symbol (`#`). The fragment identifier allows a portion of a resource to be identified in a URI. For example, you may have a very large document that is structurally broken down into sections. Using the fragment identifier in the URI, you could point to a particular section, allowing the browser to find that section on behalf of the user and save them scrolling through the document:

```
http://server.com/documents/bigdocument.html#section3
```

The relevant section in the HTML document would be tagged with an identifier equal to `section3` and would have to be unique within the document, in order for the browser to find it.

Hierarchical URIs can be either absolute or relative. A relative URI is so called because it is relative to another URI, which may itself also be relative. It is common to see links on a Web page that are relative, e.g.:

```
../images/fido.jpg
```

Typically, such a URI is relative to the location from which the document in which the URI appears was retrieved. Hence, if the above relative link occurred in a document downloaded from

```
http://server.com/pets/dogs/index.html
```

then it would be resolved against this. The resolution process would involve first getting the parent path element of the `index.html` page, i.e., `dogs`. Then, for every occurrence of `../` in the relative URI, we get the next parent path element of the absolute URI. Similar to Unix file system paths, the `../` characters mean *up one level*. In this case we would traverse upwards once to the `pets` path element. Finally we append the relative URI to the absolute URI to arrive at a new absolute URI:

```
http://server.com/pets/images/fido.jpg
```

You will have noticed that a relative URI cannot traverse beyond the first path element or across the authority component of the URI. Hence you cannot have a relative URI resolve against an absolute URI pointing to a different host.

5.3.1 URI Templates

According to Berners-Lee, URIs should be inherently opaque by design, even if the different components that make it up can be extracted and dissected:

> *"The only thing you can use an identifier for is to refer to an object. When you are not dereferencing you should not look at the contents of the URI string to gain other information."*

The argument for this approach is that the more a client understands or reads into a URI, the more brittle the system becomes, because the client may start making inferences about other similar URIs in the server's namespace which are wrong. It also makes the system more tightly coupled because there is the possibility of shared, or implied, meaning in the URIs served up by a server. This in turn exposes the internal logic of the server and makes it harder for the server to change its internal organization without affecting the external identification mechanism.

However, beyond simply being syntactic devices for defining a server-side defined reference to some resource, the various components of a URI inevitably represent relationships between parts of the URI itself in an intuitive manner. For example, the path element of a URI is a forward slash delimited series of character strings. While the relationships between the components in the path have no intrinsic meaning, the order in which they appear is reminiscent of a graph or tree structure, much like files and folders on your local machine. Hence the order in which they appear can be used to imply logical groupings resources:

```
http://server.com/media/photos
```

and

```
http://server.com/media/music
```

for example express a logical grouping called media, which in turn contains two subsets: photos and music. This does not necessarily tell me any more about the internal workings or organization of the resources at the server side. It is the server using the URIs to expose the resources in a particular way that allows me to make logical connections between them. It is no different from a supermarket arranging the aisles in such a way that I can make the assumption, having found the tea, that the coffee is probably not far away. If the supermarket has no ordering to how its resources are laid out, I get frustrated.

Likewise, query strings intuitively imply some algorithm that is going to take place at the server side in response to the particular values I put in the query. This should not be confused with imagining that I am invoking some method on the server which takes certain parameters. To return to the supermarket analogy, it is like me asking a shop attendant for coffee which is fair-trade and extra strength. The attendant takes me to the coffee aisle and shows me a pack of coffee that is fair-trade *and* extra strength. One could just as well address each coffee individually, but this may become cumbersome if the choices are numerous, and if you want clients to be able to view your products using such filtering techniques.

Recent commentators are suggesting that such logical arrangement of URIs is useful, particularly as more machine-processable services are made available on the Web. Part of this movement is the development of the URI Template specification which is currently at IETF Network Working Group Internet Draft stage [48].

URI Templates are URI strings with embedded variables in them. Variables are surrounded by curly braces (curly braces are not allowed in URIs, so the appearance of a variable cannot be confused with a valid URI). A template is converted to a standard URI by replacing the variables with actual character content which is specific to a particular situation. For example:

```
http://www.server.com/users/{userid}
```

becomes

```
http://www.server.com/users/1234
```

if the particular user's identifier is `1234`. URI Templates are particularly suited to machine-processing because they allow a service to describe how their resources are accessed in abstract terms. For every user of the imaginary service at www.server.com, their user page is of the same form and described once by the service, as long as the client knows they have to replace the variable with their actual user identifier. This in turn allows services to publish their service interface in a generic, machine readable-manner, something that the Web has in general been lacking.

URIs have proven to be incredibly versatile. The uniformity of URIs provides the Web with a single syntax for naming entities and it is flexible enough to allow virtually anything to be named. The HTTP scheme alone is today used to name a virtually infinite number of resources. Not only do they provide the glue that binds the disparate elements of the Web together by allowing content on one side of the planet to reference content on the other side, they have stepped off the computer screen and now inhabit the physical world as well. They are exchanged in conversations, written on the backs of envelopes, printed in newspapers and on billboards and are emblazoned on the sides of cars, trains and aeroplanes.

This transferral from the digital world to the physical has naturally had an impact on how we perceive and understand the Web in terms of its overall architecture. For example, one thing the Web had never been particularly focussed on is coherent, reliable resource discovery. In general, resource discovery is either highly centralized on the Web, for example via a search engine, or a service such as Technorati, which keeps a database of weblog content, or it is achieved through the informal and often fortuitous process of following links.

However, the fact that URIs appear almost anywhere means discovery can at times become so de-centralized as to be 'out-of-bounds'; while waiting in a take-away restaurant the other day, I found a catering trade brochure advertising pizza ovens — something I have always coveted. I promptly remembered the URI on the brochure, went home and typed it into my browser. I had discovered a pizza oven manufacturer. I have never come across a CORBA object reference, or even a Web Services WSDL document, under similar circumstances. Perhaps this is what Berners-Lee and Lao Tse mean by *useful*.

5.4 A Shared Representation of Things

In the spirit of *Usefulness from what is not there*, Berners-Lee defines the Principle of Least Power which states that *when expressing something, use the least powerful language you can*. The premise of this principle is that the more complex an expression is, the less likely it is to be understood by others, and the less likely it is that others will be able to convert it into a language or representation that best suits their own needs, and which itself may be complex and highly specific. When sharing representations across different communities with different conceptual views, it is important that the representation format does not enforce a centralized or exclusive paradigm.

Hypertext Markup Language (HTML) provides a very low entry point into being able to express resources. The language is primarily concerned with how to present resources in a human-readable way — not on how to model the capabilities or internal structure of the resource itself. This is very different from exchanging serialized Java objects for example, as Jini does. Here the representation is specifically designed to enable the reconstitution of the capabilities and internal structure of a resource. The price paid is that only clients with an understanding of the internal structure and the representation can reconstitute the resource. On the other hand, the structure of HTML is not tied to the structure of the resource — the two are orthogonal. Instead a resource, or the author of the representation, shoe-horns their conception of the resource (the car, the petition, the pet dog) into the limited vocabulary of HTML. What emerges is not necessarily a perfect transcription of the resource, but at least everyone will be able to access the representation, whether they are a car mechanic, a political activist, or a dog lover. And depending on their field of expertise, they may be able to extract enough information from the representation to convert it into their own proprietary format which is concerned with the internal structure of the resource. HTML acts as a kind of many-to-one meta language for resource transferral. As a result it also means it imposes many limitations.

The reason why HTML is *Hypertext* markup as to any other markup language is because HTML transcends the traditional concept of text being a linear progression of states in which content is defined by the author and is unchangeable by the reader. Instead, HTML presented to a client consists of a number of options. The implications of the use of HTML and the fact that it is a form of hypermedia are described in relation to Representational State Transfer in Section 5.6.

5.5 Hypertext Transfer Protocol

Hypertext Transfer Protocol (HTTP) has become the de facto means of exchanging resources on the Web. In fact, it is considered such a useful, flexible and ubiquitously deployed protocol that it is also used by other systems under certain circumstances, for example JXTA and Gnutella. Likewise, SOAP-based Web Services almost invariably use HTTP for tunneling SOAP envelopes.

HTTP is a simple application-level protocol. It supports a handful of methods which are analogous to operations one might perform on a database or a simple key/value-based storage facility. Some of the request methods allow resource representations to accompany them in the request while others do not. Along with the method name, a client sends an identifier for the resource and a number of HTTP headers. The resource identifier is that portion of the URI after the authority component. HTTP headers are essentially key/value pairs. The most commonly used methods are:

GET retrieves a resource from a given URI. This request contains no resource representation.

DELETE removes a resource at a given URI. This request contains no resource representation.

PUT updates or alters a resource at a given URI. If the resource does not exist on the server, the server may allow a new resource to be created at that URI. This request contains a resource representation.

POST is used differently in different contexts. In general this method implies the creation of a new resource based on the representation sent to the server in the request. The created resource is logically a subordinate resource to the resource at the URI to which the POST request is made. What 'subordinate' means in practice is up to the server to decide. This request contains a resource representation.

HEAD gets metadata about a resource. This should return all the information to the client exactly as if a GET request had been made, except that the payload, i.e., the representation of the resource, is not present in the response. This request contains no resource representation.

OPTIONS returns a list of HTTP methods that are allowed at a given URI. This request contains no resource representation.

So what does an HTTP request look like? Here is a simplified example of the HTTP request you might send to the BBC weather page at `http://www.bbc.co.uk/weather/`:

```
GET /weather/ HTTP/1.1
User-Agent: curl/7.16.3
Host: www.bbc.co.uk
Accept: */*
```

The first line of the request specifies the method — GET — the resource path, namely, the part of the full URI after the authority component, and the version of HTTP being used — in this case version 1.1. Then the headers follow. The User-Agent header tells the server what software is being used to create the request. The Host header identifies the host server and is usually the authority component of the complete URI. The Accept header tells the server what type of data the client is prepared to accept. This may be one of the common Multipurpose Internet Mail Extensions (MIME) types that are defined such as text/html, text/plain or image/jpeg and image/png. As is apparent, a MIME type has a type — the value before the slash, and a subtype — the value after the slash. Thus html and plain text are both subtypes of text, in the same way as jpeg and png are subtypes of the image type. In the header above, the wildcard character (*) is used to say any type. Hence the client above is happy to accept any type and any subtype.

Here is the simplified reply:

```
HTTP/1.1 200 OK
Date: Wed, 26 Mar 2008 16:03:01 GMT
Server: Apache/2.0.59 (Unix)
Content-Length: 12345
Content-Type: text/html
```

The first line specifies the HTTP version being used and then the response status code and an attendant 'reason phrase'. The 200 response code means everything went well and the requested resource is contained in the message. Other common response codes include 201 Created, if a resource was successfully created on the server, 404 Not Found, if the server cannot map the request path to a resource, and 403 Forbidden, if the client is not authorized to access the resource. There are 40 standard response codes covering a variety of possible conditions. In the example above the server returns headers describing the date and time the request was fulfilled, the server software, the length in bytes on the representation being returned to the client, and the MIME type of the representation. Following these headers is the actual data, if any.

The HTTP methods, and the contexts in which they are used, are often assessed in terms of two properties — whether or not they are *safe* and whether or not they are *idempotent*. A safe operation is one that produces no side effects. From a user's perspective, a side effect is some change of state in the resources with which it is interacting. By convention the GET, HEAD and OPTIONS methods should be considered safe, and should therefore not be used in circumstances where a change in state on the server may result from their use. Even if such a change takes place, the client making the request cannot be held accountable for the side effect. The other methods — PUT, POST and DELETE — are generally not safe. Their semantics imply changing resource state at the server side and so should be used in situations where this will be the case. The property of safety underpins an implicit contract between the server and the client when a particular method is used. Performing a safe method, such as a GET, implies that no contract is entered into by the client, no further requests will be expected by the server and no change will happen on the server which the client is responsible for. Therefore, if a server uses a safe method in a situation where a side effect will be produced, or some sort of obligation on the client side is implied, they are breaking the contract with the client.

Maintaining this contract helps keep the Web loosely coupled — breaking it can cause unwanted results. For example, it is common when joining a mailing list to receive an email containing an address to go to in order to confirm one's subscription. When a user clicks on this link, the browser performs a GET request to the server at the URL provided. When the content is returned to the browser, the user is surprised to see a page offering its congratulations on joining the mailing list. However, the user unknowingly confirmed that they would join — they sent a safe GET request but have as a result entered into a contract with the server. What the server should return from the GET request is a page with a button reading "Click Here to Confirm Your Subscription". When this button is clicked by the user, it should trigger a POST request to the server which adds the user to the mailing list database.

An idempotent method is one which can be invoked many times with the same effect as if it had only been invoked once. This property is generally shared by GET, HEAD, OPTIONS, PUT and DELETE. Methods that are safe are inherently idempotent. The idempotent property is particularly useful in a distributed context because it allows requests to be repeated if partial errors occur during the request process. For example, the server may go down leaving the client without a response. If a request is neither idempotent nor safe and such a condition arises, then the client has to make a difficult decision on when or if to repeat the request because repetition could induce a side effect which is unwanted.

URIs, HTML and HTTP make up the core technologies of the Web. The only thing missing is the software that understands and combines them. At the server side, this requires a Web server that can serve up content based on HTTP requests. At the client side, it needs software to render the HTML and allow users to click on links. Enter the browser.

5.5.1 HTTP and Security

Secure communications on the Web use a combination of techniques depending on their requirements. HTTP supports user/password authentication directly via certain headers and response codes. In a typical scenario, a browser will follow a link to a particular resource. If the resource is restricted to certain users then the server responds with a 401 Unauthorized status code. Along with this response code, the server includes a WWW-Authenticate header specifying the type of authentication the server expects and the *realm* associated with the credentials expected of the client. There are typically two types

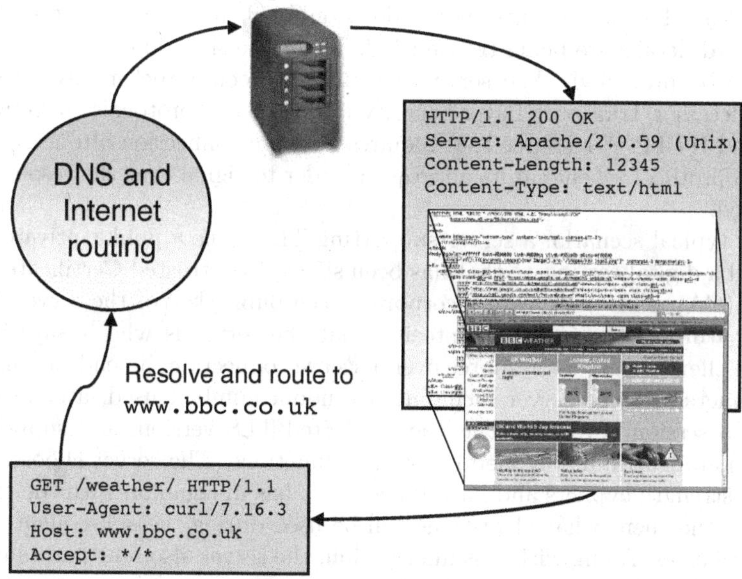

Fig. 5.2. Browser request process.

of authentication used — basic and digest. Both types expect a username and password pair. Basic authentication takes the username and password and encodes it to Base64. Base64 is a binary-to-text encoding scheme designed to safely transmit binary data using printable characters. This encoding is not secure in any way — a simple algorithm can convert the encoded string back to plain text. Digest authentication, on the other hand, uses a hash function to encrypt the credentials. Hash functions produce a non-reversible fixed-length key (see Chapter 4 for more details). Typically MD5 is used for this. The realm of the authentication challenge represents the restricted area of the Web site, usually as a URI relative to the server's domain.

When the browser receives the 401 status code, it offers the user some information on the realm and input fields for entering the username and password details. If the user fills in this information, then the browser re-transmits the original request, this time with an Authenticate header containing the type of authentication and the credentials encoded accordingly, i.e., as Base64 for basic authentication or as a hash key if digest is used. If the server accepts the credentials then the request is granted and the browser receives the content of the restricted page.

The HTTP authorization mechanism has a number of limitations. First, using basic authentication the credentials are sent, to all intents and purposes, as plain text, allowing third parties to intercept the transmission and decode the username/password pair. Second, even if a secure hashing function is used for digest authentication, the subsequent data exchanges likewise take place in the clear. This is obviously not good enough when sensitive data such as credit card details are being transmitted. To handle situations in which data needs to be protected, Web servers usually use Secure Socket Layer (SSL) or its successor Transport Layer Security (TLS). These protocols sit between TCP and HTTP. A resource that requires a secure connection often uses the HTTPS protocol scheme in its address, in order to signal that the resource is protected.

In a typical scenario, a server supporting TLS owns a public/private key pair and a digital certificate that has been signed by a trusted Certificate Authority (CA). This certificate incorporates the public key of the server with the signature of the CA, guaranteeing that the server is who it says it is. When a client requests a resource over a secure connection, it sends a number of parameters to the server including a random number, used later in generating a session key, as well as the supported TLS version, and supported encryption algorithms (cyphers) and hash functions. The server chooses the highest strength cyphers and hash functions it has in common with the client and tells the client what algorithms will be used during the subsequent message exchanges. Along with this information, the server also sends an random number. The server then sends the client its certificate.

At this stage, the client may contact the CA to verify the authenticity of the certificate. Browsers generally come with a list of well-known CAs against which they can check the signature in the certificate. If the signature is not known by the browser, for example, if the certificate is self-signed, it will usually prompt the user to either accept of reject the certificate.

If the certificate is deemed trustworthy, then the client creates a new random number, known as the *PreMasterKey*, encrypts this using the public key of the server, and sends it to the server. Only the server can decrypt the number using its private key. Then both sides generate the *master secret* from the random numbers initially sent to one another, and the PreMasterKey. This master key is then used to encrypt and decrypt all message exchanges until the session has completed.

TLS also supports mutual authentication in which a client is also required to possess a public/private key pair, although this is less common on the Web. In this circumstance, the server requests a certificate from the client and the client returns it in response. After having sent the PreMasterKey to the server, the client then sends a signature over the previous messages exchanged during the handshake process. The server can verify this signature using the client's public key proving that the client has access to the associated private key used to generate the signature, and is therefore who they say they are.

5.6 Representational State Transfer

Representational State Transfer (REST) is an architectural style developed by Roy Fielding in his PhD thesis submitted in 2000 by examining how the Web works and what makes it scalable. The acronym REST has become widely used, not always in situations where it is applicable. For example, it is often confused with HTTP, in the sense that any service or client using an HTTP interface is inherently RESTful. This is certainly not the case. REST is neither intrinsically tied to HTTP, nor do all interactions that use HTTP follow REST principles.

The REST architectural style is derived from examining the needs of a system, in particular a distributed hypermedia system such as the Web. Design constraints are applied incrementally to separate the design space and be able to understand the forces they exert on the system. The set of constraints defined by Fielding constitutes REST and is described in the following sections.

5.6.1 Client-Server

The first constraint is that the system is client-server based. A client is a software entity that triggers requests directed at a server, usually at a time and of a nature decided by itself. A server is a software entity that waits for those requests, and then responds to them. Separating out the two roles means each entity can evolve separately as long as the interface between them remains the same.

5.6.2 Statelessness

The interaction between client and server must be stateless in the sense that each request contains all the information needed for a server to generate a response. It does not mean that the server does not maintain its own state. Indeed, if it did not, it would probably provide only very uninteresting services. The main reason we connect to a server is to access the resources, i.e., state, that it maintains. This statelessness refers to communication state, the communication being the message exchanges between client and server. As a consequence of this communication statelessness, session or application, state is stored at the client side, not the server side.

This statelessness increases visibility because all information is in every request which makes firewall implementations much simpler. Reliability is increased because it simplifies recovery from events such as network failure, i.e., it allows operations to idempotent. Statelessness also increases scalability because the server does not have to maintain state between requests. This is turn means the server can free resources associated with a request, and servers can be replicated or moved without affecting interactions with the client.

A common example of interactions on the Web that break this constraint, are those that use cookies, such as the typical shopping cart. A cookie is an identifier of session state that is sent by the server in the initial HTTP response headers. The client should store the cookie and use it in subsequent requests to the same server by inserting it into its HTTP request headers.

Roy Fielding
Roy Fielding is most widely known for his doctoral dissertation "Architectural Styles and the Design of Network-based Software Architectures" in which he describes REST as a key architectural principle of the World Wide Web. He was also one of the principal authors of the HTTP specification as well as being involved in the development of HTML and URIs. That's not all, however. Fielding was also co-founder of the Apache HTTP Server, the most widely used server software on the Web.[3]

Typically a cookie contains some unique identifier, an expiry date, and a URI associated with the identifier. The reason cookies break the principle of statelessness is because they are keys to session state that are stored on the server. To the client application, the cookie is essentially opaque — the identifier means nothing to it. At the server side, however, this key is mapped to some context within which each client request is understood. This may be a shopping cart object, or a user account. As a consequence, the server is compromising its own scalability because it must track each individual client across numerous message exchanges. Furthermore, because the cookie represents the server's view of application state, rather than the client's view, the two can cease to be synchronized. In the case of a browser for example, application state can be understood in terms of the series of requests that constitute the browser's history. If a client moves back through history and continues to send the cookie in each request as it is supposed to do, the view of state becomes desynchronized. Many of us are familiar with such problems, for example when completing online purchases which require a rigid sequence of server-defined state transitions.

As Fielding points out, a more sensible shopping cart implementation would more directly reflect its manifestation in the physical world in that a client should maintain the shopping cart and its contents at the client side, and proceed to the checkout URI when and if they are ready to do so, relieving the server from being involved in the process of choosing products.

5.6.3 Caching

The Caching constraint is the next to be added to the system. Caching is the process by which a client or intermediary node stores. Caching allows requests to be partially or fully fulfilled without resorting to actual network activity. This improves perceived client performance, and scalability through reducing network traffic. It requires, however, that messages have some way

[3] Biography summarised from wikipedia `http://en.wikipedia.org/wiki/Roy_Fielding`.

of expressing whether or not a resource is cacheable, and for how long. In terms of the Web, this has been addressed through particular HTTP headers that allow such stipulations to be ascribed to requests and responses. The trade-off to such benefits is of course that cached data may become stale and not represent the current state of the data at the original source.

5.6.4 Uniform Interface

This is a key constraint of REST which sets it apart from many other distributed systems. A uniform interface means both the message exchanges and the data exchanged in those messages should be commonly understood and shared. This simplifies the overall system architecture massively. For example, imagine a Web in which every Web server has a different way of accessing the resources in its charge. This would require a different messaging client for every Web site, something that would clearly inhibit the scalability and adoption of the Web. This may seem obvious, but it is exactly the approach taken by distributed object systems and Web Services (see Chapter 7). In these systems, the service description and messaging syntax is shared, but not the actual service interface; that is, the message structure used in the request. These have to be discovered, and local bindings to them generated beforehand or on-the-fly, before communication can take place.

Enabling a uniform interface requires further constraints on the interfaces between components. REST defines these as:

- identification of resources
- manipulation of resources through representations
- self-descriptive messages
- hypermedia as the engine of application state

In terms of the Web, this first constraint is addressed through the use of URIs which act as a uniform naming scheme. The second constraint is addressed through the use of well-known media types. As described in Section 5.4, HTML is the primary resource representation format of the Web. Other formats are used in conjunction with it, such as JPEG and PNG image formats and more recently, Macromedia Flash movies. However, these are usually embedded, with HTML acting as the container representation. From the perspective of REST, HTML is a representation of the state of a resource at a given point in time, available at a given URI. The resource itself may be dynamically generated from a series of database queries, or exist in memory as a collection of programming language objects. The representation is a shared interface to a hidden entity, thus providing a layer of abstraction to the client. Combined with HTTP, it provides a restricted view on how the underlying resource can be manipulated, namely, through one of the HTTP methods alone.

This approach is quite different from Object-oriented systems. An object is essentially the encapsulation of data, or state, and operations over that state.

The operations are the interface to the object — the means by which the data, and hence state, of the object is altered. The data itself is hidden from view. A resource on the other hand exposes its state — the representation of a resource is a representation of the state of that resource. Furthermore, a representation of a resource has no operations for manipulating its state. Rather, these are defined separately. Specifically in terms of URIs, the possible operations on the state of a resource are defined by the *scheme* of the URI at which the representation is available. If a representation of a resource is available at a URI with an `http` scheme, then the HTTP methods represent the possible operations on the resource. If the resource is exposed at a URI with a `mailto` scheme, then the operations are defined by the mail transfer protocol supported by the client that wishes to interact with the resource — probably SMTP. Likewise, a resource available at a URI with an `ftp` scheme will be subject to the operations defined by the File Transfer Protocol.

The fact that representations of resources are explicit formulations of state has interesting side effects. In particular, it increases visibility in that a server can examine the state representation as it arrives. This makes both firewalling and caching much simpler. When exchanging encapsulated data, for example remote method invocations or serialized objects, it is very hard to unravel the message without having a prior knowledge of the application that is exchanging the data. This in turn makes it harder to determine equivalence, for the sake of caching, or whether the contents are malicious or not.

The fourth constraint has attracted almost as much confusion as it has interest: what does Fielding mean by *hypermedia as the engine of application state*? In the context of this constraint, the *application* is the distributed communication between client and server. The states of the application are the points before, during or after one or more request response pairs. As described in Section 5.5, hypermedia provides a non-linear path through a set of states. Hence, when a client clicks on a link, the application state changes and a new set of possibilities are presented to the client. The hypermedia, for example an HTML page containing links, acts as the engine that allows transitions through states. As Fielding says:

> *"The model application is therefore an engine that moves from one state to the next by examining and choosing from among the alternative state transitions in the current set of representations. Not surprisingly, this exactly matches the user interface of a hypermedia browser."*

The use of hypermedia as the central resource representation type of the Web has a number of advantages that are not seen in other distributed systems. First, it acts as an insulation layer between the client and the server. This allows both entities to evolve independently. For example, it allows a service to expose a single bootstrapping URI, e.g., the company's homepage, as a gateway to a series of state transitions, or conversations. The server is likely to want to change these conversations over time as it evolves. In this case, the bootstrap URI can remain the same while the hypermedia and hence the possible state transitions a client can enter, can be changed.

Second, it provides a client with a sequential view of the service. This is poorly addressed in technologies such as Web Services that have no intrinsic means of describing anything more complex or long lasting than a single request response pair. Instead, other specifications are used such as the Business Process Execution Language (BPEL) for defining workflows of Web Service interactions. However, even such modeling of service workflows is on the whole digested by clients at compile-time. The states are modeled explicitly often with conditional branches, much like a flowchart. Such static descriptions are arguably paramount in order for clients to understand the expected logic and hence be machine processable, but they impose a pre-defined set of possibilities. Hypermedia allows state transitions to be generated and presented to the client at runtime, without the client having to understand the logic that has led to the particular conversational state. While placing less burden on the client because it does not have to understand the complete server-side logic, it can make machine processing more complex, perhaps even impossible, because the machine cannot verify the current state and possible transitions against a pre-defined template.

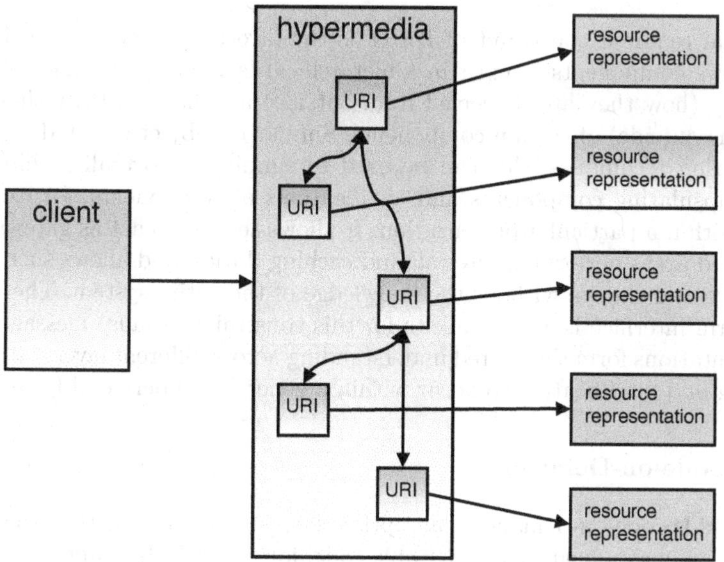

Fig. 5.3. Hypermedia providing sequential understanding of resource representations, which can themselves be hypermedia.

While hypermedia presents the client with resource state and possible transitions to other states, the temporal relationships of these states should only perceived by the client. This is because REST is stateless. Application, or session, state resides on the client side. This is possible because messages are self-descriptive. So, although a particular client request will lead to a particular resource representation being returned, with further possible states referenced in the hypermedia, the client request is independent from any other requests as far as the server is concerned. In the case of a browser, this allows a user to click the back and forward buttons without destabilizing server-side state. As a simple example, take a request to Google. The client sends a parameterized request to `www.google.com` containing the search criteria amongst other parameters. The response contains an HTML document with usually ten links that relate to the search terms. At the bottom of the page further results are available at a different URI. The client may then click on the *Next* button, to retrieve the next set of results. Here the client has experienced application state as moving from the first ten results to the next ten results. Google, on the other hand, has experienced no such thing — each request is entirely independent and directed at a different URI. Between state transitions, Google has forgotten that the client exists. (Try adding a `start` parameter to the end of the URI once you have performed the initial query, e.g., `&start=30`. Then look at the bottom of the page again.)

5.6.5 Layering

The final required constraint of REST is the layering of the system. Layering allows components to exist in a hierarchical fashion, restricting both the visibility (how they are perceived from outside) and horizon (how they perceive the outside) of certain components. Similar to Object-oriented software engineering techniques, this can be used to simplify an overall architecture by encapsulating components and aggregations of components, for example those within a particular organization. It allows servers to act as gateways to contained areas performing firewall and caching duties, and allows such areas to evolve and change without the knowledge of the entire system. The use of a uniform interface is a prerequisite for this constraint because messages and representations form the shared understanding across different layers, allowing filtering and modification to occur within a generally understood framework.

5.6.6 Code-on-Demand

REST adds code-on-demand as an optional constraint. This is the process by which clients can download executable code, for example Java applets, reducing their dependence on compile-time capabilities. The reason this constraint is optional is because it reduces visibility; that is, no longer are client and server sharing representations of resources in the form of hypermedia. Rather, binary code is being exchanged, making firewalling and caching harder to implement.

5.7 The Semantic Web

The Semantic Web is a World Wide Web Consortium (W3C) initiative based on the vision of Tim Berners-Lee that:

> *"Computers become capable of analyzing all the data on the Web — the content, links, and transactions between people and computers."*

While the resources on the Web are currently designed primarily for human consumption, the Semantic Web is about making statements about those resources in such a way that machines can, first, parse the information, and second, derive properties from it. Once the properties of a resource have been found, it is possible to make assertions about what the resource is, and once you know what the resource is, it is possible to describe its relationships with other resources.

The primary mechanism used by the Semantic Web to achieve this level of introspection over resources is the Resource Description Framework (RDF). RDF is a set of W3C specifications for describing the properties of a resource, or what it is, and the relationships it has with other resources. Underpinning RDF is a data model based on simple *triple* expressions comprising *subject*, *predicate* and *object*. By making statements about resources using this model it is possible to build up graphs of relationships between resources. Such a graph becomes a web of meaning, or semantics, complementing the web of links that currently exists.

The subject of an RDF triple is the resource about which the statement is being made. The object represents another resource, or a literal character string value. The predicate is the relationship between the subject and the object. For example, the statement *John has a pet cat* can be broken down into three constituent parts. The subject is *John*, the entity about which the statement is being made. The predicate is the relationship that *John* has with the entity *cat*. This predicate is *has a pet*. The object of the statement is the cat itself, being at the receiving end of the predicate. One could reverse the subject/object relationships which would change the predicate. For example, *The cat is owned by John* changes the predicate to *is owned by*. Therefore, predicates have a direction and the graphs produced by linking resources in this way are directed graphs.

Subjects and predicates are resources, and hence, according to Web principles, are represented by URIs. The object of the triple can either be a resource represented by a URI, or a literal character string. Several mechanisms for converting such statements into human- or machine-readable syntax exist, including XML.

On their own, such triples are of limited use to a machine, because although the syntax may be machine readable, the machine has no *a priori* knowledge about what any of the elements mean. Hence shared vocabularies are required to define the properties that resources can have. An example of such a set of well-known properties is the Dublin Core Metadata Element Set, defined by the Dublin Core Metadata Initiative [49]. These properties are useful in describing metadata about online resources, including elements such as creator, publisher, title and language, to name a few. Using sets of properties, it is possible to define a class for a certain type of resource through the properties that a resource has. By classing resources, you create types, and therefore can determine equivalence or difference between resources. The classification of resources and their properties is essentially a schema called an *ontology* in Semantic Web terminology. An ontology represents knowledge, rather than a message format, as is usually the case with schema. Because an ontology is a knowledge representation, tools can be used to derive conclusions about resources that are not physically present in the ontology itself. Let us look at a relatively simple example in order to get a clearer idea of how an ontology works. The Friend of a Friend (FOAF) is a simple ontology defining a Person class and its relation to other instances of the Person class:

```
<rdf:RDF
  xmlns:rdf="http://www.w3.org/1999/02/22-rdf-syntax-ns#"
  xmlns:foaf="http://xmlns.com/foaf/0.1/"
  xmlns:rdfs="http://www.w3.org/2000/01/rdf-schema#">
  <foaf:Person rdf:about="#AL">
    <foaf:name>Archibald Leach</foaf:name>
    <foaf:mbox_sha1sum>cf2342293...</foaf:mbox_sha1sum>
    <foaf:knows>
      <foaf:Person>
        <foaf:name>Katharine Hepburn</foaf:name>
      </foaf:Person>
    </foaf:knows>
  </foaf:Person>
</rdf:RDF>
```

The Person class represents a resource and must therefore have a URI. To this end the Person element has an about attribute defined in the RDF namespace representing the URI of the person. Here it is defined simply as a fragment identifier and cannot be presumed to be unique.

There are a number of properties a Person class can have, only a few of which are shown above. Each of these properties represents an RDF triple of which the subject is the person in which they appear. For example, the name property represents a predicate with a URI of http://xmlns.com/foaf/0.1/name and the object of the triple is a character string literal of Archibald Leach.

The knows property is an important property in a FOAF person because it links one person object with another. Here, the knows property is the predicate, the person with the name Archibald Leach is the subject and the FOAF person with the name Katharine Hepburn is the object of the triple.

The mbox_sha1sum property is a hexidecimal number (truncated above for clarity) which is the result of applying a SHA1 mathematical function to the actual email address of the person represented. This performs two roles. First, it allows the person to keep their email address hidden from spammers. Second, it can act as a unique identifier for the particular person. For example, if we came across another FOAF person such as the one below, we would be able to reason that the two are the same person:

```
...
<foaf:Person rdf:about="#CG" >
  <foaf:name>Cary Grant</foaf:name>
  <foaf:mbox_sha1sum>cf2342293...</foaf:mbox_sha1sum>
</foaf:Person>
...
```

FOAF people can be combined into a graph of nodes connected via the `knows` predicate, revealing relationships that are not modeled in the individual person classes.

The Web Ontology Language (shortened to OWL rather than WOL) is the primary ontology language at the moment. OWL extends the RDF vocabulary and provides mechanisms for defining class and property hierarchies. Classes in an OWL ontology are constrained by *axioms*. Axioms place restrictions on classes and their possible relationships with other classes. By processing the classes and axioms, for example using First-Order Logic, it is possible for a machine to deduce properties of classes that are not explicitly modeled. For example, transitive relationships can be deduced:

> *A cat is a sub-class of animal*
> *Felix is a cat*
> *therefore Felix is an animal*

And disjoint constraints:

> *A human is a sub-class of animal*
> *A human is not a cat*
> *John is a human*
> *therefore John is not a cat*

Relationships can also be constrained.

> *A car is not an animal*
> *An animal can be a pet*
> *A human can have a pet*
> *John has a pet cat*

is fine, but

> *John has a pet car*

is not.

Creating an ontology is a non-trivial task. Similar to creating an object-oriented set of software components, relationships between components have to be modeled in a suitable way. On top of this, however, an ontology has to support reasoning that is only derived or inferred from the actual modeling. The results of such reasoning can be difficult to predict. Hence extra care and knowledge is required in designing ontologies. For example, the statement

> *John has a pet human*

is also legal according to the constraints above.

While the Semantic Web has much potential and is built on a flexible data model, it has not gained wide acceptance as yet. This may be for various reasons. First, the XML representation of RDF is cumbersome. This is being addressed by a number of projects, for example RDFa [50]. RDFa defines a set of extensions to XHTML allowing RDF triples to be embedded into Web content. This means separate RDF representations of resources described in HTML do not have to be created. Instead RDF metadata can be constructed inline, alongside the data itself. Such an approach may prove to be more attractive to developers and designers.

Second, to be useful, the RDF model requires shared ontologies based on broad agreement across many domains. This may also be difficult to achieve. To date, therefore, RDF is used more in highly specialized domains, where data structures are complex and creating and agreeing upon shared ontologies has tangible benefits. These include research areas such as bio-informatics [51] and government initiatives such as the IPSV-Integrated Public Sector Vocabulary [52].

In contrast to the ontological and taxonomic approach to data adopted by the Semantic Web, recent years have seen an explosion in more informal means of associating metadata with data in the form of *tagging.* Web sites such as del.icio.us and Flickr allow users to tag data with keywords. The aggregation of these individually defined associations leads to so-called *folksonomies.* Folksonomies develop organically and require no special or previous knowledge on the part of users. Hence, they are easy to contribute to. It may be that the Semantic Web movement has concentrated too much on the rich possibilities afforded by a deep modeling of complex data structures, rather than on gaining traction by proposing modeling simple structures in a more shallow way [53]. This way, once such technologies such as RDF have gained a foothold, richer relationships can be defined on top. RDFa may in fact be the start of such a process. A more lightweight approach to metadata is also championed by movements such as Microformats (see Section 18.2.3), who align themselves with the *small S semantic Web*. These developments may lead to a convergence of technologies and approaches that can accommodate both mass uptake and high-level ontologies leading to the fruition of Berners-Lee's dream, despite its long gestation period.

5.8 Conclusion

The importance of the Web cannot be overstated, both in a social context and in its relation to other distributed systems. It has achieved a ubiquity unequalled by other systems and continues to influence them. In the following chapters we will be looking at a variety of distributed systems and architectures. Many of them use and abuse the Web drawing upon its underlying technologies to achieve their own aims. For example, the Gnutella (see Section 6.4.2) protocol is designed to achieve decentralized discovery of files. Once a Gnutella node is found with a certain file, the download of the file is achieved using the HTTP GET operation. Jini too (see Chapter 14) uses an HTTP server for sending and receiving Java class files across the network.

Bootstrapping to a P2P network is also often achieved using the Web. For example, known Web pages were used to discover Gnutella nodes, and BitTorrent commonly uses the Web for discovering torrent files. Likewise, the BitTorrent controller is an HTTP server.

Although HTTP is a request/response-based protocol, it is useful even for systems that on the face of it are asynchronous and message based. An example of this is Jxta (see Chapter 15). Jxta makes use of URIs as logical, unique identifiers for peers. A Jxta Peer id URI is not bound to a network location, or even a particular type of network. Rather the URIs are resolved to network addresses using the Jxta protocols at runtime. The default behaviour of the Jxta reference implementation is to use HTTP if the peer is connected to the Internet. Hence a Peer id URI is often resolved to an HTTP address and the peer available at that address uses the HTTP protocol to send and receive Jxta messages. Although Jxta is based on one-way messages through the *pipe* abstraction, HTTP allows Jxta to make use of the rich set of headers and response codes in its message exchanges. For example, receiving a 200 OK response code from an apparently one-way message, allows a peer to understand that a message has arrived at the remote endpoint and is being processed as expected.

Web Services (see Chapter 7) are another set of technologies that make use of the Web. Retrieval of a Web Services description document usually takes place using HTTP. Likewise, although the SOAP message container used by Web Services is essentially transfer protocol independent, Web Services almost invariably use HTTP to exchange them. When doing this they *tunnel* the SOAP message over HTTP; that is, they do not use the HTTP methods according to their intended semantics, but rather always use the POST method imposing generic *send/receive* semantics on it, irrespective of whether the message will have side effects or not. HTTP is primarily used by Web Services because it is so widely deployed meaning they can make use of existing business IT infrastructure.

6

Peer-2-Peer Environments

> *"The Internet isn't free. It just has an economy that makes no sense to capitalism."* Brad Shapcott

At the time of writing, there are 1.35 billion devices connected to the Internet worldwide (e.g., PCs, phones, PDAs, etc.), a figure which has been rising rapidly [47]. With almost a quarter of the world's populations already connected to the Internet and growth rates in Africa and the Middle East reaching almost 1000% over the past 8 years, the increases to on-line connectivity seem to be following a familiar pattern seen in other areas within the computing industry.

The computer hardware industry has also been characterised by exponential production volumes. Gordon Moore, the co-founder of Intel, in his famous observation in 1965 [54] (made just four years after the first planar integrated circuit was discovered), predicted that the number of transistors on integrated circuits would double every few years. Indeed this prediction, thereafter called *Moore's law*, remains true today and Intel predicts that this will remain true at least until the end of this decade [55].

Such acceleration in development has been made possible by the massive investment by companies who deal with comparatively short product life cycles. Each user now in this massive network has the CPU capability of more than 100 times that of an early 1990s supercomputer and surprisingly, GartnerGroup research reveals that over 95% of today's PC power is wasted. The potential of such a distributed computing resource has been in some ways demonstrated by the SETI@home project [19], having used more than two million years of aggregate computing time at the time of writing.

In this chapter, peer-to-peer (P2P) computing is introduced, which offers a combination of techniques for connecting and making use of such resources at an Internet scale. First, we provide a historical perspective into the term peer to peer, which is followed by a discussion of modern definitions and justification for P2P computing. A background into the P2P environment is given followed by several examples of P2P applications that operate within such an environment.

6.1 What Is Peer to Peer?

This section gives a brief background and history of the term "peer to peer" and describes how this definition has changed through the introduction of the World Wide Web and the change in focus on new Internet users.

6.1.1 Historical Peer to Peer

Peer to peer was originally used to describe the communication of two peers and is analogous to a telephone conversation. A phone conversation involves two people (peers) of equal status, communication between a point-to-point connection. Simply, this is what P2P is, a point-to-point connection between two **equal** participants.

The Internet started as a peer-to-peer system. The goal of the original ARPANET was to share computing resources around the USA. Its challenge was to connect a set of distributed resources, using different network connectivity, within one common network architecture. The first hosts on the ARPANET were several U.S. universities, e.g., the University College of Los Angeles, Santa Barbara, SRI and University of Utah. These were already independent computing sites with equal status and the ARPANET connected them as such, not in a master/slave or client/server relationship but rather as equal computing peers.

From the late 1960s until 1994, the Internet had one model of connectivity. Machines were assumed to be always switched on, always connected and assigned permanent IP addresses. The original DNS system was designed for this environment, where a change in IP address was assumed to be abnormal and rare, and could take days to propagate through the system. However, with the invention of Mosaic, another model began to emerge in the form of users connecting to the Internet from dial-up modems. This created a second class of connectivity because PCs would enter and leave the network frequently and unpredictably. Further, because ISPs began to run out of IP addresses, they began to assign IP addresses dynamically for each session, giving each PC a different, possibly masked, IP address. This transient nature and instability prevented PCs from being assigned permanent DNS entries, and therefore prevented most PC users from hosting any data or network-facing applications locally.

For a few years, treating PCs as clients worked well. Over time, though, as hardware and software improved, the unused resources that existed behind this veil of second-class connectivity started to look like something worth getting at. Given the vast array of available processors mentioned earlier, the software community is starting to take P2P applications very seriously. Most importantly, P2P research is concerned in addressing some of the main difficulties of current distributed computing: scalability, reliability, interoperability.

6.1.2 The Shift to New Internet Users

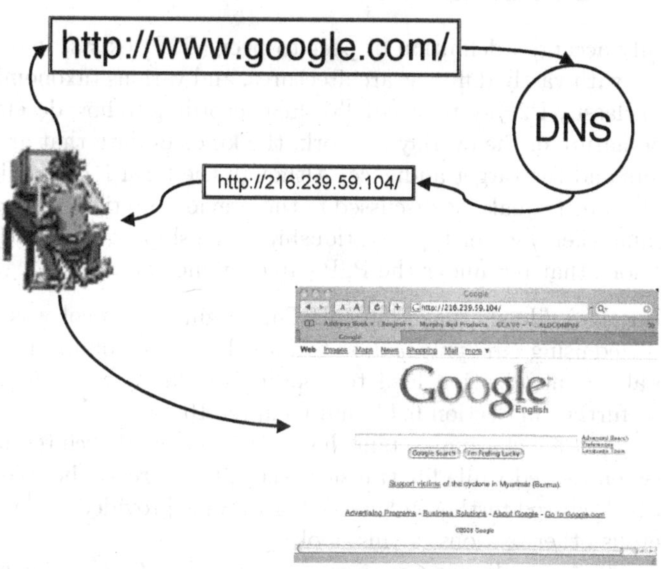

Fig. 6.1. The process whereby an Internet address is converted into the IP address for locating a Web page on the Internet.

Within today's Internet, we rely on fixed IP addresses. When a user types an address into his/her Web browser (such as http://www.google.com/), the Web server address is translated into an IP address (e.g., 216.239.59.104) by a domain name server (DNS). The Internet protocol (IP) then makes a routing decision based on the IP address. If DNS is unavailable, then typing http://216.239.59.104/ into a browser would be equivalent since, at the time of writing, one of the Google Web sites is bound to this IP address.

This is known as static or early binding. Figure 6.1 illustrates this process graphically. Early bindings form a simple architecture very similar to an address book on a mobile phone; e.g., the person's name is statically bound to his/her telephone number. This works in practice because typically people have long-term (early) bindings with their phone numbers and Web sites have long-term bindings with their IP addresses.

However, if a Web site changed its IP address several times a day, then this type of binding starts to become impractical. Within P2P networks this is the norm. Often devices do not have a fixed address as they are hidden behind Network Address Translation (NAT) systems and therefore need a **late binding** of their addresses with their network identifier.

6.2 Modern Definition of Peer to Peer

No universally accepted definition of peer to peer (P2P) exists. It is used to cover systems with vastly different architectures, and various taxonomies have been used to classify P2P systems [56] [57] [58] according to how decentralized they are, the nature of the overlay network, the kinds of data that are shared between peers and the target audience. Although the term P2P implies communication between equals, as discussed in the previous section, most systems employ unequal client/server-type relationships. Flagship examples of systems and applications that fall under the P2P category include:

- **Gnutella** [4] A file sharing protocol. The original protocol was entirely decentralized using *viral propagation* to spread queries around the network. This total decentralization lead to flooding of the network. Gnutella is discussed further in Section 6.4.2 and Chapter 10.
- **Napster** [5] A file sharing system that uses a brokered architecture. Discovery is centralized while file transfer takes place directly between peers. Napster is discussed further in Section 6.4.1 and is provided as an example in numerous other sections in this book.
- **BOINC** [20] An application framework for building CPU scavenging systems as exemplified by SETI@home [19]. Clients log into a server and download data that is processed by the system's client software. Results are returned to the server. These systems follow a centralized architecture and BOINC does not class itself as P2P. BOINC is discussed further in Section 6.6.2.
- **BitTorrent** [6] A system for downloading files which redistributes the cost of file upload by using incentives to force peers to upload while they are downloading. The process of collectively uploading and downloading is called swarming. Swarming of a particular file is managed centrally. File discovery is out of bounds. BitTorrent is discussed further in Chapter 13.
- **Distributed Hash Tables (DHTs)** These systems use a logical identifier space to deterministically map neighbour ids to network addresses or content to peers. They are sometimes referred to as *structured* overlays because of the deterministic algorithms used. DHTs are discussed further in Chapter 11.
- **Freenet** [59] A distributed content storage and retrieval system primarily designed to ensure anonymity of publishers. Freenet is fully decentralized and uses caching and routing tables to allow query routing to be optimized over time. Freenet is discussed further in Chapter 12.

- **Kazaa** [60] A file sharing system. Kazaa uses a super-peer architecture to reduce flooding the network with queries. Super-peers act as caches to groups of ordinary peers.
- **Jxta** [24] An application independent framework for developing P2P applications. Jxta specifies a number of protocols that enable the creation and maintenance of P2P networks such as joining groups, publishing adverts and queries and resolving logical addresses. Jxta is discussed further in Chapter 15.
- **Groove** [61] provides distributed, decentralized collaborative working environments and has had significant takeup in the business community. The system uses relay servers for handling bandwidth constraints and firewall and NAT traversal.
- **Instant Messaging** These systems allow users to log into the network with a registered identity and discover other identities. Typically the systems use a centralized server infrastructure to manage the logging in and mapping of IP address to identities.
- **Skype** [62] Skype has made Voice over IP (VOIP) accessible through a decentralized architecture for both managing logging in of users as well as routing conversations through the network and to firewalled or NAT bound nodes. Skype was founded by the same team that developed the FastTrack P2P protocol on which file sharing applications such as Kazaa are based.

This snapshot of well-known systems shows their diversity and the crossover between them in many dimensions including topology, intended application domain and target users. However, a common theme shared by all is that nodes at the periphery of the network contribute to the functionality of the system. With the emergence of all these new technologies in the late 1990s and the beginning of the new millennium, a new definition was proposed by Shirky [13] that attempted to extract the commonalities of the peer-to-peer applications as they began to emerge:

> *"P2P is a class of applications that takes advantage of resources e.g. storage, cycles, content, human presence, available at the edges of the Internet."*

and the often not cited part of the definition is:

> *"Because accessing these decentralized resources means operating in an environment of unstable connectivity and unpredictable IP addresses, P2P nodes must operate outside the DNS system and have significant or total autonomy from central servers."*

Computers/devices "at the edges of the Internet" are those operating within transient and often hostile environments. Devices within this environment can come and go frequently; can be hidden behind a firewall or operate outside of DNS, e.g., by NAT (see next section); and often have to deal with differing transport protocols, devices and operating systems. The number of computers in a P2P network is often enormous, consisting of millions of interconnecting peers.

The second half restricts the definition somewhat and excludes systems such as SETI and BOINC due the inherent central control of these systems. The definition also focuses far more on the environment of devices and resources rather than previous definitions that focussed on the *servent* methodology and decentralized nature of systems like Gnutella [4]. For example, in Gnutella, there are two key differences compared to client/server-based systems:

- A peer can act as both a client and a server (they call these *servents*, i.e., *serv*er and cli*ent* in Gnutella).
- The network is completely decentralized and has no central point of control. Peers in a Gnutella network are typically connected to three or four other nodes and to search the network a query is broadcast throughout the network.

Certainly, within P2P systems, peers exist as defined in Gnutella. However, P2P networks do not have to be completely decentralized. This is evident in modern Gnutella implementations [63], which employ a centralized/decentralized approach in order to be able to scale the network and increase efficiency of search. Such networks are implemented using super-peers that cache file locations so that peers only have to search a small fraction of the network in order to satisfy their search requests.

True P2P

"True P2P" is a term often used to describe the architectural ideal in a P2P network, which employs the use of a purely decentralized design, and where everyone participates equally in the network as both a client and a server.

Therefore, Shirky's definition here is more appropriate to describe a new class of applications that are designed to work within this highly transient environment (see also Section 6.3), something previously unattainable. Other authors have noted the same. For example, in [11], the authors state that they prefer Shirky's defintion because it encompasses large-scale deployed P2P systems where much experience has been gained. Completely decentralized systems like Gnutella are now often referred to as **true P2P** because of their pure decentralized approach, where everyone participates equally in the network. However, this ideal can never really be realised by a P2P system simply because certainly not all peers are equal within actual P2P networks, which has been proven by several empirical studies [64], [65] and [66].

A related definition is given by Andy Oram [67]:

> *"Any networking technology where crucial responsibility lies at the end-points."*

Both Oram's and Shirky's definitions focus on the periphery of the network. The periphery of the network constitutes those nodes that are not part of the infrastructure of the Internet; that is, they are not an integral part of any of the networks that make up the Internet, nor are they part of the DNS, resolving host names to IP addresses. Further, it outlines the fact that nodes that are not part of the fabric of the Internet now constitute the majority. Oram continues:

> *"In fact, definitional inadequacies aside, peer-to-peer isn't really a set of technologies as much as it is a set of problems."*

This is an important insight and is implicit in the second half of Shirky's quote because it posits that P2P technologies have emerged out of necessities. Questions such as 'How can I harness the vast amounts of resources (processing power, files) available on the Internet cheaply?' , 'How can I connect two **people** (not two machines)?' and 'How can I support freedom of speech in the information age?' are what have led to P2P technologies. These questions have arisen from different communities with different concerns and hence P2P is difficult to quantize. Furthermore, in answering them they have often generated a user base as the result of the technology developed. This is quite different from paradigms such as Grid computing, which have a well-defined user base, in the form of various scientific communities, placing demands on the research and development community to produce usable products [68].

Therefore it is possible to class P2P as a set of technologies that have been developed in an attempt to move storage, processing, responsibility or power to the edges of the Internet for diverse reasons. In addressing this challenge, many systems have focussed on how to maintain network stability despite the unreliable nature of nodes at the edges. This has often resulted in the use of decentralized architectures to handle node failure and mobility. Many of these decentralized architectures in turn have proven themselves to be very robust and highly scalable.

6.2.1 Social Impacts of P2P

The legal connotations and social impacts of P2P are ongoing. No doubt, it has opened the eyes and imaginations of people from numerous disciplines to the massive sharing of resources across the Internet. Even within the context of the sharing of copyrighted material, there are compulsive arguments for and against the use of such technologies. There are a number of articles and books written on the subject that support the concept of P2P and those that give legal context for it. For example, on the *Open Democracy* Web site, there are a number of articles that give a social context for P2P, both from a cultural perspective and a legal one. In this section, a very brief summary of some of the points raised is given.

Vaidhyanathan [69], in his five-part article on the new information ecosystem, paints a picturesque account of a deep cultural change that is taking place through the introduction of P2P technologies. He argues that "what we call P2P communicative networks actually reflect and amplify — revise and extend an old ideology or cultural habit. Electronic peer-to-peer systems like Gnutella merely simulate other, more familiar forms of unmediated, uncensorable, irresponsible, troublesome speech; for example, anti-royal gossip before the French revolution, trading cassette tapes among youth subcultures as punk or rap, or the illicit Islamist cassette tapes through the streets and bazaars of Cairo."

He argues against the current clampdown strategy that is being employed by companies and governments. Such a strategy involves radically redesigning the communication technologies so that information can be monitored more closely. These restrictions would destroy the openness of the current Internet and could bring about a new type of Internet which, he says, would "not be open and customisable. Content — and thus culture would not be adaptable and malleable. And what small measures of privacy these networks now afford would evaporate."

Rainsford [70] uses the term "information feudalism," which was taken from an analogy given by Peter Drahos [71]. Drahos suggests that

> *"The current push for control over intellectual property rights has bred a situation analogous to the feudal agricultural system in the medieval period. In effect, songwriters and scientists work for corporate feudal lords, licensing their own inventions in exchange for a living and the right to 'till the lands' of the information society."*

Rainsford quotes a number of authors who believe that the struggle that we are experiencing has deep underlying roots in cultural transformations, which will inevitably bring about a change in the decaying business models of today. Rainsford also notes that "the links asserted between p2p systems and terrorism, or the funding of terrorism" are "a concept which is laughably ironic as p2p by its very nature is a non-profit system."

Rimmer [72] gives a legal case for the argument and argues that "if claims by peer-to-peer distributors that they are supporting free speech and contributing to knowledge want to find a sympathetic ear in the courtroom, then they have to mean it." He discusses the current use of P2P and argues that they have not lived up to their revolutionary promise, being used mostly for circulating copyrighted media around the world. He lists several cases which have been brought against companies, which have resulted in infringements, and some that have not.

Rimmer states that P2P networks are "vulnerable to legal actions for copyright infringements because they have facilitated the dissemination of copyright media for profit and gain." He concludes that "the courts would be happy to foster such technology if it promoted the freedom of speech, the mixing of cultures, and the progress of science."

For further reading, see the articles listed on the Open Democracy Web site [73], which hosts a series of articles in response to these comments. Similar articles appear on other Web sites, such as OpenP2P [74].

6.3 The P2P Environment

This section covers the technology that makes the P2P environment so difficult to work within; that is, peers are: extremely transient (they are continually disappearing and reappearing), connections are often multi-hop (i.e., packets travel via several intermediaries before they reach their destination) and peers reside in hostile environments (i.e., they live behind NAT routing systems and firewalls). In this section, a background is given into some of the technologies behind P2P networks, which helps set a more realistic P2P scene. The first section makes a brief excursion into switching technology for networks. The second section describes a particular subset of these that contains NAT systems. Lastly, firewalls are discussed.

6.3.1 Hubs, Switches, Bridges, Access Points and Routers

This section gives a brief overview of the various devices used to partition a network, which gives the context for the following two sections on NAT and firewalls often employed within a P2P network. Briefly, the critical distinction between these devices is the level or layer at which they operate within the International Standard Organization's Open System Interconnect (ISO/OSI) model, which defines seven network layers [75].

- **Hubs:** A hub is a repeater that works at the physical (lowest) layer of OSI. A hub takes data that comes into a port and sends it to the other ports in the hub. It does not perform any filtering or redirection of data. You can think of a hub as a kind of Internet chat room. Everyone who joins a particular chat is seen by everyone else. If there are too many people trying to chat, things get bogged down.
- **Switches and Bridges:** These are pretty similar. Both operate at the Data Link layer (just above Physical) and both can filter data so that only the appropriate segment or host receives a transmission. Both filter packets based on the physical address (i.e., Media Access Control (MAC)

address) of the sender/receiver although newer switches sometimes include the capabilities of a router and can forward data based on IP address (operating at the network layer), referred to as IP switches. In general, bridges are used to extend the distance capabilities of the network while minimizing overall traffic, and switches are used primarily for their filtering capabilities to create multiple, smaller virtual local area networks (LANs) out of one large LAN for easier management/administration (V-LANs).

- **Routers:** These work at the Network layer of OSI (above Data Link) and operate on the IP address. Like switches and bridges, they filter by only forwarding packets destined for remote networks thus minimizing traffic, but are significantly more complex than any other networking device; thus they require much more maintenance and administration. The home networker typically uses a DSL or cable modem router that joins the home's LAN to the wide area network (WAN) of the Internet. By maintaining configuration information in a "routing table" routers also have the ability to filter traffic, either incoming or outgoing, based on the IP addresses of senders and receivers. Most routers allow the home networker to update the routing table from a Web browser interface. DSL and cable modem routers typically combine the functions of a router with those of a switch in a single unit.

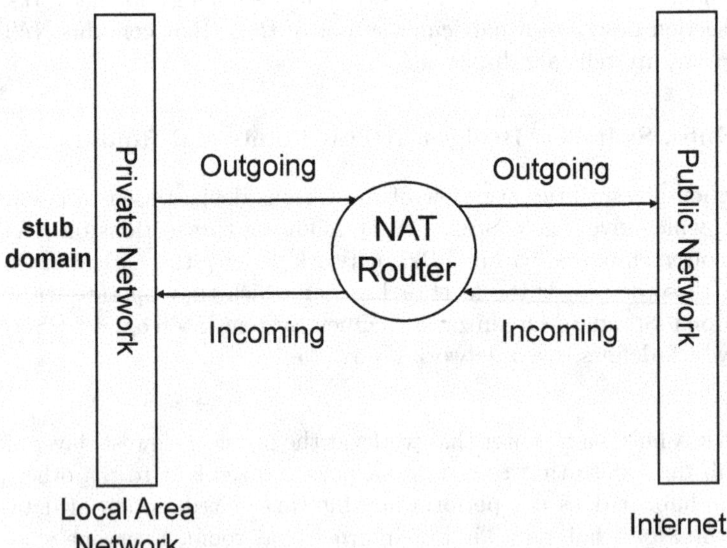

Fig. 6.2. A NAT System divides a local network from the public network and offers local-to-public mapping of addresses. This allows the number of machines on the Internet to increase past the physical limit. A NAT system converts local addresses within the *stub domain* into one Internet address.

6.3.2 NAT Systems

For a computer to communicate with other computers and Web servers on the Internet, it must have an IP address. An IP address is a unique 32-bit number that identifies the location of your computer on a network. There are, in theory, 2^{32} (4,294,967,296) unique addresses but the actual number available is much smaller (somewhere between 3.2 and 3.3 billion). This is due to the way that the addresses are separated into classes and also because some are set aside for multicasting, testing or other special uses.

With the explosion of the Internet and the increase in home networks and business networks, the number of available IP addresses is simply not enough. An obvious solution is to redesign the address format to allow for more possible addresses. This is being developed and is called IPv6, but it may take several years to deploy because it requires modification of the entire infrastructure of the Internet.

A network address translation system (see Fig. 6.2) allows a single device, such as a router, to act as an agent between the Internet (public network) and a local (private) network. This means that only a single, unique IP address is required to represent an entire group of computers. The internal network is usually a LAN, commonly referred to as the *stub domain*. A stub domain is a LAN that uses IP addresses internally. Any internal computers that use unregistered IP addresses must use NAT to communicate with the rest of the world.

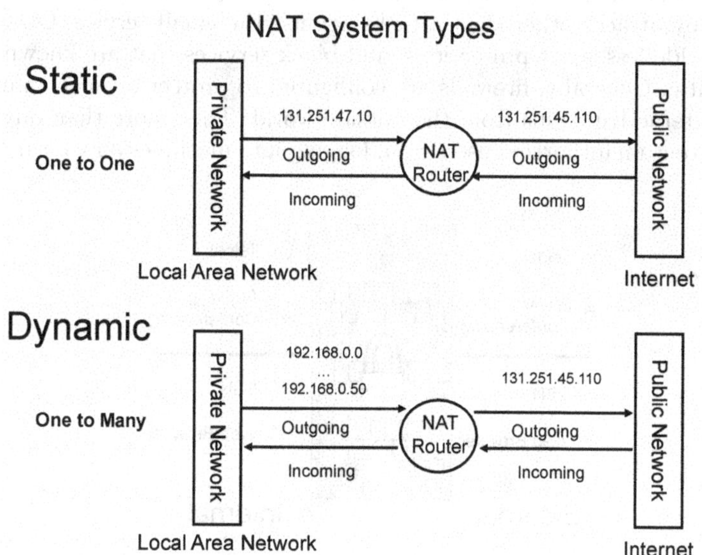

Fig. 6.3. A NAT system can be allocate dynamic address or translate from fixed stub domain address to outside ones.

There are two types of NAT translation, static or dynamic, which are illustrated in Fig. 6.3. Static NAT involves mapping an unregistered IP address to a registered IP address on a one-to-one basis. Particularly useful when a device needs to be accessible from outside the network (i.e., in static NAT), the computer with the IP address of 192.168.0.0 will always translate to 131.251.45.110 (see upper part of Fig. 6.3).

Dynamic NAT, on the other hand, maps an unregistered IP address to a registered IP address from a group of local dynamically allocatable IP addresses, i.e., the stub domain computers will be allocated an address from a specified range of addresses, e.g., 192.168.0.0 to 192.168.0.50, in Figure 6.3 and will translate these to 131.251.45.110 for the outside world. In this circumstance, it is easy to see why NAT systems are problematic since you could have potentially hundreds of stub domain computers masquerading as one external IP address.

6.3.3 Firewalls

A firewall is a system designed to prevent unauthorized access to or from a private network. All messages entering or leaving the computer system pass through the firewall, which examines each message and blocks those that do not meet the specified security criteria. Specifically, firewalls are implemented by blocking certain ports, thereby disabling certain types of services that operate on those ports.

Some firewalls permit only email traffic, thereby protecting the network against any attacks other than attacks against the email service. Other firewalls provide less strict protections, and block services that are known to be problematic. Generally, firewalls are configured to protect against unauthenticated interactive logins from the outside world. This, more than anything, helps prevent unauthorized users from logging into machines on your network.

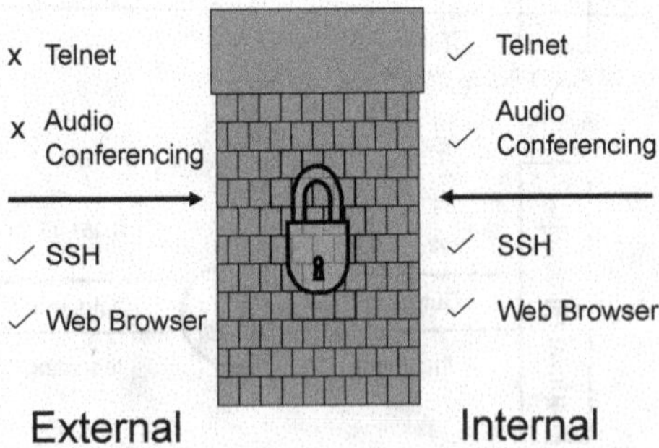

Fig. 6.4. A firewall blocks traffic to and from specified ports; here only SSH and Web browsing are allowed by external computers.

More elaborate firewalls block traffic from the outside to the inside, but permit users on the inside to communicate freely with the outside. Figure 6.4 illustrates a scenario where both telnet and audio conferencing are blocked from the outside world but Web browsing and SSH connections are acceptable. However, internal users can freely open up external connections using any of these services but, in this example, they would not be able to hear the other participants in the audio conference because incoming audio is blocked.

A firewall therefore can essentially protect you against most types of network attack. Firewalls are also important since they can provide a single choke point where security and audit can be imposed, i.e., they can provide an important logging and auditing function and provide summaries to the administrator about what kinds and amount of traffic passed through it and how many attempts there were to break into it. Within P2P applications, it is often necessary to traverse such firewalls, for example, by rerouting the data over the HTTP port.

6.3.4 P2P Overlay Networks

P2P middleware implementations frequently involve the creation of overlay networks ([10]) with a structure that is completely independent of that of the underlying network of connected devices. The purpose of overlay networks is to abstract the complicated connectivity of a P2P network to a higher-level programmatical view of the peers that make up the network. This is illustrated in Fig. 6.5 which shows the programmer's view of the network (see top cloud of peers) that simplifies and abstracts the network structure and underlying transport mechanisms (see bottom part) into a collection of cooperating peers.

There are several different types of overlay networks. For example, within Jxta ([24] and see Chapter 15) a virtual network overlay sits on top of the physical devices and is organized into transient or persistent relationships, which they call peer groups. Peers in Jxta are not required to have direct point-to-point network connections and such connections are represented through the use of virtual pipes. Virtual pipes simply define the endpoints of the connection and leave it to the underlying mechanisms to implement the appropriate behaviour for that environment; e.g., for TCP, a fixed point-to-point connection is created for the pipe, but for UDP pipes, this is not required and therefore the pipe remains connectionless. There are many other notations and structures for the creation of overlay networks, which are described further in Chapter 11 and include the use of distributed hash tables, e.g., Chord [76], Pastry [77], Tapestry [78] or CAN [79].

6.4 P2P Example Applications

This section introduces two popular file-sharing systems that employ different architectures, which provide food for thought for a number of scenarios that are presented in the following chapters.

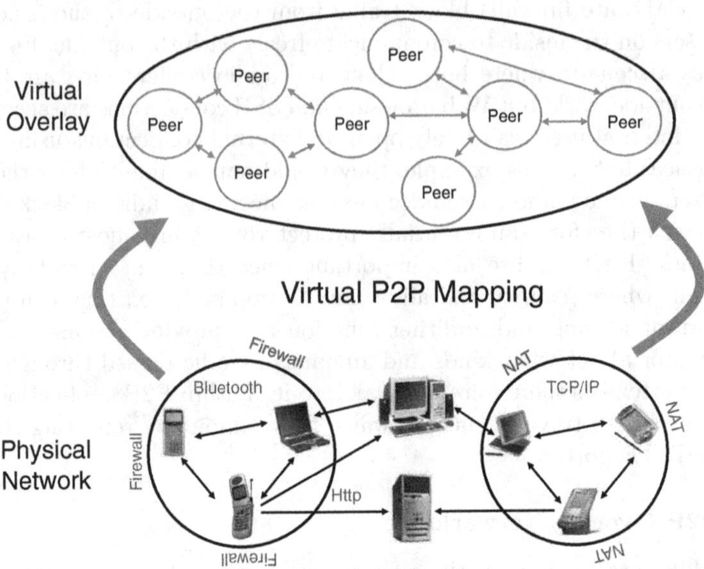

Fig. 6.5. An illustration of the notion of an overlay network. P2P infrastructures typically overlay a virtual view of the nodes on the network to abstract the underlying mechanisms that actually connect these devices; this example was taken from Jxta [24].

6.4.1 MP3 File Sharing with Napster

Napster [5], the famous MP3 file sharing program, was launched in 1999. It had a revolutionary impact on the Internet due to its infamous reputation for sharing illegal MP3 files and its unique design; i.e., after the initial centralized Napster search, clients connected to each other and exchanged data directly from one system's disk to another. Figure 6.6 illustrates this process.

Users first connect to the main Napster server and register themselves to join the network. The main server obtains a list of MP3s that the user has and adds this to the list of songs in the central database. When a user (User A) performs a search, Napster searches the local database on the main server and then returns the address of the peer that has a copy of the file. User A then connects directly to the peer who has the file (User B) and downloads the file directly from this user's disk without any further intervention from the host, unless communication is interrupted (because the peer has logged off, for example).

Napster is P2P because the Napster peers bypass DNS and because once the Napster server resolves the IP address of the PCs hosting a particular song, it shifts control of the file transfers to the nodes. However, Napster is an example of brokered P2P for the same reasons.

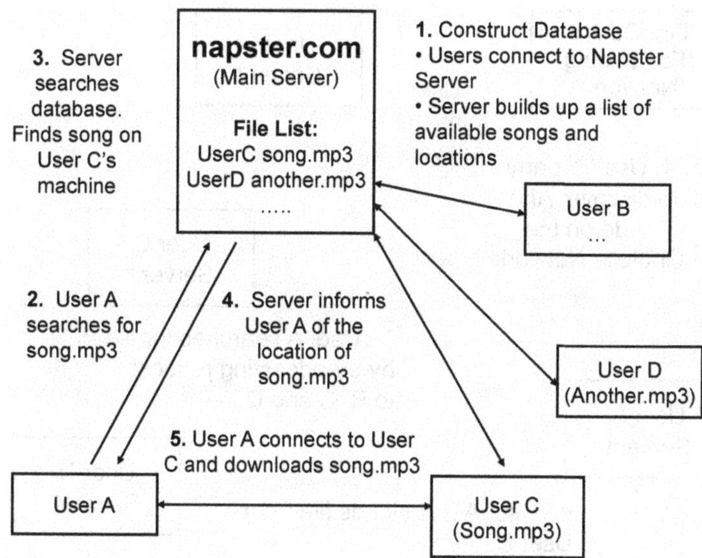

Fig. 6.6. The Napster scenario for providing a distributed file system for music files.

6.4.2 File Sharing with Gnutella

Gnutella is a 'true P2P' system. It does not rely on central control for lookup, organization and communication. The internal mechanisms of Gnutella will be discussed in detail in Chapter 10, but the scenario is given here in Fig. 6.7.

There are several ways of joining a Gnutella network. The one given in Figure 6.7 uses a *GnuCache* as a lookup server for a list of Gnutella nodes, but one could easily use another method; e.g., use newsgroups to get lists of nodes, Web sites, etc. The node joins the network by connecting initially to one Gnutella node, which can be any node on the network making it generally easy to join in a decentralized fashion.

Once it has joined, the node discovers other nodes through the first node by issuing *Ping* and receiving *Pong* descriptors from peers accepting connections. Gnutella nodes typically connect to three nodes and then search by broadcasting their search request to all connected neighbours, as illustrated here. Each neighbour repeats this search request to his/her neighbours and so on, which is known as *flooding the network.* Here, User D has the required file so User A connects directly to User D and downloads the file using this point-to-point connection.

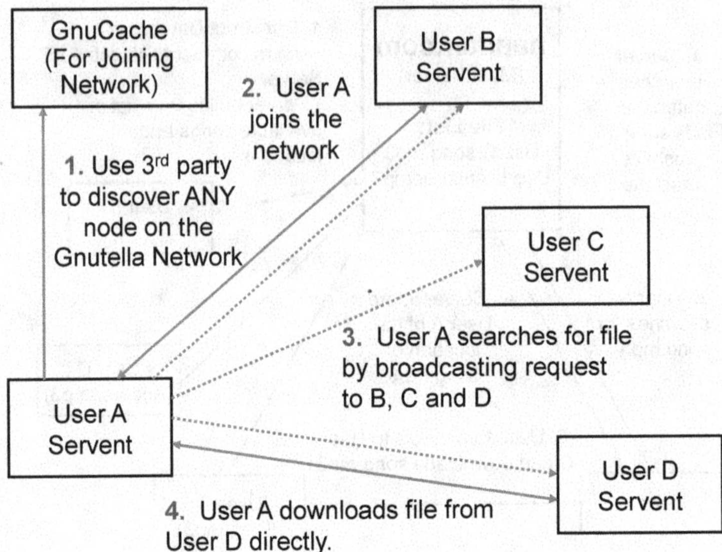

Fig. 6.7. Gnutella decentralized approach. There are two aspects to discovery: joining the network and then discovering other peers.

6.5 True P2P and Good Distributed Design

Many Internet services are distributed using the traditional client/server (centralized) architecture. In this architecture, clients connect to a server using a specific communications protocol (e.g., TCP) to obtain access to a specific resource. Most of the processing involved in delivering a service usually occurs on the server, leaving the client relatively unburdened. Most popular Internet applications, including the World Wide Web, FTP, telnet, and email, use this service-delivery model. Unfortunately, this architecture has a major drawback; that is, as the number of clients increases (and therefore load and bandwidth) the server becomes a bottleneck and can eventually result in the server not being able to handle any additional clients or results in a substantial increase in financial cost to the provider in order to support such a centralized model. The main advantage of the client/server model is that it requires less computational power on the client side. However, this has been somewhat circumvented due to ever-increasing CPU power and therefore most desktop PCs are ludicrously overpowered to operate as simple clients, e.g., for browsing and email.

P2P, on the other hand, has the capability of serving resources with high availability at a much lower cost, while maximizing the use of resources from every peer connected to the P2P network. Whereas client/server solutions rely on costly bandwidth, equipment, and location to maintain a robust solution, P2P can offer a similar level of robustness by spreading network and resource demands across the network. Note, though, that some middleware architectures used to program such systems are often capable of operating in one or more of these modes.

Further, the more decentralized the system is, the better the fault tolerance, since the services are spread across more resources. Therefore, at the far side of the scale, you have true P2P systems, which employ a completely decentralized structure, both in look up and in communication. Hong [21] gives a useful description for communication within P2P systems. He defines P2P systems as being a class of distributed systems that are biased to more of a decentralized approach, where there is no global notion of centralization. He argues that such systems are primarily concerned with smaller distributed levels of centralization with respect to communication.

When designing a P2P system, therefore, there is a trade-off between inserting the correct amount of decentralization for the network to be fault tolerant against failure but centralized enough to scale to a large number of participants. These issues are discussed in detail in Chapter 11.

6.6 Related Projects: Volunteer Computing

In this section, we briefly discuss volunteer-computing projects, such as SETI@home and the middleware infrastructure which was built from SETI, called BOINC. However, there are many other similar projects, which can be found elsewhere:

- Distributed.net [80] uses computing power to crack previously unbreakable encrypted messages.
- Companies such as United Devices [81] and Entropia [82] which solve a varied number of problems for both non-profit and commercial gains. For example, United Devices in February 2003 used their meta processor to help the United States Department of Defense (DoD) to find a cure for smallpox [83].
- XtremWeb is "an open source software to build lightweight Desktop Grid by gathering the unused resources of Desktop Computers (CPU, storage, network). Its primary features permit multi-users, multi-applications and cross-domains deployments. XtremWeb turns a set of volatile resources spread over LAN or Internet into a runtime environment executing highly parallel applications" [84].

Although projects like BOINC and SETI are not considered P2P (because they have a centralized control and do not "connect" people as such), they do take advantage of many aspects of the P2P environment and hence they are worth mentioning here within the context of this environment.

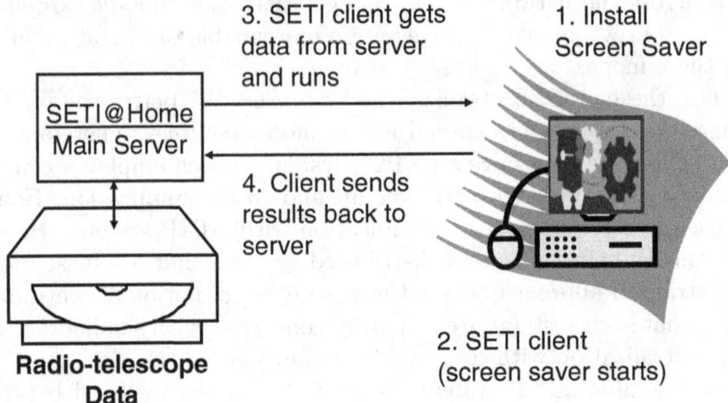

Fig. 6.8. SETI algorithm for performing distributed data analysis on radio-telescope data.

6.6.1 Distributed Computing Using SETI@home

In 1996, SETI@home [19] was launched, which is a scientific experiment that uses Internet-connected computers in the **S**earch for **E**xtra**T**errestrial **I**ntelligence. SETI distributes a screen saver-based application to users that uses various signal analysis algorithms to process radio-telescope data. At the time of writing, it had signed up more than three million users (around a half million active contributors) and had used over a million years of CPU time. The client software (i.e., the screen saver) contacts a server to download the data to process and then processes this until the problem is solved, then returns the results back to the server (see Fig. 6.8). If the run does not succeed, then this data segment is assumed to be lost and therefore ignored.

6.6.2 BOINC

The Berkeley Open Infrastructure for Network Computing (BOINC)[20][85] is a software platform for distributed computation using otherwise idle cycles from volunteered computing resources. BOINC's use is widespread, with many different and varying projects employing the core infrastructure to distribute their data processing jobs. The diverse scientific domains utilizing BOINC range from gravitational wave analysis, to protein folding, to the search for extraterrestrial life [86]. Although these projects are diverse in their scientific nature, each one has something in common with the others: they have work units that can easily be distributed to run autonomously in a highly distributed and volatile environment. To achieve this task, each project must prepare its data and executable code to work with the BOINC libraries and client/server infrastructure, and will also need to set up and maintain their own individual servers and databases to manage the project's data distribution and result aggregation.

Despite these individual server setup and maintenance tasks which separate projects from one another, BOINC users are still able to participate in multiple projects through the client interface, thereby deciding how their resources are divided. BOINC is currently the most widespread and successful volunteer computing Desktop Grid application ever, with approximately 20 distinct projects [86] and almost three million total computers from over 200 countries registered to date. For data distribution, BOINC projects generally use a single centralized server or a set of mirrors.

6.7 Conclusion

There are many aspects to categorising a system as P2P. Although a true P2P system employs a completely decentralized structure (e.g., Gnutella), there also exist other systems that have other structures, e.g., Napster has a hybrid P2P structure. Therefore, although decentralization is not a required consideration of P2P systems, it is a desired one. The real key feature of P2P that makes it a new computing paradigm is that the responsibility of the network is pushed to the edges rather than maintained centrally. And a consequence of this model is that the P2P environment becomes a key factor in circumnavigating in order to build P2P applications. Therefore, factors such as operating outside DNS, transient connectivity and deploying servers behind NAT and firewalls, become key enablers for this technology.

7

Web Services

> *"As we look forward, we are tempted to distinguish between the multimedia world of information targeted for human perception, and the well-defined world of data which machines handle.... The Web technology must allow information intended for a human to be effectively presented, and also allow machine processable data to be conveyed. Only then can we start to use computers as tools again."*
> *Tim Berners-Lee [87]*

7.1 Introduction

Up until recently, data has been exported on the World Wide Web for human consumption in the form of Web pages. Most people therefore use the Web to read news/articles, to buy goods and services, to manage on-line accounts and so on. For this purpose, we use a Web browser and access information mostly through this medium.

From a publishing perspective, this involves converting the raw information, from a database, for example, into HTML or similar language so that it can be rendered in the correct form. Further, many Web sites collate information from other sites via Web pages, which is a bizarre occurrence involving decoding and parsing human-readable information not intended for machines at all (see Fig. 7.1).

This scenario works well for many applications but it is highly redundant because the conversion from the raw data into human-readable format for publication and availability does not support software interactions very well. What we really need to do is provide a mechanism whereby the raw data can be accessed in a similar fashion by machines as humans read Web pages now. Therefore, a more efficient mechanism is required in order to enable true *machine-to-machine* communication to provide a machine-processable Web. This is illustrated in Fig. 7.1.

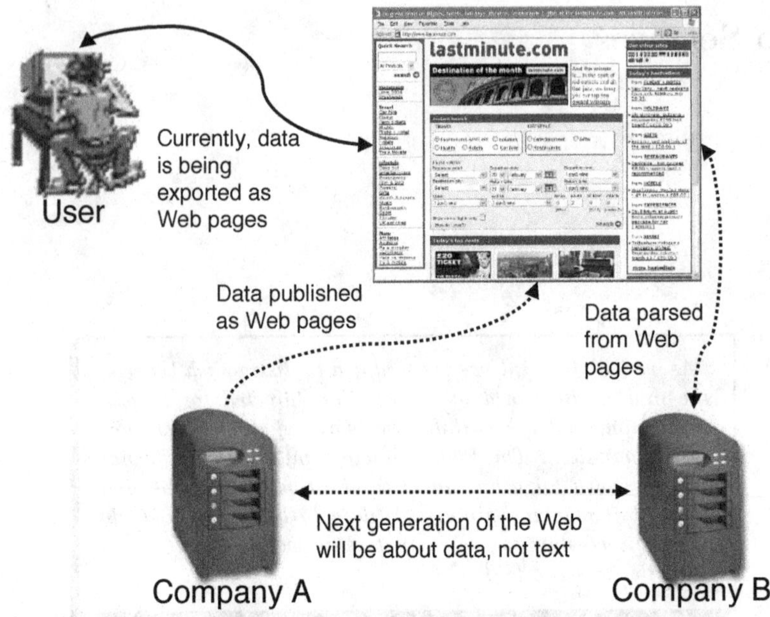

Fig. 7.1. We use the Web for Web browsing at the moment but the next generation will be more focused on machine-to-machine interaction.

Many believe, including Berners-Lee, that the next generation of the Web will be about data, not text. Providing ubiquitous mechanisms for representing and providing data in a machine-readable fashion is at the core of *Web Services*. Companies are increasingly in need of standard mechanisms to be able to publish, advertise and discover links to actual data sources, rather than Web pages.

7.1.1 Looking Forward: What Do We Need?

In order to see what we need to build a new infrastructure that allows such machine-to-machine Web communication, we need to look at what the World Wide Web actually provides. In Section 5.2, we learned how Berners-Lee had the idea of creating some imaginary information system which everyone could read.

Figure 7.2 illustrates this idea. The Web allows many disparate information systems to serve data by creating an abstract imaginary space where these differences do not exist. A Universal Resource Identifier (URI) identified the document and a suite of protocols (e.g., HTTP) and data formats

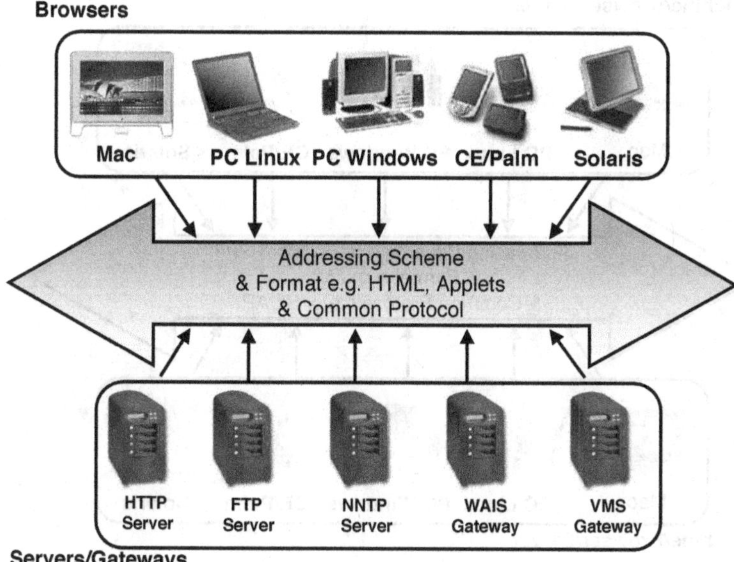

Fig. 7.2. The model for the World Wide Web. Multiple types of browsers can talk to multiple types of machines if they share common address schemes, formats and protocols.

(e.g., HTML) forms a *bus* which allows computers to exchange information by mapping from their **local formats** into **standards** that provided global interoperability. The Web therefore is deployed as a set of protocols, not a single program.

This layer provided the interface for interoperability between the diverse clients and servers that existed on the Internet. For the machine-to-machine interoperable Web, we need the same kind of group of protocols that will allow machines to interoperate at the data level. To achieve this, we must build this layer out of standardized technologies in order to gain widespread adoption.

The first step was for commercial and non-commercial sectors to agree on a common data format in order to be able to expose their functionality to others in a truly interoperable fashion. This led to the standardization of XML through W3C [88], the latest version being 1.0, Third Edition [89].

Since then, a number of other technologies have been standardized through W3C and other organizations, such as OASIS [90]. Figure 7.4 shows a list of a subset of the standards that are used at each level, ranging from the network protocols, data transport and service descriptions, through to higher-level workflow orchestration languages, such as BPEL4WS [91]. For a more complete list, see [92].

The three core technologies designed to support Web Services will be described in detail in Chapter 16, but briefly they are: SOAP, which provides

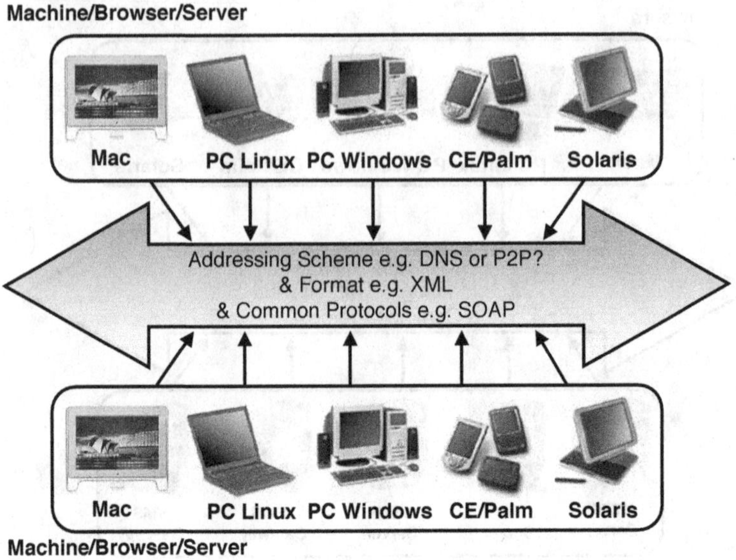

Fig. 7.3. Creating a machine-to-machine communicable Web involves building a common layer of protocols.

an *envelope* for the XML message; WSDL, which provides the description of the interface for the Web Service; and UDDI, which provides a lookup service for dynamically locating Web Services. We use the term *Web Services* with an uppercase 'S' to specifically mean components that use these technologies. We use the term *Web Services* with a lowercase 's' to mean a broader set of services that use Web technologies. This wider set can include Web servers and mashups as well as SOAP/WSDL-based Web Services.

7.1.2 Representing Data and Semantics

The focus on representing and exchanging data on the Web is based around the eXtensible Markup Language (XML), which was described in depth in Chapter 3. The focus on representing and exchanging data using XML has led to two main thrusts in this direction. These are:

- **The Semantic Web:** is an extension of the current World Wide Web in which information is given well-defined meaning, better enabling computers and people to work in cooperation [93]. It is focused on the representation of data and seeks to create a machine-processable Web. The effort is led by W3C [94] with participation from a large number of researchers and industrial partners. The Semantic Web is based on the Resource Description Framework (RDF), which integrates a variety of applications using XML for syntax and URIs for naming.

- **Web Services:** are a software system designed to support interoperable machine-to-machine interaction over a network [95]. In simple terms, Web Services provide the definitions (and infrastructure) to allow applications to exchange XML messages with each other.

BPEL	Service Flow and Composition	Semantics
Trading Partner Agreement	Service Agreement	
UDDI/WS Inspection	Service Discovery	
UDDI	Service Publication	
WSDL	Service Description	
WS Security	Secure Messaging	
SOAP	Messaging	
HTTP, FTP, SMTP, MQ etc	Transport	

Fig. 7.4. A taxonomy of the various technologies used to represent and deploy Web Services and those that can be influenced by semantics.

These two technologies do not compete, but rather they complement each other. In a keynote speech [96], Berners-Lee said, "Web Services meet immediate technology needs, while the Semantic Web has the potential for future exponential growth." Such convergence has led to a number of groups that are focusing on this integration, e.g., [97] and [98]. In a recent paper the authors noted [99], "Semantic Web Enabled Web Services (SWWS) will transform the Web from a static collection of information into a distributed device of computation on the basis of Semantic Web technology making content within the World Wide Web machine-processable and machine-interpretable."

Further, the authors define a taxonomy (see Fig. 7.4) that illustrates the various Web Services technologies with those that can be influenced by semantics. Anything from the service description upwards can be enhanced to include a rich layer of semantics that can be understood by applications.

In this chapter, we will take a look at the core infrastructure that can enable machine-to-machine interactions now using Web Services. For more information on the Semantic Web, see the references listed above, as well as Section 5.7.

7.2 Web Services

> *"Web Services are loosely coupled, reusable software components that semantically encapsulate discrete functionality and are distributed and programmatically accessible over standard Internet protocols. [100]"*

Web Services are a distributed systems technology that uses standard Internet protocols to move XML documents between service processes [101]. Simply, therefore, Web Services are software programs that enable applications to talk to each other remotely via XML messages.

Briefly, a program sends a *request* to a remote Web Service containing an XML message and (optionally) *receives* a response (see Fig. 7.5). The specifics about how such services are represented, advertised, discovered and communicated with are all defined by Web Service standards, such as WSDL, UDDI and SOAP, described in Chapter 16.

In a sense, Web Services can be thought of as Internet-oriented text-based integration adapters [102] and since any data format can be mapped in and out of text, their applicability is widespread. Since Web Services are based on XML documents and document exchange, the technological underpinning of Web Services is often called *document-oriented* computing [101].

Although Web Services are centred around documents, it does not necessarily follow that such documents should be readable by people, which is reflected in the core goal of Web Services, that is, to enable machine-to-machine communication at the same scale and using the same style of protocols as the human interface-centred World Wide Web.

7.2.1 A Minimal Web Service

A minimal Web Service has three components [101]:

1. **The Service:** a service is a software component which is capable of processing an XML document. The particular transport and application protocols, e.g., what programming language the service is written in, whether it operates as a stand-alone process or is part of a Web or application server, etc., are of no importance.
2. **The Document:** the XML document that is sent to a service which contains the application-specific information.
3. **The Address:** this describes the protocol binding (e.g., TCP or HTTP) along with the network address that can be used to access the service. The address is also called a port reference.

Even though, in principle, these should be enough to build a Web service, in practice, at least one more component is added, that is, the *Envelope* or *message encapsulation protocol*, which adds things like routing and security information to the message without the need to modify the actual XML document.

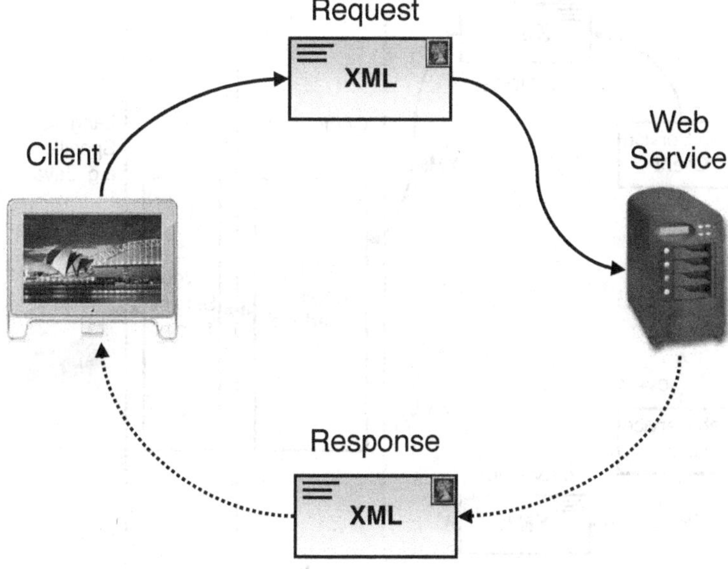

Fig. 7.5. An illustration of the role of a Web Service.

Typically, services use SOAP to define its envelope. Further, comprehensive descriptions of Web Services have also been adopted (i.e., WSDL) and if you introduce these, then it is useful to have a yellow pages for looking up such descriptions (e.g., UDDI). These three technologies provide the programming backbone for current Web Services and are outlined later in this chapter and described in detail in Chapter 16.

7.2.2 Web Services Architecture

Web Services can be used to exchange simple or extremely complex XML documents that can contain either document-oriented or procedural-oriented information. They are based on standardized XML protocols which are supported globally by most major technology firms.

Web Services are *interoperable* and *loosely coupled*, which go hand in hand to create a powerful but flexible infrastructure for document exchange that can work on all platforms. The key to this interoperability is XML which provides the message-passing and service definitions in an operating system and programming language neutral fashion. Messages, wherever they originated from, are *converted* into XML **before** being transported to the remote service.

This is illustrated in Fig. 7.6, which shows this conversion process from language-dependent clients (in C++ here) and services (in Java here), which can interoperate through a common representation of the data, i.e., XML. This leads to a many-to-one situation that is perfectly scalable; i.e., vendors

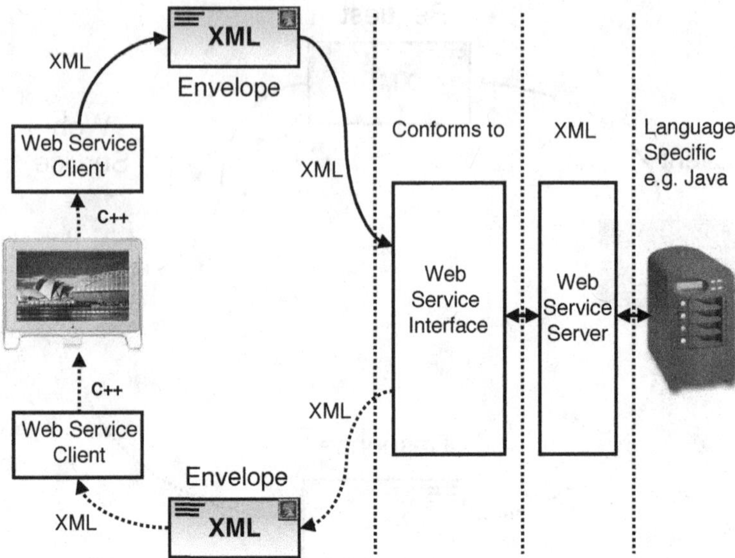

Fig. 7.6. A Web Service is loosely coupled, meaning that the Web Service interface is separated from its implementation.

only have to write data-to-XML and XML-to-data converters once for each supported language. Many already exist (e.g., for Java [103] and [104]). XML provides the common ground for all diverse service implementations. Similar architectures have been employed elsewhere; for example, Jxta uses an XML data representation [24] but the protocols implemented around this are not based on open standards.

Web Services extend this approach to decouple the logic of the client and the server by providing XML descriptions for the service interface (WSDL). This means that a Web Service can be accessed through a common-ground interface which is independent of the back-end implementation.

Figure 7.6 illustrates this by showing a C++ client talking to a Web Service written in Java. Further, each Web Service can have multiple language bindings, which makes it easy to change the back-end implementation without the client needing to update its code. For example, a company could keep the same Web Service interface but re-implement its C++ implementation of this service in Java and the client would not even realise that it had been changed.

A service model that can provide diverse implementations behind a single interface definition is defined to be a *virtual service*. The fact that Web Services are virtual was one of the compelling factors that led to the convergence of Grid computing and Web Services that will be discussed in Chapter 17.

A useful analogy of the decoupling of a Web Service interface and its implementation is a Java interface and implementation. Java interfaces are similar to abstract classes except all of their methods are automatically public and abstract. They provide an extensible mechanism for defining external interfaces to objects that are used to represent some (or all) of its functionality. Java interfaces are similar to Web Service interfaces in that they allow multiple back-end implementations of the same interface. Within Web Services, this may involve implementations from different programming languages whereas within Java, this typically involves creating objects that conform to the same interface but provide different behaviour.[1] Such an approach is fundamental to the Factory Method Design Pattern [105], which has proved to be popular and good programming practice.

Due to the structure of Web Services, they are suited to expose *coarse-grained* functionality. The overhead of converting from programming language to text and vice versa means that the functionality exposed by a Web Service must justify this process and therefore typically several components are combined. For example, a service such as a method call in a Java class is far too fine an operation for a Web Service. Further, maintaining a coarse-grained interface is also key to retaining the loose-coupling offered by Web Services. The finer the granularity, the greater the chance of introducing dependencies between services is.

7.2.3 Web Services Development

As Web Services decouple the Web Service interface from the back-end implementation, there are a number of ways that a developer can integrate applications. There have been four common development practices identified [106] that are useful to illustrate such possible scenarios:

1. **Greenfield:** the developer starts from scratch, creating not only the Web Service but also the application functionality being exposed as a Web Service.
2. **Bottom up:** the functionality being exposed as a Web Service (i.e., the back-end application) already exists and the programmer needs to design a suitable interface.
3. **Top down:** you start with an existing Web Service interface and then create the application functionality capable of implementing that interface.
4. **Meet in the middle:** this is a combination of the bottom-up and top-down scenarios. Here, the Web Services interface (abstract WSDL) and existing application code exist already and you need to integrate them. This may involve creating a bridge between the Web Service interface and the underlying operations implemented in the application.

A number of companies are now using the bottom-up approach to expose current functionality as Web Services, thus enabling better machine-to-machine communication of such services.

[1] Objects could use Java interfaces to bind to different languages also, using JNI.

7.3 Service-Oriented Architecture

The Service-Oriented Architecture (SOA) is an example of the *composite computing model*, defined as follows:

> *The composite computing model is an architecture that uses distributed, discovery-based execution to expose and manage a collection of service-oriented software assets.[107]*

At the fundamental level, an SOA is a collection of services on a network that communicate with each other. The services are loosely coupled, have well-defined interfaces and are reusable. An SOA therefore has a higher-level view of coarse-grained application development that uses standard interfaces to hide the underlying technical complexity.

In an SOA, the capabilities (i.e., software assets) should be dynamically discoverable, there should be a clear separation of the software's capabilities and its implementation and it should be possible to quickly assemble impromptu computing communities with minimal coordinated planning efforts, installation technicalities or human intervention. For more details on SOAs see [108]. It is important to note that an SOA does not require Web Services and further, Web Services can be deployed without an SOA. However, many believe that building an SOA using Web Services is the ideal approach.

7.3.1 A Web Service SOA

A service can be described, discovered and invoked using standardized XML technologies in the current Web Services technology stack. There are three main components:

1. **SOAP:** the envelope for a Web Service that contains the XML message
2. **WSDL:** an XML format for describing the interface to a Web Service
3. **UDDI:** the repository (the yellow pages) for a number of deployed Web Services

SOAP messages (when used for Web Service requests and responses) conform to the WSDL definition of available Web Services. Typically, WSDL defines the interface and location of the Web Service, the SOAP message used to access the Web Services and the protocols over which such SOAP messages can be exchanged and the WSDL descriptors can be accessed via a UDDI repository (or another directory service).

Services are implemented and published by *service providers*, discovered and invoked by *service requesters* and information about a service may be kept within a *service registry*. Therefore, we have three essential operations that you would want to perform:

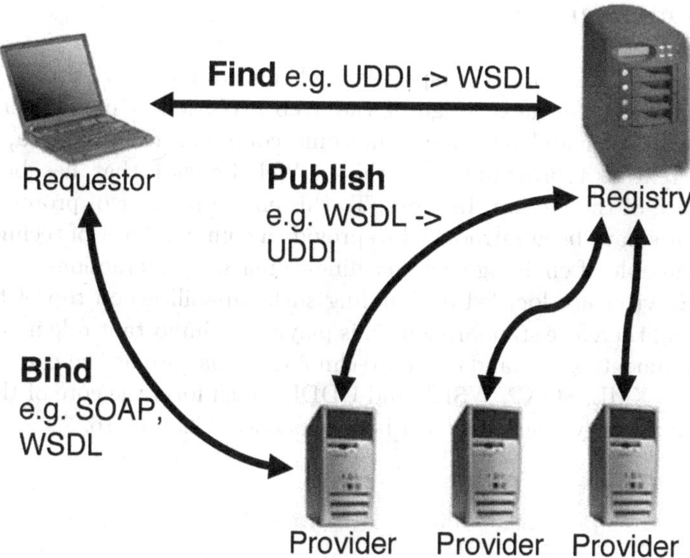

Fig. 7.7. An overview of the service-oriented architecture.

- **Publish:** Performed by the service provider to advertise the existence and capabilities of a service
- **Find or Locate:** Performed by the service requester to locate a service that meets a particular need or technology fingerprint
- **Bind or Invoke:** Performed by the service requester to invoke the service being provided by the service provider.

Figure 7.7 illustrates how these operations map to the underlying Web Service protocols. Service providers create a WDSL interface for their Web Service that specifies its functionality. The WSDL document also contains the location (address) of the service and the transport mechanism that is used to contact the service. Therefore, to publish a service, the service provider registers the WSDL document with the UDDI registry (typically by providing a link to the location of the document).

When a service requester wishes to use a service, it contacts the UDDI server, searches through its database and finds a service that closely matches the search criteria to obtain the location of the WSDL file. Then, the service requester uses the WSDL file to create a request/response invocation on the Web Service. The message for the invocation is typically wrapped in an envelope, using SOAP, and sent to the Web Service. SOAP includes various transport bindings and data encoding mechanisms, which are described in Chapter 16.

7.4 Conclusion

In this chapter, a historical perspective and conceptual overview of Web services was given. The next stage of the Web evolution is more focused on the representation and machine-to-machine communication of data, rather than the textual representation within a Web browser that has been the quintessence of the modern Internet. To this end, a number of protocols and data formats have been introduced to provide a common layer of technologies that are capable of enabling such machine-to-machine interaction.

Web Services are focused on building such capabilities on top of today's Internet and therefore standardization is playing an important role in defining this environment. The standardized technologies that are at the core of Web Services are XML, SOAP, WSDL and UDDI, which form the core of the Web Services technology stack that will be discussed in Chapter 16.

8

Distributed Objects and Agent Technologies

> *"Experience seems to be the only thing of any value that's widely distributed." William Feather (1889-1981)*

Distributed object technology has been the mainstay of many corporations for many years, providing a well-defined mechanism for enacting complex yet predictable business processes across the corporate network. It has been used to simplify client-server systems and connections to remote database through the use of object-oriented APIs, which stemmed from the popularity of the object-oriented programming paradigm. To provide this context, the concept of objects is discussed in the next section and then related to how these can be transferred across a network within distributed object systems. The two distributed object systems we focus on in this book are CORBA and Jini, although we also discuss in Section 8.3 how distributed objects relate to the popular agent paradigm.

An overview of the salient features of CORBA is discussed in this chapter in Section 8.2 but Jini is discussed separately in Chapter 14. However, the underlying Java serialization and Remote Method Invocation (RMI) mechanisms for Jini are discussed here in Section 8.5 in order to illustrate how the state of a Java object can be saved and passed across a network as an argument to a remote method on a distributed object. This mechanism is illustrative of the underlying problems that need to be addressed within any distributed object system. Further, the same serialization mechanisms also need to be addressed in systems based on XML technologies, such as Web Services, which were discussed in the previous chapter. However, distributed object technologies differ in approach to Web Services in a number of ways but primarily because they maintain *state* across the distributed entities in the system.

8.1 What Are Distributed Objects?

Before addressing what a distributed object technology is, we should be clear about what an *object* is. According to [109]:

> *"An object is an entity that encapsulates some private state information or data, a set of associated operations or procedures that manipulate the data, and possibly a thread of control so that collectively they can be treated as a single unit."*

This combination of state and logic imbues objects with identity. Apart from the singleton abstraction, the state in different objects may be different and therefore calling an operation on one object to manipulate its state may have a different outcome than calling the same operation on a different object of the same type. As a result, users of objects need to locate the object and keep track of objects and their current state in order to make repeated invocations to them. Because objects are instances, they also have a lifetime, that is, they are created, used and destroyed. Object instances are instantiations of a particular type or class and instances of the same type share their class. When combined with the notion of inheritance, this leads to class hierarchies. Classes that inherit from others have dependencies on these and can only be understood in the context of their parent class.

Object-oriented programming languages such as Java leverage the encapsulation of data and behaviour, allowing a programmer to make fine-grained decisions about access to data maintained by an object and the view presented to the outside world of that data. Java also defines a kind of global taxonomy for all objects that can be created within the bounds of the language, leading to a well-defined structured graph of inheritance and dependencies.

The 1990s saw a general trend away from mainframe computers acting as single intelligent processors and connected to by many *dumb* clients, towards a distributed network of processing, based on client/server technology. In order to facilitate more decentralized processing of multiple services, and multiple consumers, shared interfaces to software components needed to be defined. Drawing on the benefits apparent in object-oriented programming languages, in particular the encapsulation of data and logic, and the ability to break down large tasks into smaller, reusable components with well-defined behaviours, the transferral of object orientation to distributed environments was considered an appropriate approach.

A number of systems emerged that allow applications to make use of the strong data typing and structured relationships between components that object orientation encourages, while at the same time being able to communicate across a network. Examples include DCOM [3], OLE [110], CORBA [2] and Jini [23]. In the following section we look briefly at CORBA, one of the most widely deployed distributed object systems, and then take a detailed look at Jini, a Java-specific distributed object technology.

8.2 CORBA

The Common Object Request Broker Architecture (CORBA) is a well-known and sophisticated distributed object architecture and serves as a good example of the core design issues and challenges of distributed object systems. In fact, CORBA can be used to communicate between objects within the same address space, i.e., in the same application on the same host, or between applications on the same host, as well as objects residing on different hosts.

Although CORBA uses the object abstraction usually associated with object-oriented programming languages, it is programming language independent. Rather it uses an *Interface Definition Language* (IDL) to specify the public methods that can be called on object instances. The IDL is then mapped a particular programming language in order to generate executable code. There are numerous CORBA IDL mappings including Java, C, C++, Python, Lisp and Smalltalk. In the common case, a CORBA implementation comes with a compiler that takes an IDL description and generates programming language code. The language-specific code can then be compiled to binary using an ordinary compiler. In order to expose objects, therefore, a service provider must create CORBA IDL in the first place, and then make this available to the system.

In order to instantiate and invoke objects, CORBA defines the Object Request Broker (ORB). This component acts as a bridge between an application using CORBA, and the underlying infrastructures supported by CORBA. ORBs handle remote communication with other ORBs as well as object management, for example counting references to objects and object lifetime policies. The ORB registers and interacts with instances of the language- and operating system-specific generated code. To enable communication across a network, CORBA defines the abstract General Inter-ORB Protocol (GIOP) which defines how ORBs talk to one another. A number of concrete implementations of GIOP exist. The most commonly used is the Internet Inter-ORB Protocol (IIOP) which maps GIOP messages to the TCP/IP layer.

Through the definition of the ORB, CORBA makes use of a brokered architecture. An application requests an ORB to create an object and in return receives a handle, or reference, to the possibly remote object. This handle is later used by the application to invoke methods on the object, and possibly to destroy it. This brokered architecture allows for location transparency because the object reference is opaque to the application. Only the ORB is able to map to it an object existing in memory or serialized to storage at an arbitrary network location. Object references in CORBA are called Interoperable Object References (IOR). An IOR contains information to retrieve a distributed object, including the wire protocol, the host and port on which the object resides and a key to reference the object.

Figure 8.1 shows the main components of the CORBA architecture. The IDL definition acts as a shared interface to an object that is programming language independent. From this, both client- and server-side code are generated

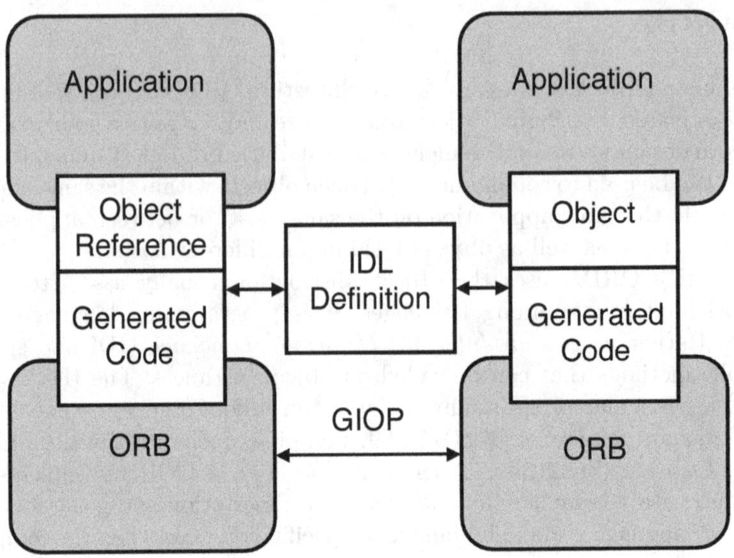

Fig. 8.1. Core CORBA architecture.

using an IDL compiler. The ORBs facilitate the communication either locally or across the network, hiding many details from the application. The client application has a handle to an object in the form of an IOR. This is used to reference and manipulate the actual object implementation on the server side.

Beyond supporting objects by reference, CORBA also supports the concept of Objects By Value (OBV). When an object is transferred from a server to a client using this mechanism, the executable code is run locally on the client. However, this code may not be present locally at the time the OBV is received and must therefore be retrieved from somewhere. The actual data that is transferred when an OBV is retrieved is a record defining the class hierarchy associated with the object as well as list of URIs at which the code is available. This allows the client to download the appropriate object implementation. This process is similar to the Code on Demand pattern in which binary code is retrieved by the client at runtime and executed locally. Code on Demand is common on the Web in the form of Java applets and Macromedia Flash movies. When a browser comes across a reference to either of these, it first checks to see whether it has access to a runtime that can support the executable to be downloaded — either a Java Runtime Environment, or a Flash plugin — and then downloads the executable from the location defined in the HTML.

While CORBA is sophisticated and highly configurable, there are a number of problems that arise from the underlying principles adopted by the system. At the root of these is the fact that CORBA, and distributed object systems in general, attempts to hide the distributed nature of communications from applications. This means applications are unaware of whether a method call is taking place locally or remotely. While this seems like a valuable quality on the face of it, it can also cause problems because distributed interactions suffer from issues not often encountered in a single address space. For example, interactions are prone to partial failure [111]. When an object within an application in a single address space fails, it leads to complete failure of the application. Partial failure is possible in a distributed environment because of network conditions or the failure of a remote host. Hence the behavior of a system modelling a distributed communication as a local one cannot easily represent this to an application. While CORBA addresses this issue through a standard exception set which provides a high level of detail about the error that has occurred, by doing so it breaks the principle of location transparency. Likewise, the combination of host address with an object reference can complicate issues such as object migration [112] because the coupling of identity with location means the reference is in danger of becoming stale if an object migrates. Therefore the infrastructure needs to keep track of migration paths. One mechanism in CORBA for achieving this is to retain the new location of the object after it has left the local address space. However, this leads to chains of references across the network, which invariably become more brittle the longer they are. In the end, overcoming problems arising from mapping a local programming paradigm to a distributed environment leads to ever more complicated solutions which couple components more tightly. While technologies such as CORBA are still used, they are most commonly found behind the corporate firewall. Many commentators are unanimous in suggesting that distributed object systems are not suitable for global-scale systems because they are too tightly coupled [113] [114] [115] [101].

8.3 Mobile Agents

Agents are a paradigm more than they are a particular technology. The concept of agents builds on that of objects; that is, agents are objects that also display certain properties, in particular a degree of *autonomy*. Associated with autonomy are also the notions of learning and adapting to the environment. A mobile agent is an agent that can also migrate between hosts on a network.

While a typical distributed object will be instantiated, manipulated and eventually destroyed by application or infrastructure code, an agent is more likely to simply be instantiated and then left to get on with its task. During the execution of its task, the agent may move to another host, communicate with other agents that it encounters and even destroy itself.

Because agents are objects, they maintain state and have a public interface which allows interaction with its environment and other agents. Similar to object references in systems such as CORBA, agents also have an identifier that uniquely identifies the agent no matter what host it is executing on at any given time. Unlike common distributed objects, however, agents can roam freely among accepting hosts and act autonomously. This in turn poses potential security hazards. Hence, agents often also maintain authentication information allowing an accepting host to determine the author and owner of the agent, for example an X.509 certificate.

The qualities that agents possess make them suitable for particular types of tasks. One example is monitoring network properties. By retaining its state between migrations, an agent can build up a global picture of a network not possible for objects that are tied to a particular host. Likewise, agents can be used to move computation to data. If an application processes large data sets, there are significant advantages in leaving the data where it is and instead transferring the computational algorithm across the network. By using agents, an application can instantiate a new agent, send it to the data and wait for it to return with the results. This approach can also be taken in situations where a process requires numerous exchanges across the network. Furthermore, if the application is a resource-constrained device, for example with limited battery life, or has only very expensive network connectivity at its disposal, then the application can shut down while the process executes, and come back online later, to retrieve the agent. Agents may also be capable of creating clones. This allows computations to be automatically spawned based on current conditions and run in parallel across a network.

Various components and environmental conditions have to exist in order for an agent to successfully transfer from one host to another. In particular, agents require a suitable environment to be present on the hosts that it may visit. This environment provides the oxygen for the agent, allowing it to be reconstituted when it arrives at a new location, as well as imposing possible restrictions on the activities that can be performed, for example reading from or writing to certain areas of the local machine.

In general, a host that accepts agents supports several key concepts:

- A runtime engine. This provides the bootstrapping of the agent environment to the underlying operating system.
- An execution environment for the agent, sometimes called a *place*. A runtime engine may support multiple places.
- A location. This is an important property for mobile agents. Agents need to know where they are, and what other locations are possible destinations.
- A set of available resources. The runtime engine and the execution environment make certain resources available to the agent.
- An authentication mechanism. Like agents, a host usually exposes public credentials so that agents can verify the authenticity of the host before transferring to it.

Mobile agents are similar to the Code on Demand pattern, and may make use of it during the migration process, for example to load class definitions required by the agent into the receiving host if they are not initially available. However, Code on Demand is essentially a client/server-based pattern in that there is a well-defined relationship between the source of the code — the server — and the host on which the code will execute — the client. Because mobile agents display autonomy, the role of the host does not have to be defined in terms of consumer and provider. In this sense mobile agents are akin to P2P technologies.

Although mobile agents have been on the scene for a number of years, research in the area is still ongoing. There are several barriers to widespread uptake of the paradigm, in particular the tight coupling between hosts through the requirement of sharing compatible execution environments for agents, as well as security concerns. Even if an agent platform supports a robust security infrastructure, allowing access to local resources by autonomous, intelligent and possibly self-replicating entities is a difficult paradigm to sell to system administrators.

8.4 Objects, Services and Resources

Any distributed system involves sending messages to some remote entity. Underlying the differences between many systems are the abstractions used to model these entities; they define the architectural qualities of the system. Three abstractions in particular — *object*, *resource* and *service* — are commonly used to describe remote entities; their definitions, however, are not always clearly distinguished. Yet the nature of these abstractions has a profound effect on the distributed communication paradigms that result from their use. One approach to identifying the similarities and differences between them, is to understand them in terms of their relationship to two properties: *state* and *behavior*.

8.4.1 Objects

As the citation at the beginning of Section 8.1 emphasizes, objects have both state and behavior. The state is maintained through the internal data and the behavior of the object is defined through the public operations on that data. A primary issue in these systems is the management of object identifiers which are global pointers to instances of objects. It has been argued that architectures based on global pointers lead to brittle systems if they scale to Internet size because of the proliferation of references and the need to maintain the integrity of the pointers [116]. As a result these systems are considered to be best suited to medium-sized networks within a single domain, with known latencies and static addressing [101] and intimate knowledge of the middleware models used [115].

8.4.2 Resources

The term *resource* is used here to specifically refer to the abstraction used by the Web and related initiative such as the Semantic Web. Such a resource is different from a distributed object in a number of ways:

- Resource state is not hidden from a client as it is in object systems. Instead, standard representations of state are exposed. In object systems the public interface of an object gives access to hidden state.
- Unlike distributed objects, resources do not have operations associated with them. Instead, manipulation and retrieval of resource representations relies on the transfer protocol used to dereference the resource identifier (URI).
- As a consequence, a resource can be viewed as an entity that has state, but not the logic to manipulate that state, i.e., no behavior.

Because resources have no behavior, they do not define how their state can be manipulated. While this could be viewed as limiting and potentially leading to ad hoc, under-specified interactions, in the case of the Web the opposite is actually true. While an object-oriented system defines proprietary behavioral interfaces for every object, leading to a proliferation of means of manipulating objects, the Web uses a single, shared interface: HTTP. The few methods defined by HTTP allow arbitrary resources to be exchanged and manipulated making interactions between entities far simpler, and hence scalable. Imagine, for example, that every Web server defined its own interface to accessing the resources in its charge. This would require a browser to digest a new service interface and generate client-side code every time you clicked on a link, a process that would severely influence the scalability of the system as a whole.

8.4.3 Services

There is no generally accepted definition of the term *service* and current understanding of the term is heavily influenced by Web Services technologies. However, while Web services technologies represent the most widely used means of exposing services, they are not synonymous. The aims of using services are generally agreed upon, including component reuse [117] [118], loose coupling [119] and ease of integration and aggregation [120]. Agreement on the properties that services should possess is not as widely shared. In the absence of a generally accepted definition of the term, the following properties, based on definitions given by a number of commentators [121][122][108][117] [120], together facilitate the aims described above:

- A service is a view of some resource, usually a software asset. Implementation detail is hidden behind the service interface. The interface has well-defined boundaries, providing encapsulation of the resource behind it.

Some commentators also stress that this interface should be programming language independent.
- Services communicate using messages. The structure of the message and the schema, or form, of its contents are defined by the interface.
- Services are stateless. This means all the information needed by a service to perform its function is contained in the messages used to communicate with it.

According to [122] there are two types of state a service comes in contact with. The first is the internal state of the service — the back-end resources behind the service interface. This is encapsulated and hidden from the outside world. The second is interaction state. This is explicitly modeled in the message exchanges. No implicit information is presumed between consumer and provider.

The service abstraction shares commonalities with the object abstraction but displays crucial differences:

- Like an object, a service can have an arbitrary interface.
- Like distributed object systems that use an IDL, services usually describe this interface in a description language.
- Unlike objects, services use a message-oriented model for communication. This has quite different semantics and implications to invoking a procedure on a remote object. In the latter, what the remote entity *is* plays a part. In the case of objects, the class of an object must be known. Once this class is known, behavior based on the class can be inferred by the consumer. Services, however, do not share class. Instead, they share contracts and schema [122]. Therefore, what an entity *is* has no bearing on communication and nothing is inferred. Furthermore, communication with an object involves addressing an instance. This is not the case with services as is discussed in the next item.
- Unlike objects, services do not have state. As noted by [121], object orientation teaches us that data and the logic that acts on that data should be combined while service orientation suggests that these two things should be separate. Therefore a service acts upon state, but does not expose its own state. Put another way, services do not have instances. You cannot create and destroy a service in the way you can an object.

The service abstraction also shares similarities with the resource abstraction but has core differences. According to the Web Services Architecture (WSA) [108], a Web service *is* a resource because it can be identified, i.e., in the usual case it had a URI associated with it. The WSA is an attempt to define Web Services in terms of the more generic Web Architecture [123] which adheres to the concept of a resource being anything that can be named. The definition of a Web service as resource is rather forced, however, because unlike a Web resource, a Web service does not necessarily have a representation of state. This representation of state is the most important characteristic of a Web resource beyond the fact that it can be identified.

The service abstraction is provably scalable. Some of the best examples of stateless service-oriented interactions can be seen in certain P2P technologies such as Gnutella. However, like the Web, these systems restrict themselves to a very limited set of behaviors, and hence to a limited amount of types of services that the system can support; in the case of file sharing application, only a single service type is supported. Infrastructures that wish to support an arbitrary amount of service types begin to look like object-oriented systems because of the proliferation of service interfaces. Figure 8.2 shows the relation of objects, services and resources to state, or data, and behavior, or operations.

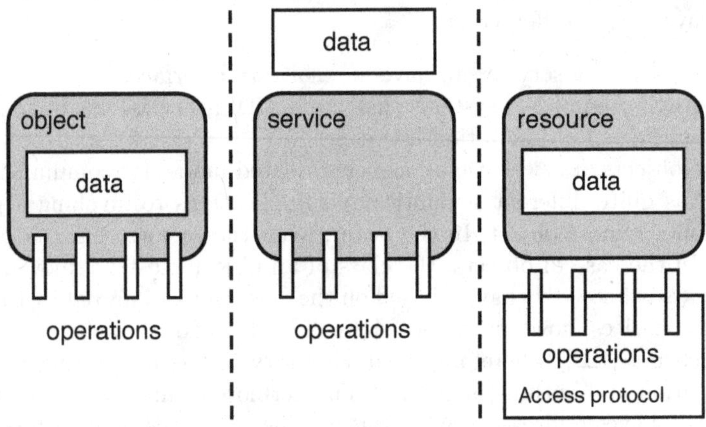

Fig. 8.2. Objects, services and resources.

8.5 Distributing Objects Using Java

If you are using the core Java SDK, you have the following options for passing a Java object and its state, around a network:

1. **Sockets:** these are one-to-one, duplex connections. With sockets you need to pack data for a socket and unpack it on the other side; i.e., you also need to agree on predefined format and internal data protocol.
2. **RMI (Remote Method Invocation):** this is similar to Remote Procedure Call (RPC), which abstracts the communication interface to the level of a procedure call. The programmer appears to be calling a local procedure but the procedure is hosted remotely. RMI is essentially the RPC for Java and it uses the Java serialization mechanism to pack objects for transportation.

8.5.1 Remote Method Invocation

RMI is a tightly coupled communication technology that requires an application to know a remote application's methods. Other more loosely coupled communication mechanisms (e.g., Web Services, Jxta pipes and JSM) are discussed elsewhere (see Chapters 7, 15 and the JMS Web site [124]). RMI provides the mechanism by which the server and the client communicate and pass information back and forth and therefore allow Java objects to be distributed across a network.

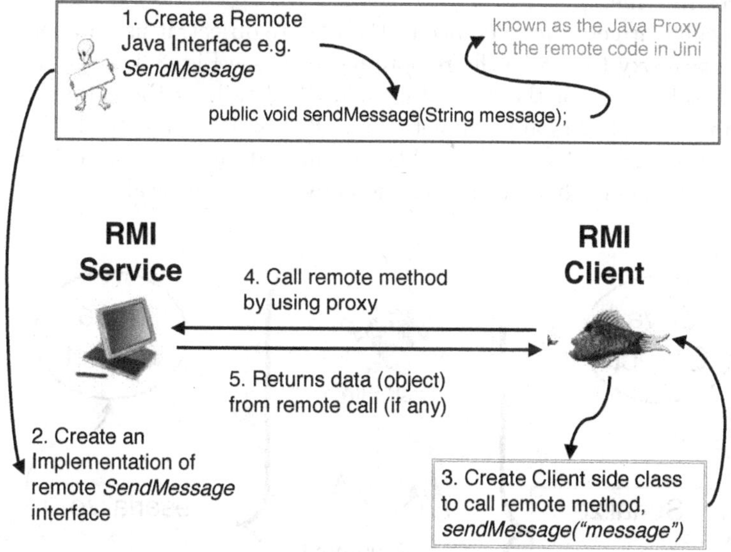

Fig. 8.3. An overview of remote method invocation (RMI).

RMI applications consist of two separate programs: a **server** and a **client**. The server application creates a number of remote objects (implementing different services), creates local references for them and then waits for clients to invoke methods on these remote objects. The remote objects are created by a two-stage process:

1. by implementing a *proxy* (using a Java Interface) to the remote code (see Fig. 8.3, stage 1);
2. and, implementing this proxy in a class that is stored on the RMI server (see Fig. 8.3, stage 2).

A client application then gets a remote reference (i.e., the *proxy* interface defined for the remote object) using one of the following methods:

- an application can register its remote objects with RMI's simple naming facility, the *rmiregistry* application;

- or the application can pass and return remote object references as part of its normal operation.

These rather simple mechanisms of discovering remote reference to objects is where Jini, described in Chapter 14, improves on the basic RMI functionality. It achieves this through the use of a Jini Lookup Service (LUS), which is a third-party application that is used to register the location of remote objects. Incidentally, the LUS is a bit like a Napster server or a super-peer in Gnutella except that these store references to the locations of remote files and an LUS stores the location of remote Java objects (which, in fact, also could be Java references to a file...).

Once a client gets the reference to the remote object, it uses its local copy of the Java proxy to invoke the remote method (see Fig. 8.3, stages 3 and 4) and RMI takes care of the rest. Within RMI, details of the communication between remote objects are completely handled by RMI; i.e., to the programmer, remote communication looks like a standard Java method call. So how does RMI transport the data across the network automatically?

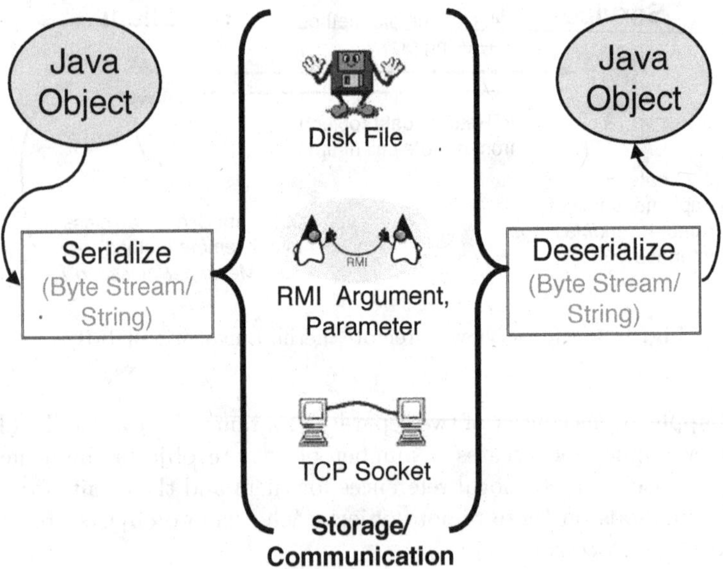

Fig. 8.4. Java serialization can be used to transport a Java object across a network or to store it to a local disk for persistence.

8.5.2 Java Serialization

Fundamental to RMI's transport mechanism is the *Java serialization* mechanism, which is used to transport any object that is passed as a parameter to or returned from a remote function. RMI uses the object serialization mechanism to transport objects by value across the network and between different Java Virtual Machines (JVMs). Serializable classes are capable of being converted into a self-describing byte stream that can be used to reconstruct an exact copy of the serialized object when the object is read back from the stream. Therefore, serialization can be used to store an object's state in such a way that later it can be completely reconstructed.

Serialized Java objects can be stored to a disk file (for persistence), can be transferred across the network using a socket and can be used within a third-party mechanism behind the scenes in order to transparently (to the programmer) pass objects between networked devices as in Jini (see Fig. 8.4).

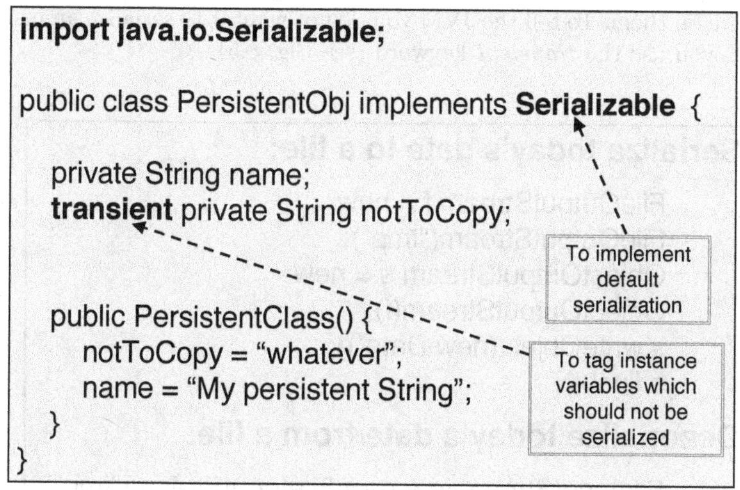

Fig. 8.5. A simple code fragment that shows how you make a Java class serializable and how you would exclude certain instance variables by using the transient key word.

In Java, the default serialization mechanism stores all (non-transient) data members of a class to a set of bytes, typically stored into a stream. This stream can then be passed across a network or stored to a local disk file. Note that serialization does not store the actual class *bytecode*; rather, it stores the name of the class needed in order to reconstruct the object. In this way, Java serialization with respect to actual classes is more of a dependency rather than part of the core serialization mechanism. In Java, there are two methods of serializing a class, by implementing either of the following *Java Interfaces*:

1. **java.io.Serializable:** simple default mechanism, where only minimal modification to the code is necessary;

2. **java.io.Externalizable:** implements a custom serialization policy. Using the Externalizable interface, you can specify precisely what, and how, you want to store and retrieve the information contained within the class.

Here, the default mechanism will be briefly illustrated using some simple Java code. For details of the *Externalizable* interface and its use, the reader is referred to the Java Tutorial [125]. Figure 8.5 illustrates, using a simple example, how you mark a class serializable. In Java, this is achieved by making the class implement the *java.io.Serializable* interface, which basically tags the class as being serializable to the JVMs. The JVM does the rest and serializes every instance variable (whether it be a simple variable, i.e., an int, double, an array, i.e., double[] or even an object). Java recursively serializes every variable by decomposing it into its constituent parts and applying the same procedure on them. To tell the JVM you do not want it to serialize an instance variable, you use the *transient* keyword (see Fig. 8.5).

Serialize today's date to a file:

```
FileOutputStream f = new
FileOutputStream("tmp");
ObjectOutputStream s = new
ObjectOutputStream(f);
s.writeObject(new Date());
s.flush();
```

Deserialize today's date from a file:

```
FileInputStream in = new FileInputStream("tmp");
ObjectInputStream s = new
ObjectInputStream(in);
Date date = (Date)s.readObject();
```

Fig. 8.6. A Java code fragment that serializes a serializable Java object (java.util.Date) to a File output stream for persistence.

The code in Fig. 8.6 shows how one would serialize any Java object to a file. In this example, we create a Java file output stream (so we can write to a file) and then stream an object output stream into this file, into which we can write our serialized Java objects. Using the same mechanism, this object output stream could be plugged into a different storage or networking device other than a file, e.g., a socket. To serialize today's date therefore, we create a new Date object (i.e., *new Date()*) and write this object to our object output stream, which in turn gets written to the file.

To load this serialized object back in from the file, we perform the inverse operation; that is, we create a Java file input stream and attach an object input stream to this in order to convert the contents of the file and to *deserialize* them into a collection of Java objects (see Fig. 8.6). The *readObject()* function returns a Java Object but since we know we have stored a Java Date object previously, we can *typecast* this into what it should be.

This simple mechanism (from the programmer's side anyway), provides a powerful way of being able to transfer objects or persist their state. Java serialization is used extensively and RMI, for the programmer, abstracts such communication to a higher level, that is, at the *method* level. Therefore, within RMI, you have to tag your objects as serializable but then thereafter you simply invoke Java methods and the associated argument objects that are passed across the network are handled for you by the RMI subsystem.

8.6 Conclusion

In this chapter, we discussed the concept of objects within object-oriented languages and showed the mechanisms and interfaces of how these can be transferred across a network in CORBA and Jini. We also showed how this technology relates to the agent paradigm in distributed systems. We provided an overview of CORBA and gave a detailed example of how Jini's underlying serialization and remote method invocation mechanisms operate in Java. We then discussed how distributed object technologies differ in approach to Web Services and provided some arguments to support these viewpoints from the community.

As an example technology, we provided an overview of Java RMI, which is the underlying communication mechanism that toolkits like Jini, described in Chapter 14, build upon to provide a network plug-and-play capability for distributed objects.

9

Grid Computing

> *"We're a superpower with a third-world grid!', Bill Richardson*[1]

Over the past decade there has been a huge shift in the way we perceive and utilize computing resources. Previously, computing needs were typically achieved by using localised resources and infrastructures and high-end scientific calculations would be performed on dedicated parallel machines. However, nowadays, we are seeing an increasing number of wide-area distributed-computing applications, which has led to the development of many different types of middleware, libraries and tools that allow geographically distributed resources to be unified into a single application. This approach to distributed computing has come under a wide number of different names, such as meta-computing, scalable computing, global computing, Internet computing and, more recently, Grid computing.[2]

9.1 The Grid Dream

The use of the term Grid derives from an analogy with an electrical *power grid.* The Grid *dream* is to allow users to tap into resources off the Internet as easily as electrical power can be drawn from a wall socket. To make this happen, not only does the underlying infrastructure (called the *power grid* for electricity and simply *the Grid* for computing) have to be pervasive, but we would need a number of levels of security and accountancy to provide transparent access, just as one has with power. For example, imagine when

[1] Bill Richardson comments to CNN in August 2003 on the state of the USA electricity grid after a series of blackouts.

[2] In the USA, Grid computing has been consumed by a more general term called "cyberinfrastructure" and in Europe, "eScience" is typically used. Other modern terms, such as Cloud computing, are discussed in Chapter 19.

you plug in your kettle, your only concern is, have you filled it with water. You should not have to worry about where the electricity comes from, whether it is bought from other countries or generated from coal, windfarms, etc. You should simply take for granted that when your appliance is plugged in, it will get the power it needs.

The Grid is trying to implement this same scenario for a different type of utility, i.e., when you sit at your computer, your only concern should be that you have a smart idea (some scientific analysis, etc.) and you want this idea to be realised without knowing (or caring) what other computer resources you are using and where they are located. Just as a power grid is a utility (i.e., you ask for electricity, you get it and pay accordingly), the Grid is also seen as a utility (i.e., you ask for computer power, storage or service capacities and you get them), and consequently you pay for it. Such issues are tackled by the Grid middleware.

Currently, however, Grid accountancy is not really practical or functional but a number of users and scientists have devoted their machines to form a prototype Grid for research development of these essential services needed for widespread adoption. In reality, however, there is not one single "Grid," rather there are many different types: some are evolving, some private, some public, some regional, some global, some specific (e.g., dedicated to one scientific application) and some generic. Such Grids have realistic goals but do not attempt to solve the whole Grid problem. It will be some time before the power grid analogy becomes reality (if ever).

Interestingly, though, there are companies [126] that are starting to offer broadband high-speed Internet access through standard electrical sockets in homes and businesses. Such connections take advantage of the extensive electricity network already in place. A specially designed modem (that consumes power of the order of one-quarter of a 40W lightbulb) transmits the broadband information across existing electricity cables to the electricity substation. From there, the data is collected and transported over a local network and onto the Internet. Trials of such systems have indicated that symmetrical speeds of up to 1 Mbit/s can be achieved. Imagine, anywhere you have a power socket, you can tap into the Internet; combine this with the Grid computing dream and then perhaps it really could become a reality!

9.2 Social Perspective

For a Grid to be successful, we not only have to tackle the huge technological problems but also address the social aspects [127] of how to engage researchers, educators, businesses and consumers in using the Grid as part of their everyday work. In describing the Grid, the authors noted [12] that the first recognisable grid was Edison's power distribution grid in New York. Its goal was to supply power to Wall Street in 1882 at the same price as the current existing technology and therefore costs needed to be kept down at every step.

At the core of Edison's economic analysis was Ohm's Law, which was used to control the cost of generating, distributing and using electricity [128]. Edison chose Wall Street because he could only compete with gas if there were a high enough population density to yield economic return, given the cost relationships defined by Ohm's Law (he also had to choose an area where he could find capital for the switching costs). Here, it is plain to see that the social good of any new infrastructure has wide social implications, i.e., if those investing in this new technology do not see an economic return, then its progress will slow down and consequently, so will its widespread availability.

This is also true for today's Grid because its adoption within the wider community is also highly dependent on social acceptance and industrial success if the cost-volume relations are to break even. Grid computing has attempted to address these issues in a number of ways, for example, by gaining large industrial backing and by *conforming* to international standards. For example, there is much support for the lower-level infrastructure, and several companies and institutions have already committed massive amounts of resources to the Grid. For example, the U.S. National Science Foundation committed $53 million on the TeraGrid [129] that included 13.6 teraflops of computing power, over 450 terabytes of data storage, and high-resolution visualization systems, interconnected by a 40 Gbps network. The actual nodes are Linux clusters of Intel-based IBM computers with Sun and Oracle also being involved. Similar initiatives are also happening elsewhere. Also, the convergence of Web services and Grid computing in the form of the Open Grid Service Architecture (OGSA) [8] and more recently the Web Services Resource Framework (WSRF) [130], [131] are clear moves in support of globally accepted standards (also see Section 9.5.2).

9.3 History of the Grid

In this section, a context is given for the introduction of how Grids came into being by taking a look at early metacomputing techniques that led to the evolution of Grid technology. The sections here form a brief summary of some of the key systems in the development of Grid technologies. The authors [132] identify three different generations in the evolution of the Grid:

1. **First Generation:** Early metacomputing environments, such as FAFNER [133] and the I-WAY [134].
2. **Second Generation:** This saw the introductions of: core Grid technologies like the Globus toolkit [9] and Legion [135]; distributed object systems, e.g., Jini [23] and CORBA [136]; Grid resource brokers and Schedulers, e.g., Condor [137], LSF [138], SGE [139]; a number of integrated systems including Cactus [140], DataGrid [141], UNICORE [142] and P2P

computing frameworks, e.g., Jxta [24]; and application user interfaces for remote steering and visualization, e.g., portals and Grid Computing Environments (GCE) [143].

3. **Third Generation:** This saw the introduction of a service-oriented approach (e.g., OGSA [7]) and the increasing use of *metadata* (giving more detailed information describing services) through Semantic Web research [94] and the introduction of collaborative technologies, such as the Access Grid [144].

The next three sections give a brief summary of the key technologies and explain the progression towards the current state of the art in Grid research.

9.3.1 The First Generation

In the early 1990s there was a shift in emphasis placed on wide-area distributed computing. A new wave of high-performance applications were being developed, which require specific requirements that were not achievable on a single computer. Two representative, yet diverse, experiments are described here that provided an infrastructure for access to computational resources by high-performance applications: these are FAFNER [133] and the I-WAY [134].

As described in detail in Section 4.3.4, the RSA algorithm for asymmetric cryptography is based on the premise that large numbers are very difficult to factorize. In 1991, RSA Data Security Inc. initiated the Factoring Challenge in order to provide a test bed for factoring implementations. FAFNER (Factoring via Network-Enabled Recursion) was set up to factor via the Web and any computer with more than 4 MB of memory could participate in this experiment. Specifically, FAFNER was set up to factor RSA130 using the Number Field Sieve (NFS) factoring method. They created a Web interface form in HTML for NFS and contributors could take this form and use it to invoke CGI scripts to perform the factoring. FAFNER is basically a collection of Perl scripts, HTML pages and associated documentation, which comprises the *server side* of the factoring effort. The FAFNER software itself doesn't factor the RSA130; rather, it provides interactive registration, task assignment and solution database services to clients that perform the actual work. FAFNER was a forerunner to systems such as SETI [19], Distributed.net [80], Entropia [82] and United Devices [81], to name a few.

The I-WAY experiment was started as a project to link various supercomputing centres and to provide the infrastructure for a metacomputing [145] environment for high computational scientific applications [134]. This connectivity involved using high-speed networks, which gave application developers access to a wide variety of resources, e.g., supercomputers, databases and scientific instruments, all potentially located at geographically distributed sites. The I-WAY environment allowed the assembly of unique capabilities that could not otherwise be created in a cost-effective manner and was the forerunner for the Globus toolkit. The I-WAY connected supercomputers and other

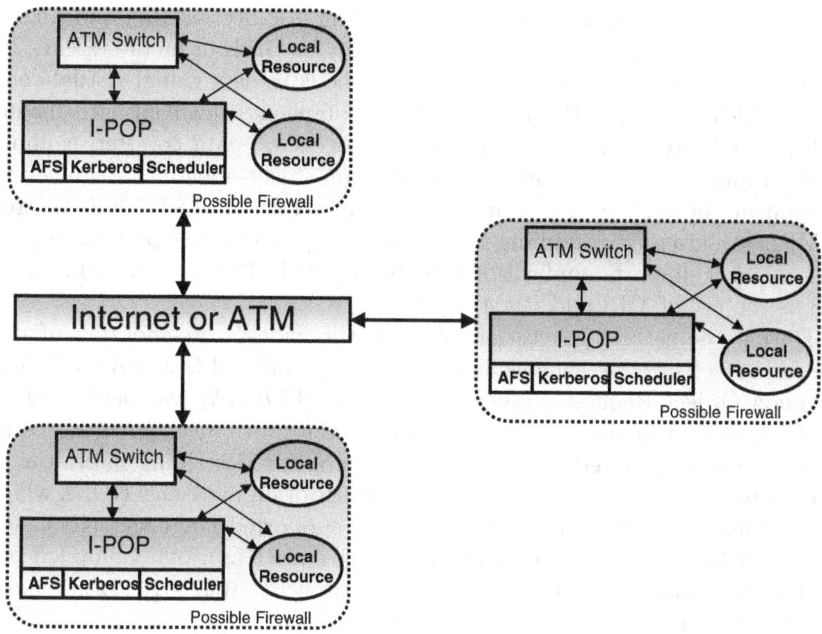

Fig. 9.1. The I-WAY network, consisting of cooperating I-POP servers that could communicate across the Internet or ATM networks.

resources at 17 sites across North America based on ATM connectivity. The I-WAY consisted of a number of I-POP (point of presence) servers [146] that were connected by the Internet or ATM networks (see Fig. 9.1). The I-Soft software infrastructure could be used to access the configured I-POP machines and provided an environment that consisted of a number of services, including scheduling, security (authentication and auditing), parallel programming support (process creation and communication) and a distributed file system (using AFS, the Andrew File System).

Sixty different groups used this network to create a diverse set of applications, for example: to construct large-scale scientific simulations [147], [148], collaborative engineering [149], [150] and supercomputer-enhanced scientific instruments [149], [151]. The I-Soft toolkit formed the basis of the Globus toolkit, which is in widespread adoption throughout the Grid computing world today.

9.3.2 The Second Generation

The I-WAY paved the path for the second generation of metacomputing technologies that aimed to provide a common infrastructure for Grid applications through the development of the Globus toolkit (see Section 9.7) and Legion [135]. Legion is an integrated operating system for Grids or meta-systems. Its focus is to give the user the impression that he is using a global virtual computer, which transparently handles all the complexity involved with having such a distributed system (scheduling on processors, data transfer, communication and synchronization). Legion has an object-oriented design; every component (hosts, files, programs) is represented as an object. It is written in MPL (Mentat Programming Language) [152], which is a parallel version of C++, and supports applications written in MPL, FORTRAN and Java as well as the use of MPI and PVM.

During the second generation, we saw the widespread adoption of *distributed object systems*, such as Jini (see Chapter 14) and CORBA [136]. The Common Object Request Broker Architecture (CORBA) was developed by the Object Management Group [153] and defines an object-oriented model for accessing distributed objects. CORBA supports describing interfaces to active, distributed objects via an Interface Description Language (IDL), which can be linked to code written in any of the supported languages (C, C++, Java, COBOL, Smalltalk, Ada, Lisp, Python and IDLscript). Compiled object implementations use the Object Request Broker (ORB) to perform remote method invocations.

For many scientists, their research is highly dependent on computing throughput, which follows the SIMD (Single Instruction, Multiple Data) parallel computing model. Here, a scientist would require that the **same program** be iterated many times over **different data**. Such a class of problem is also called High-Throughput Computing (HTC). In this generation of the Grid, we saw a number of *Grid resource brokers* and *schedulers* that supported this class of application. These were either introduced or extended for operation on the Grid, e.g., Condor, [137], LSF [138] and SGE [139]. For example, Condor is a system that takes advantage of idle machines (e.g., at night or weekends) and allows the submission of many jobs at the same time. Source code does not have to be modified in any way to use Condor and it supports transparent *checkpointing* and *migration* of jobs across the network. *Checkpointing* involves saving a job's state to disk so that it can be resumed at a later stage, either locally or remotely by *migrating* (or moving) it to another machine.

Also, in this generation, we saw a number of integrated systems including Cactus [140], DataGrid [141], UNICORE [142] and P2P computing frameworks (e.g., Jxta [24]; see Chapter 15) and application user interfaces for remote steering and visualization, i.e., portals. Briefly, Cactus is a problem-solving environment designed for scientists and engineers. It has a modular structure which can be distributed across a parallel machine and the Grid. Cactus originated in academic research and is one of the driving applications in the GridLab project [154] (Triana [39] being the other). Cactus runs on many architectures and supports checkpointing, which was demonstrated in the Cactus Worm experiment [155] that deployed Cactus on the Grid using the Globus toolkit. DataGrid's objective is to enable next-generation scientific exploration that requires intensive computation and the analysis of large-scale shared databases. Such databases range from hundreds of terabytes to petabytes and are used by widely distributed scientific communities. UNICORE attempts to make seamless Grid computing a reality for non-Grid experts. It has developed a user-friendly interface that allows easy and uniform access to distributed computing resources and provides support for running scientific and engineering applications.

9.3.3 The Third Generation

The second generation paved the way for the basic interoperability to enable large-scale distributed computation and sharing of resources. The key focus of the third generation extended this model to allow the flexible assembly of Grid resources by exposing the functionality through standard interfaces with agreed interpretation. This solution employed the use of the *service-oriented model* with increasing attention to metadata of such services. The defining paper of the Grid anatomy [156] focused on terms such as *distributed collaboration* and *virtual organizations* and identified a model based on the Open Grid Service Architecture model. OGSA represents a convergence with Web Services and allows Grid protocols to be exposed through Web Services' XML standardized technologies, such as WSDL, UDDI and SOAP, described in detail in Chapter 17. The following sections in this chapter introduce the foundations for some of these key concepts and give a broad overview of the functionality of the most widely used Grid toolkit, Globus.

Ian Foster

Ian Foster is Director of the Computation Institute at Argonne National Laboratory, where he is also an Argonne Distinguished Fellow, and the University of Chicago, where he is also the Arthur Holly Compton Distinguished Service Professor of Computer Science. His research deals with distributed, parallel, and data-intensive computing technologies and applications. He has published six books and over 300 articles and technical reports on these and related topics.[3]

[3] Photo and biography printed with kind permission from Ian Foster.

9.4 The Grid Computing Architecture

As mentioned in the previous section, Grid computing was initiated through various early efforts, most notably the I-WAY experiment in the mid 1990's. Ian Foster and Carl Kesselman were the very much behind that effort and their book entitled *The Grid: Blueprint for a New Computing Infrastructure* [12] led to a coining of the term Grid across the community and an explosion of effort in this area. They went on to write several key papers in the field, which led the design of the architecture and structure of Grid computing applications.

Carl Kesselman

Dr. Carl Kesselman is a Fellow in the Information Sciences Institute at the University of Southern California. He is the Director of the Center for Grid Technologies at the Information Sciences Institute and a Research Professor of Computer Science at the University of Southern California. He received a Ph.D. in Computer Science from the University of California, Los Angeles, a Master of Science degree in Electrical Engineering from the University of Southern California, and Bachelors degrees in Electrical Engineering and Computer Science from the University at Buffalo.[4]

In [156], the authors define Grid computing as "flexible, secure, coordinated resource sharing among dynamic collections of individuals, institutions, and resources." The emphasis here is on the flexible and dynamic environment that can be used to discover and interoperate with distributed resources. This coordinated resource sharing is undertaken via multi-institutional *virtual organizations*. Virtual organizations provide a highly controlled environment to allow each resource provider to specify exactly what she wants to share, who is allowed to share it and the conditions whereby this sharing occurs. The set of individuals and/or institutions that provides such sharing rules is collectively known as a virtual organization (VO).

In Grid computing, users can share or have direct access to computers, software, data and other resources. This transparent access to distributed resources is achieved through the use of *middleware*, e.g, Globus (see Section 9.7).

[4] Photo and biography printed with kind permission from Carl Kesselman.

VOs are not original in concept. In many ways, they are similar to Jxta peer groups (see Section 15.3.1), which also facilitate the dynamic creation of a collection of cooperating peers that have a common set of goals. In Jxta, groups share common group protocols that can provide authentication, authorization and other policies for their interaction. Sharing resources can also be set at finer levels of granularity within the peer group itself so that specific criteria can be set for each resource or person accessing that resource. The VO and peer group concepts are very similar but the terms used are different.

Figure 9.2 illustrates the Grid architecture. Here, users/clients use the standard Internet via a Grid middleware toolkit, e.g., Globus. This toolkit enables them to discover the existence of distributed resources, make reservations for their use and then gain direct access to them. The direct access is achieved via standard Internet technologies, such as FTP or the Grid-enhanced version GridFTP [157]. Therefore, the routing of the data is achieved by standard TCP/IP routing and therefore could pass through several intermediaries but is not controlled by higher-level mechanisms, e.g., like those employed by P2P infrastructures such as Jxta (see Chapter 15). Also shown here is the concept of the virtual organization which provides a blanket for every resource to define its sharing and security policies.

9.4.1 Virtual Organizations and the Sharing of Resources

VOs are dynamically accessible from a Grid application and applications are capable of spanning a number of different organizations, each running its own VO. The authors [156] identify a number of examples of different VOs and scenarios. Some of these are illustrated here:

- **Resource Providers:** application service providers, storage service providers and CPU cycle providers all can represent a VO.
- **Product Design:** for example, here, several organizations could form an industrial consortium in order to integrate sophisticated tools to simulate a next-generation supersonic aircraft. The simulation will need to integrate and aggregate multiple software and hardware resources, including sensitive proprietary software components developed by the various participants. Each component may operate on its machine but has access to the necessary design databases and related information. Security is paramount because, although such organizations have agreed to collaborate, they do not want to lose intellectual copyright on their constituent software components, which may have been developed over many years. Such a scenario could enable the collaboration to prototype and cost-estimate the production of such an aircraft even though no one partner has complete knowledge of the entire process.
- **Crisis Management:** for example, a team may be set up to respond to a chemical spill by using local weather and soil models to estimate the spread of the spill. This could determine the impact based on factors

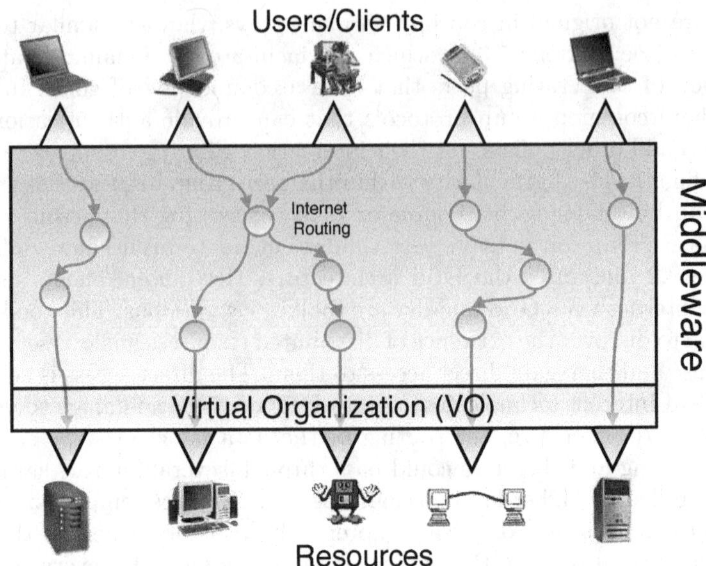

Fig. 9.2. The architecture of a computational Grid. The middleware (e.g., Globus) enables clients to access distributed resources from another administrative domain (i.e., virtual organization), whilst providing transparency across the various protocols of the underlying Internet, as shown.

such as the location of the population and environmental considerations, e.g., rivers, water supplies and create a short-term emergency plan that could evacuate and notify the relevant authorities and hospitals. Other examples here include using modules that could be developed to forecast extreme hazardous events such as avalanching, flooding, landslides, storms or forest fires. For example, for the case of a severe storm, the output from the operational meteorological forecast models could drive the suite of fine scale models for the primary target area of the storm. The fine-scale models could locally forecast maximum wind speeds, the snow loading of avalanche slopes, river run-off or landslide danger.

- **Data-Intense Applications:** for example, the members of a large, international, high-energy physics collaboration, such as DataGrid [141], described earlier, could also form a VO.

Although each of these examples differs in many ways, e.g., the number and type of participants, the activities, the duration and scale of the interaction, and the particular resources being shared, they each share a common set of goals, i.e., to collaborate. In every case, each organization will consist of a number of distrustful participants who may or may not have prior relationships with those who wish to share their resources. Further, in some cases the data could be sensitive, e.g., direct access to a sensor or an incoming physics

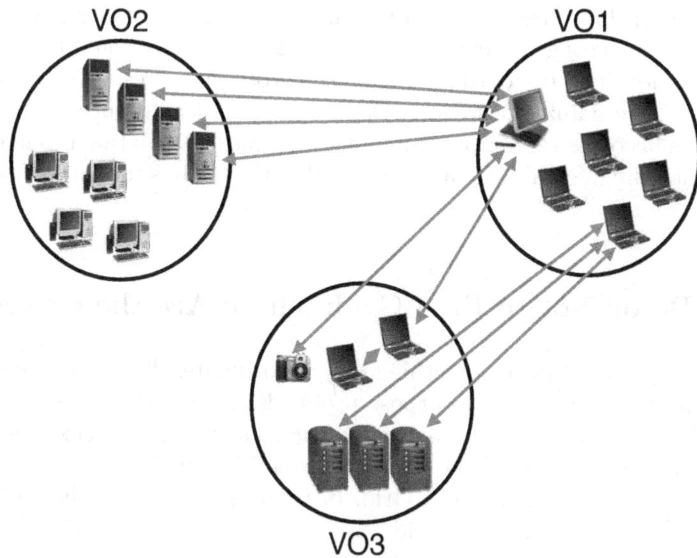

Fig. 9.3. Three virtual organizations. Users can access multiple VOs and access a number of different services across the multiple sites.

data stream. Therefore, each participant must be sure that she only shares such resources with permissible participants.

The scope for the VO can span multiple organizations but its granularity depends on the specific collaboration at hand. Therefore, it could be convenient within a multi-institutional collaboration to have a specific policy and therefore fit the entire collaboration under one VO. However, in other scenarios several VOs representing the participating institutions could be integrated. The actual designing of how many VOs you want to use is completely flexible and an organization can participate in one or more VOs by sharing some or all of its resources. Figure 9.3 illustrates an example of one organization blanketed by its own VO (VO1) simultaneously accessing resources from two other virtual organizations, VO2 and VO3.

The pooling of resources at multiple sites is a key element in aggregating functionality that exposes new services to the community that previously could not have been achieved. The actual sharing of resources is dependent on the choices made by the resource owner, i.e., when, where and what can be done. For example, a participant in a VO may only accept *secure* computational resources by some defined policy.

The implementation of a VO must be flexible and allow mechanisms for users to express policies, to establish identities (of users and resources) for authentication and to authorize the use of the particular operation. Further, such relationships can vary over time depending on various factors, e.g., the availability of resources, the access to morphed data sets, etc. Further, such sharing relationships are very much P2P in nature; e.g., providers can also be consumers and sharing can exist at many levels; e.g., there could be common sharing relationships to coordinate the use across many resources, spanning many different organizations. Here, the ability to delegate authority in controlled ways becomes very important along with the coordination mechanisms, e.g., co-scheduling. Such issues are addressed in the Globus toolkit; see Section 9.7.

9.5 To Be or Not to Be a Grid: These Are the Criteria...

The Grid is defined [158] as something that "coordinates distributed resources using standard, open, general-purpose protocols and interfaces to deliver required qualities of service" (also becoming known as "qualities of experience"). To qualify this vision, specific criteria have been identified that an application must support to be classified as a Grid. In Foster's paper [159], he outlines a three-point checklist; that is, a Grid:

1. coordinates resources that are not subject to **centralized control**
2. uses **standard, open, general-purpose protocols** and interfaces
3. delivers non-trivial **qualities of service**.

These criteria have been reiterated elsewhere [127] and form the basis for current guidelines from programming Grids.[5] The Globus toolkit, for example, supports the creation of Grids by meeting all criteria. These, perhaps somewhat contrived, criteria mean that other systems do not qualify as Grids for various reasons. For example, Jxta could not be considered a Grid because it does not use standard protocols and Condor [137] couldn't be considered a Grid because it has centralized control. In the following three sections these criteria are described in more detail.

9.5.1 Centralized Control

The first point in the checklist concerns how the resources that make up the distributed system are controlled, whether they are:

- centrally controlled by one administrator (a non-Grid) or
- consist of a number of interacting administrative domains that pull resources together using common policies.

There are a number of issues here that support these criteria. For example, resources within a collaborative development may be owned by different organizations, who would not be happy to surrender control of their resources

5 There are a number of researchers who think these criteria are too restrictive; see [160] for a collection of articles on the subject.

under some central management infrastructure. Second, since the Grid aims to join a larger number of resources, any centralized control will certainly affect its scalability.

Therefore, computational Grids should connect resources at different administrative domains. Typically, this is achieved by defining and using a virtual organization (see Section 9.4.1) that provides a controlled environment for its set of individuals and/or institutions. However, other protocols and mechanisms exist elsewhere to achieve similar desirable results; e.g., most P2P applications achieve this, although at varying degrees of granularity.

Jxta, for example, supports VO concepts but also much finer levels of granularity and has the capability of connecting a vast number of machines administered by different organizations or users. Other systems, e.g., Freenet (see Chapter 12), provide a virtual overlay that allows secure encrypted storage and retrieval across millions of computers, potentially spanning millions of different administrative domains.

There are also several examples of systems that are not Grids under this category; e.g., Sun's Grid Engine [139] or Platform's Load-Sharing Facility [138] have a centralized control of the hosts they manage.

9.5.2 Standard, Open, General-Purpose Protocols

The Grid architecture is a protocol architecture [156]. It is important that such protocols and interfaces are multi-purpose, standard and open. If not, then we are dealing with an application-specific system that will not generalize to the wider community. Within the Grid, such standards-based open protocols define the basic mechanisms of how users and resources (from within a VO) negotiate, establish, manage and exploit sharing relationships. The Grid *vision*, therefore, is about creating or using existing standards for open and generalized protocols, interfaces and policies that enable this level of resource sharing within such a distributed system.

In essence, Grid computing is aiming to help standardize the way we do distributed computing rather than having a multitude of non-interoperable distributed systems. A standards-based open architecture promotes extensibility, interoperability and portability because it has general agreement within the community. To help with this standardization process, the Grid community has the successful and popular Open Grid Forum (OGF) [161], which hosts three conferences a year with both research groups (for researching areas) and working groups (for standardization) existing in a number of different areas.

For example, the newly adopted OGSA and OGSI (see Chapter 17) by Globus [9] have working groups concentrating on their standardization throughout the whole Grid community. Further, the de facto implementation of the core Grid standards, *Globus* [9], has over six years of experience dealing with the Grid community and the new version of its toolkit has embraced

Web Services (see Chapter 7) to create a standardized interface to their Grid services (see Chapter 17).

Many systems fail on this criterion but excel in the other two categories. For example, distributed computing systems that harness idle CPU cycles, e.g., Entropia [82] and United Devices [81], and file-sharing systems, such as Gnutella [4], all deliver high levels of QoS, albeit for specialized services, but for the most part are not based on open standards, and therefore are too specific for generalized use; e.g., it would be difficult to see how the Gnutella protocol could be useful for anything but searching for files or data content.

9.5.3 Quality of Service

A key parameter in Grid systems is the *Quality of Service* (QoS). When a Grid job has QoS requirements, it is often necessary to negotiate a *service-level agreement* beforehand to enforce this certain level of service. There are three types of quality support that can be provided:

1. None: No QoS is supported at all.
2. Soft: You can specify QoS requirements and these will try to be met but they cannot be guaranteed. This is the most common form of QoS implemented in Grid applications.
3. Hard: This is where all nodes on the Grid support and guarantee the level of QoS requested.

A Grid should be able to deliver non-trivial QoS, whether, for example, this is measured by performance, service or data availability or data transfer. QoS is application specific and it completely depends on the needs of the application. For example, in a physics experiment, the QoS may be specified in terms of computational throughput, but in other experiments, the QoS may be specified in terms of reliability of file transfers or data content.

9.6 Types of Grid

Broadly speaking, there are three types of Grid:

- Computational Grids
- Data Grids
- Service Grids

A *computational Grid* is a distributed set of resources that are dedicated to aggregate computational capacity. Computational Grids are highly suitable for *task farming* or *high-throughout computing* applications where there is typically one data set and a huge parameter space through which the scientist wishes to search. The scientist will be typically searching for some phenomenon (e.g., whilst searching for gravitational wave signals) or some stabilisation or convergence of network state (e.g., teaching a neural network). Such algorithms involve little or no communication between the nodes and therefore fit excellently onto a coarse-grained processor, such as the Grid. There are many infrastructures for this, including those outlined in Section 9.3.2.

A *data Grid* is a collection of distributed resources that are specifically set up for processing and transferring large amounts of data. Here, the European DataGrid project [141] is a good example, focusing on the development of middleware services to enable distributed analysis of physics data from CERN. At its core, DataGrid uses Globus but adds a rich set of functionality on top of this to support data Grids. For example, it employs a hierarchical structure that will distribute several petabytes of data to various sites across the world. They use global namespaces to differentiate between different and replicated data sets and this huge data Grid will load balance the analysis jobs from over 700 physicists for the largest throughput for this community.

A *service Grid* is a collection of distributed resources that provides a service that cannot possibly be achieved through one single computer. In this example, therefore, the Grid will typically consist of several different resources, each providing a specific function that needs to be aggregated in order to collectively perform the desired services. For example, you could have a service that obtained its functionality by integrating and connecting databases from two separate VOs (representing two data streams from physics sensors/detectors) in order to output their correlation. Such a service could not be provided by one organization or the other since the output relies on the combination of both.

9.7 The Globus Toolkit 2.x

Over the past several years many protocols, services and tools have sprung from research and development efforts within the Grid community. Such tools have attempted to address the challenges of building scalable VOs through the use of services such as cross-institutional security management, resource management and co-allocation, information services and data management services for data replication and transfer. These tools have been implemented by the Globus toolkit [9], which enables applications to handle distributed heterogeneous computing resources as a single virtual machine. The Globus project is a U.S. multi-institutional research effort that seeks to enable the construction of computational grids and contains a core set of services that aim to provide solutions for the Grid infrastructure. These services use standards (some achieved through the OGF, formerly GGF) wherever possible and have well-defined interfaces that can be integrated into applications in an incremental fashion.

The Globus toolkit consists of four layers, as outlined in Fig. 9.4. The first layer, the Grid fabric, consists of the actual resources that you want to make available to the Grid application. The components of this Grid fabric are integrated by Grid APIs that have been implemented by the Globus toolkit.

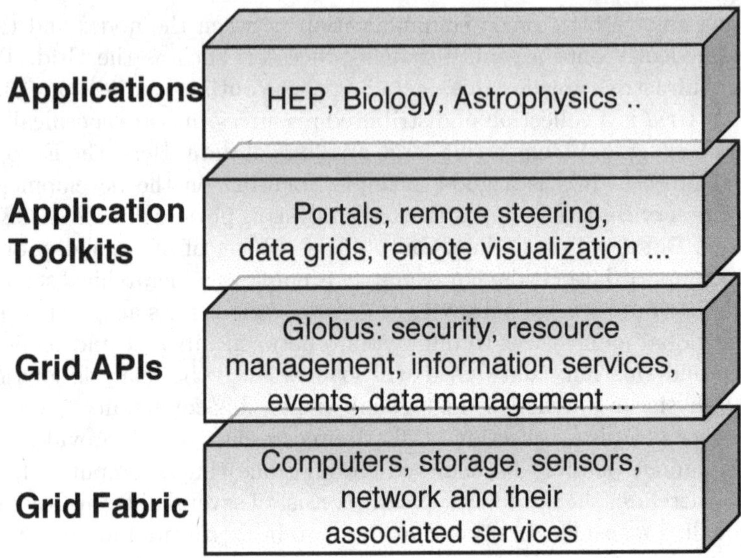

Fig. 9.4. The Globus Toolkit 2.x, showing the various layers in the Grid technology stack. The key building block for an application is the Globus toolkit.

Such APIs are now being exposed as Grid services in the Globus Toolkit 3.x (see Chapter 17). The third layer typically consists of a set of capabilities that are specific to an application or a set of applications. For example, DataGrid has created such a layer for flexible transportation of data and all DataGrid applications access the various Grid functionalities through this layer. More generalized application-level interfaces have also been recently implemented, for example, within the EU-funded Gridlab project [154]. Within these layers, other services that provide remote steering services (i.e., to dynamically change parameters of a remote application, for example) and to give access to the current state of the application are typically provided through the use of a Grid portal [143]) or another graphical interface, e.g., a visual problem solving environment [39].

Finally, the fourth layer is the actual application. A wide number of applications (i.e., hundreds) have used Globus to build multi-institutional Grids. Some examples of key worldwide projects and forums are given in Appendix A.

9.7.1 Globus Tools

This section outlines these main services provided by the 2.x version of the Globus toolkit. See Chapter 17 for details of the 3.x toolkit. The purpose of this section is to give the reader an overview of the types of services on which the Globus team has been focused. Rather than providing a uniform programming model, such as the object-oriented model, the Globus toolkit provides a bag of services that programmers developing either specific tools or applications can use to meet their needs. Such a methodology is only possible when such capabilities are distinct and have well-defined interfaces that can be incorporated into applications or tools in an incremental fashion. The Globus toolkit essentially consists of four elements:

1. **Security:** to provide authentication, delegation and authorization.
2. **Information Services:** to provide information about Grid services.
3. **Data Management:** involves accessing and managing data.
4. **Resource Management:** to allocate resources provided by a Grid.

These will be described in more detail in the following four sections.

9.7.2 Security

The Grid Security Infrastructure (GSI) provides security mechanisms, i.e., authentication and communication over an open network. GSI supports a number of features that a Grid user requires; e.g., authenticate using a single sign-on mechanism, delegation, integration with local security systems and trust-based relationships. GSI is based on public-key encryption (using X.509 certificates) and SSL but extensions have been added for single sign-on and delegation. The GSI implementation in Globus adheres to the IETF GSS-API standard [162].

X.509 certificates involve the use of the Certificate Authority (CA), which issues the certificates to the subjects (i.e., Grid users). The use of X.509 certificates therefore implies that each subject exchanging information trusts the given CA; i.e., a CA acts as a *trusted third party.*

X.509 certificates contain information about the CA as well as the subject. They contain the subject's name, along with his public key, the name of the CA and other fields such as an ID of the encryption algorithms applied and identifiers. The certificates are also signed by the CA so that users can verify that the CA specified in the certificate actually issued the certificate; i.e., they can get the public key of the CA and test if it matches the private key used to sign the certificate. Private keys are also password protected by the user. Certificates can be obtained in a number of ways depending on the particular CA-approved mechanism. For examples, see [163] and [164].

GSI allows **mutual authentication**, i.e., allows two parties across the Grid to prove to each other that they are who they say they are (for a detailed overview of the underlying security techniques, see Chapter 4). Figure 9.5 illustrates how one person, B, verifies that A is who she says she is. The steps are as follows:

1. A sends her public key to B.
2. B then verifies that the key being sent to him has been issued by the listed CA in the certificate. This is achieved by checking the signature on the certificate against the CA's public key. (Therefore B has to trust the CA.)

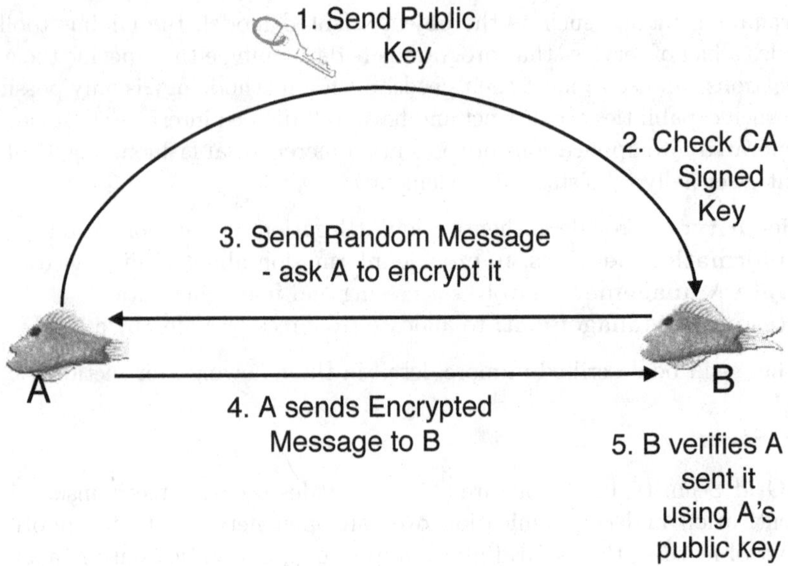

Fig. 9.5. Shows how a person verifies that the person with whom they are communicating is who she says she is; used for mutual authentication in Globus.

3. B then sends a random message to A and asks her to encrypt this message.
4. A then encrypts this message using her private key and returns this message to B.
5. B then uses A's public key to decrypt the message. If the message is the same that was sent, then B is sure that A is identified (since A is the only person can have her private key).
6. The exact same operation is then performed by A to verify that B is who he says he is.

Delegation is achieved in Globus by the use of **proxy** certificates. Proxy certificates are temporary certificates that are generated on the fly from a person's identity but bypass the need for password-protected private keys. Specifically a proxy consists of a new certificate containing a new public and private key. The new certificate is signed by the owner rather than the CA, which creates a *chain of trust*; i.e., the proxy is verified and trusted because it is signed by the certificate owner and the certificate is trusted because it is signed by the CA. For a detailed overview of the security mechanisms, see the Globus GSI Web page [164].

9.7.3 Information Services

The Monitoring and Discovery Service (MDS) is the collective interface to the various information services that are provided by Globus. Each of the information services can be accessed separately but MDS integrates these to provide a standard mechanism for publishing and discovering resource status and configuration information. The Globus team uses a so-called hourglass approach to software writing where the toolkit components (MDS, GRAM, etc.) provide an API for many underlying components and Grid protocols. Therefore, MDS here is the neck of the hourglass that has applications and higher-level services or tools above it and the lower-level mechanisms (e.g., local monitoring services) below it.

MDS consists of three main components, illustrated in Fig. 9.6:

1. **GRIS (Grid Resource Information Servers)** that collect data on each resource and can be located on a well-known port (i.e., 2135).
2. **IP (Information Providers)** which provide the interface between local data collection service and the GRIS servers.
3. **GIIS (Grid Index Information Services)** that collect information from one or more GRIS servers and act as a lookup service for resource information.

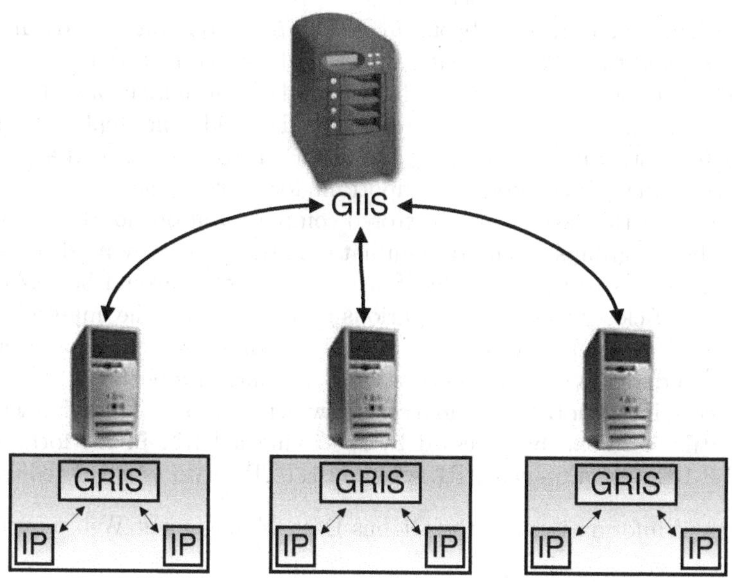

Fig. 9.6. An overview of the protocols you use within MDS.

Briefly, data flows from the local data collection services to the IPs, along to the GRIS servers and then are finally collected by the aggregate directory service, GIIS. IPs can collect data from a variety of sources, e.g., current load status, operating system type and version, file system information (free disk space, etc.), RAM and virtual memory levels. There can be several local data providers connected to one GRIS server, each interfaced through an IP as illustrated. Further, there can be several GRIS servers registered with one GIIS server and so on.

Therefore, when a request arrives at the GIIS, the GRIS checks its local cache and if the information is not there, or out of date, then it invokes the IP to gather the data and pass it along up the chain. For more information, see the Globus Information Services Web page [165].

9.7.4 Data Management

Data management in Globus consists of three distinct components:

- **GridFTP:** an extended version of the IETF's FTP (File Transport Protocol). It is secure; i.e., it authenticates via GSI security and adds new features, such as parallel data transfer, partial file transfer and server-to-server (i.e., third-party) data transfer. GridFTP is downloadable from the Web site [166] as an SDK (software development kit). There is also a community effort GGF GridFTP working group that focusses on improving the current GridFTP protocol [157].
- **Data Replication:** consists of a *Replica Catalog* component and a *Replica Management* tool. The Replica Catalog is a lookup directory that contains mappings between logical names for files and one or more copies of the files located on physical storage systems across the Grid. The Replica Management tool integrates this catalog and GridFTP to keep track of and replicate data files. Such tools are important for certain science experiments where either the data cannot be stored completely at one location or when a number of groups collaborate on data analysis and they need to obtain efficient access to the data files. Such data therefore would be replicated and moved closer to where the various groups perform the analysis.
- **GASS:** the Global Access to Secondary Storage system allows remote access to data via standard protocols. GASS includes both client libraries (for accessing remote files) and a server (which acts as a limited file server). Data therefore can be accessed by specifying a URL, in the form of an HTTP URL or an x-gass URL when an HTTP server is not accessible.

For more information, see the Globus Data Management Web page [166].

9.7.5 Resource Management

The Globus Resource Allocation Manager (GRAM) is used to allocate and monitor remote resources. The main component of GRAM is a server process, called the *Gatekeeper*, which typically runs on the machine on which the user wants to run a job. The Gatekeeper has the responsibility to authenticate the user and then satisfy the request.[6] Job requirements are specified using the Resource Specification Language (RSL). GRAM uses GASS to download the executable, to move stdin/stdout/stderr and access files to and from remote locations.

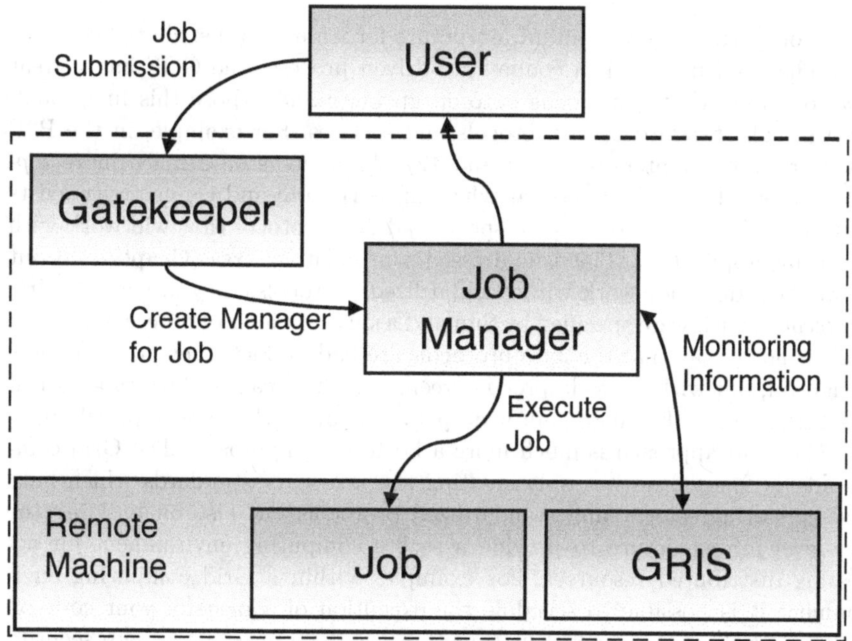

Fig. 9.7. An overview of how GRAM submits and monitors jobs.

Briefly, when a job is submitted in RSL to GRAM, the request is sent to the *Gatekeeper* for the remote computer (see Fig. 9.7). The Gatekeeper then creates a *job manager* for the job, which starts and monitors the job during its lifetime. The job manager is the interface to the user and communicates state changes during the running of the job. Then, when the remote job terminates (either normally or by failing), the job manager terminates also. For more information, see the Globus Resource Management Web page [167].

Globus has evolved from the I-Soft system, through version 1 (GT1) to version 2 (GT2) and recently, its emphasis has moved from supporting just high-performance applications towards supporting more pervasive services that can support virtual organizations. This evolution is continuing through

[6] In fact, the Gatekeeper is really part of the security infrastructure, which checks the credentials and changes the user ID to the mapped user before running the specific service. However, the only services ever implemented to work with this, at the time of writing, were GRAM and GARA.

OGSA (GT3), which is based on exposing its functionality as Web Services; see Chapter 17.

9.8 Comments and Conclusion

Grid computing provides an infrastructure for wide-area distributed computing. The Grid process is a community-driven process (the GGF has a great deal of support) and its focus is to encapsulate and expose this functionality through standard open protocols and services. For example, in the P2P chapters (see Chapters 6, 10, 11 and 12), the focus is on a much more *top-down* view; that is, let's look at what infrastructure and connectivity exists in today's Internet and adapt a specific ad hoc protocol that will work with a specific application. This is addressed somewhat by Jxta (Chapter 15) but again Jxta does not work with standardized protocols; they are simply *Jxta protocols*, which were specified by Sun and a small number of other companies. This is not to say that the Jxta protocols are bad, in fact, they are extremely insightful, but without widespread agreement, which can lead to standardization, it is more difficult to gain widespread adoption (but not impossible).

The Grid approach is much more a bottom-up approach. The Grid community is focused on not only creating the necessary standards which have widespread agreement and standardized protocols but also on building the low-level infrastructure to provide a secure computing environment for accessing distributed resources. For example, within a Grid computing environment it is possible to schedule the execution of a piece of your code on a distributed resource, which is something that requires a concrete security policy as well as the technical specification of how you describe what it is you wish to execute and how this is accomplished (via environment variables, etc.). The core toolkit, Globus, tackles a number of these key issues including security, job submission, resource allocation, reliable (and fast) file transfer, data replication and information systems.

This chapter has outlined the concepts behind Grid computing. Analogous to the power grid, Grid computing is aiming to provide computing resources as a utility, just as gas and electricity are provided to us now. To this goal, the underlying infrastructure needed to support this kind of interaction has evolved from middleware, such as I-Soft that supports wide-area high-performance computing, to Globus 1 and 2, which introduces more interoperable solutions. In Chapters 16 and 17, we'll see how these technologies move to a more service-oriented approach (see Section 7.3) that exposes the Grid protocols using Web Service standards (WSDL, SOAP, etc.), in the form of OGSA.

This continuing evolution is bringing us closer to systems for production Grids capable of running a wide range of applications. Key to this integration is the concept of virtual organizations that make it easier to establish cross-organizational sharing relationships. Today, Grids have three main properties:

they coordinate resources that are not subject to *centralized control*; use *standard, open, general-purpose protocols* and interfaces; and deliver non-trivial *qualities of service.*

Part III

Protocols and Architectures I — P2P Applications

10

Gnutella

"The World's Most Dangerous Geek," David Kushner[1]

Gnutella defined and popularised modern P2P technology through its truly decentralized design and implementation. It arrived right around the time when centrally organized solutions were being targeted and provided a mechanism that offered a much more tolerant structure, where no single entity could be isolated to bring down the entire network. The Gnutella network consists of thousands of information providers, which are not indexed in a central place. Therefore, to shut down such a network is not trivial since a vast number of peers (i.e., many hundreds) would have to be eliminated.

This chapter provides an overview of the original 0.4 version of the Gnutella network. It combines a conceptual overview and a user-friendly rewrite of the Gnutella protocol specification [168]. A historical perspective is provided, along with usage scenarios, which include joining and searching the Gnutella network. This is followed by a detailed account of its protocol specification that provides the fundamental information required for a competent programmer to build a Gnutella network from scratch.

10.1 History of Gnutella

Gnutella was born sometime in early March 2000. Justin Frankel and Tom Pepper, working under the dot-com pen name of Gnullsoft [169], are Gnutella's inventors. Their last life-changing product, Winamp [170], was the beginning of a company called Nullsoft [171], which was purchased by America Online (AOL) in 1999. Winamp was developed for playing music files. According to Tom Pepper, Gnutella was developed primarily to share cooking recipes.

[1] Headline of Rolling stone interview with Justin Frankel, co-inventor of Gnutella, `www.rollingstone.com/news/story/5938320/the_worlds_most_dangerous_geek`.

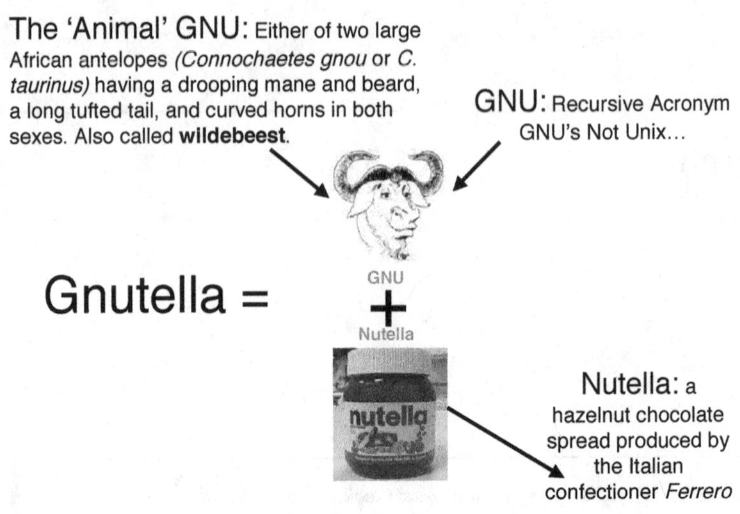
The 'Animal' GNU: Either of two large African antelopes (Connochaetes gnou or C. taurinus) having a drooping mane and beard, a long tufted tail, and curved horns in both sexes. Also called wildebeest.
GNU: Recursive Acronym GNU's Not Unix...
Gnutella =
GNU
+
Nutella
nutella
Nutella: a hazelnut chocolate spread produced by the Italian confectioner Ferrero
....

Fig. 10.1. The Gnutella name explained.

Gnutella was developed in just fourteen days by two guys without college degrees. It was released as an experiment but was then abruptly stopped by AOL shortly afterwards (see [172] and [173]). It was supposed to be released as Version 1.0 under the GNU General Public License but never actually grew beyond version 0.56. The Gnutella name is a merging of GNU and Nutella (see Fig. 10.1). GNU is short for GNU's Not Unix, open source developing and Nutella is a hazelnut chocolate spread produced by the Italian confectioner Ferrero, which the authors liked.

> **Tom Pepper**
> *Tom Pepper is best known for his collaboration with Frankel on the invention of Gnutella, releasing the first version on March 14, 2000. He and Frankel co-founded Nullsoft and later worked for AOL as the manager of SHOUTcast. He is now working on RAZZ, Inc. but continues to collaborate with Frankel on projects like Ninjam.*

Just as Gnutella was about to disappear, open source developers intervened and Bryan Mayland reverse-engineered Gnutella's communication protocol and released the findings on the gnutella's nerdherd Web site.[2] This site hosted the protocol documentation but also hosted a link to Gnutella's Internet Relay Chat (IRC) channel *#gnutella*, which had a massive response and significantly affected the future development.

[2] Originally at `http://gnutella.nerdherd.net`. For a more comprehensive history of the start of Gnutella, see `http://www.nathanm.com/gnutella/`.

10.2 What Is Gnutella?

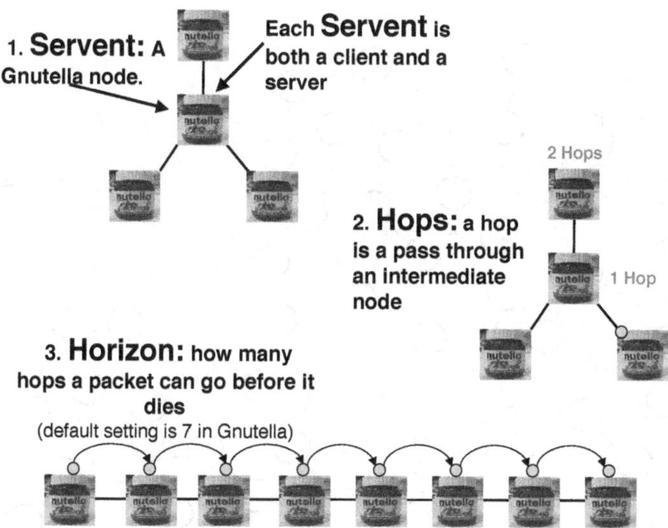

Fig. 10.2. Gnutella terms defined.

> **Justin Frankel**
> *Justin Frankel graduated high school with a 3.9 GPA. He studied Computer Science at the University of Utah in 1996 but dropped out and released the first shareware version of Winamp. At ten dollars a copy and fifteen million downloads in 2 years, Frankel was soon earning tens of thousands of dollars a month. Nullsoft was bought by AOL and soon after Gnutella was born.*

Gnutella is a protocol for a distributed search. In this model, every peer in the network is both a client and a server. This is illustrated in Fig. 10.2. These so-called Gnutella *servents* (**serv**er + cli**ent**) provide client-side interfaces through which users can issue queries and view search results, whilst at the same time they also accept queries from other servents, check for matches against their local data set and respond with applicable results. Due to its distributed nature, a network of servents that implements the Gnutella protocol is highly fault tolerant, as the operation of the network as a whole is not affected if a subset of servents goes off line.

Each Gnutella node is connected to a small number of other Gnutella nodes (typically around four) and such connections are formed on a random ad hoc basis depending on where new peers happen to join the network. This structure is shown in Fig. 10.3, which illustrates the flat nature of the Gnutella network. Gnutella nodes have no central lookup service or caching servers and therefore only see other peers to whom they are connected.

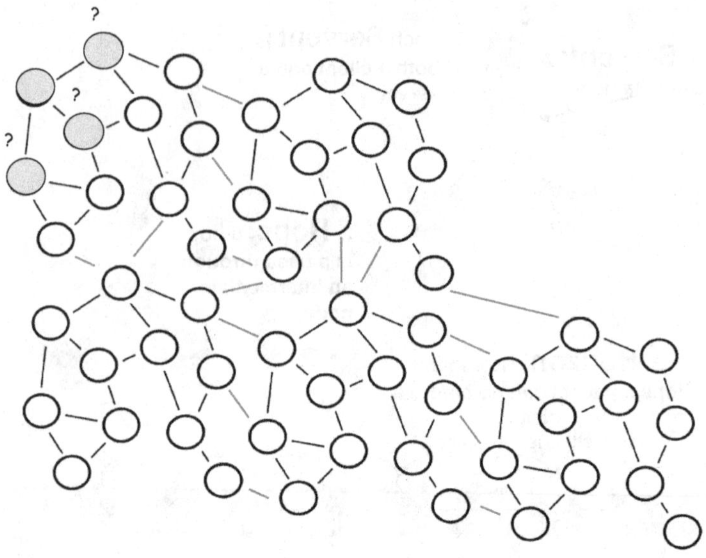

Fig. 10.3. An illustration of a basic Gnutella network containing tens of nodes.

Therefore, when a peer wishes to search the network for a file, it has to ask its neighbours. Requests are answered if the peer has a copy of the requested file, otherwise they are forwarded to all its connected peers, and so on. In this way, the network is flooded with a request in an inherently massively parallel fashion, which in theory should result in ultra-fast searching. Well it does, but in practice of course, the amount of traffic that such a request generates can often saturate the capacity of the network and leave little bandwidth left for actually retrieving files, which defeats the point of the exercise! Such limitations are discussed in great detail in Chapter 11, but it is important to understand the core Gnutella technology before understanding how these issues are addressed.

As a consequence of this method of searching a network, the Gnutella protocol defines a term to measure the number of nodes the packet travels through before it reaches its destination. This term is referred to as the *number of hops*, i.e., how many peers a request hops through (see Fig. 10.2).

In practice, a real-world Gnutella network would not be as organized as Fig. 10.3 due to the semi-random fashion that peers join the network and discover other peers. It would almost certainly be the case that peers will be connected in such a way that they will form loops. For example, peer A may connect to peer B, which may connect to peer C , which may, in turn, connect back to peer A. In this circumstance, it is important to make sure that the request doesn't loop indefinitely. For this reason, a unique identifier is attached to the message so that peers can drop requests that they have already seen. This is described in more detail in Section 10.3.3 but this principle is used in all P2P searchable networks.

Networks of this nature can become incredibly large and therefore you need a mechanism to limit the searchable area. For this reason, the Gnutella specification includes a TTL (Time To Live, see Fig. 10.2) for the request. TTL is also known as the Gnutella horizon, i.e., how far a packet can go before it dies.

The "standard" TTL is 7 hops, so, how far is that? A 7-hop radius combined with network conditions (i.e., 4 connections) means that around 10,000 nodes are reachable within a fully connected network. Another way to look at a TTL is with an analogy of a "large crowd," i.e. when you're in a large crowd (e.g., a rock/pop concert, a demonstration) you can only see so far. The crowd appears to go on forever and also, you don't know exactly where you are in relation to the rest of the crowd; that's a peer in Gnutella.

10.3 A Gnutella Scenario

This section provides an overview of how a servent joins the Gnutella network and, once joined, how it then discovers other servents available on the network. The next section illustrates this by using a typical Gnutella scenario.

10.3.1 Discovering Peers

There are various ways to discover a peer, both initially, when joining a Gnutella network, and when already connected to a Gnutella node:

1. **Out of Band Methods:** e.g., IRC and Web: In the early days, users used IRCs (Internet Relay Chat) to locate a host to which to connect. Otherwise, users checked a handful of Web pages to see which hosts were available. Users tried a number of hosts using the Gnutella software until one worked.
2. **Host Caches:** GnuCache was used to cache Gnutella hosts, which was included in Gnut software for UNIX. This gave users a permanent server for users to connect to in order to find other users on the Gnutella network.
3. **Internal Peer Discovery:** involves issuing Ping messages, waiting for Pong responses with invitations to connect.

Note: peers must be willing to receive incoming connections from "unknown" peers. Peers may be picky about accepting connections for many reasons; for example, nodes may have too many connections already or prospective nodes may not have good properties, e.g., sharing few files, slow connections and so on. Also, peers leaving a network can cause additional shuffling. Therefore, establishing a good set of connections can be haphazard.

10.3.2 Gnutella in Operation

Figure 10.4 illustrates the steps involved in connecting and searching within a Gnutella network.

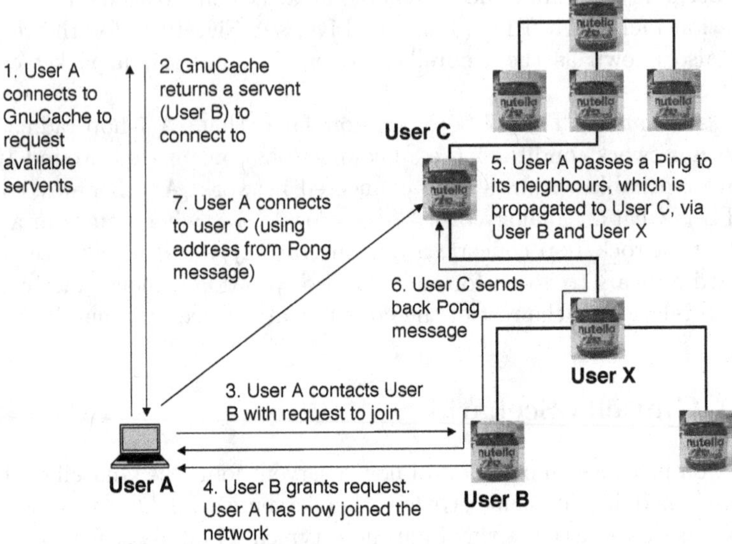

Fig. 10.4. Joining and discovering peers within a Gnutella network.

User A performs the following steps in order to join and become an active participant in the Gnutella network:

1. User A uses one of the techniques discussed in Section 10.3.1 to join the Gnutella network. In this case, the user connects to a GnuCache server.
2. GnuCache returns a list of nodes on the Gnutella network. User A chooses one of these (User B) and attempts to contact it.
3. User A sends a “Gnutella Connect” (see Section 10.4) to User B to request to join the network.
4. User B accepts and returns a "Gnutella OK" to User A, who finalises the connection. User A is now connected to the Gnutella network.
5. User A now announces its presence by issuing a *Ping* to its neighbour (User B); User B forwards this to User X, who, in turn, forwards it to User C.
6. User C returns a *Pong* message, which gets passed along the same path as the Ping descriptor travelled. *Pong* messages contain the address of the sender.
7. User A connects to User C by using the address specified in C’s Pong message to create another connection. User A continues in this fashion

until it has reached its maximum connection count (typically set to around 4).

10.3.3 Searching Within Gnutella

In order to locate a file, a servent sends a query request to all its direct neighbours, which in turn forward the query to their neighbours, and the process repeats. When a servent receives a *query request*, it searches its local files and returns a *query response* containing all the matches it finds. *Query responses* follow the reverse path of *query requests* to reach the initiating servents for the request. Servents along the path do not cache the *query responses*.

To avoid *query requests* and *responses* flooding the network, each query contains a TTL field (typically set to 7, see Fig. 10.2). When a servent receives a query with a positive TTL, it decrements it before forwarding the query to its neighbours. Queries received with a TTL of 0 are not forwarded. In other words, queries are propagated using a controlled flooding.

It is easy to see that the same query can visit a servent more than once during the controlled flooding, i.e., through different neighbours of that servent. To make sure that each node does not serve the same query more than once, each message (i.e., descriptor) is identified by a 128-bit Unique IDentifier (UID). Servents memorise these UIDs and when a servent receives a query with a UID it has encountered previously, it simply drops the query.

10.4 Gnutella 0.4 Protocol Description

This section describes the Gnutella 0.4 protocol. This was the first description of the protocol and it is important to bear in mind that several more recent implementations have extended these descriptors to impose additional rules.

The Gnutella protocol defines the way in which servents communicate over the network. It consists of a set of descriptors (i.e., packets) for communicating data between servents, and a set of rules governing how Gnutella descriptors are exchanged. An overview of the various descriptors is shown in Fig. 10.5. This figure shows how the various descriptors relate to each other and how they are packaged to create a Gnutella descriptor packet that is passed around the Gnutella network.

Briefly, a Gnutella descriptor consists of a header and a payload (i.e., message). The descriptor includes common attributes for any payload (id, TTL, hops, etc.). Then there are five payloads (messages) that can be described using this protocol. These are *Ping* (for announcing presence), *Pong* (for replying to Ping messages), *Query* (for searching the network), *QueryHit* (for replying to search messages) and *Push* (for traversing firewalls). This structure and each payload are described in more detail in the remainder of this section.

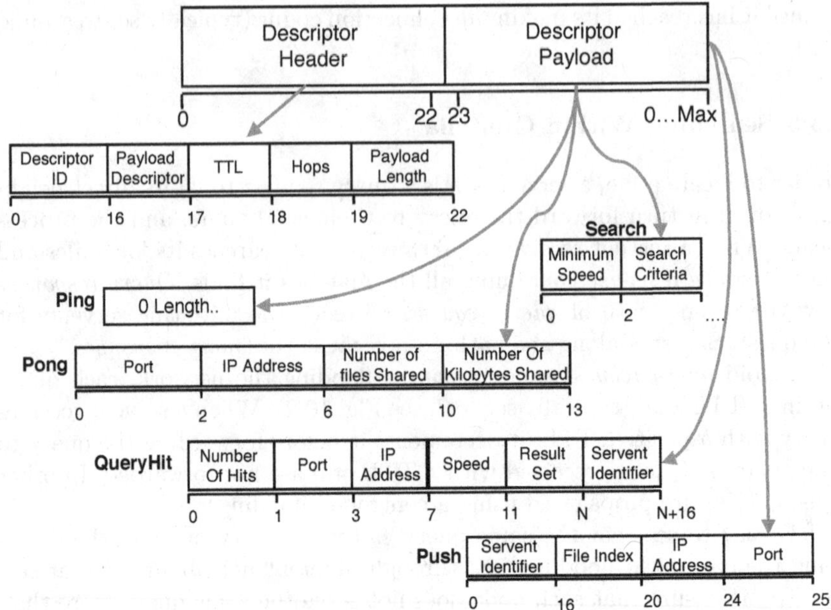

Fig. 10.5. An overview of the Gnutella specification and the descriptors it uses to define the protocol.

10.4.1 Gnutella Descriptors

Gnutella descriptors consist of a message header and a payload (see Fig. 10.6, part *I*). As listed earlier, the following five descriptors are defined:

1. ***Ping*:** is used to announce presence on the network. A servent receiving a *Ping* descriptor can respond with a *Pong* descriptor.
2. ***Pong*:** is the response for a *Ping*, which includes the servent's contact details and the number of files it is sharing on the network.
3. ***Query*:** is the search mechanism, which contains a search string, e.g., "freeSongs". A servent matching a search request returns a *QueryHit*.
4. ***QueryHit*:** contains a list of matches for the *Query* along with the servent's contact details.
5. ***Push*:** provides a mechanism for a servent behind a firewall to share its files.

To join a Gnutella network, as illustrated in Section 10.3.2, a servent opens a TCP/IP connection to a peer already on the network and issues the following command (ASCII encoded):

```
GNUTELLA CONNECT/<protocol version string>\\n\\n
```

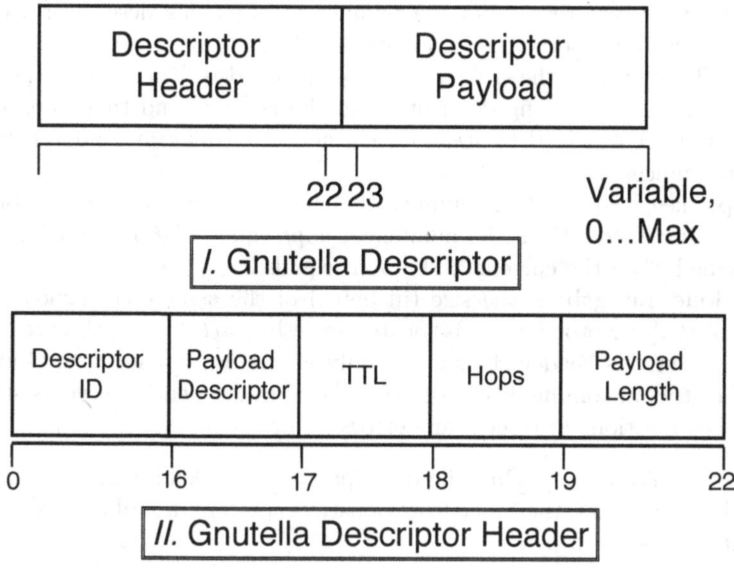

Fig. 10.6. The format of the Gnutella descriptor (I) and its header (II).

where <protocol version string> is the version of the specification (e.g., "0.4"). To accept a connection, a servent responds with:

```
GNUTELLA OK\\n\\n
```

Otherwise, it is assumed that the connection is refused, perhaps because:

1. the servent has enough connections already
2. incompatible version number

Once a servent has joined the network, Gnutella *descriptors* (i.e., messages) are used to make requests and to issue responses.

Each descriptor has a *Descriptor Header*, which is described in the next section.

10.4.2 Gnutella Descriptor Header

The Gnutella descriptor header is given in Fig. 10.6, part *II* and consists of:

1. **Descriptor ID:** a unique identifier for the descriptor on (a 16-byte string).
2. **Payload Descriptor:** contains the type of payload, i.e., 0x00 = *Ping*, 0x01 = *Pong*, 0x40 = *Push*, 0x80 = *Query*, 0x81 = *QueryHit*.

3. **Time to Live:** represents the number of hops this descriptor will be forwarded. Each servent decrements the TTL before passing it on. When the TTL equals 0, the descriptor is not forwarded. The TTL is the only mechanism for expiring descriptors on the network and therefore, abuse of this field will lead to unnecessary network traffic and poor network performance.
4. **Hops:** keeps count of the number of times (i.e., hops) the descriptor has been forwarded. When the number of hops equals the initial TTL value specified, then the current TTL count equals 0.
5. **Payload Length:** is the size (in bytes) of the associated payload: i.e., the next descriptor header is located exactly *Payload Length* bytes from the end of this header. This is the only mechanism for locating Gnutella descriptors in communication streams[3] and consequently, servents should drop connections to reset if any errors occur.

The other section of a Gnutella descriptor is its payload, which can be one of five different types, mentioned previously. These are described in detail in the next five sections.

10.4.3 Gnutella Payload: Ping

Ping payloads contain no information as they are simply used to announce a peer's presence on the network. The header contains the necessary information (i.e., the UID is used) for the peers to be able to detect *Pong* replies from other peers. They will receive the reply because *Pong* descriptors always travel along the same path as their corresponding *Ping* messages and are identifiable by the initiating *Ping* UID. Further, more than one *Pong* descriptor can be sent in response to a *Ping* descriptor. This allows certain caching servers to reply with many servents' addresses in response to a *Ping*.

A *Ping* is therefore simply represented by a header whose *Payload_Descriptor* field is 0x00 and whose *Payload_Length* field is 0x00000000.

10.4.4 Gnutella Payload: Pong

A *Pong* descriptor (see Fig. 10.7) contains the address of the replying Gnutella servent and the quantity of data it is sharing. It defines four fields:

1. **Port:** is the responding servent's IP port for incoming connections.
2. **IP Address:** is the responding servent's address (little endian).
3. **Number of Files Shared:** specifies the number of files the servent is sharing.
4. **Number of Kilobytes Shared:** is the number of kilobytes the servent is sharing.

[3] All fields in this structure are in *big-endian* byte order (unless otherwise stated) and IP addresses are in IPv4 format.

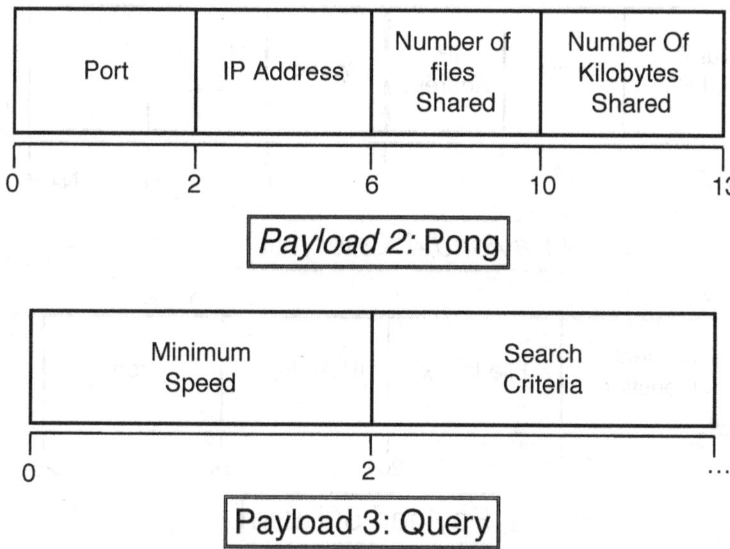

Fig. 10.7. The *Pong* descriptor, payload 2, and the *Query* descriptor, payload 3.

10.4.5 Gnutella Payload: Query

The *Query* descriptor (see Fig. 10.7) is Gnutella's search message format. It is passed to connected servents to enquire if they have the given file and has the following two fields:

1. **Minimum Speed:** the minimum connectivity speed (in kb/second) of a responding servent. Servents not passing this criterion should not respond to the message.
2. **Search Criteria:** contains the search string, which can be at most *Payload_Length* (minus 2 for *Minimum Speed* field) bytes long. This field is terminated by a *null* character (0x00).

10.4.6 Gnutella Payload: QueryHit

A servent receiving a *Query* descriptor will respond with a *QueryHit* (see Fig. 10.8, payload 4) if a match is found in its local file set. The *QueryHit* descriptor that is sent from a **responding host** defines the following fields:

1. **Number of Hits:** is the number of matches in this result set.
2. **Port:** is the port used for connecting for file transfer.
3. **IP Address:** is the IP address of the host (little-endian format).
4. **Speed:** is the speed (in kb/second) of the host's connection.
5. **Result Set:** is the set of *Numberof_Hits* hits, where each hit contains:

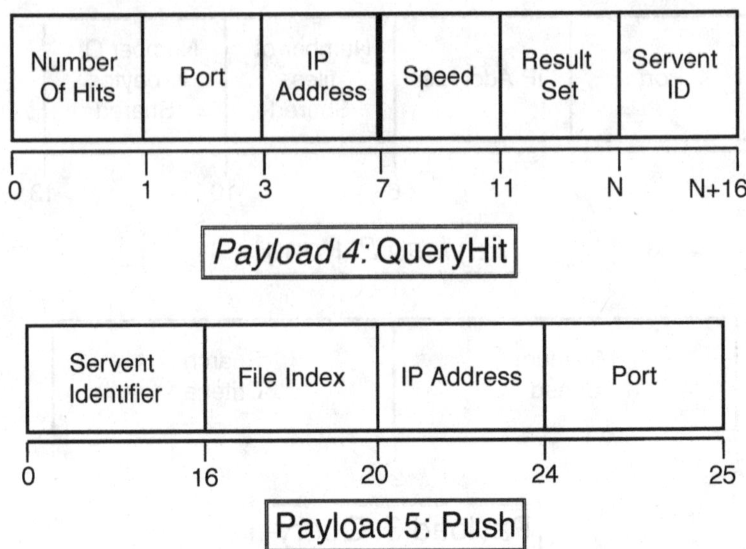

Fig. 10.8. The *QueryHit* descriptor, payload 4 and the *Push* descriptor, payload 5.

a) **File Index:** is a unique identifier for this file. This is up to the host to decide and is used for file retrieval, either directly or by using the *Push* mechanism, if required.
b) **File Size:** is the file size (in bytes).
c) **File Name:** is the name of the file matched (double-null terminated, i.e., 0x0000).

6. **Servent Identifier:** is the UID for this servent, typically calculated using some function of this servent's network address, used in the *Push* operation, if needed.

Using the same identification mechanism as the *Ping* and *Pong* messages, the *QueryHit* descriptors contain the same *Descriptor_Id* as the corresponding *Query* descriptor and since *QueryHit* descriptors may only be sent along the same path that carried the *Query* descriptor, this ensures that only those servents that routed the *Query* descriptor will see the *QueryHit* descriptor.

10.4.7 Gnutella Payload: Push

Push (see Fig. 10.8, payload 5) provides the mechanism to allow a servent hiding behind a firewall to serve files on a Gnutella network. This is illustrated below using a typical *Push* scenario:

1. A servent (A) issues a search request.
2. Servent B is contacted (via several intermediaries) and matches the search request.

3. B responds with a *QueryHit* descriptor. Imagine here that this servent is behind a firewall and consequently cannot accept incoming connections.
4. Servent A receives the *QueryHit* returned from B because it checks the *Descriptor_Id* to see if it matches the one it issued in its *Query* descriptor.
5. Servent A sends a *Push* request to servent B. The *Push* descriptor is sent along the same path as its corresponding *QueryHit*, which ensures that servent B will see it. This is achieved by a simple routing algorithm that makes a peer drop a *Push* descriptor which does not match any *QueryHit* descriptors they have seen.
6. Servent B receives this request (by matching the *Descriptor_Id*) and attempts to create a new TCP/IP connection to servent A by using the *IP Address* and *Port* fields of the *Push* descriptor; i.e., servents that cannot accept incoming connections can normally create outgoing ones.
7. A direct connection is established and the file is downloaded. If a direct connection cannot be created, then it is likely that servent A is also behind a firewall and consequently, a file transfer cannot take place.

The *Push* descriptor defines four fields. To simplify things, servents A and B from the above scenario are used to depict the originator and responder to the search request in the following description of the *Push* descriptor's internal fields:

1. **Servent Identifier:** is the UID for servent B and is set by A by using the *Servent_Identifier* for the corresponding *QueryHit*. This UID is in fact B's UID.
2. **File Index:** is set to the value of one of the *File_Index* fields from the *QueryHit* response to specify the file to be pushed.
3. **IP Address:** is the IP address of servent A, i.e., the host where the file should be pushed (little-endian format).
4. **Port:** is the port of servent A for the connection of the push.

10.5 File Downloads

In brief, after the query hits are received by the servent, it establishes a direct connection in order to download one of the files in the *QueryHit* descriptor's *Result Set*. The download request is carried out using the HTTP protocol, through an HTTP GET request with the following message format:

```
GET /get/<File Index>/<File Name>/ HTTP/1.0\\r\\n
Connection: Keep-Alive\\r\\n
Range: bytes=0-\\r\\n
User-Agent: Gnutella\\r\\n
\\r\\n
```

where *File Index* and *File Name* are the index and name for one of the files in the *Result Set*. For example, if the *Result Set* from a *QueryHit* descriptor contained the entries given in Fig. 10.9, then a download request would contain the following:

```
GET /get/1234/coolsong.mp3/ HTTP/1.0\\r\\n
Connection: Keep-Alive\\r\\n
Range: bytes=0-\\r\\n
User-Agent: Gnutella \\r\\n
\\r\\n
```

File Index	1234
File Size	5678910
File Name	coolsong.mp3\x00\x00

Fig. 10.9. An example of a result set from a QueryHit Descriptor.

The servent receiving this request replies with the following *HTTP OK* message:

```
HTTP 200 OK\\r\\n
Server: Gnutella\\r\\n
Content-type: application/binary\\r\\n
Content-length: 5678910\\r\\n
\\r\\n
```

This response is followed by the actual data, which is read according to the number of bytes specified in the *Content-length* field as illustrated. To assist with transient connectivity, the Gnutella protocol also provides support for the HTTP *range* parameter, which enables an interrupted transfer to be resumed at a later point.

10.6 Gnutella Implementations

Figure 10.10 gives a list of some examples of Gnutella-based applications, broken down into three different operating systems, which are available (or have

Gnutella Clients		
Windows	**Linux/Unix**	**Macintosh**
BearShare	Gnewtellium	LimeWire
Gnucleus	Gtk-Gnutella	Phex
Morpheus	Mutella	
Shareaza	Qtella	
Swapper	LimeWire	
XoloX	Phex	
LimeWire		
Phex		

Fig. 10.10. A list of Gnutella implementations for various platforms.

been available) on the Internet for file sharing. Some other client implementations are listed in Appendix A.

10.7 More Information

There are a number of good articles and papers on the Internet that give concise overviews of Gnutella. One in particular can be found on the LimeWire site [174]. Another [175] has a number of papers relating to Gnutella including various studies that have been and indeed still are being carried out.

10.8 Conclusion

In this chapter, Gnutella has been described. Gnutella is a search protocol that allows peers to search a network of peers without the need for any centralized control. In Gnutella, every node is both a client and a server and is referred to as a *servent*. Servents join the network using one of several techniques, e.g., the Web, IRC, GnuCache, and once joined, can discover other peers through Gnutella's discovery mechanism using *Ping/Pong* descriptors.

The Gnutella protocol defines the way servents communicate over the network. It defines a set of Gnutella descriptors and a set of rules governing their interaction. Gnutella descriptors consist of a descriptor header and a payload. The header contains a descriptor's unique identifier and its corresponding payload contains one of the following types, e.g., *Ping*, *Pong*, *Query*, *Query-Hit* and *Push*, which are used for peer discovery, searching and for traversing firewalls within the Gnutella decentralized network.

11

Scalability

> *"You can't scale better than by utilising someone elses computer."*
> *Paul James*[1]

P2P has led to a recent renewal of interest in decentralized systems and a number of scalable applications being deployed on the Internet. Although the underlying Internet itself is the largest decentralized computer system in the world, most systems have employed a completely centralized topology in the 1990s through the massive growth of the Web as discussed in Chapter 6. With the emergence of P2P in early 2000, there has been a shift into employing the use of radically decentralized architectures, such as Gnutella [4]. In practice, however, extreme architectural choices in either direction are seldom the way to build a usable system. Most current P2P file-sharing software, for example, use a hybrid of the two approaches.

In this chapter, we look at the ways in which peers are organized within ad hoc, pervasive, multi-hop networks by providing an overview of two common scalable approaches often referred to broadly as structured and unstructured P2P networks. Structured networks adopt a somewhat hierarchical approach by creating a structured overlay across the network and dividing content across the distributed network by using hash functions. An unstructured approach, however, adapts dynamically by adding caching centres (super peers) across the network in an ad hoc fashion. Both approaches have been shown to scale to large numbers of participants and both have somewhat equal popularity at the time of writing. Although the specifics of the various approaches within these categories are out of scope for this chapter, we do provide here a high-level overview of the basics of each approach and discuss their similarities and differences.

---

[1] From Paul James' blog article "Living Without Sessions" `http://www.peej.co.uk/articles/no-sessions.html`.

11.1 Performance in P2P Networks

So, how do we organize P2P networks in such a way as to get optimum performance? Well, performance in P2P networks is non-deterministic. A P2P network is often constructed in an ad hoc fashion and due to its nature and transient availability of its cooperating peers, it is therefore impossible to stabilise the network for optimal performance. However, this does not mean that we should give up; it simply means we have to devise complicated robust algorithms that make the best of this situation. Therefore, performance in P2P networks cannot be measured precisely; it rather involves taking empirical measurements such as:

- How long does it take to search for a particular file?
- How much bandwidth will the query consume?
- How many hops will it take for my package to get to a peer on the far side of the network?
- If I add/remove a peer to/from the network, will the network still be fault tolerant?
- Does the network scale as we add more peers? Such networks can rapidly expand from a few hundred peers to several thousand or even millions.

The answers to these questions have a direct impact on the success and usability of a system. Remember that P2P networks operate in unreliable environments where peers are continuously connecting and disconnecting. Resources may suddenly become unavailable for a variety of reasons: e.g., users may disconnect from the network because they do not want to participate any more. Further, there are more random failures, e.g., cable and DSL failures, power outages, hackers and attacks, as personal machines are much more vulnerable than dedicated servers. In such an environment, therefore, there need to be algorithms which can cope with this continuous restructuring of the network core. P2P systems need to treat failures as normal occurrences, not freak exceptions, and therefore P2P networks must be designed in a way that promotes redundancy with the trade-off of a degradation of performance.

There are three main factors that make P2P networks more sensitive to performance issues compared to other types of networks [21]:

1. **Communication:** An obvious fundamental necessity of any P2P network. Most users connect through dial-up, cable or DSL and so their connection speed is the main bottleneck. However, this problem is amplified by the highly parallel, multi-hop nature of a P2P network where it often takes a number of hops for a packet to reach its destination. Therefore other users' connection speeds also create a bottleneck; i.e., if one peer on your multi-hop request is running a 56K modem, then this slows things down en route. Network traffic minimization and load balancing therefore are important considerations to overall performance.

2. **Searching:** There is no central server in P2P networks so many more peers are involved in the search process, which typically occurs over several parallel network hops. Each hop of such a search adds to the total bandwidth load and therefore the time to set up a connection becomes a critical factor. Combine this with the inherently unreliable nature of the individual peers and delivery time starts to grow alarmingly; e.g., if a peer is unreachable, TCP/IP can take up to several minutes to time out the connection.
3. **Load-Balancing Peers:** In theory, true decentralized P2P networks consist entirely of *equal peers*, meaning that each peer potentially shares as much as it consumes. However, in real-world implementation, such network ideals are skewed by usage patterns. For example, studies have indicated that around 70 percent of Gnutella users share no files at all [65]. Too many free riders will degrade the performance of the network for others and therefore care must be taken to factor in the correct proportion so that measures can be taken to optimize the current topology, not assume a static and perhaps unrealistic one.

11.2 Unstructured P2P

Unstructured P2P networks are dynamically formed in an ad hoc fashion through the use of super peer nodes. Such a topology is often referred to as a centralized-decentralized topology because it combines a centralized structure of connectivity from edge peers to super-peers and then employs a decentralized connectivity between the super-peers in the network for fault tolerance. Super-peer networks have been shown to scale to millions of peers and are used in a number of well-known Internet applications, such as LimeWire, Gnutella, KaZaA and even Skype.

Where distributed hash tables, described in Section 11.3, offer a structured approach by aiming to provide efficient insertion and retrieval into a decentralized system, unstructured protocols, such as Gnutella, propagate arbitrary advertisements and queries across the overlay. Retrieval of a certain resource, or even its existence, is not guaranteed. They employ the use of super-peer caches for lesser peers, such as caching services, file locations, endpoints or advertisements, and can build their own overlay amongst themselves. This approach leads to the dynamic development of layers, reducing network flooding of messages which can happen in topologically flat systems. This layered approach can be extended through the formation of groups that form their own neighbourhoods, in systems such as Jxta, described in Chapter 15.

However, the theory of unstructured networks is not new. To illustrate this concept, let's begin our journey in the 1960s by taking a look at an experiment that shows how social networks are organized and look at the similarities between social networks and unstructured P2P networks.

11.2.1 Social Networks

Before we analyse P2P networks, let's first take a look at a unique social experiment conducted in 1967 by Harvard professor Stanley Milgram [176], with some notes from [21]. He performed a social-networking experiment within the United States to find out how many *social hops* it would take for messages to traverse through the population, which was then around 200 million people.

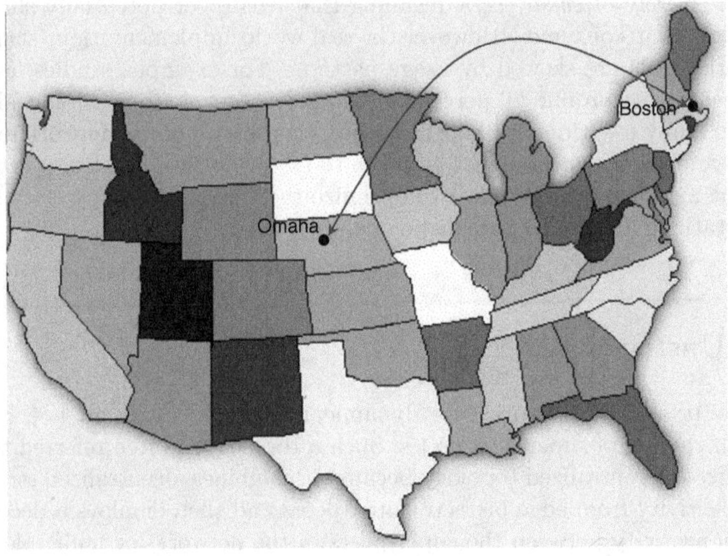

Fig. 11.1. The Milgram social-networking experiment, illustrating the distance on a map of the states that he posted the 160 letters.

He posted 160 letters to randomly chosen people living in Omaha, Nebraska, and asked them to try to pass these letters to a stockbroker he knew working in Boston, Massachusetts (see Fig. 11.1). The rules were that they could only pass the letter to intermediaries known to them on a first-name basis. Such intermediaries should be chosen intelligently so that they might bring the letter closer to the stockbroker. For example, this decision could be because they may know someone who is geographically closer to Boston — e.g., they may know someone in Illinois — or they may know someone who may know someone who lives near Boston. The friend given the letter would continue in this fashion, passing it on to another friend and so on until the letter reached a friend of the stockbroker who could give it to him personally. At each stage of the journey the intermediaries noted their details on the package.

In the end, 42 letters made it through to the stockbroker. The interesting fact was that the average number of hops (i.e., through intermediaries) each letter passed through was 5.5. The Milgram experiment demonstrated concretely for the first time what has become popularly known as the small-world effect, something we'd say when we bump into a friend from our home town on some remote beach in the middle of nowhere, using the expression, "it's a small world, isn't it!" with the infamous retort "Yes, but I wouldn't like to paint it!"

Stanley Milgram

Milgram was one of the most outstanding social scientists of our time. His untimely death at the age of 51 on December 20, 1984, ended a life of scientific inventiveness and controversy. But his research and writings continue to influence contemporary culture and thought. His research included the small-world method (the source of "Six Degrees of Separation"), the lost-letter technique, mental maps of cities, cyranoids, the familiar stranger and an experiment testing the effects of televised antisocial behavior which, though conducted 30 years ago, remains unique to the present day.[2]

This experiment was designed to explore the properties of social networks and it gave evidence that the social network of the United States could be connected with a path-length (number of hops) of around 6. This number is surprisingly low compared to the population at the time. Does this mean it takes less than 6 hops to traverse 200 million people? If so, can't we achieve the same organization in computer networks by simply modelling social networks?

It turns out that although social circles are highly clustered, some acquaintances in the group will have more wide-ranging connections and these connections form a bridge between social clusters that are geographically far away from each other. This *bridging* plays a critical role in bringing the entire network closer together. For example, in the Milgram experiment, a quarter of all letters reaching the stockbroker passed through a single person, who was the local shopkeeper. In all, half of the letters passed through just three people, who acted as gateways or hubs between the source and the wider world.

[2] Photo and biography taken from `http://www.stanleymilgram.com/`.

A small number of bridges therefore can dramatically reduce the number of hops.

P2P networks have a number of similarities to social networks. People would be peers and the intermediaries in Milgram's experiment would be known as gateways, hubs, bridges or rendezvous nodes in P2P networks. The number of intermediaries used to pass the letter from the source to the destination would be the *number of hops* in a P2P network. The similarities go on and on. In many senses, P2P networks are more like social networks than other types of computer networks as they are often self-organizing, ad hoc, employ clustering techniques based on prior interactions (like we form relationships), and have decentralized discovery and communication, which arguably are analogous to the way we have formed neighbourhoods, villages, towns, cities, etc.

11.2.2 Combining Network Topologies

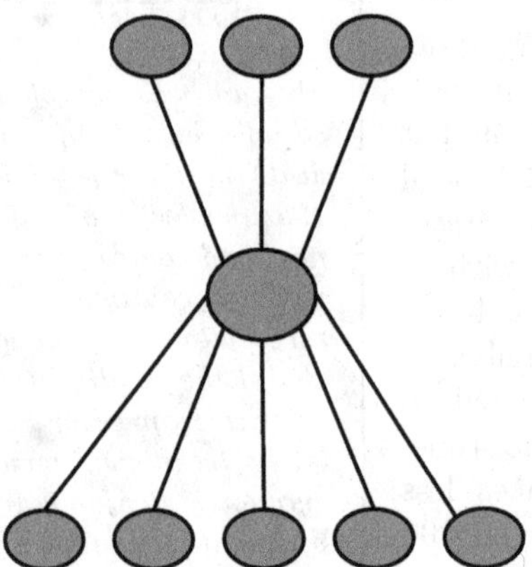

Fig. 11.2. A centralized topology.

Fundamentally, the debate between centralized and decentralized systems is about topology, that is, how the nodes in the system are connected. For P2P networks, the topology is considered in terms of the information flow of the network. Nodes in the graph are the peers and links (edges) between peers indicate a regular sharing of information. For simplicity, edges here are considered undirected. The topologies here are based on an on-line article [177]. Below, two opposite topologies are described and we show how these are combined to build the unstructured P2P approach. These are:

- Centralized
- Decentralized

Centralized client/server systems (see Fig. 11.2) are by far the most common form of topology. Communication is completely centralized with many clients connecting directly to a single server, which is illustrated in detail in Section 1.3.3. Examples of centralized systems include Web servers, databases, SETI@home, etc.

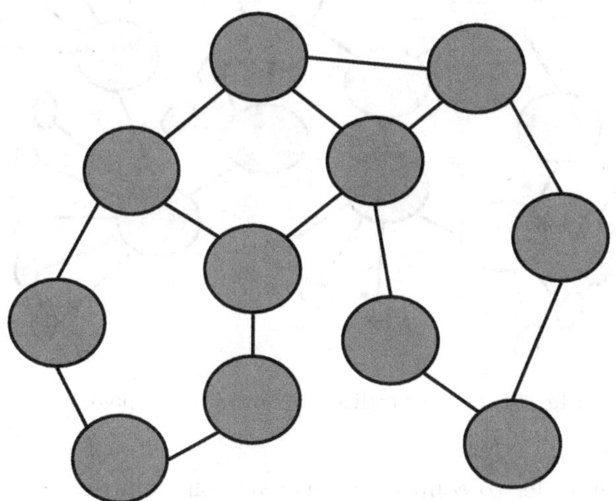

Fig. 11.3. A decentralized topology.

In a completely decentralized system on the other hand (see Fig. 11.3), there is no single point of control. Peers communicate symmetrically and have equal roles. Gnutella is a good example and has been described in detail elsewhere in this book (see Chapter 10). Pure decentralized networks are extremely fault tolerant against random peer failures but this comes at a price, which is the bandwidth required to search such a network. Later in this chapter, we will see several studies that indicate this (see Section 11.2.4). For example, in pure Gnutella networks, a quarter of the overall network bandwidth is consumed by searching alone.

In super-peer networks these two topologies are combined in order to capitalise on the speed of the centralized approach and the fault tolerance of the decentralized one. As illustrated in Fig. 11.4, the centralized/decentralized topology consists of a two-tiered structure, where a number of centralized systems are connected in a decentralized fashion. Therefore, at the higher level, you have a structure and behaviour similar to Gnutella, that is, a highly fault-tolerant decentralized set of peers that provide information to their lower-level collections of centrally organized peers.

The fault tolerance of the upper layer is highly dependent on the number of nodes present, but in structure, such networks are rather reminiscent of social networks, where many people typically use a gateway (remember the

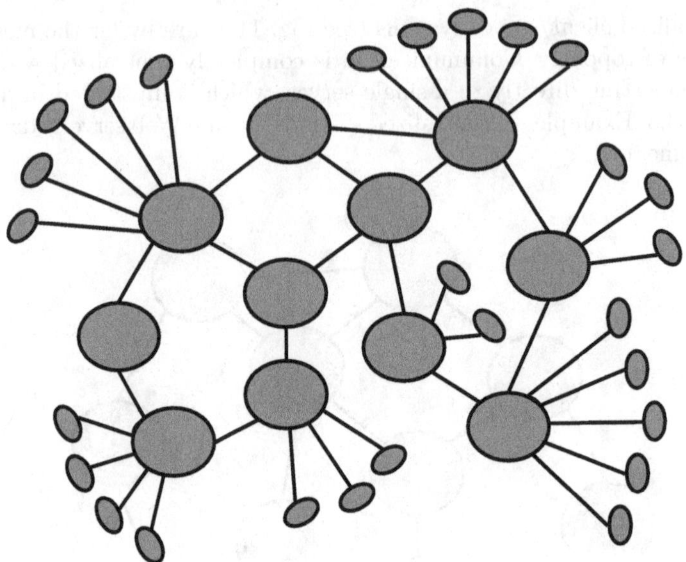

Fig. 11.4. A centralized/decentralized topology.

shopkeeper?) in order to connect to far-flung communities, i.e., the centralized/decentralized topology implements the small-world effect demonstrated by Milgram. It turns out that centralized/decentralized topologies scale remarkably well and have therefore been adopted by a number of popular P2P file-sharing systems. For example, the FastTrack file-sharing system used by KaZaA and Morpheus, which can connect hundreds of thousands of peers, use this topology.

The decentralized peers are referred to as super-nodes or Gnutella reflector nodes. Super-nodes act as caching servers to connected clients and perform a similar operation to Napster servers. So, rather than propagating the query across the entire set of nodes, the super-peer will check its own database to see if it knows the whereabouts of the requested file and if so, it returns that address to the client, just like Napster. If not, it performs a Gnutella-type broadcast across the decentralized set of super-peers to propagate this request across the network. This means that a client can search an entire network without consuming a vast amount of bandwidth. Jxta rendezvous nodes perform a similar type of service within Jxta networks.

11.2.3 The Convergence of the Napster and Gnutella Approaches

It is interesting to note that both Gnutella and Napster converged towards a centralized/decentralized topology, even though they came from completely different sides of the coin. Gnutella started its life as a decentralized system and Napster started its life as a centralized search architecture, with brokered communications. However, Gnutella inserted super-peers and Napster duplicated its centralized search engines for scalability, both resulting in a similar design topology, as illustrated in Fig. 11.5.

A Southern Side-Step

During the writing of the first edition of this book, I (being Ian) decided to get away and he took a three-week writing trip to Sicily. Interestingly (and unsurprisingly) one night, I was in a pub and they adopted a rather bizarre serving scheme.... A customer had to walk to a server by a till at the centre of this long bar, order his drink, then walk back to his barstool and pass this receipt onto the bartender who would bring him his drink. I thought this was very strange, as they turned an inherently decentralized service into a centralized one! Why, I thought to myself, could I not simply pay the bartender directly?

Anyway, after a few drinks the bar got rather packed and I soon realised that this scheme in fact was working rather well. This kind of disturbed me because there I was, writing this book about decentralized systems and these Sicilians have completely circumvented the idea! So, perhaps this is all wrong.... Sometime later though I was saved by the realisation of two facts, namely: the Italians, in general, don't drink so much, and I predicted that this could never work, for example, in Britain...; but most importantly, I then realised that they were not running a centralized system at all. They were in fact running a brokered system; i.e., they centralized discovery (i.e., and therefore payment) but the service of pouring drinks was still decentralized; hence the scalability.

Furthermore, I did notice that during the night every time the cashier wandered off for a cigarette, not only was there a non-trivial accumulating number of patrons waiting but also, the bartenders finished serving their current order and then stood around doing absolutely nothing; that is, the whole system came to a halt. Hence I conclude that the Waxies in Catania has, in fact, the same taxonomy as Napster: centralized discovery and therefore with intermittent availability (with no redundancy). However, due to its decentralized communication, services that have been discovered (and paid for here) can still be concluded as normal. Of course, we are talking about payment and beer but as social perspectives go, there are much worse analogies!

Consider both scenarios more closely:

- Gnutella is a completely decentralized search which operates on the premise that all peers are equal. In practice, however, users operate at different levels. One user may only have several files to share, whilst others might be sharing several thousand. Therefore, in a completely self-organizing way, Gnutella tends to converge into a hybrid structure. Clip2.com [3] recognised this early on and developed a program that they call the *Gnutella Reflector*. This is a proxy and index service designed to

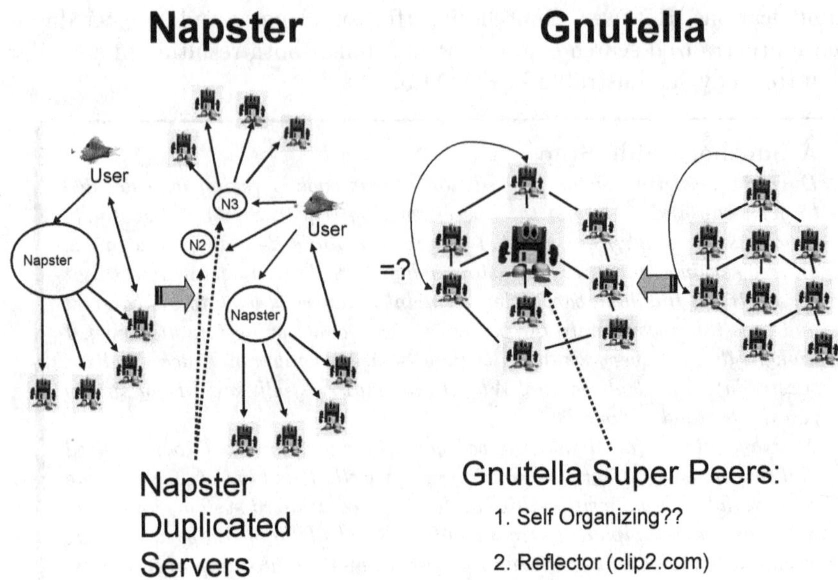

Fig. 11.5. The convergence of Naptser and Gnutella.

make Gnutella more scalable that can also make outside connections to gather other information, as described.

- Napster, on the other hand, started its life as a brokered system, centralizing the search but decentralizing the communication (downloading of the MP3 file). Napster, however, started to replicate its main server as the user base grew, thereby creating many Napster servers that served fewer clients. This, in effect, has exactly the same result as the Gnutella reflector nodes but instead, they extended the centralized approach into a decentralized arena and not vice versa.

The key difference here, as illustrated in Fig. 11.5, is that within a decentralized system, such as Gnutella, the formation of the Gnutella super-peers is self-organizing and scales proportionately and dynamically with the size of the network. The actual algorithm for achieving this is typically based on a combination of user preferences and communication resource considerations.

However, in a centralized/brokered approach, the servers have to be explicitly added by hand and therefore cannot scale dynamically with the network, without using some extra management software capable of monitoring the current usage. In essence, though, the Gnutella reflector nodes are mini-Napster servers. They maintain an index of files from peers currently connected. When a query is issued, the reflector does not retransmit it; rather, it answers the query from its own memory.

11.2.4 Gnutella Research Experiments

The centralized/decentralized architecture is arguably the most popular architecture used within today's P2P file-sharing applications. This section gives a background into some empirical studies that support this type of topology by analysing the behaviour of users and connectivity on a Gnutella network. But first, let's recap the core Gnutella model and how far this scales.

Gnutella uses a simple broadcast model to conduct queries, which does not utilize the small-world effect. Each peer tries to maintain a small number of connections (around 3 or 4). Gnutella's topology is in fact a 3- or 4-D Cayley tree [178].

Searching in Gnutella involves broadcasting a Query message to all connected peers. Each connected peer will send it to its connected peers (say 3) and so on. This search will run for a specific number of hops, typically 7. If the number of connected peers c = 3 and the hops h = 7, then the total number of peers searched (s) in a fully connected network will be:

```
s = c + c2 +c3 + ..
s = 3 + 9 + 27 + 81 + 243 + 729 + 2187 = 3279 Nodes
```

In practice, the network often converges somewhere between 3 and 4 connections per node giving around 10,000 nodes each peer can search (assuming full connectivity). In the following sections, a number of studies show how such a Gnutella network performs and evolves.

In the article [65], they considered two types of free riding in an analysis of the Gnutella network: peers free riding who only download files for themselves without ever providing files for download for others; and users who have undesirable content, i.e., they might be sharing files but the files may be corrupted and therefore lead to unnecessary network traffic.

They found that, in one experiment, 22,084 of the 33,335 peers in the network (or approximately 66%) of the peers share no files, and 24,347 or 73% share 10 or fewer files. The data also showed that the top 1% (333 hosts) represent approximately 37% of the total files shared. This quickly escalates to the top 20% (6,667 hosts) sharing 98% of the files. This experiment shows that even without Gnutella reflector nodes, the Gnutella network naturally converges into a centralized/decentralized topology with the top 20% of nodes acting as super-peers or reflectors.

Why can't there be a network full of equal peers? Well, there are a number of reasons including: users have a variety of different spec'd machines with different capabilities; users connect via different mechanisms, and hence different speeds; and each user has different interests. For example, one user may have collected a huge number of files, and although she may be willing to share these files, other users may not be interested in them at all. So, even though they are a good contributor in theory, they are not effective in the network as a whole, and therefore will simply be ignored.

Further, Clip2.com [17] performed an analysis of Gnutella based on measurements over a month. They noted an apparent scalability barrier when query rates went above 10 per second. Why? Well, a typical Gnutella query message is around 560 bits long and queries make up approximately a quarter of the traffic. A quick calculation, therefore, given that Gnutella peers are connected to an average of 3 remote peers, gives us 560 *10 * 3 = 16,800 bits per second. Now, if this is a quarter of the traffic, then the total traffic is 16,800 x 4 = 67,200 bits per second. A 56K link cannot keep up with this amount of traffic and therefore one node connected in the incorrect place can grind the whole network to a halt. It is for this reason that one of the main goals for the organization of a P2P network is to place slower nodes at the edges of the network.

A further study of the topology of the Gnutella network was undertaken [64] over a period of several months, and it reported two interesting findings:

- **Power-Law Structure:** the Gnutella network shares the benefits and drawbacks of a power-law structure [179];
- **Virtual Overlay:** the Gnutella network topology does not match well with the underlying Internet topology leading to inefficient use of network bandwidth.

In a power-law structure, a network organizes itself so that most nodes have a few links and a small number of nodes have many (i.e., like super-peers). This is equivalent to the centralized-decentralized topology described above. The article points out that the power-law networks have been found to show an unexpected degree of robustness when facing random node failures. Consequently, the ability of the network to communicate is unaffected by high failure rates. However, such error tolerance comes at a high price. For example, such networks are more vulnerable to attacks than completely decentralized networks, e.g., by selectively removing a few of the critical super-nodes, one can inflict massive damage on the structure and function of the network as a whole.

In the paper, the author suggested two directions for improvement. He suggested that an agent could monitor the network and intervene by asking servents to drop/add links to keep the topology optimal. Such agents would have knowledge of the underlying network and, therefore, be able to create a better virtual overlay for the Gnutella network. The second suggestion is to replace the Gnutella flooding mechanism with a smarter routing and group communication mechanism.

11.3 The Structured P2P Approach

So-called structured networks are typically based on the use of Distributed Hash Table (DHT) technology, which consists of a logical identifier hash key space to which peers and resources are mapped. Peers maintain neighborhood state about each other enabling application level routing of messages through the overlay network based on the identifier space. The algorithm for inserting into, or retrieving from, the network is deterministic; that is, given a certain key, the resource with that key will reside at a certain peer.

DHTs essentially provide a lookup service similar to a hash table; that is, *name* and corresponding *value* pairs are stored in the DHT, and a user can retrieve previous stored values if they know its *name* key. The keys in a DHT are generated using a hashing algorithm, such as SHA, and employ the use of a number of different sources for hash mappings. For example, for organization most DHTs organize their hash space by using identifiers that are generated from the peer itself, whilst for storing and retrieval, a hash of the content of the data is typically used.

An advantage of the DHT approach is that the nodes can be organised using a structured tree-like approach and O(logN) search algorithms[3] can be created for locating keys. This allows DHTs to scale to extremely large numbers of nodes. A disadvantage of this approach is that a user needs to know the exact *name* key in order to retrieve the desired data and therefore keyword searching is not possible. However, applications can be created on top of the DHT technology in order to perform such semantic searches. Another possible disadvantage is that the overlay requires generally more effort than unstructured in order to maintain a consistency between the nodes when peers join or leave a network.

In 2001, four DHTs were released, CAN [79], Pastry [77], Chord [76] and Tapestry [78], which all offered in-depth solutions to creating and maintaining reliable overlays based on distributed hashes. Each algorithm guarantees data will be found, typically within the order of O(logN) hops across the network. In this section, we provide a broad overview of the commonalities to these approaches and therefore the reader is advised to take a look at these four papers for specifics on the individual approaches.

At first glance, DHTs might seem to have a number of similarities with Freenet, described in Chapter 12, in that they both employ the use of hash key values to organize the distributed network. However, Freenet employed a heuristic key-based routing algorithm, where files with similar keys tended to cluster on a similar set of nodes through the updating of local routing tables, i.e., the network learns. Perhaps the major difference between these technologies, however, is that Freenet does not guarantee that data will be found.

11.3.1 Structure of a DHT Network

A DHT consists of two main components:

- A **keyspace partitioning scheme**, which attempts to divide the keyspace amongst participating nodes.

[3] N is the number of peers in the network.

- An **overlay network** that connects the nodes in such a way as to allow them to locate an "owner" of any given key in a keyspace in the minimal hops possible. The overlay network is also responsible for injecting redundancy into the network so that there are multiple paths available for locating a given key on the network in the event of node failures.

Generally, DHTs use some variant of *consistent hashing* in their **keyspace partitioning scheme**. This technique uses a distance function that is capable of measuring an abstract distance from one key to another, which is unrelated to any physical parameter, e.g., geographical distance, or network latency. Each node is typically assigned an identifier hash key (based on hashing some peer properties, e.g., network address, time and so forth). In consistent hashing algorithms, a removal or addition of one node changes only the set of keys that are "owned" by adjacent nodes (with neighbouring IDs). This is an essential property, which enables the DHT to minimize the reorganization when nodes join or leave the network.

The **overlay network** makes use of these properties in order to maintain a set of links to neighbouring nodes within their routing tables. A node chooses neighbours according to the specific DHT's connectivity policies but generally for any key, a node either owns that key or has a pointer to a node that is closer to that key. Therefore, keys can be retrieved using a greedy algorithm approach by forwarding the request to the neighbour whose ID is closest to the requested key. When there is no such neighbour, then this must be the closest node.

DHTs also define two key parameters that can tune the algorithm for maintaining the overlay. One can define the number of hops in any route (to minimize route length or number of hops); and the maximum number of neighbours for any node (maximum node degree), which can be used to reduce the maintenance overhead. The parameters are a trade-off, however, because having shorter routes requires higher maximum degree. A common choice is to define maximum degree to be O(logN) and the route length also to be O(logN).

11.4 Further Reading

Minar [177] creates a taxonomy for analysing various network topologies in his second article. Gunther [66] compares various topologies for scalability issues for networks up to two million peers. He found that the 20-dimensional hypercube performed the best. Also, Hong [21] provides an excellent overview for scalability issues within P2P networks and provides two case studies for Freenet (see Chapter 12) and Gnutella.

11.5 Conclusion

This chapter gave a background into some of the problems facing the scalability of P2P networks. Due to their extremely dynamic nature, standard network topologies do not work very well and therefore, more elaborate topologies are needed to offer scalability and robustness against random peer failures. One of the most popular topologies used in recent file-sharing applications is the centralized-decentralized model that employs the same characteristics as a power-law network. This topology is similar to social and biological networks, where most nodes have a few links and a small number of nodes have many, serving as gateways to other networks. Such a topology in Gnutella can be implemented by using super-peers or reflector nodes.

Another approach discussed in this chapter involved the use of a more structured layering across the network. Distributed Hash Tables offer O(logN) search mechanisms for retrieving data from a massively distributed hash table based on the use of hash functions, such as SHA1. Here, resources are organized by using a keyspace partitioning algorithm, which divides the keyspace amongst participating nodes, and an overlay network that connects the nodes in order to minimise the number of hops.

12

Freenet

Ian Clarke in 2003 when asked in an interview "Should file swappers have any expectation of privacy?" [180], replied:

> *"Everyone, including file swappers, should have the ability to communicate freely without someone looking over their shoulders. Free communication is essential to free thought, which is essential to democracy."*

This chapter is dedicated to the Freenet distributed information storage system. Freenet was chosen to be included because it is an excellent example of how many of the techniques discussed so far in this book can be adapted and used in a practical and innovative system. For example, Freenet works within a P2P environment (Chapter 6) and addresses the inherently untrustworthy and unreliable participants within such a network. Freenet is self-organizing and incorporates a learning algorithm that allows the network to adapt its routing behaviour based on prior interactions. This algorithm is interestingly similar to social networking and achieves a power-law (centralized-decentralized) structure (discussed in Chapter 11) in a self-organizing manner. Such a technique offers a different perspective on how to efficiently scale P2P networks (e.g., Gnutella in Chapter 10) to hundred of thousands of nodes.

Freenet was designed from the ground up to provide extensive protection from hostile attack, from both inside the network and out by addressing key information privacy issues. Freenet therefore implements various security strategies that maintain privacy for all participants, regardless of their particular role. The individual security techniques that are used collectively in Freenet were discussed in Chapter 4.

This chapter is concise but it provides a relevant real-world application that integrates many of the technologies described thus far. For a more detailed overview of Freenet see [59], [181] and [182].

12.1 Introduction

Freenet is a decentralized system for storing and retrieving files within a massively distributed network. Each Freenet participant provides some network storage space and acts as a *servent* (i.e., both clients and servers as in Gnutella), both providing storage and requesting it. Freenet differs in philosophy to Gnutella as it gives P2P participants write access to the distributed file system. Gnutella is a protocol for searching distributed networks and cannot be used to propagate files onto the network. Freenet, on the other hand, allows users to store and retrieve files but does not focus on searching the network. Therefore, to a user, Freenet can be seen as an extension of one's file system that provides one with more storage space, whereas Gnutella allows a user to search and download other users' files and therefore provides an extension to the information space.

12.2 Freenet Routing

The key novel feature of Freenet is how it self-organizes its routing behaviour. The network learns to route better by adapting local routing tables based on prior experience of successful file retrievals. In this section, the basic mechanisms are described for achieving this self-organizing behaviour. The same algorithm is used for file storage and retrieval, and the network actually learns according to usage patterns across the network's participants. For example, files that are retrieved often will generate more references across the network and therefore can be located quickly and will not expire (i.e., get deleted). Files that are not requested regularly can expire because peers can collectively decide to delete them. The next three sections describe the storage, retrieval and requesting of files, followed by a section on comparing this approach with other techniques.

12.2.1 Populating the Freenet Network

When a file is added to the Freenet network, it is assigned a **file key** (see Section 12.3). Each node keeps a local *routing table* that contains a list of such keys that are stored on neighbouring peers as illustrated in Fig. 12.1. The actual storage location for a file is calculated by comparing such keys at each peer hop to other keys in a peer's routing table in order to find the peer with the closest match (see Fig. 12.1). The winning peer, who has the closest key, is passed the file to store. This process continues for the specified TTL (see Section 10.2).

Freenet peers can make intelligent decisions about where they think the data may be. The keys in individual routing tables either identify a file **or** a region in the key space for which they are responsible. Therefore, when a peer receives a request, it redirects it to the neighbouring peer who has the

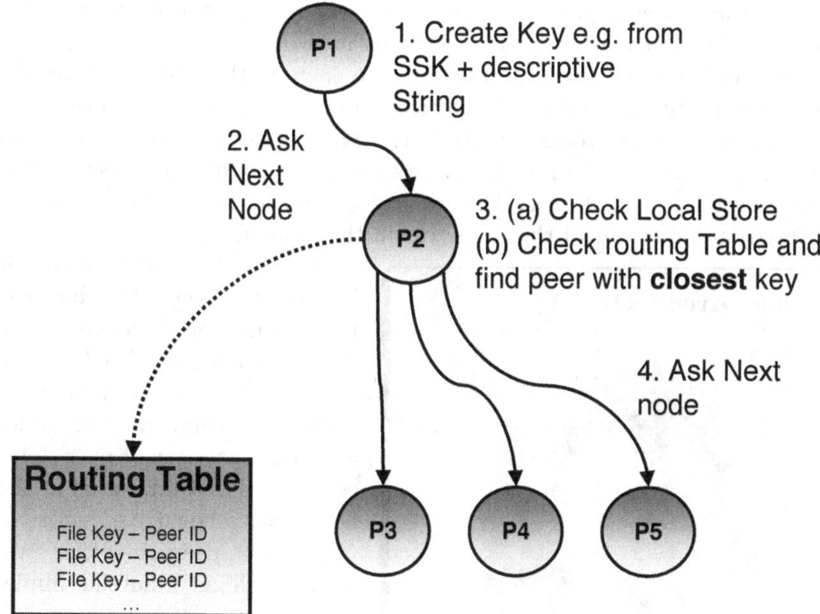

Fig. 12.1. Each peer within Freenet keeps a local routing table that stores file keys of connected peers. These are used to intelligently route the file storage or retrieval request.

closest key to the one supplied. In this way, peers become responsible for regions of the key subspace between themselves and their neighbouring peers who contain similar keys. The more nodes that join the network, the finer is the granularity of the key space.

Using this technique, similar keys get placed in similar parts of the network, but (as we will find out in the next section) although such keys are derived from a file's contents or description, comparisons in the key space are non-related. This ensures that files are evenly distributed throughout the network. The actual storage location for the file is determined by a number of factors and files can be replicated across several peers, depending on their local constraints, e.g., storage space, etc. The actual location(s) for the file is kept hidden from the user, which is achieved by employing a combination of random peer behaviour and multiple levels of encryption at each hop as the data traverses the network.

12.2.2 Self-Organizing Adaptive Behaviour in Freenet

When a file is retrieved from Freenet, it uses the same mechanism as for storage. Freenet peers adaptively update their routing tables when they successfully locate a file somewhere upstream on the network. Therefore, when a peer forwards the request to a peer who can retrieve the data, then the address of the upstream peer that contains it is included in the reply. The peer then updates its local routing table to include the peer who has the more direct route to the file. The peer can also nominate to store the data depending on current storage limitations. When a similar request is issued again, the peer routes the request more effectively. In this way, peers adapt to usage patterns; i.e., they learn, and they automatically replicate or delete files based on behaviour of the users within the system.

Freenet Architect

Ian Clarke is the architect and coordinator of The Freenet Project, and the founder of Thoof, Inc. Ian is also a co-founder and former Chief Scientist of Revver, Inc. Ian is a co-founder and formerly the Chief Technology Officer of Uprizer Inc., which was successful in raising $4 million in A-round venture capital from investors including Intel Capital. In October 2003, Ian was selected as one of the top 100 innovators under the age of 35 by the Massachusetts Institute of Technology's Technology Review magazine . Ian holds a degree in Artificial Intelligence and Computer Science from Edinburgh University, Scotland. He has also worked as a consultant for a number of companies including 3Com, and Logica UK's Space Division. He is originally from County Meath, Ireland, and currently resides in Austin, Texas.[1]

Using this mechanism, it has been shown [21] that the Freenet network converges to a centralized-decentralized model, where only a small number of nodes have large routing tables and most have small ones. This centralized-decentralized model has been shown to scale to millions of peers in other systems, such as Gnutella implementations, e.g., LimeWire [63]. This natural dynamic nature employed by Freenet to update its knowledge is analogous to the way humans reinforce decisions based on prior experiences.

Remember the Milgram experiment in Section 11.2.1? Milgram noted that 25% of all requests went through the same person (the local shopkeeper). The people in this experiment used their experience of the local inhabitants to attempt to forward the letter to the best person who could help it reach its destination. Now, the local shopkeeper was a good choice because he knew a number of out-of-town people and therefore could help the letter get closer to its destination. If this experiment were repeated using the same people, then surely the

[1] Photo and biography printed with kind permission from Ian Clarke.

word would spread quickly within Omaha that the shopkeeper is a good person to forward the letter to and subsequently, the success rate and efficiency would improve.

Another analogy, given by the Freenet authors, is deciding that since your friend George answered a question about France, then the next time around perhaps he would be a good choice to ask a question about Belgium.

12.2.3 Requesting Files

When a Freenet peer receives a request for a file, it first checks its own store. If it has the file, then it answers appropriately. If not, it forwards the request to a peer in its routing table with the closest key to the one requested (see Section 12.3 for more information on how key correlation is measured). This continues in this fashion until either the file is found or all possible avenues have been exhausted within a given radius of the requesting peer, i.e., within a TTL. Within Freenet, if a request fails, then the user has the option of choosing a higher TTL and sending the request again. Freenet also supports mix-net routing algorithms to be applied before normal routing to offer better security since the TTL can give clues about where in the chain the request is. Mix-net routing essentially repositions the start of the chain away from the requester.

Figure 12.2 shows a typical request sequence within Freenet. Here, the request initiates from peer A. Peer A asks its neighbour (peer B) if it has the requested file. B does not, so it looks in its routing table and locates the best-bet peer with the closest key, which happens to be peer F. F looks in its internal store and also does not have it, and further, it has no access to other peers. At this stage, therefore, it returns a *request failed* message back to the requester (i.e., B).

B does have further options and therefore forwards the request to the peer with the closest key (peer D). D looks in its internal store, does not find the file and so forwards the request to peer C. C doesn't have the file, so forwards the request to its closest neighbour (B). At this stage, B notices that it has seen this request and sends it back to the sending node, C, which in turn sends it back to peer D.

Peer D now explores further options and forwards the request to node E. Node E looks in its internal store and finds the requested file and so forwards this file back to the originator by hopping through all intermediaries. The intermediary peers update their routing tables accordingly and also each peer can choose to cache the file locally depending on the distance it is from the originator and local considerations.

A mixture of local caching and routing table updating is how the Freenet network *learns* to provide more effective routing. Such routing, therefore, is based on the popularity of the requested files. As more requests are processed, the network becomes better trained. The result is a dynamically formed hierarchical routing table that clusters similar keys, which helps to minimize

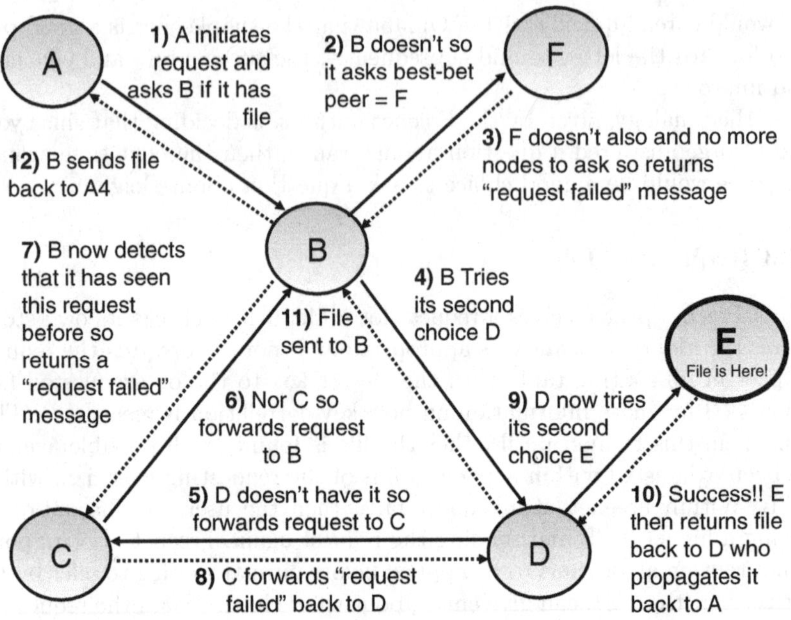
A
1) A initiates request and asks B if it has file
2) B doesn't so it asks best-bet peer = F
F
3) F doesn't also and no more nodes to ask so returns "request failed" message
12) B sends file back to A4
B
7) B now detects that it has seen this request before so returns a "request failed" message
4) B Tries its second choice D
11) File sent to B
E
File is Here!
6) Nor C so forwards request to B
9) D now tries its second choice E
5) D doesn't have it so forwards request to C
10) Success!! E then returns file back to D who propagates it back to A
C
D
8) C forwards "request failed" back to D

Fig. 12.2. A request sequence within Freenet.

the number of hops to the data. This is an interesting model, reminiscent of the ways certain artificial neural networks update their weights between connections in order to learn particular patterns.

12.2.4 Similarities with Other Peer Organization Techniques

Routing in Freenet is highly dynamic and is a departure from techniques employed by other systems discussed in previous chapters. For example, in Gnutella a user searches the network by broadcasting its request to every node within a given TTL. Napster, on the other hand, uses a central database that contains the locations of all files on the network. Gnutella, in its basic form, is inefficient and Napster, also in its simplest form, is simply not scalable and is subject to attack due to the centralization of its file indexing. As discussed in Section 11.2.3, however, both Napster and Gnutella matured into using multiple caching servers in order to be able to scale the network.

Such caching services form the basic building block of the Freenet network since each peer contains a routing table, similar in principle to Gnutella super-peers or Napster indexes. The key difference is that Freenet peers do not store locations of files at all, rather they contain file keys that indicate the direction in the key space where the file is *likely* to be stored.

The routing algorithm used in Freenet has been analysed [21] and a number of improvements are currently being integrated within Freenet's *Next Generation Routing* algorithm [183]. For example, the current algorithm does not distinguish between slow nodes at the edges of the network and fast nodes which are fault tolerant and perhaps connected by T1 or similar links.

12.3 Freenet Keys

All files within Freenet get assigned with a globally unique identifier (GUID) that uniquely identifies the file. The assigned GUID is used in both the storage and retrieval of the file and forms the basis for the comparisons used within the routing algorithm.

Freenet uses a combination of *direct* and *indirect* references to files using three distinct types of GUID keys that ensure data integrity, authentication and privacy. The keys are computed using a combination of asymmetric cryptographic techniques and hash functions. All hash functions are computed using SHA-1 secure hashes, which are described in Section 4.3.5. Freenet defines three keys:

1. **Keyword-Signed Keys (KSK):** are the simplest of Freenet keys that are derived directly from a descriptive string that the user chooses for the file.
2. **Signed-Subspace Keys (SSK):** are intended for higher-level human use, for example, to define ownership, or to make pointers to a file or a collection of files.
3. **Content-Hash Keys (CHK):** are used for low-level data storage and are obtained by hashing the contents of the data to be stored.

The three are analogous to files, directories and *inodes* on a conventional file system. For example, the KSK allows you to name a file, just as you would with a conventional file, and this name is used to store and retrieve the file. However, by only using KSKs, you limit yourself to a flat file system; i.e., it is similar to putting all of your files in one directory.

SSKs give a subspace that can act as a container for files. This is similar to the way we use directories on a conventional file system except that SSKs are used, in practice, along with the file name, giving the absolute path of the file. In practice, SSKs are used instead of KSKs to expand the user namespace.

CHKs are straight hashed versions of the file itself. They identify the contents of the file and serve as a unique pointer to the file. Similarly, there is an inode for each file and a file is uniquely identified by the file system on which it resides and its inode number on that system.

12.3.1 Keyword-Signed Keys

A KSK is the simplest type of file key, which is computed directly from the descriptive string that a user chooses for his/her file. The descriptive string is

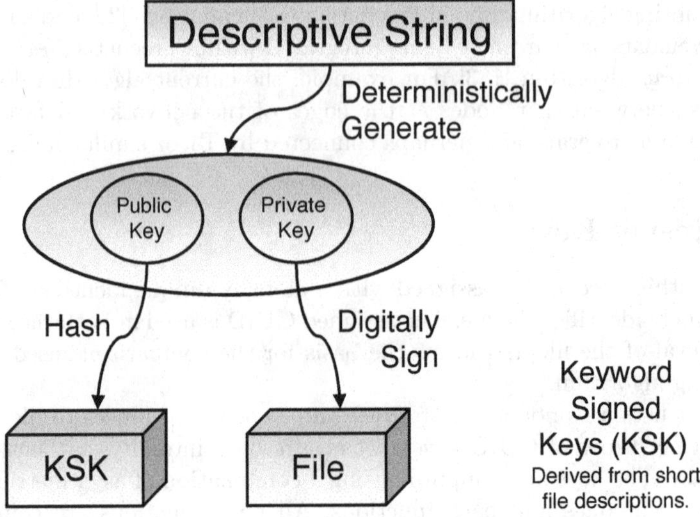

Fig. 12.3. KSKs are derived directly from a descriptive string for a file.

used to **deterministically** create a public/private key pair. The public half is hashed to give the KSK and the private key is used to sign the actual file (see Fig. 12.3). This provides a minimal integrity check, since the user can check whether the retrieved file matches its file key; i.e., from the public key, a user can compute the KSK and also check the signature for the file itself. Files are also encrypted using this descriptive string.

To retrieve the file using the KSK, the user only needs to provide the descriptive string, since he can easily regenerate the rest of the keys because they are deterministically generated from this string. However, such keys form a flat global namespace, analogous to creating a file system without any directories. The SSKs in the next section address this issue.

12.3.2 Signed-Subspace Keys

An SSK enables a personal namespace to be set up. The namespace can be used in a number of ways; for example, to store a file, to store multiple files, to store a file that is split into multiple sections or to point to other namespaces. In this way, complex multiple-level structures can be created, similar to directories on a file system. For example, you could create a subspace called *books* and make this a container for other SSKs (e.g., *fiction* and *non-fiction*), which could, in turn, be a container for a list of author SSKs, followed by a list of files containing descriptions of each book.

SSKs are created as follows. First, the user randomly generates an asymmetric key pair (public/private key) for the subspace. She keeps the private key private but the public key is made available to other users. This key pair

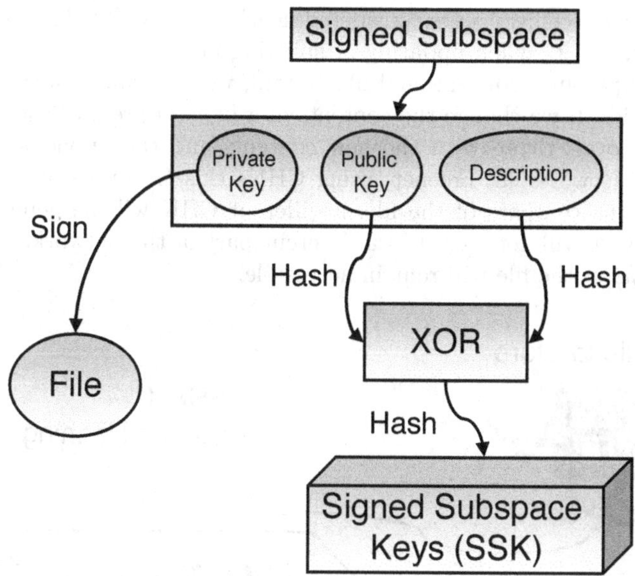

Fig. 12.4. Signed subspace keys (SSK) incorporate a description and a namespace for files.

uniquely identifies the subspace and is highly unlikely to clash with other subspace keys.

To insert a file into the subspace, the user provides a descriptive string for the file. Then, as illustrated in Fig. 12.4, the public key and the file description are hashed independently, XORed together, then hashed again to give the SSK for that file. The private key is then used to sign the file, to ensure the authenticity of the file when it is retrieved. Since SSKs are generated using hash functions, they are also one-way functions so in order to reconstruct the SSK, you need the inputs to the function, which are the public key for the subspace and the descriptive string for the file. From this, you can recalculate the SSK and locate the file within the system.

However, to store files in a subspace, a user needs to be able to sign the actual file with the subspace's private key in order to be able to generate the correct digital signature. Therefore, subspaces are set up so that anyone can read from them but only the subspace owner can write — analogous to the way we add permissions to directories in UNIX file systems.

12.3.3 Content-Hash Keys

CHKs are computed directly from the file's contents using SHA-1 secure hashes (see Section 4.3.5) and hence are called content-hash keys. A CHK gives each file a unique hash key for each file based on the contents of that file (since SHA-1 collisions are considered nearly impossible). This is useful in many contexts, e.g., when updating or splitting files.

For example, in a conventional file system, we label files using file names and directories. If we change the contents of a file and press the save button, the file gets overwritten with the new contents and the previous version is lost forever. However, in Freenet, using CHKs this is impossible because, if you change the contents of the file, a different CHK will be generated and consequently, it will get stored in a different part of the network. Therefore, both *versions* of the file will remain accessible.

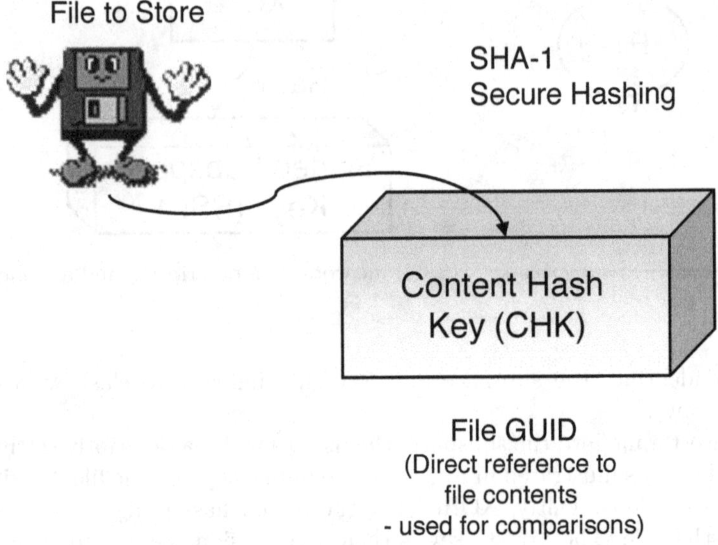

Fig. 12.5. The construction of a content-hash key is simply a secure hash of the contents of the file.

CHKs are generally used in conjunction with SSKs to create indirect files. Indirect files are created within a two-stage process. First, the user inserts the file using the CHK. He then creates an SSK by pointing to the CHK rather than to the file itself. Therefore, for retrieval, the user first obtains the CHK from the SSK subspace and then retrieves the file itself using the CHK.

CHKs are computed directly from the contents of the file and this is independent of the originator. This helps to maintain privacy, if desirable. Also, CHKs help with versioning of files. As mentioned, if a file is modified slightly, then a new CHK will be generated for that file. This ensures that old copies of the file will not get overwritten but further, if two identical files are inserted from different participants, then the same GUID will be generated and therefore be considered equivalent. This helps avoid unnecessary duplication and alongside the SSK can ensure appropriate file authentication.

12.3.4 Clustering Keys

Keys are clustered by comparing their GUID values which are created in various ways, as described in the three previous sections. However, since they are constructed using hash keys that have a good *avalanche effect* (see Section 4.3.5), key comparisons are completely unrelated to the similarities of their input. For example, if we are using CHKs and comparing two almost identical input files, their hash values will be completely different.

This non-correlation of Freenet hash comparisons is unimportant and does not adversely affect the convergence and efficiency of the network. In fact, it somewhat helps the network because it ensures that files get evenly distributed across the entire network as a quasi-random set of keys will be produced. Clustering files within the GUID space results in unbiased decisions about where the files are actually located.

This property is in practice very useful since setting up such a Freenet network will normally involve a particular type of data storage and consequently, there may be a number of files with similar content being stored on the network. If these files were correlated directly to determine where they would be stored on the network, then such files would converge to a particular network segment, resulting in a partitioning of data storage with an uneven distribution across the resource. However, using hash functions produces quasi-random representations of the data which are typically spread across the spectrum and therefore enable a more even distribution across the mass data storage network.

Such a distribution has been shown [21] to demonstrate good scaling and fault-tolerant characteristics and, in fact, converge to a power-law (centralized/decentralized) structure (see [179] and Section 11.2.4) that exhibits all the advantages of *small-world* networks. Freenet therefore has been shown to scale effectively to hundreds of thousands of nodes.

12.4 Joining the Network

This section briefly describes how a node joins the Freenet network, which is illustrated in Fig. 12.6. Initially, the new peer creates itself a public-private key pair (step 1) that is not only used to identify the peer but also to sign its current physical address reference for security; peers can keep their identities even though their physical addresses may differ.

Nodes then locate a node in the Freenet network (step 2). This is achieved in a similar fashion to the way Gnutella peers locate a node within the network (see Section 10.3.1), either by using an IRC, Web site or lists through some server. The new node sends its public key and physical address to the existing Freenet node it has discovered (FN1, step 3). FN1 now makes a note of NN's identity and forwards this information to other connected peers in a random

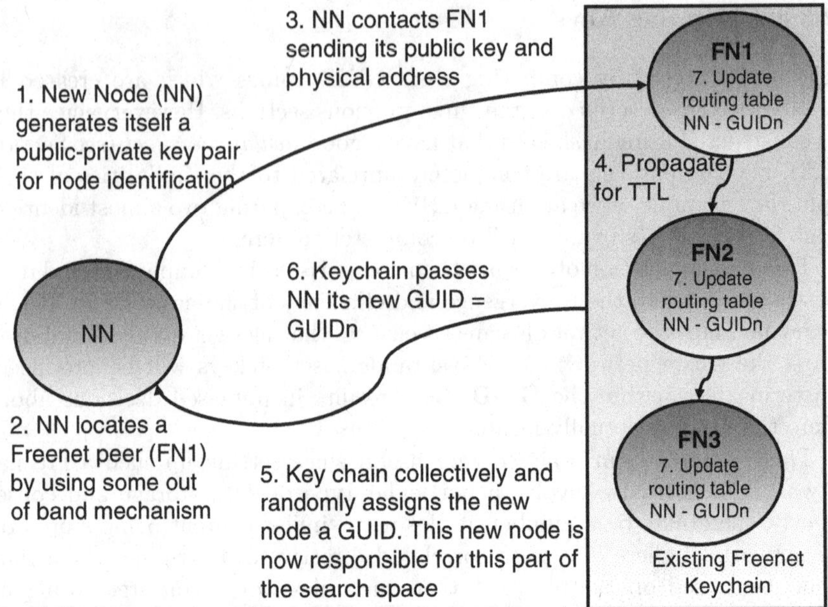

Fig. 12.6. A scenario about how a new node joins the Freenet network and gets assigned a GUID that identifies for which proportion of the CHK key space it will be responsible.

fashion by taking entries from its routing table. This continues in this fashion for the specified TTL.

Once the TTL expires, all nodes in the keychain collectively assign the new node a GUID, which assigns the new node a part of the key space for which it will be responsible. This new GUID is calculated using a cryptographic protocol for shared random number generation, which is designed to prevent any one participant from biasing the result. The new node is then passed this new GUID (GUIDn in step 6) and each peer updates its local routing tables accordingly.

12.5 Conclusion

This chapter gave a brief overview of the Freenet distributed information storage systems, with the aim of providing a concrete example of how the many techniques so far described in this book can be integrated into a single system. Freenet is designed to work within a P2P network and is fault tolerant to both random peer failures and breaches of security.

It employs an adaptive routing algorithm which updates the information cached at each peer according to its previous experience of successful queries or data inserts. The mechanism by which a peer routes queries is based on comparisons in the key-space domain, which are all calculated using a combination of hash functions and asymmetric cryptography techniques. Such keys are therefore unrelated to the input (i.e., file descriptions or file content) and therefore create a key space in a random fashion that has been shown to utilize the entire network and create a desired power-law distribution of peer connections across the peers, which can scale to hundreds of thousands of nodes.

There are three types of keys, which are calculated from: the file description for keyword-signed keys; a subspace and the file description for signed-subspace keys; and directly from hashing the contents of the file for the content-hash keys. The construction of these keys illustrates the practical use of the security mechanisms described earlier in this book.

13

BitTorrent

> *"You get so tired of having your work die," he says. "I just wanted to make something that people would actually use."*

The above quote if from Bram Cohen, BitTorrent's author, in an interview with Wired in 2005[184]. The first version of the BitTorrent protocol was presented in the first CodeCon conference[185][1] in San Francisco in February 2002 and subsequently became one of the most popular Internet file sharing protocols [184]. In essence, BitTorrent introduced two key concepts that were novel to its file-sharing competitors at the time. First, rather than providing a search protocol itself, it was designed to integrate seamlessly with the Web and made files (torrents) available via Web pages, which could be searched for using standard Web search tools. Second, it enabled so-called *file swarming*; that is, once a peer starts downloading that file, it also makes whatever portion of the file that is downloaded immediately available for sharing. The file-swarming process is enabled through the use of a tracker, which is an HTTP-based server used to dynamically synchronise and update the peers as they are downloading as to the locations and availability of pieces of the file in question on the network. The tracker also can monitor users' usage on the network and can implement a tit-for-tat scheme, which divides bandwidth according to how much a peer contributes to the other peers in the network.

The result of the file swarming techniques made BitTorrent an extremely attractive tool for sharing files because it allowed users to download files to the maximum of their download capability of their broadband connection by enabling simultaneous downloads of pieces of the same file from multiple users. This is significant because typically a broadband connection has a far lower upload bandwidth than a download one (the upload bandwidth can be typically ten times slower than the download). This means that being able to connect to, say, ten peers, will balance this mismatch and enable the full

[1] http://www.codecon.org/.

potential of your Internet link, which results in files being downloaded several times faster than other file sharing systems on the Internet at that time. The BitTorrent protocol therefore has had a massive impact on file sharing applications and similar schemes have been adopted by competitors since. Further, its use has far outgrown the illicit file-sharing arena and nowadays the BitTorrent protocol or similar techniques are used in a multitude of different applications in science and business and it has even being integrated into hardware devices. In this sense, the protocol has grown up and is now taken very seriously throughout the Internet community.

13.1 What Is BitTorrent?

Cohen[2] authored both the peer-to-peer (P2P) BitTorrent protocol and the first file sharing program that used the protocol, also called BitTorrent. He developed BitTorrent in 2001 and around the same time, he co-founded the CodeCon conference with his roommate Len Sassaman. CodeCon is a low-cost conference (i.e., less than $100) aimed at hackers and technology enthusiasts, with a focus on presentations from developers with working code, in contrast to other conferences, which they suggested focused more on companies with products to sell. The first CodeCon conference was on 24 February 2002 and BitTorrent was one of the several presentations. It continues to this day to claim the "most famous presentation" title for this conference series.

BitTorrent's Author

Cohen was born in 1975 and grew up in New York. After school, he left New York City to study at the University of Buffalo in 1993 but decided to leave and work for a number of dot-com companies in the nineties, the last of which was MojoNation, which allowed users to break up files into encrypted chunks and serve from a number of sources. Bram liked this idea and this led into his thoughts on the development of the BitTorrent protocol, which he focused on from April 2001. Cohen was the co-founder of CodeCon, the organiser of the San Francisco Bay Area P2P-hackers meeting and the co-author of Codeville. At the time of writing, he lives in San Francisco with his wife Jenna and two children.

BitTorrent is simply a protocol for distributing files [186]. It was designed to be based around the Web with content (file to be downloaded) being identified by URLs and accessed via standard Web pages. However, it differs from a typical HTTP scenario, because when a user clicks on a BitTorrent a conventional client-server download of the content between the browser and the Web server does not take place. Rather, when the link is clicked, a MIME-type mapping (from a .torrent file) takes place that results in a BitTorrent client-side application starting and joining the BitTorrent network. Thereafter, multiple downloads of the

[2] For more information, see http://en.wikipedia.org/wiki/Bram_Cohen.

same file happen concurrently by breaking the file into pieces and by exchanging these pieces between users using TCP until everyone has the complete file.

A *tracker* is used to update the network as more pieces are downloaded, which results in continuous updating of the state of a group of users downloading a particular file (a swarm), which results in massive increases in download speeds for files that are popular in the network. Therefore, the more people trading a file, the more options for obtaining its pieces. So, unlike the Web or P2P systems like Napster, popularity of a specific file does not slow down the process; rather, it allows for more simultaneous downloads and therefore makes for much faster downloads. BitTorrent trackers also keep track of how much you contribute to hosting files for the group and it further expedites a user's download speed if that peer shares files to the swarm group, by implementing policies in such a way that the more you share, the faster you can download (i.e., the more hosts the tracker notifies you of). This ensures a more even ratio of "file sharing versus file downloading," which helps to limit so-called leaches or free riders and therefore helps balance the network as a whole.

13.2 The BitTorrent Protocol

The BitTorrent protocol is an open specification that can be found in full on the BitTorrent Web site [187] and is updated periodically in order to keep various BitTorrent applications compatible. This section provides a summary of the protocol and describes the interactions between the various BitTorrent components. We begin with a description of the terminology and an overview of the entities in a typical BitTorrent application to specify the interactions, before describing the low-level messages in more detail.

13.2.1 Terminology

In this chapter, we use the following terms that are defined in the BitTorrent protocol:

- **Torrent:** a metadata file containing the information about a file to be shared on the BitTorrent network (files ending in .torrent).
- **Peer:** a participant in the network. Peers are defined as elsewhere in this book, being both consumers and providers of files on the distributed network.
- **Seed:** the peer that has a complete copy of the file (who probably created the torrent).
- **Swarm:** peers who are connected (interested) in a particular file.
- **Tracker:** server responsible for keeping track of the people in a swarm.
- **Choked:** state of a connection when a peer does not wish to upload information at this time (perhaps because he already has too many connections).

- **Interested:** a client who wishes to download a file from another BT node.
- **Piece:** is a piece of a file in Bittorrent that is distributed around t he network. Pieces typically have a length which is a power of 2 and very much depends on the size of the files that are to be distributed on the network. Common sizes in BitTorrent applications are 256K, 512K or 1MB. However, care must be taken to choose a piece size carefully as a piece size that is too small will incur much overhead in establishing TCP connections.
- **Bencoding:** is the terse format for BitTorrent messages, which is described in Section 13.2.3.

13.2.2 Entities in a BitTorrent Application

BitTorrent was designed to be interfaced seamlessly with a user's Web browser. A user launches the BitTorrent application by simply clicking on a *.torrent* hyperlink within a standard Web browser. A BitTorrent application therefore generally has the following components:

1. An 'original' **downloader**, referred to as a seed.
2. An ordinary **Web server**.
3. An end user's **Web browser**. A user clicks on a hyperlink to a **.torrent file** containing the 'metainfo', which results in the launching of:
4. An end user's **BitTorrent client application** to initiate downloading — there are typically ideally many end users for a single file.
5. A **BitTorrent tracker** for synchronising the downloading process.

The interaction between these components is illustrated in Figure 13.1, which shows a simple scenario of a professor (Ian) who makes his collection of PPT lecture slides available to his students using BitTorrent. Ian would first either start his own tracker for the file or search for an existing tracker, using one of a number of methods, for example, by searching the BitTorrent tracker sites directory.[3] Once a tracker is identified, Ian can create the metainfo (*.torrent*) file using the **maketorrent** application [188] specifying the directory containing the PPT lecture slides to be shared, the *announce URL* of the tracker and the **piece size** he would like to use on the network for his files. The contents of the resulting *.torrent* file is discussed are Section 13.2.3.

Ian would then start a downloader using BitTorrent, which has the original copy of the complete file that is being made available. This downloader is known as the 'seed' of the process, described in Section 13.2.1. He would upload the *.torrent* metainfo file to a Web server he has access to and then make an association of the extension *.torrent* with MIME-type application/x-bittorrent on this Web server. He would next add a link to the metainfo (*.torrent*) file from a Web page so that his students could click on the link to start the downloading process.

[3] http://www.torrentscan.com/torrent_trackers/.

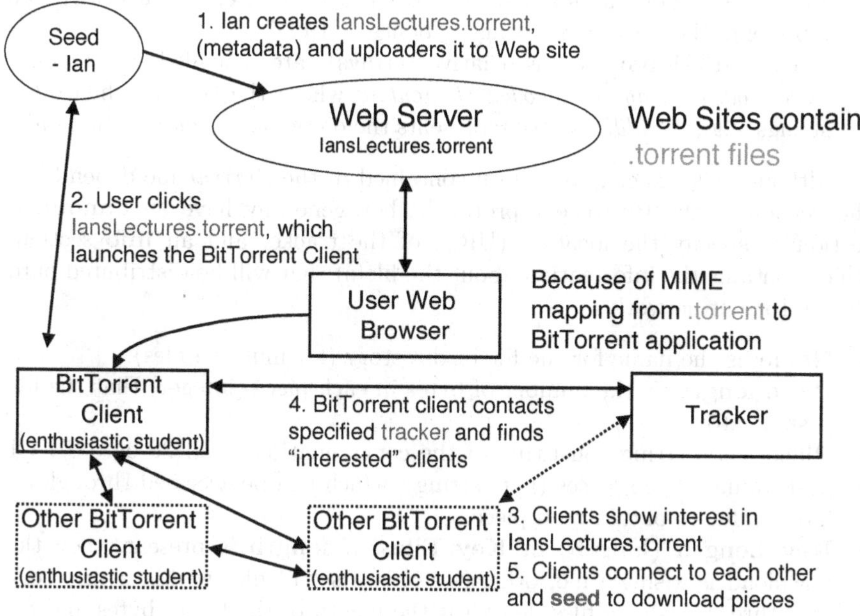

Fig. 13.1. A typical usage scenario, showing how Ian could release his lectures as an archive using BitTorrent.

Once made available, Ian's students would first install a BitTorrent client and then surf the Web to find Ian's Web page containing the *.torrent* file for the lectures. They would then select where to save the file locally and wait for download to complete. They would finally exit the BitTorrent client application, if they would like to stop sharing this file to others.

13.2.3 Bencoding and Torrent Metafiles

Bencoding (pronounced "bee-encoding") is an ASCII-based format for tersely describing data in *.torrent* metadata files. An ASCII format is obviously less efficient than binary encoding but because numbers are encoded in decimal notation, it has the advantage of being unaffected by the cross-platform problems associated with byte ordering (endianness). Bencoding supports the following four data types:

1. **Strings** are encoded as follows: *<string length>:<string data>*, e.g., *4:spam* represents the string "spam".
2. **Integers** are encoded as follows: *i<integer>e*, e.g., *i9e* represents the integer "9".

3. **Lists** are encoded as follows: *l<bencoded values>e*, e.g., *l5:bones4:tunae* represents the list of two strings: ["bones", "tuna"].
4. Finally **dictionaries** (associative arrays) are encoded as follows: *d<bencoded string><bencoded element>e* where the keys are bencoded strings, e.g., *d3:addl1:a1:bee* represents the dictionary *"add" = ["a", "b"]*.

Although the exact information contained in the *.torrent* file depends on the version of the BitTorrent protocol, they generally have an **announce** section to specify the location (URL) of the tracker and an **info** section, which contains the information about the file(s) that will be distributed onto the BitTorrent network:

- **Name**: is the name for the file or directory (for multiple files).
- **Piece length**: is the number of bytes in each piece (integer) that the file is split into.
- **Pieces**: is a string consisting of the concatenation of all 20-byte SHA-1 hash values of the pieces (byte string), which can be accessed through an index value to obtain each piece.
- **Key Length (length)** or **Key Files**. If **length** is present, then the download is a single file, otherwise it is a set of files within a directory structure. For single files, length is the length of the file in bytes and for case where there are multiple files, the key files are treated as a single file by concatenating the files in the order they appear in a file list, which is a dictionary containing:
  - **Length**: is the length of the file (in bytes).
  - **Path**: is a list of subdirectories and names for the files in the list.

As discussed in Section 13.2.2, *.torrent* files are created using an application such as *maketorrent.* They are hosted on a Web site and then when clicked the client-side application is launched, which reads the **announce** URL from the *.torrent* file and connects to the tracker to join the group and start downloading the file from other peers and seeds in the network. This process is described in the next section.

13.2.4 The Tracker and File Downloading

A BitTorrent tracker keeps track of all of the users that form the swarm for a particular file. As users join or leave the network, the tracker maintains a list of peers who are currently registered as interested in a particular file. Trackers receive information from each peer in the swarm containing their contact information and statistics on how much they have uploaded or downloaded so far. This helps the tracker to make decisions about the priority of the peers, which results in deciding the number of seeds they are given for the downloading of the file. The tracker returns an update to each BitTorrent node in the group as new pieces are downloaded within the network. This is illustrated in Figure 13.2, which shows how BitTorrent nodes make further

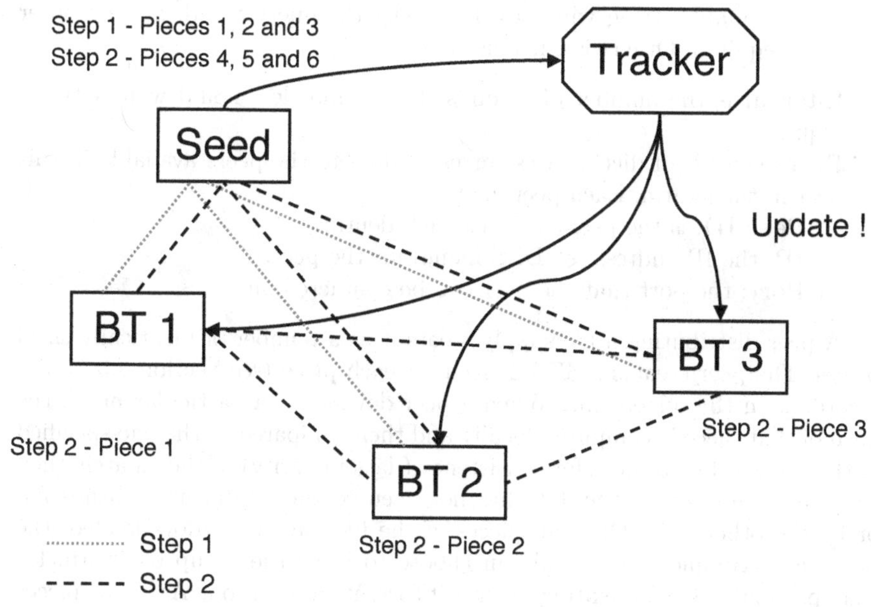

Fig. 13.2. BitTorrent tracker scenario.

connections to other BitTorrent nodes after simultaneous downloads of the different pieces from the seed result in the tracker notifying peers that new pieces are available in the network.

The communication from the peer to the tracker is an HTTP GET request, which contains the following information:

- **Info_hash**: 20 byte SHA1 hash of the bencoded form of the info value from the metainfo file.
- **Peer_id**: string of length 20 containing ID of downloader — generated at random at the start of a new download.
- **IP**: IP address or IP name for the peer.
- **Port**: port number for the peer — tries port 6881 and if that port is taken, it tries 6882, then 6883, etc. and gives up after 6889.
- **Uploaded**: total amount uploaded so far.
- **Downloaded**: total amount downloaded so far.
- **Left**: number of bytes this peer still has to download.
- **Event**: optional key which maps to started, completed, or stopped or it is empty.

The tracker then responds with either a failure reason or a bencoded dictionary containing the list of peers that the requesting peer can connect to in a swarm. If a tracker response has a key failure reason, then that maps to a human-readable string which explains why the query failed, and no other keys are required. Otherwise, it must have two keys:

- **Interval** is the number of seconds the downloader should wait between requests.
- **Peers** is a list of dictionaries corresponding to the peers available to this peer in the swarm. Each peer has:
  - **Peer ID**: is the peer's self-selected identifier.
  - **IP**: the IP address (or DNS name) for the peer.
  - **Port**: the port that the peer can be contacted on.

A peer distributing a file simply treats it as a number of identically sized pieces. The peer creates a SHA-1 hash for each piece (see Section 4.3.5) and records it in the torrent file. When a peer downloads a particular piece, the hash of that piece is computed locally and then compared to the one specified in the *.torrent* file to check for consistency (data integrity). If they match, then the peer assumes that the data has not been corrupted during transmission or by the other peer. Once all pieces of the file have been downloaded, the peer has a complete copy and can choose to leave the group or swarm for that particular file by exiting their BitTorrent application. As more pieces are downloaded, there are more options for the various pieces and therefore downloading increases in speed. Setting the piece size is key to the success of the protocol. A piece size too small will cause too much latency for opening the TCP connections whereas a piece size too large may reduce the efficiency of the protocol because less pieces (and therefore locations on the BitTorrent network) are available for simultaneous download.

13.3 BitTorrent, Inc.

BitTorrent, Inc. was founded by Bram Cohen and Ashwin Navin, who in 2007, secured funding of $28.75 million from Accel Partners and DCM (formerly Doll Capital Management) to pursue the development of a software platform based around BitTorrent that aims to help software providers and media companies to download high-resolution files faster for real-time on-line content distribution. In a Wired article in late 2007 [184], they were listed as one of the top 10 startups worth watching in 2008. The company initially employed 60 people.

At the time of writing, the company had 27 partner logos listed on their partner page and their current CEO Doug Walker stated in an interview in early 2008 [189] that the company was talking to 55 partners from the media industry, and was in active discussions about how BitTorrent could help them deliver media content and games over the Internet. These companies include 20th Century Fox, Comedy Central, Lionsgate Films, MTV, Paramount, Spike TV and Warner Brothers. The company boasts an installed base of over 160 million clients worldwide.

BitTorrent has three lines of business: BitTorrent DNA for enabling Websites to add BitTorrent technology to their current content delivery infrastructure; BitTorrent Device Partners, which is a program designed to help hardware and software companies to embed BitTorrent through the use of their Software Development Kit (SDK); and the Torrent Entertainment Network (TEN), which is an online destination for downloadable and ad-supported streaming entertainment content powered by BitTorrent DNA. The network provides fast, on-demand access to the most comprehensive catalog of licensed content on the Internet, featuring thousands of movies, TV shows, music titles and games.

13.4 Conclusion

This chapter gave an overview of the BitTorrent protocol. It described how BitTorrent uses a tracker to create a group or swarm for a particular file which dynamically updates the information about the peers in the network who have interest in downloading the particular file. As more participants join the group, more pieces are downloaded, which, in turn, create more sources for the pieces of the file on the distributed network. This provides more download sources for peers to make multiple TCP connections to in order to increase their download bandwidth for a particular file. BitTorrent also incorporates incentives for peers to share files to the network by offering a tit-for-tat scheme which ensures that peers who share more are offered more locations for pieces so they have higher download speeds than peers who do not share. These two factors make BitTorrent faster for file sharing than other protocols offered at the time of its release. BitTorrent is now used in a number of applications and has already become part of the next-generation protocols for file transfer on the Internet. BitTorrent has already been deployed widely in software but is also being integrated into many hardware network devices.

Part IV

Protocols and Architectures II — Middleware

14

Jini

This chapter gives an overview of Jini, which provides a further example of well-known distributed-object-based systems that were discussed in Chapter 8. Jini is similar in concept to industry-pervasive systems such as CORBA [136] and DCOM [3]. It is distinguished by being based on Java, and deriving many features purely from this Java basis (e.g., the use of RMI and Java serialization). There are other Java frameworks from Sun which would appear to overlap Jini, such as Enterprise Java Beans (EJBs) [190]. However, whereas EJBs make it easier to build business logic servers, Jini could be used to distribute these services in a network *plug-and-play* manner.

In this chapter, a background is given into the development of Jini and into the network plug-and-play manner in which Jini accesses distributed objects. Specifically, this chapter will build on the Java RMI description and Java serialization mechanisms, discussed in Section 8.5, which form the transportation backbone for Jini. The discovery of Jini services is described and the notion of a Jini *proxy* is introduced.

Jini implements three protocols that allow a service provider to register its service, a client to search for the service and both a client and service provider to discover the Jini lookup server. The Jini lookup server is central to the control of the Jini environment as it coordinates the discovery and registration of Jini objects. Jini runs a brokered architecture, however, in that the discovery is centralized through the lookup service but the communication thereafter between the client and the service is direct.

Finally, Jini advanced issues, such as leasing and distributed asynchronous events, are discussed. In Chapter 20, an overview of how to set up the Jini runtime and how Jini services are deployed using a simple application illustrates how these individual parts fit together.

14.1 Jini

14.1.1 Setting the Scene

> **The Conception of Jini**
> *The idea of the Jini system sprang from Sun co-founder Bill Joy at Sun Aspen Smallworks R&D lab in 1994. Under his and Jim Waldo's leadership, Ann Wollrath, the inventor and designer for RMI, Ken Arnold, the designer of JavaSpaces technology and Bob Scheifler, a principal of the X Consortium and designer of Lookup/Discovery, designed the Jini middleware. On January 25, 1999, Jini was officially launched and the technology was available for download.*

Historically, operating systems have been designed with certain assumptions; that a computer will have a processor, some memory and a disk. When a computer is booted, it looks for a hard disk and if it can't find one, then it cannot function.

In more recent times, however, computers are used within different scenarios and have fundamentally different roles. For example, a mobile phone does not contain a hard disk but it does have a processor, some memory and a network connection and when it boots up, rather than searching for a disk, it looks for the telephone network. If a network cannot be located, then it can't function as a mobile phone. This growing trend from disk-centric to network-centric within a wide range of embedded devices radically affects the way we organize software.

The main emphasis of Jini [23], [191] is to place the emphasis back onto the network and attempt to provide an infrastructure that will enable the many varied processors in devices that have no disk drive to operate and locate services. Jini therefore provides mechanisms to enable adding, removing and locating devices and services on the network.

In addition, Jini provides a programming model that makes it easier for programmers to get their devices talking to each other. Although Jini can be implemented using more verbose networking communication techniques, e.g., XML-based message passing [192], most Jini applications sit on top of two of the core Java technologies implemented in the Java SDK; that is, RMI and the Java serialization of objects, which were discussed in Section 8.5. Jini builds on top of these technologies to enable objects to move around the network from virtual machine to virtual machine and extend the benefits of object-oriented programming to the network. Instead of requiring device vendors to agree on the network protocols through which their devices can interact, Jini enables the devices to talk to each other through interfaces to objects. First, let's look at some of the technologies that Jini integrates in order to implement this distributed mechanism.

Jini development is being continued by the River project. See the project home page[1] or text box opposite for more information.

[1] http://incubator.apache.org/river/RIVER/index.html.

In the next section, a brief overview of Jini is given, which is followed by a detailed description of each part.

14.2 Jini Architecture

Jini has a brokered architecture, discussed in Chapter 1, which will become apparent in the following overview.

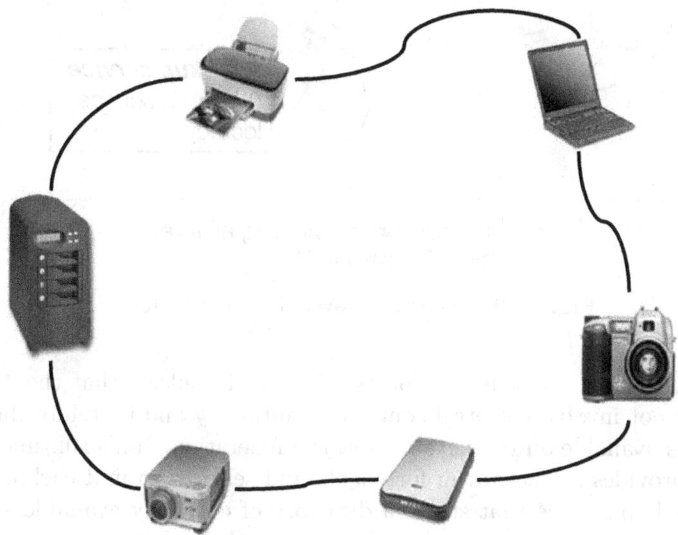

Fig. 14.1. A Jini federation.

Jini is a set of APIs and network protocols that can help you build and deploy distributed systems that are organized as federations of services. A service is a network-enabled entity that performs some function. Some examples of services include hardware devices (printers, scanners, hard drives, etc.), software, communications channels and even human users themselves. For example, a Jini-enabled disk drive could offer a "storage" service and a Jini-enabled printer could offer a "printing" service. The federation of services is a set of available services on the network that a client can utilize to help accomplish some goal.

Therefore, to perform a task, a client enlists the help of services. For example, a client program might upload an image from a scanning service, download this to a disk drive via a disk-drive service and send it to the printing service of a colour printer. In this example, the client program builds a distributed system consisting of itself, the scanning service, the disk-drive storage service and the colour-printing service. The client and services of this distributed system work together to perform this task.

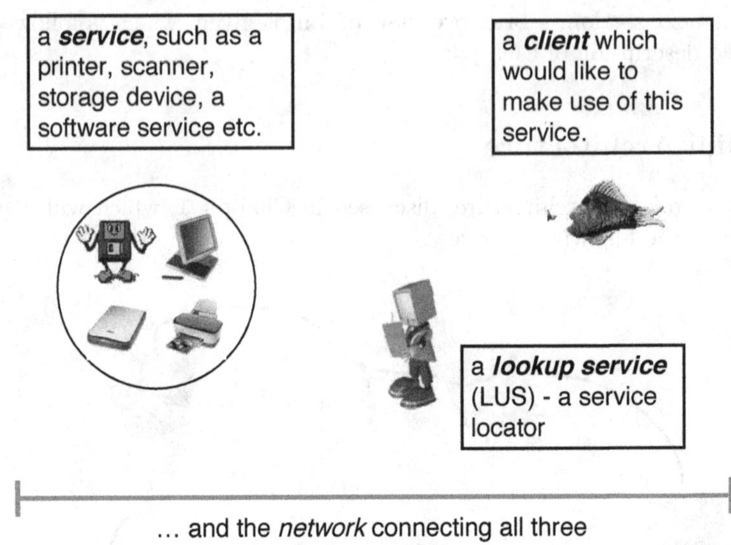
a service, such as a printer, scanner, storage device, a software service etc.
a client which would like to make use of this service.
a lookup service (LUS) - a service locator
... and the network connecting all three
- generally running TCP/IP

Fig. 14.2. The three players in a Jini system.

The concept of a Jini federation (see Fig. 14.1) reflects that the Jini network does not involve a central controlling authority and therefore the set of all services available on the network forms a federation. Jini's runtime infrastructure provides a mechanism for clients and services to find each other by using a lookup service that stores a directory of currently available services. Such a directory service allows a client to broker the task to a service available on the network.

Once services locate each other, they thereafter communicate directly and are independent of the Jini runtime infrastructure. This architecture is therefore brokered and similar in mechanism to systems such as Napster (see Section 6.4.1), although differing in functionality. As in Napster, if the Jini lookup service crashes, any clients or servers brought together via the lookup service before it crashed can continue their work.

14.2.1 Jini in Operation

Jini defines a runtime infrastructure that provides mechanisms that enable you to add, remove, locate and access services. Briefly, in a running Jini system, there are three main players (see Fig. 14.2):

1. There is a service, such as a printer, scanner, storage device, a software service, etc.
2. There is a client which would like to make use of this service.
3. And there is a lookup service (LUS). This essentially is a service locator that acts as a broker/trader/locator between services and clients.

Of course, there is also an additional component, and that is a network connecting all three of these, and this network will generally be running TCP/IP. (Note that the Jini specification is fairly independent of network protocol, but the only current implementation is on TCP/IP.)

When new services become available on the network, they register themselves with a lookup service. When clients wish to locate a service to assist with some task, they consult a lookup service.

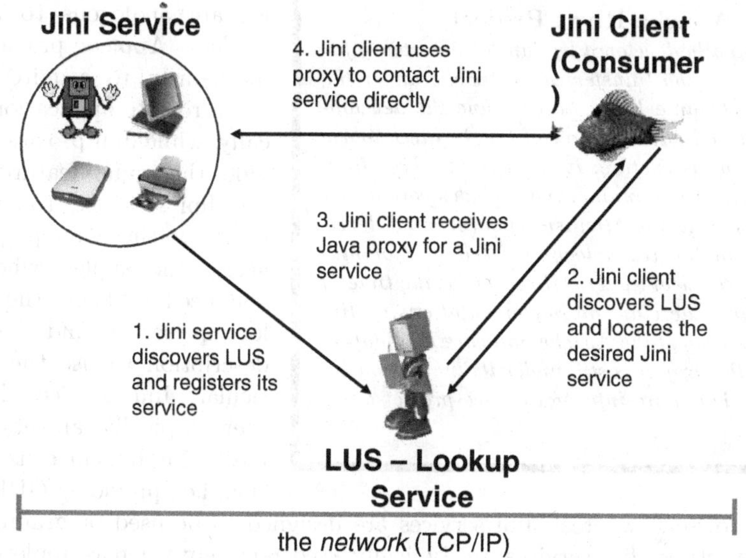

Fig. 14.3. Broad overview of Jini in operation.

The scenario of using Jini services is given in Fig. 14.3 and has the following steps:

1. The Jini service uses discovery (see Section 14.3.1) to locate the LUS and then registers its service with the LUS for use on the Jini network.
2. The Jini client uses discovery (see Section 14.3.1) to locate the LUS and then uses the LUS to find the particular Jini service(s) it wishes to use. The lookup service then returns information to the client (a proxy, see below), which allows the client to contact the service directly.
3. Thereafter, the client and service exchange information directly and the lookup server is no longer required.

Code is moved around among these three pieces, and this is done by marshalling the objects. This involves serializing the objects in such a way that they can be moved around the network and later reconstituted (deserialized) by using included information about the class files as well as instance data as discussed in Section 8.5.2.

Much of the power of Jini comes from the core nature of Java, that is, the ability to download bytecodes from the network and execute them locally, just as you do each time you use an applet. In Jini, services are always accessed via an object that is provided by the service itself, called a proxy (as in RMI; see Section 8.5). The client downloads this proxy from the lookup server and makes calls on this object just as it would on any other RMI object, in order to use the service.

> **The Apache River Project**
> *Originally developed by Sun, responsibility for Jini is being transferred to Apache under the project name River, to continue the development and advancement of the Jini technology core infrastructure. It has broad backing from the Jini Community, and includes core developers from Sun Microsystems (original developer of the technology) as well as Community technical leaders. However, at the time of writing, there are no implementations of Jini technology at the Apache Software Foundation and the project is still under its incubation period. For more information see project home page.*

In some ways, Jini proxies are analogous to Java applets. Applets provide a mechanism to acquire and use a remote application locally, while Jini proxies provide the same feature for the Jini services. You need to know the Web page to access the applet, whereas you need to know the Jini lookup server and service description to use the particular Jini service. However, typically applets are meant for human consumption, i.e., providing GUIs for Web browsers, whereas Jini services are designed to be used programmatically. Further, Jini services are typically used remotely whereas applets are always run locally. Jini services are essentially network aware, on-demand device drivers. The way proxies interact with the service is up to the creator of the service proxy. Here are some possibilities:

1. **The proxy performs the service itself:** This is very similar to an applet: the Java proxy code is downloaded to the client and the client executes the function directly on the downloadable object. When it is executed, the object is completely self-contained and does not require any remote functionality.
2. **The proxy is an RMI stub for a remote service:** Here, the proxy is a minimal piece of code which is an interface to the remote object. The client makes a call on the proxy object; then RMI transfers this call and arguments to the remote object on the service provider, where the actual execution is made.
3. **The proxy acts as a smart adapter:** Here, the proxy contains enough code to be able to make decisions about how to execute the functionality. It could use whatever communication protocol it likes, e.g., sockets, CORBA, Jxta, etc., to broker the request to a remote service. Under this scenario, Jini services can gain access to hardware devices that have their own

communication protocol or contact Jini services that are written in other programming languages.

14.3 Registering and Using Jini Services

The Jini runtime infrastructure defines one network-level protocol, called discovery, and two object-level protocols, called join and lookup. Briefly, discovery enables clients and services to locate lookup services, join enables a service to register itself in a lookup service and lookup enables a client to query a lookup service for available services.

14.3.1 Discovery: Finding Lookup Services

Discovery is the Jini mechanism that allows both clients and services to locate Jini lookup services. For a service provider, this allows their services to be registered with this LUS and made available to Jini clients/users. For a client, this enables the lookup of available Jini services on the network for use within a particular application. There are two ways of discovering Jini lookup services, by:

1. **The Unicast Discovery Protocol:** is used when the client or service already knows the location of the LUS, e.g., *jini://spectra.astro.cf.ac.uk*. This specifies the lookup service running on the host *spectra.astro.cf.ac.uk* on the default port (note that Jini uses its own protocol for this). Unicast lookup is used when static connections are needed between services and lookup services.
2. **The Multicast Request and Announcement Protocols:** use multicast to a local (or well known) network. As soon as a Jini service connects to the network, it broadcasts a presence announcement by sending a multicast packet onto a well-known address. Included in this packet is an IP address and port number where the Jini service can be contacted by a lookup service. Lookup services monitor this port using a multicast request for appropriate packets and when received, a lookup service makes a TCP connection to the IP address and port number extracted from the packet.

When the lookup service is contacted, it uses RMI to send an object (called the service registrar, *net.jini.core.lookup.ServiceRegistrar*) to the Jini service provider. The service registrar object facilitates further communication with the lookup service. It can return information about the available Jini groups, service identifiers (for Unicast lookup), notification (for asynchronous discovery of new services) and last, services can use the join protocol and clients can use the lookup protocol, as described in the next two sections.

14.3.2 Join: Registering a Service (Jini Service)

Once a Jini service provider has obtained a service registrar object, it can join the federation of services that are registered with the particular lookup service. To join, the service provider invokes the *register()* method on the service registrar object (see Fig. 14.4).

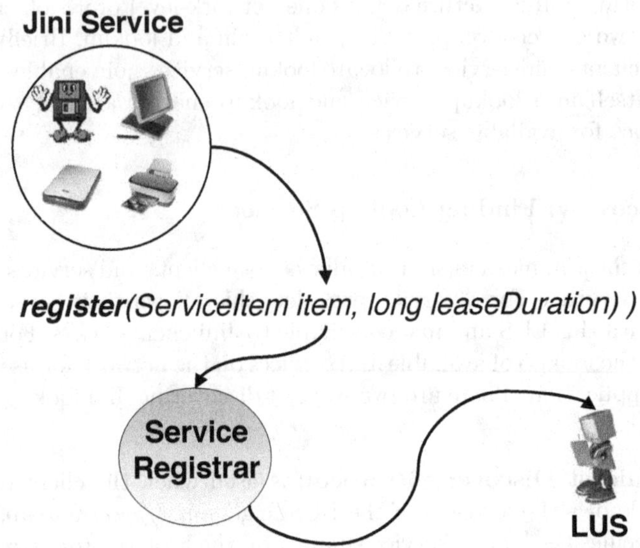

Fig. 14.4. Jini Services use the *register()* function of the *ServiceRegistar* object to join the Jini network.

There are two parameters to register: an object called a *ServiceItem* and a *lease duration.* The service item is defined as follows:

```
ServiceItem(ServiceID id, Object service, Entry[] attrSets)
```

- **id:** universally unique identifier (UUID) for registered services (128-bit value). Service IDs are intended to be generated only by lookup services, not by clients.
- **service:** the object implementing the actual Jini service, i.e., the Java proxy object.
- **attrSets:** attribute sets include extra information about the service. Examples of these are: icons; classes that provide GUIs for the service; and objects that give more information about the service.

The *leaseDuration* variable is used by Jini lookup services to keep track of active Jini services. The lease duration can be specified by the service itself or by the lookup server. Services can therefore choose either of the following defaults or set this duration themselves:

- **Lease.ANY:** the service lets the lookup service decide on the time.
- **Lease.FOREVER:** the request is for a lease that never expires.

Leasing is a way for components to register that they are alive, but allow themselves to be "timed out" if they have failed or if they are unreachable. The lookup service acts as the *granter* of the lease.

The *register()* method sends a copy of the *ServiceItem* object (using RMI) to the lookup service, where the service item is stored. This completes the *join* process and its service is now registered in the lookup service.

14.3.3 Lookup: Finding and Using Services (Jini Client)

Once a service has registered with a lookup service via the join process, it is available for use by clients who query that lookup service. To find a service, clients query lookup services via a process called *lookup*.

First, a client discovers a lookup service and obtains a service registrar object, as described. It then invokes the *lookup()* method on this object to perform a lookup:

```
Object lookup(ServiceTemplate tmpl)
```

```
public interface JiniPrinter {
   /**
   * Print the document contained in the given String or
   * throw a PrinterException explaining why the call failed
   */
   public void print(String text) throws PrinterException;
}

public class LaserPrinter implements JiniPrinter {
   public void print(String text) throws PrinterException {
// implement Laser-specific code here or throw exception
   }
}
```

Fig. 14.5. A simple example of how one might build a searchable Jini hierarchy for a definition of any printer.

The client passes a *ServiceTemplate* argument to *lookup()*, which is an object containing the search criteria for the query. The service template can include a reference to an array of *Class* objects. These objects indicate to the lookup service the Java type (or types) of the service object desired by the client. The service template can also include a *service ID*, which uniquely identifies a service, and attributes, which must exactly match the attributes uploaded by the service provider in the service item. Attributes can contain a plaintext string for describing a service, e.g., "Epson 880 Service".

The *ServiceTemplate* can also contain wildcards for any of these fields. A wildcard in the *service ID* field, for example, will match any *service ID*. The *lookup()* method sends the service template to the lookup service, which performs the query and returns the matching service objects. The client gets a reference to the matching service objects as the return value of the *lookup()* method.

In most cases, a client looks up a service by using a Java type, typically specified using a Java interface. For example, if a client wanted to use a printer, it would compose a service template that included a *Class* object for a well-known interface to printer services. All printer services would implement this well-known interface. For example, something like the code in Fig. 14.5 might be constructed to provide a generalized interface that could be implemented for any printer, whether it be a laser printer (as shown) or any other printer type.

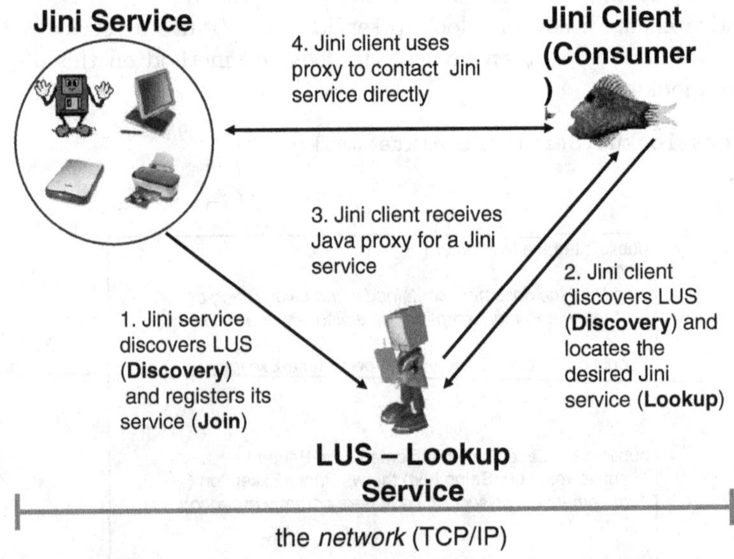

Fig. 14.6. An enhanced Jini example illustrating which Jini protocols are used at each stage of the scenario given in Fig. 14.3.

The lookup service would return a service object (or objects) that implemented this JiniPrinter interface. Attributes can be included in the service template to narrow the number of matches for such a type-based search. The client would use the printer service by invoking the service object's methods declared in the printer service interface (in this case the print() method).

14.4 Jini: Tying Things Together

In summary, therefore, in this section we insert the protocols and the relevant Java objects that are used at each stage of the Jini scenario given in Fig. 14.3. In Fig. 14.6, the actual Jini protocols that are used by the three main Jini components are illustrated. For example, here, when either the client or the service contacts the Jini LUS, it uses the *discovery* protocol; when the service wishes to add its service to the list of available Jini services, it uses the *join* protocol on the LUS; and finally, when the client wishes to search for available services that match its search criteria, it uses the *lookup* protocol.

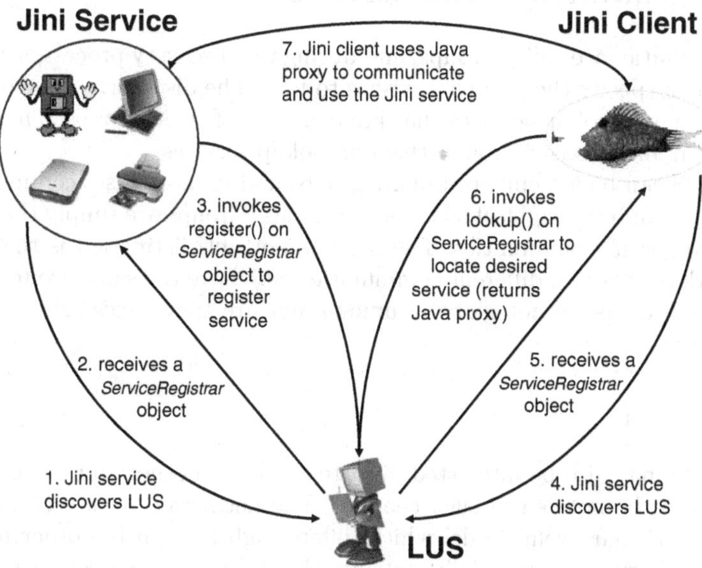

Fig. 14.7. An even more enhanced Jini example illustrating the Java objects along with the Jini protocols used at each stage of the scenario given in Fig. 14.6.

To enhance this scenario, we now add the actual Java objects that are involved at each stage of this process (see Fig. 14.7). This figure is a good overview of the entire Jini process. In Chapter 20, we will see how this is implemented and deployed within a Jini environment. Figure 14.7 gives a detailed scenario for our print example introduced in the previous section and has the following stages:

1. The Jini service uses *discovery* to locate the LUS, either by using multicast or unicast discovery.

2. The LUS returns a ServiceRegistrar object.
3. The Jini service can now use the ServiceRegistrar's register() function to register its print service with the LUS.
4. The Jini client uses discovery to locate the LUS, again either by using multicast or unicast discovery.
5. The LUS returns a ServiceRegistrar object.
6. The client uses the ServiceRegistrar's lookup() function to search for the LaserPrint service required.
7. The client receives the Java proxy (the LaserPrint interface).
8. The client executes the LaserPrint's print, which results in a remote method invocation of an implementation of the LaserPrint interface, which is connected to the remote printer and therefore the text is printed.

14.5 Organization of Jini Services

Jini communities are called groups, and during the discovery process, a service or client can specify the groups it wishes to find. The discovery protocols will then return any lookup services that are members of those groups. Therefore, grouping in Jini is based around the Jini lookup services.

An LUS can be a member of many groups and in most cases communities and groups can be thought of as the same things. Groups are simply the name used to represent communities. The most important distinction is that, due to network separation, different communities may have the same group name. Therefore, groups are not globally unique, nor are they necessarily globally accessible.

14.5.1 Events

Jini objects may also be interested in state changes in other Jini objects, and would like to be notified of such changes. The networked nature of Jini has led to a particular event model which differs slightly from the other models already in Java. Jini essentially extends the Java event model to work in a distributed environment. There are several factors which lead to this new event model design, such as: messages may be lost due to network delivery and therefore synchronous methods will fail; network delivery may delay events so events may appear in a different order than intended; and a remote listener may have disappeared by the time the event arrives so there needs to be a time-out mechanism.

Jini typically uses events of one type, the *RemoteEvent* or a small number of subclasses and conveys just enough information to allow state information to be found if needed. A remote event is *serializable* and can be moved around the network to its listeners.

In a synchronous system an interaction has the precise state and order of events. In a network system this is not so easy. Jini makes no assumptions about guarantees of delivery, and does not assume that events are delivered in order. The Jini event mechanism does not specify how events get from producer to listener (but are typically implemented by RMI calls).

The event source supplies a sequence number that could be used to construct state and ordering information if needed. This generalizes things such as timestamps on mouse events. For example, a message with id of ADD_NODE and sequence number of 3 could correspond to the state change *"added MIME type text/xml for files with suffix .tbx"*. Another event with id of REMOVE_NODE and sequence number of 4 would be taken as a later event even if it arrived earlier. The event source should be able to supply state information upon request, given the sequence number.

14.6 Conclusion

This chapter discussed the use of Jini for distributing Java objects across a network. There are three main players in Jini: a service, such as a printer, scanner, storage device, a software service, etc.; a client which would like to make use of this service; and a lookup service that is a service registration and lookup facility.

Jini clients and services discover an LUS by using the discovery protocol. Services join a Jini federation (collection of Jini services) by using the join protocol and clients locate services by using the lookup protocol. These concepts are illustrated through the use of a simple scenario which outlines the various Jini protocols and how one uses the Java objects that are used to implement these protocols.

about guarantees of delivery, and does not require that events are delivered in order. The Bully election algorithm does not specify how events get from one node to another. (This are typically implemented in MPI calls.)

Several other examples [illegible] the model [illegible] states [illegible] model, [illegible] states [illegible] (state [illegible] with id of ANODE, OK) and sequence number [illegible] corresponds to the state [illegible] (ANODE [illegible]) [illegible] MOVE, OK [illegible] event that arrived earlier. [illegible] simply state information [illegible] sequence number.

14.? Conclusion

This chapter [illegible] the use of [illegible] objects [illegible] [illegible] are [illegible] [illegible] protocol [illegible] protocol. [illegible] [illegible] to [illegible] these protocols.

15

Jxta

> *"SAN FRANCISCO, February 15 – Keynoting at the O'Reilly Peer-to-Peer Conference this morning, Bill Joy, Unix pioneer and Sun chief scientist, announced Sun's Jxta initiative to provide basic infrastructure services for P2P applications."*[1]

The Jxta[2] middleware is a set of open, generalized peer-to-peer protocols that allow any connected device (cell phone to PDA, PC to server) on the network to communicate and collaborate. Jxta is an open-source project that has been developed by a number of contributors and as such, it is still evolving. For the most recent Jxta Technology Specification, see [24].

The goal of project Jxta is to develop and standardize basic building blocks and services to enable developers to build and deploy interoperable P2P services and applications. The Jxta project intends to address this problem by providing a simple and generic P2P platform to host any kind of network services. The term Jxta is short for juxtapose, as in side by side. It is a recognition that P2P is juxtaposed to client/server or Web-based computing, which is today's traditional distributed-computing model. Jxta provides a common set of open protocols[3] and an open-source reference implementation for developing P2P applications.

15.1 Background: Why Was Project Jxta Started?

Project Jxta was originally conceived by Sun Microsystems, Inc. and designed with the participation of a small number of experts from academic institutions

[1] Bill Joy's keynote in 2001, introducing the Jxta project, can be found at `http://tim.oreilly.com/pub/a//p2p/2001/02/15/joy_keynote.html`.

[2] We use the lowercase version of Jxta to be consistent with other terms used in this book; that is, Jxta is not an acronym so we do not write it as one.

[3] The Jxta protocols are open and generalized but they are not standardized.

and industry. This team identified a number of shortcomings in many existing P2P systems and set up project Jxta in order to address these. The three main objectives were to achieve interoperability, platform independence and ubiquity.

15.1.1 Interoperability

Jxta notes that current P2P systems are built for delivering a single type of services, e.g.:

- Napster provides music file sharing.
- Gnutella provides decentralized file sharing.
- AIM provides instant messaging.
- SETI@home performs specific computations on specific data. Recently, however, the BOINC project has generalized this into a standard platform for use by other applications but even in this case it is specific to the CPU sharing class of applications.

Each software vendor tends to create specific code for each of these services, which results in incompatible systems; i.e., they cannot interoperate. Consequently, there is much duplication in the effort of creating the middleware primitives commonly used by all P2P systems. Project Jxta attempts to provide a common language that all peers can use to talk to each other.

15.1.2 Platform Independence

Jxta technology is designed to be independent of:

- programming languages, e.g., C or Java
- system platforms, e.g., Microsoft Windows and UNIX
- networking platforms (such as TCP/IP or Bluetooth)

This set of criteria solves a number of development issues including code duplication and incompatibility. For example, many P2P systems offer services through APIs that are tied to a particular operating system using a specific networking protocol; i.e., one system might use C++ APIs on Windows over TCP/IP, whilst another uses a C API hosted on UNIX systems over TCP/IP but also requiring HTTP. A P2P developer is then forced to choose which set of APIs to use and consequently, which set of P2P customers to target. Further, if the developer wants to target both communities, then he may have to develop the services twice, one for each platform (or develop a bridge system between them).

Jxta achieves programming language and platform independence through the use of the Jxta protocols being defined in a textual representation (i.e., XML) and the networking independence is achieved through the use of Jxta pipes (described in Section 15.3.3).

It should be noted that Jxta is not original in this respect. A number of distributed-systems technologies are based on exchanging XML messages, e.g., Web Services. XML represents a common format that enables applications to abstract the message format into a programming language-neutral representation. For example, a SOAP (see Chapter 16)) performs a similar operation, that is, all communications between SOAP endpoints are represented in XML. A Jxta binding or a SOAP processor converts language-specific internal representations into and out of XML, which enables various programming languages to interoperate at this textual representation level. As long as you can map into and out of text, any client or server can encode or decode the information. Therefore, XML is the key here to interoperability, not Jxta.

15.1.3 Ubiquity

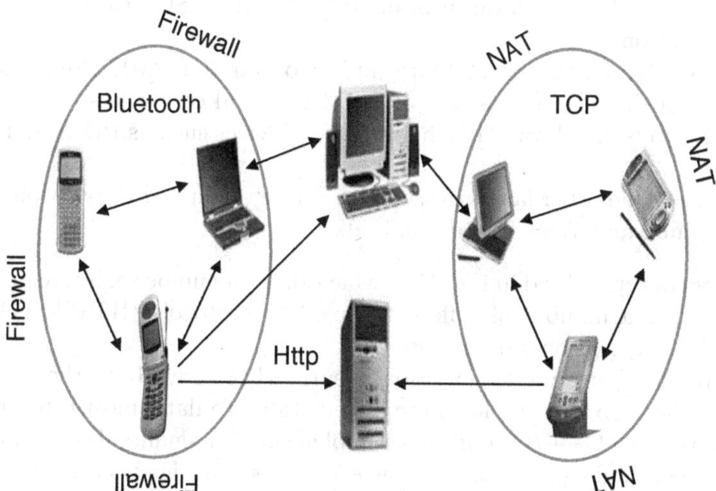

Fig. 15.1. Jxta networks are designed to work on all kinds of devices, underlying transport mechanisms and operating systems.

Another problem Jxta addresses is in the limitations of the deployment of applications to a particular set of devices either due to incompatibility issues and transport problems or that they are too complicated for particular devices due to size limitations. Jxta technology is designed to be implementable on "every device with a digital heartbeat" [24]. For example, devices that could join a Jxta network include:

- PDAs
- phones
- sensors

- consumer electronics
- network routers
- appliances
- desktop computers
- data-center servers
- storage systems

For example, currently many P2P systems tend to choose Microsoft Windows as their target deployment platform (unsurprisingly since this is the largest installed base and therefore the fastest path to profit) resulting in many Wintel-specific dependencies. Even though the earliest demonstrations of P2P capabilities are on Wintel machines, it is very likely that the greatest proliferation of P2P technology will occur at the two ends of the spectrum, e.g., large systems in the enterprise and consumer-oriented small systems. Current Jxta implementations include:

- Jxta for the Java 2 Platform Standard Edition (J2SE); the reference implementation
- Jxta (JXME) for the Java 2 Platform Micro Edition (J2ME); for MIDP-1.0 compliant devices such as cell phones, PDAs and controllers
- Jxta for Personal JavaTM technology; for devices such as PDAs and Webpads
- Jxta for C and other languages such as Perl, Python and Ruby, Mon (C#), Arm-Linux and WinCE and Smalltalk.[4]

This is conceptualised in Fig. 15.1, which shows a number of interconnected devices, using a number of different transport protocols (HTTP, TCP/IP, Bluetooth, etc.) and operating systems.

The most mature implementation is currently in Java but other versions exist. See the Web site [24] for more information. To date, most other implementations (e.g., C++/C) only have implemented a small subsection of the Jxta protocols and can only be used as *edge peers*. An edge peer is a peer that cannot function as anything more than a simple Jxta peer; i.e., it cannot be a *rendezvous* or *relay*, for example. Here, we will base our discussion on the Java Jxta version.

15.2 Jxta Overview

Project Jxta defines a set of six protocols that can be used to construct P2P systems using a centralized, brokered or decentralized approach but its main aim is to facilitate the creation of decentralized systems. In this section, we describe these protocols and other components of a Jxta application.

---

[4] Typically only implementing edge-peer functionality.

15.2.1 The Jxta Architecture

The Jxta protocols standardize the manner in which peers:

- Discover each other
- Self-organize into peer groups
- Advertise and discover network services
- Communicate with each other
- Monitor each other

The Jxta protocols do not require the use of any particular programming language or operating system; network transport or topology; or authentication, security or encryption model. The Jxta protocols therefore allow heterogeneous devices with completely different software stacks to interoperate.

Figure 15.2 shows that the common layering structure defined by Jxta is broken down into three layers:

1. **Jxta Core:** at the lower level is the core layer that deals with peer establishment, communication management (such as routing) and other low-level "plumbing."
2. **Jxta Services:** second, there is a service layer that deals with higher-level concepts, such as indexing, searching and file sharing. These services make heavy use of the plumbing features provided by the core but further, can be commonly used as components in P2P systems.
3. **Jxta Applications:** at the upper level, there is an applications layer, such as file sharing, auctioning and storage systems.

Some features (e.g., security) exist throughout the P2P system (although in different forms). Jxta technology is designed to provide a thin layer on top of which services and applications are built using powerful primitives.

Briefly, the Jxta protocols are: the *Peer Resolver Protocol* (PRP) is the mechanism by which a peer can send a query to one or more peers, and receive a response (or multiple responses) to the query. The *Peer Discovery Protocol* (PDP) is the mechanism by which a peer can advertise its own resources, and discover the resources from other peers (peer groups, services, pipes and additional peers). The *Peer Information Protocol* (PIP) is the mechanism by which a peer may obtain status information about other peers, such as state, uptime, traffic load and capabilities. The *Pipe Binding Protocol* (PBP) is used to connect pipes between peers. The *Endpoint Routing Protocol* (ERP) is used to route Jxta messages. Finally, the *Rendezvous Protocol* (RVP) is the mechanism by which peers can subscribe or be a subscriber to a propagation service. The Jxta protocols are described in more detail in Section 15.4.

15.2.2 Jxta Peers

A peer is any networked device that implements one or more of the Jxta protocols (see Fig. 15.3). Each peer operates independently and asynchronously

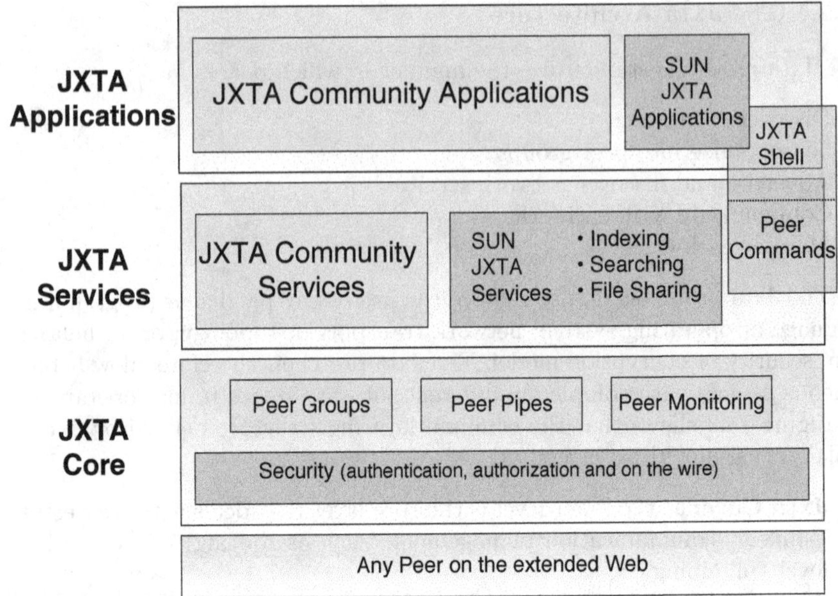

Fig. 15.2. The Jxta software architecture.

from all other peers, and is uniquely identified by a *Peer ID* (identifiers, like in Gnutella). Peers publish one or more network interfaces (advertisements) for use with the Jxta protocols, which are passed around the network in datagrams (messages). Peers can form transient or persistent relationships (peer groups). Each published interface is advertised as a peer endpoint, which is used to establish direct point-to-point (but not fixed) connections between two peers (pipes). These are discussed in more detail in the rest of this section.

A Jxta peer therefore is any entity that can speak the protocols required of a peer. This is akin to the Internet, where an Internet node is any entity that can speak the suite of IP protocols. As such, a peer can manifest in the form of a processor, a process, a machine or a user. Importantly, a peer does not need to understand all six protocols as a peer can still perform at a reduced level if it does not support a protocol.

A Jxta peer, just like a Gnutella servent, can be a client and a server. Furthermore, Jxta peers can act as rendezvous nodes, which are meeting places (or lookup servers) for other Jxta nodes.

15.2.3 Identifiers

Jxta uses UUID, a 128-bit datum to refer to an entity (see Fig. 15.3), e.g., a peer, an advertisement, a service, etc.; recall that Gnutella used the same mechanism to identify messages, albeit in a cruder form. It is easy to guarantee

JXTA Terms, at a glance

Peer: any networked device that implements **one** or **more** of the **JXTA protocols**

Advertisements: XML structured document that names, describes, and publishes the existence of a resource e.g. peer, peer group, pipe, or service

Messages: sent between peers, can be XML or binary

Identifiers: each JXTA entity e.g. peer, advert etc has a UUID identifier

Rendezvous Nodes: caching nodes for advertisements – similar to super/ reflector nodes

Pipes: messages are sent through virtual pipes

Peer Group: virtual entity that speaks the set of peer group protocols

Relay Nodes: JXTA routers – help to route messages via firewalls, NAT systems etc – i.e. they relay the message to other peers

Fig. 15.3. Brief definitions for a number of the key Jxta terms.

that each entity has a unique UUID within a local runtime environment, but because any global state is not assumed, there is no absolute way to provide a guarantee of uniqueness across an entire community that may consist of millions of peers. Jxta tackles this by binding the UUID to other information such as a name and a network address.

15.2.4 Advertisements

An advertisement is an XML structured document that names, describes and publishes the existence of a resource, such as a peer, a peer group, a pipe or a service (see Fig. 15.3). Jxta technology defines a basic set of advertisements but more advertisement subtypes can be formed from these basic types using XML schemas, or more typically by using the particular language binding, e.g., in Java, you would subclass the *Advertisement* class.

15.2.5 Messages

A message is an object that is sent between Jxta peers that can be represented in either XML or binary format (see Fig. 15.3). The Java binding uses the binary format to encapsulate the message payload. Services can use the most appropriate format for that transport. A service that requires a compact representation, for example, for sending scientific data, can use the binary representation, while other services can use XML.

A Jxta message is the basic unit of data exchange between peers. Messages are sent and received using the *Pipe Service* and routed using the *Endpoint Service*. Typically, applications interface with the *Pipe Service* directly and the routing is hidden behind the scenes.

A message is a set of name/value pairs represented as an XML document. The content can be an arbitrary type. The Jxta protocols are specified as a set of messages exchanged between peers. Each software platform binding describes how a message is converted to and from a native data structure such as a Java object or a C structure.

15.2.6 Modules

Jxta modules are an abstraction used to represent any piece of "code" used to implement a behaviour in a Jxta network (see Fig. 15.3). The module abstraction does not specify what this "code" is: it can be a Java class, a Java jar, a dynamic library DLL, a set of XML messages or a script. The implementation of the module behaviour is left to module implementers. For example, modules can be used to represent different implementations of a network service on different operating system platforms in a similar fashion to Web service implementations (see Chapter 7).

15.3 Jxta Network Overlay

Conceptually, Jxta consists of a collection of peers which interact and are organized in a number of ways. The organization of Jxta peers is independent of the underlying physical devices and connectivity (see Fig. 15.4). Here, it can be seen that Jxta peers are arranged within a virtual overlay which sits on top of the physical devices, as mentioned in Chapter 1. Peers are not required to have direct point-to-point network connections between each only (through the use of pipes) and they can discover each other on the network to form transient or persistent relationships called peer groups. These concepts are described in the following two sections.

15.3.1 Peer Groups

A peer group is a virtual entity that speaks the set of peer group protocols (see Fig. 15.3). Typically, a peer group is a collection of cooperating peers providing a common set of services; e.g., you could have a file sharing peer group, a CPU sharing peer group (see Fig. 15.5). Therefore, peer groups are typically formed and self-organized based upon the mutual interest of peers and

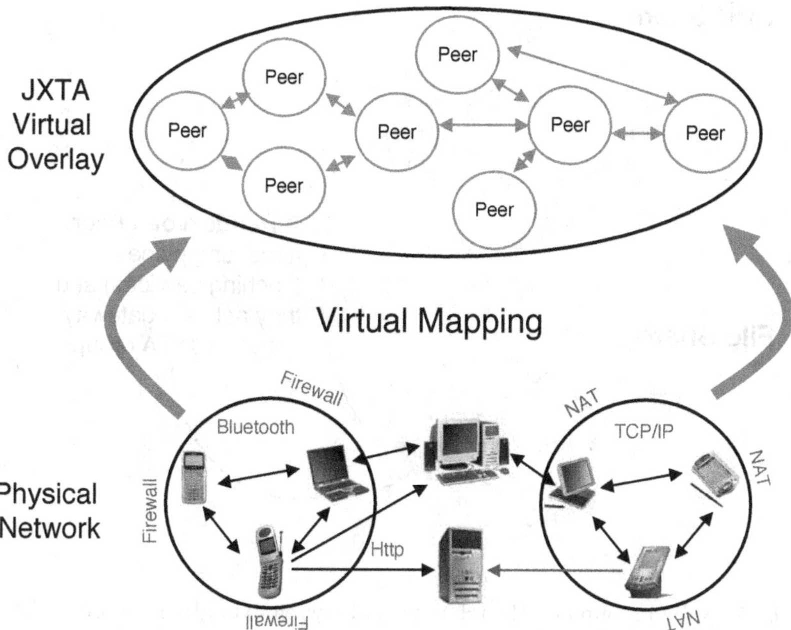

Fig. 15.4. The virtual network overlay used within Jxta providing the applications with a virtual view of the physical underlying network.

therefore provide a scoping environment for the group. Peer group boundaries define the search scope when searching for a group's content.

Peer groups can also be used to create a monitoring environment, monitoring a set of peers for any special purpose (heartbeat, traffic introspection, accountability, etc.). Peer groups can be password protected and implement local security policies if secure groups are desired. There is one special group, called the *World Peer Group* (the default peer group a peer joins), which includes all Jxta peers (see Chapter 21).

15.3.2 Rendezvous Nodes

To compensate for the absence of a central service (such as a domain name server), a Jxta network uses rendezvous peers. Rendezvous peers are volunteers who have agreed to act as a meeting point (or a caching server) for other peers. Rendezvous peers often maintain a permanent (early bound) IP address, so that other peers can contact them to check the current bindings of dynamic (late bound) peer endpoints. Rendezvous peers may also keep a record of other rendezvous peers. Therefore, if you know a rendezvous point and your friend also knows a rendezvous point, and the two rendezvous points know each other (directly or through other rendezvous points), you and your friend can find and reach each other, as illustrated in Fig. 15.5.

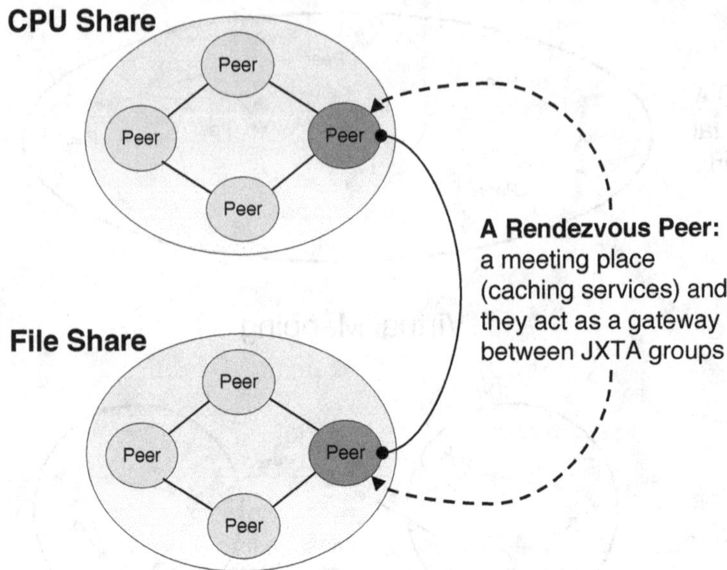

Fig. 15.5. A Jxta group and the relationship between Jxta groups through the use of rendezvous nodes.

Rendezvous nodes can be used to automatically configure intranets by using multicast but they can be configured as permanent unicast servers also. Rendezvous points are similar in concept to Gnutella super-peers in that they cache the peer advertisements (which can be anything including files) that peers use to publish the services they offer. Rendezvous nodes, therefore, are an integral part of scalability in Jxta. There can be many rendezvous nodes per group (as there are super-peers within a Gnutella network) and they allow the network to implement a centralized/decentralized network structure. Applications do not have to worry about these low-level details. Peers just send search messages to the rendezvous points they know and the Jxta network will do what's necessary by itself.

15.3.3 Pipes

Jxta peers use pipes to send messages to each other (see Fig. 15.3). Pipes are an asynchronous and unidirectional message transfer mechanism used for service communication. Pipes support the transfer of any object, including binary code, data strings and Java technology-based objects.

The pipe endpoints (see Fig. 15.6) are referred to as the input pipe (the receiving end) and the output pipe (the sending end). Messages flow from the output pipe into the input pipes.

Pipes are virtual communication channels and may connect peers that do not have a direct physical link. In the example given in the upper section of

Fig. 15.6, *Peer 1* has created a virtual Jxta pipe between itself and *Peer 2*. The actual physical route, however, that this connection travels is through a firewall, via a desktop (*Peer 3*) and a server (*Peer 4*). The number of intermediaries used to communicate a message is known as the number of *hops*.

Further, at each hop of this network a different transport protocol may be used as pipes are independent of any particular communication mechanism. To date, there are four implementations: HTTP, TCP, BEEP and Reliable Multicast. Pipes dynamically switch at runtime depending on what is available for use. In some sense, a pipe can be viewed as an abstract, named message queue that supports a number of abstract operations such as create, open, close, delete, send and receive. Pipes offer two modes of communication, point-to-point and propagate, as seen in the lower part of Fig. 15.6.

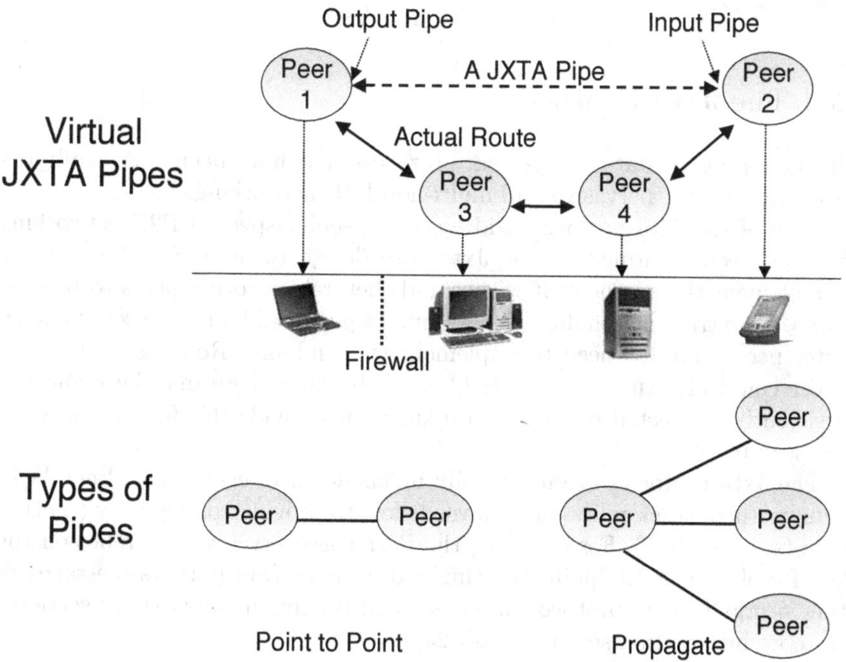

Fig. 15.6. A Jxta pipe is not a fixed one-to-one connection. It can traverse through multiple hops and networks before the message reaches its destination. Also, the two types of Jxta pipes, point-to-point and propagate, are shown.

A point-to-point pipe connects exactly two pipe endpoints: an input pipe on one peer receives messages sent from the output pipe of another peer. A propagate pipe connects one output pipe to multiple input pipes. The Jxta core also provides secure unicast pipes, a secure variant of the point-to-point pipe that provides a secure communication channel.

15.3.4 Relay Nodes

A Jxta relay peer is a kind of Jxta router for Jxta messages (see Fig. 15.3). There are many examples of why these are needed. They can be used to help traverse firewalls or to help micro-Jxta nodes. For example, the Java Jxta version for micro devices (e.g., PDAs using J2ME) simply talks to a Jxta relay (a message relaying peer), which in turn bears most of the message processing (such as XML authoring for advertisements, sending search messages across the Jxta network and so forth) and relaying burden. A J2ME-based peer, together with a Jxta relay, is functionally equivalent to a normal Jxta peer. Therefore, J2ME peers act as an edge device, sitting on the perimeter of a Jxta network.

15.4 The Jxta Protocols

The Jxta protocols are a set of six protocols that have been specifically designed for ad hoc, pervasive and multi-hop P2P networking.

Each of the Jxta protocols addresses a specific aspect of P2P networking that has been identified by the Jxta core design team. A peer can choose to implement the protocols it wishes and then rely on other peers to provide them with extra functionality. For example, a peer could rely on a set of known router peers and not need to implement the Endpoint Routing Protocol or a peer could elect not to be a *rendezvous* because there may be dedicated persistently connected peers that are known to provide this functionality for their group.

The Jxta protocols are not totally independent of each other. Each layer in its protocol stack relies on its layer below to provide connectivity to other peers (see Fig. 15.7). For example, the Peer Discovery Protocol relies on the Peer Resolver and Endpoint Routing protocols to transport its messages to other peers. The six protocols are described briefly, in the next six sections. For more information see [193] and [24].

15.4.1 The Peer Discovery Protocol

A peer uses the peer discovery protocol to discover a Jxta resource. Jxta resources are described by XML advertisements, as mentioned previously. Note that the first word, peer, is the subject and not necessarily the object. Using this protocol, peers can advertise their own resources, and discover the resources from other peers.

Jxta does not mandate exactly how discovery is done. It can be decentralized, centralized, or a hybrid of the two. There are two levels of discovery:

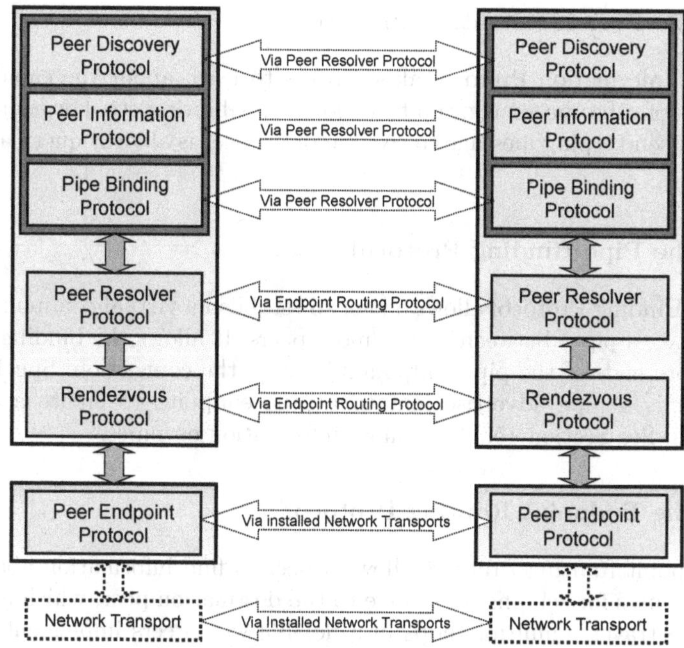

Fig. 15.7. The layering of the six Jxta protocols.

joining a Jxta network and discovering a Jxta resource within a Jxta network. Further, there are two methods of joining a Jxta network:

1. **Multicast:** which uses the multicast protocol to a local (or well known) network, i.e., as soon as a Jxta peer connects to the network, it broadcasts a presence announcement by sending a multicast packet onto a well-known port. Other peers monitor this port using multicast requests for appropriate packets and when received, make contact with the other peers.
2. **Point-to-Point, i.e., Unicast:** which is used when the peer knows the location of a Jxta peer, typically a rendezvous node (or a collection of known peers) and therefore can contact it directly. Typically, peers search for several rendezvous nodes for redundancy.

Once a peer has joined the Jxta network, it can find out about Jxta resources in several ways. For example, a peer can use cascaded discovery; that is, if a peer discovers a second peer, the first peer can view its horizon and discover other peers or rendezvous points and so on.

15.4.2 The Peer Resolver Protocol

The Peer Resolver Protocol enables a peer to implement high-level search capabilities, allowing a peer to send and receive generic queries to find or search for peers, or other generic advertisements.

15.4.3 The Peer Information Protocol

This Peer Information Protocol allows peers to learn about the capabilities and status of other peers, e.g., up time, load, capabilities, etc. For example, a peer could send a ping message to see if another peer is alive or query a peer's properties.

15.4.4 The Pipe Binding Protocol

The Pipe Binding Protocol allows a peer to establish a virtual communication channel (i.e., a pipe) between one or more peers. It allows the binding of the two or more ends of the pipe endpoints forming the connection. Specifically, a peer binds a pipe advertisement to a pipe endpoint to create a virtual connection. See Section 15.3.3 for more information on pipes.

15.4.5 The Endpoint Routing Protocol

This Endpoint Routing Protocol allows a peer to find information about the available routes for sending a message to the destination peer, which allows a message to traverse multiple hops in a flexible way. Peers implementing the Endpoint Routing Protocol respond to queries with available route information giving a list of gateways along the route.

15.4.6 The Rendezvous Protocol

The Rendezvous Protocol allows a peer to send messages to all the listeners of the service. By default, query messages only reach peers within the same physical network. The Rendezvous Protocol defines how a peer can subscribe or be a subscriber to a propagation service allowing larger communities to form. A rendezvous node's scope is a peer group. The Rendezvous Protocol allows a peer to propagate messages to all the listeners of the service.

15.5 A Jxta Scenario: Fitting Things Together

A Jxta peer, just like a Gnutella servent, can be a client and a server. Furthermore, Jxta peers can act as rendezvous nodes, which act as meeting places (or lookup servers) for other Jxta nodes. Figure 15.8 gives a scenario of how a peer joins a Jxta network, performs a search query and locates a file for download.

The various Jxta protocols involved in the operation at each stage are described below:

1. The rendezvous node (RV) accepts connection for nodes 1 to 7 and stores their advertisements locally.

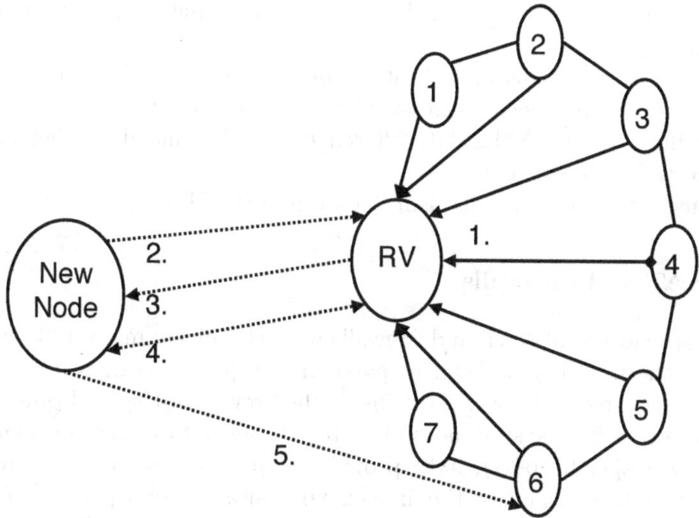

Fig. 15.8. A connection scenario for a simple file search using Jxta.

2. A *new node* then contacts the RV using a discovery mechanism, e.g., Unicast/multicast via the peer discovery protocol.
3. RV authenticates the *new node* and adds the new node to the group.
4. The *new node* performs a file search query by contacting the RV to search for local match or to propagate this query to all other members in the group. The file is eventually found on node 6. This uses the peer Discovery Protocol, the peer resolver protocol and the Endpoint Routing Protocol.
5. The *new node* and node 6 set up and communicate directly through a Jxta pipe. This connection is virtual and may actually traverse (route) through the RV node and node 7. This step uses the Pipe Binding Protocol, the Peer Resolver Protocol and the Endpoint Routing Protocol.

Note here, that peers can volunteer to become rendezvous peers. They do this when they join the Jxta network using the Jxta configurator (see Section 21.1.1).

15.6 Jxta Environment Considerations

15.6.1 Security

Jxta does not enforce specific security approaches but provides the following security primitives:

- Cryptography: hash functions (e.g., MD5), symmetric encryption algorithms (e.g., RC4) and asymmetric cryptographic algorithms (e.g., Diffie-Hellman and RSA)

- An authentication framework based on PAM (Pluggable Authentication Module)
- Password-based login scheme that can be plugged into the PAM framework
- An access control mechanism based on peer groups; i.e., members of the group have access to the data offered by another member whereas non-members do not
- A transport security mechanism, based on SSL/TLS

15.6.2 NAT and Firewalls

The widespread use of NAT and firewalls severely affects many P2P systems and hence the usability of Jxta. In particular, a peer outside a firewall or a NAT gateway cannot discover peers inside the firewall or the NAT gateway. In the absence of asking system administrators to let Jxta traffic through (e.g., by opening a specific port), Jxta provides some solutions to this problem. Specifically, Jxta peers inside the firewall can contact a relay peer, outside the firewall, in order to advertise its services. It can then periodically contact the relay peer to retrieve messages. The relay effectively acts as a broker for the firewalled peer.

15.7 Comment

It is hard to see how Jxta protocols can compete with the mass of standardized XML technologies used in Web Services and the like. Without widespread support from the community at large, the momentum will surely be difficult to sustain, or will it? Many have commented on this approach, for example, [194].

15.8 Conclusion

The Jxta protocols define how peers can locate, communicate and collaborate with other peers within multi-hop pervasive P2P networks. Jxta peers can operate on a wide range of heterogeneous devices, which can run on any programming language, computer platform or networking protocols, through the use of XML.

Jxta peers live within a virtual network overlay and are organized in peer groups. Each peer group can have one or more rendezvous nodes which act as a local propagation service for advertisements of Jxta resources (pipes, peers, services, etc.). Jxta also supports relaying which allows smaller devices with limited functionality to join the Jxta network and gives a support mechanism for traversing firewalls. A typical file-sharing scenario illustrated how these mechanisms fit together.

16

Web Services Protocols

> *"If this thing is going to be called Web Services, then I insist that it actually have something to do with the Web." Roy Fielding on the W3C TAG mailing list, April 23 2002*

The aim of the Web Service protocols is to provide a means of describing data and behavior in a machine-processable way. Web Services use XML to describe metadata for discovery purposes and to define behaviour, and in general presume that XML documents will be the payload of the messages exchanged. These XML documents are not typically descriptions of resources in the sense that the Web exchanges resource representations, but rather encoded data that can trigger operations and responses from remote hosts. As such, Web Services are akin to distributed object technologies. Indeed, SOAP originally stood for Simple Object Access Protocol and early versions influenced the XML Remote Procedure Call (XML-RPC) specification [195].

This affinity with distributed object approaches, as well as the way in which Web Services use the Web, has meant they have had their detractors, as the quote above demonstrates. The debate between the Web Services community and the Web community led to the so-called SOAP versus REST war that raged from 2002 until roughly 2007 with no outright victor. Currently, in 2008, a mood of sometimes resigned acceptance has fallen on the debate with many authors suggesting that both approaches are suitable for different kinds of systems, in terms of scale, heterogeneity and underlying purpose. Those with reservations about Web Services technologies argue that they go against the grain of the Web, because they do not use its existing infrastructure, such as URIs for identifying resources, and HTTP for modelling behaviour. Instead, SOAP and WSDL define their requirements from scratch and merely use Web technology to expose and transfer these formats. Furthermore, during the period in which a plethora of Web Services specifications were being developed (see Section 16.4 for some of the most salient), many argued that the quantity and their complexity would lead to unmanageable and brittle systems. At the core, this debate was about differences in architectural approaches, in particular between object-orientation, service-orientation and resource-orientation. The abstractions underpinning these architectures and the relationships between them are described in Section 8.4.

Despite the debates surrounding them, Web Services technologies have seen wide acceptance, particularly within the business community, in part because business processes are naturally modelled in terms of component behaviour, fine-grained data typing, and business policies such as security, something Web Service technologies are good at.

The basic building blocks underlying Web Services are the service-oriented architecture (SOA) and Internet protocols. Service-oriented architecture using Web Service technologies provides a means for achieving interoperability between businesses, as well as component reuse both within and beyond a single organization. Within an SOA, services can be represented, advertised, discovered and communicated within a dynamic environment. In this chapter, the Web Service technologies, SOAP, WSDL and UDDI that can enable such an environment, are outlined. We then look at some of the extensions to these core technologies that are used to model complex service policies and requirements.

16.1 SOAP

The submission of SOAP v1.1 to the WC3 (by 11 vendors in May 2000)[1] and the subsequent starting of the XML Protocols Working Group were significant events in Web Services history. SOAP v1.2 reached recommendation status in June 2003, which is the highest recommendation of a standard that the WC3 can give.[2] To illustrate the level of support, SOAP has currently been implemented in over 60 languages on over 20 platforms.

SOAP is a "protocol that can be used to exchange structured information in a decentralized, distributed environment" [196]. It provides an XML format for sending messages which is independent of programming language or computer platform. It also allows this communication to occur over HTTP, which simplifies things greatly; that is, it helps with firewalls and can be integrated with existing server-side infrastructure.

16.1.1 Just Like Sending a Letter

A SOAP message is analogous to a letter, as depicted in Fig. 16.1. First you write a letter and then put it in an envelope, which includes the receiver's

[1] UserLand, Ariba, Commerce One, Compaq, Developmentor, HP, IBM, IONA, Lotus, Microsoft and SAP.

[2] However, WC3 does not call its specifications standards because it does not have the official standing of a standards organization, such as the International Organization for Standardization.

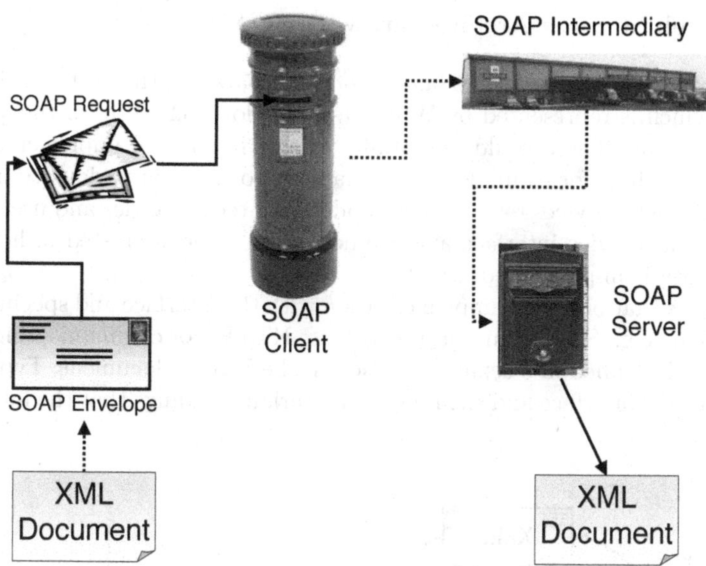

Fig. 16.1. SOAP provides an envelope for the XML message, just like a real envelope.

address and other routing information (e.g., specifying air mail), plus a stamp representing a means of payment.

In SOAP, you write a document, just like a letter, but it is written in XML. Then you pop your XML document into a SOAP envelope. The SOAP envelope contains your document (in the *body* element) along with a header that can contain optional routing and security information; it could be used to add the name or identification of the sender for example (just as real letters that are sent to the United States).

Once the envelope has been created, it is converted into a SOAP request and passed to a SOAP client for delivery; just like putting our letter in a postbox. The SOAP client takes this message and delivers it to the destination. Such a delivery may traverse several intermediate SOAP servers before it reaches its destination, just as a letter may be transported by bus and then a plane, for example. The actual route the SOAP message travels depends on the (optional) routing information that may have been included in the message header, e.g., like specifying *Air Mail* will, *it is hoped*, make your letter fly across to its destination.

When the SOAP message reaches its destination, it is handled by a receiver, i.e., a SOAP server. The SOAP server performs extra operations than our letter box counterpart, however, as it unwraps the envelope for you and passes the Web Service the message via whatever means it needs.

16.1.2 Web Services Architecture with SOAP

Web Services enable *service virtualization* by separating the Web Service interface, which is represented by WSDL (see Section 16.2.3), from the service implementation. There could potentially exist a number of implementations for a service that, for example, could enable it to work on various computer platforms. Web Services remove these underlying technicalities and users only deal with the service interface and are not aware of or interested in how the functionality is implemented.

The *glue* that binds the implementation with the interface and specifies the data format (e.g., SOAP) and protocols (e.g., HTTP) for communicating with the service is defined in a separate section in the WSDL document. Typically, you define one interface and then insert the various bindings that the interface supports.

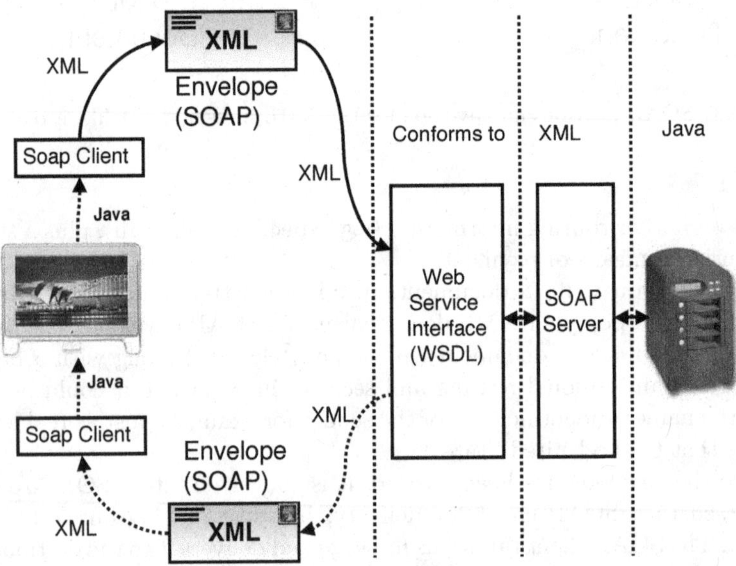

Fig. 16.2. An overview of how a message gets sent from a client to a Web service using SOAP.

This architecture is illustrated in Fig. 16.3, which builds on the model described in Section 7.2.2. Here, a C++ client is invoking a Web Service written in Java. The figure also gives the details of the various stages and how they relate to SOAP. SOAP messages are delivered from a client to a SOAP server in the following way:

- The user prepares a message that conforms to the service interface (i.e., the WSDL). For example, the service may have several input elements and therefore the message has to be formatted appropriately in order to convey this information correctly. This typically involves building up a list of variables or strings in the client's language (e.g., C++ here) in preparation.

- The user sends this message to the Web Service:
  - The client sends the request to the SOAP client, typically as a method call (in this case in C++). Programmers never really need to deal with the XML directly; there are numerous utilities that do this for you.
  - The SOAP client takes this request and converts it into an XML message.
  - The SOAP client then puts this message into the body of a SOAP envelope and populates the other elements with optional information provided by the user.
  - The SOAP client then makes a SOAP request document, which adds things like destination and transport protocols to the SOAP message and sends this to the receiving SOAP server.
  - The SOAP server then transforms this XML message back to a language-dependent representation. For example, it could convert the XML to Java to invoke a function call within a Java class that implements the service.[3]
- The SOAP server then uses the same mechanisms to send the response, if there is any, from the Web Service back to the client.

16.1.3 The Anatomy of a SOAP Message

A SOAP message is an XML document containing the following elements, as shown in Fig. 16.3:

1. An *Envelope* that identifies the XML document as a SOAP message (*required*).
2. A *Header* element that contains information about the request defined in the SOAP body. For example, it might contain security, contextual or user profile information (*optional*).
3. A *Body* element that contains the actual *Payload Document*, containing the request and response in XML format (*required*).
4. A *Fault* element that provides error information that may have occurred while processing the message (*optional*).

In the example below, a request/response message for obtaining the price of a CD from a fictional CD retailer is given. In this example, we show a SOAP message with a *Header* element and a *Body* element:

---

[3] You may have surmised by now that implementations of the Web are quite simple because the underlying infrastructure takes care of a number of housekeeping issues.

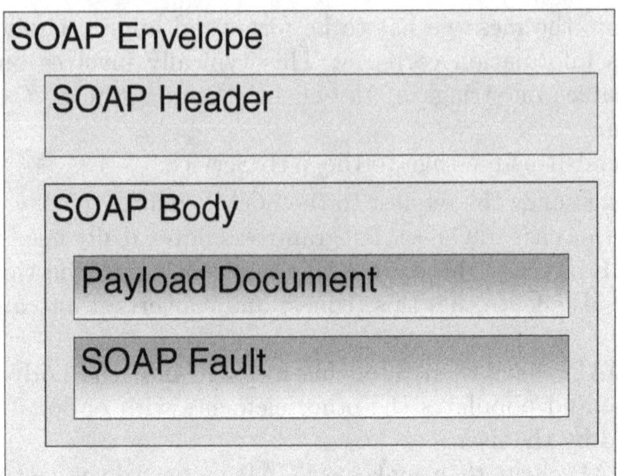

Fig. 16.3. The anatomy of a SOAP message.

```
<SOAP:Envelope
  xmlns:SOAP="http://schemas.xmlsoap.org/soap/envelope/"
  SOAP:encodingStyle="http://schemas.xmlsoap.org/soap/encoding/">

  <SOAP:Header>
    <person:mail
     xmlns:fan="//http://www.ibycds.com/">tapfan@ibycds.com
    </person:mail>
  </SOAP:Header>

  <SOAP:Body>
      <m:getCDPrice xmlns:m="http://www.islcds.com/">
            <name xsi:type="xsd:string">Smell the Glove</name>
       </m:getCDPrice>
  </SOAP:Body>
</SOAP:Envelope>
```

A SOAP *Envelope* normally requires defining two basic *namespaces* for the envelope and for the encoding, as shown. The namespace for the envelope (this is SOAP 1.1) must be included as it identifies the message as a SOAP message. Messages that do not follow this namespace declaration are considered invalid. Here, a namespace is also given for the encoding style, which represents the data used in the message.

The *Header* element is optional, but if included, must also be namespace qualified. Namespaces are analogous to Java *packages*: Java packages give a Java class a namespace in order to differentiate it from a class with the same name in a different package. Java classes are therefore grouped into packages by functionality, whereas namespaces just provide a unique context for an element. Here, the body contains information about the buyer of the CD.

The *Body* element is required and specifies the payload intended for the receiver of the message. Here it contains a procedure, called *getCDPrice*, which accepts one argument to specify the name of the CD for which you wish to obtain the price. The argument is typed as a string.

The example here provides only a brief overview. For a comprehensive description of SOAP documents, see [196] or [107].

16.2 WSDL

The Web Services Description Language (WSDL) is "an XML format for describing network services as a set of endpoints operating on messages containing either document-oriented or procedural-oriented information" [197]. WSDL describes an abstract interface for Web Services while simultaneously allowing you to bind to a specific transport mechanism, such as HTTP. WSDL functions as a reusable Web Service technology by abstracting the interface and providing a transport binding mechanism; i.e., the transport may change, but the payload persists. There are similar techniques employed in other technologies, e.g., Jxta pipes (Section 15.3.3).

WSDL was developed by Microsoft, Ariba and IBM and V1.1 of the specification was accepted by the World Wide Web Consortium (W3C) as a note [197]. Twenty-two other companies then joined the submission (the largest number to date to support a joint submission) and therefore WSDL already has broad support.

String is King
XML is an encoding mechanism in which arbitrary data structures are described using character strings. When exchanging data in XML format you need a mechanism for defining how a data type is encoded and how actual data (an instance of a data type) is mapped to the type. XML Schema are most commonly used in the context of Web Services for this purpose. XML Schema are templates defining the structures of data types allowing you to create, validate and extract information from the instance. There are a number of data types that are built-in *to XML Schema, for example booleans, integers, character strings and dates to name a few, and there are default rules for mapping these to character strings. These are not always sufficient however. Applications may need to exchange complicated, hierarchical, and domain specific structures. XML Schema allow the definition of types through containment, extension and restriction of both built-in types and other application-defined complex types. In a typical Web Services scenario, tools are used to generate XML Schema from programming language objects at the server side. At the client side, similar tools are used to generate programming language objects from XML Schema. This allows nodes using different programming languages and frameworks to share data types over the wire. For a more detailed overview of XML Schema and related technologies, see Chapter 3.*

WSDL documents can be flexibly organized by using the *import* element, which allows other files to be imported (e.g., other WSDL documents or XML schemas). When composing a WSDL document, the various sections (typically two or three) can be composed completely independently and then combined (or more importantly, reused) to form complete WSDL files. For example, two WSDL documents can import the same basic elements and yet include their own service elements to make the same service available at two physical addresses. WSDL documents are divided into two broad sections: a service description and the implementation details. The service description is an abstract definition for a set of operations and messages. The service description is reusable and contains information common to a certain category of services, such as message formats and port types (abstract interfaces). The implementation details define how the interface maps onto the underlying concrete protocol binding and a network endpoint specification for the binding.

The following two sections give an overview of the contents of these two broad sections of a WSDL file. This is followed by a more in-depth anatomical description of a WSDL file, illustrating the various XML sections.

16.2.1 Service Description

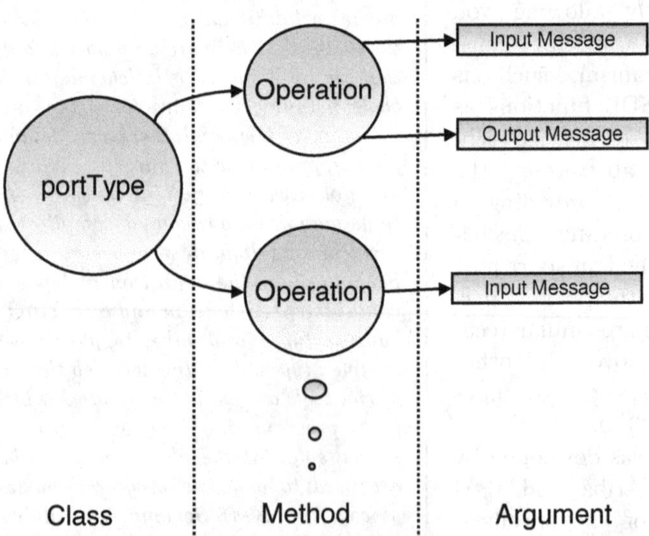

Fig. 16.4. The WSDL portType element contains operations that have input and (optionally) output arguments.

Web Service interfaces are defined in WSDL by using a *portType* XML element (illustrated in Section 16.2.3). The portType element in programming terms is analogous to an object-oriented class as shown in Fig. 16.4. PortTypes consist of a collection of *operation* elements, each of which defines a specific function of the portType. In programming terms, this would be analogous to a method in a class.

Finally, within each *operation* you have associated messages, which are defined in a separate WSDL *message* element. The message element is an abstract definition of the data along with its data types and describes a one-way message, whether it is a single message request (input) or a single message response (output). It defines the name of the message and contains zero or more message part elements, which can refer to message parameters or message return values.

Each message has a type that is specified through reference to a built-in or custom XML Schema type. Custom types are declared within the *types* WSDL element — built-in types are considered to be well-known, and therefore do not have to be declared in the *types* section. In practice, most Web Service tools have mappings to XML Schema built-in types. The message elements are analogous to arguments passed to and from a method or function call.

16.2.2 Implementation Details

There are three WSDL document elements that are used to bind the abstract interface to concrete endpoints:

- **Service:** is a collection or set of related endpoints (i.e., **ports**).
- **Port:** is a single endpoint that consists of a **binding** and a network address.
- **Binding:** is a protocol and data format specification for a particular portType.

A WSDL document defines a service as collections of network endpoints, or ports. A port is defined by associating a network address with a specific network binding or data format and different ports of a service can be located at geographically different locations. WSDL has specific binding extensions for the following protocols and message formats:

- SOAP
- HTTP GET/POST
- MIME

For example, Fig. 16.5 shows an interaction between a client and a server in a Web Services scenario. In the first case, the Web Service is invoked using a WSDL SOAP binding and the SOAP HTTP transport binding. The second scenario illustrates that the same Web Service is invoked using the the WSDL HTTP GET/POST protocol binding. The MIME binding allows abstract types to be bound to concrete messages in a MIME format. For example, using the MIME encoding *multipart-related*, a WSDL operation can

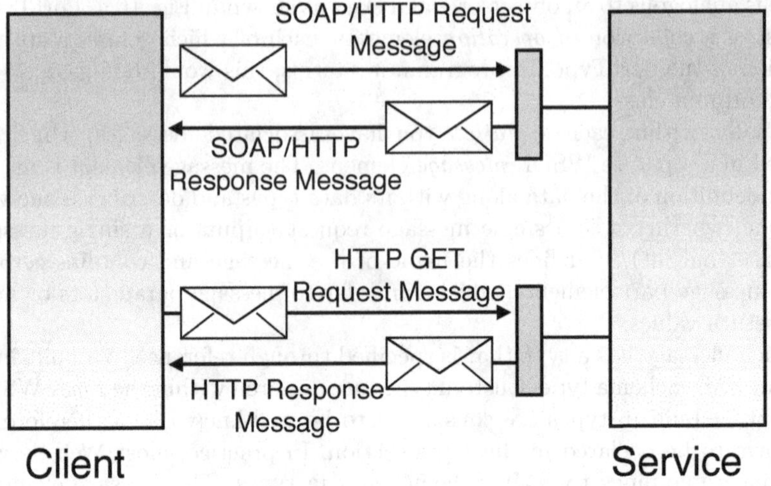

Fig. 16.5. An example of transport bindings that can be specified for WSDL.

return collections of objects with certain MIME types such as images and HTML pages.

WSDL makes a clear distinction between messages and ports. Messages define the abstract syntax and semantics of a Web Service and are required. Ports, on the other hand, are concrete as they specify the network address where the Web Service can be invoked. Ports are optional elements and therefore a WSDL file could contain just the abstract interface information and may not refer to any concrete implementation; i.e., WSDL files are decoupled from implementations and there can be multiple implementations of a single WSDL interface.

This design allows disparate systems to write implementations of the same abstract interface, thereby guaranteeing that the systems can talk to each other, as discussed in detail in Section 7.2.2.

16.2.3 Anatomy of a WSDL Document

In this section, an explanation of a simple WSDL file is given. For a comprehensive description, see [197].

Just as SOAP messages are encapsulated by an *Envelope* element, WSDL documents are encapsulated within an element called *definitions.* WSDL documents consist of a set of definitions, and although WSDL has seven definitions, a document is split into five main sections, illustrated in Fig. 16.6. The other two elements are *import*, described earlier, and *documentation*, which can be used to provide human-readable documentation and can be included inside any WSDL element.

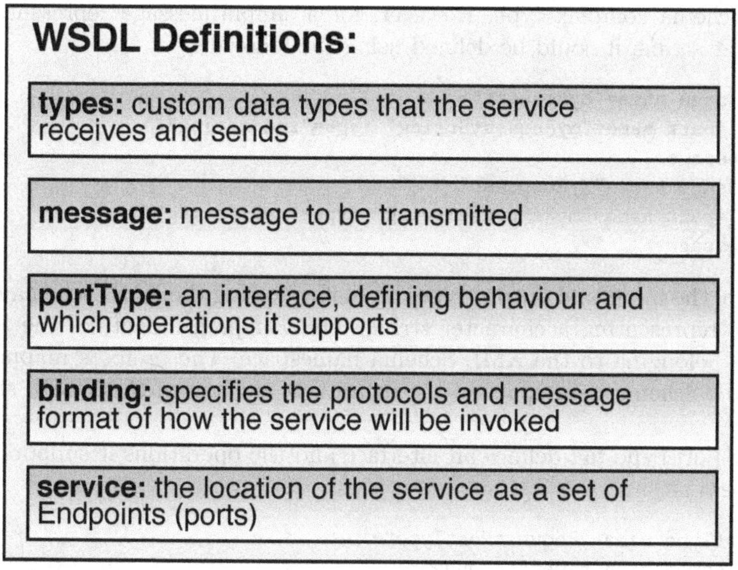

WSDL Definitions:

types: custom data types that the service receives and sends

message: message to be transmitted

portType: an interface, defining behaviour and which operations it supports

binding: specifies the protocols and message format of how the service will be invoked

service: the location of the service as a set of Endpoints (ports)

Fig. 16.6. An overview of a WSDL document.

As part of the definitions tag itself, we first need to set up the *namespaces*, which give a context for elements:

```
<definitions name="SimpleService"
  targetNamespace="http://cleverfish.co.uk/wsdl/SimpleService.wsdl"
  xmlns="http://schemas.xmlsoap.org/wsdl/"
  xmlns:soap="http://schemas.xmlsoap.org/wsdl/soap/"
  xmlns:tns="http://cleverfish.co.uk/wsdl/SimpleService.wsdl"
  xmlns:xsd="http://www.w3.org/2001/XMLSchema">
```

XML namespaces are specified as a URI. This does not mean, however, that the URI can necessarily be dereferenced. For example, the first element shown above specifies a *targetNamespace* attribute. The targetNamespace enables the WSDL document to refer to itself. However, this address, *http://cleverfish.co.uk/wsdl/SimpleService.wsdl* does not actually have to exist; it is just a placeholder for the uniqueness of this document. The definitions element also specifies the namespace (*http://schemas.xmlsoap.org/wsdl/*) of the elements types defined by the WSDL specification, such as the message and portType elements.

The *types* section contains the XML Schema of the data types used in the messages defined by the service. It is optional and depends on the complexity of the data-typing needs of the service. If you were defining a customer record, for example, then several typed fields would be needed, e.g., name, address, telephone number, etc, and therefore, this would have to be defined as an

XML Schema complex type. However, for a simple message representing a character string, it could be defined using the following:

```
<message name="MyRequest">
    <part name="myRequestString" type="xsd:string"/>
</message>
<message name="MyResponse">
    <part name="myResponseString" type="xsd:string"/>
</message>
```

Here, the input and output types are defined using the XML Schema *built-in* type representing a character string. The *xsd* prefix identifies the *string* type as belonging to the XML Schema namespace. The prefix is mapped to the XML Schema namespace in the definitions element of the WSDL shown above.

The portType tag defines an interface and the operations it supports, for example:

```
<portType name="RequestPortType">
    <operation name="aRequest">
        <input message="tns:MyRequest"/>
        <output message="tns:MyResponse"/>
    </operation>
</portType>
```

Here, the operation (`aRequest`) accepts an *input* message (`MyRequest`) and responds with an *output* message (`MyResponse`) and since we defined the types in the message definition, they are typed as strings. Note that the input and output messages to this operation are *namespace* qualified, using the *tns* prefix (short for "this namespace") defined in the definitions element.

The *binding* section of the file specifies how the portType operation will be transmitted on the wire, i.e., using any of the bindings described in Section 16.2.2. Here, we use the SOAP binding:

```
<binding name="aBinding" type="tns: RequestPortType">
<soap:binding style="document"
    transport="http://schemas.xmlsoap.org/soap/http"/>
        <operation name="aRequest">
            <soap:operation soapAction="aRequest"/>
                <input>
                    <soap:body use="literal"/>
                </input>
                <output>
                    <soap:body use="literal"/>
                </output>
        </operation>
</binding>
```

The binding is given a name (`aBinding`) and a type, which is the portType that was defined earlier; i.e., we are specifying a binding for a portType. There can be any number of bindings for a specified portType.

SOAP is specified using the *soap:binding* element, which specifies a *style* attribute. There are two styles, either RPC-oriented or document-oriented. In the RPC case, the messages contain parameter and return values, whereas in the document style, the messages contain documents. The document style is used here.

The *transport* attribute specifies the transport binding for the SOAP protocol, e.g., HTTP in this case. The *soap:operation* element defines a *soapAction* for the operations defined within the portType. SOAP action specifies that an HTTP header should be attached to the request whose key is SOAPAction and whose value is the value defined in the WSDL.

Finally, for each operation a *soap:body* is specified, which defines how the message elements appear in the SOAP body element. The *use* attribute defines whether the message element is encoded using any encoding rules. Here, we chose a literal coding, i.e., no encoding rules.

The *service* definition specifies the location of the service:

```
<service name="MyService">
   <documentation>A do-not-a-lot service</documentation>
   <port binding="tns:aBinding" name="MyPort">
       <soap:address
          location="http://localhost:8080/axis/services"/>
       </port>
</service>
</definitions>
```

The `MyService` is bound to SOAP, so therefore the *soap:address* element is used to specify the URL, in this case, to an HTTP server running on the local machine and listening on port 8080.

16.3 UDDI

Universal description, discovery and integration [198] is a service discovery protocol for Web Services. It provides an on-line electronic registry, which serves as a kind of electronic *yellow pages* that allows applications to dynamically provide information about companies and the (Web) services that they offer. It provides a similar role to the Web Service business community that a Jini lookup server does for the Jini service community but whereas Jini is designed for the intranet, UDDI and Web Services are designed for the Internet.

UDDI is a cross-industry effort driven by commercial sectors and the OASIS standards organization [90]. The UDDI standard was unveiled by Ariba, IBM, Microsoft and 33 other companies in September 2000.

The UDDI XML schema defines four core data types for business and service information each having an XML-based data structure containing mandatory and optional fields. They are called *businessEntity*, *businessService*, *bindingTemplate* and *tModel*. These core types can be used to represent three types of information:

- **White Pages:** which contain addresses, contacts and other general information about a company or individual such as a Dun and Bradstreet Universal Numbering System number (D.U.N.S) for the business. For example, you could use this to search for a company that you already know something about, e.g., its name or address. The *businessEntity* structure is used to represent this level of information.
- **Yellow Pages:** this contains industrial classifications of businesses based on some standardized taxonomies, such as the North American Industry Classification System (NAICS) [199]. The *businessService* structure is designed to represent this level of classification. A *businessEntity* may reference numerous *businessService* structures.
- **Green Pages:** contains technical information about services provided by businesses including, although not restricted to, references to specifications of interfaces for Web Services. Examples of non-Web Service binding types include communication mechanisms such as telephone, e-mail and File Transfer Protocol. A service may have multiple bindings, e.g., a Web Service binding and a telephone binding. The *bindingTemplate* and *tModel* structures are used at this level of service description.

Figure 16.7 shows the main UDDI data structures and their relationships using a fictional News Inc. business. The *businessEntity* provides a key (*ABCD*) and a name (*News Inc.*). The *businessService* structure represents the news service of News Inc. It references the *businessEntity* via its key, and provides its own service key (*EFGH*). The *businessService* structure is referenced by two *bindingTemplates*. The first of these is a Web page available at *http://news.newsinc.com*. The second is a Web Service available at *http://newinc.com/news*. Both *bindingTemplates* reference the *serviceTemplate* via its service key, and themselves provide binding keys. The Web Service *bindingTemplate* provides more information about how the service is invoked by referencing a *tModelInstanceInfo* that provides a tModel key (*QRST*). The *tModelInstanceInfo* is contained in a *tModelInstanceDetails* structure which allows multiple tModel keys to be referenced. If we look at the *tModel* structure with the matching key *QRST*, we can see it contains an overview document containing a URL. This structure points to the location of the WSDL file for the service — *http://newsinc.com/news?wsdl*.

A query for the News Inc. business might look something like this:

```
<find_business>
  <findQualifiers>
    <findQualifier>
```

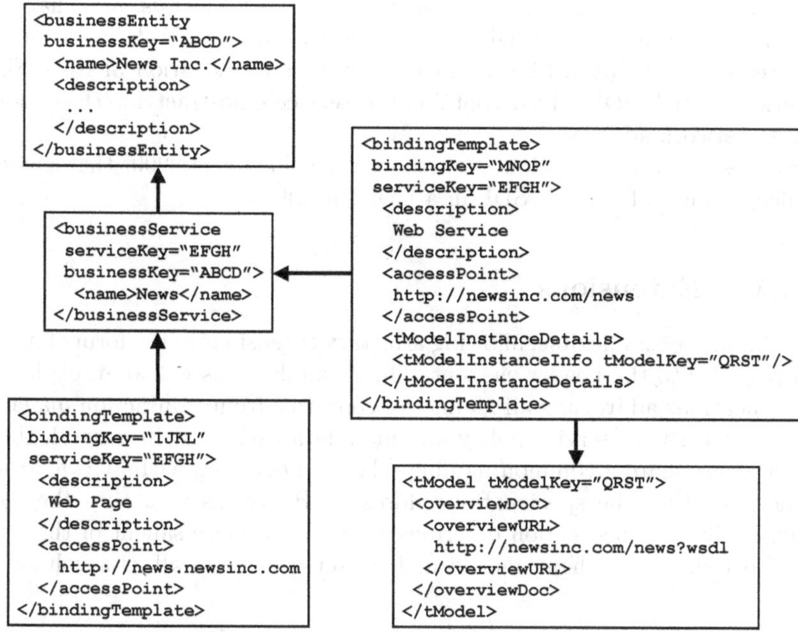

Fig. 16.7. UDDI data structures.

```
        uddi:uddi.org:findQualifier:exactMatch
      </findQualifier>
    </findQualifiers>
    <name>
      News Inc.
    </name>
  </find_business>
```

This example shows a *find_business* structure that is filtering the query to an exact match on the name of the business. Such a query is directed at the *businessEntity* structure stored by the UDDI registry. Equivalent queries for the *businessService*, *bindingTemplate* and *tModel* structures are also part of the UDDI protocol.

As is apparent from this example, there is a fair amount of XML to drill down through in order to arrive at something as useful as the location of a WSDL file, if the query begins at the White Pages level, or even the Yellow Pages level. This is because UDDI is not specifically tied to Web Services. Hence it provides a generic graph of data structures that can contain a variety of communication protocols.

Both WSDL and UDDI were designed to clearly delineate between abstract metadata and concrete implementations. In a typical usage scenario, a programmer contacts the UDDI's green pages to discover a Web Service using some search mechanism. She would then extract the location of its WSDL definition from UDDI, which contains the service's abstract interface along with its network address.

For best practice techniques, there exists a document [200] that gives a detailed account of using WSDL in a UDDI registry.

16.4 WS-Extensions

SOAP is simple and flexible, allowing arbitrary extensions in the form of metadata placed into the header element. This flexibility has led to an explosion of specifications addressing all manner of concerns, from transaction management to security, to service policy and metadata exchange. In general, these specifications share a common naming scheme, beginning with *WS-* followed by the issue that the specification addresses. Hence, as a totality they are known as *WS-**. This section describes some of the more salient of these efforts. Covering all of them, indeed making sense of them all, is a volume in itself.

16.4.1 WS-Addressing

Let us return to the analogy between SOAP and the physical envelope as described in Section 16.1.1. You will notice in Figure 16.1 that the SOAP envelope is converted into a SOAP request. What is actually happening at this point? Well, the SOAP envelope is being placed into another, outer, envelope, which almost invariably is an HTTP message. Most importantly, this outer envelope is used to route the SOAP envelope to the receiver. Unlike its physical counterpart, a SOAP envelope does not contain the address of the recipient on it. In other words, on its own, a SOAP envelope is not independent of the transfer protocol used to exchange it. This was considered unacceptable, not least because during the evangelistic REST versus SOAP debates, the argument was often leveled at the REST community that REST was flawed because it relies on a transfer protocol to do the exchanging of resources, hence tying the architecture to implementation detail beyond its control. The idea of SOAP is that it is transfer protocol independent and as a result more generic in application. At the same time, as adoption of Web Services technologies grew, system designers found that there was no standardized means of identifying or referencing services. While the Web is based on naming and linking resources, Web Services were unable to talk to each other about either themselves or others.

The WS-Addressing specification was designed to solve this. Of all the WS specifications, WS-Addressing is the most widely adopted and used because it addresses the fundamental issues of transport protocol independence and service referencing. To achieve its aim, WS-Addressing specifies an *EndpointReference* XML element. This structure is used to describe the network address of the service as well as a *Metadata* element that can contain arbitrary metadata pertaining to interactions with the service such as security policies. It also contains a *ReferenceParameters* XML element. This can be used to specify parameters expected by the service at invocation time. On top of this, WS-Addressing specifies rules for how to convert an *EndpointReference* to a series of SOAP headers. These SOAP headers include a variety of message-related fields such as sender, receiver, message identifier, as well as identifiers of previous messages that the current one relates to.

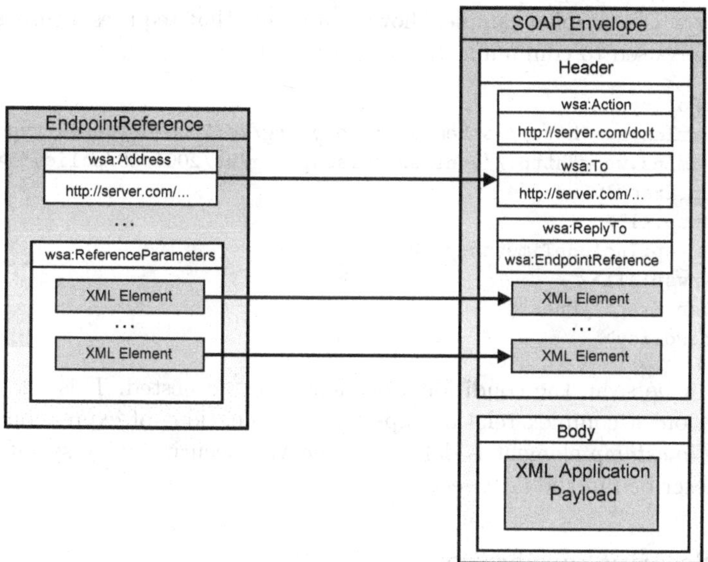

Fig. 16.8. WS-Addressing EndpointReference mapped to SOAP headers.

Figue 16.8 shows a simple EndpointReference being mapped to a SOAP envelope: The *Address* element becomes the *To* header. An *Action* header is also available, indicating to the server, what processing to perform. This header is typically defined in the service's WSDL file, as an attribute of a WSDL *Operation* element. The reference parameters are copied as-is into the SOAP header element. The figure also shows a WS-Addressing *ReplyTo* header field in the SOAP message. This is itself an *EndpointReference*, allowing the client to model itself using this construct, and the service to retain it, and use it in any further interactions. WS-Addressing also specifies a *MessageID* header field, which can be used to uniquely identify a message, and a *RelatesTo* field, allowing responses to be mapped back to the message id.

16.4.2 WS-Policy

WS-Policy [201] is designed to provide mechanisms to enable Web Services to specify policy information. To achieve this, it defines a *Policy* XML structure that can contain domain-specific policy information, as well as mechanisms to define choices and combinations of policy assertions. These expressions can then be advertised by inserting them into the *Metadata* element defined by the WS-Addressing *EndpointReference*.

WS-Policy does not define actual policies, rather it is used by other specifications, as a holding form. It defines two elements that can be used to define combinations of policies — *ExactlyOne* and *All*. These are similar to programming language conditional statements, and evaluate to either true or false. Below is a simple example, showing a policy that requires a time stamp in messages used to communicate with it.

```
<wsp:Policy
    xmlns:sp="http://schemas.xmlsoap.org/ws/2005/07/securitypolicy"
    xmlns:wsp="http://schemas.xmlsoap.org/ws/2004/09/policy" >
  <wsp:ExactlyOne>
    <wsp:All>
      <sp:IncludeTimestamp />
    </wsp:All>
  </wsp:ExactlyOne>
</wsp:Policy>
```

As can be seen, the conditional elements can be nested. This allows the construction of complex relationships and combinations of expressions. The *IncludeTimestamp* element is defined in the WS-SecurityPolicy specification briefly described in the next section.

16.4.3 Security Specifications

There are a whole raft of security-related Web Service specifications. In general, these specifications define mechanisms for leveraging existing security technologies within SOAP messages. For example, Kerberos and X.509 address authentication and X.509 also uses existing PKI for key management. XML-based specifications are also built upon, for example XML Encryption [202] and XML Signature [203].

The WS-SecurityPolicy [204] builds on WS-Policy, defining a particular set of policy assertions that can be made about security tokens and how they are used by a service. These assertions are designed to fit in with the other security-related specifications.

WS-Security [205] is a kind of umbrella specification allowing others to embed security information into the XML constructs it defines. It allows authentication, signing, and encryption of content to be described as a series of SOAP headers. It does this by defining a *Security* element that can be placed into the SOAP header. A SOAP header can contain multiple security headers and any kind of XML content can be placed into it. By default, WS-Security supports username/password tokens and binary tokens such as X.509 certificates. These can be placed into the security header to pass the data in the message. Alternatively, information used to sign or encrypt the message may reside elsewhere and not in the message at all. To allow messages to reference token, either elsewhere in the message or residing at the client or server, WS-Security provides a *SecurityTokenReference* element. This can house various types of information such as the token type, and an abstract URI that can be used to identify the token. Building on the XML Encryption and XML Signature specifications, the WS-Security elements can contain details about the encryption and signing algorithms used.

By reading the WS-Security headers, a service can decrypt encrypted data in the body of the SOAP envelope, check whether the content has been tampered with, as well as verify that the message has come from who they expected it to come from.

WS-SecureConversation builds on top of WS-Security to allow services to engage in message exchanges that are defined within a security context; that is, a security token shared between actors for the lifetime of a particular conversation. A *SecurityContextToken* element can be added to the WS-Security defined *Security* element, which is used to identify the shared secret, and thence sign or encrypt the message content for the duration of the conversation.

16.4.4 WS-Transfer

WS-Transfer [206] defines SOAP header information that can specify data transfer semantics to be applied to the body of the message. This information models operations similar to those defined by HTTP — Get, Put, Delete and Create. Specifically, WS-Transfer makes use of the WS-Addressing defined *Action* SOAP header, giving it a value associated with the particular operation being requested. Equivalent response values for each operation are also defined, that are sent by the service provider back to the client after the operation has completed. The irony of creating a Web Services specification that echoes HTTP, which is the transfer protocol almost invariably used by Web Services, has not eluded commentators. When sending a WS-Transfer decorated message to a server, for example to Get a resource, the client creates a SOAP envelope, inserts the WS-Addressing headers, giving the *Action* header a value of *http://schemas.xmlsoap.org/ws/2004/09/transfer/Get*, and then uses the HTTP POST method to send the envelope. Using HTTP directly, the client could simply send an HTTP GET request to the server.

WS-Transfer has been extended via the *WS-Resource-Transfer* [207] specification. WS-Resource-Transfer is influenced by the capabilities of the Web Services Resource Framework (WS-RF), described in detail in Section 17.3. In particular, it provides a means of applying the WS-Transfer operations to fragments or sub-sets of resources, thus alleviating the requirement of sending an entire resource which may be quite large. It does this by including content in the body of the SOAP message which uses an XML expression language such as XPath [208] to identify sub-parts of a resource. For example, a client may issue a WS-Transfer Get request to a server for a particular resource, and in return receive an XML representation of it. The client can then use WS-ResourceTransfer to Put a new value into the resource using XPath to specify the target XML element to change. The resource can thence be modified by the service provider without the entire resource being sent again.

16.4.5 WS-Eventing

WS-Eventing [209] defines a protocol that allows Web Services to subscribe to events and generate notification messages. WSDL operations defined by the specification allow services to subscribe to events generated by a notification service. In return, they receive the endpoint of a *SubscriptionManager* service, and an expiration date of the subscription. As part of the subscription process, the subscriber sends its address as a WS-Addressing EndpointReference. Typically, this contains a ReferenceParameter providing an identifier for the subscription. The EndpointReference is used by the notification service to asynchronously send event messages to the subscriber.

The *SubscriptionManager* service is used by the subscriber to perform operations related to its subscription. It can renew the subscription, get the expiration status of the subscription or terminate the subscription.

WS-Eventing is similar in spirit to WS-Notification described in Section 17.3.5, although much simpler, and is considered a rival specification. Indeed a convergence between WS-Notification and WS-Eventing called WS-EventNotification has been proposed as part of a general move towards integrating resource and subscription standards.

16.4.6 WS-ReliableMessaging

WS-ReliableMessaging [210] provides a means for services to engage in message exchanges in which the arrival of messages can be verified. If a message does not arrive for some reason, for example network failure, then the message can be retransmitted in an idempotent manner. This capability is important in the context of particular transactions, for example payments and database modifications.

To achieve reliability, the specification provides three WSDL operations to create, close and terminate *sequences* — *CreateSequence*, *CloseSequence* and *TerminateSequence*. A sequence is a container for a series of messages within a particular context and is modeled in the SOAP headers during message exchanges. It has a unique identifier and is associated with a WS-Addressing EndpointReference defining a service location to which acknowledgement messages should be sent. When a client has received a sequence identifier from a server via the *CreateSequence* operation, it can begin sending messages. In doing so, the client includes a SOAP header including the sequence identifier, and the message number. Messages are numbered sequentially in a sequence, starting with 1. When a client has sent all the messages in the sequence, it can request acknowledgment from the server. The server returns the list of messages it received to the address defined in the EndpointReference passed to it in the *CreateSequence* operation. If there is a gap in the message numbering, then both client and server know what message got lost along the way, allowing the client to retransmit those messages for which the server does not have a message number. Once all messages have been received, the client can invoke the *CloseSequence* operation on the server.

16.4.7 WS-Coordination

WS-Coordination [211] is another specification designed to be used by other specifications. It defines a way for services to enter into an activity, and then engage in the protocols defined by that activity. WS-Coordination does not specify what the particular protocols are of the activity, leaving this open for other specifications to develop. One such specification based on WS-Coordination is *WS-AtomicTransaction*, which provides a message protocol for performing database style transactions including rollbacks and commits.

WS-Coordination defines a coordination service interface made up of an *Activation* service interface, a *Registration* service interface and a set of domain-specific message protocols, for example those defined by WS-AtomicTrasaction. This service acts as a third party through which activities between the services can be coordinated in terms of security and message aggregation and notification.

Services wishing to engage in a coordinated exchange with other services use the Activation service to create a coordination context for a particular activity. Once a coordination context is acquired by an application, the application can use the Registration service to register for the activity. It can then send the context to the other services. The context contains the necessary information to register into the activity specifying the coordination behaviour that the service will follow, allowing the other services to register with the activity. Multiple coordination services can be chained together, allowing for arbitrary large and complex coordinated message exchanges to take place.

16.5 Conclusion

This chapter has discussed the three core technologies used by Web Services to support the *publish, find, bind* triad of operations defined by SOA as well as some of the most widely used Web Services specifications that extend the Web Services space to support a variety of capabilities that are deemed important to achieving secure and reliable machine-processable service interactions.

SOAP was initially associated with distributed object technology and Remote Procedure Call, but has since moved beyond this (indeed SOAP is no longer an acronym for Simple Object Access Protocol). Although its initial purpose was primarily to design a typing system, allowing applications to encode programming language-specific data types in XML, most of this area of work was addressed through the XML Schema work at the W3C. This has simplified the usage of SOAP as it is now used mostly as a generic container for service-specific data and metadata.

WSDL is heavily influenced by distributed object technologies. Abstractions such as portTypes, and operations, as well as the message exchange patterns supported by it — essentially one-way and request-response — are typical of interfaces defined for remote procedure calls. While WSDL 2.0 goes some way to addressing this, for example by supporting more message exchange patterns, it was a long time in gestation, and by the time it was standardized, WSDL 1.1 was already widely deployed.

The future of UDDI as a core component in the Web Service stack is uncertain. The initial vision of publicly accessible, mirrored UDDI registries has not come to fruition and IBM has discontinued their universal business and test registries. There are a number of possible reasons for this. Some have argued that the business model UDDI is based on, namely, empowering intermediaries between service providers, does not fit with actual business practice [212]. Another possible reason is that UDDI is complex, not least because of its separation between the abstract and concrete. And yet despite its complexity, UDDI does not easily facilitate sophisticated searching, being based on lexical matching, such as those encouraged by Semantic Web technologies. These capabilities need to be overlaid onto the API [213] [214].

As for the many Web Services specifications, some have become widely used, such as WS-Addressing, whilst others will likely fade from the map. After the rush to define every possible scenario using SOAP and WSDL as a backbone, only time will show which specifications are actually useful in practice. In fact, this is probably true of Web Services in general. Whilst the technologies are open, shared and encourage interoperability, the object orientation of WSDL and the complexity of the associated specifications are barriers to mass adoption on the scale of the Web. Hence Web Services will continue to be used in business-to-business processes and academic and scientific computing where security, reliability and the need to share complex, proprietary data types are high priorities.

17

OGSA

The Globus toolkit (GT) is the de facto open source toolkit for Grid computing. The functionality of the GT version 3.x is exposed as a collection of virtual Open Grid Services Architecture services [7]. OGSA services, or Grid services, extend Web Services, discussed in the previous chapter, to add features that are often needed within distributed applications. Specifically, OGSA adds *state* to Web Services in order to control the remote service during its lifetime. Whereas Web Services are *stateless*, OGSA-based services are *stateful*. OGSA services represent the GT's various components, e.g., GRAM, MDS, etc., described in Chapter 9, using this unified representation and can be aggregated and used within virtual organizations in a number of different ways.

However, the road to OGSA realisation has not been easy. In 2002 the Open Grid Services Infrastructure specification was announced. This specification defined the extensions to WSDL needed in order to represent and enable stateful Web Services. The designers of OGSI introduced the notion of a Grid service, which *extended* a basic Web Service to attach a number of additions to which a Grid service must adhere. Stateful resources within OGSI were modelled as Web Services that support the GridService *portType* (see Section 16.2.2), which is an extension of the WSDL portType.

This approach led to much unrest in the Web service community for several reasons discussed in Section 17.3.1 but principally because Grid services did not conform to Web Service standards. For these reasons, OGSI has been surpassed by a new specification called the Web Services Resource Framework that addresses these criticisms. In the GlobusWORLD conference at the beginning of 2004, Foster [158] described Globus as "a balancing act between addressing short-term needs (software engineering and development plus supporting user needs) and long-term needs (pushing development of standards, conducting research and keeping the project on the 'bleeding edge')." He added that "Globus must be a research and a development organization."

This chapter therefore will be split into three sections. The first section will describe the OGSA architecture, the second OGSI and the third the re-implementation of OGSI as WS-RF, upon which the Globus toolkit version 4 is based.

17.1 OGSA

The Open Grid Services Architecture Framework is the Globus and IBM vision for the convergence of Web Services and Grid computing. OGSA was presented at the Global Grid Forum (GGF, now Open Grid Forum — OGF) in February 2002 and described in the accompanying paper [7], which outlines this new architecture for distributed systems integration. The GGF has since set up an Open Grid Services working group to review and refine the architecture.

OGSA adopts the service-oriented architecture, discussed in Section 7.3, in order to expose Grid functionality as collections of service-oriented software assets. To this end, the OGSA authors define how the various Grid technologies can be implemented and applied through the use of this service-oriented approach. They noted "we view a Grid as an extensible set of **Grid services** that may be aggregated in various ways to meet the needs of VOs, which themselves can be defined in part by the services that they operate and share" [7].

In the next section, Grid services are described and put into context with the current Web Services.

17.1.1 Grid Services

At the core of the OGSA specification and implementation (see Section 17.2) is a *Grid service.* A Grid service is a Web Service that provides a set of well-defined interfaces and that follows particular conventions. More specifically, it is:

> *"a (potentially transient) stateful service instance supporting reliable and secure invocation (when required), lifetime management, notification, policy management, credential management, and virtualization." [7]*

Simply put, within the OGSA model, everything is represented as a Grid service, whether it is a computational resource, a storage resource, a network, an application, a database, etc. The difference between OGSA and Web Services is that within OGSA, the Grid services can be managed, i.e., created, monitored, destroyed, etc. The OGSA architecture therefore allows an application to obtain references to Grid service instances that can be used to monitor a service and access its local data directly, similar in principle to the functionality provided by distributed object systems. However, all of this is achieved within XML documents that are passed between the Grid services, in the same way as Web Services.

Grid services are built on Web Services for a number of reasons. First, Web Services support dynamic discovery and composition in heterogeneous environments by using WSDL to describe the Web Service in such a way that it is independent of any specific implementation of that service (see Section 16.2.3). Second, there has been a widespread adoption of Web Services technology and this helps for two reasons: first, there are a number of tools that already exist, e.g., WSDL to language convertors; and the actual uptake of the technology is vast, which helps the ubiquitous deployment needed to realise a truly global Grid (see Section 9.2). Further, Web Services are built on standards-based technology, which is necessary for such widespread adoption (see Section 9.5.2).

At the core of Grid services, the focus is on the management of transient service instances. Within a Grid computing environment, services often need to be created dynamically, as and when a service is needed. As an example, let's take a look at a simple *migration* scenario. Migration involves moving the execution of a job across the network from one machine to another, perhaps because the job is not running quickly enough at present. There are several steps needed for this simple scenario, as shown in Fig. 17.1.

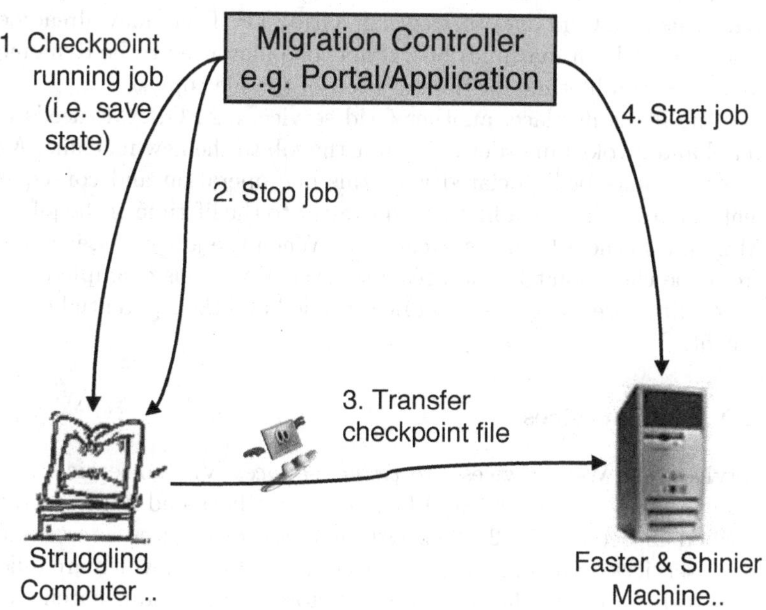

Fig. 17.1. A simple job migration scenario.

The first step is to save the current state of the job that you wish to migrate, which is called *checkpointing*. Typically, a job checkpoints by saving its state to a file. This information can be passed to another instance of the same job at a later stage in order to resume the progress. Second, the first job needs to be stopped because any further work would be redundant as it would not be *checkpointed*.

Checkpointing can be achieved in numerous ways depending on the particular scenario and the application that is controlling the migration. For example, a job could checkpoint itself and then coordinate the rest of the migration process by using the relevant services directly or a portal could manage these tasks. In this example, the migration process is controlled by a third-party migration controller, which monitors the job's progress and makes a decision on whether to migrate the job to another machine based on some quality of service requirement: e.g., perhaps the job is running too slow to complete by a given time. Such coordination could be achieved by using a communication mechanism between the controller and the job (sockets, Jxta, Jini, etc.) or it could be implemented with a Grid service directly using the stateful distributed systems mechanisms.

Once the job has been stopped, the checkpoint file needs to be moved to the machine to which the job is being migrated. This would typically be achieved by using a Grid data service, e.g., GridFTP. There may already exist such a service on both machines but, if not, one may need to be dynamically started and have a lifetime for the duration of the file copy.

Once the file is in place, another Grid service, e.g., GRAM, needs to be discovered and invoked in order to submit the job to the new machine. Again, such a service may be associated with this one operation and consequently transient in nature, having a lifetime equivalent to the lifetime of the job (since GRAM monitors the job during execution). When the job starts, it reads the data from the checkpoint file and resumes execution. This example is simple but it does illustrate the types of services needed and their potential transient deployment.

17.1.2 Virtual Services

Grid services, like Web Services, are *virtual services*. Virtual services are services that provide a consistent interface to diverse back-end implementations as described in Section 7.2.2. This virtualization of services is essential for overlaying services on heterogeneous collections of devices, which are inherent within a Grid. Access to the resources therefore becomes transparent, which allows the mapping of multiple logical resource instances onto the same physical resource, which is a necessity for providing state to the distributed OGSA services.

Virtual services appear in other systems described in this book. For example, Jxta can provide the same behaviour and have multiple back-end implementations of the same service interface. Jini, on the other hand, deals strictly with distributing Java objects and through the use of RMI and Java proxies makes it unsuitable for service virtualization.

Within the context of the Grid, the virtual Grid services help to provide a virtual overlay across the various Grid resources, providing the ability to map common service semantic behaviour onto multiple platforms; e.g., the same service could be built for Linux, Solaris and Windows machines, and the user would not realise (or care) which platform was hosting the service.

17.1.3 OGSA Architecture

OGSA uses WSDL (see Section 16.2.3) to describe Grid services. OGSA proposed several new WSDL *portTypes* that can be used to access this added functionality, which were refined by the OGSI specification. These will be described in the next section.

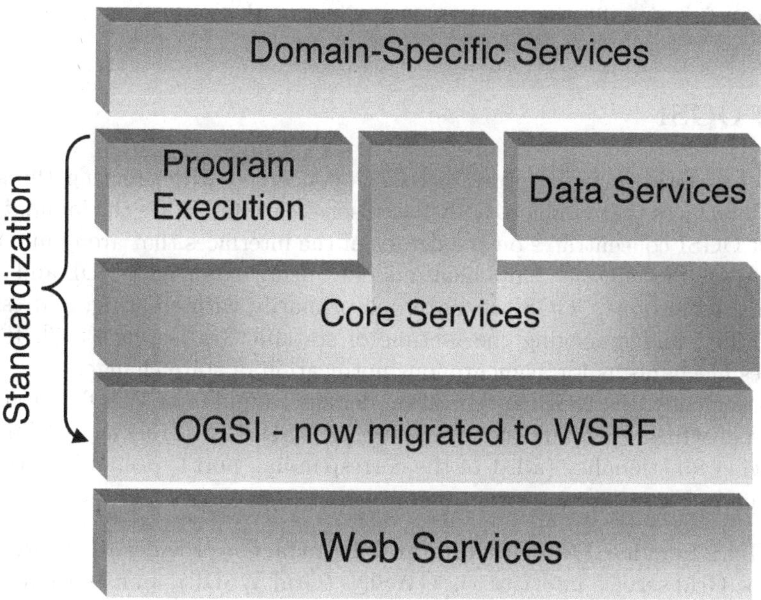

Fig. 17.2. The Open Grid Services Architecture showing the OGSI layer that provides the infrastructure to expose OGSA services.

Figure 17.2 shows how OGSI fits in with the OGSA architecture. At the core of a Grid service is the Web service framework that enables XML messages to be sent between distributed processes. At the next level there is the OGSA infrastructure that builds on Web Services to provide the stateful behaviour that a Grid service requires. Here, this is provided by OGSI but is now specified using different syntax within the WS-RF.

Even though the manner and syntax in which the OGSA services are defined has changed, this does not affect the semantic behaviour of the resulting services; i.e., both provide stateful Web Services for representing network-enabled components on the Grid. This is indicated at the left-hand side of the figure, which emphasises the fact that the middle three layers of the architecture are currently going through a standardization process, i.e., still under debate.

The core Globus services are unlikely to change significantly but their external service representation may be tuned. The fact that these may be built upon OGSI or WS-RF makes little difference to the outcome; it's really just syntax. The core services are outlined in Section 17.2.1 and the more advanced services build upon the core services to expose greater functionality and so on. At the top of the architecture, we have the domain-specific services that could be as specific as solving a particular problem or again represent common functionality for a subset of application domains.

17.2 OGSI

The open Grid services infrastructure is concerned with creating the standard interfaces that enable OGSA-based services. OGSA lays the foundations, whilst OGSI concentrates on the details of the interfaces that are required for OGSA. OGSI defines a component model by using extended WSDL and XML Schema definitions. "OGSI is concerned primarily with creating, addressing, inspecting, and managing the lifetime of stateful Grid services" [7]. It also defines mechanisms for asynchronous notification of state change.

Specifically, the OGSI specification defines a number of WSDL extensions (some of which have analogous support in WSDL 2.0 [215]) that define the following functionality (a list of the corresponding portTypes and operations is given in Fig. 17.3):

1. **Grid Service Descriptions and Interfaces:** provides descriptions of the Grid service interface via GWSDL (Grid WSDL), an extension to the WSDL standard containing the Grid extensions. OGSI allows descriptions of the actual instance of the Grid service; e.g., the instance could potentially be stateful and transient and needs to be addressable.
2. **Service Data:** OGSI extends WSDL to allow users to gain access to a service's state information, e.g., a service's internal data; analogous to access methods on a Java object, e.g., setX(), getX(), etc. OGSI defines mechanisms that allow both querying (pull model) and subscription-based (push model) access to the data. The subscription-based access is similar to attaching a *Java Listener* to an object or subscribing to a newsgroup. Within OGSI, essentially, you subscribe to a data element and thereafter

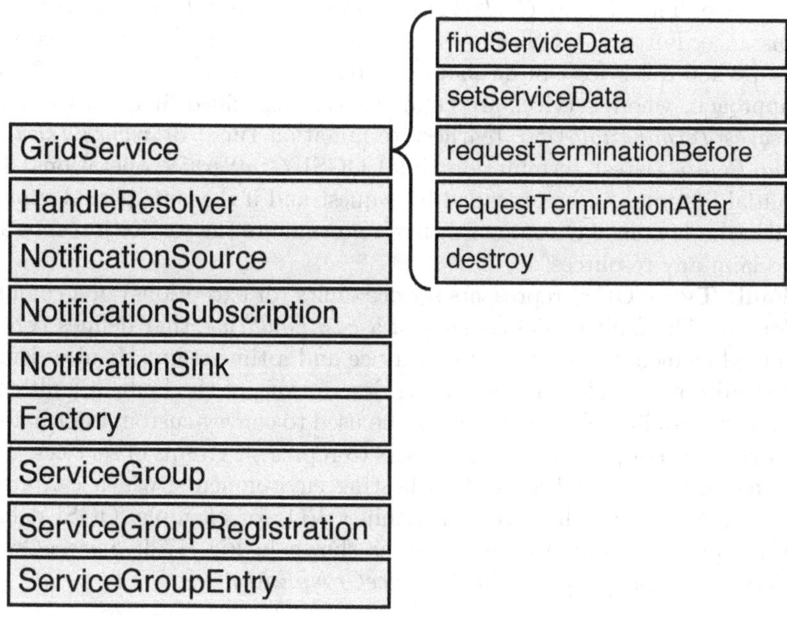

Fig. 17.3. A list of the OGSI portTypes used to define the various interfaces necessary. Also the operations defined by the Grid service portType are shown.

any change occurring on that element is sent to you (via notification). OGSI defines the *NotificationSource*, *NotificationSink* and *Notification-Subscription* WSDL portTypes for this purpose.

3. **Naming and Name Resolution:** a Grid service can be dynamically created and therefore you need to obtain a reference in order to gain access to its state information. OGSI defines a two-level naming scheme for this purpose: a Grid Service Handle (GSH) and a Grid Service Reference (GSR). The GSH is an invariant abstract globally unique name that identifies the service instance. It is guaranteed to be unique from all other service instances but has no protocol or instance-specific information. The GSR, on the other hand, encapsulates the information required to interact with a particular service instance. For example, in a SOAP environment, the GSR will typically contain the WSDL *service* and *binding* information (see Section 16.2.3). Within one execution, you could potentially have many different GSRs if the job migrates from machine to machine but it will retain the same GSH. OGSI therefore contains a resolver function to extract the current GSR from the GSH, which is performed by the *HandleResolver* OGSI portType.
4. **Service Life Cycle:** OGSI provides factories for creating transient Grid services. The *Factory* OGSI portType is used to create a Grid service

instance. The *destroy GridService* operation is used to destroy a service instance. Further, OGSI allows users to specify the lifetime of a service, i.e., when a service can or should be terminated. OGSI uses a *soft-state* approach, where services are created with a specified lifetime, using the *requestTerminationAfter* (earliest termination time) or *requestTerminationBefore* (latest termination time) OGSI *GridService* operations. The initial lifetime can be extended by request and if the time period expires, then the hosting environment is free to terminate the service instance and reclaim any resources.

5. **Fault Type:** OGSI represents service faults (or exceptions) in a common format. The fault model consists of a *ogsi:FaultType* that defines two required elements: the originating service and a time-stamp. It also defines several optional elements including descriptions of the fault, a fault code and extensibility elements that can be used to convey custom information.
6. **Service Groups:** OGSI allows users to represent groups of services. This is particularly useful for virtual hosting environments, which can group all services that it has created within a VO, for example. OGSI defines three portTypes for this purpose, as shown in Fig. 17.3: *ServiceGroup*, *ServiceGroupRegistration* and *ServiceGroupEntry*.

There exist around half a dozen independent implementations of the OGSI specification. In the next section, a brief overview of one such implementation, the Globus Toolkit, version 3, is given.

17.2.1 Globus Toolkit, Version 3

GT3, officially released in mid-2003, is based on the OGSI specification. All services from GT2, described in Chapter 9, have been adapted to conform to the OGSI specification. This section briefly outlines the structure and contents of this toolkit.

Figure 17.4 illustrates the architecture of the GT3 toolkit. At the lower level you have the GT3 core, which implements the core OGSI infrastructure to enable the other services to be exposed as Grid services. For example, the *GridService* core is implemented here, e.g., obtaining references and handles, the notification framework, the state management and service data, as described in Section 17.2.

The next layer implements the GT3 security layer, which adapts the mechanisms outlined in Section 9.7.2 to work within the service-oriented framework technology stack. For example, Globus has created a new secure protocol, called *httpg*, which is based around the transport layer security mechanisms, described in Section 4.5, e.g., TLS and SSL. They have also adapted the SOAP layer security based on *WS-Security* [205], *XML Encryption* [202] and *XML Signature* [203] standards. For mutual authentication, delegation, etc., X.509 certificates are used in a similar fashion to those described in Section 9.7.2.

The next layer consists of the GT2 components translated to Grid services, e.g., MDS, GridFTP, GRAM, etc., plus the addition of new services that have

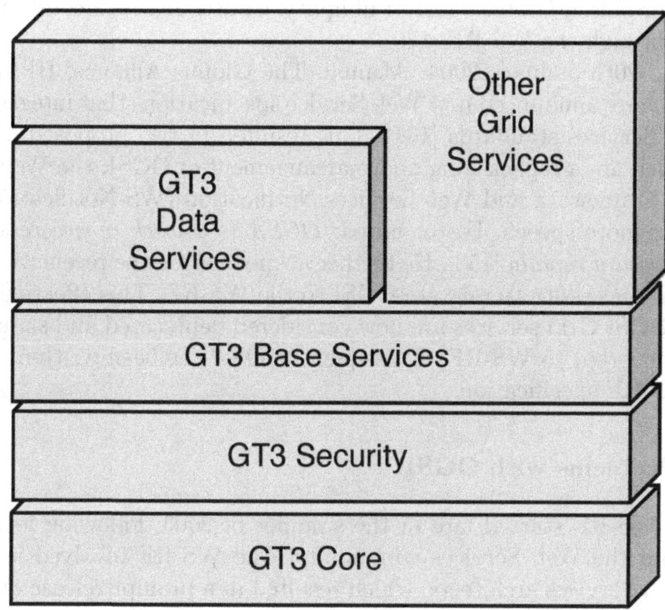

Fig. 17.4. GT3 architecture.

been developed since GT2, e.g., a file streaming service, a reliable file transfer service and a managed-job service. See [9] for more information.

The structure of the toolkit is built to reuse functionality of the lower levels and it is anticipated that many new services will be implemented, as illustrated in Fig. 17.4, by the Globus team itself and other services created by other companies and organizations. Within GT3, an example of a higher-level service is illustrated here, for replica management of data files stored across the Grid. This service utilizes other data services already implemented in order to replicate and catalogue data.

17.3 WS-RF

In parallel with the work on OGSI through the OGF, the Web services community were working on standardizing their own components which related to aspects of the OGSI specification. In particular, WS-Addressing [216] was developed that provides a transport-neutral mechanism for representing *service endpoints* to Web Services, which duplicates the work on the Grid handles and references, described in Section 17.2. Further, the OGSI specification resulted in a number of criticisms from the Web Services community, which in turn compromised Globus' goal of ubiquity. Consequently, a compromise was reached through the WS-RF [130].

On the 20th January 2004, Akamai, The Globus Alliance, HP, IBM and Sonic Software announced new Web Service specifications that integrated Grid and Web Services standards [131]. This resulted in two proposed infrastructures, which are a repackaging and rearrangement of OGSI: the Web Services Resource Framework and Web Services Notification (WS-Notification).

In a keynote speech, Foster noted: *OGSA is a work in progress, but it's moving forward rapidly* [158]. He further acknowledged the recent *bump in the road* by the necessity to migrate OGSI to the WS-RF. This effectively means that the OGSI Grid services are now considered deprecated and should therefore be converted to WS-RF. Consequently, GT4 has been written according to the WS-RF specification.

17.3.1 Problems with OGSI

Work on WS-RF started late in the summer of 2003, following feedback on OGSI from the Web Services community. The WS-RF involved input from senior Web Services architects, which resulted in a prompt release of the WS-RF specification for public comment. The Web Services community identified four main problems with the OGSI specification [217]:

- **Too Much in One Specification:** the OGSI specification defined a number of areas of functionality. Many felt that this was far too much for one specification and that a clear separation of functionality would provide a more flexible infrastructure for incremental adoption, allowing services to implement some things but not others. For example, a service may want to retain state but not implement event notification. WS-RF therefore partitions the OGSI specification into six distinct areas.
- **Incompatible with Web Services and XML Tooling:** OGSI used XML Schema which were incompatible with XML tooling, e.g., JAX-RPC, and it extended the WSDL *portType* causing compatibility problems. WS-RF uses standard XML Schema, familiar to developers and existing tooling and annotates the *portType* definition, making it compatible with WSDL 1.0.
- **Too Object Oriented:** Within OGSI, a Grid service is a Web Service that encapsulates the resources state; i.e., both the service and resource states are coupled. Therefore, current Web Services would have to be extended and rewritten to create a Grid service. In WS-RF, the service and the resource state are separated.
- **Relied on WSDL 2.0:** OGSI exploited constructs from the promised WSDL 2.0 specification, which had been delayed in coming, resulting in difficulty with existing Web Services tooling. WS-RF conforms to the WSDL 1.0 specification entirely.

17.3.2 The Specifications

The basic requirement addressed by both OGSI and WS-RF is the ability to create, address, inspect, discover and manage *stateful resources* [218]. In terms of Grid computing, stateful resources represent a variety of entities, for example:

- Machines with particular OSs, number of CPUs, amount of memory, load, network latency, etc.
- Computations/processes (jobs) that are long running, may need monitoring or checkpointing or migrating.
- Remote manipulation of instruments, e.g., a telescope.
- Group membership tokens when joining secure groups.
- Subscriptions to events allowing asynchronous notification rather than polling. These subscriptions require lifetime functionality.

However, Web Services specifications emerging from the business community did not address such scenarios particularly well. As noted previously (in Section 17.1.1), services that conform to OGSI specifications are called Grid services. Grid services in OGSI, however, *extended* Web Services in order to provide this extra functionality. Such an approach was deemed *heavyweight* by the Web Services community. Furthermore, SOA purists insisted that services should not expose resource state, arguing that the separation of functionality from data is what distinguishes a service from a remote object. Therefore WS-RF and WS-N use a different approach that separates the message processor (i.e., the Web Service) from the resource (i.e., the stateful instance).

WS-RF is a suite of specifications, breaking down the various functionalities supported by OGSI into separate components. The relationship between the specifications is hierarchical in that certain specifications rely on others.

WS-Resource The base specification on which all the others rely. This defines how to model a resource that has state using the WS-Addressing specification (see Section 16.4.1). WS-Resource is discussed in more detail below.

WS-BaseFaults Defines an extensible set of faults (errors) that may occur in relation to dealing with stateful resources. This replaces the OGSI representation for service faults or exceptions.

WS-ResourceProperties Defines how to describe, access and manipulate the properties of a resource. This specification is also described in more detail below.

WS-ResourceLifetime Defines how to model lifetime properties, e.g., how to destroy a resource, how to find out when it ceases to exist. This replaces the Grid Service life cycle operations.

WS-ServiceGroup Defines how to describe the grouping of services. This replaces the OGSI grouping mechanisms, described in Section 17.2.

17.3.3 WS-Resources

The WS-Resource specification makes use of the WS-Addressing specification which is described in detail in Section 16.4.1. Briefly, WS-Addressing defines an *EndpointReference* (EPR) XML structure that is used to describe a Web Service endpoint. The *Address* element in the EPR defines the network accessible location of the service. An EPR can be decorated with certain types of service-related information, for example metadata pertaining to the behavior, requirements and capabilities of the service. It also contains a *ReferenceParameters* element. ReferenceParameters are associated with an endpoint in order to fulfill a particular interaction. Beyond the EPR, WS-Addressing also defines a series of SOAP Header elements relating to the message's source and destination, and rules for mapping an EPR to a group of SOAP headers. This allows services to exchange addressing information about themselves and others in the body of the SOAP message, using an EPR, and then convert that information into message metadata at service invocation time, by mapping the EPR to the message headers.

The WS-Resource specification uses the EndpointReference to house an application-defined identifier to a particular resource. From the client's perspective, the identifier is opaque; that is, the client would not be able to locate the resource merely from the identifier. However, when a client is in possession of an EPR with a resource identifier, called a WS-Resource, it can connect the Web Service identified in the Address element of the EPR. The service can look at the resource identifier, and locate the particular resource it represents. The resource itself could be a machine, an instrument, a database entry — anything that has been exposed as a resource. This mechanism is shown in Figure 17.5.

A slightly simpler, though more ambiguous way of modeling the two entities is to dispense with the EndpointParameters and combine them in a single URI. This is actually the form of the example in the final WS-Resource specification.

```
http://server.com/MyService?res=xyz
```

At this point, the client has a reference to some resource, but it cannot do much with it because it does not know the nature of the resource, nor how it can manipulate it. The WS-ResourceProperties specification defines how services can expose resources, and operations for accessing and manipulating them.

17.3.4 WS-ResourceProperties

A Web Service that supports operations over stateful resources, includes an XML Schema element in the *Types* element of its WSDL document, describing the kind of resources that it can operate on. The XML Schema element, called a *Resource Properties Document*, defines the properties, or attributes, that the

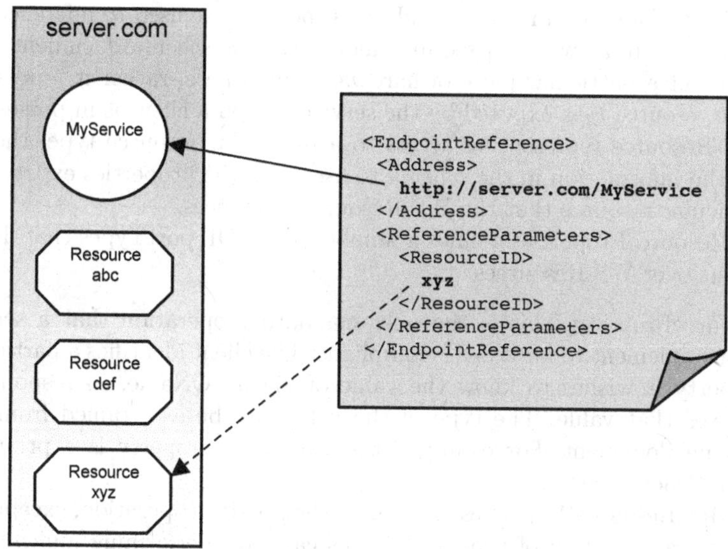

Fig. 17.5. WS-Resource referencing a stateful resource using ReferenceParameters.

service wishes to expose for the given type of resource. For example, if a service provides access to storage space, it might expose properties such as capacity and amountUsed. In terms of XML Schema, this might look as follows:

```
...
<wsdl:types>
  <xsd:schema xmlns:tns="http://example.com/storage">
    <xsd:element name="capacity" type="xsd:integer"/>
    <xsd:element name="amountUsed" type="xsd:integer"/>
    <xsd:element name="storage">
      <xsd:complexType>
        <xsd:sequence>
          <xsd:element ref="tns:capacity"/>
          <xsd:element ref="tns:amountUsed"/>
        </xsd:sequence>
      </xsd:complexType>
    </xsd:element>
  </xsd:schema>
</wsdl:types>
...
```

Here we have an element called `storage` which is defined in the namespace `http://example.com/storage`. It references two elements — `capacity` and `amountUsed` — also in the same namespace. Because the elements are defined in a namespace, the `storage` resource type can be identified using a Qualified Name, or QName — a combination of the namespace, and the element name. The QNames of a resource and its properties, are used to reference the entities elsewhere as we shall see in a moment. This schema document does not represent a particular piece of hardware somewhere, rather it represents a storage resource *type* exposed by the service. When a client is in possession of a WS-Resource representing access to a particular resource type, then it can use the information in the schema to ascertain the properties exposed by the particular resource that the WS-Resource references.

WS-ResourceProperties defines a number of WSDL portTypes that define operations over WS-Resources:

GetResourceProperty This is the only mandatory operation that a service must implement to be WS-RF compliant. The client identifies a particular property it wishes to know the value of via its QName. In response it receives that value. The type of the value can be ascertained from the Schema document. For example, the `capacity` property is a primitive XML Schema integer type.

GetMultipleResourceProperties Similar to the previous operation, except one can get a collection of properties. This can save performing multiple requests for individual properties.

GetResourcePropertyDocument Get the whole document that defines the resource, for example an instance of the XML Schema we saw above.

PutResourcePropertiesDocument Replace all the properties of the resource by supplying a new resource properties document.

SetResourceProperties Allows Insert, Update, Delete on properties in a single request, again, identifying properties via their QName.

QueryResourceProperties Allows querying over resource properties using a query expression language, e.g., XPath.

A service supporting WS-Resources implements at least one of these operations. To create a mapping between a service's WSDL portType, and resource type, the service includes an attribute in its portType declaration referencing the QName of the Resource Property Document that models the resource type. For example, if a service supported the GetResourceProperty operation for storage resource types, then it would reference the QName of the storage element defined in the XML Schema above.

The relationship between a WS-Resource, i.e., the handle a client has to a particular resource instance, and the operations defined by WS-ResourceProperties is called the *Implied Resource Pattern*. To illustrate, if we look at the signature of the GetResourceProperty operation, we find that it takes a single parameter. This parameter is the QName identifying the resource property the client wishes to get the value of, as defined in the XML Schema. The signature does not include an identifier for the particular entity the client wished to get the property of. Rather, this identifier is included in the SOAP header of the request to get the property. Hence, the action to take, in this case GetResourceProperty, and the thing to act on (e.g., a storage entity) are separated. The former resides in the SOAP body as part of the application payload. The latter resides in the SOAP header. A programming language equivalent might look something like this:

```
public Object getResourceProperty(QName qname);
```

As can be seen, there is no information being passed to the method, identifying the entity on which to act. Hence the relationship is implied.

When a service receives the request, it must extract the resource identifier from the SOAP header, map it to some local resource, and then perform the operation on a property of the local resource, based on the QName parameter of the operation. Likewise, when a client receives a response, it must extract the resource identifier from the SOAP header to ascertain what resource the server is talking about, and then look in the SOAP body to find out the result of operation.

The question arises, how does the client access a resource qualified EPR, or WS-Resource, in the first place, and how can the client be sure that the service will be able to map the identifier to a resource. Both these issues are considered out of bounds to the specification. In particular, there is no mechanism for creating WS-Resources, the logic being that the generation of a WS-Resource is too application specific. The typical scenario echoes OGSI by following the Factory design pattern. It is common for a service to act as a WS-Resource factory, returning a WS-Resource in the body of a SOAP request. The client can then extract the EndpointReference, and insert it into the SOAP header of later requests according to the mapping rules defined by WS-Addressing.

17.3.5 WS-Notification

WS-Notification builds on top of WS-RF and defines three further specifications:

WS-Topics Defines how to describe topics; that is, categories of potential interest to subscribers. Topics are defined hierarchically, allowing topics to have parent-, and sub-topics. Furthermore, dialects of topic expressions can be defined. This provides fine-grained control over subscriptions, although in practice, such subtleties have not been widely implemented yet.

WS-BaseNotification Defines how to expose notification producer services and consumer services, to support asynchronous message exchanges. A notification producer typically exposes the topics it supports as a resource, modelled in the WSDL using a Resource Properties Document as described above, and accessed using the implied resource pattern. A client may retrieve an instance of such a resource, and then query the notification producer service about the set of topics, whether they are fixed, and what dialect they are described in. The downside of this design is that a notification producer's supported topics are not immediately accessible.

Rather a new resource must be created and the topics supported by it discovered in the context of the created resource.

Once a client has the set of topics supported by the notification producer, it can send a *Subscribe* message to the notification producer. This message contains amongst other things, the topic the subscriber is interested in, and an endpoint, usually local to the subscriber, to which notification messages can be sent. When the producer receives the Subscribe message, it creates a new *Subscription* resource, mapped to the topics in the message. It then returns a WS-Resource representing the subscription back to the subscriber. The subscriber can retain this WS-Resource to manipulate the lifetime of the subscription, for example canceling it, using the WS-ResourceLifetime operations supported by the subscription resource. When the notification producer creates or receives an event that maps to a topic, it checks the list of subscriptions mapped to the topic, and sends a *Notify* message containing the event data to the endpoints defined by the subscribers when they initially subscribed. Therefore this process requires that subscribers can create a network accessible endpoint in order to receive the Notify messages. In situations where this is not possible, WS-BaseNotification also supports a *pull* model. In these circumstances, the producer can provide a *PullPoint* resource to which it sends messages, and from which subscribers can retrieve messages.

WS-BrokeredNotification Describes how to expose and subscribe to notification services that use a brokered architecture. Brokered notification is useful when services that are producing events are not directly accessible on the network, because they use the broker as a middleman between the producer and the consumer. For example, imagine a mobile temperature monitoring device that produces events when the temperature moves beyond a particular bound. This device may not have a stable network address, making it difficult for interested parties to subscribe and receive notification events directly from the device. Using a brokered architecture, the device can register itself as a producer with the network accessible broker service, whilst other nodes on the network can subscribe to the broker. When an event occurs, the device connects to the broker service passing it the event message. The broker in turn notifies any nodes that have registered an interest in the event. Because the broker has a stable address, nodes can consistently subscribe to it, and match the event messages received from it. This architecture is similar to the *PullPoint* mechanism used by WS-BaseNotification, except here the node without an accessible endpoint is the producer rather than the subscriber.

17.3.6 The Future of WS-RF

Despite having gone through the arduous process of re-specifying OGSA, the Grid community found that the future of WS-RF and WS-N was not secure.

Other Web Service specifications were being developed at the same which covered similar areas of concern. In particular, WS-Transfer and WS-Eventing (see Sections 16.4.4 and 16.4.5), two Microsoft lead specifications, deal with resource exchange and asynchronous event notification. As a result of there being rival specifications, a convergence between the various specifications was proposed in 2006 [219] by leading vendors. The new specifications absorb some of the capabilities of WS-RF, in particular the ability to modify fragments of resources, rather than requiring the movement of entire resources. This has been addressed by extending WS-Transfer with WS-ResourceTransfer (see Section 16.4.4). The Grid community has not particularly embraced the convergent specifications, no doubt in part due to a 'specification fatigue' after the upheaval of the last few years. Recent work, for example the Basic Execution Service (see below), tries to remain agnostic in terms of such specifications in order to facilitate longevity. BES currently allows two forms of event notification to be used in conjunction with its core service — WS-Notification and WS-Eventing.

17.4 Higher Level Interfaces

Beyond defining generic capabilities such as handling stateful resources and asynchronous communications, Grid computing has begun defining high-level interfaces to specific Grid-related services. The most central capability of any Grid is the ability to execute processes across a set of distributed resources. While there are numerous systems that can do this, such as the Globus Toolkit described in detail previously in this chapter, and the Uniform Interface to Computational Resources (UNICORE), these systems use data descriptions and execution commands that are specific to their own system and environment. Therefore higher level Web Service interfaces are needed to connect different domains and provide users with a homogeneous view of heterogeneous underlying environments. The Basic Execution Service (BES) is a recent specification released by the Open Grid Forum (OGF) that defines a set of WSDL portTypes designed to allow process execution by a variety of underlying systems. BES depends on another OGF specification, the Job Submission Description Language (JSDL) which provides an XML format for defining jobs and how they should be executed. The following section briefly describes JSDL, after which BES is described.

17.4.1 Job Submission Description Language

Job Submission Description Language (JSDL) is a verbose, yet straightforward language for defining an application or process, its requirements and the preferences a user might have in executing it. In short, it allows you to define everything you might want to in order to get a job run somewhere on a Grid, and get the results back. There are four primary sections to a JSDL document:

Job Identification This element provides a means of describing a particular job, e.g., its name, a human-readable summary and the project it is associated with.

Application This element describes the requirements of the executable itself — the name of the executable, the version number, a description, and the arguments it requires to run.

Resources This element describes the resources the application and the user, i.e., the human submitting the job, require, or would prefer, during the execution. For example, an application may require a particular operating system, CPU architecture, speed and number as well as a minimum amount of memory during execution. At the same time, the user may suggest particular hosts on which to run the application. Some of the elements are therefore requirements, while others are preferences particular to the submission.

Data Staging In order for an application to run, it may require local access to files before it can run. Likewise, after, or during the execution, files may be produced and dumped to the local file system. The data staging element allows a user to specify what files to pre-stage to the local machine, and where to retrieve them from. It also allows output files to be staged to another location once they are produced.

The design of JSDL means that, apart from the data staging processes, a job is essentially a black box; that is, it is modeled as an atomic act. JSDL has no facility for allowing the user to define relationships between job descriptions, either data dependencies or control dependencies. How jobs are linked together lies outside of the JSDL remit. However, JSDL allows, for better or for worse, extensibility in virtually every element it defines. This could be used to model dependencies between different jobs. However, such extensions, although syntactically legal, reduce the chances of interoperability because they are not core requirements of understanding JSDL. On the other hand, an important concept in document-oriented programming models such as those that are based on exchanging XML documents, is a *laissez-faire* approach to unrecognized content. The declarative nature of XML means it can be read, yet not all of it need be understood in order to perform some processing based on it. Hence interoperability is not compromised despite a potentially limited understanding of the content. The trick is to provide extensions that would not contradict decisions based upon the restricted understanding. The Basic Execution Service interface goes to some lengths in ensuring that clients and servers can negotiate extensibility without either one falling over.

17.4.2 Basic Execution Service

The Basic Execution Service (BES) is a Web Service interface to executing a job on a Grid. It is based on the concept of *activities*. Activities are represented using JSDL and are identified using WS-Addressing EndpointReferences. When a client submits an activity to the BES it uses a JSDL document, and in return receives an EndpointReference. This EndpointReference can be used in later invocations to refer to the particular activity.

BES also defines an extensible state model defining the states that an activity can pass through during execution. Figure 17.6 depicts the basic state model. As can be seen, an activity can either be pending, that is, waiting to begin execution, terminated, running, failed or finished. Arrows between the boxes point to the next possible states in the execution process. For example, if an activity is in a pending state, then it may either enter a terminated state, which would be the result of a client request, or a running state. Once the activity is running, it cannot re-enter a pending state.

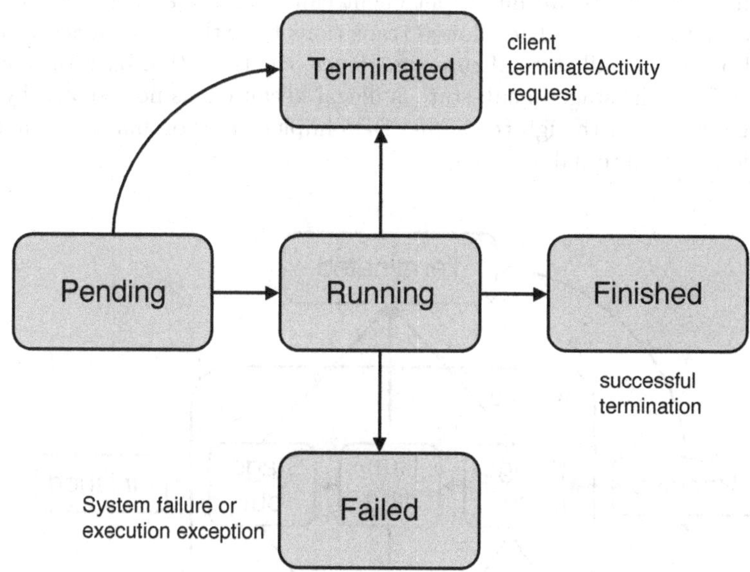

Fig. 17.6. BES basic state model.

This model is very simple, and many systems will support more complex behaviour, for example it may be possible to suspend and resume an execution, or checkpoint and migrate the job to another host. In order to be generally applicable, BES does not presume such capabilities because they may not be supported by all underlying systems. However, BES tries not to exclude these capabilities either, if they are available in particular BES implementations.

Hence the state model is extensible, allowing BES implementations to introduce sub-states that are particular to their system. Figure 17.7 shows an example extension which breaks down the running state into three separate states: the running state itself, as well as a pre-staging and post-staging phase in which data is moved to and from the locus of execution.

Although extensions are allowed to the basic BES model, they must follow certain rules. In particular, any new sub-states must replace states defined in the basic model, and those sub-states must not allow transitions to states defined in the basic model, that do not exist in the basic model. This allows BES implementations to define specializations to the basic state model for clients that are capable of understanding them, whilst allowing clients with only a knowledge of the basic model to still interoperate with the implementation. Taking the data staging extension example in Figure 17.7, the stage-in and stage-out states are sub-states defined within the overall state of running. As we shall see from the BES portTypes, the current state of an activity is modeled in XML to allow the representation of enclosing states and sub-states. Hence a client with only knowledge of the running state can just view the enclosing state, whilst an intelligent client can interpret and respond to the data staging sub-states. The allowed transitions from the sub-states are those defined by the overall state of running. Hence, the transition back to a pending state from the stage-in sub-state is illegal because it is not defined by the running state, even though the actual BES implementation may allow such a transition in its internal state model.

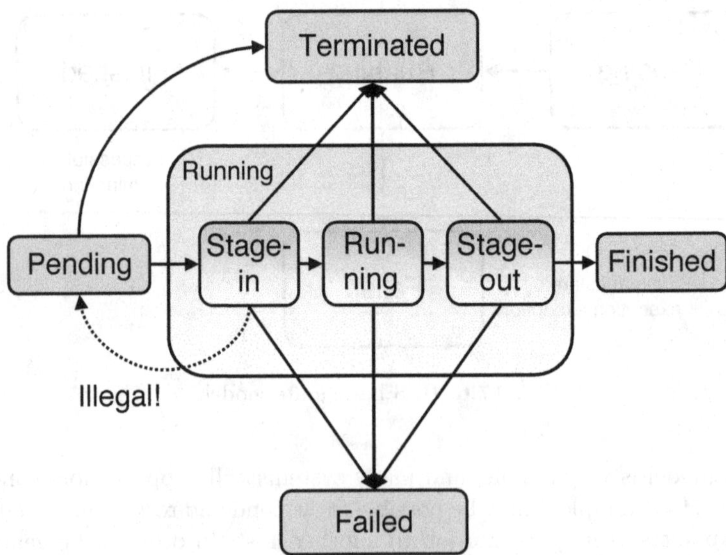

Fig. 17.7. Data staging extension to BES state model.

BES defines two WSDL portTypes. The BES-Management portType supports two operations that are targeted at system administrators, allowing the BES container to begin accepting new activities, and cease accepting new activities. The BES-Factory portType provides the interface to clients wishing to execute jobs. It provides five operations:

CreateActivity Allows a client to create a new activity — hence BES-Factory. The input to this operation is a JSDL document that has been authored by the client. The output is a WS-Addressing EndpointReference (EPR) referring to the activity created from the JSDL document. This EPR is used in subsequent calls to refer to the activity.

GetActivityStatuses This operation allows a client to retrieve the status of a collection of activities. The input to the operation is an array of EPRs that refer to the activities. The output is an array of ActivityStatus XML types. These contain an element defined in the BES namespace, encapsulating the current state of the activity, e.g., TERMINATED or RUNNING. The states defined in the BES namespace are only those in the basic state model. Extensions can add other elements to the ActivityStatus type defining their proprietary sub-states. The ActivityStatus type also contains the EPR associated with the activity (i.e., the EPR the client sent in the request).

TerminateActivities This operation allows a client to force an activity to cease, either from the pending state, or the running state. The input is an array of EPRs. The output is an array of TerminateActivityResponse XML types. These contain the EPR associated with the activity As well as a boolean indicating whether or not the activity has been terminated.

GetActivityDocuments This operation allows a client to retrieve the JSDL documents associated with particular activities. It takes as input an array of EPRs, and returns an array of GetActivityDocumentResponse XML types. These contain the EPR associated with the activity as well as the JSDL document initially sent by the client when creating the activity. The JSDL document may have been modified or extended by the service.

GetFactoryAttributesDocument This operation allows a client to examine the attributes of the BES container. It takes no input, and returns a BES-ResourceAttributesDocument XML type. This contains the attributes of the factory service, e.g., number of running activities, CPU type, OS and many others defined by BES.

One point to note about the BES operations, is their use of WS-Addressing EndpointReferences. Like WS-RF they are used to refer to stateful resources — in this case activities that pass through states — that are managed by a Web Service interface. However, their use is not *implied*, as it is in WS-RF. The operations take the EPRs as parameters, rather than inserting them into the SOAP message header.

17.5 Conclusion

In this chapter, an overview of the Open Grid Services Architecture (OGSA) and corresponding specifications were given. OGSA is primarily concerned with extending Web Services to include state information, necessary for distributed systems integration. There have been, to date, two specifications that have resulted from this architecture.

The first, the Open Grid Services Infrastructure (OGSI), extended Web Services to create Grid services and used techniques which were outside the scope of current Web Service standards and tooling but also duplicated other work within the Web Services community. This resulted in the Web Services Resource Framework (WS-RF) that addressed these shortfalls by subdividing the OGSI specification into a number of different areas and reporting to conform to current standards. Newer specifications dealing with stateful resources are also beginning to stake their claim on the areas covered by WS-RF. Hopefully this will be the final change to the core requirements of Grid computing, allowing the community to continue to move on to defining particular service and data interfaces that make use of the underlying specifications.

18

Web 2.0

> *"But most times, the whole thing still feels like a shaky early beta to me."*
> *Tim Bray*

The term Web 2.0 is applied to diverse contexts and technologies and is surrounded with varying degrees of hype. It seems to sum up a "movement," but eludes precise definition. Is it the dawning of the age of Aquarius, or a branding exercise designed to rescue the Web after the dot-com bubble burst? Is it a set of technologies, or a business model? Can it be summed up by Web pages with curvy boxes and 3D icons, or are there real insights underlying it?

In 2005, Tim O'Reilly published a now well-known article called *What is Web 2.0* [220] in which he tries to clarify what is meant by the term. He describes it as not having defined edges, but rather a centre of gravity from which a variety of principles and practices emanate that share certain themes. These include:

- Services not packaged as software. Providers are moving away from the traditional approach of encapsulating capability as a software commodity. This allows services to evolve and change in a fluid manner, existing in a state of so-called *perpetual beta*. As a result, many projects working under the Web 2.0 banner adopt lightweight, flexible programming approaches and languages such as JavaScript, PHP, Perl and Ruby.
- Architecture of participation. This allows services to scale and evolve in accordance with user adoption and non-predefined user behaviour.
- Remixable data and services. Web 2.0 encourages building small, well-defined components with limited capability. These small components can be transformed, composed, hacked and remixed to create new services. This is very different from trying to become market leader by selling a grand solution.

These themes share a view of successful Web activity that promotes agility and the ability to harness the ever-changing nature of the Web, rather than imposing a more traditional software or commercial model onto it. Underlying all these themes is the concept of The Web as Platform.

18.1 The Web as Platform

The concept of the Web as Platform is not exclusive to Web 2.0. Indeed, it was central to the initial vision of the Web, as a space in which users could consume *and* create data. As Tim Berners-Lee said in 2006 [221]:

> *"If Web 2.0 for you is blogs and wikis, then that is people to people. But that was what the Web was supposed to be all along."*

As the Web expanded, it turned from a *read/write* space into a *read-only* space in which most of the data was produced by few and consumed by many. The same was true of the software used to access it. Whilst Netscape considered the Web as a platform, their business and software model was still centred around client desktop and server-side applications that were marketed as commodities. The Web was viewed very much as a tool for supporting traditional forms of *consumerism*. However, after the dot-com bubble burst, it became clear that this consumerist model was not working. In its moment of contraction, the Web looked back to its roots and what emerged was an approach that has since been called *producerism* [222]. Now, browsers and servers are not considered commodities anymore, rather they are just infrastructure tools, two poles between which the Web is mapped. Newer companies have moved from these poles into the space between them both in terms of their business and software models. They make use of the nature of the Web itself, rather than simply as a mechanism for propagating a traditional software business model, in particular drawing on its scale, the relationships of the links across it, and most of all, the billion or so people who make up the Web.

The success of Google, for example, is based not on selling commodities. Nor does it require users to download any software. Instead Google provides a service that is free and which requires only a browser to use. Why has its core service become so predominant? Because Google draws on the interconnectedness of the Web by using page ranking as a means of assessing the likelihood that a link will be useful as a search result. It does this by counting the number of pages that link *to* the URL. This not only allows results to be ranked according to how popular, and hence potentially useful or accurate, the page is, but also discourages page authors from asserting, through metadata in the HTML, that their content is about something it is not, or that it is more accurate than it is.

Amazon uses customer preference data to make recommendations based on similarity of interest. This provides users with a far better view of available books than the traditional approach which recommends sponsored content. A list of "other books published by The Same Publisher Inc." is far less useful than a list of similar books based on the history of previous buyers. Sites like del.icio.us and Flickr have taken such recommendations further through the concept of *folksonomies*, informal and user-defined keyword associations with digital artefacts. These associations evolve organically and overlap in a semi-chaotic way, in sharp contrast to the concept of taxonomies and Semantic Web ontologies, which are highly structured means of organizing data.

Chad Hurley

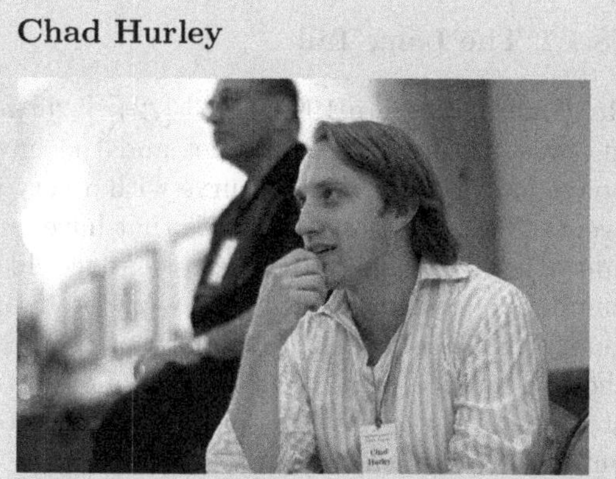

Chad Hurley is co-founder and Chief Executive Officer of YouTube. YouTube began when Hurley and two friends (Chen and Karim) wanted to share videos taken during a dinner party in January 2005. Sharing using e-mail was not working. The e-mails kept getting rejected because they were too big, whilst posting the videos online was too long-winded. So they began work on designing something simpler. YouTube soon became one of the most popular Web sites on the Internet because people can post almost anything they like on YouTube in minutes. In October 2006 he sold YouTube for $1.65 billion to Google.[1]

Other sites make use of user-generated content, sites such as MySpace, Facebook, YouTube, eBay and Wikipedia. Here, there is no intrinsic content provided by the site hosts themselves. Rather they act as content aggregators or portals. As more content is added to the portal, the more useful it becomes, and the more likely it is that other users will contribute content. Once such a site reaches a critical mass, its growth and hence usefulness snowballs.

What these examples have in common is that they leverage the characteristics of the Web. As such they benefit from scale, rather than being burdened by it. The algorithms used by Google and Amazon for providing search results are statistical, and therefore depend on large data sets. Likewise portal sites hosting user generated content attract greater interest, the more content they provide. These sites also have control over certain types of data which is what makes them powerful — shopping habits in the case of Amazon, Web links in the case of Google and vast aggregations of user-generated content in the case of portal sites. A quality that is shared by these different sites is that relationships between disparate data are generated. Data becomes more accessible, recommendations become more

[1] Photo and biography summarised from wikipedia `http://en.wikipedia.org/wiki/Chad_Hurley`.

useful, queries become more accurate. As Tim O'Reilly says: *the service automatically gets better the more people use it.*

Services that benefit from scale can reap rewards, not just from the "centre" of the network, populated by those customers who represent the average and whose likings are statistically most prevalent, but from the many users at the edges of the network — those that make up the myriad of niche communities and interests.

18.1.1 The Long Tail

Research in the late 1990s [223] [224] [225] revealed power-law distributions in the structure of the Internet and the interconnectedness of the Web. A power-law distribution is a curve with a very small number of very high-yield events (like the number of words that have an enormously high probability of appearing in a randomly chosen sentence, like 'the' or 'to') and a very large number of events that have a very low probability of appearing (like the probability that the word 'probability' or 'bafflegab' will appear in a randomly chosen sentence) [226]. The number of events with a very low probability creates a *heavy* or *long* tail, depicted in Figure 18.1, as the probability decreases but never quite reaches zero.

In his book *The Long Tail*, Wired Editor Chris Anderson [227] argues that this distribution is an important property of the Web, in particular because the content and commodities available on the Web are digital. A traditional business, constrained by storage capacity and costs, focusses on the high-frequency end of the power-law distribution in order to reap the greatest profit from every transaction. Anderson uses a music shop as an example. This music shop will focus on providing popular albums because the faster they shift them, the less time the albums remain on the shelves, which in turn means the profit margin is greater. Difficult-to-sell albums take up space and cost more the longer they idle on the shelves. Such a situation enforces the power-law distribution because it ensures that customers find it harder to buy less popular albums. However, an online music shop has only virtual shelf space and can therefore virtually stock an infinite number of albums, including the least popular. It costs Amazon no more to virtually stock a highly popular album than it does to stock a niche product. As a result the artificial barrier to users buying less popular albums is lifted and the tail of the distribution grows.

Although the number of events under the tail of the distribution is small compared to the high-frequency end, it is still a substantial amount when dealing with the numbers of users of the Web. Hence there are significant advantages to businesses in supporting the tastes of those customers who make up the tail. According to Anderson, in traditional retail, new albums account for 63% of sales (in 2005), but online that percentage is 36%.

The Long Tail is not only important for astute business people. It has significant implications for all the users of the Web. By removing the traditional

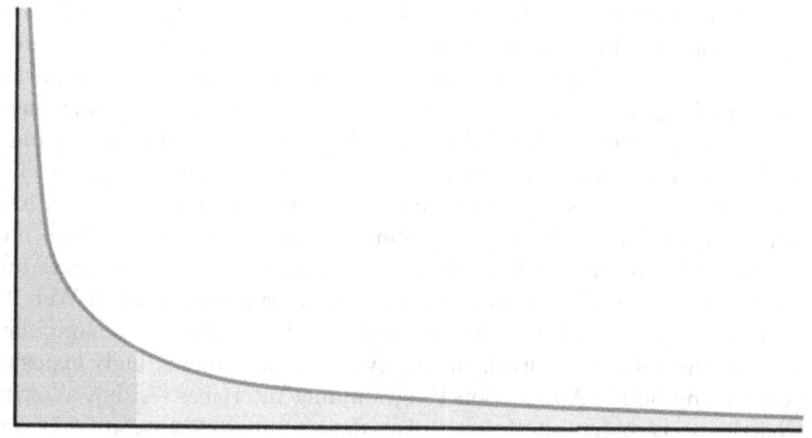

Fig. 18.1. The Long Tail (picture by Hay Kranen/PD).

barriers to content production and storage, the road is open for production by anyone — the Web becomes a *read/write* space again, but this time on a massively greater scale with infinite room for endless niche markets. This mass *producerism* creates not only a vast amount of data, but a number of possibilities that arise from the data that are exploited by savvy applications and businesses aware of its potential. In particular, they draw strength from the diversity displayed in the long tail.

Tim O'Reilly uses the slightly ambiguous term *harnessing collective intelligence* to describe the process by which individual activity and decision making are aggregated to produce something that is greater, more interesting or more reliable than the individual activities are in isolation. He uses the Cloudmark [228] collaborative spam filtering system as an example, which aggregates decisions of users about what is spam and what is not, and which apparently out-performs traditional spam filters that examine the actual messages. Likewise, Wikipedia, an experiment in radical trust, brings together the vast distributed knowledge of its users into a single portal, exemplifying exploitation of the Long Tail. Tagging and bookmarking systems such as del.icio.us are another example of aggregating individual decisions to create collections and relationships between resources far richer than could be achieved by an individual.

Many of these systems are built on what Tim O'Reilly calls an Architecture of Participation. Systems using this architecture do not just promote participation, but are designed to become more useful, and more efficient through increased participation. The example used by O'Reilly is BitTorrent (see Chapter 13). Bittorrent shares the bandwidth needed to transfer large files between the users who want the file. The more popular the file, the faster the download can be achieved. This is inverse to a centralized system, where high demand usually causes the system to slow down. Many of the systems and sites mentioned previously, such as Google's page ranking, Amazon's recommendations and eBay's reputation system, are based on a similar premise.

Web 2.0 is about people — connecting them, encouraging them to participate and making sense (and profit) from the mass of data they knowingly and unknowingly produce. But achieving this interaction and moving from a *read-only* to a *read/write* environment, also raises technological issues. The Web as Platform requires shared approaches to exposing and sharing data. A significant element of the Web 2.0 movement is about making the Web programmable to facilitate the dynamic relationships between participants and the services they use. Whilst many of the best known exponents of Web 2.0 such as Amazon, Facebook and Google use proprietary software to manipulate and analyze the data the control, these services are also increasingly exposing their data using public Application Programming Interfaces (APIs), allowing third parties to combine multiple existing data sources to generate new and novel services, called *mashups*. Likewise, there are open standards that are commonly used to distribute blog content and podcasts, and programming models and techniques used to provide dynamic content and a rich visual experience to users.

18.2 Technologies and APIs

The following sections provide an overview of some of the technologies, approaches and specifications that are or have attracted attention and usage. In keeping with the composability of Web 2.0, these examples address different issues, but can be aggregated by the developer to create new services.

18.2.1 Ajax (formerly AJAX)

Many will be familiar with the term Ajax in the context of Web 2.0 not least because of the amount of hype that came with it and the inevitable backlash against that hype. Ajax used to be an acronym for Asynchronous JavaScript and XML. But it became apparent that you do not specifically need JavaScript or XML to do what Ajax does. So what exactly is it?

Ajax is not a technology, but rather a combination of pre-existing technologies used in a particular way to achieve particular effects, primarily a smoother and more dynamic experience for the user. It is based on interaction between the scripting languages and Document Object Model (DOM) supported by browsers.

The most popular scripting language used in HTML is JavaScript. JavaScript was originally developed at Netscape. Previously named LiveScript, it was renamed JavaScript in 1995. Some suggest that the change of name was part of the agreement between Netscape and Sun Microsystems to include the Java runtime environment in the Navigator browser in order to support Java applets. Although JavaScript borrows some stylistic and syntactic elements from Java, they are not related beyond that. JavaScript is limited to working within the confines of the current document that has been loaded into the browser. It is commonly used to provide interactivity on Web pages such as image change or text color change when a user moves their mouse over a document element. It has also been widely used for basic form validation. This allows simple form errors to be detected before the data is sent to the server for processing.

The DOM is a W3C developed language and platform-independent object model for representing XML and HTML documents. The elements of a document are modelled in a hierarchical fashion with defined means of accessing parent, child and sibling elements. Browsers do not have to support the DOM when internally rendering an HTML page, but should expose the page via the DOM to scripting languages such as JavaScript. JavaScript can use the DOM to manipulate and retrieve values from the content visible in the browser. The HTML DOM has a root element representing the browser window. Using the window, child elements can be accessed using *dot notation*, for example the statement below returns the document contained by the window:

```
var doc = window.document;
```

The document object in turn has defined child elements, for example arrays of form and image objects. Individual elements within a document can also be retrieved by their *id* attribute. For example, if a document contains a table element with a unique id of *mytable*, it can be accessed using the following JavaScript statement:

```
var table = document.getElementById("mytable");
```

The DOM also allows traversal across the hierarchy of elements, for example the JavaScript snippet below accesses the table element and then iterates through its child elements:

```
var table = document.getElementById("mytable");
// get the number of child elements
int length = table.childNodes.length;
for(var i = 0; i < length; i++) {
    // get a handle to the current child element
    var child = table.childNodes.item(i);
    // do something interesting with it
}
```

In the days before the DOM was widely supported by browsers, scripts often contained many conditional branches depending on which browser had been detected by the script, in order to traverse the proprietary object model supported by the particular browser. And although the DOM is now widely supported, there are still cross browser issues stemming from implementation and rendering details. Furthermore, these idiosyncrasies are often highlighted when new technologies or coding patterns emerge. This is the case with Ajax as well.

> **JSON**
> *JavaScript Object Notation (JSON) is a data interchange format. It is often used in conjunction with JavaScript code, but can be used with any programming language, providing a simpler, more restricted and lightweight alternative to XML. It is essentially a way of describing data using name/value pairs. Data can also be nested providing a means of describing compound objects. The snippet below defines a point object containing* **x** *and* **y** *attributes.*
>
> ```
> {"point":
>   {"x":  "120",
>    "y": "250"}
> }
> ```
>
> *JSON is comprised of a subset of JavaScript data structures. This makes it very simple to convert JSON into a JavaScript object, in particular using the JavaScript* `eval()` *function. This function takes an arbitrary character string and attempts to execute it as JavaScript. Whilst this facility is useful, it also raises security issues, because potentially malicious code defined as JSON structures can be downloaded from a remote host and executed within the scripting environment of the user's browser.*

Essentially, browsers that support Ajax allow the scripting language (usually, but not necessarily, JavaScript) embedded in the HTML to access an HTTP client and make HTTP requests from within the page. The functionality has been supported by Microsoft's Internet Explorer since the late nineties, through an *ActiveXObject* available to scripts. But other browsers did not pick up on the technology, and so it did not gain much popularity. Now most browsers support it through an *XmlHttpRequest* object accessible to the scripting environment. An XmlHttpRequest object can be passed a URL of a server to contact, an HTTP method to perform, as well as optional data to send in the request, if the request method supports it. It then performs the request. During this process, the XmlHttpRequest goes through several states — uninitialized, open, sent, receiving and finally loaded, meaning the object has finished. The term *asynchronous* is used, because the XmlHttpRequest object can be assigned an event handler when it moves from one state to the next. This event handler typically takes the form of a script function that is called. When this function is called, it can check what state the XMLHttpRequest has entered and act accordingly. For example, when the request enters the receiving state, the function can access the response data of the request. Typically, it checks that no errors occurred and then processes the data in some way and inserts it into the DOM of the page at runtime. Figure 18.2 shows the process.

This process is really just a microcosm of what a browser does when loading a URL. However, performing this from within the HTML page has a number of benefits for applications. First, the content does not have to be HTML. Beyond HTML, the most common forms of data returned from an Ajax request include XML, JavaScript Object Notation (JSON) and images (as is the case with Google maps). Second, the contents of a previously loaded document can be modified dynamically. This means the browser does not have to go to a new URL in order for the rendered view to change. This allows only portions of the document to be changed, reducing the bandwidth and time spent in downloading a new page. This in turn provides the user with a smoother experience. There are now a number of Ajax libraries available written in JavaScript which shield the developer from the differences between browser implementations of the underlying technologies used by Ajax.

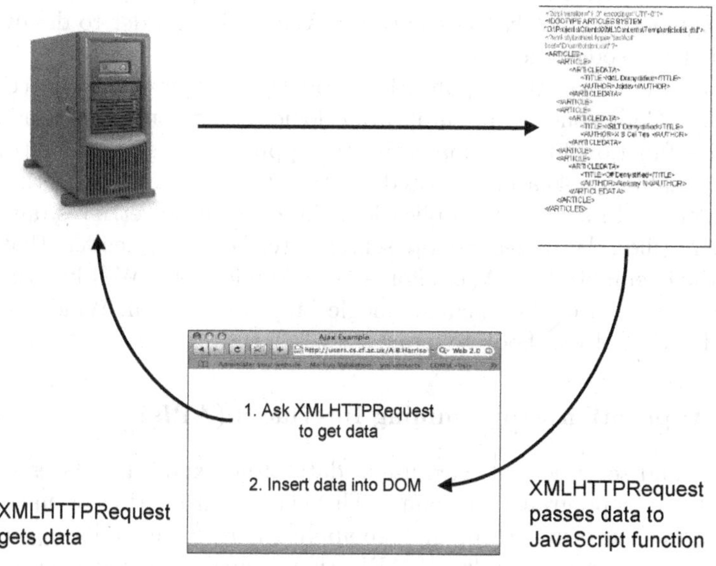
1. Ask XMLHTTPRequest to get data
2. Insert data into DOM
XMLHTTPRequest gets data
XMLHTTPRequest passes data to JavaScript function

Fig. 18.2. The Ajax process.

There are some caveats and gotchas to using Ajax. First, in most cases, browsers restrict requests to the same domain from which the request is being made. In other words, an *XmlHttpRequest* made from a page served by `http://acompany.com` cannot access a server at `http://anothercompany.com`. This restriction protects a user from receiving data from another site without their consent. To get around this, developers often insert a local proxy server between the *XmlHttpRequest*, and the externally available data they want to retrieve. When this is the case, the Ajax makes a request to the local proxy server within the same domain. The proxy server then performs the "real" request, unencumbered by the browser's security manager, and then returns the data to the *XmlHttpRequest*. There are some exceptions to the single domain restriction, including the retrieval of images.

Another issue with Ajax is that it reduces the *addressability* of URLs. Because new data can be retrieved without moving to a new URL, state changes occur which are not tracked by the browser nor modelled in the URL. Hence when a user presses the browser's *Back* button, they may end up somewhere they did not expect to be, possibly having lost all the states generated by the Ajax calls. Likewise, when a state is arrived at that has been generated by Ajax requests, the URL in the address bar of the browser may not reflect the state. If the user copies and pastes the URL into an email and sends it to a friend, the friend may not see what the sender expected them to see. This veiling of addressability is also an issue for search engines that commonly crawl the Web using the link and URL structures in the page. These engines are unlikely to execute the Ajax code in order to discover the states that the code generates.

In the traditional Web application model, the client-side code (HTML, JavaScript, CSS) contains no application logic. It acts only as a renderer of server-side functionality that maintains the application logic. Ajax introduces a more desktop application-oriented relationship between application logic and rendering. In a desktop application, the client code retrieves data from somewhere (files, databases, remote servers, etc.) and then renders that data. This is the capability that Ajax affords Web Applications. Well-known examples of sites that use Ajax include Google Maps and GMail, Windows Live's Virtual Earth and Facebook to name a few.

18.2.2 Application Programming Interfaces (APIs)

Web sites and services that have useful data often expose interfaces to their data that can be programmed against. This allows third parties to make use of that data in their own desktop or Web applications. In the following sections we will look at two examples of APIs that provide access to data stored remotely. The first is very simple and can be run from within a browser. The second is an example of a very sophisticated API requiring some client-side coding.

Technorati

Technorati [229] maintains data on the *blogosphere* — the collection of weblogs on the Web — allowing users to search for the most popular blogs, keywords, links and tags. The API exposed by Technorati is simply a URI with some query parameters, in much the same way as a Google search request. Many Web 2.0-oriented services provide a simple HTTP interface (usually advertised as a REST interface, although not all of them are RESTful), rather than requiring clients to use SOAP. Like many APIs to Web services, they require an *API key*. This is simply an identifier that associates a user with the requests they make, and allows the service to track the user's use of the service (possibly in order to store that data and expose it via another service!). When making a request to the Technorati services one of the parameters is your API key. The other parameters are used in processing the response. One of the services Technorati provides is the amount of times per day that a particular word appears in the blogs contained in their database. Below is an example of such a request:

```
http://api.technorati.com/dailycounts?
    key=1234567890&q= technorati&days=3
```

Broken down into its constituent parts, we have:

- `http://api.technorati.com` - the host
- `/dailycounts` - the resource representing the service
- `key=1234567890` - the user's API key
- `q=technorati` - the keyword being searched for
- `days=3` - how many days to receive the daily count for

The result of issuing such a request will be an XML document containing the number of times the word "technorati" has appeared in the blogosphere in the last five days:

```
<?xml version="1.0" encoding="utf-8"?>
<!-- generator="Technorati API version 1.0" -->
<!DOCTYPE tapi PUBLIC "-//Technorati, Inc.//DTD TAPI 0.02//EN"
    "http://api.technorati.com/dtd/tapi-002.xml">
<tapi version="1.0">
<document>
<result>
    <queryterm>technorati</queryterm>
    <days>3</days>
    <searchurl>http://technorati.com/search/technorati</searchurl>
</result>
<items>
    <item>
        <date>2008-04-16</date>
        <count>1921</count>
    </item>
    <item>
        <date>2008-04-15</date>
        <count>12853</count>
    </item>
    <item>
        <date>2008-04-14</date>
        <count>14698</count>
    </item>
</items>
</document>
</tapi>
```

Such a request is trivial to execute, but nonetheless displays some powerful properties. First, while one can type this address into one's browser, it is of course also possible to make the HTTP request programmatically, either using Ajax, with a proxy server, as described above, or with one of the many HTTP tools available in every programming language. Second, it provides a programmatic interface to the Technorati database because what is returned is machine readable XML rather than visually riveting, but syntactically messy html. The XML format is proprietary, which means that to do anything useful with the data, I will have to write a parser to extract the data; however, the XML structure is very simple, and can be validated against a Document Type Definition, so this task is pretty straightforward. Given the simplicity of the invocation — the use of HTTP and URIs as the means of identifying and accessing the service, and the use of XML as the response format — it is not difficult to see how this service can be easily integrated or aggregated with other services, either Web applications, or desktop applications. Web applications that aggregate such results from a variety of APIs are called *mashups* in Web 2.0 parlance. There are many available on the Web (`http://www.programmableweb.com` keeps a database on them) that draw on the APIs of services such as Technorati, Flickr and many more. Perhaps the most popular API used in this way is the Google Maps API.

Google Maps

The Google Maps API is more sophisticated than the Technorati API, allowing developers to make full use of all the functionality available in Google Maps, and extend it in a number of ways. Like Technorati, the Maps API requires the developer to sign up for an API key before they can use the service. This API key is actually mapped to the URI where your Web site that uses the API is hosted.

In order to use the API, the developer imports the Google JavaScript into their page. This is achieved using a script import HTML tag which contains the URI of the script to import into the page. It is here that the API key is included in the URL, authorizing the request for the script:

```
<script src="http://maps.google.com/maps?file=api&amp;v=2
&amp;key=1234567890 type="text/javascript"></script>
```

The script is retrieved by the browser and loaded into the scripting environment of the page, making the JavaScript objects defined in it available to other JavaScript functions on the same page. The Maps API JavaScript defines interfaces to the maps data managed by Google:

Map objects These provide various functionalities, e.g., setting the latitude and longitude of the map, setting the centre of the map and panning the map.

Map events Allow event handlers to be attached to them that are executed when particular event are detected for example the user clicking or double clicking on a map, as well as users dragging their mouse.

Map controls Provide different controls, for example, a slider zoom control.

Map overlays Allow drawing shapes and lines onto a map. An example of overlays are the direction routes available from the Google Maps site.

Map services Provide various functionalities that do not fit neatly into the other categories, e.g., reading in data files containing geo data and geo coding; that is, converting an address to a latitude/longitude pair.

The Maps API is commonly used in mashups to provide a visual geographical representation of data drawn from other services.

18.2.3 Microformats

In the words of the Microformats Web site [230]:

> *"Designed for humans first and machines second, microformats are a set of simple, open data formats built upon existing and widely adopted standards."*

As the name suggests, they are not about trying to address grand issues. Rather, they attempt to solve small problems in a way that is as non-disruptive as possible. This is a quite different approach to, say, the standardization efforts within the Web Services community. The Web Services community has seen an explosion in new standards which are generic, flexible and extensible, yet complex to implement. Microformats, on the other hand, promote *paving the cow paths*; that is, only defining new microformats to serve existing applications, rather than trying to imagine all possible scenarios and standardizing against some future possibilities. Likewise, microformats should be able to be embedded into as many different data formats as possible, rather than forcing people to change their preferred formats, or tools.

While microformats place humans first, they are also part of the movement towards making Web content more machine friendly. Hence they are associated with *lowercase semantic web*, and have coined the acronym *POSH* which stands for *Plain Old Semantic HTML.* This approach is about modelling data structures in such a way that they can viewed by humans in a browser but also parsed by a machine. The *lowercase* here refers to the Semantic Web initiative. The uppercase Semantic Web uses complex XML in its serializations of the Subject-Predicate-Predicate triple defined by Resource Description Framework (RDF). The complexity associated with RDF has meant its takeup has not been huge, despite being led by Tim Berners Lee. To achieve both human-readable and non-lossy data structures, microformats make use of XHTML. POSH advocates the use of semantic (or simply *meaningful*) class attribute names for elements and dropping the use of purely presentational HTML tags, and techniques such as transparent GIF images to position content visually. (X)HTML that is cleanly and correctly constructed allows the data structures embedded in it to be converted to formats such as XML and JSON and back again without loss of data.

Mircoformats define elemental formats that can then be used by compound formats. Currently the compound formats themselves try to model existing standards, rather than defining new, or similar ones that address the same issues, thus in effect being XHTML serializations of standards defined in other formats. Some elemental microformats include:

rel-tag This microformat defines a link relation that can be added to an anchor tag (`<a>`) to identify the URL pointed to by the `href` attribute, as being a tag space associated with the page on which the link appears. For example, given the link:

```
<a href="http://en.wikipedia.org/wiki/Technology" rel="tag">
   tech stuff
</a>
```

then the author is asserting that the page on which the link appears (or a portion of it) is tagged with the value *Technology.* Note that it is the last path component of the referenced URL that defines the value of the tag — not the text inside the anchor tag. The referenced URL should exist, but the specification does not define how the content of referenced URL should relate to the tag value. The above example would take the user to the Wikipedia page on Technology.

The benefit of including such metadata as tagging as links within an HTML document, is that they are visible. This allows users to see, and follow tag links, and authors to control their tagging easier, rather than leaving metadata generation to the vagaries of their HTML or blog editor.

rel-nofollow This microformat defines a link relation that can be added to an anchor tag, asserting that the URL referenced by the anchor's `href` attribute should not be given any weight by agents performing link analysis, such as search engines. Examples include links provided in comments to blog entries, and links which the author wishes to provide, but not endorse.

XOXO Extensible Open XHTML Outlines (XOXO) is a microformat based on the modularization mechanism defined as part of XHTML 1.1 (see Section 3.3). Its aim is to provide a means of modelling outlines, e.g., page contents and blogrolls (the list of favourite other blogs on a blog site) in both a human- and machine-readable way. The XOXO document type uses a restricted set of tags, primarily the HTML list and dictionary tags (`dl, dt, dd, ol, ul, li`) as well as the anchor tag, and the document structure tags (`html, head, body, title`), to enable a XOXO document to be stand-alone.

The following example shows a fragment of an imaginary *family* data structure might be modelled using the XOXO document type (very much for illustration purposes only!). The ordered list has a class of `xoxo` and `family`. This in turn contains list items with a class of `member`. Each member item contains a definition with a class of `member-definition`. The member structure also contains a sublist of other members this one is related to.

```
<ol class="xoxo family">
  <li class="member">dad</li>
    <dl class="member-definition">
      <dt>dad</dt>
        <dd>the weak link</dd>
    </dl>
    <ol class="related">
      <li>wife</li>
      <li>child</li>
    </ol>
  </li>
  ...
</ol>
```

The point of this example is to show how such data can be rendered in a browser, but also examined by a machine to extract the family structure from the XHTML in a non-lossy way.

Beyond these elemental structures, microformats also define compound components. The most popular of these are the *hCard* and *hCalendar* microformats. In keeping with the principles of reuse and non-disruptive integration, these are based on the respective *vCard* and *iCalendar* formats that are widely used by address book and calendar applications. These allow the embedding of identity and calendar data structures, into HTML and, of course, the extraction of those structures as well.

18.2.4 Syndication

Syndication is the process of publishing material simultaneously across a number of channels or newspapers. In terms of the Web, it is applied to the process of making site metadata or content summaries available from other Web sites, in particular content that changes frequently, and which clients may want to subscribe to and be automatically notified when content has changed. Technologies supporting updating and subscription are often called *feeds*. There were ongoing attempts to develop technologies to support this capability since the mid-nineties, which culminated in Netscape releasing RDF Site Summary (RSS 0.9) available on the My Netscape portal, and four months later Rich Site Summary (RSS 0.91). But when AOL bought out Netscape in 2001, it dropped support for RSS. Without an owner, development of RSS continued simultaneously within the RSS-DEV working group, and independently by Dave Winer of Userland Software, neither of which had official Netscape backing but both releasing different variations and version numbers of the original specification. To confuse matters further, the Userland releases stressed Really Simple Syndication as the meaning of the abbreviation.

By 2003 there were six versions of RSS in circulation and Winer's RSS 2.0, the most commonly used today, had undergone a number of changes without the version number being altered. Furthermore, Dave Winer had passed ownership of RSS 2.0 to Harvard's Berkman Center for the Internet & Society [231].

A combination of the fluctuating history of RSS as well as the fact that it was not publicly owned, was the partial reason for the development of Atom, an alternative syndication format of the RSS family. But beyond the politics, there were also technical reasons for creating not just a new syndication format, but a clearer, more flexible approach to publishing content as well [232]. Certain areas of RSS are under-specified, for example defining how content should be encoded, whilst other areas are confusing, for example duplicate elements in different namespaces describing the same concepts, like author and published date. Furthermore, publishing APIs, MetaWeblog [233] and Blogger [234], use different data formats than those used in the syndication format, making it necessary to translate between the two. Atom aimed to develop a syndication format and publishing protocol that were vendor neutral, freely extensible and cleanly specified. While RSS 2.0 is still the most used, The Atom Syndication Format 1.0 has been endorsed by the Internet Engineering Task Force (IETF) as a *proposed standard*. Hence it, and the related publishing protocol, stand to gain wider acceptance over time.

Apart from addressing various aspects of RSS that are under-specified, The Atom Publishing Protocol which builds on the syndication format, defines a protocol for retrieving, editing and publishing Atom feeds. In the following section we look at both the syndication format and the publishing protocol.

Atom Syndication Format

The Atom Syndication Format defines an *Entry* XML document. Any number of entries can be contained in a single *Feed* document. A Feed represents an entity whose content changes over time. This may be a blog, a news agency or even the conversation that ensues between two applications. Atom is good at modelling anything that has temporal or episodic qualities.

The Feed document contains various useful metadata fields including:

- A unique Identifier
- A title
- A list of authors and contributors
- The date the feed was last updated
- A feed logo and icon
- Copyright information
- Categories that the feed falls into

Atom makes use of a *category* structure for defining classification and tagging attributes, both for Feed and Entry documents. A Category element has a *term* — a character string identifying the category to which the Feed or Entry belongs — a *scheme* — an optional URI identifying a categorization scheme allowing the term to be qualified or contextualized — and an optional *label* which is a human-readable rendition of the categorization. Because the category element is very simple, and makes no assumptions about the meaning or interpretation of its values, it provides a flexible means for applications to define application-specific metadata pertaining to a Feed or Entry.

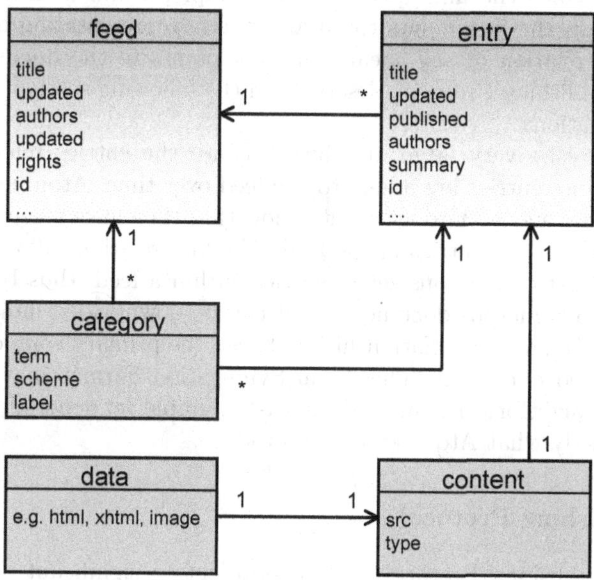

Fig. 18.3. Atom Feed document.

The Entry document contains, or references, the actual content that the producer creates and the client subscribes to. It also contains similar metadata fields to the Feed document adding a published date and an optional summary of the content in, or referenced by, the Entry. This allows Entry documents to exist outside of a Feed document and be exchanged and consumed independently.

An Entry has a single *content* element which is used to either house the content inline, or reference it at another URI. This allows large documents, as well as binary data such as images or MP3 files to be stored and retrieved independently of the Feed or Entry document. To support different media types, the content element provides a *type* attribute, defining the types of data according the Multipurpose Internet Mail Extension (MIME) type. MIME types are the de facto means of describing data formats on the Web. They consist of two character strings separated by a forward slash. The first string is the primary type of the data. The second is a subtype of the first. Common MIME types include *text/html*, *text/xml* and the various image types such as *image/png* and *image/jpg*.

The XML documents defined by Atom represent a form of hypermedia. Container documents point to other documents, which in turn point to others. To model the links and, more importantly, the relationships between resources in a machine-understandable way, Atom uses the *link* tag, also to be found in HTML, in combination with the *rel* attribute. The rel attribute, as we have seen from microformats, describes the *relation* of the hyper-reference to the document in which the link appears. For example, a link with a relation of *alternate* means the link points to an alternative representation of the same document. A relation of *self* means the link points to the document itself. The Atom Publishing Protocol, described in the following section, also makes use of link relations.

A feed may be very large, not just because the entries reference large files, but because entries are added to the feed over time. Atom uses the link relations of *next* and *prev* to let clients know that they have received a subset of the total amount of entries in the feed. The link relations allow a client to move to the next or previous set of entries within a feed, thus breaking the feed down into numerous documents that can be downloaded individually.

Figure 18.3 shows the relationships between the primary components that make up a Feed document. The Atom Syndication Format may seem very simple and straightforward, and indeed it is. A simple yet generally applicable format is exactly what Atom set out to produce.

Atom Publishing Protocol

The Atom Publishing Protocol (APP) represents a significant development in the application of REST to machine-processable service delivery. Because the Atom Syndication Format is applicable to a variety of contexts, not just Web syndication in the usual sense, it means the APP, which sits on top of the syndication format, provides a well-specified means of discovering, and manipulating arbitrary resources using a RESTful approach.

Like the syndication format, APP uses XML to expose constructs that allow clients to access and store resources on a server. The XML documents define a hierarchical relationship of entities. Figure 18.4 shows the relationship between the documents. At the root of the hierarchy is the *Service* document. A Service document has a URI associated with it, and is the top-level entry point for a client. In keeping with the use of hypermedia in REST(see Section 5.6), the Service document is analogous to a Web site address providing hyperlinks to other documents. The Service document contains *Workspaces*. These are purely logical entities, in the sense that they do not have a URI associated with them. They are merely means of grouping *Collection* documents. A Collection has a URI that can be dereferenced. When a client does

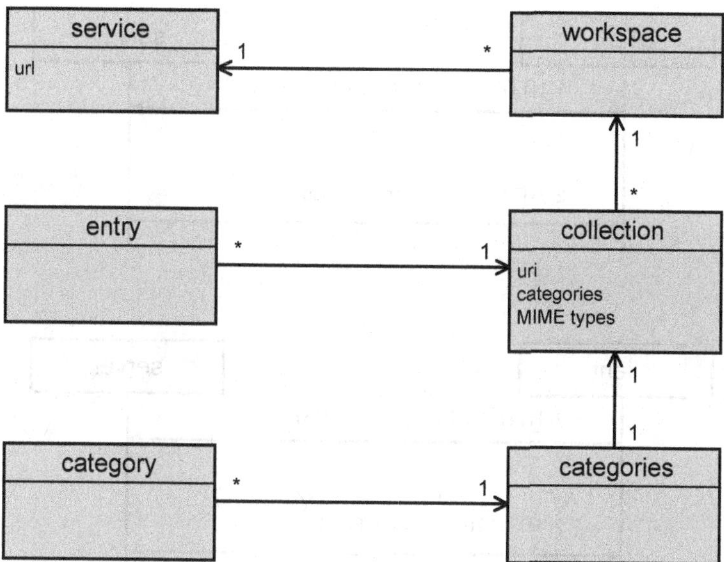

Fig. 18.4. Atom Service document.

this, they receive an Atom Feed document; that is, a Collection is an APP interface to an Atom feed. This interface provides further metadata about the feed that it represents, in particular the categories and MIME types allowed in the collection. The categories are grouped into a *Categories* document made up of Atom Category documents.

The APP is based entirely on HTTP. It uses URIs in the XML documents to point to particular resources, and makes use of link relations to clearly specify the nature of the resources. For example, when an entry is created, the server will provide both a public view of the entry, i.e., as part of the feed that clients subscribe to, as well as a URI at which the entry can be edited by the author. Likewise, an entry may point to a media resource such as an image. In this case there are actually two resources on the server — the Entry document itself with its attendant metadata, and the image resource. To model the relationship between these resources, Atom uses a link relation of *edit* to point to a URI to which an updated version of the entry document can be sent, and an *edit-media* link relation, pointing to the URI to which a new image can to sent. If a client sends a new image to the URI with a relation of *edit-media*, they will be updating the image referenced by the entry.

Figures 18.5 shows how a client retrieves an Atom Feed document in order to publish to it. There are two stages to the process. Each stage is a simple HTTP request/response pair. First the client issues an HTTP GET to the service document's URI. This service document URI has to be known in advance, or is discovered through a process not defined by the APP. The service document contains workspaces, which in turn contain collections of

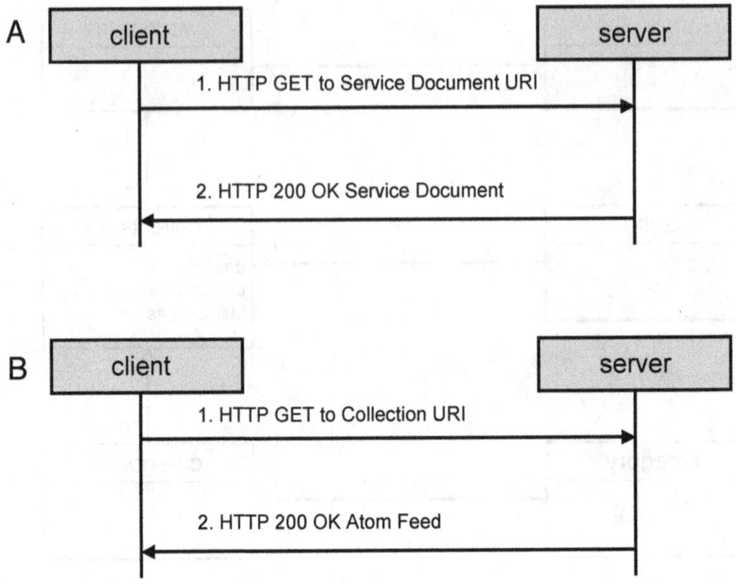

Fig. 18.5. A: Getting an Atom Service Document. B: Getting an Atom Feed Document.

feeds. Each collection has an associated URI, and hence the client can issue an HTTP GET to a particular collection URI depending on its understanding of the workspaces and the categories supported by the collections. If all goes well, then the client receives an Atom Feed document, containing any Entry documents that have previously been inserted into the feed.

Figure 18.6 depicts the Protocol by which a client manipulates the Feed document. Again, each process is modeled as a single HTTP request/response pair. In process C, the client first creates an Atom Entry locally. It then uses the HTTP POST method to publish the Entry, using the collection URI as the target of the method. In response, the server returns an HTTP status code of 201, meaning the resource has been created. The server also includes a *Content-Location* HTTP header in its response which provides the client with the URI at which the entry is now available on the server. The client can take this URI, and use it to retrieve the newly created Entry document. This is depicted in process D.

Clients can actually publish any kind of data to the Collection URI, not just Atom Entries, provided the collection supports the MIME type of the data being sent. This actually makes Atom highly flexible and generic. If a client publishes something other than an Entry document, let us say an image, then two resources are created on the server. First, the image itself is stored on the server. Second, a new Entry document is created. This entry contains a reference to the image in the Entry's content element *src* attribute, as well as a

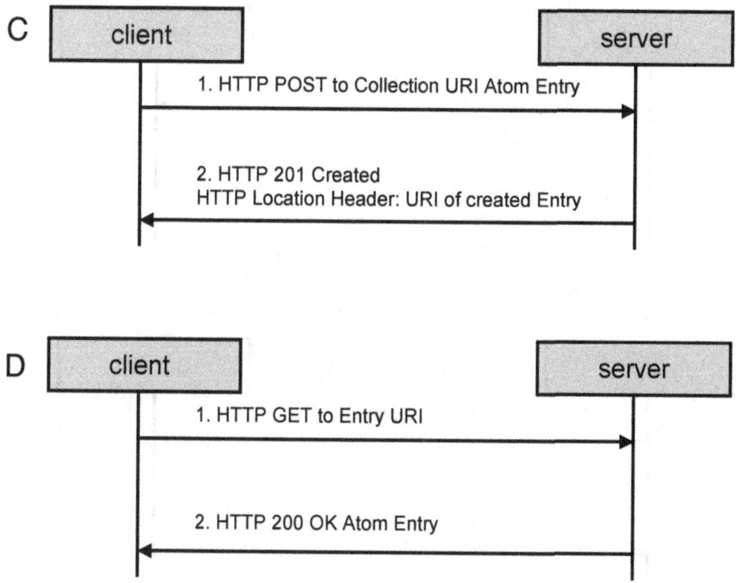

Fig. 18.6. C: Publishing an Atom Entry. D: Retrieving an Atom Entry.

link with a relation of *edit-media*, pointing to the URI at which the image can be updated. The response from the server contains an HTTP Location header, pointing to the newly created Atom Entry, allowing the client to retrieve the Entry and flesh out any contents such as a textual summary of the image.

In order to edit, or update, the entry, the client uses the same URI to send a modified Entry document to, using the HTTP PUT method. Again, all being well, the server returns a 200 OK response code. Finally, if the author wishes to remove the entry, it can send an HTTP DELETE request to the entry URI. These two interactions are depicted in Figure 18.7.

Similar to the syndication format, the APP is very simple and easy to understand. This is in part because it makes use of the HTTP methods and status codes, rather than defining Atom-specific means of transferring the data in the way the Web Services based on SOAP and WSDL do. A further benefit to using HTTP and hypermedia in the way that Atom does is that it can seamlessly accommodate binary data of any description or size.

Although Atom was primarily designed with Web syndication in mind, it is proving to be a useful technology for a variety of situations and applications. For example the Google GData service, which is a machine-oriented protocol for exchanging geo data has made use of of Atom extensibility capabilities to define geo specific extensions to the syndication format, and is using the APP to transfer the data. Likewise Windows' Application Based Storage API which allows applications to store user data on Windows Live servers uses the APP, as does the Windows Live Photo API, which provides a means to users

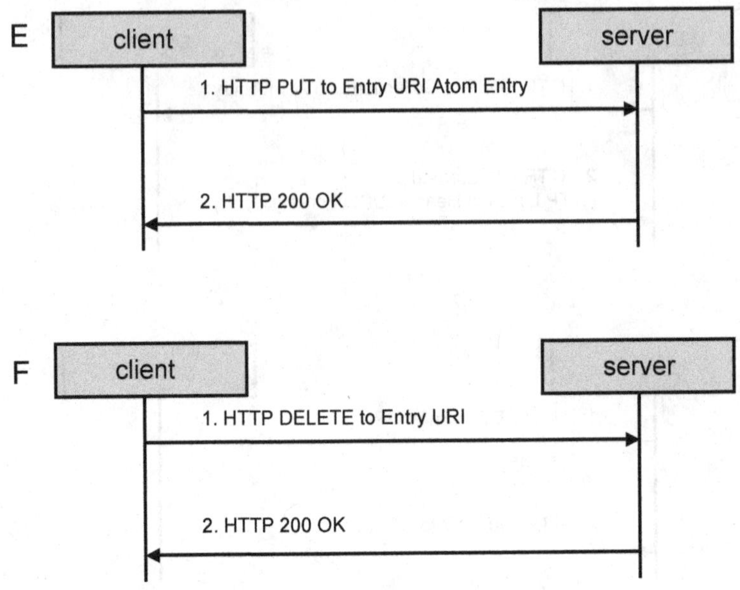

Fig. 18.7. E: Updating an Atom Entry. F: Deleting an Atom Entry.

of securely granting third parties the ability to edit their online photo store. Even Grid computing has begun looking at Atom, for example in the context of Geo Sciences [235]

18.2.5 Web Application Description Language

As the degree to which Web technologies focus on machine-to-machine interactions increases, so the need for describing them in a machine-processable way becomes more apparent. Whilst a cornerstone of Web Services technologies is Web Service Definition Language (WSDL), Web services (with a small 's') usually rely on human-readable documentation. When creating a client for a service on the Web, for example the Google Maps API, the developer will go to the developer site and start reading. Web Services developers, on the other hand, usually get hold of the service WSDL location, and run the file through a tool that will generate programming language objects that enact the SOAP message exchanges required by the service. The Web Application Description Language (WADL) — the name being a direct reference to WSDL — is designed to enable services using a resource-oriented approach and HTTP as their transfer protocol to be described in a machine-processable way. In particular, WADL targets applications that:

- Are based on existing Web architecture and infrastructure
- Are platform and programming language independent
- Promote re-use of the application beyond the browser

- Enable composition with other Web or desktop applications
- Require semantic clarity in content (representations) exchanged during their use

To facilitate this, WADL models various facets of a Web-based application using an XML vocabulary, specifically sets of resources exposed by the application and the relationships between them, including the links between them and whether the relationship is referential or causal. It also models the representation formats of resources — similar to WSDL, WADL allows representation types to be described using XML Schema — and the HTTP methods a resource responds to.

Figure 18.8 shows the relationships between the primary XML elements defined in WADL. The top-level *application* element contains a *resources* element. This provides a base URL against which contained *resource* elements relative URLs are resolved. A *resource* element can contain *method* elements representing particular HTTP methods. A *method* element in turn has a *request* and *response* child element. Requests and responses have zero or *representation* elements. The representation of a request depends on whether the HTTP method allows an entity in the request, as is the case with the HTTP PUT and POST methods. The representation of the response depends on the server's evaluation of the request at runtime.

The *resource*, *request*, *response* and *representation* elements can also have parameters associated with them through the *param* element. Parameters have *name*, *style* and *type* attributes. The style of a parameter indicates the semantics of the parameter. For example, *request* and *response* elements can have parameters with a style of *header*, indicating that the parameter represents an HTTP header. Likewise, a *resource* element may have a parameter of style *query* indicating that the parameter represents a query component to be appended to the URL of the resource. WADL also supports URI Templates (see Section 5.3) via a parameter style of *template*. Parameters also have a *name* attribute, which identifies them, and a possible *type* attribute. The type attribute is used in parameters that expect a certain data type.

To give a more concrete example of how WADL can be used to express an HTTP-based API, let us return to the Technorati example we used in Section 18.2.2. This is a simple request to the dailycounts service which returns the amount of times per day that a particular word appears in the blogs contained in their database. The form of the request is a simple HTTP GET to the URI:

```
http://api.technorati.com/dailycounts?
key=1234567890&q= technorati&days=3
```

To model this request using WADL, one might create the following document:

```
...
<resources base="http://api.techorati.com">
```

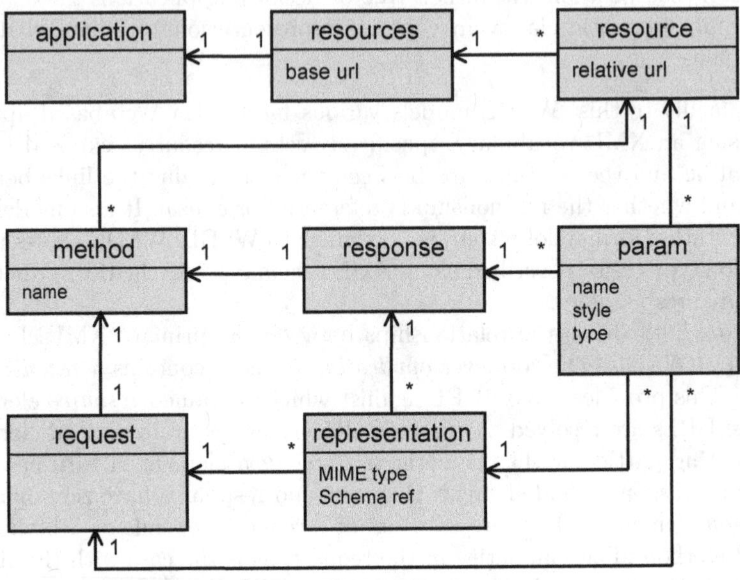

Fig. 18.8. WADL element relationships.

```
    <param name="key" style="query" required="true"/>
    <resource path="dailycounts">
      <method name="GET">
        <request>
          <param name="q" style="query" type="xsd:string"/>
          <param name="days" style="query" type="xsd:int"/>
        </request>
        <response>
          <representation mediaType="text/xml"/>
        </response>
      </method>
    </resource>
    ...
  </resources>
  ...
```

Here, the base URI is defined in the *resources* element. Also defined globally within the *resources* element is the query parameter with a name of `key`. This represents the API key query element required by all the Technorati services. The dailycounts service is represented as a *resource* element with a URI of `dailycounts`, which is relative to the absolute URI defined in the parent element. The HTTP method used to access the service is defined as the GET method. The method request has two query parameters. The first has a name of `q`, representing the keyword to search on. The second has a name of `days`, representing the amount of days to return hits for. The first parameter has a type of string, while the second has a type int, i.e., the number of days. These types are qualified by a namespace prefix (see Section 3.2). The snippet above presumes that this prefix has been mapped to the XML Schema namespace somewhere else in the document.

The response of the method contains a representation element with a *mediaType* attribute of `text/xml`, representing the MIME type of the returned data.

Using this piece of WADL (or rather a more robust and complete version), it would be possible to programmatically generate a Technorati client, in the same way that current Web Service WSDL parsing tools can do. Whilst WADL is not currently widely used by service providers, it is well placed to become more popular. And, although it is similar to WSDL in its aims, unlike WSDL it does not impose an object-oriented view on the underlying processes. WADL stays true to the concepts of REST and the Web. Whether future tooling supporting WADL does as well remains to be seen.

18.3 Conclusion

This chapter has provided an introduction to Web 2.0 and some of the technologies that are used by it. Whilst the concepts underlying Web 2.0 are about leveraging the power and nature of the Web, in particular through the adoption of architectures of participation, emerging technologies, either closely or loosely associated with Web 2.0, are commonly concerned with enabling machine-to-machine interactions to some degree. This is not a contradictory situation. In order to leverage the mass of humanity and the data generated by it, shared mechanisms need to be developed that move beyond the consumer-oriented approach taken by Web 1.0 towards one in which users can produce data that can be digested by the Web at large. In general, these technologies attempt to remain backward compatible with the Web, but are pushing the concept of the Web as Platform through defining machine-processable layers that can co-exist and integrate with existing behaviour patterns and well-understood, ubiquitous technologies.

19

On the Horizon

> *"DON'T PANIC" Douglas Adams, The Hitch-Hiker's Guide to the Galaxy*

As memory becomes more affordable, devices become more compact and networks become more ubiquitous, scenarios that were once nothing more than visions are beginning to become reality. These scenarios leverage the pervasiveness of computing devices and networking capabilities, offering possibilities in which the boundaries between human and computer, and between mobile device and supercomputer are blurred. Approaches drawing on these trends go under different names, and have different areas of focus. In this chapter we look at some of the paradigms and concepts that are defining next-generation distributed systems, beginning with systems and technologies that are already being implemented and used, and moving towards the more esoteric visions proposed by contemporary commentators.

19.1 Computing in the Cloud

Cloud computing is a term that has gained currency in recent years in the commercial sector to describe a form of *Service Grid* (Chapter 9). While Grid computing has been mainly driven by the academic sector, Cloud computing is emerging as a business paradigm. Its advocates claim it represents a major new development in the way computers are used, in particular making the current desktops redundant. Rather than storing data and executing software locally on our machines, Cloud computing allows these capabilities to be provided as services across the Internet via a Web interface by businesses supporting huge storage capacity and redundancy, and processing parallelism. For users this means they do not have to worry about losing their data or upgrading their software. Instead they can rely on the backup and security services of a professional organization. For businesses it means they can pay for storage and processing power on a pay-per-use basis. This allows the business to be insulated from the associated costs of rapid or unexpected expansion or contraction. In fact, many people are already making use of cloud computing. Google's GMail and Docs services provide users with a Web interface to their email and documents.

Such a vision also ties in with the growth in mobile computing because users can access all their data wherever they are, even from small hand-held devices. These possibilities are leading to a potential collaboration between Apple Inc. and Google in which Apple would provide the user side of the equation, in the shape of a mobile device, while Google would provide the cloud in the shape of its massive data centres [236].

The image of the cloud comes from the notion that services are available over the Internet but their whereabouts and the software and hardware used to provide them are hidden. This is very similar to the vision of Grid computing. However, Cloud computing, in general, does not try to address the issues arising from working across a large set of different administrative boundaries, as Grid computing does. Rather, the resources of a service provider are controlled by a small group of business partners. Achieving this on an Internet scale requires a massive amount of hardware and electricity to run. Hence many suggest only a few companies, e.g., Google, Amazon, Microsoft and IBM, will be able to provide such clouds because of the financial resources required to support them.

In many cases, cloud service providers use *virtualization* to provide a suitable interface to the underlying resources. For example a storage service may expose resources in a data centre via virtual servers, potentially made up of a number of actual machines. Clients only see the virtual server, and can configure it how they like. To achieve this, physical machines run a *hypervisor*. This is a platform that allows a number of virtual machines to run concurrently on the same hardware. Each virtual machine can run its own operating system and be exposed as a virtual server whilst the hypervisor ensures that the virtual machines exist in strong isolation. Clients of the service can often choose from a set of available virtual machines of a given operating system, capacity and configuration allowing them to run their applications in a (virtual) software and hardware environment that suits them. Virtual machines can also be easily replicated, saved, copied and moved to another machine allowing the service provider to manage workload and sudden rises in demand cheaply and without downtime.

The most high profile examples of cloud services are Amazon's Simple Storage Service (S3) [237] and Elastic Compute Cloud (EC2) [238]. S3 allows users to store data in *buckets*. A bucket is a virtual container which could be physically located in either Europe or the United States. Users can add, remove and manipulate data objects within their buckets via user-defined keys. S3 also supports authentication to protect data from unauthorized access and objects can be made private or public, and rights granted to specific users. Whilst S3 uses HTTP as the default download protocol, it also provides a

BitTorrent interface to support scalable, yet cost-effective content distribution. The pricing is based on a pay-per-use scheme with no minimum fee.

EC2 allows users to execute software in the cloud by allowing them to create an *Amazon Machine Image.* A machine image contains everything needed to run an application including applications, data, libraries and configuration. Amazon provides a number of predefined images that are suitable for typical tasks such as running a Web server, but users with more demanding or specific requirements can also upload their own specialist images. The images are stored in the S3 cloud. By combining S3 and EC2, a business or individual can run their software and store data it uses without ever knowing anything about the hardware they are using or even where it is.

Other cloud infrastructures are also being developed. IBM has announced the *Blue Cloud* [239] infrastructure. This will leverage virtualization and parallel processing techniques to allow instant resource provision based on client demand. Likewise, Google has released the *Google App Engine* [240]. This is a more restrictive environment than EC2, but provides specific support for quickly and easily deploying Web applications using the Google server infrastructure. Another big player in Cloud computing is 3Tera [241]. 3Tera allows clients to use a graphical workflow tool to construct their data centres and processing components. By dragging and dropping virtual images of databases, firewall servers, Web servers and load balancers onto the visual desktop, users can create a sophisticated grid in a few simple steps. All the configuration and resource allocation happens under the hood.

Beyond the core set of businesses that have the resources to act as cloud providers, there are several companies now offering services that are more client-facing, and build on top of the infrastructures provided by the large companies, for example distributed database implementations. It is likely that the number and range of these services will continue to grow as the core infrastructures become more stable. It still remains to be seen whether the Cloud computing paradigm will completely change the way we store data and run applications, but with the development of lightweight, streamlined mobile devices supporting sophisticated user interfaces combined with increasing download speeds, the opportunity to develop a new type of interface that supplants the traditional desk/laptop is certainly there.

19.2 Ubiquitous Computing

The term *ubiquitous computing* was coined as long ago as 1988 by Mark Weiser while working for Xerox PARC. Ubiquitous computing considers itself the third wave in computing. The first wave consisted of mainframes, each shared by many dumb clients. Next followed the personal computing era. This is the era we are now primarily in. Ubiquitous computing considers this a transient phase in which the human and the machine stare *uneasily at each other across the desktop* [242]. The third era, now beginning, is that of ubiquitous computing, or the age of *calm technology.* Calmness is achieved when technology ceases to be at the centre of our attention when dealing with it. Rather, it performs its tasks imperceptibly to the user, fully integrated into the environment inhabited by the human.

One of the earliest and most famous examples of ubiquitous computing was the *Dangling String*, created by artist Natalie Jeremijenko and installed at Xerox PARC. This was an 8-foot piece of plastic that hung from the ceiling, and attached to a small electric motor. The motor was electrically connected to a nearby Ethernet cable, so that every time data travelled through the cable, the motor would rotate. A very busy network would cause the string to whirl madly with a characteristic noise; a quiet network would cause only a small twitch every few seconds. The ingenuity of the installation lay in the fact that it could describe network load without taking up space on one's desk, or requiring the user to decipher network statistics; in fact without even using a computer. Rather, the string described network conditions in an intuitive manner.

Central to the concept of ubiquitous computing is the relationship of the human with the machine. Changing this relationship from one of active engagement, to one of seamless, invisible interaction requires advances in a number of areas. First, computer interfaces that we have become accustomed to such as the command line and graphical user interfaces are based on the human actively triggering events. More subtle forms of exposing computational capability need to be designed. An example of developments in this area are *e-Readers*, tablets that display digital content but behave much more like paper than a computer screen. Second, the kinds of spaces that computers inhabit need to be extended. This is happening rapidly. As computational devices become smaller they are being introduced into new environments such as the human body, for the purpose of recording physical measurements such as temperature and heart rate. Likewise, the spaces that humans move through, both public and private, are being equipped with devices that can store local information and record human activity and movement. And of course such devices are being situated on products and documents used for identification and payment purposes, for example credit cards and passports.

Developments in networking technologies are also driving computing towards ubiquity. The Internet Protocol version 6 (IPv6) supports far more addresses than the current IPv4 used on the Web. IPv6 allows for vast amounts of objects to be accessible across the Internet potentially increasing capacity by some 25,000 trillion trillion times [243]. This provides the possibility of an *Internet of Things*, in which every household device, consummable, item of clothing, car engine part are addressable, and hence can intercommunicate. Building on top of the concept of an Internet of Things is the notion of *Ambient Intelligence* which proposes embedded systems that are responsive to human presence. In a world of ambient intelligence the fridge checks its contents and their expiry dates and passes this information to the electronic shopping list, which can then notify the supermarket of a delivery request over the Internet.

Radio-frequency identification (RFID) is another important technology in this context. It enables tiny transponders, called tags, to be embedded into products, pets or even humans for the purposes of identification. RFID reader components can query for nearby transponders to receive their identification. The simplest type of tag — the passive type — requires no internal energy supply to function. When it receives a query, the radio frequency signal of the query contains enough power to enable it to respond with its identification information. This information can be used to determine an entity in order to induce payment from a bank account, or to change environmental conditions in accordance with an entity's profile (for example unlocking the cat flap for a tagged pet). Beyond simple identification data, RFID tags can also contain writable memory.

RFID is being used in a number of systems. Malaysia introduced RFID into passports in 1998 which also track when a person enters or leaves the country. Transport payment has been a popular application with the Moscow underground introducing RFID smart cards as early as 1998, whilst in Hong Kong almost all public transport is paid for using Octopus RFID Card. Co-operation between sectors has meant this card can also be used in supermarkets, vending machines and restaurants. Product identification is another common application, used in the context of tracking products through the delivery process and inventory systems. RFID tags are also being embedded into live organisms. Pets are commonly *chipped* these days and examples of employees being tagged also exist — in 2004 18 Mexican government employees were chipped in order to control access to sensitive data [244].

19.2.1 *Everyware*

Whilst this vision of ubiquity offers huge potential to change the nature of human society, health and day-to-day activity for the better, it also carries with it risks, in particular to values that many consider to lie at the heart of a free society including privacy and the right to choice. In his book *Everyware: The Dawning Age of Ubiquitous Computing* [245], Allen Greenfield addresses the challenges and dangers of a world in which digital systems are ubiquitous. In particular, he argues that, because such systems are seamlessly integrated with the environment, users are no longer aware that they are engaging with them which in turn leads to a loss of control; people are no longer users, they are subjects. Whilst the current relationship with computers may be *uneasy*, according to ubiquitous computing, the fact that it is based on the principle of active engagement means the user has complete control over how and when they interact with the system. We are already surrounded by systems that record data about us without our consent. As early as 2002, the average UK citizen was being captured on CCTV three hundred times a day [246]. More recently the Times Online reported on new technology being used to track shoppers by picking up the periodic signals sent out by their mobile phones [247]. The system provides retailers with information about how long a person stays in their shop and what shops they go to next. While such systems are arguably harmless, or, in the case of CCTV, a necessary side effect to increasing the safety of our environment, this is only the case because the data the systems are capturing is supposedly not being passed to entities that could draw conclusions from it resulting in a negative impact on those individuals whose data is being recorded. Greenfield suggests that the design of ubiquitous systems needs to follow certain guidelines to ensure that the paradise they promise does not turn into a hell. In particular, he suggests five principles:

- Systems must default to harmlessness. Any systems that inhabit every detail of human life must ensure that any errors, design flaws or degradation does not result in harm.
- Systems must be self-disclosing. Whilst seamlessness is necessary in order to not be disruptive, humans must also be able to examine a system and extract what its capabilities are, what it is used for and who it is owned by.
- Systems should be conservative of face. They must respect human dignity and not unnecessarily embarrass, humiliate or shame. Ubiquitous systems potentially handle highly private or intimate data. Furthermore, data about people might be recorded twenty-four hours a day. Whilst in our ordinary lives we have many different masks that we wear in different situations, for example at work or with our family, having data constantly being recorded about an individual means data pertaining to one mask can spill into the domain of another, potentially compromising the individual.
- Systems must be conservative of time. The design mentality of the PC era has led to rich interfaces that help the unspecialized user and increased time being spent engaging with technology. In a ubiquitous system, in which even simple tasks are being aided and monitored, such approaches would slow the activity down, making the intrusion of the system almost unbearable. Imagine the helpful kettle saying *You look like you're about to make a cup of tea. Can I help?* This principle has tensions with the other principles because the decisions about when a system should intervene to help a person are finely balanced against the need to remain seamless and default to harmlessness.
- Systems must be deniable. Users must be allowed to opt out of the system at any point with no penalty apart from not receiving the added value of the system. This is the hardest principle to follow, yet it is the most important. In the systems that exist today, for example CCTV, it is already almost impossible to opt out, yet the notions of consent and choice lie at the heart of our society.

19.2.2 Spimes

The science fiction author Bruce Sterling created the neologism *spime* to refer to

> *"Objects precisely located in space and time. They ingest their own metadata. They accumulate histories. They network with peers. They are scary, infinitely complex and almost inconceivable. But they are coming." [248]*

Sterling uses the term *blobject* [249] to refer to the *period objects of our time. They are the physical products that the digital revolution brought to the consumer shelf* [250]. A blobject is an object, typically with a curvilinear appearance, such as the original Apple iMac. Such products are more than mere consumer items. Rather, they are objects of desire, objects that induce engagement and participation from those who use them. Stirling identifies four classes of objects that have been produced by humans and that have emerged in historical succession. Artefacts emerged first. These are made and used by hunter-gatherers and farmers. Machines followed. These are made and used by customers. Then products emerged. These are used by consumers. Finally the Gizmo arrived. Gizmos are objects with huge amounts of functionality that are focussed, not on current functionality, but on trying to encapsulate the future. Gizmos begin their life on a computer screen and are used by *end-users.* An end-user is the historical evolution of the consumer and is an active participant in the development process of a Gizmo. Gizmos use end-users to guide their development process, permanently pushing the frontier of what is possible now. Blobjects are typically a subset of Gizmos.

A spime, according to Sterling, is the next generation of man-made object evolving out of the blobject. Such objects are associated with their own provenance data, their own story. They are continually recording, tracking and being recorded and tracked. People who are prepared to engage with spimes, to collaborate with them, he calls *wranglers.* Well-developed spimes will encourage people to become wranglers, for the same reasons that Amazon and Google make use of users' habits in order to provide a better service. By engendering engagement from people, the spime will become more intelligent and hence achieve market edge. In this sense, Sterling is taking the phrase *Harnessing Collective Intelligence* used in the context of Web 2.0 by Tim O'Reilly [220], to the next level. He himself calls it *open-source manufacturing.*

Physically, a spime will use technologies discussed previously in this chapter in order to exchange data over a network and store data locally such as IPv6 and RFID. But the importance of a spime is not so much the physical material object. It is the provenance, history and support system that it creates. Whilst the traditional product life-cycle involves creation, use and disposal, spimes have a more subtle relationship to their environment because they are more about process than artefact. Critically, from an environmental point of view, product disposal can be controlled because of the spime's history. Armed with the complete log of its birth and life, the spime can be destroyed, dismantled and recycled efficiently. This offers an entirely new way of understanding how artefacts relate to their environment, not just their users, breaking centuries-old habits that have resulted in the build up of detritus across our planet. As Sterling puts it:

> *"You would be able to swiftly understand: where it was, when you got it, how much it cost, who made it, what it was made of, where those resources came from, what a better model looked like, what a cheaper model looked like, who to thank for making it, who to complain to about its inadequacies, what previous kinds of Spime used to look like, why this Spime is better than earlier ones, what people think the Spime of Tomorrow might look like, what you could do to help that happen, the history of the Spime's ownership, what it had been used for, where and when it was used, what other people who own this kind of Spime think about it, how other people more or less like you have altered or fancied-up or modified their Spime, what most people use Spimes for, the entire range of unorthodox uses of Spimes by the world's most extreme Spime geek fandom, and how much your Spime is worth on an auction site. And especially — absolutely critically — where to get rid of it safely." [250]*

Of course, such developments are also a potential menace, a perfect technology for suppressive regimes. Even within a free society the challenges will be immense with a wide area of issues needing to be addressed, including spying, eavesdropping, identity theft, legal, ethical and social responsibilities and underclasses excluded from using spimes.

19.3 Conclusion

In this chapter we have moved from technologies and systems that are being developed today, to potential developments in the field of ubiquitous computing and related paradigms, with a view to providing a taster of the issues that are currently being debated. Whilst the interpretations discussed are conjectural and personal to their authors, there is widespread interest in the possibilities that current technological advances are suggesting, both inspiring and disturbing.

Part V

Deployment

20

Distributed Object Deployment Using Jini

In this chapter, two specific examples illustrate the use of RMI and Jini. The focus of this chapter is not to create complicated remote Java services and therefore give a lesson in Java programming, but rather it is to provide the reader with the core framework and components needed in order to run simple RMI and Jini services. Providing complicated services at this stage simply clouds this issue of understanding the fundamentals of running remote services.

Therefore, the source is very concise but it gives all the necessary code needed in order to run and describe remote RMI and Jini services. Such code can easily be extended to provide as complicated a service as the reader desires. The complete set of examples for this chapter and others can be found at the following Web site:

```
http://www.p2pgridbook.com/
```

On this Web site, there is a complete set of batch files that enable the reader to set up and run the various services required in order to run these examples. Such batch files are described in detail for each example. Typically though, the reader will need to set a few variables in each case specifying things such as where JINI is installed for example, which is outlined on the Web page.

Let's first look at the RMI security which is pervasive throughout the source code in the rest of this chapter.

20.1 RMI Security

This section briefly describes the role of the security manager for remote code. This is common to both Jini and RMI and is set using the code:

```
if (System.getSecurityManager() == null) {
    System.setSecurityManager(new RMISecurityManager());
```

A security manager protects access to system resources from untrusted downloaded code running within the virtual machine (i.e., provides basic sandboxing capabilities; see Section 4.6). A security manager is needed not only by the RMI server, but also by the client because it is possible that RMI could be downloading code to the client in a similar fashion to the way an *applet* works. Therefore, both *applets* and *Jini* clients have to implement a sandbox, which is a necessary restriction that ensures that all operations performed by downloaded code are passed through a security layer.

If a security manager is not set, then RMI will not function because, without a security manager, RMI will not download classes for objects in remote method calls,[1] e.g., parameters, return values or exceptions.

In the examples given here, we simply set the security manager to the default, which is a similar security policy to that adopted in applets; i.e., downloaded code is not allowed to access the local disk or to open sockets to third-party hosts, etc. This can be overridden either by using another SecurityManager or through the use of a *policy file* to grant specific permissions (see [125] for more information).

20.2 An RMI Application

We discussed in Section 8.5 that Jini is based on the RMI technology. This section provides an RMI example to outline the core transport mechanism for Jini. In the next section, this is expanded to illustrate how this fits in with Jini. You'll notice straight away how similar they are.

This example provides a simple RMI application that outputs *Hello World* on a remote machine. It consists of three files:

1. **RemoteMessageInterface.java:** is the Java RMI proxy object to the remote implementation of this code. The client calls this locally.
2. **RemoteMessage.java:** is the remote implementation of the Java proxy that is run on the remote machine.
3. **LocalObject.java:** is the local client that calls the Java proxy (*RemoteMessageInterface*), which transmits this call over the network to call the function in the remote object (*RemoteMessage*).

20.2.1 The Java Proxy

The *RemoteMessageInterface* provides a simple interface that allows the user to invoke a function containing a message argument. This code is implemented on a server and invoked using the generic RMI mechanism. To extend the service, simply extend this *RemoteMessageInterface* with the methods you require and reimplement these in the server code described in the next section.

[1] Other than from the local class path.

The rest of the code stays exactly the same. The source code for this interface is given below:

```
public interface RemoteMessageInterface extends Remote {
    public void sendMessage(String message) throws RemoteException;
}
```

Remote RMI interfaces need to extend *java.rmi.Remote*. This interface marks our *RemoteMessageInterface* as one whose methods can be called from any virtual machine and therefore has the ability to be located remotely. Further, as a member of a remote interface, the *sendMessage(String)* method is also a remote method and as such, it must be capable of throwing a *java.rmi.RemoteException*.

RMI uses exceptions to handle remote errors, indicating that a communication failure, an internal method error in *sendMessage()* or protocol error has occurred. Remote exceptions are checked at compile time, so this has to be *thrown* from any remote method.

20.2.2 The Server

The server code implements our *RemoteMessageInterface* and therefore provides the code that *sendMessage()*, line 8, will invoke on the remote machine. The source code is given below:

```
1  public class RemoteMessage extends UnicastRemoteObject
2                                implements RemoteMessageInterface {
3
4      public RemoteMessage() throws RemoteException {
5          super();
6      }
7
8      public void sendMessage(String message) {
9          System.out.println(message);
10     }
11
12     public static void main(String[] args) {
13         if (System.getSecurityManager() == null) {
14             System.setSecurityManager(new RMISecurityManager());
15         }
16         try {
17             RemoteMessageInterface rmi = new RemoteMessage();
18             String name = "//"
19                       + InetAddress.getLocalHost().getHostName()
20                                  + "/RemoteMessageInterface";
21             Naming.rebind(name, rmi);
22             System.out.println("Remote Message bound");
23         } catch (RemoteException e) {
```

```
24              System.err.println("RemoteMessage exception: "
25                                                + e.getMessage());
26          }
27      }
28  }
```

Listing 20.1. RemoteMessage object.

This class implements the *RemoteMessageInterface* (line 2) to provide the remote *sendMessage()* method implementation, which outputs the given string on the remote machine. This class also extends the class *java.rmi.server.UnicastRemoteObject*, which is a convenience RMI class that can be used as a super class for remote object implementations. This class basically supplies appropriate remote implementations for the *java.lang.Object* methods (e.g., equals, hashCode, toString) along with extra constructors and static methods used to export a remote object and make it available (via the RMI registry) to remote clients.

Note, though, that a remote object implementation does not have to extend *UnicastRemoteObject.* However, if it does not, then it must supply an appropriate implementation of the *java.lang.Object* methods; otherwise the code will not compile. It must also provide exporting functions (or link to the ones in *UnicastRemoteObject*).

The **main()** method, line 12, provides the main RMI mechanism for setting up and registering this object with the local RMI registry.

First, as in any remote Java implementation, you must set the security manager for that remote machine (see RMI Security, Section 20.1, for details). Next, we create an instance of the *RemoteMessage* and cast it as a *RemoteMessageInterface* (which it implements) so that remote clients can access this through our defined proxy interface (via the RMI Registry) and not the implementation.

```
RemoteMessageInterface rmi = new RemoteMessage();
```

The RMI registry is a basic remote object name service, which allows remote clients to gain references to a remote object by using its class name. The *java.rmi.Naming* interface is used for binding, registering or looking up remote objects. The *RemoteMessage* class creates a name for itself and registers this in the RMI registry using the following code:

```
String name = "//" + InetAddress.getLocalHost().getHostName()
                                  + "/RemoteMessageInterface";
Naming.rebind(name, rmi);
```

This name includes the host where the registry is located and a name that identifies the remote object in the registry. The *getLocalHost()* function dynamically obtains the local host name, which works well for our server class defined here (for clients, see Section 20.2.3). For more information about how such names are created, see the *RMI Trail* of the *Java Tutorial* [125].

This is added to the RMI registry by using *rebind* with the name and reference to the object associated with this name (i.e., our *RemoteMessage* object, rmi) as arguments. During this process, any *RemoteExceptions* generated are caught by the corresponding *try* and *catch* block.

20.2.3 The Client

The client code gets access to the remote object (via the *RemoteMessageInterface*) and invokes the *sendMessage* function on line 12. The mechanism of how this is accomplished is given in Fig. 20.1 and is described along with the source code given below:

```
1  public class LocalObject {
2      public static void main(String args[]) {
3          if (System.getSecurityManager() == null) {
4              System.setSecurityManager(new RMISecurityManager());
5          }
6          try {
7              String name = "//"
8                          + InetAddress.getLocalHost().getHostName() +
9                                  "/RemoteMessageInterface";
10             RemoteMessageInterface rmi =
11                         (RemoteMessageInterface)Naming.lookup(name);
12             rmi.sendMessage("Hello Remote Machine!!!");
13         } catch (Exception e) {
14             System.err.println("LocalObject exception: "
15                                 + e.getMessage());
16             e.printStackTrace();
17         }
18     }
19 }
```

Listing 20.2. LocalObject class.

At first, the client sets a security manager (see Section 20.1 for details). Now, since our RMI server program (*RemoteMessage*) has registered itself with the remote RMI registry using its implemented remote interface, *RemoteMessageInterface* (see Fig. 20.1), the client can now use the *rmi.Naming* interface to look up the reference to the remote object (see step 2, Fig. 20.1). This is achieved using the following code:

```
String name = "//" + InetAddress.getLocalHost().getHostName() +
                          "/RemoteMessageInterface";
RemoteMessageInterface rmi =
```

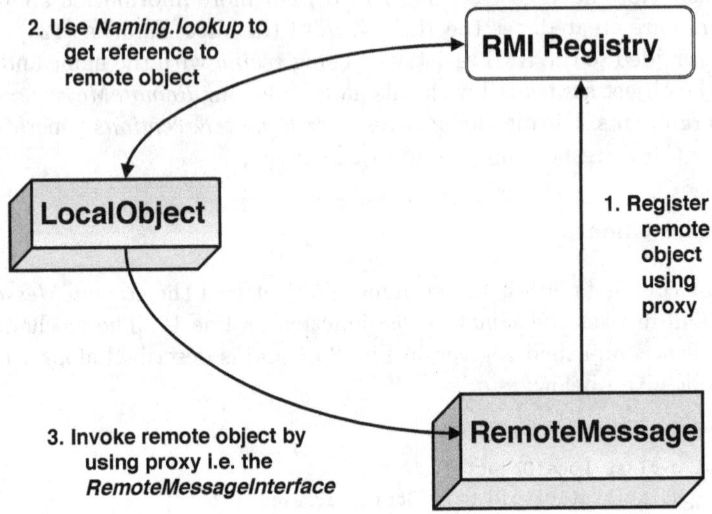

Fig. 20.1. An overview of how the client gets access to the remote object using RMI.

```
(RemoteMessageInterface)Naming.lookup(name);
```

This code is identical to the server because this example is configured to run the client and the server on **ONE** machine. Although this is not distributed in the network sense, the principles are exactly the same. It is easy to reconfigure the code to insert an IP address of a remote RMI machine if desired. To do this, the formation of the name will have to be changed to point to the remote machine directly, for example:

```
String name = "//" + "spectra.astro.cf.ac.uk"
 + "/RemoteMessageInterface";
```

or better still, pass this as a command line argument to your program:

```
String name = "//" + args[0] + "/RemoteMessageInterface";
```

Once a reference to the remote interface has been looked up, the client can invoke the remote method (see step 3, Fig. 20.1) as if it were a local method call, by using:

```
rmi.sendMessage("Hello Remote Machine!!!");
```

The next section explains what RMI services you need to run and how you execute this RMI example.

20.2.4 Setting Up the Environment

With any RMI program, you must start an *RMI Registry* on the machine that is running the remote service, using the command:

```
> rmiregistry
```

Note that before you start the rmiregistry, you must make sure no CLASSPATH is set; i.e., unset the CLASSPATH environment variable. See the Java Tutorial for a detailed explanation [125]) but briefly, if the rmiregistry can find your local stub classes, it will forget that the loaded stub class can be loaded from your server's code base and subsequently, the client will not be able to locate and load the stub class or other server-side classes.

There is a convenience batch file for running rmiregistry (*runRegistry.bat*) on the Web site. There are also batch files for: compiling and creating the local *stubs* file (*build.bat*); for setting the *java.policy* file (sets all permissions granted) and running the RMI Service, RemoteMessage (*runRemote.bat*); and for setting the *java.policy* file and running the RMI client, LocalObject (*runLocal.bat*).

Briefly, to run your service, you can use the batch file or run using the following command:

```
java -Djava.rmi.server.codebase=file:/./classes
    -Djava.rmi.server.hostname=localhost
        -Djava.security.policy=./java.policy
            -classpath ./classes
                    RemoteMessage
```

and to run the client, you would use a similar command:

```
java -Djava.rmi.server.codebase=file:/.classes/
    -Djava.security.policy=java.policy
        -classpath classes
                LocalObject
```

and now, on to Jini.

20.3 A Jini Application

This section illustrates how to create a Jini remote service and how a client might access that service. The actual service, as in the RMI example above, is very simple. In this example, the remote service method takes no parameters but returns a *String* in order to retrieve a message from the remote service.

Again, to extend these interfaces in order to make a more advanced Jini service is trivial and application specific. For a Java programmer, the framework of how you go about creating and deploying Jini services can be the majority of the learning step.

Specifically, this example returns a "Hello World" string from the remote computer. The client uses the Jini lookup service to locate the "Hello World" service and obtains a Java Proxy (essentially an RMI stub). It makes a call on this object which remotely executes the specific function in the server code. As in RMI, you need to implement three files: one interface (or proxy), one client and one server. As you will see, the actual source code is very similar to RMI. The files are:

- **MyService.java:** is the Jini service which implements the *MyServiceInterface.*
- **MyServiceInterface.java:** is the interface to the Jini service, i.e., the Java proxy.
- **MyClient.java:** is the local client that calls the *MyServiceInterface* Java proxy, which RMI transmits over the network to call the function in the remote object (i.e., *MyService*).

20.3.1 The Remote Interface

As with RMI, we start off with the Jini proxy interface for the remote object. Like RMI, the Jini proxy contains the functionality that the remote object will provide. The code for this interface is given in the following listing:

```
public interface MyServiceInterface extends Remote {
    public String sayHello () throws RemoteException;
    }
```

As you can see, the only method our remote implementation has to implement is the *sayHello()* function which returns a *String.*

20.3.2 The Server

The remote *MyService* class implements the *MyServiceInterface* interface and provides the necessary calls in order to publish its service to the Jini lookup server, using the Jini *Join* protocol (see Section 14.3.2). The source code is given below:

```
public class MyService extends UnicastRemoteObject
                                    implements MyServiceInterface {

    public MyService () throws RemoteException {
        super ();
    }

    public String sayHello () throws RemoteException  {
        System.out.println ("MyService: sayHello() called");
        return ("Hello World from MyService!");
```

```
11     }
12
13     public static void main (String[] args) {
14         MyServiceInterface myServer;
15         LookupLocator lookup;
16         ServiceRegistrar registrar;
17         ServiceItem serviceItem;
18
19         try {
20             System.setSecurityManager (new RMISecurityManager());
21
22             myService = new MyService ();
23
24             Entry[] attr = new Entry[1];
25             attr[0] = new Name("HelloWorldService");
26             serviceItem = new ServiceItem(null, myService, attr);
27
28             lookup = new LookupLocator ("jini://localhost");
29             registrar  = lookup.getRegistrar();
30
31             registrar.register(serviceItem, Lease.FOREVER);
32
33             System.out.println("Service Ready ...");
34         } catch (Exception e) {
35             System.out.println("MyService.main: Exception " + e);
36         }
37     }
38 }
```

Listing 20.3. MyService class.

As in RMI, all Jini services should subclass the server-side RMI implementation class (*java.rmi.server.UnicastRemoteObject*) unless they wish to reimplement these underlying calls themselves. The first operation of the *main* method (line 13), as in RMI, sets the security manager to the default RMI manager, since our transport is RMI. We then create an instance of our Jini service, *MyService* on line 22 that implements the *MyServiceInterface* proxy interface.

In order to add this Jini service we need to *register* it with the lookup service (see line 31). The *register* function expects a *ServiceItem* object and a lease duration (see Section 14.3.2). A *ServiceItem* object has the following parameters:

```
ServiceItem(ServiceID id, Object service, Entry attrSets)
```

where:

- **id:** is a universally unique identifier for registered services (128-bit value). Service IDs are intended to be generated only by lookup services, not by clients.
- **service:** is the object implementing the Jini Service, i.e., a **MyService** instance.
- **attrSets:** are attributes for service represented by a list of objects.

In our example, we use the following code to populate the attribute array to describe this server. This is used to identify this service when it is registered with the lookup service:

```
Entry[] attr = new Entry[1];
attr[0] = new Name("HelloWorldService");
serviceItem = new ServiceItem(null, myServer, attr);
```

Note here that the attribute used for lookup is the Jini *Name* class and we set its contents to "HelloWorldService". The service could be advertised, however, using a number of mechanisms, for example, by using the *Java proxy* name. The service item is created by ignoring the ID, using our *MyService* instance and the set of attributes that describe this service. Note that this description is much more sophisticated than in the RMI example as Jini provides much more sophisticated capabilities for searching for services.

Once we have our service item created, we can locate the lookup server and populate it with our service. This is achieved by using the Jini *LookupLocator* class as follows:

```
lookup = new LookupLocator ("jini://localhost");
registrar  = lookup.getRegistrar();
registrar.register(serviceItem, Lease.FOREVER);
```

The *LookupLocator* expects you to pass it a resource that is running a Jini lookup server address. Jini uses its own protocol for this purpose, i.e., "jini://". Following the protocol is the name of the computer hosting the lookup service. We specify this as the *localhost*, i.e., this machine. The LUS could easily be stored elsewhere and specified here in the same way.

Therefore, for this example, we are using the *Unicast Discovery* mechanism to find our lookup server. When we have a reference to the lookup server, we can then get the registrar object and publish our service using the register method. Here, we register our Jini service and allow the Jini LUS to lease it forever. The service is now deployed and waiting for use.

20.3.3 The Client

```
public class MyClient {
    public static void main (String[] args) {
        Entry[] aeAttributes;
```

```
4           LookupLocator lookup;
5           ServiceRegistrar registrar;
6           ServiceTemplate template;
7           MyServerInterface myServerInterface;
8
9           try {
10              System.setSecurityManager (new RMISecurityManager ());
11
12              lookup = new LookupLocator ("jini://localhost");
13              registrar  = lookup.getRegistrar();
14
15              aeAttributes = new Entry[1];
16              aeAttributes[0] = new Name ("HelloWorldService");
17              template = new ServiceTemplate (null, null, aeAttributes);
18              myServerInterface =
19                              (MyServerInterface)registrar.lookup(template);
20
21              System.out.println ("Calling sayHello()->"
22                      + myServerInterface.sayHello () + "<-");
23          } catch (Exception e) {
24              System.out.println ("MyClient.main() exception: " + e);
25          }
26      }
27  }
```

Listing 20.4. MyClient class.

The client code, as in the other examples, sets the security manager to access remote objects. It then discovers the Jini lookup service by creating a *LookupLocator* object in the same way as with the service (see line 12):

```
lookup = new LookupLocator ("jini://localhost");
```

After obtaining the lookup service's *ServiceRegistrar* object (line 13), it performs a search to find the service that has the attribute name of "HelloWorldService". This is accomplished in the same way as the service publishes the description of the service except that rather than creating a *ServiceItem* object, the client creates a *ServiceTemplate* object (on line 17) as follows:

```
aeAttributes = new Entry[1];
aeAttributes[0] = new Name ("HelloWorldService");
template = new ServiceTemplate (null, null, aeAttributes);
myServerInterface = (MyServerInterface)registrar.lookup(template);
```

A *ServiceTemplate* has the following parameters:

```
public ServiceTemplate(ServiceID serviceID,
                java.lang.Class[] serviceTypes,
                        Entry[] attrSetTemplates)
```

where:

- **serviceID:** service ID to match, or null
- **serviceTypes:** service types (i.e., Java Classes that the service implements) to match, or null
- **attrSetTemplates:** attribute set templates to match, or null.

Here, we use the attributes to search for all services that identify themselves with the "HelloWorldService" tag. The Jini lookup protocol is invoked by the *lookup* method on the *ServiceRegistrar* object. It service returns the Jini *proxy* object to the service, which gives the client direct access to the remote Jini service.

This is an extremely simple example but forms the basis of programming with Jini. It can be easily expanded to implement any Jini service you desire.

20.4 Running Jini Applications

To run Jini applications, you can use the Jini starter kit [191] but in fact, to run the example given here you actually only need five Jini Jar files from this kit:

- jini-core.jar, core Jini functionality
- jini-ext.jar, Jini lookup functionality (from client)
- reggie.jar, Jini lookup service
- reggie-dl.jar, Jini lookup service
- tools.jar, HTTP server

Of course, you'll also need the Java Runtime Environment (JRE) [45]. You then start three services:

- **an HTTP server:** for accessing the remote class files
- **RMID Daemon:** which starts on machines where you want to host the remote Java objects
- **Reggie:** the default Jini lookup server

These are described in more detail in the following three sections.

20.4.1 HTTP Server

To run the example, you need to start an HTTP server for communicating data files between the Jini client/service and the Jini lookup service. There is a default implementation in the *tools.jar* jar file supplied with Jini. You execute it as follows:

```
java -jar -classpath %JINI_CLASSPATH%
      %JINIHOME%\lib\tools.jar -port 8081 -dir
            %JINIHOME%\lib -verbose
```

20.4.2 RMID Daemon

The next step is to start an RMI daemon for executing remote code (if the Jini service is actually remote). This can be achieved by using the following command:

```
rmid -J-Dsun.rmi.activation.execPolicy=none
```

Also, you can use the following *rmid* command-line option to enable logging for debugging purposes:

```
-J-Djava.rmi.server.logCalls=true
```

20.4.3 The Jini Lookup Service

There is a default implementation of a Jini lookup service, called Reggie. This can be executed by using the following command:

```
java -jar -classpath %JINI_CLASSPATH%
 -Djava.security.policy=%JINIHOME%/example/lookup/policy.all
    %JINIHOME%/lib/reggie.jar
     http://localhost:8081/reggie-dl.jar
       %JINIHOME%/example/lookup/policy.all
          reggie_log public
```

The parameters here specify the various lookup policies and jar files needed. The details are beyond the scope of this book but you can find more information at [251] or the Jini Web site [23].

20.4.4 Running the Service

To run the service, you'll need to add the Jini Jar files (listed in Section 20.4) to the Java CLASSPATH, set the security policy and set the codebase to the address of the HTTP server that you started in Section 20.4.1. Therefore to run the service (which obviously needs to be started first), you would type in:

```
java -classpath %JINI_CLASSPATH%;./classes
     -Djava.security.policy=policy.all
         -Djava.rmi.server.codebase=http://localhost:8080/
             MyService
```

and to run the client the following command would be issued:

```
java -classpath %JINI_CLASSPATH%;./classes
     -Djava.security.policy=policy.all
         -Djava.rmi.server.codebase=http://localhost:8080/
                 MyClient
```

Note that, as in the RMI example, the Web site listed at the beginning of this chapter has a number of batch files to help you run these examples. These are:

1. **Compile.bat:** which compiles the example and creates the local stubs file.
2. **Setup.bat:** which sets up the local environment. This file MUST be edited to configure your platform correctly; i.e., you must insert the location of the JRE (RUNTIME_JAR in the example below).
3. **HTTP-1.bat:** which runs the HTTP server for the transportation of the Java code on the Jini network. This must be run first.
4. **RMID-2.bat:** is the RMI registry that keeps track of the RMI objects, currently available on the remote machine.
5. **REGGIE-3.bat:** is a Jini lookup server.
6. **runService.bat:** is a batch file that uses the *policy.all* file to set up the security model (all permissions are granted in this example). It then runs the RMI service, emphRemoteMessage.
7. **runClient.bat:** also uses the *policy.all* file to set up the security model for the client and then runs the RMI client, *LocalObject.*

```
set RUNTIME_JAR=c:\java\jdk1.4\jre\lib\rt.jar
set JINIHOME=.
set JINI_CLASSPATH=.;%RUNTIME_JAR%;
       %JINIHOME%\lib\jini-core.jar;
           %JINIHOME%\lib\jini-ext.jar;
               %JINIHOME%\lib\reggie.jar;
                   %JINIHOME%\lib\reggie-dl.jar;
                       %JINIHOME%\lib\tools.jar
```

20.5 Conclusion

In this chapter, two examples illustrated how one would use the Remote Method Invocation (RMI) and Jini frameworks for distributing Java objects. Both examples consist of very simple source code and services that illustrate the core building blocks necessary for applications working within these environments.

RMI and Jini are alike, except that Jini has much more comprehensive searching capabilities, which can be used to locate objects in a much more distributed and scalable fashion. Jini also integrates other mechanisms essential for writing robust distributed object-based applications, e.g., distributed event modelling and object management.

21

P2P Deployment Using Jxta

This chapter describes how to deploy applications using Jxta's Java reference implementation [24]. There are two specific examples: the first illustrates how to manually start the Jxta platform and configure it using the *Jxta Configurator* application; and the second demonstrates how to automatically set an ad doc networking environment by employing the use of the *NetworkManager* class and a client/server application using Jxta Unicast pipes can be created within that environment. The purpose of these examples is twofold: to familiarise the reader with the style of coding involved in creating Jxta applications and to discuss the tools involved in using the Jxta platform, and considerations that this environment exhibits.

Jxta is very much an evolving project and during the past four years alone, between the first edition of this book and this one, the Jxta API has changed significantly (even the stable build directory location has changed). The chapter presented here therefore is a complete rewrite of the one found in the previous edition of this book. The examples provided here are re-engineered examples from the first edition using the updated API, and many more examples can be found in the Jxta tutorial.[1] The examples provided here are representative of the Jxta API and how to program using the toolkit. Even if the API changes again, it is highly unlikely that the style of the approach will differ so much as a whole. Code for these examples can be found at the book Web site:

`http://www.p2pgridbook.com/`

There are two Jxta [24] examples illustrated in this chapter:

- A simple example that starts the Jxta platform
- Creating and using Jxta pipes.

[1] The tutorial can be found at `http://download.java.net/jxta/`.

Each of these examples is similar to those you can find on the Jxta Web site [24]. The code listed here just outlines the main methods and omits some of the details. For a complete version of the code see this book's Web site.

21.1 Example One: Starting the Jxta Platform

This simple example primarily illustrates how you can start and use the Jxta platform from a Java application. Here, we start the Jxta platform manually, meaning that no pre-configuration is performed. The example, when run, will launch the Jxta Configurator, which is described in the next section, in order to prompt you to configure the environment. Whilst this is not necessary if you use one of the pre-configured settings, it is useful to show it here in order for the reader to understand the various configuration options within the Jxta environment, to better understand how it operates.

```
public class StartJxta {
    static PeerGroup netPeerGroup = null;
    static PeerGroupAdvertisement groupAdvertisement = null;
    private DiscoveryService discovery;
    private PipeService pipe;

    public StartJxta() { }

    public static void main(String args[]) {
        StartJxta myapp = new StartJxta();
        myapp.startJxta();
        System.exit(0);
    }

   private void startJxta() {
        NetPeerGroupFactory factory=null;
        try {
            factory = new NetPeerGroupFactory();
            netPeerGroup = factory.getInterface();
        } catch (PeerGroupException e) {
            System.out.println("Fatal: Group creation failure");
            e.printStackTrace();
            System.exit(1);
        }
                   ..
    }
}
```

Listing 21.1. StartJxta class.

The functionality here is provided in the *startJxta* method on line 15, which is called from the main program. Here, we create a new *net peer group*, the default platform peer group. This function simplifies the method by which applications can start Jxta. First, we create a new *NetPeerGroupFactory* class, which instantiates the net peer group using the configuration parameters stored in the directory specified by the JXTA_HOME system property or the *.jxta/* directory if JXTA_HOME is not defined. In this example we use the default, so after you run this demonstration, a *.jxta* directory will be created within the directory from which the Jxta code was launched. Jxta always creates such a directory and stores a number of configuration parameters in this directory, along with adverts that are created and advertised during the running of the application. This explicit on-disk caching is a subject we will debate in Section 21.3.

The *NetPeerGroupFactory* returns a new factory, which we can use to get the interface to the network peer group using the *getInterface()* method. It should be noted that starting Jxta in this fashion is generally not recommended. As of Jxta version 2.5, the *preferred* way to initialise the platform is to use either the *NetworkConfigurator* or, more commonly, the *NetworkManager* class, which is described in Section 21.2. However, as mentioned previously, it is useful to understand which settings the more higher-level classes have control over and therefore, we describe the Configurator application next, which allows a user to specify these settings directly.

21.1.1 Peer Configuration Using Jxta

Configuring a local peer in Jxta has a number of connotations because there may be a number of peers running on the same host, and therefore each peer needs to be individually identifiable within this environment. In other systems, services are hosted within a container that provides a hosting environment for outside access; e.g., OGSA services can be hosted within a J2EE container.

Jxta instead has opted for an environment that allows individual peers to be self-configurable and independent of any external hosting environment. The Jxta Standard edition (2.5 or greater) includes a simple UI configurator application (called the **Jxta Configurator**) that allows it to set specific parameters about how it is hosted and what operations it can perform.

This approach can be more flexible but also has more individual administrative overhead than allowing a hosting environment to make these decisions for you. Within a P2P environment, therefore, a number of extra parameters that are extremely specific to individual peers have to be specified. For example, within the Web Services/OGSA world, services do not suddenly decide to become a lookup service, whereas, within Jxta, this is not only possible (via Rendezvous) but for some applications it may be essential (e.g., in ad hoc wireless sensor networks where a peer may change its role depending on its battery strength). Although configuration in Jxta is somewhat static, that is, it is generally specified once at start-up, it is illustrative of the types of settings one must consider within P2P environments as a whole.

21.1.2 Using the Jxta Configurator

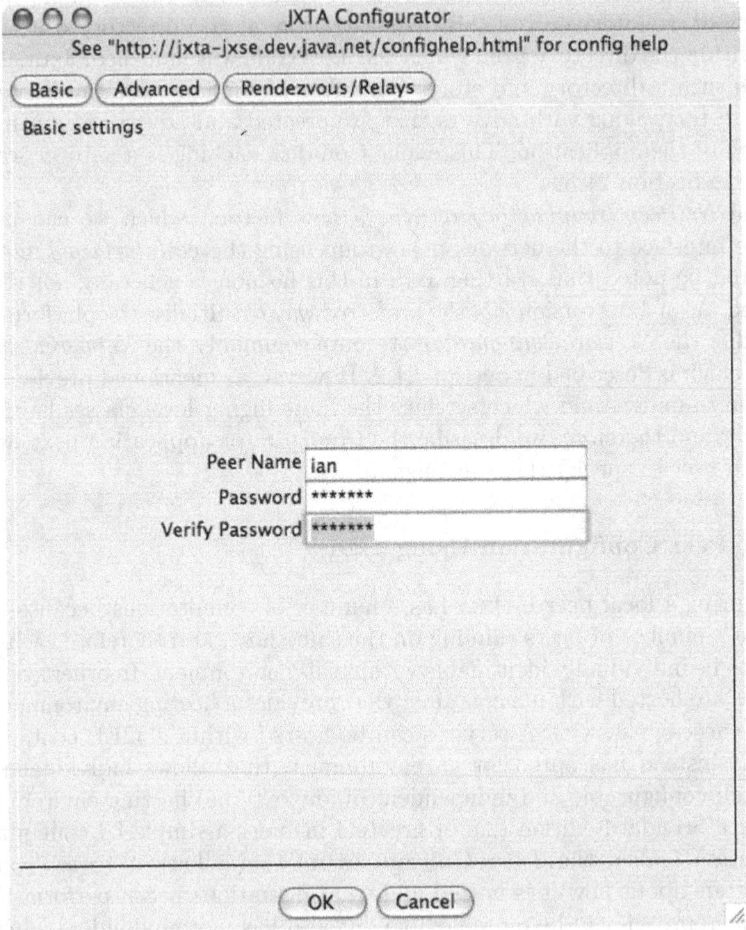

Fig. 21.1. Jxta configurator: screen 1.

The **Jxta configurator** application allows a user to specify to which port the peer listens, where Rendezvous Peers are, whether this peer will be operating as a Rendezvous and also which username and password you will be using to access the network. At the time of writing, the *Jxta configurator* consists of three screens that allow various peer settings to be configured. For detailed on-line information, see the latest documents on the Jxta Web site

[252] and [253]. The first screen is shown in Figure 21.1. Screen 1, as shown in Figure 21.1, simply allows you to enter your user name and password for this peer on the Jxta network, which allows you to protect your settings.

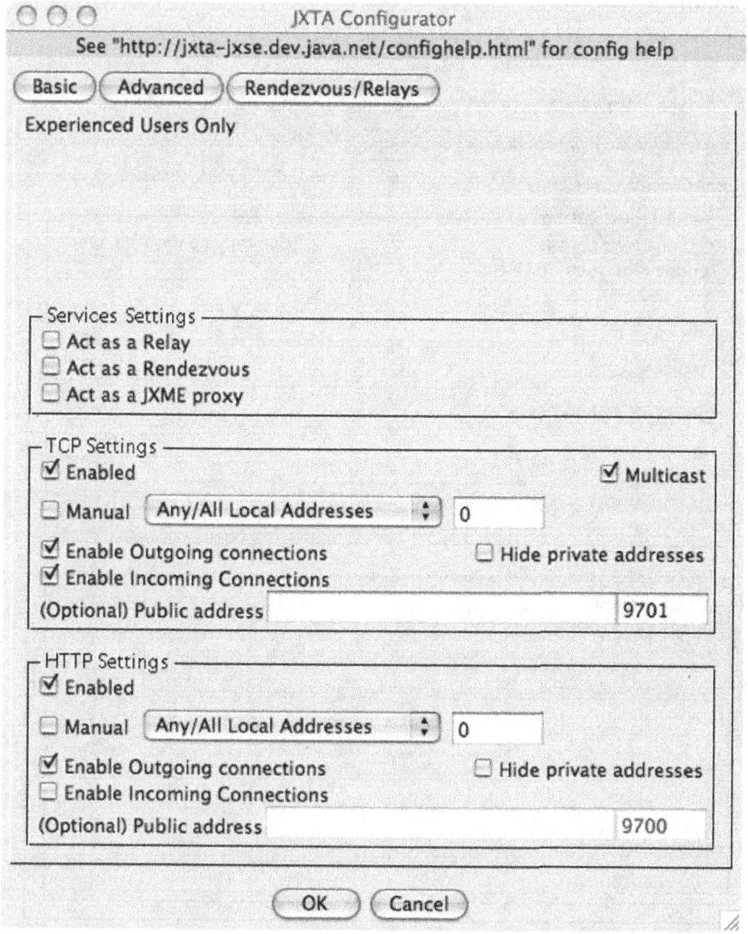

Fig. 21.2. Jxta configurator: screen 2.

The Advanced Settings (see Fig. 21.2) screen is used to set parameters about the environment in which the peer is running:

1. The **Services Settings** panel enables you to specify your rendezvous, relay and JXME (Jxta Micro Edition for constrained devices[2]) settings. By default, the Jxta peer does not act as a rendezvous node, a relay or

[2] jxta-jxme: JXTA Java Micro Edition Project, `https://jxta-jxme.dev.java.net/`.

a JXME proxy. A peer can opt to act as a Rendezvous here and perform a similar function to super-peers, described in Chapter 11, or a relay to help firewalled/NAT peers or a JXME proxy, which allows JXME applications to participate with a Jxta P2P substrate by using HTTP for its communication.

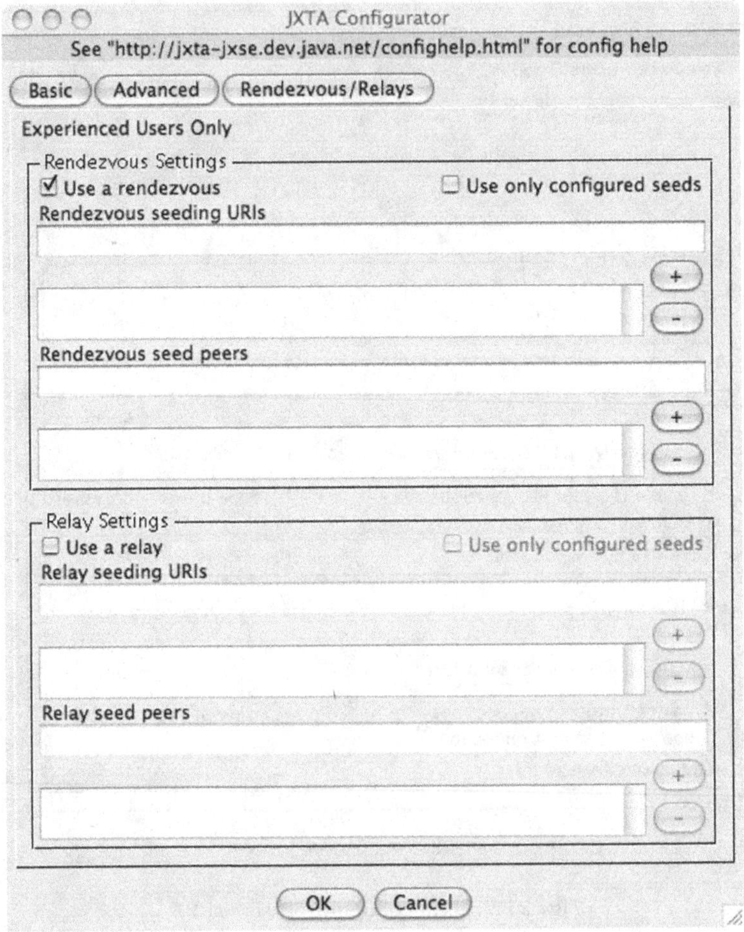

Fig. 21.3. Jxta configurator: screen 3.

2. **TCP Settings:** by default, TCP is enabled on the default network interface (port 9701). When TCP is enabled, each instance of a Jxta platform is bound to a specific TCP port number of a given peer. If you select manual configuration, the configurator screen will prompt the user to manually select the network interface for TCP each time a Jxta peer is booted. Your computer may have multiple network interfaces and you can select which

network interface should be used from the pull-down menu to the right. You can then opt to enable or disable incoming/outgoing connections and also choose to hide private addresses. At the lower part of this settings panel, you can also change the port used for TCP (multiple instances of the Jxta platform can be run on a single peer by using different TCP port numbers). To the left, if the Jxta peer is located behind NAT, you may need to specify the public NAT address for this node.

3. **HTTP Settings:** by default, HTTP is enabled on the default network interface (port 9700). HTTP must be enabled if the Jxta peer is located behind a firewall or NAT. If you want to use a different network interface for HTTP, use the pull-down menu to select the desired network interface (IP address). You can also set the port for HTTP manually as with TCP/IP. If you're running Jxta on an intranet (i.e., with no Internet connection), then this should be disabled. You can also opt to enable or disable incoming/outgoing connections and choose to hide private addresses, as with TCP.

In the third screen, shown in Figure 21.3, a peer can also specify external points for connectivity onto known rendezvous nodes on the Internet or to ones that an application may choose to set up by hand. The lower part of the screen allows you to specify a relay, if your peer is behind a NAT or firewall, for example.

21.2 Example Two: Using Jxta Pipes

This is a two-part example primarily to illustrate how to create an *OutputPipe* and *InputPipe* to send and receive messages.

1. **PipeReceiver.java:** a Jxta application that constructs an advert to create an *input pipe* and waits for messages to arrive.
2. **PipeSender.java:** an advert using the same UUID is created for binding the *OutputPipe* to the PipeReceiver with the matching advert. When the output has been bound, an asynchronous notification results in the *outputPipeEvent* being invoked to indicate that the connection is ready to use. We then send a message through the pipe.

This example is analogous to the socket client and server implementation. The input pipe is like a socket server and the output pipe is similar to a socket sender. There are two ways of creating a pipe advert in JXTA. Either you can create a dynamic advertisement that produces a different UUID for each pipe or you can generate an advert once using a fixed UUID and use this advert for the pipe. In this example we use the latter approach and generate a known UUID (which is the rather long number on line 129 defined in the PIPEIDSTR String in the listing below). Note here that all Jxta adverts are XML based (to provide the programming language independence) and that each advert has its own universally unique identifier. This UUID is crucial for several reasons, e.g., to avoid looping when routing messages. The code for the pipe receiver is as follows:

```
import net.jxta.endpoint.Message;
import net.jxta.endpoint.MessageElement;
import net.jxta.peergroup.PeerGroup;
import net.jxta.pipe.*;
import net.jxta.platform.NetworkManager;
import net.jxta.protocol.PipeAdvertisement;
import net.jxta.id.IDFactory;
import net.jxta.document.AdvertisementFactory;

import java.io.File;
import java.io.IOException;
import java.net.URI;
import java.net.URISyntaxException;


public class PipeReceiver extends Thread implements PipeMsgListener {

    static PeerGroup netPeerGroup = null;

    private NetworkManager manager;
    private PipeService pipeService;
    private PipeAdvertisement pipeAdv;
    private InputPipe inputPipe = null;
    private final Object lock = new Object();

    public static void main(String args[]) {
        PipeReceiver server = new PipeReceiver();
        server.start();
    }

    public PipeReceiver() {
        manager = null;
        try {
            manager = new net.jxta.platform.NetworkManager
                (NetworkManager.ConfigMode.ADHOC, "PipeReceiver",
            new File(new File("bookcache"), "PipeReceiver").toURI());
            manager.startNetwork();
        } catch (Exception e) {
            e.printStackTrace();
            System.exit(-1);
        }

        // Get NetPeerGroup
        netPeerGroup = manager.getNetPeerGroup();
```

```
            // get the pipe service
            pipeService = netPeerGroup.getPipeService();
            // create the pipe advertisement
            pipeAdv = PipeReceiver.getPipeAdvertisement();
        }

        /**
         * Creates the input pipe with this as the message listener
         */
        public void run() {

            try {
                System.out.println("Creating input pipe");
                inputPipe = pipeService.createInputPipe(pipeAdv, this);
            } catch (IOException io) {
                io.printStackTrace();
                return;
            }

            if (inputPipe == null) {
                System.out.println("Cannot create input pipe");
                System.exit(-1);
            } else {
                System.out.println("Waiting for Messages");

                try {
                    synchronized (lock) {
                        lock.wait();
                    }
                } catch (InterruptedException e) {
                    System.out.println("Thread interrupted");
                }
            }
        }

        public void pipeMsgEvent(PipeMsgEvent event ) {
            Message msg=null;
            try {
                msg = event.getMessage();
                if (msg == null) {
                    return;
                }
            } catch (Exception e) {
                e.printStackTrace();
                return;
            }

            // get the message element named SenderMessage
            MessageElement msgElement = msg.getMessageElement(
```

```
                                null, PipeSender.MessageLabel);
        // Get message
        if (msgElement.toString() == null) {
            System.out.println("null msg received");
        } else {
            System.out.println("Received: "+ msgElement.toString());
        }

        stopJxta(); // shutdown after receiving message
    }

    /**
     * Close input pipe shut down jxta gracefully
     */
    public void stopJxta() {
        synchronized (lock) {
            // done.
            lock.notify();
        }

        // Close the input pipe
        inputPipe.close();
        // Stop JXTA
        manager.stopNetwork();
    }

    /**
     * Creates the pipe advertisement
     * pipe ID
     *
     * @return the pre-defined Pipe Advertisement
     */
    public static PipeAdvertisement getPipeAdvertisement() {
        PipeID pipeID = null;
        // Have to generate the same pipe id for client and server
        String PIPEIDSTR = "urn:jxta:uuid-59616261646162
                                    14E5047205032503 3C0C1DE89
                                          719B456691A596B983BA0E1004";

        try {
            pipeID = (PipeID) IDFactory.fromURI(new URI(PIPEIDSTR));
        } catch (URISyntaxException use) {
            use.printStackTrace();
        }
        PipeAdvertisement advertisement = (PipeAdvertisement)
                AdvertisementFactory.newAdvertisement(
                PipeAdvertisement.getAdvertisementType());

        advertisement.setPipeID(pipeID);
```

```
143         advertisement.setType(PipeService.UnicastType);
144         advertisement.setName("Pipe Book Demo");
145         return advertisement;
146     }
147 }
```

Listing 21.2. PipeReceiver class.

The PipeReceiver code is the more complex and contains the following aspects:

1. The constructor on line 31 uses the NetworkManager class, described below to initialise the platform. We then gain access to the pipe service.
2. A *PipeAdvertisement* object (*pipeAdv*) is created in the constructor by calling the *getPipeAdvertisement* method on line 126. This method uses the *AdvertisementFactory.newAdvertisement* method to create an advertisement object and then sets the *PipeID* field to be our statically defined UUID. We then set the type for this pipe to be Unicast *PipeService.UnicastType* and set a name for the pipe to "Pipe Book Demo" to uniquely identify it. Note that the *getPipeAdvertisement* is a static method, which is also used by the *PipeSender* object in order to generate the same advert in order to connect to the receiver.
3. The *run* method is run within a separate thread and creates the input pipe by using the *createInputPipe* method of the pipe service. The arguments take the *PipeAdvertisement* object created and the *PipeMsgListener* interface that provides the asynchronous callback of *PipeMsgEvent* events through the *pipeMsgEvent* method. Our *PipeReceiver* class implements this interface (see line 80) and therefore registers itself to receive the pipe adverts. *PipeReceiver* then uses the *java.lang.Object*'s wait() method to halt and wait for incoming messages.
4. Within the *pipeMsgEvent* method, the messages are extracted via the *getMessage* method on the *PipeMsgEvent* events, which are encapsulated within the Jxta *Message* object.
5. The message can be retrieved from the *Message* object using its *getMessageElement* method that returns a *MessageElement* by providing the message *PipeSender.MessageLabel*, which is appended to the message before transmission. A *MessageElement* can then, in turn, be converted to a string using the standard *toString* Java method in order to print out the message (see line 99).
6. Finally the *stopJxta* method (line 108) is invoked, which closes the input pipe, shuts down the Jxta platform and releases the lock using the *java.lang.Object*'s notify() method, which results in the thread terminating and the program exiting gracefully.

In this example, configuration is specified programmatically by using the *NetworkManager* classes. The *NetworkManager* abstracts the configuration to one of the preset configurations:

1. **Ad-Hoc:** for deploying a stand-alone node in an ad-hoc network and connected in a peer-to-peer fashion using multicast, i.e., no rendezvous or relay services are used.
2. **Edge:** supports Ad-Hoc behaviour and also allows a peer to connect to an infrastructure peer (a rendezvous, relay, or both).
3. **Rendezvous:** allows the node to make network bootstrapping services available to others, such as discovery, pipe resolution, etc.
4. **Relay:** enables a peer to provide message relaying services to allow peers to traverse firewalls.
5. **Proxy:** enables JXME Jxta for J2ME proxy services.
6. **Super:** enables the simultaneous functionality of a rendezvous, relay and a proxy node.

The programming guide [254] states, "It is highly recommended that Jxta peers be configured through the *NetworkManager*, or *NetworkConfigurator* static configuration methods with the desired mode of operation such as newEdgeConfiguration(storeHome). Once a configuration is created, it may be tuned to the application requirements."

The pipe sender uses the same initialisation method for the Jxta platform (see the PipeSender constructor at line 27). The listing for the PipeSender is given below:

```
1  package tutorial.ians;
2
3  import net.jxta.endpoint.Message;
4  import net.jxta.endpoint.StringMessageElement;
5  import net.jxta.pipe.OutputPipe;
6  import net.jxta.pipe.OutputPipeEvent;
7  import net.jxta.pipe.OutputPipeListener;
8  import net.jxta.pipe.PipeService;
9  import net.jxta.platform.NetworkManager;
10 import net.jxta.protocol.PipeAdvertisement;
11 import java.io.File;
12 import java.io.IOException;
13
14 public class PipeSender extends Thread implements OutputPipeListener {
15
16     public final static String MessageLabel = "BookPipeDemo";
17     private PipeService pipeService;
18     private PipeAdvertisement pipeAdvert;
19     private OutputPipe outputPipe;
20     private final Object lock = new Object();
```

```
    private NetworkManager manager;

    /**
     * Create this instance and starts the JXTA platform
     *
     */
    public PipeSender() {
        try {
            manager = new net.jxta.platform.NetworkManager(
                NetworkManager.ConfigMode.ADHOC, "PipeSender",
              new File(new File("bookcache"), "PipeSender").toURI());
            manager.startNetwork();
        } catch (Exception e) {
            e.printStackTrace();
            System.exit(-1);
        }
        // get the pipe service, and discovery
        pipeService = manager.getNetPeerGroup().getPipeService();
        // create the pipe advertisement
        pipeAdvert = PipeReceiver.getPipeAdvertisement();
    }

    /**
     * Create thread and output pipe and wait for callback.
     */
    public synchronized void run() {
        try {
            pipeService.createOutputPipe(pipeAdvert, this);

            try {  // wait for sent message before shutting down
                synchronized (lock) {
                    lock.wait();
                }
            } catch (InterruptedException e) {
                System.out.println("Thread interrupted");
            }
        } catch (IOException e) {
            System.out.println("Can't create output pipe");
            e.printStackTrace();
            System.exit(-1);
        }
    }

    /**
     * Called when pipe is resolved and ready to accept data
     *
     * @param pipeEvent contains output pipe object
     */
    public void outputPipeEvent(OutputPipeEvent pipeEvent) {
```

```
        outputPipe = pipeEvent.getOutputPipe();

        Message msg;

        try {
            String message = "Hello from Pipe Sender !!!";
            msg = new Message();
            StringMessageElement sme = new StringMessageElement(
                                    MessageLabel, message, null);
            msg.addMessageElement(null, sme);
            outputPipe.send(msg);
            System.out.println("Message sent");
        } catch (IOException e) {
            System.out.println("failed to send message");
            e.printStackTrace();
            System.exit(-1);
        }
        stopJxta();
    }

    /**
     * Close output pipe shut down jxta gracefully
     */
    public void stopJxta() {
        outputPipe.close();
        manager.stopNetwork();
        synchronized (lock) {
            // done.
            lock.notify();
        }
    }

    /**
     * Kicks Things off
     */
    public static void main(String args[]) {
        PipeSender client = new PipeSender();
        client.start();        // sends message
    }
}
```

Listing 21.3. PipeSender class.

As with the *PipeReceiver* class, the *PipeSender* starts the Jxta platform and creates the same advert (in the *PipeSender* constructor), using the same static method defined in the *PipeReceiver* class, called *PipeReceiver.getPipeAdvertisement()*.

After initialisation, *PipeSender* is executed in a separate thread using the start() method (line 107), which corresponds to its run method being invoked (line 46). The *run* method uses the pipe service to create a pipe (see pipeService.createOutputPipe on line 48) by passing the pipe advert and an *OutputPipeListener* (itself) as a listener for events. This class then uses the *java.lang.Object*'s wait() method to stop the thread until the *PipeSender* finishes its task, i.e., sends data to the receiver. When the pipe has been created it notifies all listeners (i.e., our *PipeSender* class) and calls the *outputPipeEvent* method.

At the start of the *outputPipeEvent* method, we create a new message by passing a *StringMessageElement*, which attaches an *id* (i.e., the *MessageLabel* string) and a simple "Hello from Pipe Sender !!!" message, to the *Message*'s *addMessageElement* method. This message is sent using the *OutputPipe send* method. Then, the output pipe is closed and the Jxta platform is shut down gracefully in the *stopJxta* method (line 93) and the lock is released using the *java.lang.Object*'s notify() method, which results in the thread terminating and the program exiting gracefully.

21.2.1 Running the Examples

To run the Jxta example applications, you need the Jar files for the core platform, which are available at the Web site listed above,[3] or for the most recent version, you are wise to check out the main Web site [24]. Therefore, at the time of writing, you need to include the following core jar files for the Jxta platform in your classpath. These are:

- bcprov-jdk14.jar
- jxta.jar
- org.mortbay.jetty.jar
- javax.servlet.jar
- jxtashell.jar

Further, in version 2.5, the jxtashell needs to be included on your classpath, otherwise you will get a warning every time you run Jxta, stating that there is a class not found exception, although this may not be the case in future versions.

You will first need to add these jar files to your CLASSPATH[4] and then each of the demos above can be run like any other Java application, for example:

```
java PipeReceiver
```

[3] The Jxta version used for the examples provided here is 2.5. The current version of Jxta may differ in syntax and the number/names of Jar files required for running, but the basic principle is the same.

[4] See `http://java.sun.com/j2se/1.5.0/docs/tooldocs/#basic` for more details.

For the *PipeReceiver* and *PipeSender* example, you will need to run the *PipeReceiver* first and then the *PipeSender*. When you run each of the examples, a configuration directory will be created by Jxta. In the first example, it will create a ".jxta" directory as discussed and in the pipe example, it will create a bookcache directory as specified in the configuration of the *NetworkManager*. For *PipeReceiver* it will create a *PipeReceiver* subdirectory as specified in the 4th argument shown in line 36 of Listing 21.2 and line 31 of Listing 21.3 for *PipeSender*. If you run the example multiple times, then you should **delete this directory** otherwise the application will not work because it will use the old cached adverts instead of the new ones you are creating.

21.3 P2P Environment: The Jxta Approach

This section provides a discussion of some issues to deal with including the inherent transient availability of peers and how one may go about representing a number of peers on one machine. Jxta provides a solution to this but these issues outline inherent problems that any P2P middleware needs to be able to address. Therefore this section, through the use of Jxta, outlines some of these.

21.3.1 Jxta and P2P Advert Availability

When you are running a Jxta peer, both the availability of adverts and out-of-date adverts can seem extremely confusing. In this section, we examine some of the issues involved with adverts in such transient environments. Adverts may be unavailable for several reasons: e.g., the UDP connection may fail or a peer may be temporarily unavailable or has disconnected, etc. Further, out-of-date adverts can also linger around the Rendezvous caches long after the peers that advertised them have disappeared. Such issues have to be addressed by any distributed system that has transient connections.

For example, consider the following two scenarios:

1. *Intranet File Sharing Application:* A company creates a simple Jxta file sharing application that has a number of persistent servers that contain files that multiple (and transient) users wish to access on a daily basis.
2. *A Chat Application:* The same company has implemented a decentralized chat application (i.e., similar functionality to ICQ). Here all users are transient; i.e., they are continually logging on and off.

In the first case, a peer joins the network and will want to discover files in which it may be interested. Each advert it discovers contains the file name and location, with respect to the unique peer ID, on the Jxta network. Therefore, when it logs off, it will certainly want to remember its cached adverts from previous runs because files on the network will be continually available on the set of persistent peers.

Therefore, here, the *cache* directory should *not* be flushed, as the cache will remain persistent and will efficiently allow each peer to bootstrap and immediately be aware of all previously accessed files on the network. Therefore, in this case the peer itself acts as a local cache (i.e., like a super-peer) for the files in which it is interested.

In the second case however, peers can advertise themselves in a number of ways, e.g., as a chat service or a pipe.[5] When a peer joins the network, there is a high probability that the previously cached adverts are mostly out of date. For example, other peers may have logged off and then logged back onto the network. It is important here to realise that every new advert, no matter how it is advertised, is unique, due to the unique identifiers being assigned to the advert.

Therefore, when the peer logs back onto the network and reloads its cache, these adverts may well be out of date, and not resolve to a living peer. Even though the peer may advertise itself using a unique name, it will create a new advert each time it logs on, but each advert can be discovered using this unique string. This leads to several adverts being discovered for each peer, but only one will be valid.

21.3.2 Expiration of Adverts

Apart from the existence of invalid adverts, there are reasons why you may not want to expire adverts that are perceived to be no longer available. For example, a node might have been temporarily disconnected from the network but is still available because it has temporarily gone out of range of the wireless network signal. When such a node returns its advert (and functionality) will be available again.

The highly transient nature of the peers within such a network makes it impossible to retain a current set of valid adverts and therefore, it is important to account for this type of failure. This situation of out-of-date adverts is amplified with the introduction of Rendezvous points which are themselves caching services.

There will always be a trade-off because any accurate management of valid adverts will surely result in an extremely high overhead of a fine-grained temporal quantization of checking and updating cached adverts. The update quantization time would have to be so frequent (several times a second, for

[5] In some ways, the use of a Jxta service can be somewhat redundant because in most cases it can be represented as a pipe. A service provides a labelling mechanism (i.e., a chat service) along with a pipe (for connection to that chat service). However, a pipe can itself be advertised as a chat pipe and therefore we do not have to use the Jxta service framework at all. The difference is only semantic.

example) that the network would be completely flooded with update requests and render it completely useless.

Furthermore, such a mechanism could never be completely fault tolerant free because even if the problem of current availability of adverts were solved, it would be impossible to tackle the transient connectivity of the peers that they were advertising. For example, by the time a peer has retrieved this advert, the service provider for the advert may have left the network making the advert temporarily (or even permanently) unavailable.

Using systems like Jxta and gaining such experience really amplify the points raised in the P2P Environments chapter (see Chapter 6). Within P2P or transient networks, **it is far easier to deal with failure in a P2P network than it is to eliminate it.**

Invalid adverts can be highly confusing when using Jxta for the first time. For example, when you are testing your program, you may have forgotten to flush adverts from a previous run and discover these instead of the new adverts just advertised. In this case, your program may intermittently fail and seem to exhibit somewhat inconsistent behaviour, i.e., since sometimes it could work and other times not, depending on the ordering of the cached adverts.

21.4 Conclusion

In this chapter, two simple Jxta applications were illustrated to give the reader a feel for the Jxta programming environment. Due to the P2P environment Jxta is designed to work within, there are a number of configuration and inevitable failure issues with which such a system must be able to deal. To this end, each Jxta node has a configurator application and network manager utility classes that help simplify its role within the network (a peer, a Rendezvous, a relay, etc.) and how it connects to the other peers within the network.

The Jxta approach is flexible but extremely fine grained because each peer is required to manage its own settings. Other systems (e.g., Web Services, see Chapter 16) deploy services within hosting environments which perform a lot of this kind of housekeeping for you. Such systems, however, do lose the individual configurability, which may be important in certain deployment conditions.

The transient nature of P2P networks was illustrated later in this chapter when the issue of advert availability was addressed. Adverts in such highly dynamic networks are likely to fail sometimes because they may be out of date or the resource they are advertising may be temporarily or permanently unavailable. These issues illustrate the importance of dealing with failure as a normal occurrence in such networks.

22

Web Services Deployment

In this chapter we will create, deploy and invoke a Web Service. The code and scripts that we create here, along with pointers to required libraries, can also be downloaded in zip form from:

`http://www.p2pgridbook.com`

The service we will create is an event storage service. It receives calendar events from clients. Clients can add themselves as interested parties to an event, retrieve a list of interested parties for a particular event, as well as get the events that a service knows about. The service will have four operations:

createEvent(Event event):String The client sends an Event to the server and receives the id of the event in return.

addContact(EventID, Card):boolean The client sends a contact card and an event id to the server. The operation returns true if the contact has successfully be associated with the event.

getContacts(EventID):list of Cards The client can retrieve the cards associated with a particular event by sending the event id.

getEvents:list of events The client can query the service for the events it has stored.

There are numerous Web Service frameworks available for Java, and numerous ways of configuring them. We will try to keep installation simple, but we also want to see more than just simply exchanging primitive data types like strings and integers. Because we are going to need object to represent both events and contact cards for people, life will be slightly more complicated, but only a little. If we play along with the way certain libraries work, then they will do most of the work for us.

The Web Services framework we are going to use is called CXF [255]. At the time of writing, CXF is an Apache Software Foundation Incubation project. Incubation does not mean the code is no good or immature, but that the project recently moved over to Apache and is still being assessed as a project. In general, however, incubation projects are more likely to change their APIs. The reason we are going to CXF is because it is quite straightforward to use, does not require a lot of XML configuration and will allow us to explore different ways of interacting with a Web Service. In particular, most Web Service clients are statically generated before the service is invoked. In our example, we'll use some CXF functionality to see how client code can be generated at runtime, rather than being pre-compiled using a wsdl2Java tool.

The server side of the example will use some of the built-in functionality provided by some of the core Web Service APIs that are in common use, and available in different Web Service frameworks.

22.1 Data Binding

Because Web Services exchange messages encoded as XML, a process is required to convert this XML into programming language-defined objects. There are actually three levels to this conversion. First, the data that is exchanged between provider and consumer needs to be decoded and encoded. Second, an interface to a service's WSDL document needs to be generated. Third, SOAP messages need to be generated at runtime. Whilst these are conceptually three different concerns, they are of course inter-related.

The general process of converting XML-defined types to programming language objects is called *data binding*. In the common case, data types used in message exchanges are defined in the WSDL document using XML Schema. Therefore, in the case of Java, data binding for Web Services specifically means converting from XML schema documents to Java objects, and converting Java objects to XML Schema instance documents. The Java Community Process has specified a standard API for achieving this called Java Architecture for XML Binding (JAXB). JAXB works by defining a set of Java annotations. Java annotations allow metadata to be inserted into the Java code, similar to the javadoc capabilities, except that annotations are fully fledged classes associated with a Java class and can be machine processed. These annotations can be examined by the JAXB implementation to determine how the Java object should be converted to an XML Schema. When JAXB classes are generated from Schema, the annotations are generated as well. Using annotations means the generated, or prepared classes are portable between JAXB implementations.

The Java Community Process has also defined an API for mapping Java classes to WSDL constructs. This specification is called the Java API for XML-Based Web Services (JAX-WS). JAX-WS delegates the data binding elements of its specification to JAXB. On top of this, JAX-WS defines further annotations, as well as some Java interfaces supporting both exposing and consuming Web Services; that is, handling both WSDL and SOAP processing.

The two specifications work hand in hand to provide a full set of tools that can be used by Web Service container middleware.

22.2 Setup

First, let's create a working directory where we can keep all the libraries and source code we create. We'll presume it is in your home directory and called *ws*.

Next, we'll get hold of CXF and set up the container. CXF can be downloaded from:

```
http://cxf.apache.org/download.html
```

You can get the binary distribution. The example here was built using version 2.0.5. Any 2.0.x version should be compatible. You can unpack the zipped file into the *ws* directory. You can also rename it to something less verbose, for example, *cxf-2.0.5*. If you look in this directory, you'll see a bunch of files. We are interested in the *lib* directory. This contains the jar files we'll need to link to in our own code, for example, the JAXB and JAX-WS reference implementations. We won't actually need all the jar files — there are quite a few — but we won't meddle with the CXF distribution by removing ones we do not need.

Next, inside the *ws* directory; that is, at the same level as the cxf directory, create three more directories:

- *src* - this will contain our source files.
- *classes* - this is where we will compile the source files to.
- *bin* - this is where we will put scripts for running the code.

Next, *cd* into the *src* directory and create the java package directory structure like this:

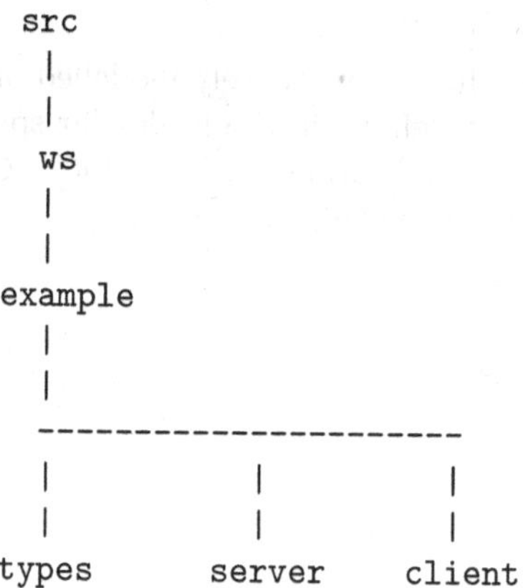

So our server-side code will live in *ws/example/server*, the client-side code will live in *ws/example/client* and the data types we will create will live in *ws/example/types*. Now we are ready to start coding.

22.3 Container Classes

First we need to create some Java classes that represent the various data types used by the service, specifically classes representing people, events, and lists of these, that can easily be converted into XML Schema by JAXB.

The easiest way to make a Java class easily convertible to XML is to create them using few simple rules. First, make sure they have a default constructor; that is, a constructor that takes no arguments. This allows the data binding system to easily generate such objects simply by knowing the class name:

```
Class clazz = Class.forName("ws.example.Container");
Object container = clazz.newInstance();
```

Next, provide *getter* and *setter* methods for the instance variables of the class following the Java Beans naming conventions. These suggest that the method name should be made up of the variable name, with the first letter capitalized, preceded by either *get* or *set*. For example, imagine we have a variable called *length* which is an int. The getter for this would be called *getLength* and the setter would be called *setLength*. The setter would also take an argument of the same type as the variable is, i.e., an int. If you have a boolean variable, the getter may also be preceded by *is*. This naming convention allows the class to be introspected using Java's reflection API to discover the properties that a Bean class exposes. We will look at the reflection API more closely near the end of this chapter.

Now, *cd* into the *types* directory and open up your favorite text editor (or IDE if you have one)

22.3.1 VEvent Class

The first class to create is the event class. This is very loosely modelled on a subset of fields defined by the VEvent object defined in the iCalendar specification. iCalendar is used by many calendar applications such as Mac's *iCal*, Microsoft's *Outlook* and Gnome's *Evolution*. The class will have:

- a start date and time
- an end date and time
- a brief summary/title
- a description
- a location
- a unique identifier

Below is the skeleton code:

```java
package ws.example.types;

import java.util.Date;
import java.util.UUID;

public class VEvent {

    private Date dtStart;
    private Date dtEnd;
    private String summary;
    private String location;
    private String description;
    private String uid = "urn:uuid:" +
      UUID.randomUUID().toString();

    public VEvent() {
    }
    public Date getDtStart() {
        return dtStart;
    }
    public void setDtStart(Date dtStart) {
        this.dtStart = dtStart;
    }
    public Date getDtEnd() {
        return dtEnd;
    }
    public void setDtEnd(Date dtEnd) {
        this.dtEnd = dtEnd;
    }
    public String getSummary() {
        return summary;
    }
    public void setSummary(String summary) {
        this.summary = summary;
    }
    public String getDescription() {
        return description;
    }
    public void setDescription(String description) {
        this.description = description;
    }
    public String getUid() {
        return uid;
    }
    public void setUid(String uid) {
        this.uid = uid;
```

```
    }
    public String getLocation() {
        return location;
    }
    public void setLocation(String location) {
        this.location = location;
    }
}
```

Listing 22.1. VEvent class.

The VEvent class will be used by the client when creating a new event. When the client wants to get hold of the events currently stored by the server, it will send the `uid` of the VEvent. As you can see above, a pseudo-random id is generated by default when a new instance of a VEvent is created. In return, the client will receive a list of event objects. Because a well-behaved SOAP message only contains a single XML element in the body of the envelope, we will create a simple event list class that is used as the return type of the method. Otherwise, if we were returning a list or array of event objects as-is, there would be more than one element in the SOAP body, and our libraries would not like that. Creating a wrapper class means an XML Schema type will be created as a container for list, meaning we will only have one XML element in our SOAP body no matter how long the list is. Here it is:

```
package ws.example.types;

import java.util.List;
import java.util.ArrayList;

public class VEventList {

    private List<VEvent> events = new ArrayList<VEvent>();

    public List<VEvent> getEvents() {
        return events;
    }
    public void setEvents(List<VEvent> events) {
        this.events = events;
    }
}
```

Listing 22.2. VEventList class.

22.3.2 VCard Class

The Java class we will create to represent a person is based on the VCard specification. VCard is, widely supported by address book applications. Again, we will create a very minimal representation. The class contains fields for a person's first name, last name, telephone number, email, etc. It also contains a separate `Address` class that encapsulates the address-specific data of a person. Below are shown just the fields of these classes. The getters and setters can be deduced from the variables — which is the whole point of having a naming convention. First the `Address` class:

```
package ws.example.types;

public class Address {

    private String streetAddress;
    private String locality;
    private String region;
    private String postalCode;
    private String countryName;

    // getters and setters
}
```

Listing 22.3. Address class.

And the VCard class:

```
package ws.example.types;

public class VCard {

    private String givenName;
    private String familyName;
    private String additionalName;
    private Address address;
    private String email;
    private String telephone;
    private String url;
    private String photoUrl;
    private String id = "urn:uuid:" +
      UUID.randomUUID().toString();

    // getters and setters
}
```

Listing 22.4. VCard class.

As you will notice, the `VCard` class contains an instance of the `Address` class. The schema generation tools are capable of recursively serializing container classes.

The VCard specification also requires a *formatted name* field. This is how the name should look for display purposes. Rather than duplicating data in the `VCard` class, we will add convenience setter and getter methods for this value, made up of the individual names:

```
public String getFormattedName() {
        String middle = getAdditionalName();
        return getGivenName() + " " +
          (middle != null ? middle + " " : "") + getFamilyName();
}
public void setFormattedName(String fullName) {
    String[] names = fullName.split(" ");
    if(names.length > 0) {
        setGivenName(names[0]);
        if(names.length == 3) {
            setAdditionalName(names[1]);
            setFamilyName(names[2]);
        } else if (names.length == 2) {
            setFamilyName(names[1]);
        }
    }
}
```

Listing 22.5. Formatted name of the VCard class.

As you can see, the implementation is not particularly robust, but will suffice for demonstration purposes. Also note that this field will not be serialized by the data binding system, because the methods do not work directly on a field defined by the class called `formattedName`. Hence the client code generated from the WSDL will not contain this method.

Because of the requirement to only have single XML element in the SOAP body, the `VCard` class will not be used directly, but instead inside container classes. The first container class will the object that is passed to the service in order to associate a card with an event. The parameters for the operation are a `VCard` object and a `VEvent` identifier. We will wrap these two parameters into an `EventAddition` class:

```
package ws.example.types;
```

```java

public class EventAddition {

    private String eventId;
    private VCard card;

    public String getEventId() {
        return eventId;
    }
    public void setEventId(String eventId) {
        this.eventId = eventId;
    }
    public VCard getCard() {
        return card;
    }
    public void setCard(VCard card) {
        this.card = card;
    }
}
```

Listing 22.6. Event Addition class.

The client will create one of these and the server will receive and wrap it to store the VCard associated with the event.

Likewise, when the client requests all the VCards associated with an event, the list will actually be wrapped in a list container class similar to the `VEventList` described above:

```java
package ws.example.types;

import java.util.List;
import java.util.ArrayList;

public class VCardList {

    private List<VCard> cards = new ArrayList<VCard>();

    public List<VCard> getCards() {
        return cards;
    }
    public void setCards(List<VCard> cards) {
        this.cards = cards;
    }
}
```

Listing 22.7. VCard container class.

That covers all the data types we will need for the service. We are now ready to write the service interface. *Cd* into the *server* directory.

22.4 Server Implementation

The server side will make use of the data types we defined earlier, as well as some simple JAX-WS annotations for defining how the Java server classes are converted into WSDL. First we need to define a Java interface. This is not strictly necessary, but good practice because the service interface is divorced from the implementation. Below is the service interface that we call EventContactService:

```
package ws.example.server;

import ws.example.types.VEvent;
import ws.example.types.VCardList;
import ws.example.types.EventAddition;
import ws.example.types.VEventList;

import javax.jws.WebService;

@WebService
public interface EventContactService {

    public VCardList getContacts(String eventId);
    public boolean addContact(EventAddition addition);
    public String createEvent(VEvent event);
    public VEventList getEvents();

}
```

Listing 22.8. Web Service interface.

As you can see, the interface imports the required data types. It also imports the JAX-WS-defined *WebService* annotation, which is associated with the Java interface. The service has four methods supporting the functionality we require.

Next we need to create an implementation of this interface. We will call this class EventContactServiceImpl:

```
package ws.example.server;

import ws.example.types.*;
import javax.jws.WebService;
```

```java
import java.util.*;

@WebService(endpointInterface =
          "ws.example.server.EventContactService",
           serviceName = "EventContactService")

public class EventContactServiceImpl
           implements EventContactService {

    private HashMap<String, List<VCard>> contacts =
                new HashMap<String, List<VCard>>();
    private List<VEvent> events = new ArrayList<VEvent>();


    public boolean addContact(EventAddition addition) {
        String eventId = addition.getEventId();
        if(eventId == null) {
            return false;
        }
        VCard card = addition.getCard();
        if(card == null) {
            return false;
        }

        List<VCard> cards = contacts.get(eventId);
        if(cards == null) {
            return false;
        }
        if(cards.contains(card)) {
            return false;
        }
        cards.add(card);
        contacts.put(eventId, cards);
        System.out.println("***********");
        System.out.println("Adding VCard " +
          "associated with event id " + eventId);
        System.out.println("VCard first name=" +
          card.getGivenName());
        System.out.println("VCard last name=" +
          card.getFamilyName());
        System.out.println("VCard email=" +
          card.getEmail());
        System.out.println("***********");
        return true;
    }

    public VCardList getContacts(String eventId) {
        VCardList list = new VCardList();
        List<VCard> cards = contacts.get(eventId);
```

```
        if (cards != null) {
            list.setCards(cards);
        }
        return list;
    }

    public String createEvent(VEvent event) {
        List<VCard> cards = contacts.get(event.getUid());
        if(cards != null) {
            return event.getUid();
        }
        contacts.put(event.getUid(), new ArrayList<VCard>());
        events.add(event);
        System.out.println("***********");
        System.out.println("created event with id " +
          event.getUid());
        System.out.println("***********");
        return event.getUid();
    }

    public VEventList getEvents() {
        VEventList list = new VEventList();
        list.setEvents(events);
        return list;
    }
}
```

Listing 22.9. Web Service implementation.

This class contains the implementation of the four methods defined by the service. The class keeps track of the events it receives in a list, and keeps associations between VCard objects and VEvent unique ids in a hash map. The methods perform some simple checks before either adding to, or retrieving from, the list and map.

The class uses the *@WebService* annotation again, this time with some of the values defined by the annotation:

- endpointInterface — defines the interface that is being used. In this case it is the Java interface we defined above.
- serviceName — this specifies the name of the service as it will appear in the *service* element in the WSDL document.

Finally we need to define a class that will deploy this service, and has a main method we can call from the command line. We just call this Server:

```
package ws.example.server;

```

```
import javax.xml.ws.Endpoint;

public class Server {

    public Server() throws Exception {
        EventContactServiceImpl implementor =
          new EventContactServiceImpl();
        String address =
          "http://localhost:8080/EventContactService";
        Endpoint.publish(address, implementor);
    }

    public static void main(String args[]) throws Exception {
        new Server();
        System.out.println("Server ready...");
    }
}
```

Listing 22.10. Web Service server.

This class makes use of the JAX-WS-defined *Endpoint* class. It could not be simpler. We pass it an address, and the annotated service implementation class to publish. Behind the scenes, the Endpoint class takes care of locating a provider for the particular address scheme (HTTP), generating the WSDL when requested and starting up a server socket to listen for the invocations. The *main* method simply creates a new `Server` instance.

That's it for the server side. Now we need to create a script to launch the server and link in with all those jar files that make our life so easy. Let's *cd* to the *bin* directory.

Depending on your operating system, you will either want to create a batch file (for Windows) or a shell script (for Unix and Mac OS X). Here is an example batch called *build.bat*:

```
@ECHO OFF

set CP=..\classes
setlocal ENABLEDELAYEDEXPANSION
FOR /R ..\cxf-2.0.5\lib %%G IN (*.jar) DO set CP=!CP!;%%G
ECHO compiling types classes
javac -classpath "%CP%" -d ..\classes ..\src\ws\example\types\*.java
ECHO compiling server classes
javac -classpath "%CP%" -d ..\classes ..\src\ws\example\server\*.java
```

Listing 22.11. build.bat.

The equivalent shell script called *build.sh* looks like this:

```
#!/bin/sh

CP=../classes/
for i in ‘find ../cxf-2.0.5/lib -name ’*.jar’‘; do
    CP="$CP:$i"
done
echo "compiling types classes"
javac -classpath $CP -d ../classes ../src/ws/example/types/*.java
echo "compiling server classes"
javac -classpath $CP -d ../classes ../src/ws/example/server/*.java
```

Listing 22.12. build.sh.

It is important that you have the directory structure correctly set up for these scripts to work because the paths are defined relative to where the script is executing from. Also, you will notice that both files loop through the *lib* directory of the CXF distribution, adding all the files with a *.jar* extension to the class path, before invoking the Java compiler. Therefore it is important that the name of the directory containing the CXF distribution is named the same as in the build file. In the examples above, this is *cxf-2.0.5*.

Once you have created one of these files, you can open the terminal and *cd* to the *bin* directory. On Windows type:

```
build.bat
```

On Unix and Mac OS X, type:

```
./build.sh
```

This will run the scripts. If all goes well, you should see some output saying it is compiling types and server classes. That means you have compiled the java classes in the *types* directory and the *server* directory. Now you are ready to start the server. Again we'll write a script to do this, because we do not want to get all the CXF jars by hand. Here are examples of batch and shell scripts to kick off the server:

```
set CP=..\classes
setlocal ENABLEDELAYEDEXPANSION
FOR /R ..\cxf-2.0.5\lib %%G IN (*.jar) DO set CP=!CP!;%%G
java -classpath "%CP%" ws.example.server.Server
```

Listing 22.13. run-server.bat.

The equivalent shell script called *run-server.sh* looks like this:

```
#!/bin/sh

CP=../classes/
for i in 'find ../cxf-2.0.5/lib -name '*.jar''; do
    CP="$CP:$i"
done
java -classpath $CP ws.example.server.Server
```

Listing 22.14. run-server.sh.

Again, make sure the directory name of the CXF distribution is the same as in the script.

Once you have created one of these, you are ready to go. Go back to the terminal. On Windows type:

```
run-server.bat
```

On Unix or Mac OS X type:

```
./run-server.sh
```

If all goes well, you should see a load of logging information scroll past the screen. The final line should read:

```
Server ready...
```

This means everything is good.

NOTE: To shut down the server, hold down the Ctrl key and press C.

Now you are ready to admire the results of your efforts, even though it means staring at a WSDL file. Open your browser, ideally one that supports XML, such as Mozilla Firefox. Type into the address bar:

```
http://localhost:8080/EventContantService?wsdl
```

This will take you to the page where the service WSDL can be found. You should see lots of XML.

22.5 Service WSDL

Let us look at the WSDL that has been generated. In the WSDL `definitions` element we see it has a name attribute of `EventService`. This is one of the values we passed the JAX-WS *@WebService* annotation in the implementation class. We can also see that the WSDL definition as a whole, and indeed the `schema` element below it have a `targetNamespace` attribute of

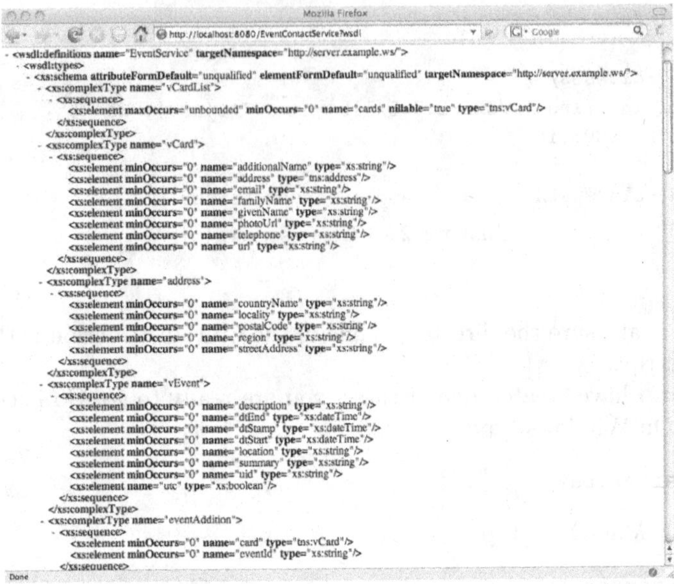

Fig. 22.1. EventContactService WSDL.

`http://server.example.ws/`. This has been generated by JAX-WS based on the package name of the implementation class. Essentially it has reversed the package name order, and prepended the HTTP scheme to it, thus creating a URI.

Next in the `types` element below the `definitions` element we have the XML Schema declaration that defines our container classes we created. The fields of these classes have been converted into XML Schema types. Strings and primitive types are mapped to XML Schema primitive types. The `vCard` element references the complex `address` type, just as the Java equivalent contains a Java address class. The date fields of the `vEvent` schema type have been mapped from the *java.util.Date* class to the built-in *dateTime* XML Schema type.

As you scroll down, you can see the schema types being referenced in the `message` elements, and the messages in turn being referenced by `operation` elements in the `portType` and `binding` elements.

Finally, the `service` element has a name of `EventService` — again the value we passed to the JAX-WS annotation, and a SOAP address of `http://localhost:8080/EventContactService`.

As we saw above, the XML Schema types are defined as being in the namespace `http://server.example.ws/`, a URI generated by JAX-WS. The *@WebService* annotation allows a targetNamespace value to be defined. If we return to the implementation class, we can add a target namespace to the annotation:

```
@WebService(endpointInterface =
    "ws.example.server.EventContactService",
    serviceName = "EventService",
    targetNamespace = "http://ws.example.contact-service-interface")
```

However, this has the effect not just of changing the target namespace of the WSDL document, it actually separates the abstract WSDL service definition from the concrete implementation. If you kill off the server, run the build script and then start the server again, with these annotation changes, you will see the WSDL looks a bit different now. Rather than defining the XML Schema types, the messages and the portType, the WSDL document only defines the service binding and endpoint. Instead, the abstract WSDL definitions are defined in a separate WSDL document which referenced via an *import statement* and pointing to:

```
http://localhost:8080/EventContactService?wsdl=EventContactService.wsdl
```

If you go to this address, you will see the abstract definitions of the WSDL document.

22.6 Client Implementation

At the server side, we used the nice interfaces provided by the Java Web Service and XML APIs. On the client side we are going to do things in two ways. The first will use the *wsdl2java* tool that comes with CXF. This tool allows you to pre-compile the data types before invoking the service. You will have noticed that, although we downloaded CXF, we did not reference it once in the server code. This is because we used the annotations to define the service, and the *Endpoint* class to deploy the service. CXF is there, but it is behind the scenes, tying everything together. It will play a similar role on the client-side when we use the pre-compiled classes.

The second client we will create we will call the *dynamic* client because we won't have to pre-compile the classes that are referenced in the WSDL. This client will make use of particular classes provided by CXF. To do this, however, we will have to use some basic interfaces to Java class objects provided by the *java.lang.reflect* package. This is because the classes we will be manipulating, namely, container classes as defined by the XML Schema in the server's WSDL document, will not actually exist at compile time. Therefore we cannot make any direct references to them. This makes the code a little less intuitive and long-winded, but provides an interesting insight into how Web Services can be used in more dynamic situations. After all, this is one reason for having a machine-readable interface like WSDL.

22.6.1 Standard Client

In order to use a standard client we need to read the data types from the WSDL and compile them. This is easily done with the *wsdl2java* tool that comes with CXF. If you *cd* into the CXF directory (we are presuming here it is called *cxf-2.0.5*) from the terminal, and then into the *bin* directory, you will see the wsdl2java listed. Depending on your operating system you will either want to invoke *wsdl2java* if you are on Unix or Mac OS X, or *wsdl2java.bat* if you are windows. On either of the former, type:

```
./wsdl2java -p gen.ws.example.server
  -d ../../src -classdir ../../classes -compile
    http://localhost:8080/EventContactService?wsdl
```

or on Windows type:

```
wsdl2java.bat -p gen.ws.example.server
   -d ..\..\src -classdir ..\..\classes -compile
      http://localhost:8080/EventContactService?wsdl
```

Type this all as one line. As before, it is important that your directory structure is correct.

NOTE: make sure you have started the server process from another terminal because the wsdl2java needs to retrieve the WSDL document in order to parse it.

This incantation has a few parameters:

- `-p` means use the specified Java package name for generated types. We set this, so that the generated classes do not clash with any existing classes we have created.
- `-d` is the destination directory in which to put the generated source files. This points to our *src* directory.
- `-classdir` is the directory to compile source files to. This points to our *classes* directory.
- `-compile` requests that the source files are compiled by the tool.
- Finally, *wsdl2java* needs to know the endpoint of the WSDL file that it should parse.

If all goes well, you should now have generated source files in the *src* and compiled class files in the *classes* directory. If you look at the source files, you will see that these echo the container classes we created before for the server. The classes are annotated with further JAX-WS annotations. These are used by the system when invoking the service. There are also some service classes that have been generated. The *EventContactService* Java Interface represents the interface to the service and echoes the *EventContactService* we created in the *ws.example.server* package. The generated *EventService* extends a JAX-WS-defined *Service* class that provides boilerplate code for getting a handle to a WSDL*portType* implementation. This class is the client's hook into invoking the service, as we shall see when we write the client code.

We are now ready to write the client side of the Web Service. *Cd* into the *client* directory under the *ws/example* directory and create a file called *EventClient.java*. Below is the code to populate the file:

```
package ws.example.client;

import gen.ws.example.server.*;

import javax.xml.datatype.DatatypeFactory;
import javax.xml.datatype.XMLGregorianCalendar;
import javax.xml.datatype.DatatypeConstants;
import java.util.List;
import java.net.URL;

public class EventClient {

    private String endpoint;

    public EventClient(String endpoint) {
        this.endpoint = endpoint;
    }
    public void invoke() throws Exception {

        EventContactService eventService = createClient();
        DatatypeFactory factory = DatatypeFactory.newInstance();
        XMLGregorianCalendar start =
          factory.newXMLGregorianCalendar();
        start.setYear(2008);
        start.setMonth(DatatypeConstants.AUGUST);
        start.setDay(4);
        start.setTime(11, 0, 0);
        XMLGregorianCalendar end =
          factory.newXMLGregorianCalendar();
        end.setYear(2008);
        end.setMonth(DatatypeConstants.AUGUST);
        end.setDay(4);
        end.setTime(18, 0, 0);

        VEvent event = createEvent("Ursula's 6th Birthday Party",
          start, end);
        String id = eventService.createEvent(event);
        System.out.println("****************");
        System.out.println("Invoked createEvent " +
```

```
            "on server with id " + id);
          System.out.println("Event start=" +
            event.getDtStart().toXMLFormat());
          System.out.println("Event end=" +
            event.getDtEnd().toXMLFormat());
          System.out.println("Event summary " +
            event.getSummary());
          VCard card = createCard("Sue", "Smith",
            "s.smith@fabrikam.com");
          EventAddition addition = createAddition(id, card);
          eventService.addContact(addition);

          card = createCard("Dave", "Jones",
            "d.jones@example.com");
          addition = createAddition(id, card);
          eventService.addContact(addition);

          VCardList list = eventService.getContacts(id);
          List<VCard> cards = list.getCards();
          for (VCard vCard : cards) {
              System.out.println("Retrieved Vcard " +
                "associated with event id " + id);
              System.out.println("Vcard first name=" +
                vCard.getGivenName());
              System.out.println("Vcard last name=" +
                vCard.getFamilyName());
              System.out.println("Vcard email=" +
                vCard.getEmail());
          }
          System.out.println("***************");
      }

      public EventContactService createClient() throws Exception {
          EventService service = new EventService(new URL(endpoint));
          return service.getEventContactServiceImplPort();
      }

      public VEvent createEvent(String summary,
        XMLGregorianCalendar start,
        XMLGregorianCalendar end) throws Exception {
          VEvent event = new VEvent();
          event.setDtStart(start);
          event.setDtEnd(end);
          event.setSummary(summary);
          return event;
      }

      public VCard createCard(String firstName, String lastName,
            String email) {
```

```
89          VCard card = new VCard();
90          card.setGivenName(firstName);
91          card.setFamilyName(lastName);
92          card.setEmail(email);
93          return card;
94      }
95
96      public EventAddition createAddition(String id, VCard card) {
97          EventAddition addition = new EventAddition();
98          addition.setEventId(id);
99          addition.setCard(card);
100         return addition;
101     }
102
103     public static void main(String[] args) throws Exception {
104         new EventClient("http://localhost:8080/" +
105             "EventContactService?wsdl").invoke();
106     }
107 }
```

Listing 22.15. Event Client class.

The `EventClient` class takes a WSDL document endpoint as a parameter. This is used to pinpoint the service that is going to be invoked. Actually, this parameter is not required, because the generated code has stored the WSDL endpoint during the generation process. By having a parameter, we can reuse this client if there are different *EventServices* at other endpoints that implement the same interface.

The class contains a few utility methods for creating the types needed to invoke the service — `createEvent`, `createCard` and `createAddition`. These take some basic parameters but could be easily extended to construct more complete objects.

The `createClient` method on lines 61-64 first creates a new `EventService` object. This is the generated class that extends the JAX-WS-defined `Service` class. It then requests the event service to create a concrete implementation of the `EventContactService` interface. It does this by using the functionality built into the JAX-WS `Service` class. This concrete implementation is what the code in the `invoke` method uses to invoke the Web Service.

The `invoke` method first creates an `EventContactService`. It then creates two `javax.xml.datatype.XMLGregorianCalendar` objects. When JAXB comes across an XML Schema date type, it binds this class to it, rather than the `java.util.Calendar` or `java.util.Date` class that we used when we created the `VEvent` class on the server side. This is because the `XMLGregorianCalendar` is easier to manipulate, and has built-in functionality in terms of how it generates a character string for XML serialization. As can be seen from the code, the `javax.xml.datatype` package provides a factory class for creating these calendar objects. The calendar objects will be the start and end time of our event. The method then creates a VEvent and then sends this to the Web Service. In return it receives a String which is the unique id for the event. Then the method creates two `VCard` objects, and sends these to the Web Service, associated with the event via an `EventAddition` object.

Finally the client requests a `VCardList` from the service, passing it the event id. It then iterates over the list and prints out the people who are associated with the event. These should be the two people we created `VCards` for earlier in the `invoke` method.

To build the client, you will need to add some lines to your build script, as well as create a new script to run the client. If you are running Windows, open the *build.bat* in the *ws/bin* directory and add the following to the end of the file:

```
ECHO compiling client classes
javac -classpath
            "%CP%" -d ..\classes ..\src\ws\example\client\*.java
```

Listing 22.16. build.bat additions.

If you are running Unix or Mac OS X, open the *build.sh* file you created, add these lines:

```
echo "compiling client classes"
javac -classpath $CP -d ../classes ../src/ws/example/client/*.java
```

Listing 22.17. build.sh additions.

This will allow you to compile all the source code, including the new client you have created. We then need to write a script to launch the client. On Windows, create a text file called *run-client.bat*, and type this into it:

```
set CP=..\classes
setlocal ENABLEDELAYEDEXPANSION
FOR /R ..\cxf-2.0.5\lib %%G IN (*.jar) DO set CP=!CP!;%%G
java -classpath "%CP%" ws.example.client.EventClient
```

Listing 22.18. run-client.bat.

On Unix or Mac OS X, create a run-client.sh file and populate it with this:

```
set CP=..\classes
setlocal ENABLEDELAYEDEXPANSION
FOR /R ..\cxf-2.0.5\lib %%G IN (*.jar) DO set CP=!CP!;%%G
java -classpath "%CP%" ws.example.client.EventClient
```

Listing 22.19. run-client.sh.

To test the whole thing, first run the build script, then the run-server script and then the run-client script. When you run the server script you will see some logging output ending with the statement:

```
Server ready...
```

At this point you can run the client script. When you run the client script you will see output in both client and server terminal windows. The server prints out when a new event is created and when VCards are associated with the event:

```
***********
created event with id
  urn:uuid:a3431f5c-4b97-4e78-aee0-8e49eb0af3b4
***********
***********
Adding VCard associated with event
   urn:uuid:id a3431f5c-4b97-4e78-aee0-8e49eb0af3b4
VCard first name=Sue
VCard last name=Smith
VCard email=s.smith@fabrikam.com
***********
***********
Adding VCard associated with event
   urn:uuid:id a3431f5c-4b97-4e78-aee0-8e49eb0af3b4
VCard first name=Dave
VCard last name=Jones
VCard email=d.jones@example.com
***********
```

Listing 22.20. Server output.

The client prints out the event identifier which is the server's response to creating an event. It then prints out the details of cards associated with the event after an invocation to the `getContacts(id)` server operation.

```
****************
Invoked createEvent on server with id
```

```
  urn:uuid:a3431f5c-4b97-4e78-aee0-8e49eb0af3b4
Event start=2008-08-04T11:00:00
Event end=2008-08-04T18:00:00
Event summary Ursula's 6th Birthday Party
Retrieved vcard associated with event id
  urn:uuid:a3431f5c-4b97-4e78-aee0-8e49eb0af3b4
Vcard first name=Sue
Vcard last name=Smith
Vcard email=s.smith@fabrikam.com
Retrieved vcard associated with event id
  urn:uuid:a3431f5c-4b97-4e78-aee0-8e49eb0af3b4
Vcard first name=Dave
Vcard last name=Jones
Vcard email=d.jones@example.com
****************
```

Listing 22.21. Client output.

22.6.2 Dynamic Client

While the example above is simple and easy to use, it does require that the service WSDL location is known beforehand so that the *wsdl2java* tool can run its magic. It also requires that the tool has been run before you can start writing the client. This means there is a development phase between service discovery and service invocation, making the system not as flexible as a SOA should apparently be. A SOA should provide the ability to discover and bind to a service at runtime. The following example shows a client that gets closer to this capability. While it still involves knowing what the WSDL and the XML types look like, it is not such a great step from the code below, to creating an application that can introspect the data types created at runtime from WSDL and return meaningful input choices to a user, for example via a graphical user interface.

This client does exactly the same thing as the previous one, only the data types do not exist at the time the code is written. This was another reason for specifying the package name to generate when running *wsdl2java*. As you will see from the code below, the classes being created are neither from the server classes in the package *ws.example.types*, nor from the generated classes in *gen.ws.example.server*. Rather they are created in a package called *ws.example.server*, which is the default package mapping that the JAX-WS does from the namespace *http://server.example.ws*. Below is the code for the `DynamicClient` class.

```
package ws.example.client;

```

```
import org.apache.cxf.endpoint.Client;
import org.apache.cxf.endpoint.dynamic.DynamicClientFactory;

import javax.xml.datatype.DatatypeFactory;
import javax.xml.datatype.XMLGregorianCalendar;
import javax.xml.datatype.DatatypeConstants;
import javax.xml.namespace.QName;
import java.lang.reflect.Method;
import java.util.List;

public class DynamicEventClient {

    Client client;
    private String endpoint;

    private DynamicEventClient(String endpoint) {
        this.endpoint = endpoint;
    }

    public void invoke() throws Exception {

        createClient();

        DatatypeFactory factory = DatatypeFactory.newInstance();
        XMLGregorianCalendar start =
          factory.newXMLGregorianCalendar();
        start.setYear(2008);
        start.setMonth(DatatypeConstants.AUGUST);
        start.setDay(4);
        start.setTime(11, 0, 0);
        XMLGregorianCalendar end =
          factory.newXMLGregorianCalendar();
        end.setYear(2008);
        end.setMonth(DatatypeConstants.AUGUST);
        end.setDay(4);
        end.setTime(18, 0, 0);
        Object event = createEvent("Ursula's 6th birthday party",
          start, end);
        String id = (String) invoke("createEvent", event);
        System.out.println("****************");
        System.out.println("Invoked createEvent " +
          on server with id " + id);
        System.out.println("Event start=" +
          event.getDtStart().toXMLFormat());
        System.out.println("Event end=" +
          event.getDtEnd().toXMLFormat());
        System.out.println("Event summary " +
          event.getSummary());

```

```
        Object card = createCard("Sue", "Smith",
          "s.smith@ex.com");
        Object addition = createAddition(id, card);
        invoke("addContact", addition);

        card = createCard("Dave", "Jones", "d.jones@ex.com");
        addition = createAddition(id, card);
        invoke("addContact", addition);

        Object contacts = invoke("getContacts", id);
        System.out.println("contacts=" + contacts);
        List cards = (List) get(contacts, "getCards");
        for (int i = 0; i < cards.size(); i++) {
            Object vCard = cards.get(i);
            System.out.println("retrieved vcard associated " +
              "with event id " + id);
            System.out.println("vcard first name=" +
              get(vCard, "getGivenName"));
            System.out.println("vcard last name=" +
              get(vCard, "getFamilyName"));
            System.out.println("vcard email=" +
              get(vCard, "getEmail"));
        }
        System.out.println("****************");
    }

    public static void main(String args[]) throws Exception {
        new DynamicEventClient("http://localhost:8080/" +
          "EventContactService?wsdl").invoke();
    }

    public Object createAddition(String id,
      Object card) throws Exception {
        Object addition =
          createObject("ws.example.server.EventAddition");
        set(addition, "setEventId", id);
        set(addition, "setCard", card);
        return addition;
    }

    public Object createEvent(String summary,
      XMLGregorianCalendar start,
      XMLGregorianCalendar end) throws Exception {
        Object event =
          createObject("ws.example.server.VEvent");
        set(event, "setSummary", summary);
        set(event, "setDtStart", start);
        set(event, "setDtEnd", end);
        return event;
```

```
    }

    public Object createCard(String firstName,
      String lastName,
      String email) throws Exception {
        Object card =
          createObject("ws.example.server.VCard");
        set(card, "setGivenName", firstName);
        set(card, "setFamilyName", lastName);
        set(card, "setEmail", email);
        return card;
    }

    public void createClient() throws Exception {
        DynamicClientFactory f = DynamicClientFactory.newInstance();
        client = f.createClient(endpoint,
                Client.class.getClassLoader());
    }

    public Object createObject(String className) throws Exception {
        return Thread.currentThread().getContextClassLoader()
          loadClass(className).newInstance();
    }

    public Object get(Object target, String method)
        throws Exception {
        Method m;
        try {
            m = target.getClass().getMethod(method, new Class[0]);
        } catch (NoSuchMethodException e) {
            return null;
        }
        Object ret = m.invoke(target, new Object[0]);
        return ret;
    }

    public void set(Object target, String method,
      Object value) throws Exception {
        Class cls = value.getClass();
        Method m = null;
        while (cls != null) {
            try {
                m = target.getClass().getMethod(method, cls);
                break;
            } catch (NoSuchMethodException e) {
                cls = cls.getSuperclass();
            }
        }
        if (m == null) {
```

```
                return;
            }
            m.invoke(target, value);
        }
        public Object invoke(String operation, Object value)
          throws Exception {
            return client.invoke(operation), value)[0];
        }
    }
```

Listing 22.22. Dynamic Event Client class.

The structure of this class is very similar to the previous client, with only a few crucial differences. First, it uses some of the CXF classes directly, in particular the `DynamicClientFactory`. This can return an instance of the CXF-defined `Client` interface, that works with java code that is generated at runtime and stored in memory as opposed to on file. CXF uses some aspect-oriented programming techniques to generate these Java classes dynamically.

Second, the class has three methods for processing objects that do not exist at compile time. These methods — `createObject`, `set` and `get` — use the Java reflection API to create Java classes, objects and their methods, accessing them by their names. In particular, you will see the `newInstance` method of a class being called to create an object, the `getMethod` method being used to retrieve a `Method` object defined by the class, and the `invoke` method of the `Method` class. Because these classes and their methods are accessed using strings, the compiler is none the wiser about whether they exist or not.

Now create a script to run the dynamic client. On Windows, create a text file called *run-dynamic-client.bat*, and type this into it:

```
set CP=..\classes
setlocal ENABLEDELAYEDEXPANSION
FOR /R ..\cxf-2.0.5\lib %%G IN (*.jar) DO set CP=!CP!;%%G
java -classpath "%CP%" ws.example.client.DynamicEventClient
```

Listing 22.23. run-dynamic-client.bat.

On Unix or Mac OS X, create a run-client.sh file and populate it with this:

```
set CP=..\classes
setlocal ENABLEDELAYEDEXPANSION
FOR /R ..\cxf-2.0.5\lib %%G IN (*.jar) DO set CP=!CP!;%%G
java -classpath "%CP%" ws.example.client.DynamicEventClient
```

Listing 22.24. run-dynamic-client.sh.

You can now re-run the build script to compile the dynamic client. Then start the server, and then run the run-dynamic-client script you have just created. You should see the same output as with the standard client.

JAX-WS provides many other ways of building both server-side and client-side applications, including the ability to manipulate the XML on the wire directly via Java XML APIs. Look in the *samples* directory of your CXF distribution.

22.7 Conclusion

In this chapter, we have built a relatively complex Web Service and client using complex types and providing a number of operations. We have seen how the Java standards for dealing with data binding and exposing classes through a WSDL interface make life reasonably simple for a developer. We also showed how you can create a more dynamic client that uses runtime generated code to communicate with a service.

We should remember, however, that the server and client we created use the same underlying library and are written in the same programming language. Life is not always so simple if you apply these libraries and standards to services written in other languages with possibly more complex objects that are exchanged. There are still interoperability problems lurking between Web Services implementations.

23

Web Deployment Using Atom

In this chapter we will look at how to deploy onto the Web using the Atom Syndication Format and Publishing Protocols. As described in Chapter 18, Atom provides both a feed format for enabling clients to subscribe to frequently updated content, as well as a publishing protocol, to allow an author to edit and create new content that clients can receive.

We are going to create an Atom version of the Event service that we made in the Web Services Deployment chapter. This is partly for comparative reasons, and also to show how Atom can be used for more than just a traditional syndication service. We will be able to reuse some of the container classes we defined for the Web Service, specifically the `VEvent` and `VCard` classes. We will also create a class that can generate HTML content from them. In doing this, we will convert these classes into their microformat equivalents of hCalendar and hCard. This will make our data types available for machine processing, as well as humanly readable in a browser.

The code and scripts that we create here, along with pointers to required libraries, can also be downloaded in zip form from:

`http://www.p2pgridbook.com`

There are a number of tools for managing feeds — both RSS and Atom. We are going to use the Abdera [256] project. Abdera is another Apache Incubation project (see Chapter 22). The aim of Abdera is to be a fully functional, high-performance Atom library, and is therefore a library worth becoming acquainted with if one is interested in Atom.

Let us remind ourselves of the Web Service WSDL operations we defined to support the event service:

createEvent(Event event):String The client sends an Event to the server and receives the id of the event in return.

addContact(EventID, Card):boolean The client sends a contact card and an event id to the server. The operation returns true if the contact has successfully be associated with the event.

getContacts(EventID):list of Cards The client can retrieve the cards associated with a particular event by sending the event id.

getEvents:list of events The client can query the service for the events it has stored.

Achieving the same capabilities using Atom will involve a slightly different approach. Feeds are conceptually collections of entries. This means that operations like *getEvents* and *getContacts* come for free if we model the list of events and list of contacts as feeds, available at a certain URI. Likewise, the *createEvent* and *addContact* can be modelled as creating a new entry in a feed. The only area where we digress from the typical feed scenario is when we create a new event. This is because the creation of a new event has to trigger the creation of a new feed, namely, the feed that will contain the list of contacts that are interested in a particular event. We should also be able to allow the user to find out where the contact feed for a particular event is, so they can sign up to it. So we need to create a mapping between an event feed and the corresponding contact feed.

23.1 Setup

Abdera can be downloaded from:

```
http://incubator.apache.org/abdera/
```

The examples here use version 0.4.0. The API may change over time, so try to use this version, or at least another 0.4.x version. Choose a binary version as opposed to a source file version.

As before, we will create a working directory in which to place all the libraries and code we create. We will presume this directory is called *web*, and will refer to it by this name throughout this chapter. Once you have downloaded the Abdera distribution, unzip it in the *web* directory. You can rename the distribution directory to something shorter, for example *abdera-0.4.0*.

Next, inside the *web* directory, at the same level as the Abdera distribution, create three more directories for the source code, classes and scripts to run the code:

- src - this will contain our source files.
- classes - this is where we will compile the source files to.
- bin - this is where we will put scripts for running the code.

Next, *cd* into the *src* directory and create the java package directory structure like this:

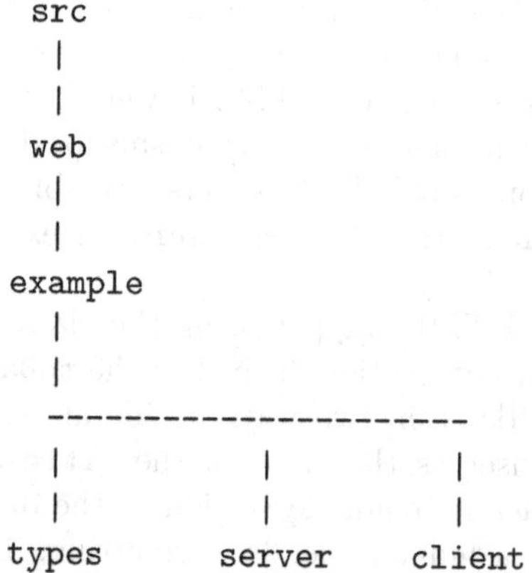

The Atom server code will live in *web/example/server*, the Atom client code will live in *web/example/client* and some utility types used by both will live in *web/example/types*. Now we are ready to start coding.

23.2 Utility Classes

Abdera provides some classes that allow you to map a domain-specific entity — in our case VEvent and VCard — to an Atom Collection, and hence Atom Feed Document. Each entity becomes an Atom Entry in the Atom Collection/Feed. Chapter 22 describes the container classes used by the Web Service deployed in that chapter. In particular, we created `VEvent` and `VCard` classes which are very minimal Java implementations of the vCard specification [257] and the events used by the iCalendar [258] specification. You can look at the description of these types in Section 22.3.

We are going to take these classes and extend them in a few ways. First, we will add an `updated` field to both of them, and corresponding getter and setter methods. This is because we are mapping our domain specific-data types to Atom Entries, which have the built-in concept of having changed at some time.

Second, we are going to add an `html` field that is a string, containing an HTML representation of the object. Specifically we will create microformat representations from the VEvent and VCard classes. These will appear as the content of the Atom Entry that is published by the client. To achieve the serialization, as well as parsing the HTML, we will add a utility class called `HtmlUtil` that does the necessary conversion. A more complete implementation would provide a `fromHTML` method as well, so that the data type can be fully re-constituted at the server side. We'll leave this as an exercise for the reader. For now, the server receives some basic data about the data type, and leaves the HTML content pretty much untouched. Listing 23.11 shows the `HtmlUtil` class. It is given at the end of this chapter, as it is quite long.

As you will see, the class contains a variety of methods for creating HTML strings and extracting values from it. It is by no means complete, or even robust, for example, the parsing methods presume the HTML is well-formed. But it will provide our server and client with some basic mechanisms for dealing with HTML. There are a number of complete HTML parsers available for Java (see `http://java-source.net/open-source/html-parsers` for examples).

The `eventToHtml` method creates an HTML snippet using the class attributes defined by the *hcalendar* microformat. Notice the call to the `toDate` method. This formats the start and end dates in two ways, inside an `abbr` HTML tag. The first, hidden from the user as the value of the `title` attribute defined by `abbr`, contains the machine readable version of the date. The second, visible to the user, contains a human friendly formatting. The `cardToHtml` method returns an HTML snippet using the class attributes defined by the *hcard* microformat. These two methods will be used by the client to set the value of the `html` field we added to the classes.

23.3 The Atom Server

The Atom Server maintains a single events feed that clients can publish events to. When a client publishes an event, the server generates a new feed for that particular event. Clients interested in the event publish their interest to this latter feed. The classes created in this section should be placed in the *web/examples/server* directory under the *src* directory. Abdera provides an `AbstractEntityCollectionAdapter` class that does most of the work of mapping from domain-specific entities to Atom Collection, Feed and Entry documents. We will use this class to create VEvent collection and VCard collection adapters. Below is the EventCollectionAdapter class that handles clients publishing and getting a list of events. All the methods are concrete implementations of abstract methods defined in the `AbstractEntityCollectionAdapter` class.

```
package web.example.server;

import org.apache.abdera.Abdera;
import org.apache.abdera.factory.Factory;
import org.apache.abdera.i18n.iri.IRI;
import org.apache.abdera.i18n.text.Sanitizer;
import org.apache.abdera.model.*;
import org.apache.abdera.protocol.server.RequestContext;
import org.apache.abdera.protocol.server.context.*;
import org.apache.abdera.protocol.server.impl.*;
import web.example.types.HtmlUtil;
import web.example.types.VEvent;
```

```
import java.util.Date;
import java.util.HashMap;
import java.util.List;
import java.util.Map;

public class EventCollectionAdapter extends
  AbstractEntityCollectionAdapter<VEvent> {

    private SimpleWorkspaceInfo workspace;
    private Map<String, VEvent> events =
      new HashMap<String, VEvent>();
    private Factory factory = new Abdera().getFactory();

    public EventCollectionAdapter(SimpleWorkspaceInfo
      workspace) {
        this.workspace = workspace;
    }

    public VEvent postEntry(String title, IRI iri, String summary,
      Date date, List<Person> persons, Content content,
      RequestContext context) throws ResponseContextException {
        VEvent event = new VEvent();
        event.setUpdated(date);
        event.setUid(iri.toASCIIString());
        event.setSummary(title);
        event.setDescription(summary);
        event.setHtml(content.getValue());
        CardCollectionAdapter cca =
          new CardCollectionAdapter(getAuthor(context),
            event.getSummary());
        String href = Sanitizer.sanitize(event.getSummary(),
          "-", true);
        cca.setHref(href);
        String text = content.getText();
        String contactsUri = context.getBaseUri()
          .toASCIIString() + href;
        String link = HtmlUtil.toAnchor("Contacts Feed",
          "contacts", contactsUri);
        text = HtmlUtil.insertInto(text, link);
        content.setValue(text);
        event.setHtml(content.getValue());
        workspace.addCollection(cca);
        events.put(event.getUid(), event);
        return event;
    }

    public Text getSummary(VEvent entry, RequestContext context)
      throws ResponseContextException {
```

```
        Text text = factory.newSummary();
        text.setValue(entry.getDescription());
        return text;
    }

    public void deleteEntry(String s, RequestContext context)
      throws ResponseContextException {
        events.remove(s);
    }

    public Object getContent(VEvent event,
      RequestContext context)
      throws ResponseContextException {
        Content content = factory.newContent(Content.Type.HTML);
        content.setValue(event.getHtml());
        return content;
    }

    public Iterable<VEvent> getEntries(RequestContext context)
      throws ResponseContextException {
        return events.values();
    }

    public VEvent getEntry(String s, RequestContext context)
      throws ResponseContextException {
        return events.get(s);
    }

    public String getId(VEvent event
       throws ResponseContextException {
        return event.getUid();
    }

    public String getName(VEvent event)
      throws ResponseContextException {
        return Sanitizer.sanitize(event.getSummary(),
          "-", true);
    }

    public String getTitle(VEvent event)
      throws ResponseContextException {
        return event.getSummary();
    }

    public Date getUpdated(VEvent event)
      throws ResponseContextException {
        return event.getUpdated();
    }

```

```
    public void putEntry(VEvent event, String s, Date date,
      List<Person> persons, String s1, Content content,
        RequestContext context)
          throws ResponseContextException {
        event.setSummary(s);
        event.setDescription(s1);
        event.setUpdated(date);
        event.setHtml(content.getValue());
        events.put(s, event);
    }

    public String getAuthor(RequestContext context)
      throws ResponseContextException {
        return "The Event Manager";
    }
    public String getId(RequestContext context) {
        return "tag:example.web,2008:events:feed";
    }
    public String getTitle(RequestContext context) {
        return "Available Events";
    }
}
```

Listing 23.1. EventCollectionAdapter class.

The getters and setters of this class are used by Abdera to generate feed information such as the title, author and identifier. `VEvent` objects are stored in a map, keyed to their identifier. The most important method is the `postEntry` method. This is invoked when a client publishes an entry to the collection. The method does several things:

- It creates a new VEvent based on the parameters of the method — authors, title, summary and id. The latter is modeled in Abdera using an *IRI*. This is an internationalized URI which allows characters from non-English alphabets.
- It creates a new `CardCollectionAdapter` instance, passing it the title and summary. This class represents the contacts feed. We will look at this next. You will notice that the event adapter takes a `SimpleWorkspaceInfo` object as a parameter in its constructor. This gives it access to the workspace to which it belongs, allowing it to add the new contacts feed to the workspace when the new event is published.
- It then calculates a URI for the newly created feed using the title field and gives the new feed this URI.
- Next it takes the content parameter. This is an HTML string generated by the client, representing the event. It modifies the HTML content, adding a link to the newly created feed. It gives the link a class attribute of

contacts. A programmatic client will have to understand this class attribute as meaning a reference to the VCard feed.
- Finally it sets the HTML on the event and stores it under its unique identifier, ready to be retrieved, edited or deleted.

The CardCollectionAdapter class is very similar, and simpler, because it performs no extra capability such as creating a new feed. Instead it simply allows Abdera to map VCard objects to Atom entries.

```
package web.example.server;

import org.apache.abdera.Abdera;
import org.apache.abdera.factory.Factory;
import org.apache.abdera.i18n.iri.IRI;
import org.apache.abdera.i18n.text.Sanitizer;
import org.apache.abdera.model.*;
import org.apache.abdera.protocol.server.RequestContext;
import org.apache.abdera.protocol.server.context.*;
import org.apache.abdera.protocol.server.impl.*;
import web.example.types.VCard;

import java.util.*;

public class CardCollectionAdapter extends
  AbstractEntityCollectionAdapter<VCard> {

    private Map<String, VCard> cards =
      new HashMap<String, VCard>();
    private Factory factory = new Abdera().getFactory();
    private String author;
    private String id;
    private String title;

    public CardCollectionAdapter(String author,
      String title) {
        this.author = author;
        this.id = "urn:uuid:" +
          UUID.randomUUID().toString();
        this.title = title;
    }

    public VCard postEntry(String title, IRI iri,
      String summary,
      Date date, List<Person> persons, Content content,
      RequestContext context)
      throws ResponseContextException {
        VCard card = new VCard();
        card.setFormattedName(s);
```

```
        card.setId(iri.toASCIIString());
        card.setUpdated(date);
        card.setHtml(content.getValue());
        cards.put(card.getId(), card);
        return card;
    }

    public void deleteEntry(String s, RequestContext context)
      throws ResponseContextException {
        cards.remove(s);
    }

    public Object getContent(VCard vCard, RequestContext context)
      throws ResponseContextException {
        Content content = factory.newContent(Content.Type.HTML);
        content.setValue(vCard.getHtml());
        return content;
    }

    public Iterable<VCard> getEntries(RequestContext context)
      throws ResponseContextException {
        return cards.values();
    }

    public VCard getEntry(String s, RequestContext context)
      throws ResponseContextException {
        return cards.get(s);
    }

    public String getId(VCard vCard)
      throws ResponseContextException {
        return vCard.getId();
    }

    public String getName(VCard vCard)
      throws ResponseContextException {
        return Sanitizer.sanitize(vCard.getFormattedName(),
          "-", true);
    }

    public String getTitle(VCard vCard)
      throws ResponseContextException {
        return vCard.getFormattedName();
    }

    public Date getUpdated(VCard vCard)
      throws ResponseContextException {
        return vCard.getUpdated();
    }
```

```

    public void putEntry(VCard card, String s, Date date,
      List<Person> persons, String s1, Content content,
        RequestContext context)
        throws ResponseContextException {
        card.setId(s);
        card.setUpdated(date);
        card.setHtml(content.getValue());
        cards.put(card.getId(), card);
    }

    public String getAuthor(RequestContext context)
      throws ResponseContextException {
        return author;
    }

    public String getId(RequestContext context) {
        return id;
    }

    public String getTitle(RequestContext context) {
        return title;
    }
}
```

Listing 23.2. CardCollectionAdapter class.

Now we can create the Server that will host the collections. This class, listed below, provides an extension to the `AbderaServlet` class, which itself extends `javax.servlet.http.HttpServlet`. The Java Servlet API provides a standard way to deploy server-side code, particularly HTTP, using a Servlet Container. The container manages much of the housekeeping required in providing efficient, robust and scalable services, and calls on particular Servlets that have been deployed into it based on the request URI of a client. By adhering to the Servlet API, your code can, in theory, be deployed into any container supporting the API. The server listed in Listing 23.4 uses the Jetty [259] container.

The `AbderaServlet` manages all the invocations for us. All we have to do is subclass its `createProvider` method to return an instance of an Abdera `Provider`. We return the default provider, but first we set up a workspace and add an instance of our `EventCollectionAdapter` class to it. We also pass the workspace itself into the constructor of our adapter, so that the adapter can add new `CardCollectionAdapter` instances to the workspace when clients create new events. Finally we add the workspace to the provider. When we invoke the `main` method of the `Server` class, the container will initialize our Servlet and make the event collection available.

```
package web.example.server;

import org.apache.abdera.protocol.server.Provider;
import org.apache.abdera.protocol.server.impl.DefaultProvider;
import org.apache.abdera.protocol.server.impl.SimpleWorkspaceInfo;
import org.apache.abdera.protocol.server.servlet.AbderaServlet;
import org.mortbay.jetty.servlet.*;

public class Server {

    public static void main(String... args) throws Exception {
        int port = 8080;
        org.mortbay.jetty.Server server =
          new org.mortbay.jetty.Server(port);
        Context context =
          new Context(server, "/", Context.SESSIONS);
        ServletHolder servletHolder =
          new ServletHolder(new EventContactProviderServlet());
        context.addServlet(servletHolder, "/*");
        server.start();
        server.join();
    }
    public static final class EventContactProviderServlet
      extends AbderaServlet {

        protected Provider createProvider() {
            SimpleWorkspaceInfo wi = new SimpleWorkspaceInfo();
            wi.setTitle("Event Contact Workspace");
            EventCollectionAdapter ca =
              new EventCollectionAdapter(wi);
            ca.setHref("events");
            wi.addCollection(ca);
            DefaultProvider provider = new DefaultProvider("/");
            provider.addWorkspace(wi);
            provider.init(getAbdera(), null);
            return provider;
        }
    }
}
```

Listing 23.3. Server class.

23.4 Atom Client

We are now ready to create the client. Whilst Atom supports creating, retrieving, updating and deleting feed entries, this client will concentrate on creating entries. We will be able to retrieve the entries from within a browser that supports Atom, such as Safari and Internet Explorer. Firefox supports Atom as well, but does not display the content of entries in the feed list, which means you will not see the beautiful HTML content we create for our events and cards. Rather, we would have to deploy the HTML content elsewhere, and link to it from within the Atom Entry. While this is possible, and is indeed the typical mechanism for syndication, the added complexity means we leave it as an exercise for the reader. Below is the `EventClient` class. This should be placed into the *web/example/client* directory under the *src* directory.

```
package web.example.client;

import org.apache.abdera.Abdera;
import org.apache.abdera.factory.Factory;
import org.apache.abdera.i18n.iri.IRI;
import org.apache.abdera.model.*;
import org.apache.abdera.protocol.client.AbderaClient;
import web.example.types.*;

import java.util.*;

public class EventClient {

    Abdera abdera = new Abdera();
    AbderaClient abderaClient = new AbderaClient(abdera);
    Factory factory = abdera.getFactory();

    public void populateFeeds() throws Exception {
        abderaClient.setMaxConnectionsPerHost(10);
        Document<Service> introspection =
                abderaClient.get("http://localhost:8080/")
                .getDocument();
        Service service =
                introspection.getRoot();
        Collection collection =
                service.getCollection(
                        "Event Contact Workspace",
                        "Available Events");
        VEvent event = new VEvent();
        Calendar start =
                new GregorianCalendar(2008,
                Calendar.AUGUST, 4, 18, 0, 0);
        Calendar end =
                new GregorianCalendar(2008,
                Calendar.AUGUST, 5, 0, 0, 0);
        event.setDtStart(start.getTime());
        event.setDtEnd(end.getTime());
```

```
        event.setSummary("Party");
        event.setDescription("Ursula's 60th Birthday Party.");
        event.setLocation("Southerdown Beach");
        Entry entry = createEntryFromEvent(event);
        Document<Entry> doc = abderaClient.post(
                collection.getResolvedHref().toString(),
                entry).getDocument();
        String content = doc.getRoot().getContent();
        List<String> hrefs =
          HtmlUtil.getAttributesWithClass("contacts",
            "href", content);
        if (hrefs.size() == 0) {
            return;
        }
        String contactsFeed = hrefs.get(0);
        VCard card = new VCard();
        card.setGivenName("Sally");
        card.setAdditionalName("Sue");
        card.setFamilyName("Smith");
        card.setEmail("sss@ex.com");
        Address address = new Address();
        address.setStreetAddress("384 Stacey Road");
        address.setLocality("Cardiff");
        address.setRegion("Wales");
        address.setCountryName("UK");
        card.setAddress(address);
        entry = createEntryFromCard(card);
        doc = abderaClient.post( contactsFeed, entry)
          .getDocument();

        card = new VCard();
        card.setGivenName("David");
        card.setFamilyName("Jones");
        card.setEmail("dj@ex.com");
        address = new Address();
        address.setStreetAddress("23 Orbit Street");
        address.setLocality("Cardiff");
        address.setRegion("Wales");
        address.setCountryName("UK");
        card.setAddress(address);
        entry = createEntryFromCard(card);
        doc = abderaClient.post(contactsFeed, entry)
          .getDocument();
    }
    private Entry createEntryFromEvent(VEvent event) {
        Entry entry = factory.newEntry();
        entry.setId(event.getUid());
        entry.setTitle(event.getSummary());
        entry.setSummary(event.getDescription());
```

```
        entry.setUpdated(new Date());
        entry.addAuthor("Event Author");
        entry.setContentAsHtml(HtmlUtil.eventToHtml(event));
        return entry;
    }
    private Entry createEntryFromCard(VCard card) {
        Entry entry = factory.newEntry();
        entry.setId(card.getId());
        entry.setTitle(card.getFormattedName());
        entry.setSummary("An interested person");
        entry.setUpdated(new Date());
        entry.addAuthor(card.getFormattedName());
        entry.setContentAsHtml(HtmlUtil.cardToHtml(card));
        return entry;
    }
    public static void main(String[] args) {
        try {
            new EventClient().populateFeeds();
        } catch (Exception e) {
            e.printStackTrace();
        }
    }
}
```

Listing 23.4. Server class.

Most of the code in the `EventClient` class is taken up with creating our objects to publish. The actual functionality is performed by the `AbderaClient` class provided by the Abdera library. The `EventClient` keeps an instance of this class to publish the entries.

The `createEntryFromCard` and `createEntryFromEvent` methods take a `VCard` and `VEvent` respectively and return an Atom Entry that can be published. The Entry fields are determined by the object passed into the method. In particular, the `HtmlUtil` class is used to generate HTML from the object, and provide this as the content for the entry. The `populateFeeds` method is where the client publishes entries. First it creates a new event, and an Entry based on it. Then it invokes the `AbderaClient`'s `post` method which takes the resolved URI of the event collection, and the Entry object. This method returns the newly created Entry. At this point, the client looks for a link with the class attribute `contacts`, pointing to the newly created feed for adding interested people. If you remember, this link with this class attribute was added by the server class when the new event arrived. The client uses `HtmlUtil` to do this search. If a link is not found, then the method exits. Otherwise, two new `VCard` objects are created and published to the new feed.

23.5 Running the Service and Client

Now that we have built both sides of the application, we need to compile and run them. Below are scripts for building the classes. If you are running Windows, create a *build.bat* file and drop it into the *bin* directory we created.

```
@ECHO OFF

set CP=..\classes
setlocal ENABLEDELAYEDEXPANSION
FOR /R ..\abdera-0.4.0\lib %%G IN (*.jar) DO set CP=!CP!;%%G
FOR /R ..\abdera-0.4.0 %%G IN (*.jar) DO set CP=!CP!;%%G
ECHO compiling types classes
javac -classpath "%CP%" -d ..\classes ..\src\web\example\types\*.java
ECHO compiling server classes
javac -classpath "%CP%" -d ..\classes ..\src\web\example\server\*.java
ECHO compiling client classes
javac -classpath "%CP%" -d ..\classes ..\src\web\example\client\*.java
```

Listing 23.5. build.bat.

If you are running Mac OS X or Unix, create a *build.sh* file and drop it into the *bin* directory we created.

```
#!/bin/sh

CP=../classes/
for i in ‘find ../abdera-0.4.0/lib -name ’*.jar’‘; do
    CP="$CP:$i"
done
for i in ‘find ../abdera-0.4.0 -name ’*.jar’‘; do
    CP="$CP:$i"
done
echo "compiling types classes"
javac -classpath $CP -d ../classes ../src/web/example/types/*.java
echo "compiling server classes"
javac -classpath $CP -d ../classes ../src/web/example/server/*.java
echo "compiling client classes"
javac -classpath $CP -d ../classes ../src/web/example/client/*.java
```

Listing 23.6. build.sh.

Note that your directory structure must be correct for these scripts to work, because they look for jar files relative to where the script is located. Also note that the directory name of the Abdera distribution must match the search path in the scripts. This is *abdera-0.4.0* in the examples above.

You can now run the build script. Open a terminal and *cd* to the *web/bin* directory. On Windows type:

```
build.bat
```

On Mac OS X or Unix type:

```
./build.sh
```

If all goes well, you should see some output saying the types, client and server classes are being compiled.

Below are scripts for running the server and client. Again, create the appropriate files and drop them into the *bin* directory. If using Windows, create the *.bat* files. If using Mac OS X or Unix, create the *.sh* versions.

```
set CP=..\classes

setlocal ENABLEDELAYEDEXPANSION
FOR /R ..\abdera-0.4.0\lib %%G IN (*.jar) DO set CP=!CP!;%%G
FOR /R ..\abdera-0.4.0 %%G IN (*.jar) DO set CP=!CP!;%%G
java -classpath "%CP%" web.example.server.Server
```

Listing 23.7. run-server.bat.

```
#!/bin/sh

CP=../classes/
for i in ‘find ../abdera-0.4.0/lib -name ’*.jar’‘; do
    CP="$CP:$i"
done
for i in ‘find ../abdera-0.4.0 -name ’*.jar’‘; do
    CP="$CP:$i"
done
java -classpath $CP web.example.server.Server
```

Listing 23.8. run-server.sh.

```
set CP=..\classes
setlocal ENABLEDELAYEDEXPANSION
FOR /R ..\abdera-0.4.0\lib %%G IN (*.jar) DO set CP=!CP!;%%G
FOR /R ..\abdera-0.4.0 %%G IN (*.jar) DO set CP=!CP!;%%G
java -classpath "%CP%" web.example.client.EventClient
```

Listing 23.9. run-client.bat.

```
#!/bin/sh

CP=../classes/
for i in ‘find ../abdera-0.4.0/lib -name ’*.jar’‘; do
    CP="$CP:$i"
done
for i in ‘find ../abdera-0.4.0 -name ’*.jar’‘; do
    CP="$CP:$i"
done
java -classpath $CP web.example.client.EventClient
```

Listing 23.10. run-client.sh.

Now you are ready to start the server. from the *bin* directory, in the terminal, type `run-server.bat` on Windows, or `./run-server.sh` on Mac OS X or Unix. Then open your browser and go to:

`http://localhost:8080/events`

You should see a feed called *Available Events.* At the moment the list is empty because we have not run the client yet. To run the client, execute the appropriate script. On Windows, type *run-client.bat* from the terminal. On Mac OS X or Unix, type *run-client.sh.*

This should execute the client, creating a new event in the Available Events feed, as well as two contacts in the new contacts feed. Refresh your browser. You should now see a single event, including a link to the contacts feed for the particular event.[1] Figure 23.1 shows what this looks like in the Safari browser.

The browser has rendered the HTML that we used to populate the content of the entry. If you click on the *Contacts Feed* link at the bottom of the event Entry, you will be taken to the feed that displays the people who have signed up for the event. The Safari rendition of this is shown in Figure 23.2.

---

[1] Remember Firefox does not display Entry content in the feed list so you will not be able to see the event details or the link to the contacts feed. You can install a feed reader such as Sage (`http://sage.mozdev.org/`) which is integrated with Firefox and very easy to install using Firefox's plugin mechanism.

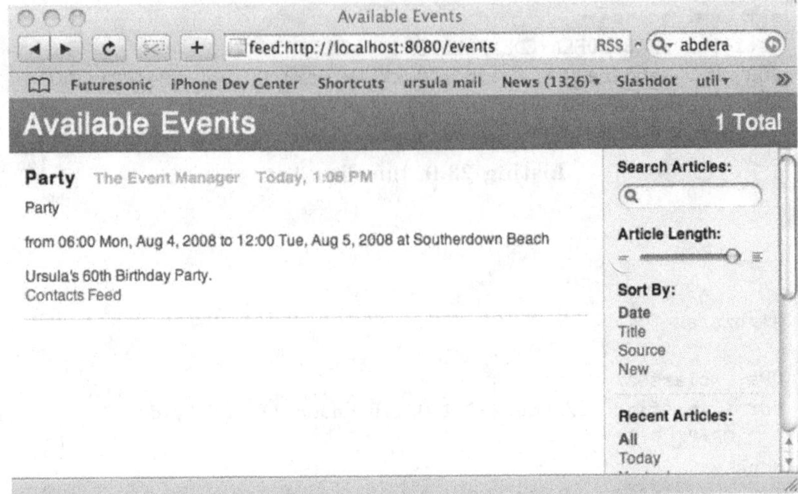

Fig. 23.1. The Event feed with a single entry.

The use of objects representing the common specifications of *VEvent* and *iCalendar*, and the fact that we have serialized them to HTML using the Microformats specifications means one could further process the entries in a number of ways. For example, the events could be extracted from the feeds and converted into renditions suitable for calendar applications such as Mac's *iCal*, Microsoft's *Outlook* and Gnome's *Evolution*. These accept *.ics* files. The same is true for the VCard objects.

23.6 Conclusion

In this chapter we have taken the Web Service we created in Chapter 22, and exposed it using the Atom protocols. By providing a mechanism by which the addition of content to one feed can generate a new feed on the fly, we were able to replicate the capabilities of the WSDL interface to the event service. Whilst Atom was primarily designed for content syndication in a more traditional context, we can see how Atom can be used in other, less obvious ways. By doing so we have shown that Atom is more than a syndication format. Rather it can operate as a generic RESTful API for a wide variety of applications.

23.7 Ancillary Code

For completeness, a full listing of the `HtmlUtil` class used by the example in this chapter is given. As mentioned before, this class is really just for example purposes and should not be considered a complete HTML generator or parser.

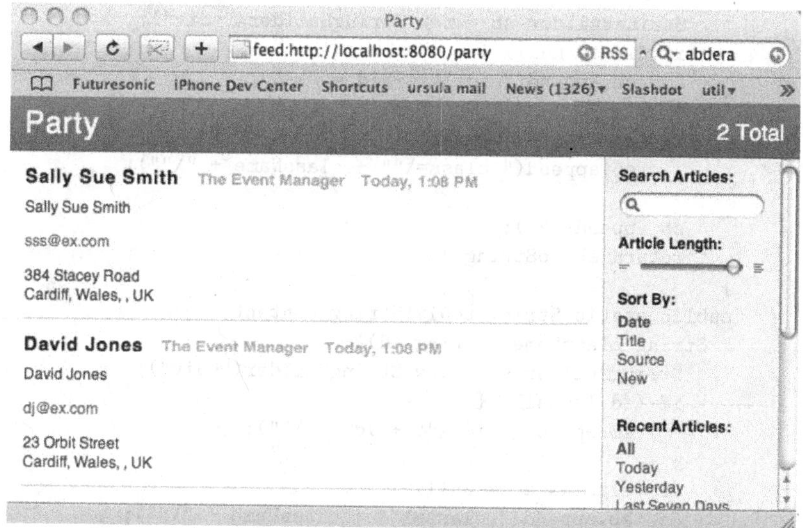

Fig. 23.2. The Contacts signed up to the event.

```
package web.example.types;

import org.w3c.dom.*;
import org.xml.sax.*;
import javax.xml.parsers.*;
import java.util.*;
import java.io.IOException;
import java.io.StringReader;
import java.text.SimpleDateFormat;

public class HtmlUtil {

    private static SimpleDateFormat machine =
      new SimpleDateFormat("yyyyMMdd'T'HHmm");
    private static SimpleDateFormat human =
      new SimpleDateFormat("hh:mm EEE, MMM d, yyyy");

    public static String closeP() {
        return "</p>";
    }
    public static String openP() {
        return "<p>";
    }
    public static String closeDiv() {
        return "</div>";
    }
    public static String openDiv(String className, String id) {
```

```
        StringBuilder sb = new StringBuilder("<div");
        if (id != null) {
            sb.append(" id=\"" + id + "\"");
        }
        if (className != null) {
            sb.append(" class=\"" + className + "\"");
        }
        sb.append(">");
        return sb.toString();
    }
    public static String toDiv(String content,
      String className, String id) {
        StringBuilder sb = new StringBuilder("<div");
        if (id != null) {
            sb.append(" id=\"" + id + "\"");
        }
        if (className != null) {
            sb.append(" class=\"" + className + "\"");
        }
        sb.append(">" + content + "</div>");
        return sb.toString();
    }
    public static String toDiv(String content,
        String className) {
        return toDiv(content, className, null);
    }
    public static String toSpan(String content,
        String className) {
        StringBuilder sb = new StringBuilder("<span");
        if (className != null) {
            sb.append(" class=\"" + className + "\"");
        }
        sb.append(">" + content + "</span>");
        return sb.toString();
    }
    public static String toAnchor(String content,
      String className, String href) {
        StringBuilder sb = new StringBuilder("<a");
        if (className != null) {
            sb.append(" class=\"" + className + "\"");
        }
        sb.append(" href=\"" + href + "\"");
        sb.append(">" + content + "</a>");
        return sb.toString();
    }
    public static String toAnchor(String content,
        String className) {
        return toAnchor(content, className, content);
    }
```

```
    public static String toDate(Date date, String className) {
        String title = machine.format(date);
        String content =  human.format(date);
        StringBuilder sb = new StringBuilder("<abbr");
        if (className != null) {
            sb.append(" class=\"" + className + "\"");
        }
        sb.append(" title=\"" + title + "\"");
        sb.append(">" + content + "</abbr>");
        return sb.toString();
    }
    public static String[] getClasses(String attribute) {
        if (attribute.trim().length() == 0) {
            return new String[0];
        }
        return attribute.split("\\s");
    }
    public static List<String>
        getAttributesWithClass(String clazz,
          String attribute, String html) throws IOException {
        Document doc = newDocument(html);
        Element root = doc.getDocumentElement();
        List<String> hrefs = new ArrayList<String>();
        List<Element> els = getElementsWithClass(clazz, root);
        for (Element el : els) {
            if(el.hasAttribute(attribute)) {
                hrefs.add(el.getAttribute(attribute));
            }
        }
        return hrefs;
    }
    public static String insertInto(String div,
      String content) {
        if(div.startsWith("<div") && div.endsWith("</div>")) {
            String trunc = div.substring(0, div.length() - 6);
            StringBuilder sb = new StringBuilder(trunc);
            sb.append(content).append("</div>");
            return sb.toString();
        }
        return div;
    }
    public static List<Element>
      getElementsWithClass(String clazz,
        Document doc) {
        Element root = doc.getDocumentElement();
        return getElementsWithClass(clazz, root);
    }
    public static List<Element>
      getElementsWithClass(String clazz,
```

```
        Element root) {
        List<Element> list = new ArrayList<Element>();
        String entry = root.getAttribute("class");
        String[] clss = getClasses(entry);
        for (String aClass : clss) {
            if (aClass.equals(clazz)) {
                list.add(root);
            }
        }
        NodeList nl = root.getChildNodes();
        for (int i = 0; i < nl.getLength(); i++) {
            Node n = nl.item(i);
            if (n instanceof Element) {
                Element c = (Element) n;
                List<Element> l = getElementsWithClass(clazz, c);
                list.addAll(l);
            }
        }
        return list;
    }
    public static Document newDocument(String html)
      throws IOException {
        try {
            StringReader reader = new StringReader(html);
            DocumentBuilderFactory dbf =
              DocumentBuilderFactory.newInstance();
            DocumentBuilder db = dbf.newDocumentBuilder();
            return db.parse(new InputSource(reader));
        } catch (ParserConfigurationException e) {
            throw new IOException(e.getMessage());
        } catch (SAXException e) {
            e.printStackTrace();
            throw new IOException(e.getMessage());
        }
    }
    public static String cardToHtml(VCard card) {
        StringBuilder sb = new StringBuilder();
        sb.append(openDiv("hcard", card.getId()));
        String name = toSpan(getValue(card.getGivenName()),
          "given-name") + " " +
                toSpan(getValue(card.getAdditionalName()),
                  "additional-name") + " " +
                toSpan(getValue(card.getFamilyName()),
                  "family-name");
        if (card.getUrl() != null) {
            sb.append(toAnchor(name, "fn, n, url",
              card.getUrl()));
        } else {
            sb.append(toDiv(name, "fn, n, url"));
```

```
        }
        if (card.getEmail() != null) {
            sb.append(openP())
            .append(toAnchor(card.getEmail(), "email",
              "mailto:" + card.getEmail()))
            .append(closeP());
        }
        if (card.getAddress() != null) {
            sb.append(openDiv("adr", null));
            Address a = card.getAddress();
            sb.append(toDiv(getValue(a.getStreetAddress()),
              "street-address"))
            .append(toSpan(getValue(a.getLocality()),
              "locality"))
            .append(", ")
            .append(toSpan(getValue(a.getRegion()),
              "region"))
            .append(", ")
            .append(toSpan(getValue(a.getPostalCode()),
              "postal-code"))
            .append(", ")
            .append(toSpan(getValue(a.getCountryName()),
              "country-name"))
            .append(closeDiv());
        }
        sb.append(toDiv(getValue(card.getTelephone()),
          "tel"))
        .append(closeDiv());
        return sb.toString();
    }
    public static String eventToHtml(VEvent event) {
        StringBuilder sb = new StringBuilder();
        sb.append(openDiv("vevent", event.getUid()))
        .append(toDiv(getValue(event.getSummary()),
          "summary"));
        String time = "";
        if (event.getDtStart() != null) {
            time += "from " + toDate(event.getDtStart(),
              "dtstart");
        }
        if (event.getDtEnd() != null) {
            time += " to " + toDate(event.getDtStart(),
              "dtend");
        }
        String loc = getValue(event.getLocation());
        String at = " at " + toSpan(loc, "location");
        sb.append(openP()).append(time).append(at)
          .append(closeP());
        String desc = getValue(event.getDescription());
```

```
        sb.append(toDiv(desc, "description"))
        .append(closeDiv());
        return sb.toString();
    }
}
```

Listing 23.11. HtmlUtil class.

A

Want to Find Out More?

This appendix contains a list of links to the core organizations and umbrella projects for many of the distributed systems discussed in this book. This list is by no means exhaustive but it does provide some pointers to on-line information for further reading.

A.1 The Web

- **The W3C, http://www.w3.org/** is the World Wide Web consortium, which is the foremost forum for information, commerce, communication and collective understanding for the Web-related technologies. The W3C develops interoperable technologies and releases specifications, guidelines, software and tools. For example, the W3C has developed the specifications for XML, SOAP and WSDL. It is the first stop on discovering standardized Internet technologies.
- **The W3C, http://www.w3.org/2002/ws/** is a starting point on the W3C Web site that lists Web service-related technologies on which W3C is currently working.
- **Fielding's Dissertation, http://www.ics.uci.edu/~fielding/pubs/dissertation/top.htm** *Architectural Styles and the Design of Network-based Software Architectures.* Chapter 5 describes Representational State Transfer.
- **HTTP, http://www.w3.org/Protocols/** W3C gateway to documents relating to the HTTP protocol.
- **Berners-Lee page at the W3C, http://www.w3.org/People/Berners-Lee/** provides links, biographies and some nice questions and answers.
- **W3C Semantic Web Activity http://www.w3.org/2001/sw/** is a gateway to various Semantic Web technologies.

- **Web Design Issues http://www.w3.org/DesignIssues/** A series of essays and thought by Tim Berners-Lee on the Web, the Semantic Web and general architectural and philosophical points. Some of these writings are now ten years old, but they still make insightful reading.

A.2 Web 2.0

- **http://www.oreillynet.com/pub/a/oreilly/tim/news/2005/09/30/what-is-web-20.html**. The concept of "Web 2.0" began with a conference brainstorming session between O'Reilly and MediaLive International. Dale Dougherty, Web pioneer and O'Reilly VP, noted that "far from having crashed, the web was more important than ever, with exciting new applications and sites popping up with surprising regularity." This Tim O'Reilly on-line article is a good start to the Web 2.0 discussions and how the term was coined.
- **Microformats homepage http://microformats.org/** links to news, mailing lists and wiki.
- **Mashups and APIs, http://www.programmableweb.com/** is a great collection of the latest developments in the world of mashups and service APIs.
- **Atom Syndication Format http://tools.ietf.org/html/rfc4287** Atom from the horse's mouth. This is the Request for Comments.
- **Atom Publishing Protocol http://tools.ietf.org/html/rfc5023** This is the current state of the APP proposal.
- **Web Application Description Language https://wadl.dev.java.net/** This is the WADL project page.
- **The blogosphere** There are a host of discussions on the themes of Web and Web 2.0 across the blogosphere. A starting point into the mesh of opinions and developments are the blogs of those working in the field.

A.3 Web Services

- **OASIS, http://www.oasis-open.org/** is a non-profit consortium, which attempts to drive the development and adoption of e-business standards. For example, it has developed specifications for ebXML and UDDI.
- **XML.com, http://www.xml.com/** provides various resources for XML including a section on Web Services.
- **WebServices.org, http://www.webservices.org/** is a portal for finding out about Web Services. It contains newsletters, introductions to Web services, news and numerous articles.
- **Web Services Architect, http://www.webservicesarchitect.com/** hosts a collection of articles and links for Web Services from both a business and a technical perspective.

- **Microsoft's Web Services Developer Center, http://msdn.microsoft.com/webservices/** is a site dedicated to providing information to Web Service developers. It hosts many useful articles on the use of various Web Service technologies and lists the new Web service specifications.
- **IBM Developer Works for Web Services, http://www-136.ibm.com/developerworks/webservices/** contains a number of technical articles and specifications about Web Services and related technologies. It also has a download section and learning resources.
- **WS-I, http://www.ws-i.org/** is "an open, industry organization chartered to promote Web Services interoperability across platforms, operating systems, and programming languages." It works with industry and standards organizations to respond to customer needs.
- **XMethods, http://www.xmethods.com/** lists the publicly available Web Services. You can access the lists of Web Services by using their UDDI server, for example, to dynamically discover and connect to available resources.
- **Web Services Journal, http://www.sys-con.com/webservices/** is an on-line resource that lists real-use cases of how various companies and organizations are deploying and using Web Services. There is a news section that lists new incentives that are happening within the Web Services world.
- **Java Technology and Web Services, http://java.sun.com/webservices/index.jsp** covers the various Java tools and packages that can support the development and deployment of Web Services.

A.4 Grid Computing

- **Open Grid Forum (OGF), http://www.ogf.org/** contains information about Grid-related events. The OGF is a forum of some 5000+ individual researchers and practitioners working on distributed computing or Grid technologies, and has a wide range of technical groups working on aspects of Grid technology and deployment.
- **GridForge, http://forge.gridforum.org/** is the working respository for OGF Working and Research Groups, housing the related documents through an open public comment process.
- **Globus: http://www.globus.org/** hosts the Globus middleware for Grid computing and all associated documentation.
- **GRIDSTART, http://www.gridstart.org/** contains information about the EU Framework 5 IST-funded Grid research projects. You can find links to CrossGrid, DAMIEN, DataGrid (EDG and EGEE), DataTAG, EGSO, EuroGrid, GRIA, GridLab and GRIP, along with a number of other projects that form the GRIDSTART cluster. The project's intention is to stimulate the widespread deployment of Grid technology by raising the awareness of potential users of the solutions already developed

or being developed. They also organize IST Concertation Meetings on Grid Research, twice yearly, which host a number of plenary talks and European technical working groups.

- **UK e-Science, http://www.rcuk.ac.uk/escience/** Here you can find more information about the UK e-Science program.
- **National e-Science Center: http://www.nesc.ac.uk/** is a site containing links to a number of projects within the UK e-Science program.
- **GridCafe, http://gridcafe.web.cern.ch/gridcafe/** is a place to learn various aspects of Grid computing, from the name and the dream to a list of concrete projects around the world.
- **Grid Technology Repository (GTR), http://gtr.globus.org/** was set up as a place for people to publish and discover work related to Grid technology.
- **The Grid Computing, http://www.gridcomputing.com/** information center is designed to promote the development of technologies which provide seamless and scalable access to wide-area distributed resources.
- **Grid Today, http://www.gridtoday.com/** provides daily news and information for the Grid community.
- **The Grid Report, http://www.thegridreport.com/** is a collection of news items about distributed and Grid computing. It contains the latest news and information about Grid computing; it's run by software engineers and its focus is for software engineers.
- **Grid Computing Planet, http://www.gridcomputingplanet.com/** is one of many sites run by JupiterWeb, the on-line division of Jupitermedia, which is a leading global provider of information, images, research and events for information technology, business and creative professionals. The Grid Computing Planet is in the EarthWeb information section and provides numerous articles, news events and so on, for Grid computing.
- **CCGrid, http://www.ccgrid.org/** is a yearly IEEE International Symposium on Cluster Computing and the Grid. It also hosts a number of workshops.

A.5 P2P Tools and Software

- **P2P and XML in Business, http://www.xml.com/pub/a/2001/07/11/xmlp2p.html** provides an article discussing the integration of P2P and XML for businesses.
- **Peer-to-Peer Computing, http://p2p.ingce.unibo.it/** is a popular yearly conference on Agents and P2P Computing (AP2PC).
- **P2P4B2B, http://www.stratvantage.com/directories/p2pworkgroups.htm** is a site listing non-commercial peer-to-peer efforts. The sites listed are non-profit, open source or informational and have relevance to the business use of P2P technology. The sites also represent standards efforts.

- **O'Reilly OpenP2P.com, http://www.openp2p.com/** is a site dedicated to various articles on P2P-related technology. Always interesting!
- **Global and Peer-to-Peer Computing, http://gp2pc.lri.fr/** is an international yearly workshop held in conjunction with CCGrid.
- **Intel P2P Developer Center, http://www.intel.com/cd/ids/developer/asmo-na/eng/technologies/peertopeer/index.htm** is a site dedicated to technologies that can leverage the power of the existing end-user's resources on the Internet.
- **Distributed Hash Tables, http://en.wikipedia.org/wiki/Distributed_hash_table** is the wikipedia page for DHT technology.
- **BitTorrent:**
  - **BitTorrent, Inc., http://www.bittorrent.com/** is the home page of BitTorrent, Inc. and provides a number of BitTorrent related resources.
  - **Wired, http://www.wired.com/techbiz/startups/news/2007/12/YE_10_startups**, *Wired* magazine 2003 interview with Bram Cohen, author of BitTorrent.
  - **BitTorrent Protocol, http://www.bittorrent.org/beps/bep_0003.html** is the location of the Official BitTorrent Protocol Specification.
  - **Doug Walker Interview, http://gigaom.com/2008/03/09/bittorrent-ceo-doug-walker-interview/** - video interview with new CEO for BitTorrent.
- **Gnutelliums, http://www.gnutelliums.com/** provides a comprehensive directory of Gnutella clients for Windows, Linux/Unix and Macintosh, some of which are provided below:
  - **BearShare, http://www.bearshare.com** is a Windows file sharing program from Free Peers, Inc.
  - **Gnotella, http://www.gnotella.com** is a clone of Gnutella for Windows.
  - **Gnucleus, http://gnucleus.sourceforge.net/** is an open Gnutella client for Windows.
  - **LimeWire, http://www.limewire.com** is a very popular Java-based Gnutella client.
  - **Phex, http://www.konrad-haenel.de/phex/** is also a Java client, based on William W. Wong's Furi.
  - **Toadnode, http://www.toadnode.com** is an extensible platform for P2P networks. Its core functionality revolves around the ability to find, retrieve and distribute data between users across multiple networks.
  - **Gnut, http://www.gnutelliums.com/linux_unix/gnut/** is a command-line client which implements the Gnutella protocol. It will run on a wide range of POSIX-compliant systems including: SunOS, Linux, FreeBSD, HP-UX and Win32.

A.6 Distributed Object Systems

- **Jan Newmarch's Guide to JINI Technologies, http://pandonia.canberra.edu.au/java/jini/tutorial/Jini.xml** provides an on-line extensive guide to Jini Technologies.
- **The Distributed Component Object Model (DCOM), http://www.microsoft.com/com/tech/DCOM.asp** is a Web site for finding out about distributed DCM technology, which enables software distributed components to communicate in a reliable, secure and efficient manner. It was previously called "Network OLE" and was based on the Open Software Foundation's DCE-RPC specification.
- **CORBA, http://www.corba.org/** is the home page for the Common Object Request Broker Architecture (CORBA) middleware. It contains a number of resources, CORBA success stories and pointers to the Object Management Group.
- **Object Management Group (OMG), www.omg.org** which is establishing a model-driven architecture through its worldwide standard specifications including CORBA, CORBA/IIOP, the UML, XMI, MOF, Object Services, Internet Facilities and Domain Interface specifications.
- **Jini, http://www.jini.org/** is a central place for finding information about Jini. It contains new information, has discussion groups and allows users to exchange code and ideas.
- **Distributed Object Computing, http://www.yy.ics.keio.ac.jp/~suzuki/object/dist_comp.html** is a useful page containing a number of links and information about distributed object systems including CORBA, Jini, MOMs and distributed agents.

A.7 Underlying Transport and Discovery Protocols

- **IANA, http://www.iana.org/**, home page for the Internet Assigned Numbers Authority (IANA), responsible for the assigned IP address range.
- **Multicast Protocol, http://www.ietf.org/rfc/rfc1112.html** is the request for comments (RFC) Web site for the original Multicast protocol.
- **UDP Protocol, http://www.ietf.org/rfc/rfc768.html** is the RFC Web site for the UDP protocol.
- **TCP Protocol, http://www.ietf.org/rfc/rfc793.html** is the RFC Web site for the TCP protocol.
- **SLP Protocol, http://www.ietf.org/rfc/rfc2608.html** is the RFC Web site for the Service Location Protocol.

B

RSA Algorithm

Figure B.1 shows an outline of the RSA algorithm for encryption, taken from Tanenbaum and van Steen [16]. For more information, see the original text.

Find ***P*** and ***Q***, two large (e.g., 1024-bit) prime numbers:

1. Choose ***E*** such that ***E*** is greater than 1, ***E*** is less than ***PQ***, and ***E*** and ***(P-1)(Q-1)*** are *relatively prime*, which means they have no prime factors in common. *E* does not have to be prime, but it must be odd. ***(P-1)(Q-1)*** can't be prime because it's an even number.
2. Compute ***D*** such that ***(DE - 1)*** is evenly divisible by ***(P-1)(Q-1)***. Mathematicians write this as ***DE = 1 (mod (P-1)(Q-1))***, and they call ***D*** the *multiplicative inverse* of ***E***. This is easy to do -- simply find an integer **X** which causes ***D = (X(P-1)(Q-1) + 1)/E*** to be an integer, then use that value of ***D***.
3. The encryption function is ***C = (T^E) mod PQ***, where ***C*** is the ciphertext (a positive integer), ***T*** is the plaintext (a positive integer), and ^ indicates exponentiation. The message being encrypted, ***T***, must be less than the modulus, ***PQ***.
4. The decryption function is ***T = (C^D) mod PQ***, where ***C*** is the ciphertext (a positive integer), ***T*** is the plaintext (a positive integer), and ^ indicates exponentiation.

...and now:

- The *public key* is the pair ***(PQ, E)***.
- The *private key* is the number ***D***.
- The product ***PQ*** is the *modulus* (often called **N** in the literature).
- ***E*** is the *public exponent*. ***D*** is the *secret exponent*.

Fig. B.1. An outline of the RSA public-key system, which is based on the difficulty of factoring large numbers that are the product of two prime numbers. This factoring problem has been studied for hundreds of years and still appears to be intractable.

References

1. T. Berners-Lee, Universal Resource Identifiers – Axioms of Web Architecture, December 1996. See: *http://www.w3.org/DesignIssues/Axioms.html*
2. J. Siegel, OMG overview: CORBA and the OMG in enterprise computing, *Communications of the ACM*, vol. 41, no. 10, pp. 37–43, 1998.
3. The Distributed Component Object Model (DCOM). See: *http://www.microsoft.com/com/tech/DCOM.asp*
4. Gnutella. See: *http://www.gnutella.com/*
5. Napster. See: *http://www.napster.com/*
6. BitTorrent. See: *http://www.bittorrent.com/*
7. I. Foster, C. Kesselman, J. Nick, and S. Tuecke, The Physiology of the Grid: An Open Grid Services Architecture for Distributed Systems Integration, Open Grid Service Infrastructure WG, Global Grid Forum, Tech. Rep., 2002.
8. IBM and Globus Announce Open Grid Services for Commercial Computing. See: *http://www.ibm.com/news/be/en/2002/02/211.html*
9. The Globus Alliance. See: *http://www.globus.org*
10. J. Touch, Overlay Networks, *Computer Networks*, vol. 36, pp. 115–116(2), July 2001. See: *http://www.ingentaconnect.com/content/els/13891286/2001/00000036/00000002/art00171*
11. I. Foster and A. Iamnitchi, On Death, Taxes, and the Convergence of Peer-to-Peer and Grid Computing, in *Proceedings of the* 2nd *International Workshop on Peer-to-Peer Systems (IPTPS '03)*, 2003.
12. C. Kesselman and I. Foster, *The Grid: Blueprint for a New Computing Infrastructure.* Morgan Kaufmann Publishers, November 1998. See: *http://www.amazon.ca/exec/obidos/redirect?tag=citeulike09-20\&path=ASIN/1558604758*
13. C. Shirky, Modern p2p definition, 2000. See: *http://www.openp2p.com/pub/a/p2p//11/24/shirky1-whatisp2p.html*
14. MySpace. See: *http://www.myspace.com/*
15. Facebook. See: *http://www.facebook.com/*
16. A. S. Tanenbaum and M. van Steen, *Distributed Systems: Principles and Paradigms.* Upper Saddle River, NJ, USA: Prentice Hall PTR, 2001.
17. Clip2, Gnutella Reflector Nodes. See: *http://www.clip2.com*
18. Youtube bandwidth: terabytes per day. See: *http://blog.forret.com/2006/05/youtube-bandwidth-terabytes-per-day/*

19. The SETI Project. See: *http://setiathome.ssl.berkeley.edu/*
20. BOINC - Berkeley Open Infrastructure for Network Computing. See: *http://boinc.berkeley.edu/*
21. T. Hong, *Peer-To-Peer: Harnessing the Power of Disruptive Technologies.* O'Reilly & Associates, Inc. Sebastopol, CA, USA, 2001, ch. 14.
22. J2EE. See: *http://java.sun.com/j2ee/*
23. The Jini Web site. See: *http://www.jini.org/*
24. D. Brookshier, D. Govoni, N. Krishnan, and J. C. Soto, *JXTA: Java P2P Programming.* Sams Publishing, Indianapolis, 2002.
25. The UDP RFC. See: *http://www.ietf.org/rfc/rfc768.txt*
26. The TCP RFC. See: *http://www.ietf.org/rfc/rfc793.txt*
27. The Multicast RFC. See: *http://www.ietf.org/rfc/rfc1112.txt*
28. Internet Assigned Numbers Authority (IANA). See: *http://www.iana.org/*
29. Glop Addressing. See: *http://www.ietf.org/rfc/rfc2770.txt*
30. PIN-SM. See: *http://www.ietf.org/rfc/rfc2362.txt*
31. The Service Location Protocol. See: *http://www.ietf.org/rfc/rfc2608.txt*
32. J. Kempf and J. Goldschmidt, RFC 3082 Notification and Subscription for SLP, March 2001. See: *http://www.faqs.org/rfcs/rfc3082.html*
33. Apache Ant. See: *http://ant.apache.org/*
34. Openlaszlo. See: *http://www.openlaszlo.org/*
35. XML User Interface Language (XUL). See: *http://www.mozilla.org/projects/xul/*
36. W3C, XML Schema. See: *http://www.w3.org/XML/Schema*
37. J. Clark and M. MURATA, RELAX NG Specification, OASIS, Tech. Rep., 2001. See: *http://www.oasis-open.org/committees/relax-ng/spec-20011203.html*
38. Public-Key Infrastructure (X.509) (pkix). See: *http://www.ietf.cnri.reston.va.us/html.charters/pkix-charter.html*
39. The Triana Project. See: *http://www.trianacode.org/*
40. Data Encryption Standard. See: *http://csrc.nist.gov/publications/fips/fips46-3/fips46-3.pdf*
41. RSA Cryptography Standard. See: *http://www.rsasecurity.com/rsalabs/pkcs/pkcs-1/index.html*
42. MD5. See: *ftp://ftp.umbc.edu/pub/unix/rfc/rfc1321.txt.gz*
43. White Paper 8: 1-Wire SHA-1 Overview, Dallas Semiconductor, Maxim. See: *http://www.maxim-ic.com/appUrls.cfm/appUrl_number/1201*
44. Transport Layer Security (TLS): IETF Draft. See: *http://www.ietf.org/internet-drafts/draft-ietf-tls-rfc2246-bis-02.txt*
45. The Java Programming Language™. See: *http://java.sun.com*
46. S. Feizabadi, History of the Web. See: *http://www.prenhall.com/abrams/demo/chap1/*
47. World Internet Users and Population Stats. See: *http://www.internetworldstats.com/stats.htm*
48. URI Template IETF Internet-Draft. See: *http://tools.ietf.org/html/draft-gregorio-uritemplate-03*
49. Dublin Core Metadata Initiative. See: *http://dublincore.org/*
50. RDFa. See: *http://www.w3.org/TR/xhtml-rdfa-primer/*
51. BioMOBY. See: *http://www.biomoby.org/*
52. IPSV-Integrated Public Sector Vocabulary. See: *http://www.esd.org.uk/standards/ipsv/*

53. N. R. Shadbolt, W. Hall, and T. Berners-Lee, The Semantic Web Revisited, *IEEE Intelligent Systems*, pp. 96–101, May/June 2006. See: *http://eprints.ecs.soton.ac.uk/12614/1/Semantic_Web_Revisted.pdf*
54. G. E. Moore, Cramming More Components Onto Integrated Circuits, *Proceedings of the IEEE*, vol. 86, no. 1, pp. 82–85, 1998. See: *http://dx.doi.org/10.1109/JPROC.1998.658762*
55. Intel Comment on Moore's Law. See: *http://www.intel.com/research/silicon/mooreslaw.htm*
56. S. Androutsellis-Theotokis and D. Spinellis, A Survey of Peer-to-Peer Content Distribution Technologies, *ACM Computing Surveys*, vol. 36, no. 4, 2004.
57. K. Kant, R. Iyer, and V. Tewari, A Framework for Classifying Peer-to-Peer Technologies, in *2nd IEEE/ACM International Symposium on Cluster Computing and the Grid (CCGRID'02)*, 2002.
58. D. S. Milojicic et al., Peer-to-Peer Computing, Hewlett-Packard, Tech. Rep. HPL-2002-57R1, 2003. See: *http://www.hpl.hp.com/techreports/2002/HPL-2002-57R1.html*
59. I. Clarke, O. Sandberg, B. Wiley, and T. W. Hong, Freenet: A Distributed Anonymous Information Storage and Retrieval System, *Lecture Notes in Computer Science*, vol. 2009, pp. 46–66, 2001. See: *citeseer.ist.psu.edu/clarke00freenet.html*
60. Kazaa. See: *http://www.kazaa.com/us/index.htm*
61. Groove Virtual Office. See: *http://www.groove.net*
62. Skype. See: *http://www.skype.com*
63. LimeWire. See: *http://www.limewire.com*
64. M. Ripeanu, Peer-to-Peer Architecture Case Study: Gnutella Network, 2001. See: *citeseer.ist.psu.edu/ripeanu01peertopeer.html*
65. A. Adar and B. Huberman, Free Riding on Gnutella, First Monday 5 (10), 2000. See: *http://firstmonday.org/issues/issue5_10/adar/index.html*
66. N. Gunther, Hypernets, Good (G)news for Gnutella. See: *http://www.perfdynamics.com/Papers/Gnews.html*
67. A. Oram, From P2P to Web Services: Addressing and Coordination. See: *http://www.xml.com/pub/a/2004/04/07/p2p-ws.html*
68. J. Ledlie, J. Shneidman, M. Seltzer, and J. Huth, Scooped, Again, in *Peer-to-Peer Systems II: Second International Workshop, IPTPS 2003*, 2003.
69. S. Vaidhyanathan, The New Information Ecosystem, pp. 1–4. See: *http://www.opendemocracy.net/debates/article-8-101-1319.jsp*
70. M. Rainsford, P2P: Revolution or Evolution? pp. 8–101. See: *http://www.opendemocracy.net/debates/article--1666.jsp*
71. P. Drahos and J. Braithwaite, *Information Feudalism: Who Owns the Knowledge Economy?* New Press, 2003.
72. M. Rimmer, The Genie's Revenge: A Response to Siva Vaidhyanathan, 2003. See: *www.opendemocracy.net/content/articles/PDF/1639.pdf*
73. Open Democracy: Free Thinking for the World. See: *http://www.openDemocracy.net*
74. OpenP2P. See: *http://www.openp2p.com/*
75. International Standard Organization. See: *http://www.iso.ch/*
76. I. Stoica, R. Morris, D. Karger, F. M. Kaashoek, and H. Balakrishnan, Chord: A scalable peer-to-peer lookup service for internet applications, in *SIGCOMM '01: Proceedings of the 2001 conference on applications,*

technologies, architectures, and protocols for computer communications, vol. 31, no. 4. ACM Press, New York, NY, USA, October 2001, pp. 149–160. See: *http://portal.acm.org/citation.cfm?id=383071*

77. A. Rowstron and P. Druschel, Pastry: Scalable, Decentralized Object Location, and Routing for Large-Scale Peer-to-Peer Systems, *Lecture Notes in Computer Science*, vol. 2218, pp. 329–350, 2001. See: *http://citeseer.ist.psu.edu/620683.html*
78. B. Y. Zhao, L. Huang, J. Stribling, S. C. Rhea, A. D. Joseph, and J. D. Kubiatowicz, Tapestry: A Resilient Global-scale Overlay for Service Deployment, *IEEE Journal on Selected Areas in Communications*, vol. 22, no. 1, January 2004.
79. S. Ratnasamy, P. Francis, M. Handley, R. Karp, and S. Schenker, A Scalable Content-Addressable Network, in *SIGCOMM '01: Proceedings of the 2001 conference on Applications, technologies, architectures, and protocols for computer communications*, vol. 31, no. 4. ACM Press, October 2001, pp. 161–172. See: *http://portal.acm.org/citation.cfm?id=383072*
80. Distributed. See: *http://www.Distributed.net*
81. United Devices. See: *http://www.ud.com/*
82. Entropia. See: *http://www.entropia.com*
83. IBM, United Devices and Accelrys Aid U.S. Department of defence in search for Smallpox Cure. See: *http://goliath.ecnext.com/coms2/gi_0199-2521136/IBM-United-Devices-and-Accelrys.html*
84. The XtremWeb Home Page. See: *http://www.xtremweb.net/*
85. D. P. Anderson, BOINC: A System for Public-Resource Computing and Storage, in *GRID*, 2004, pp. 4–10.
86. BOINC Projects. See: *http://boinc.berkeley.edu/projects.php*
87. T. Berners-Lee, The World Wide Web, Past Present and Future: Exploring Universality, 2002. See: *http://www.w3.org/2002/04/Japan/Lecture.html*
88. W3C Home Page. See: *http://www.w3.org/*
89. W3C, eXtensible Markup Language. See: *http://w3.org/XML/*
90. Organization for the Advancement of Structured Information Standards (OASIS). See: *http://www.oasis-open.org/home/index.php*
91. T. Andrews, F. Curbera, H. Dholakia, Y. Goland, J. Klein, F. Leymann, K. Liu, D. Roller, D. Smith, S. Thatte, I. Trickovic, and S. Weerawarana, Business Process Execution Language for Web Services Version 1.1.
92. Web Services Specifications Index Page, MSDN. See: *http://msdn.microsoft.com/library/default.asp?url=/library/en-us/dnglobspec/html/wsspecsover.asp*
93. T. Berners-Lee, J. Hendler, and O. Lassila, The Semantic Web: A new form of Web content that is meaningful to computers will unleash a revolution of new possibilities. See: *http://www.sciam.com/article.cfm?id=the-semantic-web*
94. The W3C Semantic Web Home Page. See: *http://www.w3.org/sw/*
95. W3C Working Group Note. Web Services Architecture, 11 February 2004. See: *http://www.w3.org/TR/2004/NOTE-ws-arch-20040211/*
96. E. Dumbill, Semantic Web and Web Services can live together, says Berners-Lee. See: *http://www.xmlhack.com/read.php?item=1978*
97. The Semantic Web Services Initiative (SWSI). See: *http://www.swsi.org/*
98. Semantic Web Enabled Web Services (SWWS). See: *http://swws.semanticweb.org/*

99. C. Bussler, A. Maedche, and D. Fensel, A Conceptual Architecture for Semantic Web Enabled Web Services. See: *http://www.acm.org/sigmod/record/issues/0212/SPECIAL/4.Bussler1.pdf*
100. The Stencil Group, Defining Web Services. See: *http://www.stencilgroup.com/ideas_scope_06wsdefined.pdf*
101. W. Vogels, Web Services Are Not Distributed Objects, *IEEE Internet Computing*, vol. 7, no. 6, pp. 59–66, 2003.
102. E. Newcomer and G. Lomow, *Understanding SOA with Web Services (Independent Technology Guides).* Addison-Wesley Professional, 2004.
103. JSX. See: *http://www.jsx.org/*
104. CERN Advanced Storage Manager, 2005. See: *http://castor.web.cern.ch/castor/*
105. E. Gamma, R. Helm, R. Johnson, and J. Vlissides, *Design Patterns: Elements of Reusable Object-Oriented Software.* Addison-Wesley Professional, 1995.
106. IBM, Web Services ToolKit for Dynamic E-business (WSTK). See: *http://www-4.ibm.com/software/solutions/webservices/overview.html*
107. R. Nagappan, R. Skoczylas, and R. P. Sriganesh, *Developing Java Web Services.* John Wiley & Sons, Inc., New York, NY, USA, 2002.
108. D. Booth et al., Web Services Architecture, W3C. See: *http://www.w3.org/TR/ws-arch/*
109. R. S. Chin and S. T. Chanson, Distributed Object-Based Programming Systems, *ACM Computing Surveys*, vol. 23, no. 1, pp. 91–124, 1991.
110. Object Linking and Embedding. See: *http://support.microsoft.com/kb/122263*
111. J. Waldo, G. Wyant, A. Wollrath, and S. Kendall, A Note on Distributed Computing, Sun Microsystems, Inc. Mountain View, CA, USA, Tech. Rep. TR-94-29, 1994.
112. M. Henning, Binding, Migration, and Scalability in CORBA, *Communications of the ACM*, vol. 41, pp. 62–71, 1998.
113. S. Baker, Web Services and CORBA, in *On the Move to Meaningful Internet Systems 2002: CoopIS, DOA, and ODBASE : Confederated International Conferences CoopIS, DOA, and ODBASE 2002*, 2002.
114. S. Vinoski, Web Services Interaction Models, *IEEE Internet Computing*, vol. 6, no. 3, pp. 89–91, May/June 2002.
115. H. Hildebrand, A. Karmarkar, M. Little, and G. Pavlik, Session Modeling for Web Services, in *The 3rd IEEE European Conference on Web Services (IEEE ECOWS 2005)*, 2005.
116. M. Little, J. Webber, and S. Parastatidis, Stateful interactions in Web Services: a comparison of WS-Context and WS-Resource Framework, *SOA Web Services Journal*, May 2004. See: *http://webservices.sys-con.com/read/44675.htm*
117. K. Channabasavaiah, K. Hlloey, and E. Tuggle Jr., Migrating to a Service-Oriented Architecture, Part 1, IBM Corporation, December 2003. See: *http://www-128.ibm.com/developerworks/webservices/library/ws-migratesoa/*
118. M. Dodani, From Object to Services: A Journey in Search of Component Reuse Nirvana, *Journal of Object Technology*, 2004.
119. S. Hashimi, Service-Oriented Architecture Explained. See: *http://www.ondotnet.com/pub/a/dotnet/2003/08/18/soa_explained.html*
120. M. Papazoglou, Service-Oriented Computing: Concepts, Characteristics and Directions, in *Fourth International Conference on Web Information Systems Engineering (WISE '03)*, 2003.

121. H. He, What is Service-Oriented Architecture? September 2003. See: *http://www.xml.com/pub/a/ws/2003/09/30/soa.html*
122. S. Parastatidis, J. Webber, P. Watson, and T. Rischbeck, The Web Services Grid Application Framework (WS-GAF), North-East Regional E-Science Centre and Arjuna Technologies. See: *http://www.neresc.ac.uk/ws-gaf/documents.php*
123. W3C Recommendation: Architecture of the World Wide Web, Volume One. See: *http://www.w3.org/TR/webarch*
124. JMS. See: *http://java.sun.com/products/jms/*
125. The Java Tutorial: A Practical Guide for Programmers. See: *http://java.sun.com/docs/books/tutorial/*
126. Broadband from Power Sockets, Scottish Hydro-Electric. See: *http://www.hydro.co.uk/broadband/*
127. I. Foster and C. Kesselman, *The Grid 2: Blueprint For a New Computing Infrastructure, Second Edition.* Morgan-Kaufmann, 2003.
128. T. P. Hughes, *The Social Shaping of Technology: How the Refrigerator Got Its Hum.* Milton Keynes: Open University Press, 1985, ch. Edison and electric light.
129. S. Withers, An Overview of Distributed Grid Computing, *Grid Today*, vol. 1, no. 21, November 2002. See: *http://www.gridtoday.com/02/1104/100635.html*
130. K. Czajkowski, D. F. Ferguson, I. Foster, J. Frey, S. Graham, I. Sedukhin, D. Snelling, S. Tuecke, and W. Vambenepe, The WS-Resource Framework, The Globus Alliance, Tech. Rep., 2004. See: *http://www.globus.org/wsrf*
131. Grid and Web Services Standards to Converge. See: *http://www.marketwire.com/mw/release_html_b1?release_id=61977*
132. D. de Roure, M. Baker, N. R. Jennings, and N. Shadbolt, The Evolution of the Grid, pp. 65–100, 2003. See: *http://eprints.ecs.soton.ac.uk/6871/*
133. Fafner. See: *http://www.npac.syr.edu/factoring.html*
134. I. Foster, J. Geisler, B. Nickless, W. Smith, and S. Tuecke, Software Infrastructure for the I-WAY High-Performance Distributed Computing Experiment, in *HPDC '96: Proceedings of the 5th IEEE International Symposium on High Performance Distributed Computing.* IEEE Computer Society, 1996, p. 562.
135. A. S. Grimshaw, A. Nguyen-Tuong, M. J. Lewis, and M. Hyett, Campus-Wide Computing: Early Results Using Legion at the University of Virginia, *International Journal of Supercomputing Applications*, vol. 11, no. 2, pp. 129–143, 1997.
136. Object Management Group (OMG), The Common Object Request Broker Architecture (CORBA). See: *http://www.corba.org*
137. M. Litzkow, M. Livny, and M. Mutka, Condor — A Hunter of Idle Workstations, in *Proceedings of the 8th International Conference on Distributed Computing Systems.* IEEE Computer Society, New York, June 1988, pp. 104–111.
138. Platform Computing, Load Sharing Facility. See: *http://www.platform.com/*
139. Sun Grid Engine. See: *http://wwws.sun.com/software/gridware/sge.html*
140. T. Goodale, G. Allen, G. Lanfermann, J. Masso, T. Radke, E. Seidel, and J. Shalf, The Cactus Framework and Toolkit: Design and Applications, in *Vector and Parallel Processing VECPAR 2002, 5th International Conference*, vol. 2565. Springer, Berlin, 2003, pp. 197–227.

141. F. Gagliardi, B. Jones, M. Reale, and S. Burke, European DataGrid Project: Experiences of Deploying a Large Scale Testbed for e-Science applications, in *Performance 2002 Tutorial Lectures Book Performance Evaluations of Complex Systems: Techniques and Tools*, 2002. See: *http://www.eu-datagrid.org/*
142. J. Almond and D. Snelling, UNICORE: Uniform Access to Supercomputing as an Element of Electronic Commerce, *Future Gener. Comput. Syst.*, vol. 15, no. 5-6, pp. 539–548, 1999.
143. G. Fox, D. Gannon, and M. Thomas, A Summary of Grid Computing Environments, 2002. See: *citeseer.ist.psu.edu/fox02summary.html*
144. Access Grid. See: *http://www.accessgrid.org/*
145. L. Smarr and C. E. Catlett, Metacomputing, *Commun. ACM*, vol. 35, no. 6, pp. 44–52, 1992.
146. T. A. DeFanti, I. Foster, M. E. Papka, R. Stevens, and T. Kuhfuss, Overview of the I-WAY: Wide-Area Visual Supercomputing, *The International Journal of Supercomputer Applications and High Performance Computing*, vol. 10, no. 2/3, pp. 123–131, Summer/Fall 1996. See: *citeseer.ist.psu.edu/article/defanti96overview.html*
147. J. Nieplocha and R. J. Harrison, Shared Memory NUMA Programming on I-WAY, in *Proc. of the Fifth IEEE Int'l Symp. on High Performance Distributed Computing (HPDC-5)*, 1996. See: *citeseer.ist.psu.edu/nieplocha96shared.html*
148. M. Norman et al., Galaxies Collide on the I-WAY: An Example of Heterogeneous Wide-Area Collaborative Supercomputing, *nternational Journal of High Performance Computing Applications*, vol. 10, no. 2-3, pp. 132–144, 1996.
149. D. Diachin, L. Freitag, D. Heath, J. Herzog, B. Michels, and P. Plassmann, Remote Engineering Tools for the Design of Pollution Control Systems for Commercial Boilers, *International Journal of Supercomputing*, vol. 10, no. 2, pp. 208–218, 1996.
150. T. Disz, M. Papka, M. Pellegrino, and R. Stevens, Sharing Visualization Experiences Among Remote Virtual Environments, in *International Workshop on High Peformance Comuting for Computer Graphics and Visualization*, 1995, pp. 135–142.
151. C. A. Lee, C. Kesselman, and S. Schwab, Near-Real-Time Satellite Image Processing: Metacomputing in CC++, *IEEE Comput. Graph. Appl.*, vol. 16, no. 4, pp. 79–84, 1996.
152. The MENTAT Project. See: *http://www.cs.virginia.edu/~mentat/*
153. OMG, Object Management Group. See: *http://www.omg.org/*
154. GridLab: A Grid Application Toolkit and Testbed Project home page. See: *http://www.gridlab.org*
155. G. Allen, D. Angulo, I. Foster, G. Lanfermann, C. Liu, T. Radke, E. Seidel, and J. Shalf, The Cactus Worm: Experiments with dynamic resource discovery and allocation in a Grid environment, *The International Journal of High Performance Computing Applications*, vol. 15, no. 4, pp. 345–358, 2001. See: *citeseer.ist.psu.edu/article/allen01cactus.html*
156. I. Foster, C. Kesselman, and S. Tuecke, The Anatomy of the Grid: Enabling Scalable Virtual Organization, *The International Journal of High Performance Computing Applications*, vol. 15, no. 3, pp. 200–222, 2001.
157. W. Allcock, J. Bester, J. Bresnahan, A. Chervenak, I. Foster, C. Kesselman, S. Meder, V. Nefedova, D. Quesnel, and S. Tuecke, Data Management and Transfer in High-Performance Computational Grid Environments, *Parallel Computing*, vol. 28, no. 5, pp. 749–771, 2002.

158. I. Foster, Globus: What Will Come, Grid Today, February 2004. See: *http://www.gridtoday.com/04/0202/102590.html*
159. I. Foster, What is the Grid? - A Three Point Checklist, *GRIDtoday*, vol. 1, no. 6, July 2002. See: *http://www.gridtoday.com/02/0722/100136.html*
160. J. Giddy, What is Grid Computing? The Great Debate, 2002. See: *http://www.cs.cf.ac.uk/user/J.P.Giddy/debate.html*
161. Open Grid Forum (OGF), Open Grid Forum. See: *http://www.ogf.org/*
162. Generic Security Service Application Program Interface, Version 2. See: *http://www.ietf.org/rfc/rfc2078.txt*
163. E-Science Certificate Authority. See: *http://ca.grid-support.ac.uk/*
164. The Globus Grid Security Infrastructure. See: *http://www-unix.globus.org/security/*
165. MDS Features in the Globus Toolkit 2. See: *4.Release.http://www.globus.org/mds/mds2/*
166. Data Management in Globus. See: *http://www-unix.globus.org/developer/data-management.html*
167. Resource Management in Globus. See: *http://www-unix.globus.org/developer/resource-management.html*
168. J. Frankel and T. Pepper, The Gnutella Protocol Specification V0, 2000. See: *4,revision1.2.http://www.clip2.com,protocols@clip2.com*
169. Open Source Napster: Gnutella. See: *http://slashdot.org/articles/00/03/14/0949234.shtml*
170. Winamp. See: *http://www.winamp.com/*
171. Nullsoft. See: *http://www.nullsoft.com/*
172. AOL's Nullsoft Creates Software for Swapping MP3s. See: *http://news.com.com/-237974.html?legacy=cnet*
173. Did AOL Eat Gnutella for Lunch? See: *http://dir.salon.com/tech/log/2000/03/15/gnutella/index.html*
174. Gnutella Overview on Limewire. See: *http://www.limewire.com/index.jsp/learn*
175. Gnutella Miscs and Links. See: *http://www.oreillynet.com/topics/p2p/gnutella/*
176. S. Milgram, The Small World Problem, *Psychology Today*, vol. 2, pp. 60–67, 1967.
177. N. Minar, Distributed Systems Topologies, Parts 1 and 2, 2001. See: *http://www.openp2p.com/pub/a/p2p//12/14/topologies_one.html*
178. M. Rains and N. Sloane, On Cayley's Enumeration of Alkanes (or 4-Valent Trees). See: *http://www.research.att.com/~njas/sequences/JIS/cayley.html*
179. L. A. Adamic, R. M. Lukose, A. R. Puniyani, and B. A. Huberman, Search in Power-Law Networks.
180. Ian Clarke Quote During 2003 Interview with News.com. See: *http://www.news.com/2010-1071-1023325.html*
181. I. Clarke, S. Miller, T. Hong, O. Sandberg, and B. Wiley, Protecting Free Expression Online with Freenet, 2002. See: *citeseer.ist.psu.edu/clarke02protecting.html*
182. The Freenet home page. See: *http://freenetproject.org/*
183. I. Clarke, O. Sandberg, B. Wiley, and T. Hong, Freenet's Next Generation Routing Protocol, 2003. See: *http://freenet.sourceforge.net/index.php?page=ngrouting*

184. Wired 13.01: The BitTorrent Effect. See: *http://www.wired.com/techbiz/startups/news/2007/12/YE_10_startups*
185. The Code Con Conference. See: *http://en.wikipedia.org/wiki/CodeCon*
186. The Official BitTorrent Protocol Specification. See: *http://www.bittorrent.org/beps/bep_0003.html*
187. The BitTorrent Web site. See: *http://www.bittorrent.com/*
188. MakeTorrent home page. See: *http://krypt.dyndns.org:81/torrent/maketorrent/*
189. Doug Walker interview — CEO Bittorrent Inc. See: *http://gigaom.com/2008/03/09/bittorrrent-ceo-doug-walker-interview/*
190. EJB. See: *http://java.sun.com/products/ejb/*
191. Jini Starter Kit. See: *http://www.jini.org/downloads/*
192. D. Sag, Crudlets: Making Peace Between Extreme Jini and XML Viewpoints. See: *www.onjava.com/pub/a/onjava/2001/02/08/jini_xml.htm*
193. e. Wilson B, Que press. freely available on-line, 2002. See: *http://www.brendonwilson.com/projects/jxta/*
194. A. Langley, The Trouble with JXTA. See: *http://www.openp2p.com/pub/a/p2p/2001/05/02/jxta_trouble.html*
195. XML-RPC. See: *http://www.xmlrpc.com/spec*
196. W3C XML Protocol Working Group, Simple Object Access Protocol (SOAP) 1.2, W3C, Tech. Rep., 2003. See: *http://www.w3.org/TR/soap/*
197. E. Christensen et al., Web Services Description Language (WSDL) 1.1, W3C, Tech. Rep., 2001. See: *http://www.w3.org/TR/wsdl*
198. UDDI Spec TC, UDDI Version 3.0.2, September 2004. See: *http://uddi.org/pubs/uddi_v3.htm*
199. North American Industry Classification System. See: *http://www.census.gov/epcd/www/naics.html*
200. Using WSDL in a UDDI Registry, 2002. See: *http://www.uddi.org/pubs/wsdlbestpractices-V1.07-Open-20020521.pdf*
201. Web Services Policy 1.2 - Framework (WS-Policy). See: *http://www.w3.org/Submission/WS-Policy/*
202. XML Encryption. See: *http://www.w3.org/TR/xmlenc-core/*
203. XML Signature. See: *http://www.w3.org/TR/xmldsig-core/*
204. Web Services Security Policy (WS-SecurityPolicy). See: *http://docs.oasis-open.org/ws-sx/ws-securitypolicy/200702*
205. OASIS, Web Services Security (WS-Security). See: *http://www.oasis-open.org/committees/wss*
206. J. Alexander et al., Web Services Transfer (WS-Transfer). See: *http://www.w3.org/Submission/WS-Transfer/*
207. Web Services Resource Transfer (WS-ResourceTransfer). See: *http://schemas.xmlsoap.org/ws/2006/08/resourceTransfer/WS-ResourceTransfer.pdf*
208. XML Path Language (XPath). See: *http://www.w3.org/TR/xpath*
209. D. Box, L. F. Cabrera, C. Critchley, F. Curbera, D. Ferguson, A. Geller, S. Graham, D. Hull, G. Kakivaya, A. Lewis, B. Lovering, M. Mihic, P. Niblett, D. Orchard, J. Saiyed, S. Samdarshi, J. Schlimmer, I. Sedukhin, J. Shewchuk, B. Smith, S. Weerawarana, and D. Wortendyke, Web Services Eventing (WS-Eventing), W3C, Tech. Rep., August 2004. See: *http://www.w3.org/Submission/WS-Eventing/*
210. Web Services ReliableMessaging (WS-ReliableMessaging). See: *http://www.oasis-open.org/committees/tc_home.php?wg_abbrev=wsrm*

211. Web Services Coordination (WS-Coordination). See: *http://docs.oasis-open.org/ws-tx/wscoor/2006/06*
212. S. Loughran, Talk:Universal Description Discovery and Integration. See: *http://en.wikipedia.org/wiki/Talk:Universal_Description_Discovery_and_Integration*
213. J. Luo, B. Montrose, and M. Kang, An Approach for Semantic Query Processing with UDDI, in *Agents, Web Services and Ontologies Merging, Agia Napa, Cyprus*, 2005.
214. N. Srinivasan, M. Paolucci, and K. Sycara, An Efficient Algorithm for OWL-S Based Semantic Search in UDDI, in *Semantic Web Services and Web Process Composition*, vol. 3387/2005, 2005, pp. 96–110.
215. W3C, Web Services Description Language (WSDL) Version 2.0 Part 2: Adjuncts. See: *http://www.w3.org/TR/2005/WD-wsdl20-adjuncts-20050803*
216. M. Gudgin and M. Hadley, Web Services Addressing 1.0 - Core (WS-Addressing), W3C, Tech. Rep., 2005. See: *http://www.w3.org/TR/ws-addr-core/*
217. K. Czajkowski et al., From Open Grid Services Infrastructure to WS Resource Framework: Refactoring and Evolution, Version 1.0. See: *http://www.globus.org/wsrf/specs/ogsi_to_wsrf_1.0.pdf*
218. Mark Baker and Ian Foster on Recent Changes in the Grid Community, Distributed Systems Online, February 2004. See: *http://csdl2.computer.org/comp/mags/ds/2004/02/o2004.pdf*
219. K. Cline et al., Toward Converging Web Service Standards for Resources, Events, and Management, Hewlett Packard Corporation, IBM Corporation, Intel Corporation and Microsoft Corporation, March 2006. See: *http://devresource.hp.com/drc/specifications/wsm/index.jsp*
220. Tim O'Reilly, What Is Web 2.0 Design Patterns and Business Models for the Next Generation of Software, September 2005. See: *http://www.oreillynet.com/pub/a/oreilly/tim/news/2005/09/30/what-is-web-20.html*
221. developerWorks Interviews: Tim Berners-Lee, Laningham, S. (ed.), 22nd August 2006. See: *http://www.ibm.com/developerworks/podcast/dwi/cm-int082206.html*
222. Doc Searls Weblog. See: *http://doc-weblogs.com/2006/01/15*
223. R. Albert, H. Jeong, and A. L. Barabasi, Diameter of the World Wide Web, *Nature*, vol. 401, pp. 130–131, September 1999.
224. J. Kleinberg et al., The Web as a Graph: Measurements, Models, and Methods, in *5th Annual International Conference on Combinatorics and Computing, LNCS 1627*. Springer Verlag, 1999, pp. 1–18.
225. B. Huberman and L. Adamic, Growth Dynamics of the World Wide Web, *Nature*, vol. 401, pp. 131–133, September 1999.
226. Y. Benkler, *The Wealth of Networks: How Social Production Transforms Markets and Freedom*. Yale University Press, 2006.
227. C. Anderson, *The Long Tail: Why the Future of Business is Selling Less of More*. Hyperion, 2006.
228. Cloudmark Spam Filtering. See: *http://www.cloudmark.com/*
229. Technorati. See: *http://technorati.com/*
230. Microformats. See: *http://microformats.org/*
231. RSS 2.0 Specification moves to Berkman. See: *http://cyber.law.harvard.edu/rss/announceRss2.html*

232. Why We Need Echo. See: *http://www.sixapart.com/about/news/2003/06/why_we_need_ech.html*
233. MetaWeblog API. See: *http://www.xmlrpc.com/metaWeblogApi*
234. Blogger API. See: *http://code.blogger.com/*
235. G. Fox and M. Pierce, Web 2.0 and Earthquake Science, in *6th ACES International Workshop, Cairns, Australia*, 2008.
236. Text of Wired's Interview with Google CEO Eric Schmidt. See: *http://www.wired.com/techbiz/people/news/2007/04/mag_schmidt_trans*
237. Amazon Simple Storage Service (Amazon S3). See: *http://aws.amazon.com/s3*
238. Amazon Elastic Compute Cloud (Amazon EC2) - Beta. See: *http://aws.amazon.com/ec2*
239. IBM Introduces Ready-to-Use Cloud Computing. See: *http://www-03.ibm.com/press/us/en/pressrelease/22613.wss*
240. What Is Google App Engine? See: *http://code.google.com/appengine/docs/whatisgoogleappengine.html*
241. 3Tera. See: *http://www.3tera.com/*
242. Ubiquitous Computing. See: *http://www.ubiq.com/ubicomp/*
243. Internet addresses 'for all'. See: *http://www.abc.net.au/news/stories/2004/07/21/1158544.htm*
244. Statements by Mexican justice official Marco Huitrón October 22, 2004. See: *http://www.spychips.com/press-releases/mexican-translation.html*
245. A. Greenfield, *Everyware: The Dawning Age of Ubiquitous Computing.* New Riders, 2006.
246. CCTV: Does it work? See: *http://news.bbc.co.uk/1/hi/uk/2071496.stm*
247. Shops Track Customers Via Mobile Phone. See: *http://technology.timesonline.co.uk/tol/news/tech_and_web/article3945496.ece*
248. P. Morville, A Garden of Forking Paths. See: *http://www.asis.org/Bulletin/Feb-06/morville.html*
249. Blobject. See: *http://en.wikipedia.org/wiki/Blobject*
250. B. Stirling, When Blobjects Rule the Earth. See: *http://www.boingboing.net/images/blobjects.htm*
251. Understanding Reggie. See: *http://www.kedwards.com/jini/reggie.html*
252. JXTA Programmers Guide: See Chapter 6 for System Requirements, Setting Up and Compiling JXTA Programs and Appendix B for Use of the JXTA Configuration Tool. See: *http://www.jxta.org/project/www/jxtaprogguide_final.pdf*
253. Configure Your Platform Using the Jxta Configurator. See: *http://platform.jxta.org/java/configuration.html*
254. Jxta Programming Guide. See: *https://jxta-guide.dev.java.net/*
255. Apache CXF: An Open Source Service Framework. See: *http://cxf.apache.org/*
256. Apache Abdera - An Open Source Atom Implementation. See: *http://incubator.apache.org/abdera/*
257. vCard The Electronic Business Card Version 2.1. See: *http://www.imc.org/pdi/vcard-21.txt*
258. RFC 2445 Internet Calendaring and Scheduling Core Object Specification (iCalendar). See: *http://tools.ietf.org/html/rfc2445*
259. Jetty Servlet Container. See: *http://www.mortbay.org/jetty-6/*

Index

.torrent files, 230, 232
Everyware, 344

access points, 116
ACK, 31
ad hoc network, 199
advertisements, 259
adverts, 378
AFS, 159
Ajax, 318
Amazon, 314
AOL, 181
applet, 75, 245, 349
Architecture of Participation, 318
ARPANET, 108
ATM, 159
Atom, 328
Atom Publishing Protocol, 330, 411
Atom Syndication Format, 328, 411
auditing, 63
authentication, 63
authorization, 63
avalanche effect, 70

Bencoding, 230–232
Berners-Lee, Tim, 127, 131
binding of peers, 109
BitTorrent, 61, 110, 227, 229, 318
BitTorrent protocol, 228, 229
BitTorrent terminology, 229
BitTorrent tracker, 229, 232
BitTorrent, Inc., 228
Blobject, 345
Bluetooth, 7, 256
BOINC, 20, 110
BPEL4WS, 130
bridge, 115
bridging, 202
broadband from power sockets, 156
brokered communication, 13
brokered systems, 9
Bush, Vannevar, 83

C, 134, 256
C++, 134, 256
CA, 171, 172
caching, 97
Cactus, 157, 160
Cactus worm, 160
CAN, 119, 209
centralized control, 166
centralized systems, 9
centralized topology, 203
centralized/decentralized topology, 203, 218, 223, 262
CERN, 83
certificate authority, 171, 172
checkpointing, 293
CHK, 221, 223
choked, 230
Chord, 119, 209
ciphertext, 67
client, 7
client/server, 203
Cloud computing, 340
CodeCon, 228
Cohen, Bram, 228

composite computing model, 136
computational Grid, 168
Condor, 158, 160
confidentiality, 62
content-hash key, 221, 223
cookies, 95, 96
copyright infringements, 114, 115
CORBA, 25, 140–144, 158, 160
cryptography, 61, 67
cryptosystem, 68
CXF, 383

DA, 28
data Grid, 168
data grid, 169
data replication, 174
DataGrid (EDG/EGEE), 158, 160, 164, 169
decentralized, 112
decentralized systems, 9
decentralized topology, 203
definition of a distributed system, 5
delegation, 172
DES, 69
descriptor header, 189
descriptors, 188
deserialization, 151
DHT, 110, 119
Diffie-Hellman key exchange, 74
digital signature, 71
direct files, 219
Directory Agent (DA), 35
directory services, 28
discovery, 10, 185, 243, 245, 265
discovery services, 27
distributed hash tables, 119, 199
distributed system definition, 5
distributed system examples, 17
distributed systems taxonomy, 9
Distributed.net, 123, 158
DNS, 11, 83, 108, 109
Document Object Model, 319
Document Type Definition, 48
document-oriented computing, 132
DoD, 123
DOM, 319
Drahos, Peter, 114
DSL, 116
DTD, 48
dynamic IP address, 110

early binding, 109
edge peers, 256
edges of the Internet, 111
Edison, Thomas, 157
email, 122
encryption, 63
Endpoint Routing Protocol, 257
endpoint routing protocol, 266
Entropia, 123, 158, 168
equal peers, 199, 207
ERP, 257, 266
examples of distributed systems, 17
examples of middleware, 23

fabrication, 63
Facebook, 315
FAFNER, 158, 168
FastTrack, 204
fault tolerance, 123, 198, 223
file downloads, 193
file swarming, 227
firewall, 112, 118
firewalls, 268
fixed IP address, 109
flooding the network, 121
FOAF, 102
focus of data control, 64
Foster, Ian, 291, 300
Frankel, Justin, 181
free riders, 199, 207
Freenet, 110, 213
Freenet, clustering, 223
Freenet, keys, 219
Freenet, requesting files, 217
Freenet, routing, 214, 218
Freenet, scenario, 217
Freenet, self-organization, 215
Freenet, SHA-1, 219
Friend of a Friend, 102
FTP, 66, 122, 174

GARA, 175
GASS, 174
Gatekeeper, 175
GGF, 169, 292
GIIS, 173, 174
global computing, 155

Globus, 158, 160, 162, 166, 168–170, 176, 298, 300
Globus, data management, 174
Globus, GRAM, 174
Globus, GSI, 171
Globus, MDS, 173
Globus, security, 171
GNU, 182
GnuCache, 121, 185, 186
Gnullsoft, 181
Gnutella, 4, 12, 21, 110, 112, 121, 181, 199, 205
Gnutella news group (#gnutella), 182
Gnutella, connect, 188
Gnutella, descriptors, 188
Gnutella, discovery, 185
Gnutella, file downloads, 193
Gnutella, header, 189
Gnutella, hops, 184
Gnutella, horizon, 185
Gnutella, implementations, 194
Gnutella, jargon, 183
Gnutella, Ping, 190
Gnutella, Pong, 190
Gnutella, protocol (0.4), 187
Gnutella, Push, 192
Gnutella, Query, 191
Gnutella, Query Hit, 191
Gnutella, scenario, 185
Gnutella, searching, 185, 187
Google, 11, 314
Google Maps, 324
GRAM, 174, 294, 299
Grid, 155, 170
Grid computing, 4, 61, 365
Grid portals, 158
Grid security infrastructure, 171
Grid services, 292
Grid, history, 157
Grid, portal, 170
Grid, security, 171
Grid, social perspective, 156
GridFTP, 163, 174, 294, 299
GridLab, 160, 170
GRIS, 173, 174
Groove, 111
groups, 250, 298
GSH, 297
GSI, 171
GSR, 297
GT2, 169
GT3, 298
GUID, 219, 223, 224
GWSDL, 296

hash function, 70
hash key, 70
hCalendar, 327
hCard, 327
header descriptor, 189
heterogeneous devices, 6
hops, 184, 202, 262
host caches, 185
hostile environment, 115
HTC, 160, 169
HTML, 40, 82, 89, 127
HTTP, 31, 82, 90, 129, 174, 229, 256, 270
HTTP security, 93
httpg, 298
HTTPS, 94
hub, 115
hybrid topology, 199, 203
hypertext, 83
Hypertext Markup Language, 82, 89
Hypertext Transfer Protocol, 82, 90

I-POP, 159
I-Soft, 159, 176
I-WAY, 158, 159
IANA, 33
ICalendar, 384
IDL, 141, 160
IETF, 88, 171, 174, 328
indirect files, 219
information feudalism, 114
integrity, 62
intellectual property, 114
interception, 63
Internet computing, 155
interruption, 63
IP, 109
IP Addressing, 28
IPv6, 343
IRC, 182, 185
ISP, 108

J2EE, 13, 23

J2ME, 256
Jar, 360
Java, 256
Java, bytecode, 151
Java, deserialization, 151
Java, Remote class, 351
Java, RemoteException class, 351
Java, RMI, 148, 349
Java, sandbox, 349
Java, security manager, 76, 349
Java, serialization, 150, 151
Java, transient keyword, 151
Java, UnicastRemoteObject class, 352
JavaScript, 318
JAX-WS, 383
JAXB, 383
Jini, 8, 23, 25, 28, 158, 239, 349
Jini, architecture, 241
Jini, discovery, 243, 245, 358
Jini, events, 250
Jini, federation, 241
Jini, installation, 355
Jini, join, 246, 358
Jini, leasing, 247
Jini, lookup, 247, 359
Jini, programming, 355
Jini, protocols, 245
Jini, proxy, 149, 239, 245, 350, 356
Jini, scenario, 243, 249
Jini, security, 349
JMS, 13, 23
JNI, 134
JSON, 320
JVM, 151
JXME, 256
JXTA, 84
Jxta, 8, 25, 28, 61, 158, 163, 166, 176, 204
Jxta configurator, 365
Jxta relay, 264
Jxta, advertisements, 259
Jxta, adverts, 378
Jxta, architecture, 257
Jxta, environment, 267
Jxta, IDs, 258
Jxta, installation, 377
Jxta, messages, 259
Jxta, modules, 260
Jxta, overlay network, 260
Jxta, peer, 257
Jxta, peer group, 260
Jxta, peer groups, 163
Jxta, pipes, 262, 369
Jxta, programming, 363
Jxta, protocols, 264
Jxta, rendezvous, 261
Jxta, scenario, 266
Jxta, security, 267

KaZaA, 204
Kazaa, 111
Kerberos, 74
key clustering, 223
keyword-signed key, 219
KSK, 219, 220

LAN, 116
late binding, 110
layering of security, 65
leasing, 247
Legion, 158, 160
LimeWire, 195
lookup service, 243
loose-coupling, 135
LSF, 158, 160, 167
LUS, 243, 250

MAC address, 116
machine-processable Web, 83, 128
machine-readable data, 128
machine-to-machine interoperable, 129
Mayland, Brian, 182
MD5, 71
MDS, 173, 299
messages, 259
metacomputing, 155
metadata, 158
microformats, 325
middleware, 6, 23, 162
middleware examples, 23
migration, 293
Milgram, Stanley, 200
MIME, 91, 230, 277, 329, 330
Mobile Agents, 143–145
modification, 63
Moore's Law, 107
Morpheus, 204
Mosaic, 83

MP3.com, 12
MPI, 160
MPL, 160
multi-hop network, 115, 199
multicast, 32, 245, 265
multicast distribution trees, 34
multicast grouping, 33
mutlicast, 28
mutlicast rendezvous point (RP), 34
mutual authentication, 171
MySpace, 315

namespaces, 46, 48, 279
Napster, 12, 21, 28, 110, 120, 205
NAT, 110, 117, 268
Nelson, Ted, 83
network flooding, 121
network topologies, 202
NFS, 158
node, 7
Nullsoft, 181

OASIS, 130
OGF, 26, 167–169, 292, 300
OGSA, 4, 158, 161, 168, 176, 291–294, 296, 365
OGSA, architecture, 295
OGSA, portTypes, 295
OGSI, 168, 291, 295, 296, 298
OMG, 160
Open Democracy Web site, 114
Open Grid Forum, 167
OpenP2P, 115
ORB, 141, 160
OSI model, 115
out of band discovery, 185
overlay networks, 119, 260
OWL, 103

P2P, 4, 26, 107, 122, 163, 167
P2P definition, 111
P2P, centralized/decentralized topology, 203
P2P, communication, 198
P2P, decentralized topology, 203
P2P, environment, 267, 378
P2P, load balancing, 199
P2P, performance, 198
P2P, searching, 199
P2P, security, 267
Pastry, 119, 209
PBP, 257, 266
PDP, 257, 264
peer, 7
peer discovery, 185
Peer Discovery Protocol, 257, 264
peer group, 260
Peer Information Protocol, 257, 266
Peer Resolver Protocol, 257, 265
peer to peer, 4, 108
peer topologies, 202
Pepper, Tom, 181
PERL, 256
persistence, 151
Personal JavaTM, 256
pervasive network, 199
PGP, 70
piece, 230
PIM, 34
PIM Bidirectional Mode (Bdir), 34
PIM Dense Mode (DM), 34
PIM Sparse Mode (SM), 34
PIM Specific Mode (SSM), 34
Ping, 121, 185, 190
Ping descriptor, 190
PIP, 257, 266
Pipe Binding Protocol , 257, 266
pipes, 262, 369
point-to-point communication, 13
Pong, 121, 185, 190
Pong descriptor, 190
portal, 170
portals, 158
POSH, 325
power grid, 155
power-law, 208, 223, 316
Protocol Independent Multicast (PIM), 34
proxy, 149, 350, 356
proxy certificates, 172
PRP, 257, 265
public key pairs, 69
Push, 192
Push descriptor, 192
PVM, 160
Python, 256

QoS, 166, 168

Quality Of Service, 168
Query, 191
Query descriptor, 191
QueryHit, 191
QueryHit descriptor, 191

Rainsford, Miriam, 114
RDF, 101, 131, 325
RDFa, 104
reflector node, 204
rel-nofollow, 326
rel-tag, 326
RELAX NG, 56
relay, 256, 264
Remote class, 351
remote proxy, 149
RemoteException class, 351
Rendezvous, 28
rendezvous, 256, 261
rendezvous node, 204
rendezvous point (RP), 34
Rendezvous Protocol, 257
rendezvous protocol, 266
replica catalog, 174
Representational State Transfer, 95
resource, 7
resource availability, 11
resource broker, 160
resource communication, 13
Resource Description Framework, 101, 325
resource discovery, 10
resource management, 175
REST, 95, 323
reverse path forwarding (RPF), 34
RFID, 343
Rimmer, Matthew, 114
RISC, 66
RMI, 148, 349, 350
RMI, programming, 350
routers, 116
RPF, 34
RSA, 69, 70, 158
RSL, 175
RSS, 328
Ruby, 256
RVP, 257, 266

SA, 28
SAAdvert, 36
sandbox, 75, 349
scalable computing, 155
scheduling, 159
secure channel, public/private keys, 74
secure channels, 72
secure mobile code, 75
Secure Socket Layer, 94
security, 61
security manager, 349
security policy, 63
security simplicity, 66
security threats, 62
Semantic Web, 101, 131, 158, 315
serialization, 150
servent, 13, 112, 183, 187
server, 7
ServerSocket, 32
service, 8
Service Agent (SA), 35
service endpoints, 300
service Grid, 168
service groups, 298
Service Location Protocol (SLP), 28, 35
service virtualization, 272, 292
service-oriented architecture, 136, 161, 270
session keys, 74
SET, 70
SETI, 20, 107, 124
SGE, 158, 160, 167
SGML, 39
SHA-1, 71, 219, 221, 233
shared keys, 69
shared secret keys, 73
Shirky, Clay, 111
signed applet, 77
signed-subspace key, 220
signing messages, 71
SIMD, 160
Skype, 111
small-world effect, 201, 204, 223, 262
SOA, 136, 161, 270
SOAP, 24, 130, 132, 133, 136, 161, 270, 273
SOAP, body, 273
SOAP, document, 271
SOAP, envelope, 133, 271, 274
SOAP, header, 274

SOAP, message, 270, 273
social hop, 200
social impacts of P2P, 113
social network, 200
socket, 32
spime, 345
SSH, 66, 73
SSK, 220–222
SSL, 66, 70, 94, 298
standardization, 83, 168
super-node, 204
supercomputing, 159
swarm, 230
switch, 115
SWWS, 131
symmetric cryptosystem, 69
symmetric keys, 69
SYN, 31
syndication, 328

Tapestry, 119, 209
TCB, 66
TCP, 28, 30, 36, 83, 122, 229, 245
TCP/IP, 7, 109, 163, 256
Technorati, 322
telnet, 118, 122
terminology, 7
The Long Tail, 316
the Web, 17
The Web As Platform, 314
TLS, 73, 94, 298
Torrent metafiles, 232
tracker, 230, 232
transient environment, 112
transient network, 115, 199, 380
transient services, 293
Transport Layer Security, 94
Triana, 66, 160, 170
true P2P, 112, 121
TTL, 185, 187, 189, 217, 224

UA, 28
Ubiquitous Computing, 342
UDDI, 24, 28, 130, 132, 133, 136, 161, 270, 281, 365
UDDI, green pages, 282
UDDI, white pages, 282
UDDI, yellow pages, 282
UDP, 7, 28, 30
UID, 187, 193
unicast, 28, 245, 265
UnicastRemoteObject class, 352
UNICORE, 158, 160
Uniform Resource Identifier, 82, 84
Uniform Resource Locator, 84
Uniform Resource Name, 84
United Devices, 123, 158, 168
URI, 82, 84
URI Templates, 86
URL, 84, 174
URN, 84
Usenet, 22
User Agent, UA, 35
utility computing, 156
UUCP, 22
UUID, 246, 258

V-LAN, 116
Vaidhyanathan, Siva, 114
VCard, 387
virtual organization, 162, 163, 165
virtual organization , 298
virtual overlay, 7, 260
virtual pipes, 119, 262
virtual service, 134, 272, 294
VO, 162, 163, 165, 292, 298

W3C, 81, 83, 270
WADL, 334
WAN, 116
Web 2.0, 4, 313
Web Application Description Language, 334
Web browser, 83
Web Ontology Language, 103
Web server, 18
Web Service semantics, 130
Web Services, 4, 24, 131, 132, 161, 168, 365
Web Services, architecture, 133, 272
Web Services, deployment, 135
Web Services, installation, 381
Web Services, minimal, 132
Web Services, SOA, 136
Web Services, stateful, 291
Wikipedia, 317
Winamp, 181
World Wide Web Consortium, 81

WS-RF, 4, 291, 300
WS-RF, resources, 301
WS-Security, 298
WSDL, 24, 130, 132–134, 136, 161, 270, 272, 275, 293, 295, 335, 383
WSDL, binding, 281
WSDL, document, 275, 278
WSDL, implementation details, 277
WSDL, namespaces, 279
WSDL, portType, 276, 291
WSDL, service description, 276
WWW, 83, 122, 127

X.509, 70, 171
XHTML, 46, 104
XML, 24, 43, 129, 130, 132, 133, 136, 254, 259, 264, 270, 273, 296
XML Encryption, 298
XML Schema, 51, 280, 290
XML Signature, 298
XOXO, 326

YouTube, 315

Zeroconf, 28

DOI 10.1007/978-1-84800-123-7

ERRATA

From P2P and Grids to Services on the Web

Evolving Distributed Communities

Ian J. Taylor
Andrew Harrison

The title of the book *From P2P and Grids to Services on the Web: Evolving Distributed Communities* has been incorrectly referred to as *From P2P and Grids and Services on the Web Evolving Distributed Communities* on page vii of the Preface. We regret this error.